ethical
space

Journal with a difference: Celebrating 20 Years

Volume 1.

Published 2023 by Abramis academic publishing

www.abramis.co.uk

ISBN 978 1 84549 817 7

© Ethical Space 2023

All rights reserved

This book is copyright. Subject to statutory exception and to provisions of relevant collective licensing agreements, no part of this publication may be reproduced, stored in a retrieval system, or transmitted in any form or by any means, without the prior written permission of the author.

This book is sold subject to the conditions that it shall not, by way of trade or otherwise, be lent, re-sold, hired out, or otherwise circulated without the publisher's prior consent in any form of binding or cover other than that which it is published and without a similar condition including this condition being imposed on the subsequent purchaser.

Abramis is an imprint of arima publishing.

arima publishing
ASK House, Northgate Avenue
Bury St Edmunds, Suffolk IP32 6BB
t: (+44) 01284 700321

www.arimapublishing.com

Ethical Space – Journal with a difference: Celebrating 20 Years
Volume 1.

Foreword

'An inspiring model of moral realism' – by Clifford Christians — Page 1

Introduction

After 20 years, time for celebration, reflection – and thanks — Page 6
– by the ES editorial team

Section 1. Communication ethics: Philosophical and theoretical reflections

Chapter 1. Open discourse: Media theory for the twenty-first century – by Denis Muller — Page 13

Chapter 2. John Stuart Mill: Freedom of expression and harm in the 'post truth' era – by Tom Bradshaw — Page 26

Chapter 3. Towards 'mindful journalism': Applying Buddhism's Eightfold Path as an ethical framework for modern journalism – by Mark Pearson — Page 45

Chapter 4. Journalists and emotions: The theory of balance – by Lyn Barnes — Page 60

Chapter 5. 'It's not easy to do a WikiLeaks': A cypherpunk approach to global media ethics – by Patrick D. Anderson — Page 74

Chapter 6. A Gandhian conundrum: The ethical dilemma in the Indian sustainability discourse – by Prithi Nambiar — Page 100

Chapter 7. Close travel: On the ethics of writing about the near-at-hand – by Ben Stubbs — Page 115

Section 2. New media, new ethical challenges

Chapter 8. 'Here come the girls': Examining professional golf organisations' online media representations of female professional golfers in a mixed gender event – by Ali Bowes and Niamh Kitching — Page 129

Chapter 9. Astroturfing in online comment: An investigation – by Murray Dick — Page 144

Chapter 10. News as conversation, citizens as gatekeepers: Where is digital news taking us – by Luke Goode — Page 157

Chapter 11. Privacy in Social Network Sites (SNS): The threats from data mining – by Yeslam Al-Saggaf and Md Zahidul Islam — Page 171

Section 3. Professionalisation and media ethics: Beyond the rhetoric

Chapter 12. Accountable sports journalism: Building up a platform and a new specialised code in the field – by Xavier Ramon-Vegas and José-Luis Rojas-Torrijos — Page 189

Chapter 13. Ofcom: An evaluation of UK broadcast journalism regulation of news and current affairs – by Chris Frost — Page 202

Chapter 14. A better death in a digital age: Post-Leveson indicators for more responsible reporting of the bereaved – by Sallyanne Duncan and Jackie Newton — Page 220

Chapter 15. Towards responsible journalism: Code of practice, journalist oath and conscience clause – by Raphael Cohen-Almagor — Page 232

Chapter 16. Reporter power: News organisations, duty of care and the use of locally-hired news gatherers in Syria – by Richard Pendry — Page 244

Chapter 17. Spies and journalists: Towards an ethical framework? – by Paul Lashmar — Page 262

Chapter 18. The ethical turn in considering hidden children's Holocaust testimony as historical reconstruction – by Julie Wheelwright — Page 278

Section 4. Communication ethics and pedagogy

Chapter 19. Can trolling be taught? Educating journalism students to identify and manage trolling – an ethical necessity – by Jay Daniel Thompson — Page 293

Chapter 20. How ethics is taught at leading institutions in the Pacific region – by Tom Cooper — Page 307

Chapter 21. Supervisors' perspectives on the ethical supervision of long form writing and managing trauma narrative within the Australian tertiary sector – by Sue Joseph and Carolyn Rickett — Page 327

Chapter 22. Communication and globalisation: A justification for critical pedagogy – by Andrea Patterson-Masuka and Omar Swartz — Page 346

Chapter 23. Journalism education after Leveson: Ethics start where regulation ends – by David Baines and Darren Kelsey — Page 364

And finally: Speaking out on ethics

Chapter 24. Angela Rippon on consumer journalism — Page 379

Chapter 25. Fernando J. Ruiz argues that Latin American communication scholars have relied for too long on Anglo-Saxon theoretical texts — Page 385

Chapter 26. Jake Lynch defends John Pilger's journalism on Israel and Palestine — Page 388

Chapter 27. John Mair on Boris and the press dogs that didn't bark — Page 401

Index — Page 407

Foreword

'An inspiring model of moral realism'

Clifford Christians

Ethical rationalism has been the dominant paradigm in media ethics. Through reason the human species is distinctive and through rationality moral canons are considered legitimate. In this paradigm, timeless moral truths are rooted in human nature and independent of the conventions of particular societies.

The idea of a common morality known to all rational beings had its detractors, already in the eighteenth-century Occident. David Hume's *Enquiries concerning human understanding and concerning the principles of morals* (1748) took seriously the multiplying discoveries of other cultures, recognising within the framework of empirical philosophy that these diverse conceptions of the good life may have nothing in common with his Scottish homeland.

But it was Friedrich Nietzsche (1844-1900) who developed in the nineteenth century a totalising attack on ethical rationalism. His assault was directed not only against a rational foundation for values, but in opposition to Kantian-style moral values *per se*. In his first book, *The birth of tragedy*, Nietzsche insisted that 'only as an aesthetic phenomenon are life and the world justified eternally' (1967a [1872]: 5). He announced a philosophy beyond good and evil that 'places morality itself not only in the world of appearances but even among deceptions, as semblance, delusion, error, interpretation, art' (1966 [1886]: Preface; cf. Nietzsche 1967b [1887]).

Ethical rationalism postulated a moral order, but Nietzsche argued that morality had become meaningless. In his *Will to power*, there is no longer an answer to the human 'why' and this nihilism means the 'end of the moral interpretation of the world' (1967c [1880]: 1-2). Because he was questioning God's existence, and with it the viability of moral commands, Nietzsche turned to aesthetic values ...

> ... which are not so firmly associated with a supernatural sanction and are conceivable without any element of obligation. One can speak of beauty without implying that anything ought to be beautiful or that anybody ought to create anything beautiful. Beauty can be construed as a factual quality which either is or is not present (Kaufmann 1968: 130).

In Nietzsche's best-known *Human all too human: A book for free spirits* (1878), the analytical awareness he called 'psychological observation' enables humans to control the narrative of their own existence.

These oppositional voices in eighteenth and nineteenth-century Europe have burgeoned into a wholesale attack internationally, so that immutable and universal morality has been generally discredited. Though presumably based on shared features of human beings as a whole, ethical rationalism has been exposed as the 'morality of a dominant gender and class' (Outka and Reed 1993: 4). Defending an abstract good is no longer seen as beneficent, but rather as imperialistic control over the moral judgments of diverse communities. Moral philosophies feeding from the Nietzschean worldview face a crisis of validation. What counts as legitimate morality, if ethical principles are presumed to have no constructive application independently of the societies within which they are constituted? Nietzsche was a philologist, and in post-modernity's world, his conundrums with metaphysical certitude typically become concentrated in language theory, semiotics and mediated symbol systems.

This sophisticated book works compellingly in this difficult terrain. As a literary composite, benefitting from two decades of authoritative scholarship, *Ethical Space: Journal with a difference* presents an intellectual alternative to the rational *cogito* of Descartes and the sceptical anti-*cogito* of Nietzsche. In its competent theorising and keen applications to technological phenomena, this volume proffers a moral realism that refuses ethical rationalism's subject-object polarity of individuated consciousness and that contradicts Nietzsche's fallacy of misplaced concreteness in which unspecified abstractions are circumscribed within the existential.

The axial core of this volume's moral realism is the common good. The academic reflections and professional analyses of these chapters are isomorphic with the common good, thus making the concept distinctive for twenty-first century media ethics. Despite Nietzsche's bombastic negation of ethical rationalism, he presumed its autonomous individuality. His psychological-observation modality directing human existence is identical conceptually to moral construal rooted in independentism. Moral realism of the common good grounds its perspective in lived experience as existentially intersubjective, rather than in the reductionism of individuated rationality. Establishing goods instead of rights as the meaning centre of the common good contrasts with John Rawls's individual autonomy as the first principle in his otherwise celebrated *A theory of justice*: 'Each person has an equal right to the most extensive total system of basic liberties compatible with similar liberty for all' (1971: 302). Consistent with John Locke, John Stuart Mill and Adam Smith, individual liberties have priority in the public domain. We are constituted as selves antecedently, that is, in advance of our engagement with others. Public life is a possible aim of individuated entities, but is not constitutive of their identity. Social goods are primary to claims of personal rights. Goods in their articulation define the scope and content of rights.

This volume with its world-wide compass for ethics theory, classroom pedagogy and instrumental purview structurally transforms moral realism from its North Atlantic parochialism into global solidarity. It does not preclude the morality of earlier cultures and of non-Western peoples, as true of Descartes and of Nietzsche and their trajectories until today. The moral norms of the six continents represented here affirm the common life of associations, definitive of all societies since the associational is indigenous to humanity's being. As illustrative, Confucius features the common good by emphasising the dependence of individual flourishing on group welfare. The common good with its content of relational values is the presupposition of African social morality. In the classic idea of Buddhist ethics, by engaging in positive actions for others, people nourish their own positive qualities. In identifying the universal values of human experience, social cohesion is given priority. A stable social order is considered a mandatory ideal for the human race. The relational obligation of the common good is presumed essential to all forms of public life, developed as well as developing, post-colonial and emerging nations, regions, tribes and territories. The relational reality is to be understood ontologically, as a category of human existence. In other words, the conception of the common good as humans-in-relation characterises our universal humanity.

Responsibility understood relationally is the productive framework for knowing what people around the globe owe one another. The necessary and sufficient conditions of membership in the human species include social stability as a primary value, the survival of identifiable communities as non-negotiable and intersubjective humans possessing the reflective knowledge needed for *eudaimonia*. As this book's authors develop global moral realism they synchronise the universal with the particulars of their case studies and urgent problematics on the street. They demonstrate that the recursive turn to the particular is only viable after establishing generalisations that are credible. The professional modality herewith is both 'univocal and imminent – with neither having priority over the other, and without claiming essentialism' (Sher 2004: 7).

The scholars of this book in their dealing with mediated reality are astute on the political structures and mechanistic instrumentalism that organise public life in cosmopolitan post-modernity. For Charles Taylor's *Sources of the self* (1989), human engrossment with life's significance is best understood by immersing ourselves within moral goods rather than be obsessed with political institutions *per se*. Our very being constitutes an obligatory claim on our humanity to respect and enhance life. Obligation is the content of human agency, without reducing obligation to autonomy. Relational obligation as the centrepiece of moral realism differs categorically from notions of the good that are prominent in consequentialist economics, where policy mandates make no substantial reference to the requirements of dialogic relationships.

Since the moral dimension of the common good is definitive, if the public face issues of policy, they can appeal to the moralist common good as the normative standard. When living in the moral aspect, humans know that they have free will, and that they are not victims of their existence, and that the survival of identifiable communities is non-negotiable. The moral goods idea means that lives can be called good only if they are morally meritorious – a reformulation of Kant's admonition that the moral life consists of making oneself 'worthy to be happy'. Within a moral understanding of the common good, the authors recognise the chasms of exclusion and incapacitation as morally outrageous. With its commitment to moral goods, this volume represents a different model than the ethical systems of rational choice centred on deontology or consequences.

To establish an alternative paradigm, this book puts Nietzsche in historical perspective. Nonetheless, it recognises that normative foundations are a permanent issue of systematic ethics. Jean-Jacques Rousseau (1712-1778) understood correctly that the universal problem in moral philosophy is integrating freedom with the moral order; and it is commonly agreed since his *The social contract* (1762) that epistemological abstractions and metaphysical command theories are inadequate for addressing the normative question. Moreover, the moral realism attended to in these chapters is not deterred into Nietzsche's expressivism beyond good and evil, where truth discourse is a purely semantic account of non-cognitive mental valuations. The source of normativity is not a preoccupation by itself in any of the four sections below, but normed phenomena are embedded within their history, culture, politics and theorems. The intellectual foundations of media ethics are considered the universal hallmarks, properties and aptitudes of human reality past and present. Transcendental criteria are not positioned into a vertical hierarchy, but seen as ordering relations within community, world and being.

Following Charles Sanders Peirce's (1940) triadic abduction, this volume replaces the dyadic methodology of foundationalism, contending that reflection on norms with highly abstract deductivist procedures obscures their concrete character. Abduction accounts for the creativity of presuppositions and hypotheses, with its realism that relational obligation can interact with domains outside the particular, such as with Paul Tillich's 'ground of being'. One's ability to act responsibly to others is not an empty affirmation, but indicates something primordial about human agency without the pretense of wilful desire as in idealism.

William Schweiker, in reflecting on Paul Ricoeur's *Fallible man: Philosophy of the will* (1960) represents the intersubjective moral agency of *Ethical Space: Journal with a difference*: 'Fallible creatures who work evil and yet can be responsible before the demands of justice, incomplete beings who face death and yet can exceed our timeliness through imagination and hope, speaking (with its vagaries) beings who can promise to abide within the bonds of fidelity…' (Schweiker 2020: 498). These twenty-seven chapters are an inspiring model of moral realism that is historically aware and theoretically precise, while knowing its full meaning demands continual assessment, a book demonstrating reflective equilibrium of worldwide scope though being suspicious of finalities.

REFERENCES

Hume, David (1963 [1748]) *Enquiries concerning human understanding and concerning the principles of morals,* Oxford, UK, Clarendon Press

Kaufman, Walter (1968) *Nietzsche: Philosopher, psychologist, anti-Christ,* Princeton, Princeton University Press

Nietzsche, Friedrich (1966 [1886]) *Beyond good and evil,* trans. Kaufman, W., New York, Random House

Nietzsche, Friedrich (1967a [1872]) *The birth of tragedy,* trans. Kaufman, W., New York, Random House

Nietzsche, Friedrich (1967b [1887]) *On the genealogy of morals,* trans. Kaufman, W. and Hollingdale, R.J., New York, Random House

Nietzsche, Friedrich (1967c [1880]) *Will to power: Attempt at a revaluation of all values,* trans. Kaufman, W., New York, Random House

Nietzsche, Friedrich (1986 [1878]) *Human, all too human: A book for free spirits,* trans. Hollingdale, R.J., Cambridge, UK, Cambridge University Press

Outka, Gene and Reeder, John P., Jr. (1993) *Prospects for a common morality,* Princeton, Princeton University Press

Peirce, Charles Sanders (1955 [1940]) *Philosophical writings of Peirce,* New York, Dover

Rawls, John (1999 [1971]) *A theory of justice,* Cambridge, MA, Harvard University Press

Ricoeur, Paul (1986 [1960]) *Fallible man: Philosophy of the will,* trans. Kelby, C.A., New York, Fordham University Press

Rousseau, Jean-Jacques (2020 [1762]) *The social contract,* trans. Cole, G.D.H., independently published, ASIN, BO8GVGM583

Schweiker, William (2020) Groundwork for the hermeneutics of morals: Paul Ricoeur and the future of ethics, *Journal of Religion,* Vol. 100, 4 October pp 481-498

Sher, Gila (2004) In search of a substantive theory of truth, *Journal of Philosophy,* Vol. 101 pp 5-36

Taylor, Charles (1989) *Sources of the self: The making of the modern identity,* Cambridge, MA, Harvard University Press

NOTE ON THE CONTRIBUTOR

Clifford Christians (PhD, Litt.D, DHL) is Research Professor of Communications, Professor of Journalism, Professor of Media Studies Emeritus at the University of Illinois, Urbana-Champaign, where he was director of the Institute of Communications Research and head of the PhD programme for 16 years. He has been a visiting scholar in philosophical ethics at Princeton University, Oxford University and the University of Chicago. His recent books are *Media ethics and global justice in the digital age* (Cambridge) and (co-authored) *Media ethics: Cases and moral reasoning,* now in its eleventh edition.

Introduction

After 20 years, time for celebration, reflection – and thanks

The *ES* editorial team

Following the launch of the Institute of Communication Ethics (largely thanks to funding by Robert Beckett), in July 2002, the first issue of its journal, *Ethical Space: The International Journal of Communication Ethics*, was published in late 2003. The opening editorial spelled out its stance clearly, stressing that it was 'an academic quarterly with a difference. At its core are the academic papers which over the years will embrace the diverse disciplines and issues that fall under the substantial communication ethics umbrella. But it is also committed to keeping abreast of the news in the field and providing a space for lively, opinionated pieces on topical subjects'. The journal was to be inter-disciplinary, international, philosophically and theoretically eclectic and rooted in a determination to approach in original ways the pressing communication, political, cultural and environmental issues of the day.

Now, after 20 years' publishing, it is a time for not only celebration but reflection.[1] To what extent has the journal achieved its ambitions? Perhaps at the heart of the journal's uniqueness is the professional experience of all its editors and many of the contributors. Richard Lance Keeble (then of City University, London, and more recently of the University of Lincoln), its first editor, was later joined by Donald Matheson (of Canterbury University, New Zealand) and more recently by Sue Joseph (University of South Australia) and Tom Bradshaw (University of Gloucestershire) – with joint reviews editor David Baines (Newcastle University) joining the monthly editorial meetings on Zoom. All editors have substantial journalistic experience behind them – and not surprisingly a 'journalistic edge' animates both the journal's pages and operations.

So over the years, *ES* has been quick to respond to major controversies and events – with academic rigour and philosophical originality. Significantly, the opening section in this anniversary collection is titled 'Communication ethics: Philosophical reflections'. In that first issue of 2003, for instance, Professor Anne

Gregory, of Leeds Metropolitan University, responded in critical detail and with theoretical insight to the recently published Report of the UK government's Communications Review Group from the public relations perspective, focusing on the relationship and advocacy models of communication practice. More recently, a special, guest-edited double issue exploring the global media's response to Covid-19 appeared in 2020 (Vol. 17, Nos 3 and 4), while in 2022 an issue (guest-edited by Barbara Henderson and David Baines) examined the many questions, theoretical complexities and ethical dilemmas thrown up by the recent surge in popularity of the true crime genre. Moreover, in keeping with its mission to stay up-to-date, the ethical issues surrounding new media are regularly examined by contributors: the second section here is suitably titled: 'New media, new ethical challenges'.

But the journal is not fixed on carrying only academically rigorous papers (mostly of around 7,500 words). It regularly publishes shorter articles ('think-pieces' in the journalistic jargon) which provide a space for contributors to sound off on an issue of concern. So a special 2007 issue on 'Communication ethics and the internet' (Vol. 4, Nos 1 and 2) was able to feature not only four papers on the central theme but six 'Views' (such as Anne Dunn on ethical crises and broadcasting training and Karen Sanders on a convicted bomber's call for peace) plus an editorial by Donald Matheson ('Why ethics should be at the heart of the internet debate') together with the text of Valeria Alia's inaugural lecture at Leeds Metropolitan University and a book review by Sarah Maltby. A more recent issue, with pieces in a wide range of genres, appeared in 2021 (Vol. 18, Nos 1 and 2); it included four papers, an article by colleagues at the University of Florida, a review essay on Paul Lashmar's *Spies, spin and the fourth estate*, an obituary for the great war correspondent Robert Fisk, penned by Huseyin Kishi – and ended with eight book reviews.

The journal operates a rapid peer-review process which helps give this 'newsy'/up-to-date feel. In 2014, due to unforeseen circumstances, the editorial team was suddenly without any copy for the upcoming issue. Quickly, joint editor Sue Joseph contacted her colleagues (Matthew Ricketson, Fiona Giles, William Roberts, Carolyn Rickett, Mark Pearson, Willa McDonald and Bunty Avieson) and in a matter of weeks a special Australia-focused issue was peer-reviewed, edited and produced. Remarkable!

Helping us in our mission to be always as up-to-date as possible are brothers Richard and Pete Franklin who run the Bury St Edmunds-based Abramis Publishing so graciously and so efficiently. If we send them copy on, say, a Monday, by Wednesday we will have the first PDF proof back. The editorial team may spend ten days checking the PDF and collating the proofing responses from the contributors. A revised PDF is then sent to Abramis who will return, again, extremely quickly for a final check. We doubt there is a publishing company anywhere who could match that efficiency! So special thanks to Richard and Pete.

Another feature of the journal worth highlighting is its international focus. To give an idea, a special, double issue on 'The ethics of local media across the globe' (Vol 18, Nos 3 and 4), edited by Tom Bradshaw and guest editor Paul Wiltshire, covered Denmark, Russia, the USA, UK, Australia, Brazil and France. In 2017, a special issue on 'Ethics of covering vulnerable people' (guest-edited by Sallyanne Duncan and Jackie Newton) had a piece written by officers for the Mental Health Foundation in Scotland plus papers by academics from the University of Melbourne, AUT University in Auckland, New Zealand, the University of Vienna, the University of Iowa, Massey University, Oslo School of Arts, Communication and Technology, the University of Technology Sydney, Avondale College of Higher Education (now Avondale University) and Murdoch University, Perth.

A special issue on 'UNESCO and the information society' (Vol. 7, Nos 2 and 3), in 2010, included papers by academics from Belgium, Germany, New Zealand, Australia, Denmark, the UK and the United States. Or otherwise, to take one publishing year (Vol. 9: 2011/2012) as an example, contributions were carried from academics in Australia, England, Hungary, Ireland, New Zealand, Scotland, South Africa, Wales, the UK and the USA.

PROFESSIONALISATION AND MEDIA ETHICS: BEYOND THE RHETORIC

Since its launch, one of the journal's major strands has been to explore critically the many aspects of professionalism. Here, a seven-chapter section, 'Professionalisation and media ethics: Beyond the rhetoric' takes in issues as diverse as sports reporting, the performance of UK broadcasting regulation, the responsible reporting of the bereaved, the debate over a journalist conscience clause, the controversial use of locally-hired news gatherers in Syria – and the ethics of reporting on spies.

The journal draws content from a wide variety of sources. Every year, from 2003 until its closure in 2019 (with Abramis taking over the administration and distribution of *ES*), the Institute of Communication Ethics held an annual conference during the autumn term, somewhere in the UK, and papers from them were collected in the first *Ethical Space* issue of the new year. For instance, Vol. 6, No. 1 in 2009 drew from presentations on the conference topic 'The ethics of scandal' including Michael Ford on the ethics of reporting gay stories, Karen Sanders on the rituals of scapegoating, Tessa Mayes on the politics of scandal coverage and PR expert Kevin Maloney on the ethical dilemmas of a whistleblower. The following year's conference focused on the media's obsession with celebrities and, on that theme, Judith Townend examined the Popbitch celebrity newsletter while Nicholas Jones explored the part apologies play in the hyper-personalisation of political coverage. Taking a typically critical line, an editorial in the same issue stressed: 'While obscenely rich celebrities are constantly in the headlines, it's equally pertinent to examine the coverage of those usually marginalised by the media: people in poverty, for instance.' A recent, worthy report had been published by the Society of Editors, Media Trust and Joseph Rowntree Foundation. The editorial continues:

> It fails to highlight the underlying ideological bias of the corporate media which inevitably leads to such discriminatory coverage. Moreover, the report is too utopian in its suggestion that improvement in professional routines and reforms in journalism education can bring about significant changes. Change will, in fact, only come if based on a radical political analysis of the media and society. This will incorporate an awareness of the possibilities of journalistic activities both within and outside the corporate media and as part of a broader political project to democratise the media and society in general.

Vol. 12, No. 1, in 2015, featured pieces on the conference theme 'Celebrating and questioning great minds' with Julian Petley on Richard Hoggart, Paul Hoggart on his father and Richard Lance Keeble on his friend and University of Lincoln colleague, John Tulloch, in a paper titled 'On the importance of mischief-making'. Keeble writes: 'John was the quintessential journo: looking closely, witnessing with an ever critical, intelligent eye, curious about everything. I always remember as we went walking through the streets of New Delhi, Paris or London he appeared to know the histories of every building we passed.' Tulloch, who died in 2013, was for many years book reviews editor of *Ethical Space* and he contributed papers and articles to the journal regularly.

PEDAGOGY AT THE HEART OF *ES*'S MISSION

Also at the 2014 conference, Florian Zollmann presented a paper 'Celebrating John Pilger's early journalism' while John Mair, a dynamic chair of the Institute of Communication Ethics for many years, gave a talk provocatively titled 'Stuart Hall: The reluctant Caribbean'. Pedagogy is at the heart of *ES*'s mission – a separate section in this volume being devoted to it – and students were often invited to attend the annual conferences at a token rate. But the editorial following the 2014 conference commented appropriately: 'Apart from Hayley Cook, who gave an appreciation of John Tulloch as an academic and inspirational tutor, the event was a very "male event". The role of prominent women as public intellectuals was sadly marginalised.'

In addition, the journal has benefited from a close link-up with the Lugano-based European Observatory of Journalism (EOJ). For many years, EOJ director, Stephan Russ-Mohl and his colleagues contributed fascinating articles to the journal; for instance, in Vol. 4, No. 3, in 2007, a piece titled 'An overview of media research in an era of globalisation'. The recent special issue on the global coverage of Covid-19 followed on from a conference jointly organised by the EOJ (with City, University of London, operating now as its UK base) and *ES*. The journal has close ties with many universities and research establishments across the globe: the 2022 conference on the ethics of true crime emerged from a collaboration between *ES* and Newcastle University.

An eclectic mix of topics in the journal provides constant interest. This first anniversary volume of pieces ends with a section, 'Speaking out on ethics', including the journalist and television personality, Angela Rippon, on consumer journalism and Jake Lynch defending John Pilger's reporting on Israel. We end with a typically robustly argued piece by John Mair on how the press dogs didn't bark – critiquing the corporate media's handling of former (and now disgraced) UK PM Boris Johnson.

A second anniversary volume, appearing later in 2023, will have four sections: 'Directing a critical spotlight on the mainstream', 'Alternative voices', 'Public relations: Beyond propaganda', 'And finally: Speaking out on ethics'.

It is fitting that the Foreword in this text is composed by Clifford Christians. Considered by many as the world's leading authority on communication ethics, Professor Christians gave the keynote speech at the London conference that launched the Institute of Communication Ethics all those years ago, had a paper 'The media and moral literacy' in *ES*'s first issue and since then has been a regular contributor and outspoken supporter of the journal. The special issue (Vol. 19, No. 2), of 2022, that served as a tribute to Brian Winston, the first chair of ICE who died in April 2022, began with a foundational paper by Professor Christians: 'Humans as cultural beings in theory and practice'. He ends with a wonderful celebration of Winston: 'As a world class critical theorist, his hermeneutical depth on mediated symbolic systems demonstrates how interpretive scholarship ought to be done in a global era of cross-cultural complexity.' We are honoured to carry Professor Christians's Foreword – and look forward to many more creative collaborations with him in the future.

We are also hugely grateful to those who have contributed pieces to the journal throughout the last 20 years: to you all – sincere thanks.

NOTE

[1] Two books edited by Richard Keeble were brought out by *ES*'s original publishers, Troubador, of Leicester, based on the papers in the journal's first two volumes: *Communication ethics today* (2005), with a Preface by Clifford Christians, and *Communication ethics now* (2008), with a Preface by Cees Hamelink. So the papers featured in the two anniversary volumes are drawn from 2007 onwards

The ES editorial team: Tom Bradshaw, Sue Joseph,
Richard Lance Keeble and Donald Matheson

SECTION 1

Communication ethics: Philosophical and theoretical reflections

Chapter 1

Open discourse: A media theory for the twenty-first century

Denis Muller

Western democracy stands at a moment in time when new thinking about political communication is needed. Social media, made possible by digital technology, has given rise to the echo-chamber phenomenon, in which participants are able to communicate with like-minded individuals and exclude themselves from exposure to other perspectives. There is substantial evidence (see Sunstein 2017, for example) that this contributes to, and intensifies, political partisanship, and to a corresponding weakening of consensus politics. It also contributes to a fragmenting of public conversation. It is this common conversation that allows citizens to identify, prioritise, and propose responses to, issues of common concern and thus have a critical influence on political, economic and social life. The professional mass media remains the vehicle that carries this common conversation in which a plurality of perspectives can be debated. It has been made all the more urgently necessary by social media's fragmentation effect, by the demonstrated unreliability of social media as a source of news, by its echo-chamber effect and by its consequent contribution to political polarisation. To counter these effects, this paper proposes a new normative theory of the media, open discourse theory. It builds on existing theories (Siebert et al. 1956; McQuail 1983; Christians et al. 2009) and requires a renewed commitment by professional mass media to certain ethical norms, in particular verification, impartiality, editorial independence, pluralism and respect for persons.

Keywords: professional mass media, ethical norms, verification, impartiality, editorial independence, pluralism, respect for persons, media theory

INTRODUCTION

The world is living through a great digital communications paradox. Technology that enables all who have access to the internet and the skills of basic literacy to participate in public discourse has also become the means by which public discourse has become fragmented and debased. The democratisation of public discourse has become a means by which democracy itself is undermined. The vision so passionately argued for in John Milton's *Areopagitica* (1644) and John Stuart Mill's *On liberty* (1859) – that truth would infallibly emerge from a free contest in the marketplace of ideas – lies now in ruins. Yet free speech must survive if democracy is to survive. So democratic societies are confronted with a great challenge: how, in the digital world, might the blessings of free speech be maximised while the curses of its excesses be minimised?

Libertarian notions of free speech, exemplified by the arguments of Milton and Mill, have been challenged on the grounds that they are fundamentally elitist and serve to silence public utterances of a majority of individuals (see, for example, Roberts 2004). On this reading, Miltonian and Millian concepts of free speech have limited application even to a public sphere as limited as that conceived of by Habermas (1991: 27). The Habermasian concept was of a bourgeois public sphere in which large numbers of middle-class individuals participated in reasoned public discussion over matters of general public interest. By the standards of today's digitally networked public sphere, the Habermasian concept looks – and is – out of touch with reality. What is not touched by digital technology is the core Habermasian idea of a public sphere as a place of mediation between individuals and the state. In democracies, this place remains essential.

Goode (2005: 21) states that Habermas feared the immediacy of electronic media, lamenting the loss of what he saw as the time and space for reflectiveness possible with the printed word. Goode sees in Habermas's thesis regrettable effects of a citizenry bereft of space and time combined with a reduction of the citizen to a ratings, box office or circulation statistic (ibid: 22-23). These concerns find their echo today in the professional mass media's fixation on analytics and the consequent attraction of clickbait as a means of generating 'eyeballs'.

Goode refers to the 'classic dilemma of balancing openness with the demands of mutual respect and care for the other incumbent on an egalitarian discourse ethic' (ibid: 28). He later refers to Habermas's distaste for the online world (ibid: 106), which Habermas describes as a series of global villages that, far from contributing towards the emergence of a global public sphere, reflect and exacerbate the fragmentation of public life and the proliferation of cultural enclaves.

Fragmentation and cultural enclaves run counter to two social conditions that have long been widely identified as necessary to democratisation: the need for a rich associative life of civil society, and the need for a communicative infrastructure of the public sphere that permits the expression and diffusion of public opinion (Bohman 2007: 60). Bohman states (ibid: 63) that digital technological phenomena have transformed the public sphere from a unitary forum to a *distributive* public of the type best exemplified in computer-mediated network forms of communication (his italics). He notes the importance of having communication in the public sphere that cuts across social spheres (ibid: 70). He points to the constructive possibilities offered by digital technology to extend the public forum by providing a new unbounded space for communicative interaction (ibid: 73), but goes on to argue that at present there is a lack of congruity between existing political institutions and these expanded forms of communicative interaction (ibid: 74).

Open discourse theory is proposed as one part of the media's institutional response to this lack of congruity. The professional mass media, as an institution, needs to adjust to its existence alongside, and as part of, this new type of public sphere that encompasses social media as well as professional mass media. Bohman (ibid: 80-81) argues that while the internet as a tool promotes a vibrant civil society and extends the public sphere, in order to transform the public sphere, something more is needed: the use of the internet to create public spaces in which free, open and responsive dialogue occurs.

A further dimension of public-sphere communication is that between publics and democratic institutions, in respect of which Dewey (1941) argues for the necessity of an ongoing interaction between the two. Without the adjustments by the institution of the professional mass media argued for in this paper, this interaction is unlikely to flourish.

BACKGROUND TO MEDIA THEORY

For more than sixty years, theorising about the role and function of the press has rested on the foundations laid by Fred Siebert, Theodore Peterson and Wilbur Schramm in their seminal work, *Four theories of the press* (1963 [1956]). Their thesis was that the press – by which they meant all media of mass communication – always takes on the form and coloration of the social and political structures within which it operates (ibid: 1). At their time of writing, extant social and political structures had developed alongside communications technologies over 500 years. The process had begun with the political responses by those in authority to the technological revolution represented by the invention of moveable type and the printing press by Gutenberg of Mainz in the 1450s. The ideals of the Enlightenment, the emergence of ideologies, specifically communism, and the corrosive effects on public trust caused by the behaviour of industrialised mass media organisations in the nineteenth and twentieth centuries provided further sources of impetus for the development of press theory (ibid: 6).

From this history, they distilled their four theories. They saw each of them as grounded in certain basic beliefs and assumptions held by different societies about the nature of individuals, the nature of society and the state, the relationship between individuals and the state, and the nature of knowledge and truth (ibid: 10). They saw these theories as a pair of pairs: authoritarian theory and its derivative Soviet communist theory (now generally referred to as revolutionary theory); libertarian theory and its derivative: social responsibility theory.

Siebert et al. proceeded on a basic assumption that also underpins this paper: that for journalistic purposes there is such a thing as 'truth'. Journalistic truth is contingent and usually incomplete but represents the best verified version of the subject-matter available at the time of publication. Thus, the existence of postmodernist theories problematising the notion of truth (see, for example, Rorty 1998: 96) is acknowledged but set aside for present purposes.

The oldest theory and, as Siebert observes, the most pervasive historically and geographically (1963 [1956]: 9) is authoritarian theory. It provided an intellectual justification for the Roman Catholic Church's Inquisition and Index of Forbidden Books. In the secular world, it supplied the basis for the ruthless system of press licensing introduced during the 16th century by the Tudors in England, which survived, albeit in an attenuated form, until 1695 (Hallam 1864: Vol. 1: 238-240). This theory holds that it is for the rulers to decide what the people should know. Moreover, the power of the state enables individuals to achieve more than they could on their own and hence the state takes precedence over the individual. The theory was also grounded in an assumption that the most valuable knowledge and truth would come from an intellectual elite, and that the masses, once properly instructed, would arrive at a unity of thought. To give effect to these assumptions, the press is a servant of the state and ought to be subject to the state's surveillance and control. The apotheosis of this theory was expressed by the Nazis: 'Our truth – truth for us' (Siebert et al. 1963 [1956]: 16).

Revolutionary theory adopts the premises of authoritarian theory and builds on it in two main ways. Firstly, it posits that the platforms of mass communication properly belong to the state and the ruling party and not to private individuals. Secondly, as such they exist to be used for state and party purposes: to educate the masses in correct doctrine; to ensure that they are not exposed to ideas that are incompatible with that doctrine; to promote unity of thought and purpose among the masses, and to propagandise on behalf of the state and party (ibid: 121). Wilbur Schramm, who wrote the chapter on what was then called Soviet communist theory in *Four theories*, captured the essence of the theory – and its effects on human reasoning – in this question put to him by a Russian: 'How could one of your elections possibly be free if the wrong side won?' (ibid: 107).

To someone schooled in libertarian theory, the question is absurd, intellectually impossible. As the name itself suggests, the foundations of libertarian theory are grounded in the ideals of the Enlightenment. Chief among these was the ideal of man as a rational being, eager to seek the truth through reasoned argument. It was an ideal passionately advocated by Milton in *Areopagitica*, his address to parliament in 1644 arguing for an end to press licensing. To the libertarian, the individual person is the prime unit of civilisation (ibid: 40), and so the fulfilment of the individual's aspirations becomes the ultimate goal of society and the prime purpose of the state. The value of individualism was given its most familiar expression in the US Declaration of Independence: '… that all men are created equal, that they are endowed by their Creator with certain unalienable Rights, that among these are Life, Liberty and the Pursuit of Happiness'.

The relationship between individuals and the state was that described by John Locke in his *Second treatise of government* (1976 [1689]) in which he asserted that all legitimate political power resided in the will of the 'sovereign people'. The nature of knowledge and truth, for the libertarians, was a Cartesian distillation of reason, logic and scientific experimentation liberated from religious dogma and superstition and discoverable by the contestation of ideas. The strength of faith among Enlightenment thinkers in the ultimate triumph of reasoned truth is powerfully captured in Thomas Jefferson's polemic on intellectual freedom and progress, as recorded by Dewey in his compilation of Jefferson's writings:

> Reason and experiment have been indulged, and error has fled before them. Truth can stand by itself (Dewey 1941: 97).

This faith was later to be echoed by Mill (1998 [1859]: 21) in his celebrated argument in support of free speech:

> ...[T]he peculiar evil of silencing the expression of opinion is, that it is robbing the human race; posterity as well as the existing generation; those who dissent from the opinion still more than those who hold it. If the opinion is right, they are deprived of the opportunity of exchanging error for truth; if wrong, they lose what is almost as great a benefit, the clearer perception and livelier impression of truth produced by its collision with error.

A further role of the press in libertarian theory was as a bulwark against tyranny, in particular by government. Today we call it the fourth-estate or watchdog function of the press. Despite his detestation of what he called a licentious press and its 'abandoned prostitution to falsehood' as recorded by Dewey (1941: 105), Jefferson nonetheless retained enough regard for its institutional necessity to say:

> ...[W]ere it left to me to decide whether we should have a government without newspapers or newspapers without a government, I should not hesitate a moment to prefer the latter (ibid: 110).

Yet in Jefferson's strictures on the 'prostitution' of the press lay the seeds of what, in the nineteenth and early twentieth centuries would grow into widespread disaffection with a press that had become not only industrialised but habituated to putting its own interests ahead of the public interest. Its debasement was exemplified by the New York circulation 'wars' of the 1890s between William Randolph Hearst's *Journal* and Joseph Pulitzer's *World*, the crude sensationalism of which spawned the term 'yellow journalism' (Campbell 2001: 26-27).

It was against this background of abuse of power and public disgust that in 1943 Henry Luce, publisher of *Time* magazine, initiated and largely paid for an inquiry into press functions and standards. It was called the United States Commission on Freedom of the Press and in 1947 it produced its report, *A free and responsible press*.

From this as well as from the associated volume by the commission's intellectual leader, William Ernest Hocking, *Freedom of the press*, came the foundations of social responsibility theory.

Concerning the nature of man and the relationship between individuals and the state, this theory rests solidly on the foundations laid by libertarian theory. Concerning the nature of truth and knowledge, however, bitter experience had shown that in the competitive frenzy of nineteenth and twentieth-century capitalism, the vision of Milton and Mill – that truth would emerge from the open contest of ideas – belonged to the distant past. Social responsibility theory asserted that the first function of the press was to provide the citizenry with a bedrock of reliable information on which they could participate in political, economic and social life: what Hocking called 'the necessary grist for the thinking of the reader' (1947: 161). To this he added what has come to be called the investigative function of the press: to reveal to the people information on matters they have a right to know about (ibid: 179-180).

For Hocking, truth-telling and impartiality in news reporting lay at the heart of the press's social responsibility (ibid: 197). Conversely, a view of press freedom as having nothing to do with truth-telling, justice and non-partisanship 'wears the aspect of social irresponsibility' (ibid: 230).

The role of the state in social responsibility theory was that of residual legatee entrusted to hold the ring between press freedom and accountability; of ensuring 'an adequate press performance' without intruding on press activities (ibid: 182-183). The commission argued that this consisted in there being no prior censorship, while holding the press answerable at law for the consequences of what it published where wrongful harm was done (ibid: 186).

In the 62 years since the exposition of *Four theories*, there has developed what Christians et al. (2009) call a 'fairly rich reservoir of ideas' about how the theories might be extended, added to or improved upon (ibid: 7). They note, however, that despite its limitations, *Four theories* continues to enjoy considerable respect and wide use. Among the more notable attempts to enlarge the field were those of McQuail, who has revisited the issue several times. Among the many theories he has reviewed and proposed are democratic-participant theory (1983: 84-98), functionalist theory (ibid: 98-99), social constructionist theory (ibid: 100-101) and communication technology determinism (2010: 101-103). Democratic-participant theory proposes that digital technology, especially the internet, empowered citizens at large to participate in public debate in a way that previously had been impossible because of high-cost barriers to entry and the consequent monopoly control of mass communication by large media organisations. Functionalist theory is concerned with identifying and prioritising for democratic purposes the various functions of media and the possibilities offered by communications technology. Social constructionist theory focuses on the role of the media in constructing people's social reality concerning matters that lie beyond their personal experience.

Communication technology determinism is concerned with the effects of the interaction between media technologies and human beings. It has been given extra vigour by the development of interactivity in digital communications.

Another contribution that has received considerable attention is development theory, which assigns to the press a role as collaborative partner with the state in promoting economic development in nations seeking to develop from a position of underdevelopment. Shah (1996: 143) described it as 'independent journalism that provided constructive criticism of government and its agencies, informed readers how the development process was affecting them, and highlighted local self-help projects'. As Christians et al. point out (2009: 202), this theory leaves many questions unresolved, even unasked. How does an ostensibly independent press confine itself to 'constructive' criticism of government? What are the consequences when government and media have a mutual interest in maintaining a national consensus?

OPEN DISCOURSE THEORY

Against that background, this paper proposes open discourse theory. It draws on elements of libertarian, social responsibility and democratic-participant theories, but it specifies a role for the professional mass media that in the past has understandably been taken for granted: the provision of a common conversation among the citizenry on matters of public interest broadly defined. In the pre-digital age, the professional mass media had a monopoly on providing news and a forum for debate open – theoretically, at any rate – to all. With all its faults, that body of news was what the community based its public discourse upon, and that was the forum where opinions among the citizenry were publicly exchanged. The rise of social media as a source of news and forum for opinion has fragmented the body of news and public argument, leading to a fragmentation of public discourse in what are now referred to as echo chambers. Open discourse theory is proposed as an antidote to this fragmentation.

The effect of fragmentation and echo chambers has been the subject of considerable research, powerfully summarised by Sunstein (2017). He begins with the prophecy of Negroponte (1995) that digital technology would enable individuals to curate their own news in a 'Daily Me'. As Sunstein says (ibid: 2), this prophecy is now looking astoundingly good. The algorithms of Facebook and Google do the curating for their users according to the preferences, interests and associations that those users reveal in their social media activities. In the light of this development, Sunstein (ibid: 5) poses four inter-related questions concerning the functioning of democracy:

1. What are the social pre-conditions for a well-functioning system of democratic deliberation?

2. Might serendipity (in exposure to news and opinion) be important, even if people do not want it?
3. Might a perfectly controlled communications universe – a personalised feed – be its own kind of dystopia?
4. How might social media, the explosion of communications options, machine learning and artificial intelligence alter the capacity of citizens to govern themselves?

He argues that instead of an architecture of individual control over exposure to news and opinion, democracy – as well as personal well-being – needs 'an architecture of serendipity' (ibid: 5), in other words, a means by which people stumble across material that would not make it through their personalised news-filtration system. He sees this as necessary to counter what may be thought of as the second face of censorship. There has long been a pre-occupation with the first face of censorship, being government restraints on free speech, but he argues that failure to perceive and respond to this second face of censorship leads to fragmentation, polarisation and extremism (ibid: 6, 7).

He also argues for the necessity of citizens having a wide range of shared experiences, without which a heterogeneous society will find it hard to identify and find solutions to social problems such as the risks of terrorism, climate change and the spread of infectious diseases (ibid: 7). Democracies, he says, may or may not be fragile, but polarisation can be a serious problem, and it is heightened if people live in different communications universes (ibid: 25).

Fragmentation in news and opinion creates these different communications universes, and the evidence showing the extent of this fragmentation is strong. A powerful factor in the development of fragmentation has been the creation of hashtags. A study of two competing hashtags, #BlackLivesMatter and #AllLivesMatter, was conducted by Gallagher et al. in 2016 and published in 2018. The first sprang up as a protest after the notorious shooting of an African-American man, Michael Brown, by a white policeman in Ferguson, Missouri, in 2014, and the second as a counter-protest.

The researchers found significant differences in the way the issue of violence between African-Americans and police were framed by each hashtag. One difference was that #BlackLivesMatter carried a proportionally higher discussion of African-American deaths than did #AllLivesMatter. By contrast, within #AllLivesMatter the only lives that were significantly discussed were those of law enforcement officers.

The contribution social media makes to the fragmentation and polarisation phenomenon is intensified when mass media also become politically polarised. Martin and Yurukoglu (2014) made estimates of both the influence of slanted news on voting behaviour and the taste for like-minded news in the context of cable television news in the US. They found that watching Fox News Channel

(FNC) increased the probability of voting Republican in presidential elections. They stated that these estimates implied large effects of FNC on presidential elections. Furthermore, they estimated that cable news could increase polarisation and that this increase depended on both a persuasive effect of cable news and the existence of tastes for like-minded news. They also found that between 2000 and 2008, FNC and another cable news service, MSNBC, had each become more politically polarised, with Republican voters increasingly likely to watch FNC and Democrat voters increasingly likely to watch MSNBC (2014: 37). Levitsky and Ziblatt argue that extreme partisan polarisation weakens democratic norms (2018: 9). They assert that a necessary response to this is the reinvigoration of institutional gatekeeping, including by the media (ibid: 56) and, in the 'fake news' environment created by the presidency of Donald Trump, a recommitment to truth-telling (ibid: 181-203).

Open discourse theory posits that, in the face of these developments, the professional mass media have a responsibility to recognise that it is they who, because of long-established experience, extensive reach, market power, brand identification and privileges, are called upon to provide a reliable and respectful informational basis for a common conversation among citizens, and to exert a gatekeeping function nowadays much despised. Carrying out these functions effectively requires renewed commitment to certain norms of professional ethics. None of these is new, but each has become weakened in the scramble by established media to find ways of surviving the digital revolution's onslaught on their business model.

The first is prior verification of facts. A common conversation based on erroneous facts is worse than no common conversation at all. It turns out that the Miltonian and Millian ideal that truth would be distilled from a free contest in the marketplace of ideas is, in the twenty-first century, as quaint as it is romantic. The concepts of 'fake news' and 'alternative facts' never entered their heads. To fulfil open discourse theory, the professional mass media must reassert the fundamental importance of being right, and prioritise it ahead of being first. The second is a recommitment to impartiality. This has six elements (Muller 2014: 73-81), all of which are necessary to the fulfilment of open discourse theory.

- The first of these is factual and contextual accuracy where facts are not only verified as true but are presented in a way that accurately and fairly reflects the context within which those facts exist.
- The second is fairness, which requires that the portrayal of people, events, ideas and organisations creates an impression similar to what an independent observer would see, hear and understand.
- The third element is balance. This much-misunderstood concept concerns following the weight of evidence and apportioning time, space and prominence accordingly. It is false balance to accord equal time, space or prominence to

two sides of an argument where the available evidence is clearly in favour of one and not the other. Climate change is an example. To give equal time or space to the conclusions of the peer-reviewed work of climate scientists and to the propositions of climate-change deniers is to create false balance. It is a failure to follow the weight of evidence.
- The fourth element is open-mindedness, an approach to reporting that includes the full range of principal relevant perspectives on an issue.
- The fifth is the absence of conflict of interest.
- And the sixth is decision-making based on established news values of the kind defined at various times by scholars such as Galtung and Ruge (1965), McQuail (1983) and Harcup and O'Neill (2001).

Adding significantly to the concept of impartiality is Ward's idea of pragmatic objectivity (2004: 261-316). This approach accepts that in journalism, as in many other fields of human endeavour, there can be no final truth. Instead, there is a contingent version of events based on verified facts that will stand as truth unless and until it is modified by subsequent events or new knowledge.

Closely allied to impartiality is the requirement to promote pluralism in public discourse. Shutting out voices or viewpoints purely on the basis of prejudice has no place in a truly common conversation, particularly at a time when professional media need to provide an alternative to the highly prejudiced and frequently offensive clamour of social media echo chambers.

A further ethical requirement of open discourse theory is the reassertion of editorial independence. This has become compromised in several ways. At the commercial level, there has been a breakdown in the separation between news and advertising content. This breakdown goes under the general name of hybrid journalism (Muller 2016). It is fundamentally deceptive because it presents advertising as if it is news, and typically any declaration that it is in fact advertising is hard to find. 'Advertorial', the analogue forerunner of digital hybrid journalism, typically was presented in typography and layout that made it clearly distinguishable from news content, and commonly was clearly labelled 'advertising'. Editorial independence has also become compromised at the political level and has led to the polarisation of news outlets that has both reflected and magnified political and social polarisation in the wider society, as shown by the work of Martin and Yurukoglu referred to above.

Editorial independence is also demonstrated by the separation of news from opinion and by treating the interests of the platform's proprietor no differently from the treatment of others' interests. The essentials of editorial independence were captured in the charter of editorial independence adopted by the *Age*, Melbourne, in 1988 when the newspaper faced the prospect of falling into the hands of the British newspaper robber baron, Robert Maxwell. In 1991, Maxwell disappeared from his yacht in the Bay of Biscay and was later, in November 1991, found dead at sea. He never secured ownership of the newspaper, but the charter still stands. It states that the proprietors acknowledge that journalists, artists and photographers must record the affairs of the city, state, nation and the world fairly, fully and regardless of any commercial, political or personal interests, including those of any proprietors, shareholders or board members. It also states that full editorial control of the newspaper, within a negotiated, fixed budget, is vested in the editor, and that the editor alone shall determine the editorial content.

A further consideration is that open discourse theory is being developed under global political and communications circumstances where online communications exchanges are global and transcend the borders of nation states. This expands the bases on which people develop a sense of identity to include global affiliation with others of like mind, shared interests or shared belief systems. It follows that a necessary element in open discourse theory is respect for persons regardless of nationality, ethnicity, race, colour, sexual orientation, religion or political persuasion. The Kantian value of respect for persons is built into journalistic codes of ethics around the world (see, for example, Keeble 2001).

CONCLUSIONS

Open discourse theory posits that adherence to these five ethical norms will enable the press to provide a shared body of reliable information necessary to democratic life, provide a platform on which a range of opinions can be expressed, and so become a means by which communities engage in a common conversation on matters of common interest and concern, countering social media's echo-chamber effect and the fragmentation of the public conversation.

Open discourse theory builds on libertarian and social responsibility theories. It assumes, as do those two theories, that the individual takes primacy over the state. Its principal objective is to give effect to the Lockean concept of the sovereign people by providing citizens with that bedrock of reliable information on which to base participation in political, economic and social life. However, the provision of shared information and opinions on which a common conversation may proceed is not to be confused with collective thought. Each individual is free to draw his or her own conclusions from the common conversation and make his or her personal contributions to it.

- This paper was first published in *Ethical Space*, Vol. 16, No. 1 pp 3-10

REFERENCES

Bohman, J. (2007) *Democracy across borders: From Demos to Demoi*, Cambridge, Massachusetts, MIT Press

Campbell, J. (2001) *Yellow journalism: Puncturing the myths, defining the legacy*, Praeger, Westport CT

Christians, C., Glasser, T., McQuail, D., Nordenstreng, K. and White, R. (2009) *Normative theories of the media*, Chicago, University of Illinois Press

Crossley, N. and Roberts J. M. (eds) (2004) *After Habermas: New perspectives on the public sphere*, Oxford, Blackwell

Dewey, J. (1941) *The living thoughts of Thomas Jefferson, selected from the writings of Thomas Jefferson*, Washington, H. A. (ed.) London, Cassell

Gallagher, R. J., Reagan, A. J., Danforth, C. M. and Sheridan Dodds, P. (2018) Divergent discourse between protests and counter-protests: #BlackLivesMatter and #AllLivesMatter. Available online at https://doi.org/10.1371/journal.pone.0195644, accessed on 4 June 2018

Galtung, J. and Ruge, M. (1965) The structure of foreign news: The presentation of the Congo, Cuba and Cyprus crises in Norwegian newspapers, *Journal of International Peace Research*, Vol. 1 pp 64-91

Goode, L. (2005) *Jürgen Habermas: Democracy and the public sphere*, London, Pluto Press

Grayling, A. C. (2017) *Democracy and its crisis*, London, Oneworld Publications

Habermas, J. (1991) *The structural transformation of the public sphere: An inquiry into a category of bourgeois society* (Burger, T. and Lawrence, F. trans.), Massachusetts, MIT Press

Hallam, H. (1864) *The constitutional history of England, Vol. 1*, Boston, William Veazie

Harcup, T. and O'Neill, D. (2001) What is news? Galtung and Ruge revisited, *Journalism Studies*, Vol. 2, No. 2 pp 261-280

Hocking, W. E. (1947) *Freedom of the press: A framework of principle*, Chicago, University of Chicago Press

Keeble, R. (2001) *Ethics for journalists*, London, Routledge

Levitsky, S. and Ziblatt, D. (2018) *How democracies die*, London, Viking Penguin Random House

Locke, J. (1976 [1689]) *Second treatise of government*, Gough, J. W. (ed.) Oxford, Basil Blackwell

Martin, G. and Yurukoglu, A. (2014) Bias in cable news: Persuasion and polarization, Working Paper 20798, Cambridge, Massachusetts, National Bureau of Economic Research. Available online at http://www.nber.org/papers/w20798, accessed on 4 June 2018

McQuail, D. (1983) *Mass communication theory*, London, Sage, third edition

Mill, J. S. (1998 [1859]) *On liberty*, Gray, J. (ed.) Oxford, Oxford University Press

Muller, D. (2014) *Journalism ethics for the digital age*, Melbourne, Scribe Publications

Muller, D. (2016) Conflict of interest: Hybrid journalism's central ethical challenge, *Ethical Space*, Vol. 13, Nos 2/3 pp 95-109

Negroponte, N. (1995) *Being digital*, New York, Vintage Books

Roberts, J. M. (2004) From populism to political dialogue in the public sphere: A Bakhtinian approach to understanding a place for radical utterances, 1684-1812, *Cultural Studies*, Vol. 18, No. 6 pp 882-908

Rorty, R. (1998) *Achieving our country: Leftist thought in twentieth-century America*, Cambridge MA, Harvard University Press

Shah, H. (1996) Modernisation, marginalisation and emancipation: Toward a normative model of journalism and national development, *Communication Theory*, Vol. 6, No. 2 pp 143-166

Siebert, F., Peterson, T. and Schramm, W. (1963 [1956]) *Four theories of the press*, Chicago, University of Illinois Press

Sunstein, C. (2017) *#Republic: Divided democracy in the age of social media*, Princeton, Princeton University Press

The *Age* (1991) Charter of editorial independence. Available online at https://www.smh.com.au/national/fairfax-media-charter-of-editorial-independence-20120619-20l4t.html, accessed on 27 June 2018

United States Commission on Freedom of the Press (1947) *A free and responsible press*, Chicago, University of Chicago Press

Ward, S. J. A. (2004) *The invention of journalism ethics*, Montreal, McGill-Queens University Press

NOTE ON THE CONTRIBUTOR

Dr Denis Muller, a former journalist, is a Senior Research Fellow in the Centre for Advancing Journalism at the University of Melbourne. He is author of *Journalism and the future of democracy* (Palgrave Macmillan, 2021), *Journalism ethics for the digital age* (Scribe Publications, 2014) and *Media ethics and disasters: Lessons from the Black Saturday bushfires* (Melbourne University Press, 2011)

Chapter 2

John Stuart Mill: Freedom of expression and harm in the 'post-truth' era

Tom Bradshaw

This paper contends that John Stuart Mill's arguments for freedom of expression – despite being first published in 1859 – remain a powerful framework through which contemporary issues of free speech can be explored and taught. As part of an analysis of Mill's On liberty, *the notion of intolerance being the default condition of mankind and restrictions on free speech being a trans-generational wrong are delineated. The issue of on-campus censorship is discussed, as are the prominence and causes of self-censorship in both the media and wider society. The usefulness of Mill's* On liberty *as a means of exploring these contemporary problems of free speech is expounded, particularly the enduring usefulness of his Harm Principle, and a phenomenon that is called the Paradox of Liberal Inheritance is identified. The concept of alethic disruption is developed to investigate the emergence of 'post-truth' news, and a Mill-inspired response to this is outlined. It is argued that Mill articulates principles that modern media students can use as an accessible means of approaching questions of media ethics, and that* On liberty *also makes powerful points about the etiquette of intellectual debate.*

Keywords: John Stuart Mill, freedom of expression, harm, 'post-truth' era

INTRODUCTION: FREEDOM OF EXPRESSION – OLD QUESTIONS, NEW QUESTIONS

What are the limits of freedom of expression in a democracy? Is there even a limit? If there is one, who polices it – the legal system, public opinion or a hybrid of the two? Are either consequentialism or deontology adequate ethical frameworks through which to produce coherent answers to issues about free expression?

Since Milton's 17th-century plea for unlicensed publication, *Areopagitica*, the first three of these questions have been defining ones for the West (Berlin 2012; Cohen-Almagor 2005; O'Rourke 2003). And the importance of all four questions has been underscored by incidents in both newsrooms and the corridors of power during the opening years of the new millennium. The death threats and killings that followed the publication of cartoons of the Prophet Mohammed in the Danish newspaper, *Jyllands-Posten* (2005-2006) and the French satirical magazine, *Charlie Hebdo* (2015), illustrate that freedom of expression is not just a matter for the debating chamber, but is potentially a matter of life and death to members of the media and wider society (Rose 2006).

Elsewhere, the prospect of state-backed press regulation in the UK arising from the Leveson Inquiry (2011-2012) prompted vociferous opposition from the mainstream media, who have argued that such a move is tantamount to pulling away a pillar of open society that has been steadily buttressed since Milton's 17th-century essay (Nelson 2016). Yet freedom of speech is far from being an absolute right in the UK and is limited by laws of defamation and contempt and, until as recently as 2008, blasphemy. Moreover, as Frost (2016) explains, a range of legislation has a restrictive effect on what can be broadcast or published in the UK on grounds of offence, from the Obscene Publications Acts 1959 and 1964 to the Race Relations Act 1976 and the Communications Act 2003. The free speech ramifications of such legislation are contentious – both for the media and wider society – as illustrated by the variety of mainstream polemics about freedom of expression (Garton Ash 2016; Hume 2015).

Long-established questions about the boundaries of free speech, therefore, remain prevalent. But to these questions can be added another layer of complexity. This complexity is provided by what can be termed the *alethic disruption* within the emerging media ecosystems of the 21st century that are dominated by social media and the algorithms that power the content distribution on those social media platforms (Knight 2013; Smith 2016). It has been contended by the new editor of the *Guardian* that in a 'post-truth' culture propelled by social media, the currency of online information is no longer truth but virality (Viner 2016). Audience engagement (by which is meant high unique visitor numbers and the sharing of content) becomes the altar on which 'good' journalism is potentially sacrificed. On this understanding what engages people online and prompts them to consume and share content is not its veracity but its 'affective' – or emotional – power (Hermida 2016). This leads to the propagation – unwittingly, but sometimes wittingly – of misinformation in an era in which 'facts become secondary to feeling; expertise and vision to *ersatz* emotional connection' (Smith 2016). Truth is in some instances relegated to being an optional extra. The prevalence and traction of 'fake news' in the coverage of the 2016 US Presidential election and the Brexit referendum are cited as an example of truth's relegation (Hermida 2016; Viner 2016). Reflecting on the US Presidential election, Hermida describes how Donald Trump's supporters 'became the media themselves, spreading and amplifying subjective and emotional affective news – news designed to provoke passion, not inform'. This is 'affective news', a diet of content that is 'designed to stir up passions, feed prejudices and polarise publics'. Moreover, people will share false information if it fits their view of the world. Even if some don't quite believe it, they will share an article with the aim of entertaining, exciting or enraging friends and acquaintances. Fake news spreads so fast that potentially hundreds of thousands of people could have seen it by the time it gets debunked (Hermida 2016).

The growth of 'fake news' and how to stem its flow – or at least nullify its penetration – has become a central concern for world leaders as well as social media company executives, with the integrity of democracy itself potentially being in jeopardy (Yuhas 2016).

The concept of alethic disruption is not equivalent to the concept of 'post-truth', but the post-truth milieu should instead be regarded as the most recent and vivid illustration of alethic disruption. Alethic disruption is the wider phenomenon of the networked society's increasingly strained and complex relationship with social reality and how the truth of that reality is to be mediated, grasped and verified in a multimedia world. Churnalism (Davies 2008) is another manifestation of alethic disruption. Churnalism – the passive, desk-bound regurgitation of content by journalists from press releases or rival media – has particularly affected newsrooms and social media channels and, as a consequence, those platforms' audiences. Churnalism and the emergence of post-truth fake news illustrate the evolution of alethic disruption.

What implication does the most recent aspect of alethic disruption, the post-truth milieu, have for freedom of expression? Many of the traditional arguments for unfettered – or at least largely unfettered – free expression have been developed on the basis that the free flow of debate enables truth to emerge (Milton 1973 [1644]; Mill 1989). This was the thought motivating one of the most memorable figures of speech in *Areopagitica*:

> And though all the winds of doctrine were let loose to play upon the earth, so Truth be in the field, we do injuriously by licensing and prohibiting to misdoubt her strength. Let her and falsehood grapple; who ever knew Truth put to the worse, in a free and open encounter (ibid: 35).

But if the evolution of alethic disruption means that the emergence of truth is no longer of primary importance to a proportion of online audiences then where does that leave those old arguments upon which free speech has been founded? Is such a Miltonic argument just a quaint relic from the era of the quill that is rendered redundant by the age of the meme?

There is a further element that complicates the contemporary debate around freedom of expression. This is the issue of censorship and self-censorship in the very places where freedom of thought is – or is often assumed to be – *sine qua non*: universities. In November 2016, the students' union at City University London – a university with one of the most distinguished schools of journalism in the UK – voted in favour of a campus ban on the *Sun*, *Daily Mail* and *Daily Express*. The motion, 'Opposing fascism and social divisiveness in the UK media', stated that the ban could be extended to other media outlets and that the three specified titles were 'merely used as high-profile examples' (Sweney and Jackson 2016). In passing the motion, City was the latest UK students' union to approve a campus-ban on national press titles.

Online magazine *Spiked* has ranked universities on the basis of their restrictions on free speech, awarding each university a 'red', 'amber' or 'green' status depending on the policies and actions of both students' unions and university administrators (Slater 2016). The 2016 survey had a sample of 115 universities. While a green rating is conferred on institutions which place no restrictions on lawful free speech, a red rating is for those universities which are 'hostile' to freedom of expression by mandating 'explicit restrictions on speech, including but not limited to, bans on specific ideologies, political affiliations, beliefs, books, speakers or words' (ibid). The amber rating is for an institution which 'chills free speech and free expression by issuing guidance with regard to appropriate speech and conduct' (ibid). The 2016 Free Speech University Rankings (FSUR) refers to an 'epidemic of campus censorship'. Ninety per cent of institutions were given either a red (55 per cent) or amber (35 per cent) grading for 2016, an increase of 10 per cent on 2015. Thirty students' unions have banned newspapers, 25 have banned songs, 20 have banned societies, and 19 have banned speakers or events. The coordinator of *Spike*'s rankings, Tom Slater, argues that such policies are inimical to universities' quest for discovering the truth. 'Today, in a time when campus bureaucrats see students as too vulnerable – or too easily led – to listen to difficult ideas, the entire purpose of the academy is being undermined, and the bar for censorship is only getting lower' (Slater quoted in Ali 2016).

While *Spiked*'s language is arguably unhelpfully sensationalist – references to an 'epidemic' and 'campus bureaucrats' is redolent of tabloidisation – it is the case that a new lexicon now frames the debate over freedom of expression in universities. 'Safe space', 'trigger warning' and 'no platforming' are terms frequently used by universities to justify restrictions on the expression of controversial views or content. And they have led to claims that current students, as part of 'Generation Snowflake' (Fox 2016), are being cosseted and deprived of robust intellectual development (Bromwich 2016; Scruton 2016). The debate around this issue has also reached mainstream literary culture. A notable example is a novel by a Booker Prize-winning author which adopts the conceit of having as a narrator an unborn child with a satirical tongue. On the education he can expect, the foetus-narrator writes:

> I'll be an activist of the emotions, a loud, campaigning spirit fighting with tears and sighs to shape institutions around my vulnerable self. My identity will be my precious, my only true possession, my access to the only truth. The world must love, nourish and protect it as I do. If my college does not bless me, validate me and give me what I clearly need, I'll press my face into the vice chancellor's lapels and weep. Then demand his resignation (McEwan 2016: 146).

Social commentators have echoed the perspective of McEwan's foetus, criticising the safe spaces and trigger warnings of the modern university campus as a form of intellectual sabotage. A vigorous case is presented by Scruton, who argues that open, Western society is itself being undermined by what he perceives to be on-campus censorship.

> Those who wish to maintain the student mind in a condition of coddled vulnerability, unhardened by opposition and unpractised in argument, now police the campus, with the result that these places which should have been the last bastion of reason in a muddled world, are instead the places where all the muddles come home for nourishment. The example vividly illustrates the way in which the attacks on free speech can go so far as to close off the route to knowledge. And in the end that is why we should value this freedom, and why John Stuart Mill was so right to defend it as fundamental to a free society. Without it we will never really know what we think (Scruton 2016).

Scruton's reference to J. S. Mill at the end of the passage suggests the enduring power of Mill to inform debates around freedom of expression. This paper is focused on extending this idea by exploring in detail the manifold ways in which Mill's ideas, particularly those from *On liberty*, can be used as a trenchant means of analysing contemporary issues of free speech, even though *On liberty* was first published in 1859. As argued above, an up-to-date discussion of the boundaries of freedom of expression needs to acknowledge and incorporate both the issues posed by alethic disruption and contemporary manifestations of censorship in Western society, one species of which is the climate of on-campus restriction. This paper uses Mill as a prism through which to explore the on-going debates about offence and harm, and proposes what is called the Paradox of Liberal Inheritance. This paradox is focused on exploring how many of the beneficiaries of Mill's powerful vision of a liberal, tolerant society in which people are free to pursue what he termed 'new and original experiments in living' (1989: 81) are now attempting to stifle the very freedom of expression that is a precondition of such a tolerant society. In addition, the paper will explain why the study of Mill's ideas is vital for modern students of journalism and media ethics. It is argued that Mill is a powerful lens through which tomorrow's custodians of the flow of information can consider the limits of freedom of expression and media regulation.

The paper also proposes a potential solution to the issues of misinformation arising from alethic disruption, arguing with Jarvis (2016a, 2016b) that the appropriate response by both the media and regulators is not to attempt to shut down the various channels of (mis)information but rather to target those same channels with truth. This, it is argued, is a Millian response that is firmly entrenched in the tradition of English liberal thought. To rephrase it in a Miltonic idiom, such a response to the rising tide of fake news and post-truth content is to enable 'Truth to be in the field' so it at least has a fighting chance to put falsehood 'to the worse, in a free and open encounter'.

ON *ON LIBERTY*

As a founding credo of modern liberal thought, *On liberty* has been – and continues to be – the focus of debate and re-interpretation (Berlin 2012; Cohen-Almagor 2005; Gray 2012; O'Rourke 2003; Rees 2012; Ryan 2012; Steel 2012). While this paper is not the place to contrast and evaluate all these interpretations, it is worth expanding on two points, neither of which has arguably received enough attention in the secondary literature. The first is that Mill argues that intolerance – and by implication censored speech – is the *default condition* of human societies. The second is that restricting free speech is what can be termed a *trans-generational wrong*, affecting not just the present generation but posterity too.

On liberty is an ardent plea for the individual to be free from constraints imposed by both the state and by majority opinion, where those constraints go beyond restricting behaviour that causes harm to other people. Freedom of expression is one facet of this wider freedom that Mill regards as so vital for people to flourish, both individually and collectively. But Mill does not contend that humankind has a benign nature, if only it were allowed to be free. Indeed, on occasion Mill's statements regarding human nature possess an almost Hobbesian tone, as when he claims that 'the disposition of mankind, whether as rulers or as fellow citizens, to impose their own opinions and inclinations as a rule of conduct on others, is so energetically supported by some of the best and by some of the worst feelings incident to human nature, that it is hardly ever kept under restraint by anything but want of power' (1989: 17).

Tolerance, moreover, does not come easy to humans, 'so natural to mankind is intolerance in whatever they really care about' (ibid: 11). The emergence of toleration is for Mill, therefore, a central element to the emergence of civilisation. As such, a society which acknowledges the legitimacy of his Harm Principle – that 'the only purpose for which power can be rightfully exercised over any member of a civilised community, against his will, is to prevent harm to others' (ibid: 13) – is one where the thirst for power is overcome, or at least contained. Freedom of expression is thus an unnatural position; acknowledging the right for another person to say something that is repellent or hateful to me, or which I believe to be plain wrong, is something that goes against the grain of human nature. And for that reason, once achieved, the acknowledgment is all the more precious. Another way of phrasing it is to say, as Bromwich does, that free speech is an 'aberration' and that 'In most societies throughout history and in all societies some of the time, censorship has been the means by which a ruling group or a visible majority cleanses the channels of communication to ensure that certain conventional practices will go on operating undisturbed' (Bromwich 2016). For

Mill, convention is a deadening, creativity-sapping burden – referred to him in one place as the 'despotism of custom' (Mill 1989: 70) – and freedom of expression is a means of weakening its influence.

A restriction on freedom of speech does not simply create an absence of opinion; it is an act of intellectual deprivation. Mill argues that it is a restriction on the spread of intellectual capital that can deprive subsequent generations. As such, it can be termed a trans-generational wrong. In an attempt to convey his point with as much rhetorical force as possible, Mill invokes imagery of physical violence, describing censorship as a robbery afflicting not just the present generation but also future ones.

> The peculiar evil of silencing the expression of an opinion is that it is robbing the human race, posterity as well as the existing generation, those who dissent from the opinion, still more those who hold it. If the opinion is right, they are deprived of the opportunity for exchanging error for truth: if wrong, they lose what is almost as great a benefit, the clearer perception and livelier impression of truth, produced by its collision with error (ibid: 20).

Mill's commitment to free speech stems from a broader commitment to diversity – diversity of belief, diversity of lifestyle, diversity of thought – which is connected to his belief that diversity enables individuals to flourish, which in turn enables individuals to achieve a state of happiness (or as Mill, reflecting his utilitarian background, often refers to it, utility). As commentators have noted, an underlying theme of *On liberty* is how diversity is essential to progress (Collini 1989: xiv). This animating sprit of the essay – and of Mill's thinking in general – is powerfully captured by Berlin:

> What he [Mill] came to value most was ... diversity, versatility, fullness of life – the unaccountable leap of individual genius, the spontaneity and uniqueness of a man, a group, a civilization. What he hated and feared was narrowness, uniformity, the crippling effect of persecution, the crushing of individuals by the weight of authority or of customs or of public opinion (2012: 134).

It is the dissident and heretic, therefore, who need protecting. For Mill, society has a duty to enable those who hold minority opinions to feel they can express them without fear of being silenced.

SELF-CENSORSHIP AND THE 'SPIRAL OF SILENCE'

Before exploring in detail how Mill's ideas in *On liberty* can illuminate contemporary issues of freedom of expression, it is important to acknowledge another important aspect of contemporary communication in the West, which is the extent and nature of self-censorship in the social media-driven era. There is a significant corpus of evidence to suggest that self-censorship is prevalent among both the news media (Preston 2009; Rose 2006; Sefiha 2010; Sturges 2008) and the public more generally (Dans 2014; Das and Kramer 2013; Hampton et al. 2014). This is, perhaps, in some ways counter-intuitive, because self-censorship would seem to be an activity at odds with the click-happy culture of 'over-sharing' that some believe is characteristic of digital-native social media users (Bromwich 2016). However, self-censorship and over-sharing are arguably two sides of the same coin, both being techniques relating to the development by social media users of an online persona.

But why be so concerned by self-censorship, a slippery phenomenon which, by definition, is difficult to quantify because its defining characteristic is an absence – namely, silence? Self-censorship is important from a Millian perspective because, for Mill, the muzzling of one's own opinion – whether through fear of upsetting conventional or majority opinion, or through fear of provoking a response from the state – is an evil, in so far as it inhibits the spread of ideas and inhibits diverse opinion (and thereby diversity itself). For Mill, freedom of thought and freedom of speech/expression are intellectually indivisible; inhibit one and you inhibit both (1989: 17). As such, self-censorship – and the reasons that cause it to happen – are another means by which the intellectual life of present and future society is impoverished. Sturges (2008) offers a quadripartite taxonomy of the reasons for self-censorship, the first of which – the fear of breaking the 'constraints of conformity' – is phrased in distinctly Millian terms, invoking as it does the spectre of the tyranny of majority opinion.

Self-censorship is defined by Sedler as 'the decision by an individual or group to refrain from speaking and the decision by a media organization to refrain from publishing information' (2012). While a useful starting point, this is too narrow a definition. It is not just 'speaking' that individuals refrain from, but publishing social media updates, while media organisations might refrain from broadcasting as well as 'publishing'. Writing from a US perspective, Sedler regards self-censorship as compromising the values of the First Amendment due to it being a phenomenon that inhibits the dissemination of information or ideas to the public.

However, one response to this is to argue that most instances of self-censorship in the social media age are something less concerning – they are merely a form of self-defence that prevent one's remarks being misconstrued. This is in the position of Dans who, reflecting on his own use of Twitter, says that his behaviour on the platform was very different when he had 200 followers to when he had tens of thousands – and that the explanation for the difference is 'simply one of survival' (2014). He contends that self-censorship is inherent in the way social media functions.

> Anybody who has spent time sharing information on a social network understands the dynamic, and that self-censorship is alive and well: as

one's perceived or real audience grows, the amount of information about ourselves that we are prepared to share diminishes. … The fewer people I am talking to, and the better I know them, the less I have to explain myself in detail, just to make sure there is no chance of any misunderstanding (ibid).

The autoethnographic, qualitative nature of Dans's reflections on the nature of self-censorship on social media contrasts with the quantitative data gathered by Das and Kramer (2013). Through data provided by Facebook, their study attempts to capture the extent to which users of Facebook self-censor at the 'last minute' (2013: 120). Their study defines self-censorship in this social media environment as the failure to post a status update that has been drafted. However, this is a questionable definition, as a user might opt not to post an update for a host of reasons other than self- censorship – such as lack of time, the realisation of multiple mistakes of grammar or spelling etc. However, in a similar manner to Dans's notion of self-censorship being a means of digital 'survival', Das and Kramer introduce the concept of how self-censorship on social media can preserve a user's 'social capital' by not alienating their online friends, or at least a subset of them.

As Hampton et al. (2014) discuss, the hope of some social media pioneers was that the proliferation of digital platforms would open the channels of communication so that those holding minority views would be willing to voice their opinions, in a way that they had not been in the pre-internet era due to the 'spiral of silence' phenomenon. The spiral of silence tendency refers to people's reluctance to publicly air their views on policy issues when they think their view is a minority opinion. However, research by the Pew Center in the United States has provided evidence that the internet has achieved no such thing. The research, which consisted of a survey of more than 1,800 adults, concluded that the growth of social media platforms had not reduced the spiral of silence tendency and that people are less willing to discuss policy issues on social media than they are in person. Moreover, in both face-to-face and digital settings, people are more prepared to share their views if they believe their audience will be in agreement (ibid).

It is important to make the distinction between censorship of *facts* and censorship of *opinions*. Research into the extent of self-censorship among the general public can implicitly focus on self-censorship of opinion (Das and Kramer 2013; Hampton et al. 2014), while research into self-censorship by the media often – again implicitly – focuses on self-censorship of facts (Preston 2009; Sefiha 2010), although not always (Rose 2006; Sturges 2008). But what constitutes the greater wrong – censorship or self-censorship? Sturges is unequivocal. He contends that self-censorship is 'much more insidious' because 'if others suppress our freedom of expression it is bad, but if we allow ourselves to censor our own opinions it is worse' (2008: 256). Such a position is implicit in the argument of Flemming Rose, culture editor of Danish newspaper *Jyllands-Posten*, who oversaw the publication of the cartoons of the Prophet Mohammed that resulted in death threats. Explaining his reasoning behind the publication of the contentious cartoons he wrote:

> I commissioned the cartoons in response to several incidents of self-censorship in Europe caused by widening fears and feelings of intimidation in dealing with issues related to Islam. Our goal was simply to push back self-imposed limits on expression that seemed to be closing in tighter (Rose 2006).

The notion of resisting 'self-imposed' limits in order to express a view is in the Millian tradition. Biting one's tongue for the sake of 'survival' (Dans 2014) or in order to foster 'social capital' (Das and Kramer 2013) would be anathema to Mill. While arguments in *On liberty* suggest that he would probably regard a phenomenon such as the spiral of silence as a naturally occurring one given humankind's innate intolerance (Mill 1989: 17), he would not regard it as inevitable but, instead, a symptom of the fact that the roots of tolerance in society were not extending deeply enough. Contemporary manifestations of censorship and self-censorship, and the appropriate response to them, are thus potentially amenable to a Mill-inspired analysis. This paper now turns to the most powerful concept that Mill offers those who seek to understand current issues of free expression.

THE HARM PRINCIPLE REVISITED

Mill's position on freedom of expression flows from what has become known as his Harm Principle, a deceptively simple ethical proposition which has generated much debate regarding its practical application. The principle states that 'The only purpose for which power can be rightfully exercised over any member of a civilised community, against his will, is to prevent harm to others' (ibid: 13). Mill makes this statement because of an absolute commitment to self-determination, in so far as that autonomy does not harmfully affect others. 'Over himself, over his own body and mind, the individual is sovereign' (ibid).

Since the essay was first published, critics have claimed that it is bogus to suggest there is a workable distinction between actions that affect only the individual agent and actions that affect others. The history of this line of argument is well-documented by Rees (2012), who quotes a leading article from *The Times Literary Supplement* of 10 July 1948:

> The greater part of English history since his [Mill's] day has been a practical commentary on the fallacy of this distinction. No action, however intimate, is free from social consequence. No human being can say that what he is, still less what he does, affects no one but himself (ibid: 171-172).

Whether or not the distinction between purely private actions or other-regarding actions can be soundly drawn is a question that goes to the heart of debates about liberal versus conservative approaches to social policy. But the distinction does have a plausibility to it, a plausibility which Mill helps establish by differentiating between 'definite' damage and 'contingent' damage. No man should be punished for simply being drunk, he argues, but a policeman, for example, should face legal and social sanction for being drunk on duty because there is 'a definite damage, or a definite risk of damage, either to an individual or to the public' (1989: 82). But where there is 'contingent' injury, by which Mill means behaviour that does not breach a specific public duty or cause hurt to anyone but himself, 'the inconvenience is one which society can afford to bear, for the sake of the greater good of human freedom' (ibid).

'Damage' here is being used as a synonym for 'harm', and in providing an analysis of contemporary issues relating to freedom of expression it is vital there is lexical precision. The key distinction that needs to be drawn is between 'harm' (or 'damage') and 'offence', and it has been argued that another important distinction is that between freedom of speech and freedom of the press. Cammaerts (2015) contends that the two freedoms are not equivalent, with freedom of the press arguably carrying a greater burden of social responsibility than the former. He further argues that freedom of expression 'is not necessarily a primary right in all circumstances, it has to be balanced out with other rights and protections, for example the right not to be discriminated against, the right not to be racially abused' and uses the concept 'Intricate Freedom' to capture the complexity surrounding free expression (ibid). It is a contention of this paper that, while freedom of expression is, indeed, intricate in this way, a Mill-inspired delineation of the distinctions between offence and harm continues to provide a useful frame through which to disentangle debates around freedom of expression.

Frost describes the issue of harm and offence as one of 'constant controversy', contending that freedom of expression 'must include the right to offend, but does it include the right to harm, and when does offence turn to harm?' (Frost 2016: 198). Underpinning Frost's question is the issue of how exactly we define 'harm'. But despite the clear need for precision in drawing distinctions between harm and offence, the line between the two concepts still often appears blurred. For example, in a recent study of how members of the public understand offence (Das and Graefer 2016) the authors write:

> On the one hand are those who champion free speech, who argue that we all have the right (some say, the duty) to express sometimes unpopular opinions without fear of censure. On the other are those who say that with that right comes a responsibility not to needlessly offend. For many who take this latter viewpoint, mocking religious symbols of two religions equally may seem equivalent on paper. But if one of those religions links to a culture, and very often an ethnicity, that already faces widespread discrimination and hardship, then perhaps free speech has crossed the line into offensiveness (ibid).

The use of the word 'offensiveness' here is confused with 'harm' or 'harmfulness'. Free speech does not 'cross a line' into offensiveness; offensiveness is part of the sphere in which free speech is deployed – the ability to say things that offend is what makes speech 'free'. The line that should be avoided being crossed is the line into harmfulness. Das and Graefer (2016) later acknowledge this when they write that 'the umbrella of "harmful and offensive material" needs more nuanced, focused and critical research'. But where does the distinction between the two lie, and what sort of harm is it that justifies restriction on free expression? Mill adopts a hard line on this point.

Steel believes Mill sets a high threshold for the circumstances in which the state can legitimately restrict freedom of speech. This is because, on his reading, harm is understood by Mill to mean a physical hurt; perceived emotional or mental 'harm' are not sufficient to justify restriction.

> For Mill, these circumstances are those in which life and liberty come under an imminent threat of harm. ... Harm here ... is understood as physical assault or at least the threat of assault on a person or property. As such for Mill, the limits of freedom of speech are very specific indeed (Steel 2012: 22).

Collini, too, sets the threshold high, summarising Mill's position as being one where the only legitimate ground for restricting a person's activities is that they 'are likely to produce *definite* harm to some *identifiable* other person or persons' (Collini 1989, xiv, my emphasis). The adjectives 'definite' and 'identifiable' are important here. On Collini's reading of the Harm Principle, vague notions of possible harm being caused to some potential group or other are not acceptable to justify state interference in individual behaviour. The harm needs to be clear and specific. Mill's principle might not always allow immediate, definite conclusions to be drawn about the rightness or wrongness of societal interference over individual behaviour. But Mill's point is that the onus of proof for the occurrence of harm lies with the institution or person proposing the restriction (ibid: xvii).

Mill's arguments here relating to harm and freedom of expression are not conclusive for the simple reason that what should be meant by 'harm' can be – and is – contested, for all the attempts at lexical precision. Cohen-Almagor believes Mill deals with the limits of free speech in a 'hasty' manner, claiming that, like other philosophers in the liberal tradition, including Milton, Dewey and Rawls, he wants to focus on 'principles, not the exceptions to them' (2005: 15-16), while Berlin alleges that 'rigour in argument is not among his [Mill's] accomplishments' (2012: 145). However, even Mill's critics, such as Cohen-Almagor, who argue that hurt should in some cases encompass emotional impact (or 'offense to sensibilities'), frame their position in Millian terms, as when Cohen-Almagor states that 'generally speaking – there is a need to strike a balance between the right to freedom of expression and harms that result from a certain speech. It is argued that the right to exercise free expression does not include the right to do unjustifiable harm to others' (2005: 6). Despite 'harm' and 'offence' remaining contested terms, it remains the case that Mill frames the debate with clarity.

'EXPERIMENTS IN LIVING' AND THE PARADOX OF LIBERAL INHERITANCE

Through *On liberty*'s espousal of diversity, toleration and support of dissenting voices, Mill produced arguably the most powerful credo of modern liberal thinking (Berlin 2012; Collini 1989). This credo helped set the intellectual and social climate that has since enabled previously oppressed groups – women, LBGT people and people from black and ethnic minorities – to benefit from both progressive legislation and changing social views; it is no coincidence that Mill, eight years after the publication of *On liberty*, proposed an (unsuccessful) amendment to the Reform Bill that would have extended the franchise to women (Collini 1989: xxviii). Mill, as the arch-proponent of the right to dissent, is committed to the right for people to conduct their 'experiments in living' provided those experiments do not harm others.

Yet some of the beneficiaries of Mill's intellectual inheritance – universities and their unions – now seek to stifle some of the central tenets of *On liberty*. This is the Paradox of Liberal Inheritance. The City University students' union motion discussed above, and the no-platforming of controversial speakers at universities, is not only contrary to the spirit of *On liberty* but in outright contradiction. 'If all mankind minus one, were of one opinion, and only one person were of the contrary opinion, mankind would be no more justified in silencing that one person, than he, if he had the power, would be justified in silencing mankind' (Mill 1989: 20). This is a statement by Mill, the arch-liberal. But how many professed liberals would concur with the statement now? Is it, as Bromwich suggests (2016), too liberal a sentiment for contemporary liberals to swallow? This points to the radical nature of *On liberty*, a radicalness that is sometimes overlooked. Mill is opposed to tyranny in all its forms: the tyranny of the state and the tyranny of the law, but also the tyranny of public opinion. From the following passage, it is more than tempting to think that Mill would view the modern campus as a form of tyranny.

> Protection, therefore, against the tyranny of the magistrate is not enough: there needs protection also against the tyranny of the prevailing opinion and feeling; against the tendency of society to impose, by other means than civil penalties, its own ideas and practices as rules of conduct on those who dissent from them; to fetter the development, and, if possible, prevent the formation, of any individuality not in harmony with its ways, and compel all characters to fashion themselves upon the model of its own (1989: 8).

Mill has a tonic – or perhaps, rather, a challenge – for the students' union and the no-platformers: if you cannot defend your position in the teeth of challenge and contradiction from those whose views you disagree with or even detest, then you do not know the grounds for your position. If you cannot stand up and defend your position then your belief is little better than a superstition; an unsupported tenet drifting about in the intellectual ether. It is a prejudice, underpinned by no understanding or rational basis. 'There is the greatest difference between presuming an opinion to be true, because, with every opportunity for contesting it, it has not been refuted, and assuming its truth for the purpose of not permitting its refutation' (1989: 23). Mill, therefore, serves to provide an electric shock for debates about freedom of expression on campus. *On liberty* also challenges professed liberals to ponder what it truly means to be a liberal.

WHY SHOULD MEDIA STUDENTS STUDY MILL?

Mill's ideas can challenge thinking on campus in another way. Through his arguments about what constitutes harm, Mill is a powerful lens through which today's media students – tomorrow's custodians of the flow of information – can debate the limits of freedom of expression and regulation, and as such a strong case can be made for his works being a cornerstone for classes on media ethics. *On liberty* is not the only work of Mill's to consider in this regard. His *Utilitarianism* (Mill 2011 [1861]) and its refined version of the 'greatest happiness of the greatest number' principle (Gray 2012) is another work that provides an accessible ethical principle from which questions of media ethics can be approached.

There are two other reasons why it is important to use Mill as a means of teaching ethics to students. As a committed reformer and progressive, the starting point of Mill's thinking in many ways chimes with the instinctive intellectual position of many students. Among other causes, Mill argued in favour of votes for women, for the right of public meeting in Hyde Park and for proportional representation (Berlin 2012: 137). Explaining this to students can serve to make Mill seem real and relevant – and therefore worth a listen. Moreover, Mill informs the etiquette and ethics of intellectual debate. Students have been accused of belonging to 'Generation Snowflake' and of 'melting' at the slightest challenge to their opinions (Fox 2016). But Mill presents powerful arguments for why opinions should be held up to ongoing and vigorous scrutiny, and these arguments can be used to emphasise the importance of lively debate in the classroom. Mill believes that it is necessary for even the most secure and sacrosanct beliefs to be held up to scrutiny, otherwise the meaning of such doctrines becomes 'enfeebled', and the risk is that 'living beliefs' become 'dead dogma' (1989: 37). 'Both teachers and learners go to sleep at their post, as soon as there is no enemy in the field' (ibid: 44). Mill is also wary of how the call for 'fair discussion' is open to abuse by being used to shut down vigorous debate. This Millian point has arisen more recently with concerns that pleas for 'civility' in intellectual debate are potentially tantamount to shutting down that debate (Bromwich 2016). Considering the proposition that there should be freedom of opinion on the condition that the delivery should 'not pass the bounds of fair discussion', Mill is cautious.

> Much might be said on the importance of fixing where these supposed bounds are to be placed; for if the test be offence to those whose opinion is attacked, I think experience testifies that this offence is given whenever the attack is telling and powerful, and that every opponent who pushes them hard, and whom they find it difficult to answer, appears to them, if he shows any strong feeling on the subject, an intemperate opponent (1989: 54).

As such, Mill has much to say about the tone of healthy debate as much as the content of healthy debate.

MILL AND ALETHIC DISRUPTION

Earlier, this paper identified and elaborated on two aspects to Mill's thinking in *On liberty*. Firstly, the notion that stifling free expression is potentially a transgenerational wrong and, secondly, how intolerance – and therefore the restriction of free speech – is the default condition of mankind. The paper also invoked the concept of alethic disruption to describe and account for the spread of 'fake news', affective news and misinformation. Having discussed the application of Mill's arguments to issues of censorship and self-censorship, the paper now ends with a suggestion of how a Millian approach can be applied to the regulation of information in a 'post-truth' era. This argument builds on points made by Jarvis (2016a, 2016b).

As has been discussed, Mill sets a high threshold for what constitutes harm. If an action will cause a physical harm, or in all reasonable likelihood cause a physical harm, to a specific individual or group, then the action can be restricted on that basis. While some malicious items of fake news that equate to incitement might be restricted under this criterion, most would not. To censor such content could be to raise the spectre of a return to the 'default condition of mankind'. Indeed, the presence of falsehood is sometimes welcomed by Mill as a means of jolting truth into life (Mill 1989: 44). But how should the spread of bogus information and demagoguery be countered? For Mill, the answer would be to pro-actively question the falsehoods; to demand that evidence and opinion be given to back them up. Vigorous questioning, after all, is how Mill believes we are able to keep alive 'a living truth' rather than allowing such statements to ossify into 'dead dogma' (ibid: 37).

A Millian approach would, therefore, be to take on the purveyors of misinformation in their own arena; to take to the social media platforms with facts. As Jarvis puts it, the answer is to 'flood the zone with good information' (2016a) rather than seeking to censor what is misinformation. But to do this, journalists can no longer just produce content in traditional column inches or long-form articles on web pages, otherwise they – and their fact-checking endeavours – face irrelevance. Instead, traditional media 'must adapt to their new reality and bring their journalism – their facts, fact-checking, reporting, explanation and context – to the public where the public is, in a form and voice that is appropriate to the context and use of each platform' (Jarvis 2016b). This means utilising memes, GIFs, video and other online techniques that engage social media users. Jarvis contends that it is impossible to play 'Whac-A-Mole' with inaccurate information, by which he means scouring the web and trying to delete each and every piece of bogus content when it pops up.

> Instead of mourning the creation of fake-news memes and putting the onus on Facebook to kill them… we should be pouring out our own truth memes – with facts, fact-checking, context, explanation, education, reporting, watch-dogging: journalism, in short. We should be arming fair-minded, intelligent, curious, rational, fact-loving citizens … with the weapons, the truth bullets, to fire at will in their conversations. They won't win all the wars but they will win some fact battles alongside us if only we enable them (Jarvis 2016b).

Although Jarvis does not mention Mill in his argument it is, nonetheless, Millian with its emphasis on truth doing battle in an unrestricted market place of ideas. As such, it is another illustration of how Mill's legacy continues to indirectly inform contemporary issues of free expression.

CONCLUSION

Despite writing in Victorian times, Mill outlines positions and arguments that modern academe can usefully ponder amid concerns over on-campus censorship and self-censorship more widely. This paper has suggested that, while contentious in its application in particular instances, the Harm Principle remains a powerful starting point for contemporary debates about free expression. Moreover, it has been argued that Mill articulates principles that modern media students can use as an accessible means of approaching questions of media ethics. He also makes powerful points about the etiquette of intellectual debate. In addition, it has been argued that Mill's vision for a liberal society and the implications of that liberal creed on free expression pose challenging questions for those who currently profess to be liberals. Despite his arguments having been made more than a century-and-a-half ago, the paper has explored how Mill speaks engagingly to current debates over freedom of expression.

- This paper was first published in *Ethical Space*, Vol. 14, No. 1 pp 15-25

REFERENCES

Ali, A. (2016) Student-led #Right2Debate campaign calls for universities to 'challenge', not ban, controversial speakers, *Independent*, 26 February. Available online at http://www.independent.co.uk/student/news/student-led-right2debate-campaign-calls-for-universities-to-challenge-not-ban-controversial-speakers-a6898341.html, accessed on 31 October 2016

Berlin, I. (2012) John Stuart Mill and the ends of life, Gray, J. and Smith, G. W. (eds) *J. S. Mill's* On liberty *in focus*, London, Taylor and Francis pp 131-161

Bromwich, D. (2016) What are we allowed to say?, *London Review of Books*, 22 September

Cammaerts, B. (2015) *Charlie Hebdo* and the Other within, 1 December. Available online at http://eprints.lse.ac.uk/63807/1/blogs.lse.ac.uk-Charlie%20Hebdo%20and%20the%20Other%20Within%20 guest%20blog.pdf, accessed on 8 November 2016

Cohen-Almagor, R. (2006) *The scope of tolerance: Studies on the costs of free expression and freedom of the press*, Abingdon, Routledge

Collini, S. (1989) Introduction in *On liberty*, Cambridge, Cambridge University Press pp vii-xvi

Das, R. and Graefer, A. (2016) What really makes something offensive? *The Conversation*, 2 November. Available online at http://theconversation.com/what-really-makes-something-offensive-66706?utm_medium=email&utm_campaign=Latest%20from%20The%20Conversation%20for%20November%202%202016%20-%205948&utm_content=Latest%20from%20The%20Conversation%20for%20November%202%202016%20-%205948+CID_8b928484999677706a6a7eec158afdce&utm_source=campaign_moni-tor_uk&utm_term=What%20really%20makes%20something%20 offensive, accessed on 9 November 2016

Das, S. and Kramer, A. (2013) Self-censorship on Facebook, *Proceedings of the Seventh International AAAI Conference on Weblogs and Social Media* pp 120-127. Available online at http://www.aaai.org/ocs/index.php/ICWSM/ICWSM13/paper/viewFile/6093/6350, accessed on 1 March 2016

Dans, E. (2014) Social networks and self-censorship, *medium.com*, 28 August. Available online at https://medium.com/enrique-dans/social-networks-and-self-censorship-f78401980ce1#.nv02j8nut, accessed on 20 September 2016

Davies, N. (2008) *Flat earth news*, London, Chatto & Windus

Fox, C. (2016) Generation Snowflake: How we train our kids to be censorious cry-babies, *Spectator*, 4 June. Available online at http://www.spectator.co.uk/2016/06/generation-snowflake-how-we-train-our-kids-to-be-censorious-cry-babies/, accessed on 29 November 2016

Frost, C. (2016) *Media ethics and regulation*, Abingdon, Routledge, fourth edition

Garton Ash, T. (2016) *Free speech: Ten principles for a connected world*, London, Atlantic

Gray, J. (2012) Mill's conception of happiness and the theory of individuality, Gray, J. and Smith, G. W. (eds) *J. S. Mill's* On liberty *in focus*, London, Taylor and Francis pp 190-211

Hampton, K., Raine, L., Lu, W. et al. (2014) *Social media and the 'spiral of silence'*. Report by Pew Research Center, 26 August. Available online at http://www.pewinternet.org/2014/08/26/social-media-and-the-spiral-of-silence/, accessed on 22 September 2016

Hermida, A. (2016) Trump and why emotion triumphs over fact when everyone is the media, *The Conversation*, 16 November. Available online at http://theconversation.com/trump-and-why-emotion-triumphs-over-fact-when-everyone-is-the-media-68924, accessed on 20 November 2016

Hume, M. (2015) *Trigger warning: Is the fear of being offensive killing free speech?* London, William Collins

Jarvis, J. (2016a) Fake news: Be careful what you wish for, *medium.com*, 14 November. Available online at https://medium.com/whither-news/fake-news-be-careful-what-you-wish-for-7246da863a40#.9zo0t2h1q, accessed on 20 November 2016

Jarvis, J. (2016b) A call for cooperation against fake news, *medium.com*, 18 November. Available online at https://medium.com/whither-news/a-call-for-cooperation-against-fake-news-d7d94bb6e0d4#.dx71xtdcw, accessed on 20 November 2016

Knight, M. (2013) *Social media for journalists: Principles and practice*, London, Sage

Kohut, A. (2000) Self-censorship: Counting the ways, *Columbia Journalism Review*, Vol. 39, No. 1 (May/June) pp 41-43

McEwan, I. (2016) *Nutshell*, London, Jonathan Cape

Mill, J. S. (1989) On liberty *and other writings*, Cambridge, Cambridge University Press

Mill, J. S. (2011 [1861]) *Utilitarianism*, London, Broadview

Milton, J. (1973 [1644]) *Areopagitica: A speech for the liberty of unlicensed printing*, Cambridge, Deighton, Bell & Co

Nelson, F. (2016) The value of our threatened free press is the real Sam Allardyce exposé, *Daily Telegraph*, 29 September. Available online at http://www.telegraph.co.uk/news/2016/09/29/the-value-of-our-threatened-free-press-is-the-real-sam-allardyce/, accessed on 29 November 2016

O'Rourke, K. C. (2003) *John Stuart Mill and freedom of expression: The genesis of a theory*, Abingdon, Taylor and Francis

Preston, P. (2009) *Making the news: Journalism and news cultures in Europe*, Abingdon, Routledge

Rees, J. C. (2012) A re-reading of Mill's *On liberty*, Gray, J. and Smith, G.W. (eds) *J. S. Mill's* On liberty *in focus*, London, Taylor and Francis pp 169-189

Rose, F. (2006) Why I published those cartoons, *washingtonpost.com*, 19 February. Available online at http://www.washingtonpost.com/wp-dyn/content/article/2006/02/17/AR2006021702499.html, accessed on 4 November 2015

Ryan, A. (2012) John Stuart Mill's art of living, Gray, J. and Smith, G.W. (eds) *J. S. Mill's* On liberty *in focus*, London, Taylor and Francis pp 162-168

Scruton, R. (2015) Why we should defend the right to be offensive, *BBC News Magazine*, 25 October. Available online at http://www.bbc.co.uk/news/magazine-34613855, accessed on 16 November 2016

Scruton, R. (2016) Self-censorship and the loss of reasoned argument, *eurozine.com*, 2 March. Available online at http://www.eurozine.com/articles/2016-02-03-scruton-en.html, accessed on 16 November 2016

Sedler, R. (2012) Self censorship and the First Amendment. Available online at http://scholarship.law.nd.edu/cgi/viewcontent.cgi?article=1042&context=ndjlepp, accessed on 4 November 2015

Sefiha, O. (2010) Now's when we throw him under the bus: Institutional and occupational identities and the coverage of doping in sport, *Sociology of Sport Journal*, Vol. 27 pp 200-218

Slater, T. (2016) The epidemic of campus censorship, *spiked-online*. Available online at http://www.spiked-online.com/free-speech-university-rankings#.WBe4DTvPzq, accessed on 31 October 2016

Smith, A. (2016) The pedlars of fake news are corroding democracy, *Guardian*, 25 November. Available online at https://www.theguardian.com/commentisfree/2016/nov/25/pedlars-fake-news-corroding-democracy-social-networks, accessed on 30 November 2016

Steel, J. (2012) *Journalism and free speech*, Abingdon, Routledge

Sturges, P. (2008) Save police time, beat yourself up: The problem of self-censorship. Available online at http://edoc.hu-berlin.de/conferences/bobcatsss2008/sturges-paul-256/PDF/sturges.pdf, accessed on 3 November 2015

Sweney, M. and Jackson, J. (2016) City University students vote for campus ban on *Sun*, *Mail* and *Express*, *Guardian*, 18 November. Available online at https://www.theguardian.com/media/2016/nov/18/city-university-students-vote-for-campus-ban-sun-daily-mail-express, accessed on 23 November 2016

Viner, K. (2016) How technology disrupted the truth, *Guardian*, 12 July. Available online at https://www.theguardian.com/media/2016/jul/12/how-technology-disrupted-the-truth, accessed on 2 November 2016

Yuhas, A. (2016) Facebook announces new push against fake news after Obama comments, *Guardian*, 19 November. Available online at https://www.theguardian.com/technology/2016/nov/19/facebook-fake-news-mark-zuckerberg, accessed on 21 November 2016

NOTE ON THE CONTRIBUTOR

Dr Tom Bradshaw is Associate Professor of Media Ethics and Practice at the University of Gloucestershire and Employer Engagement and Employability Lead in the School of Creative Industries. Joint editor of *Ethical Space: The International Journal of Communication Ethics*, he is the joint author of *Sports journalism: The state of play* (Routledge, 2019). He studied philosophy at the University of Cambridge and then journalism at the University of Central Lancashire before becoming a news and sports journalist. He has worked as a print, online and radio journalist for organisations across the UK and South Africa. He currently works as a freelance journalist and broadcaster for the BBC and *The Times*, among others, and has contributed to *The Times Literary Supplement*. His research interests include uses of technology in education and media ethics, particularly self-censorship.

Chapter 3

Towards 'mindful journalism': Applying Buddhism's Eightfold Path as an ethical framework for modern journalism

Mark Pearson

Religious codes of morality have informed professional ethical principles, particularly with regard to fairness, truth and honesty. Buddhism has a growing relevance in Western societies, prompted by migration and a developing interest in Eastern religions and philosophies. This paper considers Buddhism's 'Noble Eightfold Path' and explores its applicability to Fourth Estate journalism in the modern era. It takes each of its elements – understanding free of superstition, kindly and truthful speech, right conduct, doing no harm, perseverance, mindfulness and contemplation – and uses modern examples to illustrate their potential usefulness to the journalist seeking to practise responsible truth-seeking and truth-telling. It assesses whether such an approach would allow the reporting of such topics as celebrity gossip and official corruption and examines the ethics of subterfuge, deception and treatment of vulnerable sources in this light.

Keywords: journalism, ethics, Buddhism, mindful journalism, philosophy, Eightfold Path

INTRODUCTION

This paper explores the possibility of applying the fundamental precepts of one of the world's major religions to the practice of truth-seeking and truth-telling in the modern era and asks whether that ethical framework is compatible with journalism as a Fourth Estate enterprise. The recent inquiries into media ethics and regulation in the UK, Australia and New Zealand have necessarily involved a deeper exploration of the role of the news media in society and appropriate press regulatory systems to control the ethical behaviour of journalists. These have prompted a re-examination of sacrosanct principles such as 'freedom of the press' and 'free expression', particularly in the context of converged and globalised communications and the damaged economic foundations of the so-called 'legacy' media. They have also forced a questioning of the morality of news reporting as a profit-making business model in the light of the unethical and illegal practices that prompted the closure of the *News of the World* and the Leveson Inquiry (2012).

It is broadly accepted that religious codes of morality have informed professional ethical principles, particularly with regard to fairness, truth and honesty. Buddhism has a growing relevance in former majority Anglo-Saxon societies, prompted by migration and a developing interest in Eastern religions and philosophies expressed by Western citizens. This paper considers Buddhism's 'Noble Eightfold Path' and explores its applicability to Fourth Estate journalism in the modern era. It takes each of its elements – understanding free of superstition, kindly and truthful speech, right conduct, doing no harm, perseverance, mindfulness and contemplation – and uses modern examples to illustrate their potential usefulness to the journalist or blogger seeking to practise responsible truth-seeking and truth-telling. It asks whether such an approach would allow the reporting of such topics as celebrity gossip and official corruption and examines the ethics of subterfuge, deception and treatment of vulnerable sources in this light.

THE PROBLEM: THE NEED FOR A NEW PERSPECTIVE

Journalism ethics has been viewed through many lenses, but most of the developed world's approach has drawn upon the thinking of Western philosophers and statesmen from the United States and the United Kingdom in the post-Gutenberg era. The very concept of the 'Fourth Estate' embodies Western libertarian notions espoused by such thinkers as John Milton (1608-1674), Thomas Jefferson (1743-1826) and John Stuart Mill (1806-1873), often stemming from government attempts to license and muzzle the press.

Gunaratne (2005: 81-82) demonstrated how the originators of the *Four theories of the press* (Siebert, Peterson and Schramm 1963) anchored their theories firmly in Western philosophical thought and political history. They categorised press systems into 'authoritarian', 'libertarian', 'Soviet-Communist' or 'social responsibility'.

Even their 'social responsibility theory', which added an ethical dimension of social consciousness (to temper the 'publish and be damned' approach of their libertarian theory) was drawn from the report of the Commission on the Freedom of the Press (Hutchins 1947). Others have criticised the Siebert approach for its simplicity and outdatedness, with Denis McQuail (1987) adding two further categories: the development model and the democratic-participant model. Social responsibility theory in the mid-20th century added an ethical dimension to the basic libertarian theory and the concept of 'development journalism theory' evolved in Asia over the past 30 years seemed to excuse government intervention in press activities in the interests of national economic growth and societal stability (Dutt 2010: 90).

There have been many developments of such theories over the past six decades, most of which have also been Western-centric, and it is not surprising that even most recent reviews of media regulation in the UK (Leveson 2012), Australia (Finkelstein 2012) and New Zealand (Law Commission 2012) were driven by Western approaches to media given their briefs to review the mechanisms in place in those jurisdictions. Each of them found shortcomings with the *status quo* libertarian approach to publishing at any cost. The Finkelstein report detailed the shortcomings of the libertarian model and the refinements of the social responsibility model in its second chapter 'The democratic indispensability of a free press' (Finkelstein 2012: 23-54). That inquiry decided there was a 'gulf' between the ethical standards of the news media and those of the public, a perception central to the actions of the *News of the World* and other London tabloids that triggered the Leveson inquiry in the UK: 'In particular, there is a wide difference in what the media and the public consider ethically acceptable concerning privacy and deception' (ibid: 124).

This necessitates a discussion of the ethical frameworks for journalism impacting upon the ways in which journalists investigate, report and comment upon news. Communication scholars' theories of press systems provide mechanisms to help us contextualise journalism ethics and to help explain why actual media laws and regulatory frameworks condone or prohibit certain news media practices. However, those very ethical codes of practice were born of an Anglo-American approach to journalism, shaped largely by the libertarian positioning of the press in those countries (truth, the public's right to know and source confidentiality) and refined somewhat by the social responsibility pressures of the latter half of the twentieth century (with concerns over privacy and discrimination).

The problem is that a predominantly Western libertarian model of journalism and its accompanying ethical guidelines may be an anachronism in a 21st-century context of an increasingly globalised media era where large scale immigration has forced cultural re-evaluation within former colonial powers, traditional media are commercially vulnerable, and Web 2.0 has put publishing technology in the hands of millions who do not ascribe to journalistic values. In such a changed context, where do we turn for guidance in reinventing journalism ethics to accommodate more universally accepted cultural values and new publishers or 'citizen journalists'?

Useful work has been conducted in this regard. Romano (2010) has considered journalism practices and ethics in an international context with her compilation of models of civic engagement. This builds upon decades of important contributions by Jay Rosen in the field of 'public journalism' (Rosen 1999) and 'citizen journalism' (Rosen 2003-2013) and by numerous others in the domain of 'peace journalism' (Galtung and Ruge 1965; Lynch 2010) and its application to other cultures (Robie 2011). These hold great promise and are, indeed, complementary to the attempt here to map a new ethical framework of 'mindful journalism' which might be applied by anyone with a motivation to incorporate core human moral values into their truth-seeking and truth-telling endeavours – whether journalists, citizen journalists or bloggers – reporting in times of peace or conflict, at home or abroad.

WHY BUDDHISM'S EIGHTFOLD PATH?

Professional ethical codes are not religious treatises, and holy scriptures were not spoken or written as codes of practice for any particular occupation. This paper aims to build upon the work of Gunaratne (2005, 2007 and 2009) to explore whether the foundational teachings of one religion focused upon living a purer life – Buddhism – might inform journalism practice. At some junctures it becomes apparent that some elements of the libertarian model of journalism as we know it might not even be compatible with such principles – particularly if they are interpreted narrowly. The teachings of other religions might also be applied in this way. Within Christianity (via the *Bible*), Islam (the *Koran*), Hinduism (the *Bhagavad Gita*), Judaism (the *Torah*) and the Confucian canon you can find common moral and ethical principles journalists might reasonably be expected to follow in their work, including attributes of peace journalism identified by Lynch (2010: 543): oriented towards peace, humanity, truth and solutions. The Dalai Lama's book – *Beyond religion: Ethics for a whole world* (2011) – explored his vision of how core ethical values might offer a sound moral framework for modern society while accommodating diverse religious views and cultural traditions. It is in that spirit that this paper explores the possibilities of applying some of Buddhism's core principles to the secular phenomenon of journalism. It also must be accepted that Buddhist practices such as 'mindfulness' and meditation have been adopted broadly in Western society in recent decades and have been embraced by the cognitive sciences, albeit in adapted therapeutic ways (Segal et al. 2012).

The Noble Eightfold Path attributed to the Buddha – Siddhartha Gautama (563 BCE to 483 BCE – but disputed) – has been chosen because of its longevity as a moral code, its relative brevity and the fact that its core elements can be read at a secular level to relate to behavioural – and not exclusively spiritual – guidelines. Former *New York Times* reporter and blogger Doug McGill (2008) has suggested Buddhist ethics sit comfortably with journalism as an endeavour:

> Indeed, in its relentless quest to observe without filter or distortion the nature of daily human existence – the fact and flavor of the simple ordinary present, the living now – Buddhism seems, in a certain way, quintessentially journalistic.

Gunaratne (2005: 35) offered this succinct positioning of the Noble Eightfold Path (or the 'middle way') in Buddhist philosophy:

> The Buddhist *dharma* meant the doctrine based on the Four Noble Truths: That suffering exists; that the cause of suffering is thirst, craving, or desire; that a path exists to end suffering; that the Noble Eightfold Path

is the path to end suffering. Described as the 'middle way', it specifies the commitment to *sila* (right speech, action and livelihood), *samadhi* (right effort, mindfulness, and concentration) and *panna* (right understanding and thoughts).

It is also fruitful to explore journalism as a practice amidst the first two Noble Truths related to suffering (*dukkha*), and this is possible because they are accommodated within the first step of the Eightfold Path – 'right views'. The Fourth Noble Truth is also integrative. It states that the Noble Eightfold Path is the means to end suffering. Here we consider its elements as a potential framework for the ethical practice of journalism in this new era.

APPLICATION OF THE NOBLE EIGHTFOLD PATH TO ETHICAL JOURNALISM PRACTICE

Each of the constituent steps of the Noble Eightfold Path – understanding free of superstition, kindly and truthful speech, right conduct, doing no harm, perseverance, mindfulness and contemplation – has an application to the modern-day practice of truth-seeking and truth-telling – whether that be by a journalist working in a traditional media context, a citizen journalist or a serious blogger reporting and commenting upon news and current affairs. Smith and Novak (2003: 39) identified a preliminary step to the Buddha's Noble Eightfold Path that he saw as a precondition to its pursuit – the practice of 'right association'. This, they explained, acknowledged the 'extent to which we are social animals, influenced at every turn by the "companioned example" of our associates, whose attitudes and values affect us profoundly' (ibid: 40).

For journalists this can apply at a number of levels. There is the selection of a suitable mentor, an ethical colleague who might be available to offer wise counsel in the midst of a workplace dilemma. There is also the need to acknowledge – and resist – the socialisation of journalism recruits into the toxic culture of newsrooms with unethical practices (McDevitt et al. 2002). Further, there is the imperative to reflect upon the potential for the 'pack mentality' of reportage that might allow for the combination of peer pressure, competition and poor leadership to influence the core morality of the newsgathering enterprise, as noted by Leveson (2012: 732) in his review of the ethical and legal transgressions by British newspaper personnel.

We will now concentrate on a journalistic reading of the steps of the Eightfold Path. Kalupahana (1976: 59) suggests its constituent eight factors represent a digest of 'moral virtues together with the processes of concentration and the development of insight'. Mizuno (1987: 160) argues that, although the precepts were originally portrayed as the path to liberation for a sage, they could apply equally to an ordinary person as guidelines for moral living.

RIGHT VIEWS

Smith and Novak (2003: 42) explained that the very first step in the Eightfold Path involved an acceptance of the Four Noble Truths. Suffice it to say that much of what we call 'news' – particularly that impacting on audiences through its reportage of change, conflict and consequence – can sit with Smith and Novak's (ibid: 33) definition of *dukkha*, namely 'the pain that to some degree colors all of finite existence'. Their explanation of the First Noble Truth – that life is suffering – is evident when we view the front page of each morning's newspaper and each evening's television news bulletin:

> The exact meaning of the First Noble Truth is this: Life currently is dislocated. Something has gone wrong. It is out of joint. As its pivot is not true, friction (interpersonal conflict) is excessive, movement (creativity) is blocked, and it hurts (ibid: 34).

This is at once an endorsement of accepted news values and a denial of the very concept of there being anything unusual about change. As Kalupahana (1976: 36) explains, a fundamental principle of Buddhism is that all things in the world are at once impermanent (*anicca*), unsatisfactory (*dukkha*) and nonsubstantial (*anatta*). News, too, is about the impermanent and the unsatisfactory. It is premised upon identifying to audiences what has changed most recently, focusing especially on the most unsatisfactory elements of that change. Yet given Buddhism's premise that all things are subject to change at all times and that happiness is achieved through the acceptance of this, it might well erode the newsworthiness of the latest upsetting accounts of change in the world since we last looked. In some ways this step supports the model of 'deliberative journalism' as explained by Romano (2010: 11), which encourages reports that are 'incisive, comprehensive and balanced', including the insights and contributions of all relevant stakeholders. Most importantly, as Romano suggests:

> Journalists would also report on communities as they evaluate potential responses, and then investigate whether and how they have acted upon the resulting decisions (ibid).

Thus, the notion of 'right views' can incorporate a contract between the news media and audiences that accepts a level of change at any time, and focuses intention upon deeper explanations of root causes, strategies for coping and potential solutions for those changes prompting the greatest suffering.

RIGHT INTENT

The second ingredient relates to refining and acting upon that very 'mission', 'calling' or drive to 'make a difference' which is the very human motivation for selecting some occupations. For some, it is a religious calling where they feel spiritually drawn to a vocation as a priest, an imam, a rabbi or a monk. But for others it is a secular drive to aid humanity by helping change society in a positive way – a career motivation shared by many teachers, doctors and journalists. It becomes the backbone to one's professional enterprise. Smith and Novak (2003: 42) describe it thus:

> People who achieve greatness are almost invariably passionately invested in some one thing. They do a thousand things each day, but behind these stands the one thing they count supreme. When people seek liberation with single-mindedness of this order, they may expect their steps to turn from sliding sandbank scrambles into ground-gripping strides.

In journalism, this might necessitate a change in mindset from bringing news 'first' in a competitive sense to 'best' and most meaningfully to an audience in a qualitative sense. Of course, it would not be 'news' if it were not delivered relatively soon after its occurrence, but in this era of instant communication this step reinforces the notion of 'responsible truth-seeking and truth-telling' – authoritative and credible news, obtained ethically, and delivered as soon as possible to retain its relevance and utility without losing its veracity.

RIGHT SPEECH

This step relates to both truthful and charitable expression and, interpreted narrowly, that second element of 'charitable expression' could present a fundamental challenge to the concept of journalism as we know it. It certainly poses serious questions about the celebrity gossip orientation of many news products today. The notion of telling the truth and being accurate lies at the heart of journalism practice and is foremost in most ethical codes internationally. While a single empirical fact might be subject to scientific measurement and verification, any conclusions drawn from the juxtaposition of two provable facts can only constitute what a scientist would call a 'theory' and the rest of us might call 'opinion'. In defamation law, collections of provable facts can indeed create a meaning – known as an 'imputation' – that can indeed be damaging to someone's reputation (Pearson and Polden 2011: 217). Thus, it becomes a question of which truths are selected to be told and the ultimate truth of their composite that becomes most relevant.

Smith and Novak (2003: 42) suggest falsities and uncharitable speech as indicative of other factors, most notably the ego of the communicator. In journalism, that ego might be fuelled in a host of ways that might encourage the selection of certain facts or the portrayal of an individual in a negative light: political agendas, feeding populist sentiment, peer pressure and corporate reward. They state:

> False witness, idle chatter, gossip, slander, and abuse are to be avoided, not only in their obvious forms, but also in their covert ones. The covert forms – subtle belittling, 'accidental' tactlessness, barbed wit – are often more vicious because their motives are veiled (ibid).

This calls into question the essence of celebrity journalism for all the obvious reasons. Gossip about the private lives of the rich and famous, titillating facts about their private lives and barbed commentary in social columns all fail the test of 'right speech' and, in their own way, reveal a great deal about the individual purveying them and their employer, discussed further below under 'right livelihood'. Taken to its extreme, however, much news might be considered 'uncharitable' and slanderous about an individual when it is, in fact, revealing their wrongdoing – all calling into question their public actions. If the Eightfold Path ruled out this element of journalism we would have to conclude it was incompatible even with the best of investigative and Fourth Estate journalism.

Indeed, many uncomfortable truths must be told even if one is engaging in a form of 'deliberative journalism' that might ultimately be for the betterment of society and disenfranchised people. For example, experts in 'peace journalism' include a 'truth orientation' as a fundamental ingredient of that approach, and include a determination 'to expose self-serving pronouncements and representations on all sides' (Lynch 2010: 543).

RIGHT CONDUCT

The fourth step of 'right conduct' goes to the core of any moral or ethical code. In fact, it contains the fundamental directives of most religions with its Five Precepts which prohibit killing, theft, lying, being unchaste and intoxicants (Smith and Novak 2003: 44). Many journalists would have problems with the final two, although the impact upon their work would of course vary with individual circumstances. And while many journalists might have joked that they would 'kill' for a story, murder is not a common or accepted journalistic tool. However, journalists have often had problems with the elements of theft and lying in their broad and narrow interpretations. The Leveson Report (2012) contains numerous examples of both, and the extension of the notion of 'theft' to practices such as plagiarism and of 'lying' to deception in its many guises have fuelled many adverse adjudications by ethics committees and courts.

Importantly, as Smith and Novak (2003: 43) explain, the step of right conduct also involves 'a call to understand one's behavior more objectively before trying to improve it' and 'to reflect on actions with an eye to the motives that prompted them'. This clearly invokes the strategic approach developed by educationalist Donald Schön, whose research aimed to equip professionals with the ability to make crucial decisions in the midst of practice. Schön (1987: 26) coined the expression 'reflection-in-action' to describe the ability of the professional to reflect upon some problem in the midst of their daily work. The approach was adapted to journalism by Sheridan Burns (2013: 76) who advised student journalists:

> You need a process for evaluating your decisions because a process, or system, lets you apply your values, loyalties and principles to every new set

of circumstances or facts. In this way, your decision making will be fair in choosing the news.

Even industry ethical codes can gain wider understanding and acceptance by appealing to fundamental human moral values and not just offering a proscriptive list of prohibited practices. A recent example is the *Fairfax media code of conduct* (undated) which poses questions employees might ask themselves when faced with ethical dilemmas that might not be addressed specifically in the document, including:

- Would I be proud of what I have done?
- Do I think it's the right thing to do?
- What will the consequences be for my colleagues, Fairfax, other parties and me?
- What would be the reaction of my family and friends if they were to find out?
- What would happen if my conduct was reported in a rival publication?

While this specific approach seems to focus on the potential for shame for a transgressor, it offers an example of a media outlet attempting to encourage its employees to pause and reflect in the midst of an ethical dilemma – what Schön (1987: 26) called 'reflection-in-action'. Such a technique might offer better guidance and might gain more traction if it were founded upon a socially and professionally acceptable moral or ethical scaffold, perhaps the kind of framework we are exploring here.

RIGHT LIVING

The Buddha identified certain livelihoods that were incompatible with a morally pure way of living, shaped of course by the cultural mores of his place and time. They included poison peddler, slave trader, prostitute, butcher, brewer, arms maker and tax collector (Smith and Novak 2003: 45). Some of these occupations might remain on his list today – but one can justifiably ask whether journalism would make his list in the aftermath of the revelations of the Leveson Inquiry (2012). That report did, of course, acknowledge the important role journalism should play in a democratic society, so perhaps the Buddha might have just nominated particular sectors of the media for condemnation. For example, the business model based upon celebrity gossip might provide an avenue for escape and relaxation for some consumers, but one has to wonder at the overall public good coming from such an enterprise. Given the very word 'occupation' implies work that 'does indeed occupy most of our waking attention' (Smith and Novak 2003: 44), we are left to wonder how the engagement in prying, intrusion and rumour-mongering for commercial purposes advances the enterprise of journalism or the personal integrity of an individual journalist who chooses to ply that trade.

The same argument applies to the sections of larger media enterprises who might sometimes produce journalism of genuine social value, but who on other occasions take a step too far with intrusion or gossip without any public benefit. This is where journalists working in such organisations might apply a mindful approach to individual stories and specific work practices to apply a moral gauge to the actual tasks they are performing in their work and in assessing whether they constitute 'right living'.

RIGHT EFFORT

The step of 'right effort' was directed by the Buddha in a predominantly spiritual sense – a steady, patient and purposeful path to enlightenment. However, we can also apply such principles to the goal of ethical journalism practice in a secular way. Early career journalists are driven to demonstrate success and sometimes mistake the hurried scoop and kudos of the lead story in their news outlet as an end in itself. There can also be an emphasis on productivity and output at the expense of the traditional hallmarks of quality reportage – attribution and verification. Of course, all news stories could evolve into lengthy theses if they were afforded unlimited timelines and budgets. Commercial imperatives and deadlines demand a certain brevity and frequency of output from all reporters. Both can be achieved with continued attention to the core principle of purposeful reflection upon the ethics of the various daily work tasks and a mindful awareness of the underlying mission – or backbone – of one's occupational enterprise – striving for the 'right intent' of the second step.

Institutional limitations and pressure from editors, reporters and sources will continually threaten a journalist's commitment to this ethical core, requiring the 'right effort' to be maintained at that steady, considered pace through every interview, every story, every working day and ultimately through a full career. As the Dalai Lama wrote in *Beyond religion* (2011: 142): 'The practice of patience guards us against loss of composure and, in doing so, enables us to exercise discernment, even in the heat of difficult situations.' Surely this is a useful attribute for the journalist.

RIGHT MINDFULNESS

This is the technique of self-examination that Schön (1987) and Sheridan Burns (2013) might call 'reflection in action' and is the step I have selected as central to an application of the Eightfold Path to reportage in the heading for this article – 'mindful journalism'. Effective reflection upon one's own thoughts and emotions is crucial to a considered review of an ethical dilemma in a newsgathering or publishing context. It is also essential to have gone through such a process if journalists are later called to account to explain their actions. Many ethical decisions are value-laden and inherently complex. Too often they are portrayed in terms of the 'public interest' when the core motivating factor has not been the greater public good but, to the contrary, the ego of an individual journalist or the commercial imperative of a media employer. Again, the Leveson Report (2012) detailed numerous instances where such forces were at play, often to the great detriment of the lives of ordinary citizens.

As Smith and Novak (2003: 48) explain, right mindfulness 'aims at witnessing all mental and physical events, including our emotions, without reacting to them, neither condemning some nor holding on to others'. Buddhists (and many others) adopt mindfulness techniques in the form of meditation practice – sometimes in extended guided retreats. The extent to which individuals might want to set aside time for meditation in their own routines is up to them, but at the very least there is much to be gained from journalists adopting the lay meaning of 'being mindful'. In other words, journalists might pause briefly for reflection upon the implications of their actions upon others – the people who are the subjects of their stories, other stakeholders who might be affected by the event or issue at hand, the effects upon their own reputations as journalists and the community standing of others, and the public benefits ensuing from this particular truth being told in this way at this time. Most ethical textbooks have flow charts with guidelines for journalists to follow in such situations – but the central question is whether they have an embedded technique for moral self-examination – a practised mindfulness they can draw upon when a circumstance demands.

There is a special need for journalists to be mindful of the vulnerabilities of some individuals they encounter in their work. Many have studied the interaction between the news media and particular 'vulnerable groups', such as people with a disability, those with a mental illness, children, the indigenous, the aged or those who have undergone a traumatic experience. For example, Pearson et al. (2010) reviewed that research and examined how journalists interacted with those who might belong to such a 'vulnerable group' or who might simply be 'vulnerable' because of the circumstances of the news event. They identified other types of sources who might be vulnerable in the midst or aftermath of a news event involving such a 'moment of vulnerability' and assessed the question of 'informed consent' to journalistic interviews by such individuals. Ethical journalists are mindful of such potential vulnerabilities and either look for alternative sources or take considered steps to minimise the impact of their reportage.

This concern for others also invokes the notion of compassion for other human beings, a tenet central to the teachings of all major religions, and a hallmark of Buddhism. The Dalai Lama has explained that it is often mistaken for a weakness or passivity, or 'surrender in the face of wrongdoing or injustice' (Dalai Lama 2011: 58). If that were the case, then it would be incompatible with Fourth Estate journalism which requires reporters to call to account those who abuse power or take unfair advantage of the system. However, the Dalai Lama explains that true compassion for others requires that sometimes we must do exactly that:

Depending on the context, a failure to respond with strong measures, thereby allowing the aggressors to continue their destructive behaviour, could even make you partially responsible for the harm they continue to inflict (ibid: 59).

Such an approach is perfectly compatible with the best of foreign correspondence and investigative journalism conducted in the public interest – and is well accommodated within the peace journalism model explained by Lynch (2010: 543).

RIGHT CONCENTRATION

Some have compared 'right concentration' to being in 'the zone' in elite sporting terminology – so focused on the work at hand that there is a distinctive clarity of purpose. Smith and Novak (2003: 48) explain that concentration exercises – often attentive to a single-pointed awareness of breathing – are a common prelude to mindfulness exercises during meditation. Initial attempts at concentration are inevitably shredded by distractions; slowly, however, attention becomes sharper, more stable, more sustained (ibid).

It is such concentrated attention that is required of consummate professionals in the midst of covering a major news event. At this time top journalists actually enter 'the zone' and are able to draw on core ethical values to produce important reportage and commentary within tight deadlines, paying due regard to the impact of their work upon an array of individual stakeholders and to the broader public interest. It is in this moment that it all comes together for the 'mindful journalist' – facts are verified, comments from a range of sources are attributed, competing values are assessed, angles are considered and decided and timing is judged. And it all happens within a cool concentrated focus, sometimes amidst the noise and mayhem of a frantic newsroom or a chaotic news event.

TOWARDS A SECULAR 'MINDFUL JOURNALISM'

This paper does not propose a definitive fix-all solution to the shortcomings in journalism ethics or their regulation. Rather, it is an acknowledgment that the basic teachings of one of the world's major religions can offer guidance in identifying a common – and secular – moral compass that might inform our journalism practice as technology and globalisation place our old ethical models under stress.

Leveson (2012) has identified the key ethical and regulatory challenges facing the British press and Finkelstein (2012) has documented the situation in Australia. One of the problems with emerging citizen journalism and news websites is that their proponents do not necessarily ascribe to traditional journalists' ethical codes. The journalists' union in Australia – the Media Alliance (MEAA) – has attempted to bring them into its fold by developing a special charter of excellence and ethics and by the end of April 2013 had 12 news websites ascribe to its principles, which included a commitment to the journalists' code of ethics (Alcorn 2013). This might be a viable solution for those who identify as journalists and seek a union affiliation, but many do not, and in a global and multicultural publishing environment the challenge is to develop models that might be embraced more broadly than a particular national union's repackaging of a journalists' code. However, codes of ethics have often failed to work effectively in guiding the ethics of the traditional journalists for whom they were designed, let alone the litany of new hybrids including citizen journalists, bloggers and the avid users of other emerging news platforms. Core human moral principles from key religious teachings like the Noble Eightfold Path could form the basis of a more relevant and broadly applicable model for the practice of 'mindful journalism'.

The recent inquiries triggered by poor journalism ethical practices have demonstrated that journalism within the libertarian model appears to have lost its moral compass and we need to explore new ways to recapture this. We should educate journalists, serious bloggers and citizen journalists to adopt a mindful approach to their news and commentary accommodating a reflection upon the implications of their truth-seeking and truth-telling as a routine part of the process. They would be prompted to pause and think carefully about the consequences of their reportage and commentary for the stakeholders involved, including their audiences. Truth-seeking and truth-telling would still be the primary goal, but only after gauging the social good that might come from doing so.

- This paper was first published in *Ethical Space*, Vol. 11, No. 4 pp 38-46

REFERENCES

Alcorn, G. (2013) Want to be a journalist? Bloggers, online media sites invited to sign on to journalism code of ethics, *The Citizen*, 29 April. Available online at http://www.thecitizen.org.au/media/want-be-journalist-bloggers-online-media-sites-invited-sign-journalism-code-ethics, accessed on 14 July 2014

Allan, S. (ed.) (2010) *The Routledge companion to news and journalism*, London, Routledge

Dalai Lama (2011) *Beyond religion: Ethics for a whole world*, London, Rider

Dutt, R. (2010) The Fiji media decree: A push towards collaborative journalism, *Pacific Journalism Review*, Vol.16, No. 2 pp 81-98

Fairfax Media (undated) *Fairfax code of conduct*. Available online at http://www.fairfax.com.au/resources/Fairfax_Code_of_Conduct. pdf, accessed on 14 July 2014

Finkelstein, R. (2012) *Report of the independent inquiry into the media and media regulation*, Canberra, Department of Broadband, Communications and the Digital Economy. Available online at http://www.archive.dbcde.gov.au/data/assets/pdf_file/0006/146994/Report-of-the-Independent-Inquiry-into-the-Media-and-Media-Regulation-web.pdf, accessed on 14 July 2014

Galtung, J. and Ruge, M. (1965) The structure of foreign news: The presentation of the Congo, Cuba and Cyprus crises in four foreign newspapers, *Journal of International Peace Research*, No. 1 pp 64-90

Gunaratne, S. A. (2005) *The Dao of the press: A humanocentric theory*, Cresskill, NJ, Hampton

Gunaratne, S. A. (2007) Let many journalisms bloom: Cosmology, Orientalism and freedom, *China Media Research*, Vol. 3, No. 4 pp 60-73

Gunaratne, S. A. (2009) A Buddhist view of journalism: Emphasis on mutual causality, *Javnost: The Public*, Vol. 16, No. 2 pp 61-75

Hutchins, R. M. (1947) *A free and responsible press: A general report on mass communication: Newspapers, radio, motion pictures, magazines and books* (Report of the Commission on Freedom of the Press), Chicago, University of Chicago Press

Kalupahana, David J. (1976) *Buddhist philosophy: A historical analysis*, Honolulu, University Press of Hawaii

Law Commission (New Zealand) (2013) *The news media meets 'new media': Rights, responsibilities and regulation in the digital age* (Law Commission report 128). Wellington, Law Commission. Available online at http://www.lawcom.govt.nz/project/review-regulatory-gaps-and-new-media/report, accessed on 14 July 2014

Leveson, B. (2012) *Report of an inquiry into the culture, practice and ethics of the press*, London, Stationery Office. Available online at http://www.official-documents.gov.uk/document/hc1213/hc07/0780/0780.asp, accessed on 14 July 2014

Lynch, J. (2010) Peace journalism, Allan, S. (ed.) *The Routledge companion to news and journalism*, London, Routledge pp 542-553

McDevitt, M., Gassaway, B. M. and Perez, F. G. (2002) The making and unmaking of civic journalists: Influences of professional socialization, *Journalism and Mass Communication Quarterly*, Vol. 79, No. 1 pp 87-100

McGill, D. (2008) The Buddha, the dharma, and the media, *McGill Report*, 20 February. Available online at http://www.mcgillreport.org/buddhamedia.htm, accessed on 14 July 2014

McQuail, D. (1987) *Mass communication theory: An introduction*, London, Sage Publications

Mizuno, K. (1987) *Basic Buddhist concepts*, Tokyo, Kosei Publishing Company

Pearson, M., Green, K. Tanner, S. and Sykes, J. (2010) Researching journalists and vulnerable sources: Issues in the design and implementation of a national study, Pasadeos, Y. (ed.) *Advances in communication and mass media research*, Athens, Atiner pp 87-96

Pearson, M. and Polden, M. (2011) *The journalist's guide to media law*, Sydney, Allen & Unwin, fourth edition

Robie, D. (2011) Conflict reporting in the South Pacific: Why peace journalism has a chance, *The Journal of Pacific Studies*, Vol. 31, No. 2 pp 221-240. Available online at http://www.academia.edu/1374720/ Conflict_reporting_in_the_South_Pacific_Why_peace_journalism_has_a_chance, accessed on 14 July 2014

Romano, A. R. (ed.) (2010) *International journalism and democracy: Civic engagement models from around the world*, New York and London, Routledge

Rosen, J. (1999) *What are journalists for?* New Haven, CT, Yale University Press

Rosen, J. (2003-) PressThink, Ghost of democracy in the media machine, weblog. Available online at http://pressthink.org

Schön, D. (1987) *Educating the reflective practitioner: Toward a new design for teaching and learning in the profession*, San Francisco, Jossey-Bass

Segal, Z., Williams, M., Teasdale, J. and Kabat-Zinn, J. (2012) *Mindfulness-based cognitive therapy for depression*, New York, Guilford Publications, second edition

Sheridan Burns, L. (2013) *Understanding journalism*. London, Sage, second edition

Siebert, F. S., Peterson, T. and Schramm, W. (1963) *Four theories of the press*, Urbana, University of Illinois Press

Smith, H. and Novak, P. (2003) *Buddhism: A concise introduction*, New York, Harper San Francisco

NOTE ON THE CONTRIBUTOR

Mark Pearson is Professor at Griffith University, Australia, and is a media law and ethics educator, blogger and author. He has written and edited for *The Australian* and has been published internationally in a range of outlets including the *Wall Street Journal*. His fields of expertise are media law and mindful journalism ethical practice. He has written or co-authored more than 100 academic works. His 12 books include *Social media risk and the law: A guide for global communicators* (with Susan Grantham, Routledge, 2021), six editions of Australia's leading journalism law text, *The journalist's guide to media law* (with Mark Polden, Allen & Unwin, 2019), *Blogging and tweeting without getting sued* (Allen & Unwin, 2012) and *Mindful journalism and news ethics in the digital era* (with Shelton A. Gunaratne and Sugath Senarath, Routledge, 2015). His new book, *The communicator's guide to media law and ethic*, is scheduled for publication by Routledge in 2023. He acknowledges funding from the Australian Research Council for the collaborative ARC Linkage Project LP0989758 which contributed to this study and to the Griffith University Arts, Education and Law Group for funding to present an earlier version to the International Association for Media and Communication Research Conference, Dublin City University in 2013. He acknowledges the insightful suggestions of the late Professor Emeritus Shelton Gunaratne, the pioneer of this perspective.

Chapter 4

Journalists and emotions: The theory of balance

Lyn Barnes

The changing media landscape and the demand for news 24/7 can make some journalists vulnerable to stress, especially those who often cover trauma. Whether it is death knocks or covering courts, the repetitive nature of trauma work can affect their mental health. By carrying out 20 in-depth, semi-structured interviews with New Zealand journalists and media managers, and using grounded theory analysis to interpret the data, a theory of balance emerged. The theory provides a framework for understanding how journalists deal with trauma and the related emotions. It identified what can be a continuum for some journalists, from attaining balance to maintaining balance through to potentially losing balance. The model can be used as a teaching device for self-care and serve as a self-assessment tool for journalists covering trauma on a regular basis, to check their mental stability. The investigation identified two key hurdles: the traditional unspoken 'rules' in newsrooms and the tendency of journalists to adopt the bystander position, that is, a reluctance to acknowledge colleagues who may not be coping with their work. It also confirmed that editors might not be fully aware of the risks of trauma work.

Keywords: journalism, trauma, grounded theory, emotional labour, bystander effect, gender, mental health

Novice journalists often carry out death knocks whereby they are expected to interview the family or friends of a victim immediately after a tragedy. Journalists throughout New Zealand are dispatched daily to cover trauma-related events and there is nothing in the journalists' codes of ethics to prevent senior staff sending out inexperienced reporters without proper support, or about providing counselling and/or debriefing them afterwards (Hollings 2005). Barnes (2016) addressed the fact that there is often minimal education about how to carry out these interviews, or support afterwards. The study considered both direct trauma (experiencing the event first hand) and indirect trauma (hearing the details second hand). Previous research has demonstrated that the denial of emotions and psychological damage from repetitive trauma work can have a cumulative effect on journalists. Moreover, because of a traditionally stoic culture and the socialisation process in many newsrooms, novice journalists feel the pressure to try to remain objective and suppress any emotions.

Any traumatic event, such as a fatality, is a shock to the system and can affect a person's equilibrium (Newman and Nelson 2012). International research has shown that graduates are particularly susceptible to strong emotional and psychological reactions (Dworznik and Grubb 2007). This becomes an issue when young journalists are being dispatched by senior staff to cover traumatic incidents as a form of initiation to see if they can handle the job (Barnes 2017). Figures are not available to indicate the turnover of staff in newsrooms in New Zealand but it becomes problematic when three-quarters of the journalism graduates now are female and the editors and managers are male (Barnes 2015). Graduates also face other stresses, in particular an unpredictable and insecure future with changes in the political economy, including contracted media ownership globally and fewer jobs (Berrington and Jemphrey 2003). These factors are combined with the demand for round-the-clock news on multi-platforms, produced on tighter budgets (Örnebring, Möller and Grip 2015).

Amidst all this uncertainty, the traditional hierarchical structure of newsrooms remains as the most common model, although organisational factors can affect operational factors, particularly in relation to covering trauma (Barnes 2016). Traditionally, editors advocated objective reporting, which was fact-based and feelings-free. Emotion in public discourse has historically been denigrated, considered the polar opposite of rationality, where facts and reason prevail (Wahl-Jorgensen 2013a). Now, however, journalists are expected to empathise with interviewees to extract emotive quotes.

This study contends that journalists covering trauma function on a continuum of balance, whereby the tension between objectivity and emotionality creates a push-pull effect. The tension between not becoming involved emotionally yet being expected to empathise with victims or people who are grieving can be intensified by internal or intrinsic pressures. These may relate to a journalist's desire to do a good job, which is usually guided by their moral compass, versus external or extrinsic pressures from editors. Using data gathered from in-depth interviews with 20 journalists, the grounded theory study identified three theoretical concepts or stages that journalists can move through when reporting trauma on a regular basis – attaining balance, maintaining balance and losing balance.

First, novice journalists need to attain balance. As part of this introductory stage, they must learn and accept the professional ideology and implicit rules of the newsroom as they come to terms with any conflicting emotions. To do so, at this stage, some adopt strategies (with varying degrees of success) to help them manage their work. Second, to maintain balance, they strive to deliver emotionally-laden stories to earn rewards in the newsroom and avoid punishment. Some journalists devise duplicitous ways to stay in control. Sometimes that control requires emotional labour, or 'putting on a mask' and, over time, some become emotionally detached (Hochschild 1979). Third, if they lose the drive to cover trauma-related incidents and feel they have no control over their work, they may burn out and subsequently lose balance.

JOURNALISM AND TRAUMA

With the commoditisation of news, violent and traumatic events have become news staples (Coté and Simpson 2000), to the point where Kitch (2009: 29) suggested that current journalism has been 'saturated with tears and trauma'. This change of focus, which Kitch termed the 'emotional shift' (ibid: 30), has also infiltrated more conservative media, which were traditionally more objective. The argument for publishing trauma-based stories has been that 'raw emotion makes the best copy' and, therefore, sells news (Berrington and Jemphrey 2003: 237). As budgets have tightened in newsrooms worldwide, news managers are giving preference to stories that will attract larger audiences, and thus increase profits (McManus 2009). These stories are market-driven topics, as opposed to topics defined by editors as newsworthy. The ubiquitous 'death knock' narrative could, therefore, be viewed as a way in which news organisations have adapted to social, economic and political contexts within which they now operate, by supplying more content specifically to meet audience demands (Allan 2004).

As a result, journalists are confronting increasing pressure to meet the requirements of their editors and media managers, as well as their audience. Yet there is a gap between the expectations of editors and what journalists are expected to deliver in terms of subjective content. Moreover, the swing towards more subjectivity in news stories has caused conflict in newsrooms. As Wahl-Jorgensen (2013b) described it, journalists are caught in the middle of change. Emotionality, or subjectivity, is gaining ground in news reporting, becoming a news value of its own (Meyer 2003). Pantti (2010) found emotions engaged by story-telling can make 'serious' news categories more interesting and intelligible. Disasters, accidents, violent episodes and child abuse are all emotional topics which lend themselves to a specific type of narrative. Rather than threatening the institutionalised ideals, Wahl-Jorgensen (2013b) considers them complementary because she regards emotionality as central to journalistic story-telling. She found that emotional story-telling was the driving force behind award-winning journalism by studying Pulitzer Prize-winning articles between 1995-2011.

Covering trauma presents a number of challenges to journalists. Most importantly, they must not connect emotionally with people because there is a concern that they risk losing their 'professional' objectivity (Novak and Davidson 2013). For example, there is a 'general prohibition' on journalists talking about the emotional aspects of their work (Richards and Rees 2011: 863). This investigation wanted to further the existing work by finding out how journalists learn to deal with trauma on the job and manage their emotions.

LOOK AND LEARN

The topic of journalism and trauma is relatively new and unexplored in New Zealand. While both Hollings (2005) and Scanlon (2014) addressed natural disasters, namely tsunamis and earthquakes, there was no research regarding day-to-day trauma. International research tended to focus on the effects of trauma on war correspondents and relatively few studies considered the everyday, domestic journalist (Keats and Buchanan 2009; Rees 2007).

New Zealand journalists regularly attend tragedies and are exposed to unpleasant incidents alongside police, fire crews and paramedics with high incidences of vehicle fatalities, suicides, child abuse and drownings. In New Zealand, the same journalists often cover police or crime rounds for years at a time, with very little preparation (Hollings 2005). There is an expectation that journalists will react 'professionally' to events as they happen, amid chaos and emotionally charged circumstances (Berrington and Jemphrey 2003: 239). Rather than being formally taught, journalists tend to rely on watching experienced journalists and learning along the way (Duncan and Newton 2010; Hopper and Huxford 2015). That includes learning about how to deal with emotions. Hopper and Huxford interviewed 20 journalists: 'Many felt suppressing emotions while covering events was simply a requirement of the job' (ibid: 35).

Empirical reports have shown that journalists' experiences of trauma can put them at risk of both direct and indirect stress, post-traumatic stress disorder, or more long-term difficulties such as depression, generalised anxiety, or struggles with relationships (Keats 2012; McMahon 2001). Novak and Davidson (2013) found that journalists who suppressed their emotions and identified with their 'professional' detached role appeared to have a protective factor in difficult situations. But there could be other reasons for striving for detachment. Emotions have been seen as a liability in the newsroom (Berkowitz 2000) so the lack of acknowledgement of such a problem could act as a form of social control (Benson 2006). Therefore, norms, routines and rules, some spoken and others unspoken, can be enforced to regulate behaviour.

The 2015 study by Hopper and Huxford found that there were ongoing risks to emotional suppression or control – as a result, some journalists might suffer long-term repercussions. They found several of the respondents were still suffering some years later from long-term guilt and self-hatred. Specific aspects of their job have been shown to make journalists more vulnerable to guilt, such as the pressure to sensationalise an article or to pressure distressed people for an interview (Browne, Evangeli and Greenberg 2012). Guilt as a risk factor for psychological impairment was the focus of research by Backholm and Idås (2015). They surveyed 371 journalists who covered the Norwegian terror attacks in Oslo and Utøya in 2011. The researchers identified ethical dilemmas caused by inner conflicts between acting as 'good human beings' versus 'professional journalists' (ibid: 143).

Although most journalists are resilient (Smith, Newman and Drevo 2015), burn-out is a psychological risk associated with covering trauma. Burn-out has been described as 'the physical, emotional and mental exhaustion that occurs when one can no longer cope with his or her everyday environment' (Dworznik 2011: 23). Other studies have looked at financial costs. An Australian study investigated the number of journalists who had claimed stress leave. Lyall (2012) found in the 10 years to June 2010 that 135 mental health claims were lodged with workers' compensation authorities from journalists and related professionals, leading to an average time off work of 26.4 weeks. During that time, around $A4.2 million was paid out in compensation, according to WorkSafe[1] information (ibid: 33). There are other implications to losing staff to stress: 'When experienced reporters leave, they take the knowledge of their communities or beats with them, which can lead to less critical and less informed coverage. If coverage suffers, news organisations may lose their audiences' (Jones 2014). Such figures for mental health claims by journalists are not readily available in New Zealand. Instead, the Accident Compensation Corporation sub-contracts to accredited employers and private companies, including publishing companies. Publishers are not required to supply information under the New Zealand Official Information Act 1982.

GROUNDED IN THE DATA

Twenty in-depth, semi-structured interviews were carried out with 16 females and four males. Four were novice journalists (graduates with up to two years in the workplace); six mid-range journalists (two to five years' experience), eight senior journalists (more than five years' in the job), and two former editorial managers.

Following grounded theory protocols, transcripts were analysed after each interview and coded, initially line by line, looking for repetition or key words and recurring actions (Charmaz 2014) as data. For example, 'feeling uncomfortable' clearly became a code early on. Constructing a grounded theory can be challenging. There is always a concern with grounded theory that the data is fragmented, which suggests it could lose its meaning. Because of the process of analysing line-by-line and coding, phrases and sentences are processed in chunks rather than in complete paragraphs. This issue was addressed by including full participant comments to illustrate the coding process that focused on actions, using gerunds, or action words ending in 'ing', and identifying key words. By incorporating a wide selection of participant comments to illustrate various arguments, journalists were given a voice and the outline of the theory formed its own narrative.

Categorisation followed more focused coding: categories can be conceptual, abstract, analytical and precise. Each category needs to be defined and its properties explored. For example, a person's years of experience as a journalist is a property, because experience influences consequences and outcomes. Alternatively, conditions, which also affect outcome, need consideration as well: for example, the amount of preparation or trauma training a young journalist has had, or what support is available after an event.

Grounded theory is not a linear process; it involves constant comparative analysis, whereby the researcher revisits the data and continually questions it, thereby refining the concepts. Sometimes this means reinterviewing participants. The voices of the journalists injected a sense of reality and helped to exemplify each category that was identified as the theory emerged. Participant comments also proved to be the best way to keep the theory grounded. For example, novice journalists appeared to test out a range of approaches to help them avoid any unpleasant feelings associated with death knocks:

> P. 2: I wasn't used to being so intrusive and I was probably a bit too apologetic, and a bit too, probably not detached enough so it affected me quite a lot. You always get that dread when you get asked to do any sort of death knock or whatever.

Others went through noticeable turmoil in their efforts to manage their emotions. They seemed to be aware that repressing their emotions was not good for them but they also wanted to be able to have some control over them:

> P. 4: You want to kind of become as cynical and weathered as the senior reporters as soon as possible, you know? You see them with a 'don't give a toss' kind of attitude and that's probably the stereotype of a hardened journalist but it's probably not the healthiest thing to aspire to.

Coping strategies were categorised under three key areas: emotion-focused, avoidance-focused or problem-focused, based on a study by Buchanan and Keats (2011).

Emotion focused: Many of the participants in this study expressed their need to share their experiences. Sharing the narrative is an emotion-focused strategy because talking, emailing or blogging helped to deal with emotions. Talking it out or sharing the story was the strategy most often used by participants after a traumatic encounter, whether it was with colleagues or other journalists elsewhere in the country.

Avoidance focused: Attempting to disengage from emotions was classified as avoidance-focused. The use of black humour and drinking alcohol were popular options here. Drinking helped one young woman share her emotions and feelings of disillusionment in the short term, as she weighed up 'the good with the bad' aspects of her job. There was also evidence of journalists who tried to deny or repress their responses and not to dwell on them. This suggested disassociation:

> P. 16: No, I was more silent, I think. ...I haven't really thought about it in-depth in terms of how I've dealt with it but I presume it's compartmentalised or something.

Some would simply give in to their emotions at times and finding a safe space to let them out was a last resort for some. This is probably because journalists who display emotions fear losing the respect of their peers. Or as Wouters (1992) surmised, they lack or lose status. Instead, they learn that containing emotions earns prestige.

> P. 11: I would end up just outside the building; I found this little corner on a concrete driveway or something. I just had a little cry and [would] go back up and get on with whatever I was doing. It was ridiculous.

Problem focused: Some participants would position themselves within their 'professional' role and focus on their work. This distracted several participants from what they described as 'uncomfortable' feelings. It often meant simply obeying instructions, as that made life easier for them and they could reconcile any inner turmoil if they did as they were told.

> P. 1: I mean, in a way having an instruction, like a decree that you will do this, makes you not have to agonise over it. You've just got to do it.

> P. 4: I think how I sort of cover, for example, a child abuse murder case is completely different to how I probably did it, probably a year ago. Now it's like, okay, focus on the story, you know, just get your lead, get the basics in. A few more details and then it's sort of like at the break you can stop and be like, okay, that's what's happened. Sweet, what am I going to do next? Just kind of deal with it in chunks in a way.

By doing as they were told and not questioning their instructions, some journalists abdicated their ethical decision-making to their editors. In so doing, they put the importance of the story first and paid less attention to 'minimising harm' to the people in the story. This approach could also be viewed as doing a disservice to their audience as well, because they avoided investigating the trauma too deeply. This comment exemplifies that:

> Researcher: Why did you feel you couldn't say no?

> P. 8: I don't know, you just ... it wouldn't be good. If you said you didn't want to do a door-knock, then I think they'd be thinking: 'Then what are you doing here?' It was that attitude that we all had to do it. You just do it.

Based on the grounded theory approach of using action words to name categories, three distinct concepts or stages emerged from the data – attaining balance, maintaining balance and losing balance. Within each of these key concepts, three sub-categories emerged that all relate to social processes. The sub-categories of attaining balance are 'being professional', 'confronting emotions' and 'learning the rules'. The sub-categories of maintaining balance are 'getting the get', 'managing emotions' and 'reading the newsroom'. The sub-categories of losing balance are 'hitting the limit', 'juggling emotions' and 'losing control'.

Each stage of Barnes' theory[2] of balance (2016) is dependent on three underlying conditions: the level of preparation, support for covering trauma work and cogitation. Preparation may relate to prior knowledge of an incident or court case. The more information the journalist had in advance, the better they felt they coped. Support can relate to having someone to share the experience with or knowing that counselling is not discouraged. The third condition is a term that evolved to encapsulate the rationalising that goes on internally. Cogitation can be described as a self-maintenance and self-aligning process, for example, when confronting an ethical dilemma. This process can be influenced by how much time there is between trauma-related assignments and how much time off a person has to 'rebalance'.

The term balance implies a level of fluctuation. For journalists, constant movement or pressure came from the push-pull phenomenon that kept them perpetually on edge. For example, being sent on a job without being fully briefed and the inner turmoil of trying to prepare on the way. This exemplifies the ongoing extrinsic pressures and the intrinsic pressures.

Figure 1: The theory of balance in trauma reporting is dependent on the three conditions: preparation, support and cogitation. Equilibrium is constantly challenged by the push/pull phenomenon, intrinsic and extrinsic factors that journalists encounter with trauma work

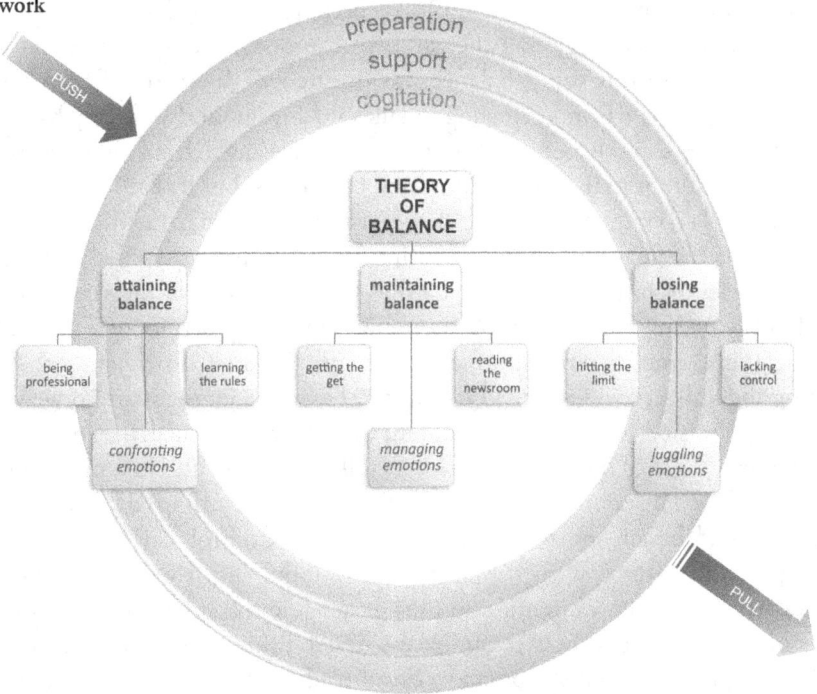

First, journalists had to learn how to attain balance when dealing with trauma. 'Being professional' implies adhering to the newsroom rules. For example, the expectation of remaining objective and not getting personally involved. Some of these rules are spoken and others are unspoken, for example, adhering to the code of ethics are spoken. Yet some journalists felt that although they were aware of how they should behave, there were unspoken expectations to break the rules at times rather than return to the newsroom without a story. 'Confronting emotions' and 'learning the rules' of the newsroom are, therefore, self-explanatory sub-categories.

Some young journalists opted out early in their careers if they could not move to the next stage, although this was based on anecdotal comments rather than hard data (Barnes 2015). However, if they achieved all three sub-categories, usually by adopting various coping strategies, they moved on to the next stage, maintaining balance. This is where they were regularly covering trauma and felt a sense of satisfaction from 'getting the get', that is, pursuing people for interviews and enjoying the challenge of getting them to talk. They had to learn to 'play the game' by 'reading the newsroom', for example, figuring out whether they should share any concerns about their work or keep them to themselves; what the accepted behaviours were and how to work around them, if necessary. This stage was dependent on learning how to 'manage emotions'. Balance was constantly tested because of the reluctance to admit disquiet or suppress it. Some journalists displayed signs of loneliness, insecurity and stress as they strived to maintain balance in a competitive work environment. Others became emotionally disconnected.

If the exhilaration of 'getting the get' began to dissipate, as it did for some of the participants in this study, balance was threatened. The thrill of the chase in 'getting the get' came from managing to talk someone around who may have been reluctant to speak to the media or finding an exclusive angle. It may also have come from recognition or praise from editors and colleagues, but if that did not sustain the sense of elation, then there were clear warning signs that something was amiss.

Therefore, the final core category is losing balance. This was typified by the three sub-categories of 'hitting the limit', 'battling emotions' and 'lacking control'. The word 'hit' as in 'hit the limit' implies a sudden, impulsive action, or a point of no return. 'Limit' implies a maximum number and finality. Consequently the term 'hitting the limit' provides a vivid definition. For some journalists interviewed, it was a snap decision to leave the newsroom, whereby the cumulative experiences or drip-by-drip effect of trauma work took its toll and they could no longer function effectively. 'Lacking control' can intensify the effects of 'battling emotions', which, in turn, could hasten someone 'hitting the limit'. 'Control' can be described as feeling valued, earning a say, or having some input into the news production process. The study drew attention to the adverse role that a lack of control in the newsroom can play and how it can have a destabilising effect. For example, one mid-range journalist said she began to dread reading the newspaper the morning after covering a death knock story because she was worried that her story may have been reduced to a news brief 'because a better death came along'. She would feel guilty because she felt she was letting the family down, especially if she had to convince members to speak openly and see them genuinely distressed as they retold their story of grief. Their emotional investment could thus be completely minimised and she would feel as though she had betrayed them if the story had been edited substantially.

> P. X (This person asked not to be numbered in case she was identifiable from other comments and jobs she had covered): Whereas now I've gone from at the beginning of the job absolutely loving that adrenaline, all that sort of stuff that I used to enjoy and now having a panic attack every time there is a big story. Getting the shakes, feeling sick, vomiting on the side of the road, proper panic attacks.

It was evident early in the data analysis that a number of the participants felt 'uncomfortable' with trauma work right from the start. Part of this could be, as several expressed, because they did not expect to have to carry out death knocks as part of their job. This implies that they were not taught as part of their journalism programmes about the reality of daily life as a journalist. Once on the job, they were generally expected to hide their emotions, although there were no guidelines or instructions on how to do this, and in spite of research demonstrating that this could be psychologically damaging. Instead, they assimilated rules for appropriate and inappropriate displays of emotions, usually through adapting to the 'professional' norms of behaviour.

Preparation and support: Preparation refers to how much information a journalist has before covering a traumatic incident or court case, for example, or what guidance the editor provides before setting off to cover a job. As one journalist commented, the only time they usually had to prepare was in the car on the way to the scene. Feeling 'unsupported' can be interpreted as having no outlet for their conflicting emotions, or no one to talk to about 'feeling uncomfortable' or 'when you feel like you're the only person who really knows' in the newsroom. This sense of isolation from a lack of support came through repeatedly. One young woman admitted that as a last resort she sought support from victims:

> P. 5: You know, I found myself feeling, which is weird, seeking solace in some way from your sources or your interview subjects…

This final stage in the theory of balance – losing balance – highlighted three key issues: newsroom hierarchy, gender and self-responsibility. Although some changes have been made in the media industry towards providing help for stressed journalists, such as free counselling sessions through the Employee Assistance Programme, which provides up to three sessions with a counsellor, respondents were sceptical and some referred to it as 'tokenism', plus, the responsibility to seek support has been left to journalists. There is also concern that few counsellors available through the EAP have specialised in trauma.

There was also a lack of genuine acknowledgement by senior staff and management of the impact of traumatic stress. Unlike a physical illness or injury, journalists were reluctant to talk about trauma in newsrooms. Being stressed, traumatised or needing time out because of work-related issues were topics that were not discussed openly, implying stoicism is still revered and there is still some shame involved. Some comments suggested that management considered changes in technology to be more distressing for journalists than covering trauma-related incidents. They also highlighted another important finding in the study, the assumption that media managers would automatically recognise symptoms of stress, or be able to differentiate different types of stress or abnormal patterns of behaviour. Perhaps more importantly, there was the assumption that they would know how to respond, or would consider traumatic stress worthy of attention. This, in itself, is a form of control and demonstrates power imbalance. As a former editorial manager commented, he had never had any training about how to identify the effects of trauma on his staff. Instead, it was assumed that, as a former journalist, he would inherently know – and it was up to him whether he chose to do anything about it or not.

The point at which some journalists lost balance was when they were put on the spot by editors who could be intimidating. Several female participants recalled newsroom incidents where they felt openly bullied by male editors. One former senior reporter vividly recalled behaviour she felt should not have been allowed to occur.

> Participant 16: Bullying is just rife though ... it is acceptable because it is accepted.

Bullying appears to have been fostered by newsroom culture and, therefore, is ultimately endorsed by senior management. One participant commented about how observers turned a blind eye when they heard screaming and swearing. And those who did, made a deliberate decision to ignore such behaviour, which is a form of 'bystander effect', or 'bystander apathy' (Darley and Latané 1968). It appears that editors and colleagues, rather than acknowledge when someone is being bullied, ignore such irrational behaviour and outbursts, perhaps in the hope that it might be contained. Managers and editors who foster the traditional hierarchical structure of newsrooms can be seen as indirectly endorsing this behaviour.

A FUTURE OF EMOTIONS?

This grounded theory study was the first investigation in New Zealand into how journalists deal with emotions when covering everyday trauma. It identifies a self-assessment scale so that journalists can check where they sit on the spectrum, from attaining balance, maintaining balance to losing balance. Awareness of the three distinct phases may alert other journalists to the importance of retaining balance: if they detect indicators of stress or witness inappropriate behaviour, rather than ignore it, they may more readily step in and offer or organise support for colleagues.

This study was limited in that the participants were self-selecting. Rather than approach possible interviewees and risk triggering any unpleasant reminders from the past, journalists were invited to contact the researcher. The study is also restricted by the size and population of New Zealand and the number of journalists who cover trauma reporting in the country. It is only in the larger centres where there are dedicated court reporters or staff allocated to cover emergency stories. In some areas, journalists cover all rounds. This is mostly the case for radio and television reporters in rural areas who cover all aspects of news.

Finally, balance in trauma journalism is a psycho-social phenomenon, a dynamic interrelationship of social factors and journalists' thoughts and behaviours as they strive to carry out their job and manage their emotions. This is because emotionality has destabilised a traditional mode of practice (Barnes 2016). And it is not likely to change as news adapts to become part of social media (Beckett 2016). First, because competition in the media has become intense, Beckett viewed the inclusion of emotions as an economic necessity, especially when there were many distractions from the news. Second, he argued that emotional cues helped attract attention and prolonged engagement with the reader, listener or viewer. Emotions might also encourage people to share content, which Beckett proposed would become increasingly important for the survival of the media. Third, he argued that people responded more favourably to emotion than to facts. He also predicted the end of objectivity as it existed because journalism was reinventing itself as a 'powerful mix of emotion and relativism'. Since emotions in story-telling are becoming more prevalent, it will be important to monitor changes in newsrooms, to ensure they align in time.

- This paper was first published in *Ethical Space*, Vol. 14, Nos 2 and 3 pp 15-24

NOTES

[1] Worksafe, now known as Safe Work Australia, is a statutory body set up to develop national policy related to work health and safety and related workers' compensation

[2] I would like to thank the peer reviewer who suggested I call this Barnes's theory

REFERENCES

Allan, Stuart (2004) *News culture*, New York, Open University Press, second edition

Backholm, Klaus and Idås, Trond (2015) Ethical dilemmas, work-related guilt and post-traumatic stress reactions of news journalists covering the terror attack in Norway in 2011, *Journal of Traumatic Stress*, Vol. 28, No. 2 pp 142-148

Barnes, Lyn (2015) An inexplicable gap: Journalism and gender in New Zealand, *Journalism*. Available online at DOI:10.1177/1464884915620231

Barnes, Lyn (2016) *Journalism and everyday trauma: A grounded theory of the impact from death-knocks and court reporting*, PhD thesis, AUT University, Auckland, New Zealand

Barnes, Lyn (2017) *Preparing journalists for the inevitable*, Leiden, Netherlands, Brill Publishers

Beckett, Charlie (2016) Navigating a complex media landscape, The London School of Economics and Political Science, 3 February. Available online at http://blogs.lse.ac.uk/communications/2016/02/03/navigating-a-complex-media-landscape/

Benson, Rodney (2006) News media as a journalistic field: What Bourdieu adds to new institutionalism, and vice versa, *Political Communication*, Vol. 23, No 2 pp 187-202

Berkowitz, Dan (2000) Doing double duty: Paradigm repair and the Princess Diana what-a-story, *Journalism*, Vol. 1, No. 2 pp 125-143

Berrington, Eileen and Jemphrey, Ann (2003) Pressure on the press: Reflections on reporting tragedy, *Journalism*, Vol. 4, No. 2 pp 225-248

Browne, Tess, Evangeli, Michael and Greenberg, Neil (2012) Trauma-related guilt and post-traumatic stress among journalists, *Journal of Traumatic Stress*, Vol. 25, No. 2 pp 207-210

Buchanan, Marla and Keats, Patrice (2011) Coping with traumatic stress in journalism: A critical ethnographic study, *International Journal of Psychology*, Vol. 46, No. 2 pp 127-135

Coté, William and Simpson, Roger (2000) *Covering violence: A guide to ethical reporting about victims and trauma*, New York, Columbia University Press

Charmaz, Kathy (2014) *Constructing grounded theory*, London, Sage Publications, second edition

Darley, John and Latané, Bibb (1968) Bystander intervention in emergencies: Diffusion of responsibility, *Journal of Personality and Social Psychology*, Vol. 8, No. 4 pp 377-383

Duncan, Sallyanne and Newton, Jackie (2010) How do you feel? Preparing novice reporters for the death knock, *Journalism Practice*, Vol. 4, No. 4 pp 439-453

Dworznik, Gretchen (2011) Factors contributing to PTSD and compassion fatigue in television news workers, *International Journal of Business, Humanities and Technology*, Vol. 1, No. 1 pp 22-32

Dworznik, Gretchen and Grubb, Max (2007) Preparing for the worst: Making a case for trauma training in the journalism classroom, *Journalism & Mass Communication Educator*, Vol. 62, No. 2 pp 190-210

Hochschild, Arlie R. (1979) Emotion work, feelings, rules and social structure, *American Journal of Sociology*, Vol. 85, No. 3 pp 551-575

Hollings, James (2005) Reporting the Asian tsunami: Ethical issues, *Pacific Journalism Review*, Vol. 11, No. 2 pp 139-155

Hopper, K. Megan and Huxford, John F. (2015) Gathering emotion: Examining newspaper journalists' engagement in emotional labour, *Journal of Media Practice*, Vol. 16, No. 1 pp 25-41

Jones, Megan (2014) Mental health: Why journalists don't get help in the workplace, *Ryerson Review of Journalism*, 9 December. Available online at http://rrj.ca/mental-health-why-journalists-dont-get-help-in-the-workplace/

Keats, Patrice (2012) Journalism, Figley, Charles R. (ed.) *Encyclopedia of trauma: An interdisciplinary guide*, Thousand Oaks, CA, Sage Publications pp 337-340

Keats, Patrice and Buchanan, Marla (2009) Addressing the effects of assignment stress injury, *Journalism Practice*, Vol. 3, No. 2 pp 162-177

Kitch, Carolyn (2009) Tears and trauma in the news, Zelizer, Barbie (ed.) *The changing faces of journalism: Tabloidization, technology and truthiness*, Oxon, Routledge pp 29-39

Lyall, Kimina (2012) Covering traumatic events without traumatizing yourself and others, Ricketson, Matthew (ed.) *Australian journalism today*, Melbourne, Palgrave Macmillan pp 28-44

McMahon, Cait (2001) Covering disaster: A pilot study into secondary trauma for print media journalists reporting on disaster, *Australian Journal of Emergency Medicine*, Vol. 16, No. 2 pp 52-56

McManus, John (2009) The commercialisation of news, Wahl-Jorgensen, Karin and Hanitzsch, Thomas (eds) *The handbook of journalism studies*, New York, Routledge pp 218-236

Meyer, Philip (2003) The proper role of the news media in a democratic society, Harper, Joe and Yantek, Thom (eds) *Media, profit and politics: Competing priorities in an open society*, Kent, Ohio, Kent State University Press pp 11-77

Newman, Elana and Nelson, Summer (2012) Reporting on resilience and recovery in the face of disaster and crime: Research and training implications, *Australian Journalism Review*, Vol. 34, No. 1 pp 17-32

Novak, Rosemary and Davidson, Sarah (2013) Journalists reporting on hazardous events: Constructing protective factors within the professional role, *Traumatology*, Vol. 19, No. 4 pp 313-322

Örnebring, Henrik, Möller, Cecilia and Grip, Lena (2015) Journalism as livelihood: Gender, space and mobility. Paper presented at Geomedia: Spaces and Mobilities in Mediatised Worlds, Karlstad, Sweden, May

Pantti, Mervi (2010) The value of emotion: An examination of television journalists' notions on emotionality, *European Journal of Communication*, Vol. 25, No. 2 pp 168-181

Rees, Gavin (2007) Weathering the trauma storms, *British Journalism Review*, Vol. 18, No. 2 pp 65-70

Richards, Barry and Rees, Gavin (2011) The management of emotion in British journalism, *Media, Culture & Society*, Vol. 33, No. 6 pp 851-867

Scanlon, Sean (2014) Quake aftermath: Christchurch journalists' collective trauma experience and the implications for their reporting, *MediaNZ*, Vol. 14, No. 1 pp 83-95

Smith, River, Newman, Elana and Drevo, Susan (2015) *Covering trauma: Impact on journalists*, Dart Center for Journalism and Trauma, Columbia University, July. Available online at https://dartcenter.org/content/covering-trauma-impact-on-journalists

Wahl-Jorgensen, Karin (2013a) The strategic ritual of emotionality: A case study of Pulitzer Prize-winning articles, *Journalism*, Vol. 14, No. 1 pp 129-145

Wahl-Jorgensen, Karin (2013b) Subjectivity and story-telling in journalism, *Journalism Studies*, Vol. 14, No. 3 pp 305-320

Wouters, Cas (1992) On status competition and emotion management: The study of emotions as a new field, *Theory, Culture & Society*, Vol. 9, No.1 pp 229-252

NOTE ON THE CONTRIBUTOR

Dr Lyn Barnes retired in 2019 from her position as a senior lecturer in journalism at AUT University in Auckland, New Zealand. Her PhD focused on trauma journalism and everyday journalists. Her other areas of interest included magazine journalism and magazine history. She worked as a sub-editor, editor and writer on a number of magazines before joining academia. Before that she has worked for newspapers, radio, television news and current affairs in New Zealand and Australia.

Chapter 5

'It's not easy to do a WikiLeaks': A cypherpunk approach to global media ethics

Patrick D. Anderson

Julian Assange, the founder of WikiLeaks, has been studied as a hacker, a journalist and an activist, but scholars have not given sufficient attention to his broader ethical theory. Assange's cypherpunk ethics emphasises justice while advocating the widespread use of digital cryptography to defend individual privacy and promote institutional transparency. This paper places Assange's cypherpunk ethics into conversation with contemporary global media ethics through a comparative study with the ethical theory of Clifford Christians. Christians and Assange offer different foundations for metaethics, and these differences give shape to their respective conceptions of cosmopolitanism, their divergent critiques of professional journalism and advocacy for convivial tools. By bringing a non-academic like Assange into the conversation, this paper practises ethical listening as a part of open media ethics, establishes a descriptive account of Assange's ethical theory and introduces a justice-centred ethical paradigm into the field of global media ethics.

Keywords: WikiLeaks, media ethics, justice, cryptography, journalism

INTRODUCTION

> Theories are a problem of axiology rather than epistemology.
> **Clifford Christians (2013: 278)**

> But there is another way of leading, and that is leading through values instead of command and control. When you lead through values you don't need to trust people, and there is no limit on the number of people who can adopt those values and the speed at which they can adopt them. It all happens very quickly.
> **Julian Assange (2016: 167)**

Over the last decade, two areas of communication studies and media ethics have emerged: a body of literature about WikiLeaks, a whistleblowing system and publishing website created by Julian Assange, and the field of global media ethics, which seeks to construct an adequate communication ethics for the global, digital age. In the literature on WikiLeaks, scholars have tended to focus on Assange's status as a hacker (Villena Saldaña 2011; Marechal 2013) or activist (Sifry 2011; Marmura 2018), the journalistic (Lynch 2012, 2013) and legal (Benkler 2011) status of WikiLeaks's publishing practices, the implications of WikiLeaks for whistleblowing ethics (Delmas 2015; Boot 2019) and the meaning of WikiLeaks for professional journalism (Brevini et al. 2013). In the literature on global media ethics, Clifford Christians (2013) has identified four emerging paradigms: Lee Wilkins's (2010, 2011a) neuroscientific approach, Stephen Ward's (2010, 2015) contractualist approach, Patrick Plaisance's (2011, 2014, 2016) moral psychology approach and Christians's (2010, 2019) own philosophical anthropology approach. These emerging paradigms offer distinctive, competing metaethical frameworks, each of which, it is argued, might provide the most adequate basis for global media ethics in the twenty-first century.[1]

Taken together, communication scholars generally and media ethicists specifically have primarily taken WikiLeaks and Assange to be *objects* of study rather than *sources* of theory. Damian Tambini (2013: 250), for example, offers one of the most insightful and sustained engagements with WikiLeaks from the perspective of global ethics, concluding: 'WikiLeaks has not yet articulated ethical practices for global publication.' Tambini reaches this conclusion after citing only a handful of remarks from Assange's public appearances and from the WikiLeaks website. Similarly, in *The WikiLeaks paradigm*, Stephen Marmura (2018) cites only *two* sources for which Assange is credited as the author: an interview about *Collateral murder* (a classified US military video, distributed by WikiLeaks in 2010, showing the indiscriminate killing of over a dozen people near Baghdad) and an essay posted to Assange's blog in 2006. The former receives a one-sentence summary; the latter receives approximately half of a paragraph. It is unclear why so many scholars fail even to examine and explain Assange's own views when discussing WikiLeaks. Consequently, neither the literature on WikiLeaks nor the field of global media ethics has adequately explored the distinctive ethical insights and theoretical claims developed in Assange's communication theory and moral philosophy.

From one perspective, scholarly inattention to Assange's media ethics is a symptom of the closed disposition of media ethics, its tendency to restrict its scope to a narrow group of professional practitioners and exclude other voices (Ward and Wasserman 2010). This paper contributes to the recent trend of opening media ethics through the practice of ethical listening by authentically including a new voice from outside academic and professionalised circles (Ward and Wasserman 2015). Likewise, this paper follows Lee Wilkins and Renita Coleman (2004) in assuming that if practitioners – including technologists and publishers like Assange

– build their moral worlds through action *and* reflection, then the theoretical aspects of Assange's work should not be neglected. More broadly, this project also answers scholars who have called for greater attention to be paid to questions of professionalism in journalism (Borden 2007; Christians 2011), journalism's audiences (Singer 2011), empire and imperialism (Innis 1950; Li 2014), theories of emerging technologies (Fortner 2011; Christians 2014b) and the connections between global and local issues in communication, journalism and whistleblowing (Rao 2011; Fortner 2011; Löwstedt 2018).

From another perspective, scholarly inattention to Assange's media ethics must be understood in the context of the United States and United Kingdom governments' persecution of Assange. Shortly after the launch of WikiLeaks, the Cyber Counter-intelligence Assessments Branch of the United States Defense Department issued a report that articulated a general strategy of attacking WikiLeaks by destroying Assange's reputation and undermining the public's trust in WikiLeaks's publications (Pilger 2018). What followed was over a decade of anti-WikiLeaks propaganda labelling Assange with a range of pejorative terms: hacker (Leigh and Harding 2011), terrorist (MacAskill 2010), rapist (Burns and Somaiya 2010) and Trumpist (Mackey 2017), among others. This propaganda campaign was promoted not only by governments (Strobel and Hosenball 2017) but also by corporate news media outlets (Macleod 2019; O'Day 2019) and academics (Anderson 2020a, 2020b). Beyond systematic defamation, the United States and United Kingdom have collaborated to silence and even eliminate Assange through judicial and extrajudicial means. In public, the United States has sought to have Assange extradited so he can be tried under the draconian Espionage Act, but in private, it has secretly surveilled Assange and even contemplated kidnapping or assassinating him (Blumenthal 2020; Quinn 2020; Dorfman, Naylor and Isikoff 2021). For over a decade, Assange has been incarcerated in some form: first under house arrest, then trapped in the Ecuadorian embassy in London, and now locked away in Belmarsh maximum security prison. Having been subject to such treatment, it is no surprise that a United Nations evaluation of Assange's mental state concluded that he has been the victim of psychological torture (Cumming-Bruce 2019). Thus, viewed from within the broader political context, the scholarly inattention to Assange's global media ethics appears even more egregious than a mere oversight.

To understand Assange's theory of global media ethics, it is necessary to recognise that his moral 'worldview' (Christians 2013) is fundamentally shaped by his participation in the cypherpunk movement (Levy 2001; Manne 2011; Greenberg 2012, Assange et al. 2012). The cypherpunk movement emerged in the early 1990s, advocating the widespread use of strong digital cryptography – or crypto – as the best means for defending individual privacy and resisting authoritarianism in the digital age. 'At the core of the cypherpunk philosophy,' Robert Manne (2011) explains, 'was the belief that the great question of politics in the age of the internet was whether the state would strangle individual freedom and privacy through its capacity for electronic surveillance or whether autonomous individuals would eventually undermine and even destroy the state through their deployment of electronic weapons newly at hand'. 'The cypherpunks,' according to Suelette Dreyfus, 'believed in the right of the individual to personal privacy – and the responsibility of government to be open, transparent and fully accountable to the public' (Dreyfus and Assange 2012: xii). Some commentators have interpreted WikiLeaks as a 'radical transparency' organisation, concluding that WikiLeaks's reliance on secrecy and its use of anonymous sources implies a 'double standard' (Marechal 2013). Yet when we acknowledge the cypherpunk roots of Assange's call for government and corporate transparency, we see that Assange is not enacting a double standard but upholding 'the traditional cypherpunk juxtaposition': 'privacy for the weak, transparency for the powerful' (Assange et al. 2012: 7). Ultimately, Assange's ethical paradigm is best understood as a philosophy of *cypherpunk ethics* (Anderson 2021).

This paper contextualises Assange's media ethics within the field of global media ethics through a comparative analysis between his cypherpunk approach and the philosophy of Clifford Christians. Christians has been recognised as a 'leading theorist' (Plaisance 2011) of global communication ethics and, as such, has been largely responsible for establishing the parameters of the field; thus, Christians's work provides a satisfactory starting point for situating Assange in the field. Furthermore, because Assange's philosophy has been articulated in disparate interviews, essays and manifestos, it is necessary to reconstruct his moral philosophy and give it systematic expression. Christians's approach of (1) identifying the most pressing problem or challenge facing media ethics, (2) presenting a metaethical solution to that problem or challenge, and (3) insisting on a cosmopolitan application of the meta-ethical solution provides a useful framework for exploring and reconstructing the details of Assange's philosophy. In addition, because Christians and Assange each interrogate and criticise nationalism, critique professionalism and analyse emerging technologies, it is helpful to use the overarching similarities of their philosophies to highlight further their deeper disagreements. Finally, the project of reading Assange as a theorist of global media ethics follows three of Christians's (2008a) recommendations for bringing the field of media ethics into the global digital age. First, it represents a 'creative construction of paradigms' that are 'grounded in the action of public life' (Christians 2008a: 5). Second, it redefines the canon by introducing theory that originates outside the social milieu of professional academic work, thus provoking and enabling new conceptions of communication ethics. And third, it contributes to the development of a much-needed 'ethics agenda for computer-based systems' (Christians 2008a: 10). Christians (2014a: 243) has noted 'the need for creative theorizing within communication ethics' and 'in media and press theory', and it is precisely because Assange is *not* an academic that his theories catalyse creative thinking, thereby enlivening and expanding academic and public debates about global media ethics through the practice of ethical listening.

By undertaking a comparative analysis of Christians and Assange, this paper takes a purely descriptive approach to understanding their respective ethical theories. As a result, it refrains from making any evaluative claims or normative assessments regarding the truth or feasibility of their ethical theories.

In the spirit of Christians, this study is an exercise in presuppositional thinking, in that it seeks to identify the basic ethical presuppositions of both Christians and Assange and show how those presuppositions give shape to the other aspects of their ethical theories (Christians 2013; Cortes 2016). Assange is one of the most controversial figures of the last decade, having sparked debates about national security, journalistic practice, digital ethics and freedom of the press. Christians (2013) himself has praised WikiLeaks's cosmopolitanism while expressing some reservations about WikiLeaks's use of anonymous sources (Christians 2016). Thus, a comparative analysis of Christians's and Assange's media ethics may provide important insights regarding the ongoing debates sparked by Assange and WikiLeaks.

This paper contributes to both the literature on WikiLeaks and the field of global media ethics by reading Julian Assange as a cypherpunk theorist of media ethics. On the one hand, the scholarship on WikiLeaks benefits from this analysis of Assange's media ethics because it highlights the ways in which Assange's basic ethical concerns about justice inform his views on cosmopolitanism, nationalism, journalistic professionalism and the promises and perils of emerging technologies. On the other hand, Assange's distinctive brand of cypherpunk ethics represents a possible fifth paradigm of global media ethics that relies on a conception of justice as the basic measure of all other moral questions. At the very least, this discussion provides one example of how justice can be the basis of a global media ethics paradigm. Given Assange's status as an activist and his frequent use of political language rather than ethical language, it is important to remember that his media ethics paradigm emerges from the intimate, reciprocal connection between theory and practice (Wilkins 2018) as well as the mutual importance that communication studies and political theory have for each other (Wilkins 2011b).

The paper is organised into four sections. The first section establishes the meta-ethical or pre-suppositional differences between Christians and Assange by showing that Christians seeks to overcome relativism with the 'sacredness-of-life' proto-norm, while Assange seeks to promote justice through the implementation of cypherpunk principles. The second and third sections demonstrate that these presuppositional differences lead Christians and Assange to offer quite different commentaries on the nature of cosmopolitanism and the shortcomings of professional journalism. The final section explores the ways in which both Christians and Assange take up Jacques Ellul's analysis of *la technique* and Ivan Illich's call for convivial tools. Again, Christians's concern about sacredness and Assange's concern about justice inform their respective understandings of what convivial technology looks like. In this comparative analysis, Christians's conceptual apparatus is used to elucidate Assange's ethics, but this approach concludes that, despite their attention to similar issues, they provide radically different assessments of them. By bringing together the scholarly conversations about both WikiLeaks and global media ethics, this paper provides the former with new insights about the structure of Assange's moral worldview and presents the latter with a possible cypherpunk paradigm of global media ethics that takes justice as its starting point.

THE CHALLENGES AND FUTURES OF GLOBAL MEDIA ETHICS

A comparative analysis of Clifford Christians and Julian Assange's respective media ethics begins with an examination of their proto-normative commitments. Both thinkers identify what they see as the biggest challenge to contemporary media ethics and present a solution to that challenge, but there are important differences between Christians and Assange. For Christians, the central challenge for global media ethics is the threat of moral relativism, and he argues that we should meet this challenge with the establishment of the universally acceptable proto-norm that human life is sacred, from which other moral principles follow. This approach assumes a subtle metaphysical contour: the particular stands as the challenge while the universal promises to help us overcome that challenge. For Assange, however, the central challenge for global media ethics is the abundance of global injustice, and he argues that we should meet this challenge by applying normative principles that redistribute power in a manner that promotes justice and mitigates injustice. This approach rejects the particular/universal opposition that structures Christians's thought, instead prioritising a conception of what we owe each other. Importantly, both thinkers advocate an axiological approach to ethics and both thinkers place the value of humanity at the centre of their thinking. But Christians emphasises that we need to reorganise the way that we think about norms, while Assange emphasises that we need to reorganise the way that we live according to justice.

For Christians (2009), moral relativism is the most important challenge for communication ethicists in the twenty-first century, a position necessarily informed by his Christian worldview (Cortes 2016). Christians (2009) distinguishes between cultural relativism and philosophical (or moral) relativism. On the one hand, he acknowledges that cultural relativism as cultural pluralism is not only a fact to be acknowledged but also a norm to be praised. Cultural pluralism, Christians (2013) argues, places much needed limits on ethnocentrism and nationalism, reminding the peoples of the world that their cultures are not supreme but rather one among many. On the other hand, he criticises philosophical relativism as an unjustifiable extrapolation from cultural pluralism. In Christians's view, the meta-ethical claim that there are not and can be no universal moral truths threatens to eliminate not only any shared normative standards but normative standards as such. Without normative standards, there is no measure of right and wrong; without transcultural normative standards, cultures or societies would be unable to reflect critically on their own standards and practices (Christians 2009).

Ultimately, Christians insists that cultural pluralism ought not be conflated with moral relativism, for if that happens, ethics – in any meaningful sense of the term – becomes impossible. To solve the problem of philosophical relativism, Christians (2009) calls for a meta-ethical intervention that takes ethics out of the realm of epistemology, where utilitarians tend to place it (Christians 2007), and places ethics in the realm of axiology or presuppositional thinking (Cortes 2016). As Christians (2013: 278) puts it: 'Theories are a problem of axiology rather than epistemology.' Taking inspiration from Aristotle's notion of the unmoved mover, Christians says that no philosopher can theorise in an infinite regression; instead, they must start with some first principles, some axioms, that form the basis of their worldview but which cannot be justified by that worldview. Such presuppositions are values that are asserted and that motivate and make possible philosophical and moral reasoning. Other philosophers have called this a 'teleological suspension of philosophy', an approach that acknowledges that philosophical reflection is not a self-justifying enterprise but is motivated by pre-philosophical value commitments (Gordon 2002; Tunstall 2013).

For Christians (2009), presuppositional thinking not only rejects the epistemic metaethics of utilitarianism but also reveals a contradiction in the metaethics of the moral relativists. Drawing on Karl Mannheim (1936), he notes that when the relativist claims 'truth depends on culture', she is making a claim that necessarily transcends culture, a paradox the relativist cannot escape. In bringing meta-ethics back to the realm of axiology, Christians suggests that value theory opens the way for the emergence – or in the language of his ontological moral realism (Christians 2016), the *discovery* – of universal moral norms that transcend culture.

With meta-ethics firmly in the realm of axiology, Christians (1997; 2015c; Christians and Nordenstreng 2004) offers one proto-norm as the foundation to a universal ethics, and that norm entails three universal moral principles. For Christians (2015b), one unquestionably universal value that may serve as a foundational proto-norm for contemporary international communication ethics is the 'sacredness-of-life'. 'Reverence for life on earth,' Christians (2015c) argues, 'establishes a level playing floor for cross-cultural collaboration on the ethical foundations of responsible communication' (ibid: 342). Christians suggests that there is empirical evidence that all peoples value the notion of the sacredness-of-life thus making it a suitable candidate for the basis of a universal ethics.

Following from this proto-norm are three universal principles (Christians, 1997; Christians and Nordenstreng, 2004). First, there is the principle of respect for human dignity, which requires all people to acknowledge the intrinsic moral worth of every human individual. Second, there is the principle of truth-telling, which requires honesty in all communicative acts. And third, there is the principle of non-violence, which requires a commitment to peace and is captured by the commandment from the Abrahamic tradition: 'Thou shalt not kill.' Like the sacredness-of-life, Christians argues that these three universal principles are empirically and logically justified and, because they necessarily follow from a single universal proto-norm, they expand the foundations of the universal ethics so desperately needed by global media ethics today.

While Christians approaches global media ethics from the perspectives of norms, Assange approaches global media ethics from the perspective of justice. In Assange's view, the growing prevalence of injustice around the world is the central challenge for media ethics. In fact, Assange (2016: 68-69) explains that he was motivated to create WikiLeaks – a communication platform that poses questions for technology, journalism and politics, among other things – precisely because he perceived that there was too much injustice in the world. 'I looked at something that I had seen going on with the world,' he says, 'which is that I thought there were too many unjust acts. And I wanted there to be more just acts, and fewer unjust acts.' The Iraq War of 2003 serves as a paradigmatic example of the unjust acts that Assange has in mind, and it is no coincidence that WikiLeaks was founded at the height of the George W. Bush administration's 'Global War on Terror'. Assange was heavily influenced by his parents' participation in the anti-Vietnam War movement (Assange 2011), and he has repeatedly denounced wars that he perceives as unjust (Assange 2011, 2015, 2016; Assange et al. 2012). Drawing upon Harold Innis's (1950) analysis of empires and communication technologies, Assange (2015) concludes United States imperialism is one of the chief causes of injustice in the twenty-first century.

Like Christians, Assange approaches ethics from an axiological perspective, but unlike Christians, Assange does not seem interested in explicitly articulating his presuppositional thinking as it regards justice. As Assange (2016: 69) once stated regarding his reasons for founding WikiLeaks: 'And one can ask: "What are your philosophical axioms for this?" And I say: "I do not need to consider them. This is simply my temperament. And it is an axiom because it is that way." That avoids getting into further unhelpful philosophical discussion about why I want to do something. It is enough that I do.' Elsewhere, however, Assange is quite clear that the principal animating concept in his moral philosophy is justice. 'I have a single goal, not a very original one but a definite goal to my life,' Assange (2011: 119) explains, 'which is to help in the creation of a more just society to live in. I am not for transparency all round, or even democracy all round, but I am for justice.' Thus, to use Christians's language, justice is a type of proto-norm for Assange, and it is based not in knowledge (epistemology) but in values (axiology). Assange (ibid) suggests that being motivated by justice is not idiosyncratic but a basic human disposition, and he argues that humans have 'an innate yearning for justice'.

Assange does not seem to provide any explicit definition or detailed explanation of how he conceives of justice, but it is possible to approximate his conception of justice based on his other statements and actions.[2] Given his willingness to critique, violate and even undermine existing norms and institutions, Assange's conception of justice seems to be more ideal and substantive than it is conservative and procedural. Likewise, given that equality (especially equality of outcome) does not play a major role in his ethical thinking, Assange seems to adhere to a non-comparative form of justice that seeks to allocate treatment based on the threshold of inherent human needs. Assange's conception of justice also seems to have retributive characteristics because he believes wrongdoers deserve punishment and that the innocent ought to be protected from undeserved punishment. This view is evidenced by Assange's statement that he enjoys both 'helping people who are vulnerable' and 'crushing bastards' (*Spiegel* 2010). Finally, Assange seems to view justice as a virtue of persons rather than a characteristic of institutions, which means that whatever formal requirements of justice might exist must follow from the normatively prior virtue (see LeBar 2014). Assange, therefore, often shies away from getting into the minute details regarding the principles at the basis of his 'worldview' (Christians 2013), but it is clear that some ideal, substantive, retributive and non-comparative conception of justice as a virtue is at the basis of his moral worldview.

In Assange's view, if global media ethics is to meet injustice with justice, then it requires the central normative principle of cypherpunk ethics: privacy for the weak, transparency for the powerful. Assange is often described as a 'radical transparency activist' who hypocritically holds a double standard for himself and WikiLeaks (Marechal 2013), but this interpretation overlooks the ways in which Assange understands the connection between information and power. As Assange (2006) argues, powerful institutions and organisations that seek to do harmful, unjust acts use secrecy to hide their plans and thus prevent the development of oppositional forces. By imposing a condition of non-consensual transparency on such organisations through the creation of 'a worldwide movement of mass leaking', it becomes possible to redistribute information and foster the development of forces that will oppose unjust actions and institutions (see Greenberg 2012: 131). However, such transparency must be supplemented with greater privacy for relatively powerless individuals and groups. In an age of public and private sector mass surveillance and ever-expanding permanent databases, forces that would oppose injustice also require means of information self-defence. Assange (2014b) is clear that privacy is not an end in itself but a means to redistributing power relations and transforming the ratio of injustice to justice. When it comes to WikiLeaks, Assange is clear that 'The method is transparency. The goal is justice' (see Hayase 2016), but we must also acknowledge the whole cypherpunk perspective, which insists that expanded privacy is also necessary for justice.

As a result of this comparative sketch of Christians's and Assange's moral philosophies, we can see not only that Assange offers an axiologically-grounded conception of global moral challenges, but also that Assange presents a possible alternative to Christians's approach. For Christians, moral relativism threatens to undermine cross-cultural dialogue and co-operation and eliminate any basis for normative critique, and he answers this challenge by articulating a universal proto-norm and the universal principles that follow from it. For Assange, cross-cultural dialogue and cooperation are not threatened by problematic meta-ethical commitments but by global actions of injustice, often perpetrated by large, powerful, secretive organisations – especially Western governments like the United States. For Christians, when it comes to global media ethics, the problem and the solution are in the realm of ideas, in the conflict between the particular and the universal. For Assange (2014b), the problem and the solution are in the realm of justice, of correcting the disparity between what people are getting and what they are actually owed. The difference, then, between Christians's meta-ethical approach and Assange's justice approach provides the basis for understanding how their shared concerns about nationalism, professionalism and technology are rooted in competing ethical paradigms and take fundamentally different forms.

FROM NATIONALISM TO COSMOPOLITANISM ... AND BACK?

Given the contrasting starting points for their respective conceptions of global media ethics, Christians and Assange approach other issues in media ethics from quite different perspectives. Even when they seem to agree on general conclusions, the details of their arguments lead them in separate directions. Christians and Assange both advocate a cosmopolitan perspective on communication ethics, but Christians advocates cosmopolitanism as the universalist answer to the nationalist particularism, while Assange advocates cosmopolitanism because it is the only way we can properly account for what we owe all other people according to the demands of justice. Likewise, Christians and Assange would both like to see professional journalism reformed, but for Christians such reform entails broadening journalists' conception of their place in the world, while for Assange such reform entails holding journalists accountable to the requirements of justice on a global scale. This section deals with Christians's and Assange's approaches to cosmopolitanism, and the next section deals with their critiques of professional journalism.

In his rejection of nationalism, Christians (1988, 1997, 2008) frequently cites Sigmund Freud's (1952 [1913]) *Totem and taboo*, which argues that every society simultaneously prohibits some values and behaviours while promoting others; the promoted ones stand as a society's ego ideal, the image to which it ostensibly aspires to embody. For Christians (1988: 6), the problem with nationalism is connected to the problem of moral relativism, for when a community or nation lacks external standards with which they can critique their own society and through which they can communicate with other communities and nations, international and cross-cultural relationships devolve into competing claims of narcissistic exceptionalism and power-driven decisions. In some ways, Christians seems to view nationalism as relativism in practice, a situation in which 'parochial ethics' impede 'international understanding'.

To overcome the limitations of nationalism, Christians draws upon his meta-ethical conceptions and insists upon a distinctively cosmopolitan disposition. 'Cosmopolitanism,' Christians (2008: 8) states, 'sets the highest and most accurate standard for our theoretical work at present as the socio-political context for understanding the ethics of news.' Because respect for human dignity is in many ways an antidote to the violent excesses of nationalism (Christians 2015b), Christians argues that human solidarity, not petty tribalism, is the only adequate basis for a global ethics. Thus, he challenges media professionals to ensure that 'all ethical theory done in whatever national context revivify the normative dimension in order to confront the ruling ideologies and to wrest the permanently valuable from our isolated posturing and flurry of activity on the treadmill' (Christians 1988: 11). While the universal proto-norm of the sacredness-of-life provides the intellectual foundations for global media ethics, cosmopolitanism provides the experiential foundation for those ethics.

Assange similarly condemns nationalism as an impediment to global ethics and adopts a cosmopolitan disposition as a means of transcending that impediment. In a way, WikiLeaks is a product of the globalisation of media. As Geoffroy de Lagasnerie (2019: 294) has observed, WikiLeaks embodies 'a practical critique of all forms of nationalism', for it is 'a project that transcends the idea of nations, and it works to dissolve the nationalistic basis at the root of all conservatisms'. WikiLeaks has this character, de Lagasnerie adds, because Assange is 'one of those rare contemporary political figures to adopt truly global perception of the world'. Assange's (2011: 148-149) own words support de Lagasnerie's commentary. On the one hand, Assange eschews the slogan 'Think Globally, Act Locally', favouring instead the alternative: 'Think Globally, Act Globally'. Assange also refuses to confine those who might benefit from or contribute to WikiLeaks's journalistic enterprise to this or that nation-state. Instead, when he conceived of WikiLeaks, Assange (2011: 114) believed that 'the flow of information would not be a matter for single journalists alone, or for individual media organisations, but for societies working together'. WikiLeaks has partnered with dozens of media outlets around the world, providing leaked primary documents to local reporters who publish the information for their respective publics (Lynch 2013; Avila et al. 2017).

Though Assange shares with Christians a cosmopolitan outlook, Assange's cosmopolitanism is grounded not in the particular/universal opposition embraced by Christians but in justice. By understanding the ways in which Assange connects his conception of justice to his conception of cosmopolitanism, we can better understand both. On the one hand, Assange seems committed to a type of global justice, which emphasises justice among individual human beings. For example, he explains his reaction to *Collateral murder* – a 2007 video of two United States AH-64 Apache helicopters gunning down unarmed Iraqi civilians, including two Reuters journalists, released by WikiLeaks in 2010 – in terms of injustice done to particular human beings. 'I must have seen the video hundreds of times,' Assange (2011: 188) writes, 'but, on each occasion, my blood ran cold when I saw those children coming under attack. ... I came to feel a large moral responsibility for exposing the bastards who did this.'

On the other hand, Assange also seems committed to a type of international justice, which conceives of justice as a relational situation between nations. In 2014, for example, *The Intercept* reported: 'Documents show that the NSA has been generating intelligence reports from MYSTIC surveillance in the Bahamas, Mexico, Kenya, the Philippines, and one other country, which *The Intercept* is not naming in response to specific, credible concerns that doing so could lead to increased violence' (Devereaux et al. 2014). Within a week, WikiLeaks published a statement charging *The Intercept* with censorship and revealing that the unnamed country was Afghanistan. Implying a connection between justice and national autonomy, Assange (2014a) argued that 'Such censorship strips a nation of its right to self-determination on a matter which affects its whole population.' Interestingly, Assange expresses a concern for not only international justice but also global justice, adding: 'By denying an entire population the knowledge of its own victimisation, this act of censorship denies each individual in that country the opportunity to seek an effective remedy, whether in international courts, or elsewhere.' For this reason, WikiLeaks has been described as a publisher advocating for national self-determination and perhaps even certain varieties of anti-colonial nationalism (Avila et al. 2017). For Assange, therefore, cosmopolitan justice means both global justice for individuals and international justice for entire national communities.

DIVERGENT CRITIQUES OF JOURNALISTIC PROFESSIONALISM

Christians and Assange both lament the shortcomings of professional journalism, especially in the English-speaking world (Christians 1988; Assange 2011, 2016), but their respective critiques of journalism differ because they follow from their respective meta-ethical presuppositions. Christians identifies at least four basic problems with contemporary professionalised journalism. First, professional journalism in the United States has been dominated by the idea that the journalist's epistemological – and therefore moral – obligation was to remain objective, writing in such a manner as to present readers with an unbiased reporting of facts (Christians 1977). Second, professional journalism is riddled with 'routines and cognitive conventions' that stifle creativity and self-criticism while promoting conformity and self-censorship (Christians and Nordenstreng 2004: 17). In other words, the training and education of professionals in the news media are designed to socialise and acculturate journalists into an institutionally predetermined way of being instead of being designed to help them cultivate a philosophical disposition. Third, professional journalism remains largely held captive by nationalist sentiments and commitments which prevent the profession from moving toward a more cosmopolitan understanding of its mission. Finally, professional journalism is guided by the economic interests of the economic elites who control the media industry, and economic incentives tend to push journalistic activity away from its democratic function and towards profitability (Christians 1985).

In Christians's view, all of these problems result from the 'profession-based' paradigm that dominates journalism, and the remedy is a paradigm shift to a 'citizen-based' paradigm (Christians and Nordenstreng 2004: 19). Christians's call for a paradigm shift in professional journalism reflects his call for a paradigm shift in meta-ethics. In the realm of meta-ethics, the particularism of moral relativism impedes self-criticism while universal ethics enables it; likewise, in the realm of professional journalism, the particularism of the profession-based paradigm impedes self-criticism while the citizen-based paradigm enables it. By constantly reminding themselves that they have a truth-telling duty and a mission to serve democracy and humanity, professional journalists can overcome the ethical limitations of their training and socialisation and establish a basis upon which they can work not only to defend the prestige and power of their profession but also improve their profession through critique and reflection. Thus, we can see that Christians's meta-ethics form the basis of his critique of professionalism in journalism. Just as relativism is the problem with global media ethics, parochialism is the problem with professional journalism and, in each case, Christians advocates a wider, cosmopolitan perspective as the remedy, one built upon the sacredness of life and advancing the principle of truth-telling.

While Christians argues that journalistic truth-telling follows from the sacredness of life, Assange argues that journalistic truth-telling is a necessary condition of justice. For Assange, one of the conditions of justice is that all people have free access to as much information as possible for, in his view, there can be no justice without truth. Assange (2011: 119) argues that every person has 'the right to know' and 'the right to speak', which together constitute 'the right to communicate knowledge'. In his words, these are 'the basic rights that underpin justice'. Importantly, Assange is not saying that these rights are metaphysically or conceptually prior to justice. On the contrary: just as the cypherpunk principle 'privacy for the weak, transparency for the powerful' follows from the proto-norm of justice, so too do these communicative rights. Alongside the 'innate yearning for justice' that he finds in human nature, Assange also believes that humans have 'an innate aversion to censorship'. Assange is concerned that 'concealment, secrecy and lies' are so prevalent in our digital world that it is becoming increasingly difficult to realise these rights, which is why, in his view, anyone fighting for justice must fight censorship and concealment – and, by extension, anyone complicit in censorship and concealment is guilty of impeding the realisation of justice.

Assange's critique of professional journalism follows from his stance on justice, truth and anti-censorship, for, in his perspective, too many people in professional journalism are willing to impede the flow of information and deny global publics the truth – and therefore justice. Returning to two previous examples, *Collateral murder* and *The Intercept* failing to name Afghanistan, Assange cites these as examples of the media using a form of censorship to impede justice. Assange (2011: 188) says he felt a moral responsibility to expose the 'bastards' responsible for the killings in *Collateral murder*, and, in part, 'the bastards were the US military'. But he adds that 'those elements of the media who had seen fit to join them in covering the thing up' were complicit in this injustice. Likewise, in WikiLeaks's criticism of *The Intercept*'s reporting on National Security Agency (NSA) surveillance in Afghanistan, Assange (2014a) unequivocally stated: 'We do not believe it is the place of media to "aid and abet" a state in escaping detection and prosecution for a serious crime against a population. ... Consequently WikiLeaks cannot be complicit in the censorship of victim state X.' While *The Intercept* cited what they called credible national security reasons not to name Afghanistan, Assange argues that those journalists actually covered for the crimes of the United States government.

When it comes to their mutual appreciation for cosmopolitanism and their shared critiques of professional journalism, Christians and Assange provide interesting and sometimes provocative insights regarding global media ethics. But because they each begin from different presuppositional concepts – the sacredness of life and justice – they offer completely different reasons for their conclusions. For Christians, just as the particularism of philosophical relativism is to be overcome with the universalism of shared proto-norms, so too are nationalism and 'profession-based' conceptions of journalism to be overcome with the universalism of cosmopolitan thinking and 'citizen-based' journalistic paradigms. For Assange, on the other hand, injustice is to be overcome, in part, by promoting open access to information and allowing all peoples to act freely on the truth. This aproach entails both a cosmopolitan perspective that recognises the role that nationalism might play in pursuing justice against empire states and a critique of professional journalism that finds journalists complicit in injustice when they fail to disclose *all* available information. It matters, therefore, whether we begin with the sacredness of life, as Christians does, or with a conception of justice, as Assange does, for those competing starting points for global media ethics lead to very different perspectives on nationalism, professionalism and truth.

BEYOND PROPAGANDA: TECHNOLOGY, *TECHNIQUE*, TOOLS

Having explored the ways in which Christians's and Assange's respective meta-ethics inform their divergent stances on cosmopolitanism and professional journalism, it is now necessary to explore the ways in which their seemingly similar positions on ethics and communication technologies take on quite different forms in light of their presuppositional commitments. Christians and Assange each argue that the technological *context* is the challenge and that we need to cultivate new or creative technologies that empower average persons (Christians 1995; Assange et al. 2012). They both explicitly draw upon Jacques Ellul's (1964) notion of *la technique* to identify the hegemonic imperatives of efficiency and propaganda as major challenges, and Christians (explicitly) and Assange (implicitly) take up Ivan Illich's (2009) notion of 'convivial tools', arguing that technologies should resist *la technique* and facilitate human coexistence. But that is where the similarities end. For Christians, *la technique* is dangerous because it violates the principles of human dignity, truth-telling and non-violence, which means it disregards the sacredness of life. Convivial tools, in his estimation, are meant to do the opposite, upholding his universal proto-norm and its corresponding principles. By contrast, Assange views *la technique* – in the form of surveillance and institutional secrecy – as a cause of injustice and convivial tools – especially digital cryptography – as a means promoting justice.

Inspired by his long-term engagement with the work of Ellul (Christians 1976), Christians (1995: 163) argues that the imperative of the communication age is not to identify individual groups who misuse technology for their own propagandistic aims but to understand how technological efficiency now dominates our very understanding of society and self. In his interpretation of Ellul, Christians suggests that public opinion – as required by the democratic ethos – is no longer an independent causal mechanism. Public opinion does not spontaneously emerge and then inform government policy; instead, the overwhelming flood of information paralyses even the most seemingly informed citizens, producing a kind of sensory overload through which perceptions and attitudes 'become crystallised'. Members of the public are dragged along in the relentless stream of information, and the journalists who incessantly demand more government disclosure and endlessly proclaim the public's 'right to know' enable rather than resist *la technique* and its propagandistic results. While Christians (1995: 170) cautions that Ellul's 'analysis of mass communication tends to be reductionist', he nevertheless believes that Ellul's analysis inspires a 'critical consciousness' (ibid: 166) of technology and 'offers a more sure-handed direction for social change than one based on the received view' (ibid: 158). The social change that Christians seems to have in mind here is the promotion of the sacredness of life.

Christians does not, however, succumb to what he sees as Ellul's pessimistic 'apocalypticism' (Christians et al. 1986). Instead, Christians (1995, 2009) turns to Ivan Illich and calls for 'convivial tools' as the best means for overcoming *la technique* and its efficiency imperative. 'Convivial technology,' Christians (1995: 168) explains, 'arises from a critical consciousness; it respects the dignity of human work, needs little specialised training to operate, is generally accessible to the public, and emphasises personal satisfaction and creative ingenuity.' For Christians (ibid: 169), there are many examples of people using convivial tools to free publics from efficiency: '… independent film companies, underground presses, people's radio, and popular theatre can go for efficienacy's jugular and provide an alternative media system from below.' (Interestingly, Christians's mention of underground presses suggests that questions of power reside just under the surface of his media ethics.) Considering Christians's (2019b: 50) analysis, we should also add *Al Jazeera* to this list, for in his view, *Al Jazeera* is convivial because it is oriented toward social change and challenges the hegemony of Western corporate media. *Al Jazeera* is anti-propaganda because it makes space for dialogue and issues of the oppressed without succumbing to overly simplified narratives of good and evil, aiming to 'reveal genuine meaning beneath the surface'. Thus, Christians (2009: 14) sees a way out of *la technique*, and the way out does not reject technology but instead distinguishes between those technologies designed to impose efficiency and those technologies that 'nurture communities of resistance against the technological mystique'. Thus, for Christians, convivial tools can help us uphold human dignity, truth and non-violence in the face of dehumanising *technique*.

In a similar fashion, Assange contrasts the dangers of *la technique* with the moral possibilities of convivial tools, but he articulates these concerns specifically within the context of digital communication and information technologies and explains their meanings as regards their relationship to justice. For Assange, the contemporary threat of *la technique* is defined by technologically enabled conspiracy and surveillance. In Assange's (2006: 1) philosophy, 'conspire' is a technical term that means to 'make secret plans jointly to commit a harmful act'. Authoritarian governments, for example, achieve their power by using secrecy to conceal their nefarious plans from unsuspecting publics, at least until the state has so much power that resistance becomes nearly impossible. Traditional authoritarian conspiracies could only be as strong as their analogue communication networks, but contemporary digital communication networks enable conspiracies to be more powerful and efficient. 'Literacy and the communications revolution have empowered conspirators with new means to conspire,' Assange (2006: 5) observes, 'increasing the speed of accuracy of … their interactions and thereby the maximum size a conspiracy may achieve before it breaks down. Conspirators who have this technology are able to out-conspire conspirators without it.'

While conspiratorial powers seek secrecy for their own communications and activities, they also seek total information awareness about their environment, especially information pertaining to possible challenges to the conspiracy's designs. Thus, surveillance is a necessary component of authoritarian power, or as the cypherpunk Jacob Appelbaum puts it, 'the more you have the ability to surveil, the more you have control' (Assange et al. 2012: 107). Echoing Ellul, Assange (2014b) is clear that surveillance is not a problem caused by this or that group but the result of the fundamental logic of our time: 'We live not only in a surveillance state, but in a surveillance society.' Thus, even before in 2013, when Edward Snowden revealed the NSA's mass surveillance practices to the world, the cypherpunks warned of an emerging 'transnational surveillance dystopia' (Assange et al. 2012: 5).

In response to the twin threats of secrecy and surveillance, Assange aligns his philosophy of technology with his emphasis on justice, advocating the use of digital cryptography and works to make the cypherpunk slogan 'privacy for the weak, transparency for the powerful' a reality (ibid: 7). In his view, cryptography promotes justice by allowing users to modify the flow of information and thereby push the world into 'a greater state of justice' (Assange 2011: 114).

On the surveillance side of the issue, the importance of cryptography seems obvious. Given that government officials are among the key architects of the surveillance apparatus, Assange argues issues of privacy cannot be left to the legal system. Instead, we must turn to mathematics. 'Encryption is an embodiment of the laws of physics, and it does not listen to the bluster of states, even transnational surveillance dystopias,' he writes. 'Strong cryptography can resist an unlimited application of violence. No amount of coercive force will ever solve a math problem' (Assange et al. 2012: 5). Assange's (2014b) concern about privacy is motivated not by a rights-based conception of ethics but in 'the calculus of power', for 'the destruction of privacy widens the existing power imbalance between the ruling factions and everyone else'. Thus, privacy is a means to justice, not an end in itself, and because cryptography preserves privacy and promotes justice, it is a convivial tool.

On the secrecy side of the issue, crypto helps advance WikiLeaks's distinctive journalistic mission, which is to increase the flow and availability of information in respect of the right to communicate knowledge. Assange (2011b: 22) explains that the fourth estate should operate as 'an intelligence agency of the people', that it should, in a sense, be observing powerful political and economic actors, gathering intelligence and reporting that intelligence to the proper audience. According to Assange, there are only two minor differences between journalists and intelligence agents: whom they are watching and whether they publish (Scahill 2017), with 'to publish' defined as making something public (Assange et al. 2012: 50). But Assange (2016: 17) also has a very distinctive notion of what it means for a news agency to publish. According to his philosophy of 'scientific journalism', it is not enough for journalists to publish their analysis of primary documents; they must make 'the primary source material public'. Assange reminds us that it is not WikiLeaks's policy to verify sources or even verify facts. WikiLeaks's policy is, instead, to verify that the documents they receive are authentic. Assange's intent is not to deliver facts but to 'let people fight with the truth' (ibid: 184). Thus, scientific journalism, the practice of publishing primary sources, gives global publics the ability to check the work of journalists. 'Scientific journalism allows you to read a news story, then to click online to see the original document it is based on,' Assange (2010) explains. 'That way you can judge for yourself: Is the story true? Did the journalist report it accurately?'

Without encryption, WikiLeaks's style of journalism would be much more difficult. On the front end of WikiLeaks's intelligence-gathering system, whistleblowers – the people inside the conspiracy who see the injustices being carried out – can submit documents using an encrypted digital drop box, which hides the whistleblower's identity not only from snoopers but also from WikiLeaks personnel. By using anonymity as a defensive manoeuvre, Assange (ibid: 143) says that 'the courage threshold' is lowered and therefore more insiders are willing to act. 'We have come to the conclusion,' Assange wrote at the moment of WikiLeaks's founding, 'that fomenting a worldwide movement of mass leaking is the most effective political intervention available to us' (see Greenberg 2012: 131). On the back end of WikiLeaks, the website is tunnelled through the Tor network – an encrypted network of relays that mask user identity – to hidden servers, using a sophisticated caching system to ensure that the website is extremely difficult to take down permanently without dismantling the entire internet (Assange 2016). In other words, WikiLeaks represents a nearly censorship-proof system.

While the most explicit connections between the issues of justice, *la technique* and conviviality emerge in Assange's discussions of using cryptography to promote privacy for the weak and transparency for the powerful, he also views cryptography as relevant to global and international justice. In the wake of the Edward Snowden revelations regarding the NSA's global mass surveillance programmes, Assange (2013) argued that cryptography could contribute to justice both at the individual level and the national level. 'Mass surveillance is not just an issue for democracy and governance,' he notes, 'it's a geopolitical issue. The surveillance of a whole population by a foreign power naturally threatens sovereignty.' Citing 'the struggle for Latin American self-determination', Assange insists that cryptography is a necessary tool for those nations seeking to resist empire. In one passage, Assange expresses the core meaning of cryptography as a convivial tool of justice: 'Cryptography can protect not just the civil liberties and rights of individuals, but the sovereignty and independence of whole countries, solidarity between groups with common cause and the project of global emancipation. It can be used to fight not just the tyranny of the state over the individual but the tyranny of the empire over smaller states.'

Not surprisingly, when it comes to ethics and technology, the convergences and divergences between Christians and Assange follow a familiar pattern: while they both warn of the dangers of *la technique* and champion the promises of conviviality, their assessments take on radically different forms because their respective ethical theories have radically different presuppositional starting points. Christians cautions us about *la technique* because it ignores the sacredness of life and violates the principles of dignity, truth and non-violence, while Assange cautions us about *la technique* because it causes injustice. Christians advocates for a range of seemingly convivial tools that ought to promote the sacredness of life, while Assange claims that cryptography is the single most convivial tool of the digital age because it promotes justice in a variety of ways. Just as with cosmopolitanism and journalism, Christians and Assange come to very different conclusions on technology, even though they conceive of the central problem in similar language. As we have seen here, their disagreements stem almost entirely from their respective proto-norms: sacredness and justice.

CONCLUSION

This paper offers contributions to both the scholarly literature on WikiLeaks and to the development of the field of global communication ethics. By considering Julian Assange a theorist of media ethics, rather than merely an activist or publisher, this paper models ethical listening, promotes an open media ethics and, most importantly, provides a detailed description of the ways in which Assange's presuppositional thinking about justice inform his broader moral, political, journalistic and technological project. This paper pushes the conversation beyond the anti-WikiLeaks propaganda that has obfuscated our understanding of Assange's moral philosophy and into the realm of theoretical analysis. As a result, it becomes possible to recognise that Assange's distinctive moral paradigm, which here is called cypherpunk ethics, offers a possible fifth paradigm for global media ethics oriented around a conception of justice.

To elucidate Assange's ethical theory, this paper presents a comparative analysis of Assange's thought and the work of Clifford Christians. Because Christians and Assange begin their ethical reasoning from different fundamental principles, they approach questions of nationalism, professional journalism and technology from very different perspectives – even though they are engaged in the same broader conversations. For Christians, moral relativism ought to be met with a universal proto-norm establishing the sacredness of life. He sees cosmopolitanism, citizen-based paradigms of professional journalism and convivial technologies as means of promoting the sacredness of life against the threats of nationalism and *la technique*. For Assange, injustice ought to be corrected through the wide application of the cypherpunk principle 'privacy for the weak, transparency for the powerful'. He sees the duties of journalism as best understood through the lens of what global and international justice require, and he identifies digital cryptography as an indispensable tool of justice.

While this paper offers a new look at Assange as a theorist of global media ethics, future research is needed to clarify lingering questions raised by this project. First, scholars should explore the implication of Assange's moral theory for our understanding of WikiLeaks and revise criticisms of WikiLeaks's journalistic methods. Second, Assange's views on justice should be more deeply explored and place into conversation the emerging scholarship on virtue ethics and communication. Third, Assange's understanding of technology, especially the potential of cryptography to help resist surveillance and secrecy and thereby promote justice, should be more deeply investigated; such a project should explore that topic in the context of the broader cypherpunk movement. Finally, Assange's concern about unjust wars and imperialistic aggression should be taken as a starting point for a new ethics of anti-imperialism. If the persecution of Assange is any indication, this justice-based paradigm of cypherpunk global media ethics provides us with a useful basis for confronting empire. As Christians (2009: 15) observes: 'The challenge is to build the conditions of public life so that publics always in the process of making themselves might also make themselves good. The press plays a vitally important role in the process of self-governance, not merely as the provider of information but as the facilitator of public opinion. A journalism of conversation views public opinion as the consequence of a social and public inquiry into common goods.' If Assange is correct that the major threats to global communication today stem from the injustices of war and imperialism, then media ethics generally and journalism ethics specifically could use a healthy dose of anti-imperialism.

- This paper was first published in *Ethical Space*, Vol. 19, No. 1 pp 4-18

ACKNOWLEDGEMENT

This paper received the Clifford G. Christians Ethics Research Award at the 2021 Association for Practical and Professional Ethics Conference. It also received the 2021 Graduate Dean's Citation for Outstanding Research Project at Grand Valley State University. Thank you to Melba Vélez-Ortiz, Alex Nesterenko, Rocio Alvarez, John C. O'Day and Clifford G. Christians.

NOTES

[1] To insure against changing URLs and disappearing content, most of the web sources cited in this paper are referenced using the archive.today service. Going to the URLs in the References will allow you to access the archived webpage and also access the original link

[2] I have suggested elsewhere that Assange may be using the term 'justice' in a rhetorical rather than theoretical manner (Anderson 2022). That argument, however, was made not because there is reason to believe that Assange is using the term rhetorically but because the editor made the inclusion of that argument a condition for publication of the article

REFERENCES

Anderson, Patrick D. (2020a) Review essay: Christian Cotton and Robert Arp (eds) *WikiLeaking: The ethics of secrecy and exposure, Logos: A journal of modern society and culture*, Vol. 19, No. 1. Available online at http://logosjournal.com/2020/cotton-arp-wikileaks-review/, accessed on 15 September 2021

Anderson, Patrick D. (2020b) The execution of Julian Assange, *Mint Press News*, 11 May. Available online at https://www.mintpressnews.com/opinion-media-execution-julian-assange/267393/, accessed on 15 September 2021

Anderson, Patrick D. (2021) Privacy for the weak, transparency for the powerful: The cypherpunk ethics of Julian Assange, *Ethics and Information Technology*, Vol. 23 pp 295-308. Available online at https://link.springer.com/article/10.1007/s10676-020-09571-x

Anderson, Patrick D. (2022) On moderate and radical whistleblowing: Edward Snowden and Julian Assange as theorists of whistleblowing ethics, *Journal of Media Ethics*, Vol. 37, No. 1.

Assange, Julian (2006) Conspiracy as governance, *Cryptome.org*, 3 December. Available online at http://archive.fo/kr8Pr, accessed on 15 September 2021

Assange, Julian (2010) Don't shoot messenger for revealing uncomfortable truths, *Australian*, 7 December. Available online at http://archive.fo/SmXpG, accessed on 15 September 2021

Assange, Julian (2011a) *Julian Assange: The unauthorised autobiography*, Edinburgh, Canongate Books

Assange, Julian (2011b) Of the people and for the people, *New Statesman*, 11 April, pp 20-22

Assange, Julian (2013) How cryptography is a key weapon in the fight against empire states, *Guardian*, 9 July. Available online at http://archive.fo/Mbsx4, accessed on 15 September 2021

Assange, Julian (2014a) WikiLeaks statement on the mass recording of Afghan telephone calls by the NSA, *WikiLeaks.org*, 23 May. Available online at https://wikileaks.org/WikiLeaks-statement-on-the-mass.html, accessed on 15 September 2021

Assange, Julian (2014b) Who should own the internet?, *New York Times*, 4 December. Available online at https://archive.fo/BrY5t, accessed on 15 September 2021

Assange, Julian (2015) Introduction: WikiLeaks and empire, *The WikiLeaks files: The world according to US empire*, New York, Verso

Assange, Julian (2016) *When Google met WikiLeaks*, New York, OR Books

Assange, Julian, Appelbaum, J., Müller-Maguhn, A. and Zimmermann, J. (2012) *Cypherpunks: Freedom and the future of the internet*, New York, OR Books

Avila, Renata, Harrison, Sarah and Richter, Angela (2017) *Women, whistleblowing, WikiLeaks: A conversation*, New York, OR Books

Benkler, Yochai (2011) A free irresponsible press: WikiLeaks and the battle over the soul of the networked fourth estate, *Harvard Civil Rights-Civil Liberties Law Review*, Vol. 46 pp 311-397

Blumenthal, Max (2020) 'The American friends': New court files expose Sheldon Adelson's security team in US spy operation against Julian Assange, *The Grayzone*, 14 May. Available online at https://archive.md/IWjkH, accessed on 15 September 2021

Boot, Eric R. (2019) *The ethics of whistleblowing*, New York, Routledge

Borden, Sandra (2007) *Journalism as practice: MacIntyre, virtue ethics and the press*, Burlington, VT, Ashgate

Brevini, B. Benedetta, Hintz, Arne and McCurdy, P. Patrick (eds) (2013) *Beyond WikiLeaks: Implications for the future of communications, journalism and society*, New York, Palgrave Macmillan

Burns, John F. and Somaiya, Ravi (2010) Confidential Swedish police report details allegations against WikiLeaks founder, *New York Times*, 18 December. Available online at https://archive.md/U1MKw, accessed on 15 September 2021

Carey, James W. (1987) Journalists just leave: The ethics of an anomalous profession, Sagen, Maile-Gene (ed.) *Ethics and the media*, Iowa City, Iowa Humanities Board pp 5-19

Christians, Clifford G. (1976) Jacques Ellul and democracy's vital information premise, *Journalism Monographs*, Vol. 45

Christians, Clifford G. (1977) Fifty years of scholarship in media ethics, *Journal of Communication*, Vol. 27, No. 4 pp 19-29

Christians, Clifford G. (1985) The news profession and the powerless, *Calvin Theological Journal*, Vol. 20, No. 2 pp 229-254

Christians, Clifford G. (1988a) Can the public be held accountable?, *Journal of Mass Media Ethics*, Vol. 3. No. 1 pp 50-58

Christians, Clifford G. (1988b) Ethical theory in a global setting, Cooper, Thomas (ed.) *Communication ethics and global change*, New York, Longman pp 3-19

Christians, Clifford G. (1995a) Communication ethics as the basis of genuine democracy, Lee, Philip (ed.) *The democratization of communication*, Cardiff, University of Wales Press pp 75-91

Christians, Clifford G. (1995b) Propaganda and the technological system, Glasser, Theodore and Salmon, Charles (eds) *Public opinion and the communication of consent*, New York, Gilford Press pp 156-174

Christians, Clifford G. (1997) The common good and universal values, Black, Jay (ed.) *Mixed news: The public/civic/communitarian journalism debate*, Mohwah, NJ, Lawrence Erlbaum pp 18-33

Christians, Clifford G. (2007) Utilitarianism in media ethics and its discontents, *Journal of Mass Media Ethics*, Vol. 22, Nos 2 and 3 pp 113-131

Christians. Clifford G. (2008) Media ethics on a higher order of magnitude, *Journal of Mass Media Ethics*, Vol. 23, No. 1 pp 3-14

Christians, Clifford G. (2009) Theoretical frontiers in international media ethics, *Australian Journalism Review*, Vol. 31, No. 2 pp 5-18

Christians, Clifford G. (2010) The ethics of universal being, Ward, Stephen J. A. and Wasserman, Herman (eds) *Media ethics beyond borders: A global perspective*, New York, Routledge pp 6-23

Christians, Clifford G. (2011a) Universalism versus communitarianism in media ethics, Fortner, Robert S. and Fackler, P. Mark (eds) *The handbook of global communication and media ethics, Vol. I*, Malden, MA, Blackwell Publishing pp 393-414

Christians, Clifford G. (2011b) Conclusion: Ethics in a new key, Ross, Susan D. and Lester, Paul M. (eds) *Images that injure: Pictorial stereotypes in the media*, third edition, Santa Barbara, CA, ABC-CLIO, LLC pp 421-432

Christians, Clifford G. (2013) Global ethics and the problem of relativism, Ward, Stephen J. A. (ed.) *Global media ethics: Problems and perspectives*, Malden, MA, Blackwell Publishing pp 272-294

Christians, Clifford G. (2014a) The impact of ethics on media and press theory, Fortner, Robert S. and Fackler, Paul M. (eds) *The handbook of media and mass communication theory, Vol. I*, Malden, MA, John Wiley & Sons, Inc. pp 225-247

Christians, Clifford G. (2014b) The philosophy of technology and communication systems, Fortner, Robert S. and Fackler, Paul M. (eds) *The handbook of media and mass communication theory, Vol. II*, Malden, MA, John Wiley & Sons, Inc. pp 513-534

Christians, Clifford G. (2015a) The problem of communitarianism in Western moral philosophy, Shan Bo and Christians, Clifford G. (eds) *The ethics of intercultural communication*, New York, Peter Lang pp 35-55

Christians, Clifford G. (2015b) The ethics of dignity in a multicultural world, Shan, Bo and Christians, Clifford G. (eds) *The ethics of intercultural communication*, New York, Peter Lang pp 337-355

Christians, Clifford G. (2016) Social justice and Internet technology, *New Media & Society*, Vol. 18, No. 11 pp 2760-2773

Christians, Clifford G. (2019a) *Media ethics and global justice in the digital age*, Cambridge, Cambridge University Press

Christians, Clifford G. (2019b) Truth as an ethical principle, Sadig, Haydar Badawi (ed.) *Al Jazeera in the Gulf and the world*, Gateway East, Singapore, Palgrave Macmillan pp 35-65

Christians, Clifford G. and Nordenstreng, Kaarle (2004) Social responsibility worldwide, *Journal of Mass Media Ethics*, Vol. 19, No. 1 pp 3-28

Cortez, Robert Z. (2016) Colloquy with Clifford G. Christians in Urbana-Champaign, *Church, Communication and Culture*, Vol. 1, No. 1 pp 135-161

Cummings-Bruce, Nick (2019) Julian Assange is suffering psychological torture, UN expert says, *New York Times*, 31 May. Available online at https://archive.md/gf3JM, accessed on 15 September 2021

de Lagasnerie, Geoffroy (2019) Julian Assange for the future, Ali, Tariq and Kunstler, Margaret (eds) *In defense of Julian Assange*, New York, OR Books pp 244-250

Delmas, Candice (2015) The ethics of government whistleblowing, *Social Theory and Practice*, Vol. 41, No. 1 pp 77-105

Devereaux, Ryan, Greenwald, Glenn and Poitras, Laura (2014) The NSA is recording every cell phone call in the Bahamas, *Intercept*, 19 May. Available online at https://archive.fo/swflk, accessed on 15 September 2021

Dorfman, Zach, Naylor, Sean D. and Isikoff, Michael (2021) Kidnapping, assassination and a London shoot-out: Inside the CIA's secret war plans against WikiLeaks, *Yahoo! News*, 26 September. Available online at https://archive.md/2sX3Q, accessed 15 September 2021

Dreyfus, Suelette and Assange, Julian (2012) *Underground*, Edinburgh, Canongate Books

Ellul, Jacques (1964) *The technological society*, trans. Wilkinson, John, New York, Knopf

Fortner, Robert S. (2011) Journalism ethics in the moral infrastructure of a global civil society, Fortner, Robert S. and Fackler, Paul M. (eds) *The handbook of global communication and media ethics, Vol. I*, Malden, MA, Blackwell Publishing pp 481-499

Freud, Sigmund (1952 [1913]) *Totem and taboo*, trans. Strachey, James, New York, Norton

Greenberg, Andy (2012) *This machine kills secrets: How WikiLeakers, cypherpunks, and hacktivists aim to free the world's information*, New York, Dutton

Gordon, Lewis R. (2002) Making science reasonable: Peter Caws on science both human and 'natural', *Janus Head: Journal of Interdisciplinary Studies in Literature, Continental Philosophy, Phenomenological Psychology, and the Arts*, Vol. 5, No. 1

Hayase, Nozomi (2016) WikiLeaks, 10 years of pushing the boundaries of free speech, *Common Dreams*, 4 October. Available online at https://archive.fo/GRn4u, accessed on 15 September 2021

Hughes, Eric (2001) A cypherpunk's manifesto, Ludlow, Peter (ed.) *Crypto anarchy, cyberstates, and pirate utopias*, Cambridge, MIT Press pp 81-84

Illich, Ivan (2009) *Tools for conviviality*, New York, Marion Boyars

Innis, Harold (1950) *Empire and communications*, New York, Oxford University Press

Keller, Bill (2011) Dealing with Assange and the WikiLeaks secrets, *New York Times*, 26 January. Available online at http://archive.fo/PIze0, accessed on 15 September 2021

LeBar, Mark (2014) The virtue of justice, revisited, van Hooft, Stan (ed.) *The handbook of virtue ethics*, Durham, Acumen Publishing pp 265-275

Leigh, David and Harding, Luke (2011) Julian Assange: The teen hacker who became insurgent in information war, *Guardian*, 30 January. Available at https://archive.md/L7u45, accessed 15 September 2021

Levy, Steve (2001) *Crypto: How the code rebels beat the government – saving privacy in the digital age*, New York, Penguin

Li, Mingsheng (2014) Nationalism and imperialism, Fortner, Robert S. and Fackler, Paul M. (eds) *The handbook of global communication and media ethics, Vol. II*, Malden, MA, Blackwell Publishing pp 667-689

Löwstedt, Anthony (2018) Communication ethics and globalisation, Plaisance, Patrick (ed.) *Communication and media ethics*, Berlin, De Gruyter Mouton pp 367-390

Lynch, Lisa (2012) 'That's not leaking, it's pure editorial': Wikileaks, scientific journalism, and journalistic expertise, *Canadian Journal of Media Studies*, Fall pp 40-69

Lynch, Lisa (2013) The leak heard round the world? Cablegate in the evolving global mediascape, Brevini, B. Benedetta, Hintz, Arne and McCurdy, P. Patrick (eds) *Beyond WikiLeaks: Implications for the future of communications, journalism and society*, New York, Palgrave Macmillan pp 56-77

MacAskill, Ewen (2010) Julian Assange like a hi-tech terrorist, says Joe Biden, *Guardian*, 19 December. Available at https://archive.md/ rLUr7, accessed on 15 September 2021

Mackey, Robert (2017) Julian Assange's hatred of Hillary Clinton was no secret. His advice to Donald Trump was, *Intercept*, 15 November. Available at https://archive.md/GvecB, accessed on 15 September 2021

Macleod, Alan (2019) Media cheer Assange's arrest, *Fairness & Accuracy in Reporting*, 18 April. Available online at https://archive. md/gNm1c, accessed on 15 September 2021

Mannheim, Karl (1936) *Ideology and utopia*, New York, Routledge

Manne, Robert (2011) The cypherpunk revolutionary, *The Monthly*. Available online at http://archive.fo/kwI60, accessed on 15 September 2021

Marechal, Natalie (2013) WikiLeaks and the public sphere: Dissent and control in cyberworld, *The International Journal of Technology, Knowledge, and Society*, Vol. 9 pp 93-106

Marmura, Stephen M. E. (2018) *The WikiLeaks paradigm*, Cham, Switzerland, Palgrave Macmillan

Monsma, Stephen V., Christians, Clifford G., Dykema, Eugene, R., Leegwater, Arie, Schuurman, Egbert and Van Poolen, Lambert, *Responsible technology: A Christian perspective*, Grand Rapids, MI, William B. Eerdmans Publishing Company

O'Day, John C. (2019) Corporate media have second thoughts about exiling Julian Assange from journalism, *Fairness & Accuracy in Reporting*, 5 June. Available online at http://archive.fo/ry6Ik, accessed on 15 September 2021

Pilger, John (2018) The urgency of bringing Julian Assange home, *johnpilger.com*, 18 June. Available online at https://archive.md/ IBFhu, accessed on 15 September 2021

Plaisance, Patrick (2011) Moral agency in media: Toward a model to explore key components of ethical practice, *Journal of Mass Media Ethics*, Vol. 26 pp 96-113

Plaisance, Patrick L. (2014) Virtue in media: The moral psychology of US exemplars in news and public relations, *Journalism and Mass Communication Quarterly*, Vol. 91, No. 2 pp 308-325

Plaisance, Patrick L. (2016) Media ethics theorizing reoriented: A shift in focus for individual level analyses, *Journal of Communication,* Vol. 66 pp 454-474

Quinn, Ben (2020) US intelligence sources discussed poisoning Julian Assange, court told, *Guardian,* 30 September. Available online at https://archive.md/jAHYf, accessed on 15 September 2021

Rao, Shakuntala (2011) Glocal media ethics, Fortner, Robert S. and Fackler, Paul M. (eds) *The handbook of global communication and media ethics, Vol. I,* Malden, MA, Blackwell Publishing pp 154-170

Sifry, Micah L. (2011) *WikiLeaks and the age of transparency,* New York, OR Books

Singer, Jane B. (2011) Journalism ethics in a digital network, Fortner, Robert S. and Fackler, Paul M. (eds) *The handbook of global communication and media ethics, Vol. II,* Malden, MA, Blackwell Publishing pp 845-863

Scahill, Jeremy (2017) WikiLeaks vs the CIA, *Intercept,* 19 April. Available online at https://archive.fo/ODOuv, accessed on 15 September 2021

Spiegel (2010) WikiLeaks founder Julian Assange on the 'war logs': 'I enjoy crushing bastards', 26 July. Available online at https://archive.fo/yLNN, accessed on 15 September 2021

Strobel, Warren, and Hosenball, Mark (2017) CIA chief calls WikiLeaks a 'hostile intelligence service', *Reuters,* 13 April. Available online at https://archive.md/nX6mX, accessed on 15 September 2021

Tambini, Damian (2013) WikiLeaks, national security, and cosmopolitan ethics, Couldry, Nick, Madianou, Mirca and Pinchevski, Amit (eds) *Ethics of media,* New York, Palgrave Macmillan pp 232-254

Tunstall, Dwayne (2013) *Doing philosophy personally: Thinking about metaphysics, theism, and antiblack racism,* New York, Fordham University Press

Villena Saldaña, David (2011) Julian Assange: Periodismo, científico, conspiración y ética hacker [Journalism, science, conspiracy and hacker ethics], *Quehacer,* Vol. 181 pp 58-69

Ward, Stephen J. A. (2010) *Global journalism ethics,* Montreal, McGill-Queen's University Press

Ward, Stephen J. A. (2015) *Radical media ethics: A global approach,* Malden, MA, Wiley-Blackwell

Ward, Stephen J. A. and Wasserman, Herman (2010) Towards an open ethics: Implications of new media platforms for global ethics discourse, *Journal of Mass Media Ethics,* Vol. 25, No. 4 pp 275-292

Ward, Stephen J. A. and Wasserman, Herman (2015) Open ethics: Towards a global media ethics of listening, *Journalism Studies,* Vol. 16, No. 6 pp 834-849

Wilkins, Lee (2010) Connecting care and duty: How neuroscience and feminist ethics can contribute to understanding professional moral development, Ward, Stephen J. A., and Wasserman, Herman (eds) *Media ethics beyond borders: A global perspective,* New York, Routledge pp 24-41

Wilkins, Lee (2011a) Journalism's sentiments: Negotiating between freedom and responsibility, *Journalism Studies,* Vol. 12, No. 6 pp 804-815

Wilkins, Lee (2011b) Ethics and ideology: Moving from labels to analysis, Fortner, Robert S. and Fackler, P. Mark (eds) *The handbook of global communication and media ethics, Vol. I,* Malden, MA, Blackwell Publishing pp 119-132

Wilkins, Lee (2018) A history of media ethics: From application to theory and back again, Plaisance, Patrick (ed.) *Communication and media ethics,* Berlin, De Gruyter Mouton pp 15-30

Wilkins, Lee and Coleman, Renita (2004) *The moral media: How journalists reason about ethics,* Mahwah, NJ, Lawrence Erlbaum Associates, Inc.

CONFLICTS OF INTEREST
The author received no funding in support of this research.

NOTE ON THE CONTRIBUTOR
Patrick D. Anderson is an Assistant Professor of Philosophy in the Department of Humanities at Central State University, Ohio. His research focuses on the anti-colonial tradition of Black radical thought and the connections between technology, ethics and imperialism. He is editor-in-chief at the WikiLeaks Bibliography and the author of *Cypherpunk ethics: A radical ethics for the digital age* (Routledge, 2022).

Chapter 6

A Gandhian conundrum: The ethical dilemma in the Indian sustainability discourse

Prithi Nambiar

While environment and sustainability are rapidly gaining currency within global discourse, fundamental constraints continue to obstruct the meaning negotiation of these terms at the community level. Drawing on symbolic interactionism, which postulates that meaning is negotiated and not inherent in objects or terms, a qualitative interpretive study was undertaken to analyse the views of opinion leaders from diverse sectors of the Indian English-speaking community. The study suggests that environment and sustainability communication needs to be synchronous with national historical and cultural narratives and value systems in order to encourage public engagement in the meaning negotiation of these terms.

Keywords: sustainability, environment, environmental communication, ethics and values, public discourse

With rising recognition of the need for sustainable development at the national and global level, there is growing interest in exploring processes of contextual negotiation of meaning relating to the terms 'environment' and 'sustainability' within public discourse. In the years after the Brundtland declaration (of 1987), many questioned the advisability of the term 'sustainable development' which appeared to inspire an ongoing battle between positive and normative propositions for optimal development in its apparent attempt to fuse technical characteristics with moral injunctions (Beckerman 1994). Terms such as sustainability and the environment being socially constructed narratives, their meanings are unstable and changing, reflecting not only the natural but also the social, cultural, economic and political context of each society (Benton and Short 1999).

While the language of the sustainability discourse is characterised by ambiguity and uncertainty, the concept is said to have spawned 'a sprawling network of politically active rhetoric' (Borne and Martell 2010: 27). The sustainability discourse has been called a discourse of modernity (Cheney, Nheu et al. 2004), while the language of sustainability has assumed the institutional authority of the international development industry that debates the relevance and appropriateness of multi-tiered societal goals on local, national and global fronts (Ratner 2004). The discourse has also been viewed as being primarily responsible for papering over the conflict between conservation and development goals with players in the development industry focusing on the sharing of the discursive vocabulary relating to sustainability rather than the values or beliefs that underscore it (Beder 2006). Nevertheless, there is a consensus that the sustainability discourse must essentially be a dialogue of values relevant to each society. Presently the discourse has also served as a platform where critical sustainability tenets are obfuscated in the constant reification of market processes, values and ideals by mainstream economic, social and political interests (Alexander 2009).

Sustainable development engenders the imbrication of individual and societal needs within global resource realities that include both inter-generational and intra-generational equity concerns. Sustainability questions the neo-classical market-centred justification of unlimited personal or group greed in a global context of fast depleting resources and unmet basic needs of the vast majority of humanity. Unsustainable attitudes, values and aspirations as expressed in lifestyle choices remain one of the greatest challenges in all societies. However, creative responses in terms of values, techniques and technologies that may serve to address this challenge could just as easily originate from old societies as from the most developed nations of the world (Atkinson, Graetz et al. 2008).

Media scholars have suggested that there exists a developmental sub-text that could encourage ethics and value-based communication in media-led discourse in new nations (Steenveld 2012). Thus a study that is focused on India's discursive experience with mediating sustainability could be of particular value and interest in view of its complex and dynamic socio-cultural heritage and traditions that continue to evolve in response to massive socio-economic, political and environmental change.

SUSTAINABLE DEVELOPMENT

The concept of sustainable development is prescriptive, directional and aspirational in nature, calling for the development of 'resonant' indicators that need to be developed and negotiated within societies and communities (Levett 1998).

The desire to improve the standards of living of their people to the much higher levels enjoyed by citizens of the developed world inspired many new nations freed from colonialism in the 1940s and 1950s to adopt the development strategies used in the successful reconstruction of post-war Western Europe. That the strategies were employed without much reference to the particular socio-cultural, economic and environmental realities that constituted each national context meant that things did not go to plan. It became clear that developing nations needed uniquely tailored and self-generated plans and strategies rather than the broad universality of the mainstream development paradigm (Haynes 2008: 8). Over time, the ideal of development as a goal has been gradually commuted to that of sustainable development, incorporating multi-layered contextual considerations into the articulation of directions and goals for individual societies (Blewitt 2008).

Sustainable development can be uniquely defined by each society in terms of vision, values, skills, attitudes, action plans, policies and practices while drawing best practices from developing as well as developed societies. Accordingly, developing a blueprint for sustainability would necessitate a discursive process of articulating a common future which is of interest and significance for each society.

THE GLOBAL ENVIRONMENTAL DISCOURSE

Initially, the global environmental discourse revolved around the realist view that saw environmental damage as an inevitable consequence of unsustainable growth and development. The realist position was then overtaken by a constructionist approach emerging from research that suggested that perceptions about environmental issues were socially defined and constructed.

Sustainable development is considered a discourse of and for global civil society (Dryzek 1997). Sustainable development has also been viewed as the subject of a fluid discourse covering issues that range from changing consumer attitudes and values to deep changes in society and economy in ways that have significantly influenced ecological thoughts, consumption habits and structural practices over the past several years since the first global conference in Rio (Koch 2006). The global sustainability discourse turns on the need for public understanding of the basic fact that global problems and concerns are caused by all and affect all and that it is only through consultative discussion between stakeholders and actors at every level that the common future of all can be secured (Ferguson and Thomas-Hope 2006).

System theory experts including Ludwig von Bertalanffy, Howard T. Odum, Fritjof Capra and Margaret Mead have been in the forefront of scholars advocating the need for trans-disciplinary, inter-disciplinary and multi-perspectival understanding that constitutes the foundation of sustainability thinking (Bausch 2001). The systems view of reality as a complex multi-layered process directly challenges the one-way causality that dominates the Western world view while accommodating Eastern and Buddhist notions of mutual causality and self-organisation that govern physical and mental phenomena as well as the dynamics of natural systems (Macy 1991).

The values and attitudes emanating from the recognition of the fundamental causal interconnectedness of all phenomena are being seen as more appropriate to the understanding and practice of sustainability, even as ecological crisis is increasingly being viewed as a corollary of the insular one-way causality inherent in mainstream development strategies that were once popular across the globe.

The issue of values and attitudes that are appropriate to sustainable development is of particular relevance to the Asia-Pacific cluster of nations which, while widely diverse in ethnicity, language, religion and culture, constitute a region that has recovered strongly from the global financial crisis (Heyser 2011). Sustainability experts warn that ongoing industrialisation and modernisation are continuing to compromise traditional lifestyles, value systems and cultural practice that had once ensured a form of social and ecological stability by bringing in ill-planned urbanisation and industrialisation and with them the disastrous repercussions of environmental and social instability (Fien and Tilbury 2002).

INDIA AND SUSTAINABLE DEVELOPMENT

As the world's largest democracy and one of the fastest growing economies of the Asia-Pacific region, India was one of the first nations to acknowledge the rising challenge posed by its environmental problems with particularly disastrous consequences for the majority of its poor citizens. Indira Gandhi, India's then-Prime Minister, was the only head of state to attend the 1972 Human Environment Conference at Stockholm and the first to formally use an international platform to publicly articulate the worrying link between increasing poverty and environmental degradation against the dismal backdrop of inequitable growth.

Exploring the discourse on sustainable development in the context of a country like India enables the identification of the political, economic or cultural origins of various discursive themes that could aid the understanding of what has been termed the heuristic value of non-Western value systems, experiences and knowledge systems to processes of social change (Melkote and Steeves 1952). This is doubly pertinent in the light of the impact that the choices made by 17 per cent of the world's population are likely to have on the global sustainability of this planet. The problem was succinctly and effectively articulated by Mahatma Gandhi when he said: 'God forbid if India were to take to industrialism after the manner of the West … keeping the world in chains. If [India] took to similar economic exploitation, it would strip the world bare like locusts' (Gandhi 1928).

However, the significance and value of studying the public discourse on sustainability in India cannot be limited to the undoubted impact of India's developmental choices for or against sustainability but can, in fact, be extended to the more universal issue of how different societies approach and develop their own unique values-based responses to global policy imperatives through internal processes of dialogue and communicative action.

METHODS AND CONCEPTUAL FRAMEWORK

The study is based on qualitative interpretive research drawing from symbolic interactionism (Blumer 1969) which postulates that meaning in discourse is an essentially contested domain dependent upon negotiation in the Habermasian tradition of mutually respectful dialogue (Habermas 1987). The research questions of the study were: What does sustainability mean to the Indian public and how can sustainability be reframed to gain greater public support and involvement for sustainable development within the country. Using elements of grounded theory and strategic frame theory, the research questions were addressed through the qualitative interpretive content analysis of data gathered from intensive semi-structured interviews of influential communicators and experts representing media, government, not-for-profit, academic and corporate sectors of Indian English-speaking society on environment and sustainability-related issues.

Experts were interviewed based on the reasoning that their access to information and knowledge through a range of networks including media makes them best placed to gauge the multiple public mind. Being engaged in a co-dependency relationship with their peers, media, the public and the state, experts are generally well apprised of the entire range of views on the subjects about which they are experts (Chitty 2011). The study was limited to English-speaking respondents based on the rationale that English in India has long been the language of the elite, the administration and of the pan-Indian press. English-language newspapers continue to enjoy an influential readership while the English-speaking community has always led opinion in India (Hohenthal 2003).

The selection criteria for the interviewees included visibility and prominence in their field and particular sector, equal representation of different sections of the English-speaking community as well as adequate regional coverage with the interview locations including the four major Indian cities of Delhi, Bangalore, Ahmedabad and Hyderabad.

DATA

Experts and policy elites were interviewed for opinions regarding the meanings attributed to sustainability and the environment in public discourse and the ways in which media, government, academia, business and the non-governmental sector framed these concepts as well as opinions on whether the current discourse served to create an understanding of sustainability that was locally relevant. The data was contextualised to enable an analysis of interlinkages between the views of participants. The interview process sought to enable reflexive thinking through the mining of personal views and attitudes on the subject of sustainability in public discourse in India. With regard to the objectivity of the interview process, care was taken to ensure that there was, as far as was possible, freedom from bias and inter-subjective consensus on questions being asked even while interviewees were encouraged to express any view they cared to with no prior knowledge or discussion of the researcher's own views on the subject.

ANALYSIS

All interviewees were invited to offer their opinions on what constituted the problematics that inhibit contemporary discourse on environment and sustainability in India. Themes and patterns emerging from the interview transcripts were identified across the range of responses to each question. Recurring themes were shortlisted and interpreted. Following an inductive approach, coding was developed based on elements of grounded theory and the data was then re-examined to establish the dominant themes that emerged from the analysis.

WHAT AILS THE SUSTAINABILITY DISCOURSE IN INDIA?

Respondents were requested to broadly discuss general factors that inhibited the sustainability discourse in India as a way to identify and further explore underlying conceptual barriers. Credibility and lack of depth were recurrent themes.

'The main problem is the lack of credible and hard facts that are seen to come from a relatively unbiased source. Whom do we trust – the UN or the local NGO? The credibility of raw data is the main problem,' said M22 from the media sector. According to N28 from the NGO sector: 'The discourse is shallow.' N30 from the NGO sector had a similar view and put the shallowness of the discourse down to the superficial, sporadic and event-based coverage of environmental issues: 'I think there is the problem that there is a lot of focus on events. A deeper engagement is required and not tokenism. Mostly the coverage is just about showcasing events.'

From the government sector, G18 said: 'As far as environmental issues are concerned we should not have personal opinions. It is more important to have scientific evidence and facts – factual data is needed. Research-based analysis is not being presented.'

Emerging from the general discussion on the inadequacy of media treatment of sustainability in terms of credibility and depth was the strikingly unique constraint that we termed the Gandhian conundrum. The Gandhian conundrum, which was explicitly mentioned by one of the interview respondents, at once appeared to encapsulate the unspoken expectation of the Indian public for values-based leadership while showing recognition of the intensely moral nature of the sustainability challenge which required change in lifestyles at the personal level.

LACK OF SINCERITY IN COMMUNICATORS AND COMMUNICATION OF ENVIRONMENT AND SUSTAINABILITY ISSUES: THE GANDHIAN CONUNDRUM

Seven respondents suggested that in the Indian context the lack of sincerity or depth in media representation of environmental and sustainability issues encouraged a deeply dismissive treatment of these issues by the public. Describing the discourse as shallow, N28, CEO of a well-known not-for-profit organisation, went on to say: 'This idea of tree planting – now, that's an expression of an attitude to the environment which is easy and not challenging. There is no discussion about lifestyles. Media has a concern for tigers but there are much bigger issues. What do you need to do to preserve tigers? Who benefits? Is it just for tourism?'

But for M20 from the media sector, it was the NGO sector which was guilty of insincerity and lack of commitment. 'It's ended up being a discourse and nothing else. [We have] more seminars, workshops and publications from the NGO sector, and still no change. Still, trees are being chopped and no NGO really cares. People may be familiar with the term "sustainability" but that is not equal to understanding it.'

Academic A2, the vice-chancellor of a major Indian university, felt that insincerity was widespread and palpable among those involved in the sustainability discourse in India from all sectors and he attributed this to what he called the Gandhian conundrum. He said:

> The Gandhian conundrum is when the professional and the personal values and behaviours of an individual are in conflict with each other, whereas, in a non-Gandhian frame, there is room for such inconsistency. In a non-Gandhian situation, I can be a heavy smoker and write articles on the problems that smokers and tobacco cause for others without feeling guilty about the inconsistency. I can write about the need for prohibition [of alcohol] and drink in private. My lifestyle really harms the environment but I can continue writing against what I do without changing anything I do. Intellectually and professionally raising issues and acting as though your lifestyle and behaviour is not part of the problem is considered acceptable in the West. But this is a Gandhian conundrum that must be resolved if we want to bring sincerity into the discourse on sustainability. This is what I mean by inter and intra self-harmony which is required for sustainability. Those in the forefront talk as if they are not part of the problem. But when Gandhi spoke of *swadeshi* or of any principle for that matter, he practised before he preached.

From the corporate sector, C9 spoke of the self-contradictory nature of the messages delivered by media: 'There is a dilemma, a contradiction. On the one hand you are being persuaded to consume, consume, use, use and dump, dump. On the other, sustainability implies care, to be aware, to think about tomorrow and about the next generation. You get the feeling from the way people act in supermarkets that only greed is being promoted today. Greed is market-sponsored and strategy-driven while sustainability is innocently or rather naively promoted.'

N30 from the NGO sector said: 'Deeper engagement is required. Not tokenism.' Seven respondents said there was a problem with the way environmental and sustainability issues were being approached. From the corporate sector, C7 called it myopia. 'There is severe myopia in looking at the issue. You need an integrated approach because a piecemeal approach is so much more expensive. The root cause is the way we approach sustainability. We can't do an end of pipe approach.' From the government sector, a high powered advisor, G15 said:

> The main problem is the import of methods that are developed in the West. When I say the West, I mean largely the American milieu where, for instance, you have the idea that you can buy and sell carbon. That is a very American concept. It is essentially driven by the market, that you can exchange carbon credits for money, exchange carbon credits for profits and so on. The idea that everything should be driven by the market is fundamentally, in my opinion, a wrong concept. Nature does not intend a surplus that can be transacted. Nature has only complete systems. Nature has a system of generation and degeneration so intrinsically linked that it doesn't create surpluses. The whole application of a Western business-driven transactional analysis is one of the main maladies in India now.

The internationally known CEO in the not-for-profit sector, N29 said:

> The public obviously goes by what the media says. I don't think the media understands it. They don't understand the holistic nature of sustainability. In India we have people in a village who think they can throw their waste out. This didn't create problems in a situation when the waste was largely organic. But when they moved to an urban area, the same practices became problematic. The transition from rural to urban sustainability hasn't happened. The leapfrog issue is to avoid making the mistakes of the West.

Also from the NGO sector, N28 said: 'I don't think we can begin to change lifestyles unless we change deep values. I am afraid I don't see an easy way to make a transition to a different world view. I don't see how it can be done easily or without pain. I think we have to keep at it. I think environmental educators have to address deep attitudinal change and the deep underlying assumptions. We need to focus on that.'

Media expert M23 suggested that the approach was incorrect because it appeared to largely involve an evangelical element with the developed world advocating sustainability to the developing world. 'The main problem is that the wrong people are teaching us sustainability,' he said.

Five respondents were of the view that the sustainability discourse was most negatively circumscribed by the lack of prioritisation of sustainability and environmental concerns in national policy and practice. Academic A6 said:

> At the IUCN meeting, the Addis Ababa principle of sustainability was discussed. Many countries are signatories but not many have followed up. Absolutely nothing has happened, not just in India, but also in the developed nations. In the IUCN, even among the different commissions – the education commission has done very little – it is no one's problem.

> There is more focus on conservation. Have they been able to influence or impact any of the issues to an extent that media or intelligentsia will look into it? I don't think so.

From the corporate sector, C8 said: 'Sustainability is not getting disseminated properly. It is only discussed within closed walls. Actionable points are not happening. Local people need to be engaged. Lay people must understand.' G16, a senior bureaucrat from the central government, also spoke of the fact that matters relating to the environment are on the concurrent list and come under the purview of the state government. 'The central government can only remind the state government and can't take action. By the time action is taken, it is too late.'

Also, a senior public servant from the central government, G14 discussed the problems with prioritising sustainability at the policy level. 'Unless you integrate sustainable development across all sectors it cannot have the desired effect. Sustainability is not just the baby of the concerned ministry of the central government. It is the concern of every ministry. All policies and projects have to mainstream and integrate sustainable development into their concerns.'

Several issues related to the discursive construction of sustainability were also raised and discussed during the interviews. These were:

PREMATURE POLARISATION OF ISSUES

Three respondents offered the opinion that the sustainability discourse remained stunted primarily as a result of the Indian media's tendency to present issues in a way that prematurely polarised them along familiar environment versus development battle-lines. From the corporate sector, C12 said:

> I see the main problem as being the sense that it is an 'either/or' situation. You can have more electricity connections or save a thousand trees. The frame is always 'either/ or' and there is an ideological framing which does not allow rational debate. Equally, it takes away from looking at innovative or new solutions, technological solutions or the social dimensions of the debate. The media just polarises the issue even before solutions are looked at.

NGO respondent N29 agreed that there was clearly a problem with media 'keeping the discourse at a contradictory level and promoting confusion'. NGO respondent N27 suggested that if issues were presented in a reasonable and comprehensive manner with careful avoidance of polarisation or the 'either/or' frame, the discourse would gain depth and wider public involvement.

> When coastal issues were considered by media, it was always the poor who lost out in the economic race. That's particularly so because in the country today, with 9 per cent growth, no one wants to talk about stopping anything. They say 'be positive'. Everyone wants to deal with solutions

without polarising issues. There was a time when people wanted to listen to another point of view. Now you are considered a loser if you are talking about the negative aspects of growth.

POVERTY IS A MORE PRESSING CONCERN FOR INDIA

One respondent, a CEO from the corporate sector, C11 was unequivocal in his insistence that the discourse on environment and sustainability was a luxury in a country like India which could not be considered ready to address sustainable development before it addressed its most pressing concern which was to feed its poor through education, training and the creation of job opportunities. C11 was of the firm view that job opportunities and the skilling of the masses could only be accomplished through industrial growth and governmental initiatives. As Brulle (2010) comments:

> How do you resolve poverty? Self-reliance is the key issue. It's a step-by-step process. Give people the type of education that makes them self-reliant. The financial discipline will come when the person is happy. Then he can understand softer issues like sustainability. First things must come first. Policies need to address what's at the bottom. Conferences on the environment should not be held at five star hotels. There is a need to make people happier at the grass root level.

DISCUSSION

As part of an interpretive, qualitative analysis, the study takes the approach that all articulated themes are valid and significant (Lincoln and Guba 1985; Mitchell and Jolley 2010) within the carefully chosen rich and representative sample. The views of experts that constitute the rich data of this study need to be considered in the context of the leadership role played by critical communities or critical thinkers who generate new values and approaches that initiate cultural and social change (Rochon 1998). Critical communities and social movements constitute the social authority that is critical to the creation of an alternative social map for advocacy and the mobilisation of individuals (Brulle 2010).

The themes and issues identified from the data appear to endorse the view that there are elements of a values-based culturally and historically constructed developmental sub-text within media-led discourse on sustainability.

Table 1. The Developmental Sub-text of Media-led Discourse on Sustainability in India

Themes identified in the sustainability discourse	Elements of the developmental sub-text
Credibility/ lack of trust/ shallowness	Divergence from acceptable ethical norms and expectations
Western neo-liberal approach makes media treatment of sustainability superficial	Sustainability is consistent with Indian spiritual traditions, values and ethics and needs to be treated as such rather than as a Western-generated reformist movement
Absence of leadership that is acceptable to the public	Need for individual leadership to steer and spearhead change for sustainability
Guidance needed at the personal level to change lifestyles	Leadership must demonstrate core values and personally exemplary behaviour
Public cynicism about governance, corruption and inconsistencies in policy	Sustainability leadership must address the need for a high standard of ethics and values in the public sphere

The themes identified from data testify to the existence of the Gandhian conundrum. It was apparent from the study that Gandhian standards are still used to measure leadership competence in the public sphere in India. The moral and intellectual inadequacy implied in the Gandhian conundrum was variously alluded to by all respondents in one way or another during the course of the interviews and seemed to echo a familiar cultural theme ubiquitous in ancient Indian proverbs and parables that underscores the dangers of inadequate leadership and guidance. As evident from Table 1 above, the themes and issues identified from the data reveal elements of a culturally generated values-based sub-text that could contribute to better public acceptance of sustainability. Running through the opinions of all respondents was the central concern that the ideals and values inherent in the concept of sustainability needed not only to resonate at a personal level for the Indian public but that sincerity and commitment needed to form an essential element of the discourse.

Gandhi and his lived ideals connect modern India with its ancient heritage of myth and history populated by exemplary folk heroes and saints who taught generations of Indians their lived lessons of integrity and wisdom while continuing to inspire an often expressed yearning for similar spiritual and ethical leadership in contemporary public life. Gandhi's own preoccupations with sustainability, decades ahead of the Brundtland commission, inspired economists like Schumacher into considering alternative economic models based on integrated community development rooted in shared democratic, socio-cultural values.

Deploring the fact that the world chose to listen to Keynes rather than Gandhi, Schumacher quotes Gandhi on the issues of constraints to economic growth: 'The earth has enough for every man's needs but not for anyone's greed' (Schumacher 1999: 20). Gandhi had rejected the concept of limitless generalised growth, which was widely accepted before 1950, as being entirely invalid and even dangerous.

However, not even Gandhi's political allies, closest friends and contemporaries chose to listen to his world views (Cox 2008), resulting in India embarking on the path of large scale state-sponsored industrialisation based entirely on the Western development model under the leadership of Jawaharlal Nehru (Rothermund 1993). Yet Gandhi appears to persist as India's spiritual leader, haunting virtually every sphere of public discourse with his non-violent methods of resistance constituting standard political practice to this day.

Recent research reveals that leadership prototypes in India tend to draw from ideals and values that are reflective of a complex amalgam of myth and history in India with the predominant style being that of benevolent paternalism based on the ideals of spiritualism and duty rather than materialistic individualism (Kessler and Wong-MingJi 2009). Benevolent paternalism implies the derivation of authority through the demonstration of personally exemplary and morally scrupulous behaviour such that compels trust and compliance from followers (Pellegrini and Scandura 2008). Pellegrini and Scandura (ibid) also cite recent research evidence that points to the widespread acceptability and acceptance of benevolent paternalism in non-Western cultures where those vested with authority are followed unquestioningly largely due to the cultural and traditional familiarity and trust implicit in this familial style of leadership.

It is unsurprising in the Indian context, therefore, that the issue of insincerity or lack of commitment appeared central to the core concerns of personal lifestyles, ideals and values as part of the sustainability discourse in India. The perception that political leadership was unconcerned with the values and ideals inherent in sustainability troubled all respondents at some level. The identification of the Gandhian conundrum needs to be viewed in the light of the benevolent paternalistic style of leadership exemplified by Gandhi in India. Gandhi consciously crafted his own style of persuasive, albeit authoritarian, leadership through the personal demonstration of benevolent concern which was additionally buttressed by moral virtue and the self-sacrificing behaviour of Indian spiritual leaders and sages of bygone eras. The current study suggests that the impact of Gandhi's leadership continues to reverberate with the Indian public in a way that has sharp implications for the sustainability discourse.

Brulle (2010) concurs with Habermas (1996) and Rochon (1998) in the need to engage rather than manipulate public opinion while asserting that there can be no separation of ends and means in the area of democratic politics. Gandhi's stringent personal ethic rejected the justification of the means by the ends. Calling the ends and the means completely convertible in his philosophy, he considered the relationship between them inviolable and binding as that between the seed and the tree (Avery 2008). The need for ethics and sincerity in the discursive construction of sustainability goals and agenda within the organic context of a society appears compelling. All respondents spoke as well of the global discourse being coloured by the irony that sustainability was being advocated by the developed world after high standards of living and prosperity had been achieved at the expense of the environment and the welfare of the colonised nations of the world. Nevertheless, while the issue of sustainable lifestyles may yet remain politically unpalatable in first world societies (Death 2010), the study reveals that personal ethics and values are regarded as being central to the sustainability discourse in India.

CONCLUSION

That the environment and sustainability discourse in India is considerably limited in scope and nature at the policy and practical level is reasonably apparent from the study. As a nation with a rich history of culture surrounding the interpretation of ethics and values, there is clearly a role for 'countervailing cultural power' (Curran 1996) as expressed by strong idealistic and charismatic opinion leaders that could serve to modulate the discursive arena and steer it towards sustainability outcomes.

However, existing constraints encompass the absence of adequate discursive opportunity, weak policy commitment and inadequate media representation resulting in a gap between global and local discourses due to what was perceived as a failure by environmental communicators and opinion leaders to contextualise and personalise issues and concerns. The study also suggests that core values such as sincerity, commitment to ethical perspectives and lifestyles are already embedded in the meanings attributed to sustainability within current public discourse thus constituting the litmus test that will determine whether communication relating to environment and sustainability rings true for the public in India.

- This paper was first published in *Ethical Space*, Vol. 10, No. 4 pp 16-24

REFERENCES

Alexander, R. J. (2009) *Framing discourse on the environment: A critical discourse approach,* New York, Routledge

Atkinson, A., Graetz, M and Karsch, D. (eds) (2008). *Techniques and technologies for sustainability,* Berlin, Technische Universität Berlin

Avery, J. (2008) Gandhi's solutions to today's problems. Available online at http://www.fredsakademiet.dk/library/solutions.pdf, accessed on 7 May 2012

Bausch, K. C. (2001) *The emerging consensus in social systems theory,* New York, Kluwer Academic

Beckerman, W. (1994) Sustainable development: Is it a useful concept?, *Environmental Values,* Vol. 3, No. 3 pp 191-209

Beder, S. (2006) The changing face of conservation: Commodification, privatisation and the free market, Lavigne, D. and Guelph, M. (eds) *Gaining ground: In pursuit of ecological sustainability,* IFAW and the University of Limerick, Ireland pp 83-97

Benton, L. M. and Short, J. R. (1999) *Environmental discourse and practice,* Oxford, Blackwell Publishing

Blewitt, J. (2008) *Understanding sustainable development,* London, Earthscan

Blumer, H. (1969) *Symbolic interactionism: Perspective and method,* Englewood Cliffs, NJ, Prentice-Hall Inc.

Borne, G. and Martell, L. (2010) *A framework for sustainable global development and effective governance of risk*, Lewiston, NY, Edwin Mellen Press

Brulle, R. J. (2010) From environmental campaigns to advancing the public dialog: Environmental communication for civic engagement, *Environmental Communication*, Vol. 4, No.1 pp 82-98

Cheney, H., Nheu, N. et al. (2004) Sustainability as social change: Values and power in sustainability discourse, *Sustainability and social science*, Sydney and Melbourne, Australia, Round Table Proceedings pp 225-246

Chitty, N. (2011) Public diplomacy: Courting publics for short-term advantage or partnering publics for lasting peace and sustainable prosperity, Fisher, A. and Lucas, S. (eds) *Projection of power: Trials of public diplomacy*, Leiden, Brill/Martinus Nijhoff Publishers pp 251-268

Cox, P. (2008) Gandhian values and post development: Models for social transformation, R. Ghosh, K. Gupta, R. and Maiti, P. (eds) *Development studies*, New Delhi, Atlantic Publishers and Distributors, Vol 2 pp 150-189

Curran, J. (1996) Rethinking mass communications, Curran, J. Morley, D. and Walkerdine, V. (eds) *Cultural Studies and Communications*, London, Arnold pp 119-168

Death, C. (2010) *Governing sustainable development*, Oxford, Routledge

Dryzek, J. S. (1997) *The politics of the earth: Environmental discourses*, Oxford, Oxford University Press

Ferguson, T. and Thomas-Hope, E. (2006) Environmental education and constructions of sustainable development in Jamaica, Hill, J. L., Terry, A. and Woodland, W. A. (eds) *Sustainable development: National aspirations, local implementation*, Farnham, Surrey, Ashgate Publications pp 91-115

Fien, J. and Tilbury, D. (2002) The global challenge of sustainability, Tilbury, D. Stevenson, R. Fien, J. and Schreuder, D. (eds) *Education and sustainability: Responding to the global challenge*, Gland, Switzerland, Commission on Education and Communication, IUCN

Gandhi, M. K. (1928) Mahatma Gandhi's views. Available online at http://www.tinytechindia.com/gandhi3.htm, accessed on 1 October 2010

Habermas, J. (1987) *The theory of communicative action: Lifeworld and system: A critique of functionalist reason*, Boston, Beacon Press

Haynes, J. (2008) *Development studies*, Cambridge, Polity Press

Heyser, N. (2011) Re-balancing Asia-Pacific growth, *Economic Times*, New Delhi, India, Bennett, Coleman and Co.

Hohenthal, A. (2003) English in India: Loyalty and attitudes, *Language in India*, Vol. 3. Available online at http://www.tinytechindia.com/gandhi3.htm, accessed on 1 May 2010

Kessler, E. H. and Wong-MingJi, D. J. (eds) (2009) *Cultural mythology and global leadership*, Cheltenham, Edward Elgar Publishing House

Koch, M. H. (2006) Telling the feel-good story of the decade: The potentials and pitfalls of education for sustainable development, *Global Media Journal*. Available online at http://lass.calumet.purdue.edu/cca/gmj/sp06/graduatesp06/gmj-sp06gradinv-koch.htm, accessed on 12 February 2011

Levett, R. (1998) Sustainability indicators: Integrating quality of life and environmental protection, *Journal of the Royal Statistical Society: Series A (Statistics in Society)*, Vol. 161, No. 3 pp 291-302

Lincoln, Y. S. and Guba, E. G. (1985) *Naturalistic inquiry*, Beverly Hills, CA, Sage

Macy, J. (1991) *Mutual causality in Buddhism and general systems theory*, New York, State University of New York

Melkote, S. R. and Steeves, H. L. (1952) *Communication for development in the Third World: Theory and practice for empowerment*, New Delhi, Sage

Mitchell, M. L. and Jolley, J. M. (2010) *Research design explained*, Belmont, USA, Wadsworth Cengage Learning

Pellegrini, E. K. and Scandura, T. A. (2008) Paternalistic leadership: A review and agenda for future research, *Journal of Management*, Vol. 34, No. 3 pp 566-593

Ratner, B. D. (2004) 'Sustainability' as a dialogue of values: Challenges to the sociology of development, *Sociological Inquiry*, Vol. 74, No.1 pp 50-69

Rochon, T. R. (1998) *Culture moves: Ideas, activism and changing values*, Princeton, New Jersey, Princeton University Press

Rothermund, D. (1993) *An economic history of India: From pre-colonial times to 1991*, New York, Routledge

Schumacher, E. F. (1999) *Small is beautiful: Economics as if people mattered 25 years later*, Vancouver, Hartley and Marks

Steenveld, L. (2012) The pen and the sword: Media transformation and democracy after apartheid, *Ethical Space: The International Journal of Communication Ethics*, Vol. 9, Nos 2/3 pp 125-140

NOTE ON THE CONTRIBUTOR

Dr Prithi Nambiar is Executive Director at the Centre for Environment Education (CEE), Australia, Senior Programme Director at CEE, India, and Editor of the *Journal of Education for Sustainable Development*. Her research interests are in the area of environment and sustainability communications. She is the author of the book, *Media construction of environment and sustainability in India* (New Delhi, Sage, 2014). Email: prithinambiar@gmail.com.

Chapter 7

Close travel: On the ethics of writing about the near-at-hand

Ben Stubbs

The idea of travel is changing. While once the thrill of adventure and exploration into the unknown propelled travellers to explore the world on the Grand Tour in the 17th Century, the overland journey from Europe to Asia and more recently the gap year, only now is there a renewed focus on the ethical notion of what we should do as travellers. Travel writers, as influential muses whose journeys often open up the world and its possibilities to travellers, are central to this concern and, as such, further investigation into how to think about travel and travel writing more imaginatively is required. This paper will examine the practice of 'close' travel, and of exploring the near-at-hand as a way of embracing a creative and more ethically nuanced notion of travel and travel writing.

Keywords: travel writing, tourism, mobility, ethics

INTRODUCTION

Travel in the modern era has become increasingly easy. During the 21st century the opening up of experiences due to the simplicity of travel, the ever presence of technology and the availability of tours venturing to the most far-flung destinations now permits unexpected travel to the most unlikely places.

In the Australian outback, for example, more than 1,300 kilometres west of South Australia's capital city, Adelaide, there is an area called Maralinga. It was once isolated by both infrastructure and geography and concealed from the public because of nuclear tests in the 1950s and 1960s. Travellers can now camp on the abandoned nuclear test site at Maralinga by night, take hot showers in the morning and enjoy the free WiFi now available. Low cost airlines allow us to travel across oceans and continents for a few hundred dollars, tourism is now worth $1.7 trillion per year to the global economy (Blackall 2019) and even the relaxation of regulations for climbers of Mount Everest, once feared and revered because of the physical stamina and extreme cost a summit expedition to the highest mountain on earth would entail, has resulted in 'an anxiety-inducing conga line in the death zone above 8,000 metres' (Beaumont 2019). This has resulted in 11 deaths in a single climbing season for 2019 due to the opening up of travel experiences to all who have the financial means to attempt it.

So, while the nature of what we *can* do as travellers has become easy, only now is there a renewed focus on the ethical notion of what we *should* do as travellers, and further investigation into how we can think about this more imaginatively is required.

Historically, the first major expansion of travel came during the Grand Tour, according to Youngs (2013), which enabled well-heeled European travellers to go on religious and cultural pilgrimages from the 17th century onwards. Travel writers have historically been the muses who have opened up the world and helped the travelling public discover how and where they can utilise their travel imaginations most effectively. These date from Harkuf, who left a written account of his travels on an Egyptian tomb in the third century BCE (ibid), through to the Grand Tour, the overland journeys from Europe to Asia of the 1960s and 1970s and the more recent international adventures of school leavers enjoying a 'gap year' before taking up their university places. Each of these stages is reflected and well represented within travel literature.

While travel is easier than ever before as journeys are charted through social media, GPS and mobile phones, this does raise the question of 'why' travellers, and travel writers as their instruments of inspiration, need to keep pushing the limits of safety, good taste and responsibility.

While heightened insecurity around the world and political changeability can be initial prompts for travellers to reconsider their journeys in the 21st century, they also now need to consider the ethical issues involved in everything from dark tourism, which is the tourist's (and travel writer's) interest in death, recent atrocities and conflict (Creech 2014); thana-tourism, which refers to real or symbolic encounters with death (Sharpley and Stone 2009) and overcrowding due to the ease of tourism-focused travel for the masses. To concentrate momentarily on the theme of overcrowding, as a community-led solution to this, creative initiatives such as Amsterdam's 'marry a local' programme have emerged, in part to also address the ethics of tourism and local community relations. The Amsterdam initiative pairs visiting tourists with local residents to guide them to observe lesser-known parts of the city in an effort to spread the impact of local tourism and to foster a more sustainable and immersive experience (Adams 2019). Alongside this is the increasing awareness of the environmental impact of travel and the 'environmental footprint' it leaves – where travellers can offset the carbon emissions of their travel or choose 'slow travel' options such as walking, rail and local transport instead of flight connections.

This does not mean that overseas travel should cease, though it does suggest that focusing our attention more readily on where we live and minimising the span of our travel and how we write about it is an increasingly ethical and responsible option.

From this prompt comes the notion of 'close travel' as a mode of looking around us and within our environments more thoroughly before venturing across the globe in search of adventure, encounters with the 'other' and cultural immersion far from the places we call home.

NOTIONS OF THE VERTICAL

Joanne Lee sees close travel as a way for writers to attempt to 'uncover hidden aspects of familiar places, often their native town or region' (2012: 203). Lee cites the travel writing of Italy as an example of this, where the focus previously has been on the writings of Anglo-Americans which has, in turn, shaped the way that both outsiders and Italians view themselves. Today, domestic writers are better able to capture the essence of Italian 'localities, regions, towns and cities', she argues (ibid: 204).

This notion of close travel is also broadly identified by Michael Cronin as 'vertical travel', being 'the temporary dwelling in a location for a period of time where the traveller begins to travel down into the particulars of place either in space (botany, studies of micro-climate, exhaustive exploration of local landscape) or in time (local history, archaeology, folklore)' (2000: 19). Cronin examines the two different modes of travel – deep or cursory – as he labels them and finds commonality with our understanding of language as we travel. For Cronin, cursory language is that which we interpret in our everyday lives on a surface level, whereas a deep understanding of language relates to the sub-languages we are exposed to while travelling in a slower and more vertical sense. This includes slang, abbreviations and regional dialects. Cronin gives the example of the 'horizontal voyage' into and across a foreign country not being a substitute for the 'vertical' understanding of its culture, customs, slang and formalities – where simple exchanges such as dining at a foreign restaurant (as writer Jonathan Raban does during his river explorations in his 1999 book *Passage to Juneau*) seem perplexing and strange because of their tone and hyperbole, of the expectation for tips and the strange titles for dishes. Cronin writes that due to Raban's lack of 'vertical understanding' of the intertextual experience of dining in the United States he was unable to engage or understand the encounter sufficiently (ibid: 18).

Alasdair Pettinger writes in *Keywords for travel writing studies* that the call is not so much a literal re-thinking of the travel within travel writing (as in Robert Macfarlane's *Underland* or Ian Vince's *The lie of the land* where the authors literally go beneath the surface of the earth) but a more thoughtful and introspective deceleration and 'microspection' focusing on the depth of the experience (2019: 277). This does not suggest that all manifestations of this form of travel writing should be philosophical rather than geographical in nature either. Pettinger writes that this form of introspective travel may have its roots in the fieldwork nature of modern anthropology, where the intensive focus on small communities was preferenced and the anthropologists practised 'thick description', as Clifford Geertz (cited in Pettinger 2019: 278) called it.

Pettinger writes that this form of writing utilises two lenses: the idea of 'proximate ethnography' focusing on the everyday nature of the places we visit; and the 'deep mapping' and intense concentration on places that outsiders would otherwise consider ordinary and not worthy of the travellers' attention (ibid). This rediscovery of seemingly mundane or over-looked places is at the centre of both Cronin's and Pettinger's interpretations of the vertical rather than the horizontal and more conventionally tourism-oriented journey. Charles Forsdick highlights the importance of the writer's relationship with space within their writing so that they no longer 'fetishise' the exotic of the horizontal journey and more readily embrace the notion of the 'endotic' experience (2019: 101), and the awareness of everyday occurrences as a proximate traveller.

This new notion of rethinking space and valuing the mundane as an ethical and creative choice acts as a counter to the previously assumed notion of the importance of distance and the predominance of the surface experiences of many travel writers from the 18th and 19th centuries. This type of travel writer was labelled by Mary Louise Pratt in her seminal travel writing studies text *Imperial eyes* as the 'monarch-of-all-I-survey' trope (2002: 201), where the travel writer aimed to obtain a more omniscient view of their location, from a more elevated and 'above the subject' position, rather than preferring a closer and more engaged position. As an example of this 'vivid imperial rhetoric' (2002: 202) Pratt cites Richard Burton in *Lake regions of Central Africa* (1860) as a prime example of this all-conquering, colonial perspective, where Burton vies to 'win' these locales for the mother country and he over-dramatises the discovery and description of mundane places as exotic and momentous.

It is the 'geometry' of the journey rather than the geography which is the most important consideration with vertical travel writing, irrespective of the literal or metaphoric focus (Forsdick 2019: 103). Forsdick uses the example of concentric circles to explain the geometry of travel as a way to divide up and expand focus within vertical writing more slowly and methodically. 'Vertical travel reflects the experimental potential of travel writing to propose new and often defamiliarising ways of viewing and engaging with elsewhere' (ibid: 110).

CLOSE TRAVEL AND HISTORY

These ideas of vertical attention and close travel writing are actually not new – and can be traced back as far as Turin in the 18th century. Xavier de Maistre wrote *A journey around my room* (1794) while being imprisoned in his bedroom for six weeks after he was caught fighting a duel in the north Italian city in 1790. Rather than sulk through his imprisonment he decided to write a travel book about the contents of his chamber. 'Room travel involves a type of detachment, which involves pulling back from the realm of the habitual to explore and describe it anew,' writes Berndt Stiegler (2013: 2). De Maistre observed his surroundings through a different lens to give the reader an alternative perspective on what travelling could be and that there are things all around us to which we do not normally pay attention.

> What a comfort this new mode will be to the sick; they need not fear bleak winds or change of weather. And what a thing, too, it will be for cowards; they will be safe from pitfalls and quagmires. Thousands who hitherto did not dare, others who were not able, and others to whom it never occurred to think of such a thing as going on a journey, will make up their minds to follow my example (1794: 4).

De Maistre was so taken by the journey around his room that he subsequently wrote a follow-up book titled *Nocturnal journey round my room* in 1829 which narrowed the focus of his inquiry even further. 'De Maistre is thus the opposite of the immensely popular "Robinsonade" of the late eighteenth and early nineteenth centuries,' continues Stiegler (2013: 12), referring to the grand adventures and remote discoveries which typified the travel writing of the 18th century. Carl Thompson writes that the 'proliferation of accounts of voyages and travels reflects the fact that this was an era of ever-increasing mobility' (2011: 45), which makes the imagination and boldness of de Maistre's close travel writing even more pronounced. The lines on the floor become hidden trails, the paintings and tapestries on the walls become windows into other places and the bed becomes a vessel for imaginative transportation and travel. Stiegler writes of de Maistre's influence: 'The room is an interior world that is in many ways charged with history and an encyclopaedic knowledge of the world. A room can be described as a country: with a climate, a location, a form of governance, a people, flora, and fauna' (2013: 44).

Indeed, Stiegler's enthusiasm for observing those who 'travel in place' continues in his book *A history of armchair travel* (2013) which observes those who are inspired by de Maistre's writing. Stiegler focuses on historical examples of the Enlightenment possible for travellers when embracing the verticality of a voyage rather than the horizontal ambition of those cited by Pratt. Stiegler does this to illuminate 'the world of the near-at-hand in order to explore the many facets of room travel and traveling in place', according to Stubbs (2016: 317). This fascination with looking closer at the familiar prompts Stiegler to look also at 'travel into the near distance and the distantly near: traveling without traveling' (2013: 1).

Thus Stiegler takes the reader on a spiritual journey across the notion of religious experiences and travel, from the pilgrimage to the metaphysical journey of the 'Christian room traveler' (2013: 20) who uses travel to prepare and reflect on the next, much more significant, journey to come in the after-life. Indeed, as the French Oratorian priest Abbé Perreyve (1831-1865) claims, 'within all journeys it is the hermit, and those who look closer at things, who attain the real value from travel' (see Stubbs 2016: 317).

Stiegler also illuminates the writing and travel of Heinrich Seidel in the 19th century. Seidel re-focused the gaze on his apartment into a microcosm, where each item has a history and an interconnected story. Similarly Alphonse Karr, in his *Tour round my garden* ('Voyage autour de mon jardin') (1851) produced two volumes and seven hundred pages focused solely on his garden where he lived in Montmarte with his pet monkey Emmanuel.

In the period after de Maistre's journey there was a slew of imitations of this style, though two in particular stand out because of their influence. In Henry David Thoreau's *Walden* (1854), the author lives alone and in seclusion in a log cabin at Walden Pond. As Youngs writes, Thoreau 'deliberately turns his attention from the exotic to the local' (2013: 64) as he focuses on the simplicity of experiences and on slowing down as an antidote to the anxiety he sees being created from modern industrialism. Youngs suggests that Thoreau's promotion of micro-travel and the stress on introspection and deceleration has influenced many travel writers – most directly this includes Graham Greene's *Journey without maps* (1936) and William Least Heat-Moon's *PrairyErth* (1991); Thoreau's influence can also be seen with modern nature writers such as Robert Macfarlane and Chris Yates with his *Nightwalk: A journey to the heart of nature* (2014) in particular.

Secondly, Mark Twain – the journalist and celebrated author of *The adventures of Tom Sawyer* (1876) and *The adventures of Huckleberry Finn* (1884) – became the first cruise travel writer when, in 1867, he took the *Quaker City* steam ship from New York to Europe and the Holy Land with a ship full of American tourists for company. 'It was a novelty in the way of excursions – its like had never been thought of before, and it compelled that interest which attractive novelties always command' (2010 [1869]: 7). This is the first example in modern travel writing where the mode of transport becomes not only part of the pleasure of the trip but also a key part of the story. Twain's resulting book, *The innocents abroad*, originally published in 1869, became the best-selling travel book of the century and Twain's most popular book. 'They were to scamper about the decks by day, filling the ship with shouts and laughter – or read novels and poetry in the shade of the smokestacks, or watch the jellyfish and the nautilus over the side' (ibid). Twain writes of his companions on their voyage. While the shore excursions (and Twain's lampooning of his fellow passengers and those they encounter along the way) are a large part of the story, the close travel perspective of the *Quaker City* and the experiences onboard are ever present throughout the narrative.

CONTEMPORARY CLOSE TRAVEL

While much of the initial experimentations and examples of close travel concentrate on those periods bracketing the Romantic Era from the 17th century onwards (such as those examples cited by Stiegler), surprisingly, this has not been a style or sub-genre which has diminished in this modern era of increased technology and shorter attention spans. When many travel books (such as guidebooks) have become largely superfluous due in large parts to technology and the prevalence of travellers using portable devices such as phones and tablets to gain instant reviews and directions rather than relying on cumbersome and out-dated guide books, the focus on new and more considered forms of travel narratives has brought about a fresh interest in the more thoughtful, ethical and engaged traveller and travel writing. The modern era has also seen a continuation of travel writing which focuses on the inner self of the travel writer as well as the journey they are taking – Peter Mathiessen's *The snow leopard* (1978), Robyn Davidson's *Tracks* (1980) and Robert Macfarlane's *The old ways* (2012) are prime examples. But this is an area which has been well covered in studies of travel writing (see Thompson 2011; Youngs 2013).

De Maistre's motivation, in part, was to present travel as something attainable for those who were sick, destitute, timid or lazy. As a counterpoint, with so much choice for the traveller in the 21st century, from package tours to Antarctica to thana-tourism experiences, some modern travel writers have been prompted to pause their wanderlust and re-focus their gaze on the things around them as de Maistre did.

A WEEK AT THE AIRPORT

In his book, *A week at the airport: A Heathrow diary* (2009), Alain de Botton inhabits London Heathrow's Terminal 5 as a writer in residence. He does so to try to understand the airport as a destination in itself and as a location with a distinct culture and 'home' to many intriguing people. 'I arrived at the airport on a train from central London early on a Sunday evening, a small roller case in hand and no further destination for the week' (2009: 16).

De Botton sets up a desk in the departure hall to pen his close travel narrative, confined, just like de Maistre, in his chosen enclosure for the duration of his stay. And so he reflects on people's body language and the 'politeness' of forced encounters at the airport; the first during a room service delivery in his airport hotel room: 'It is a strange moment when two adult men meet each other, one naked save for a complimentary dressing gown, the other (newly arrived in England from the small Estonian town of Rakvere and sharing a room with four others in nearby Hillingdon)' (ibid: 20).

He also investigates the journey of the inflight meals to their planes, the backstories of the luggage carried by passengers through departures – from flat screen TVs for relatives in Accra, to six dark green suitcases full of souvenirs bound for Kashmir. De Botton reflects on the hope and anger he witnesses as people go about their business – leaving for holidays, returning from business trips, boarding flights to meet family or working shifts in British Airways' check-in counter, all together for a few brief moments before departing again – with his immersed and stationary presence there to witness it all.

This gives his experience and the more significant thoughts as to why we travel and how we treat one another during these encounters much more time than a traditional 'horizontal' voyage would permit. De Botton comes to understand that the loudspeaker announcements every few minutes come from two women, either Juliet or Margaret, that Ana-Marie from Transylvania is the cleaner assigned to his section and that after chatting to the head of British Airways as they wander through the terminal, he decides that in another life he and Willie Walsh, 'might have become good friends' (ibid: 80) because of their unusual travel encounter.

De Botton clearly relishes the experience, though it does instil a sense of fear in the writer, that this new focus will lead him further into the notion of close experiences and domestic adventure: 'I worried that I might never have another reason to leave the house' (ibid: 106). This rethinking of the focus of travel writing as demonstrated by de Botton, revisits Forsdick's idea of the concentric circles of attention possible with vertical travel. There is an '(in)exhaustibility' (2019: 110) to this travel approach as it presents more layers, perspectives and ideas around place, the deeper the writer is immersed within the experience.

Despite this excitement over the potential of close travel, de Botton comes to an interesting conclusion: that the notion of travel is always loaded in the modern era with our rationale for travelling in the first place – that travel becomes a space for time out, recharge, reconnection, exploration, generosity and emotion as much as it does a voyage to a new destination.

Travel agents would be wiser to ask us what we hope to change about our lives rather than simply where we wish to go. The notion of the journey as a harbinger of resolution was once an essential element of the religious pilgrimage, defined as an excursion through the outer world undertaken in an effort to promote and reinforce an inner evolution (ibid: 104).

'ANOTHER LIFE IN PARIS'

Another example of modern close travel comes from Meg Watson in her article 'Another life in Paris' for the Australian *Saturday Paper* which focuses on her experience inhabiting another person's space as an Airbnb guest in Paris. 'On my first night in Canelle's bed, I watch *Midnight in Paris* and drink rosé from one of her stained teacups' (2014).

The emergence of Airbnb has undoubtedly changed the way many people travel. But, as displayed in Watson's writing, it also affords travel writers the opportunity to utilise this closeness and sense of focus in a novel manner by embracing the changes in the way people travel and write about it. 'I can't help but think of it as someone living a version of my own life with different faces around them, different words to express the same emotions' (ibid).

Within the intimacy of the apartment Watson shows the reader a closer and more nuanced perspective of Paris. The voyeurism of this close approach also allows the reader to appreciate the sameness of travel experiences once they concentrate on more 'endotic' encounters:

> Travel is really equal parts curiosity and delusion. By buying a plane ticket and taking leave from work, in some small way we step out of ourselves. We try the local cuisine and create new shapes with our tongues to form words we've never heard before. We roam strange city streets and try to tessellate ourselves into crowds. As Marcel Proust said, 'The real voyage of discovery consists not in seeking new landscapes, but in having new eyes' (ibid).

From a contemporary perspective Watson's close writing embraces the affordances of the 21st century by utilising a technological and touristic advancement such as Airbnb in order to obtain this new, closer perspective. While it does give the author a more nuanced and personal experience (in Paris, in this example), Watson writes of the conflicted ideas around authenticity this perspective also raises. She writes about the ethics of both Airbnb, as it creates imbalances in the tourist economy of cities such as Paris and Barcelona where locals rent out family homes and offer sub-par accommodation to meet the growing tourist demand to 'live like a local'. Watson remarks: 'In my mind, the heavy brass key in my pocket guarantees me access to the coveted inner life of this secretive city' (2014), yet at the same time she notes the contradictions to this idea – there is an identical Ikea blanket on her bed back in Australia and her time in Canelle's apartment is bookended by the prompt to fill in a visitor's book for the next Airbnb guests to read – loosening this notion of the unique and authentic nature of the experience.

ISOLARION: A DIFFERENT OXFORD JOURNEY

In his book, James Attlee extends the notion of close travel, or a 'home tour' as Kinsley calls it (2019: 119), when he decides that he needs a break from the everyday monotony of his life, and a pilgrimage 'too insistent to ignore' (2007: xiii) presents itself to him. Attlee's issue is that because of work, family and general life commitments he no longer has the means nor the desire to pack a bag, book a ticket to a far-off location and toil for months on end away from his familiar life as his travels once compelled him to do. As such, he arrives at a compromise: 'Gradually it dawned on me that the voyage I needed to make began in my own neighbourhood, within a few minutes' walk of my front door' (ibid: xiv). And so he goes exploring his local environment in suburban Oxford, a city mostly known for its past and the prestige of its university. 'This city has dispatched anthropologists, explorers, scientists, authors, and poets to every nation represented on Cowley Road' (ibid: xvi). So he commits to flip his gaze and see Cowley Road through their eyes.

He walks past Asian grocery stores, transfixed by the stories revealed from the litter on the pavement – of boxes of Spanish oranges, radishes from Lazio and Indian fruit boxes. He revels in the answers to questions he poses – about the origin of fresh sugarcane stalks at the counter, yellow dates offered during Ramadan and the stories of *patra* leaves used by the Cambodian and Gujarati communities instead of plates to eat their meals. As further examples of close travel encounters along Cowley Road, Attlee visits immersion tank facilities, jewellers, tailors, restaurants, former leper institutions and churches – places he had never stopped to examine closely before, though these are all on this one stretch of road and now part of his vertical travel experience.

This type of close travel, though peeling back layers of the familiar, is not without its ethical challenges. Attlee discovers that as he seeks to understand Cowley Road, it does not afford him the usual anonymity that many travel encounters allow. Attlee writes about his attempts to enter the notorious blue door of Cowley Road's adult sex store, which is adjacent to a local bus stop: 'Whenever I pass and think about entering, the queue waiting for a bus appears inordinately long and made up almost exclusively of people known to me' (ibid: 67).

What makes Attlee's journey a valuable contribution to vertical travel writing is its imaginative use of psychogeography by demonstrating a novel way of 'apprehending our urban environment', as Coverley (2006: 13) writes. Attlee focuses on encounters 'that atomise and defamiliarise everyday spaces, and encourage attention to their unexpectedly fractal details' (2019: 101) according to Forsdick's definition, where he revisits locations he has walked past for years, and uses this new technique to look closer at people and places he has not considered previously. Attlee is challenging his own notion of travel and the popular assumption of what is worth visiting in Oxford as an outsider. He draws these experiences out in slow, methodical detail to demonstrate the verticality possible in somewhere so familiar to him.

CONCLUSION

While the notion of close travel writing began with the room-scale introspection of Xavier de Maistre in the 18th century, surprisingly it has not diminished as technology, style and altered reading habits influence the way travel literature is both read and produced. As a foil to the adaptations of modern travel life, close travel writing, with its renewed focus on the close at hand and the layers of our familiar surroundings, has increased the validity and creativity of the travel writing genre while also adding a deeper ethical component to travel.

As Pettinger says: 'To describe "dwelling" as "travel" is to transform it into something worth writing about' (2019: 277). This paper has illuminated historical and contemporary examples where the notion of 'dwelling' as a travel writing technique allows for more nuanced and thoughtful perspectives. Forsdick (2019) and others have expanded this idea further by suggesting that some travel writing involves the intersections of the horizontal journey and the vertical sense of depth, 'reflecting the experimental potential of travel writing to propose new and often defamiliarising ways of viewing and engaging with elsewhere' (ibid: 110), as can be seen in the work of Macfarlane, Sinclair and Attlee.

This approach of utilising the vertical more evidently within travel writing challenges the expectations of the genre and holds the reader's attention because it presents something new and engaging, thus meeting important creative and ethical standards of the form. Cronin reinforces the value of this approach, where the vertical and horizontal, or macroscopic and microscopic journeys can co-exist, in the process adding both depth and experience to the traveller and travel writers' trips. Kinsley writes that close travel encounters do, indeed, focus our attention and curiosity: 'Travellers can and do experience foreignness and defamiliarization on the home tour' (2019: 119).

While the initial premise of this paper, of not moving, not seeking adventure or physical challenge by staying close to home may run counter to what travel writing has traditionally been seen as, it is this challenge – to acknowledge and explore a different way of writing travel – which can ultimately expand its boundaries and its lasting impact.

- This paper was first published in *Ethical Space*, Vol. 17, No. 1 pp 11-17

REFERENCES

Adams, Cathy (2019) Tourists can 'marry' a Dutch local in new tourism initiative, *Independent*, 31 May. Available online at https://www.independent.co.uk/travel/news-and-advice/amsterdam-marry-tourist-local-dutch-untourist-guide-a8938, accessed on 12 October 2019

Attlee, James (2007) *Isolarion: A different Oxford journey*, Chicago, University of Chicago Press

Beaumont, Peter (2019) Why I won't be joining the queue at the top of Everest, *Guardian*, 26 May. Available online at https://www.theguardian.com/world/2019/may/26/i-wont-be-joining-queue-everest-overcrowding-summit, accessed on 21 October 2019

Blackall, Molly (2019) Global tourism hits record high, but who goes where on holiday? *Guardian*, 19 July. Available online at https://www.theguardian.com/news/2019/jul/01/global-tourism-hits-record-highs-but-who-goes-where-on-holiday, accessed on 15 October 2019

Burton, Richard (1860) *Lake regions of central Africa*, London, Longman & Roberts

Coverley, Merlin (2006) *Psychogeography*, Harpenden, Pocket Essentials

Creech, Brian (2014) The spectacle of past violence: Travel journalism and dark tourism, Hanusch, Folker and Fürsich, Elfriede (eds) *Travel journalism: exploring production, impact and culture*, London, Palgrave Macmillan pp 249-266

Cronin, Michael (2000) *Across the lines: Travel, language, translation*, Cork, Cork University Press

De Botton, Alain (2009) *A week at the airport: A Heathrow diary*, London, Vintage

De Maistre, Xavier (2015 [1794 and 1829]) *A journey round my room (and a Nocturnal expedition round my room)* (trans. Attwell, Henry), New York, Hurd & Haughton

Forsdick, Charles (2019) Vertical travel, *The Routledge research companion to travel writing*, Youngs, Tim and Pettinger, Alasdair (eds) London, Routledge pp 99-112

Karr, Alphonse (1851) *Voyage autour de mon jardin* [Voyage around my garden], Paris, Calmann Levy

Kinsley, Zoë (2019) Home tour, Forsdick, Charles, Kinsley, Zoë and Walchester, Kathryn (eds) *Keywords for travel writing studies: A critical glossary*, New York, Anthem Press pp 119-121

Lee, Joanne (2012) Alternative urban journeys: Italian travel writing and the Contromano series, *Studies in Travel Writing*, Vol. 16, No. 2 pp 203-214

Pettinger, Alasdair (2019) Vertical travel, Forsdick, Charles, Kinsley, Zoë and Walchester, Kathryn (eds) *Keywords for travel writing studies: A critical glossary*, New York, Anthem Press pp 277-279

Pratt, Mary-Louise (2002) *Imperial eyes: Travel writing and transculturation,* London, Routledge

Raban, Jonathan (1999) *Passage to Juneau: A sea and its meaning,* London, Picador

Sharpley, Richard and Stone, Phillip (2009) *Darker side of travel: The theory and practice of dark tourism,* Bristol, Channel View Publications

Stiegler, Berndt (2013) *Traveling in place: A history of armchair travel* (trans. Filkins, Peter) Chicago, University of Chicago Press

Stubbs, Ben (2016) Review of *Traveling in place: A history of armchair travel, Studies in Travel Writing*, Vol. 20, No. 3 pp 316-318

Thompson, Carl (2011) *Travel writing (The new critical idiom),* London, Routledge

Twain, Mark (2010 [1869]) *The innocents abroad,* London, Wordsworth Editions

Watson, Meg (2014) Another life in Paris, thanks to Airbnb, *Saturday Paper*, No. 32, 4-10 October. Available online at https://www.thesaturdaypaper.com.au/2014/10/03/another-life-paris-thanks-airbnb/14122957881047, accessed on 1 October 2019

Youngs, Tim and Pettinger, Alasdair (2019) Vertical travel, *The Routledge research companion to travel writing*, London, Routledge pp 99-112

Youngs, Tim (2013) *The Cambridge introduction to travel writing,* Cambridge, Cambridge University Press

NOTE ON THE CONTRIBUTOR

Ben Stubbs is a senior lecturer in journalism and writing at the University of South Australia. He has written numerous academic articles and book chapters exploring the plurality of travel writing. Dr Stubbs has written five books on immersive travel and non-fiction writing and he was previously a features and travel writer for *The New York Times,* the *Guardian,* the *Sydney Morning Herald* and the *Toronto Star* among others.

SECTION 2

New media, new ethical challenges

Chapter 8

'Here come the girls': Examining professional golf organisations' online media representations of female professional golfers in a mixed-gender event

Ali Bowes and Niamh Kitching

It is widely accepted that golf participation is on the decline and that golf clubs are exclusive environments, in response to which the European Tour launched the short golf format GolfSixes. In May 2018, male and female professional golfers competed against each other at the European Tour's GolfSixes event, following the invitation of five female players from the Ladies European Tour. Both organisations used the social networking site Twitter to promote the tournament. Using a neoliberal feminist perspective, this study examines the depiction of the five competing female professional golfers through both golf organisations' Twitter accounts, before, during and after the event. Thematic analysis revealed the way in which the GolfSixes was depicted as a stage to showcase women's golf and promote narratives around gender equality, whilst in some cases still framing women in problematic ways. Results highlight the role that female golfers can play as empowered and entrepreneurial agents of change.

Keywords: women's golf, neoliberal feminism, social media, sport media, media analysis

Research has confirmed the discriminatory environment in which golf takes place for females of all abilities both on and off the golf course (Reis and Correia 2013). While there are exceptions, golf is widely recognised as a male domain, which has led to a persistent struggle for women in terms of equality of access, participation, employment and decision-making (Kitching 2017). In golf settings, women are considered to be slower, less able, less competitive (and more social) and less powerful (in terms of driving distance) players (McGinnis and Gentry 2002;

McGinnis et al. 2005). Different tee boxes alter the length of the hole and are often imbued with gender codes such as the shortest 'ladies' tee' (Hundley 2004) which marks women as different or 'other' (McGinnis et al. 2009) and, significantly, inferior. This is translated on to the course, with women reporting feeling ignored, overlooked or unimportant, particularly in their on-course interactions with males (McGinnis et al. 2005; McGinnis and Gentry 2006). To this day, golf participation figures indicate the low visibility of female participants and some golf clubs still obstruct membership by women (Kitching 2017).

When women were historically excluded from full membership and playing rights, they were forced to form female-only sections, initiated by the St. Andrew's Ladies' Golf Club in 1867 (George 2009). Subsequently, women's golf developed independently from the men's game, with gender-segregated golf governing bodies forming at amateur level and later at professional level. While competitive professional golf for men started as early as 1860 in the United Kingdom through the Professional Golf Association, the professionalisation of the women's game occurred much later. The Ladies Professional Golfers' Association (LPGA), in America, was formed in 1950, followed by the Ladies European Tour (LET) in 1978. Subsequently, disparities exist between male and female professional golf, in terms of visibility, endorsements and prize money. It has been found that only one third of LPGA players will break even or make a profit in an average tournament once they have accounted for expenses, caddy fees and entry fees (Crosset 1995), and many European-based female golfers work on part-time jobs alongside their professional golf career (Scrivener 2018).

Ethnographic research on the LPGA tour has highlighted women's status as outsiders within the world of professional golf (Crosset 1995), something that is pertinent today. In April 2019, the European Tour and the LET played concurrent tournaments on different courses in Morocco, hosted at the Royal Golf Dar Es Salam, in Rabat. These tournaments, held at the same time, highlighted stark differences: the winner of the men's tournament, Jorge Campillo, earned €416,660 in comparison to Nuria Iturrios on the LET, earning €67,500 (Cooper 2019). In 2018, when Francesco Molinari earned £3,652,504 on the European Tour, the top earner on the LET (Georgia Hall) accumulated £456,110 (*Golf World* 2019). This was only marginally more than the 75th ranked European Tour player, Ashley Chesters (£450,231), whereas finishing 75th on the LET earned Kelsey MacDonald £14,508 (ibid).

Women's subordinate position in golf is perpetuated in the golf media which has been shown to replicate the same exclusionary practices evidenced within the game. However, technological advancements have led to a new media landscape in sport, with athletes and sport organisations using social media sites such as Twitter to engage and interact with fans. Sheffer and Schultz (2013) highlight that the growth in social media more broadly has had a 'profound impact on the way sports are created, delivered and consumed'. Allison (2018) specifically describes the role that Twitter can play as a communication medium in women's sport, most notably as a potential marketing tool. She highlights how social media use becomes a 'free way of circumventing mainstream media outlets to communicate with and expand the fan base' (ibid: 215). Sports organisations are now taking ownership of their own media and promotion and creating their own content.

The aim of this paper is to investigate how professional golf organisations represented female professional golfers in online media before, during and after a mixed-gender professional golf tournament, the GolfSixes. Examining representations through Twitter should illustrate the lens through which female professional golfers are viewed by golf itself and reveal the intentions of golf governing bodies in their promotion or otherwise of female professional golfers. The GolfSixes tournament presents a unique opportunity to explore the representation of female professional athletes in direct competition with male professionals, and through the Twitter accounts of both the male and female golf organisations. One further goal of the research is to contribute to the growing literature on new and online representations of female athletes.

THE GOLFSIXES EVENT

The GolfSixes, featuring on the men's professional European Tour, was hailed as a 'revolutionary and novel short form of the game' presenting a modern image of golf and illustrating the Tour's desire 'to embrace innovation and originality in professional golf' (European Tour 2017). Data from the inaugural GolfSixes tournament in 2017 found a 42 per cent increase in new golf fans at the event who were, on average, 14 per cent younger than those seen during the rest of the golfing calendar (European Tour 2018a). For 2018's version, four wildcard teams were selected alongside twelve qualifying teams from the European Tour. Within these wildcard teams, European Tour chief executive Keith Pelley invited five professional female players from the LET: Carlota Ciganda and Mel Reid formed a European Women's team, Georgia Hall and Charley Hull formed an England Women's team, and Catriona Matthew (2019 European Solheim Cup captain) combined with Thomas Bøjrn (2018 European Ryder Cup captain) in a European Captains team. In the end, 27 European Tour male professionals and five LET female professionals competed. Not only was this the first time the European Tour had included women in a team golf event, the European Captains team became the first male and female professionals to play together in a competitive match play format event worldwide (European Tour 2018b).

TRADITIONAL MEDIA REPRESENTATIONS OF FEMALE ATHLETES

Traditional media outlets such as newspapers and television have been found to privilege male athletes over females in both the quantity and depth of the coverage (Bernstein and Kian 2013). Sport, including golf, is often constructed as a male domain in the mass media, with gendered practices in the sport media devaluing female athletes and emphasising cultural equivalents of hegemonic masculinity. Women's inclusion within the sports media is, thus, problematic; when women do find themselves on the sports pages of the popular press, they are often represented in ways that restrict our imagination about women's sport and retain the hegemonic position of men in sport (Bruce 2015). While McClearen (2018) suggests that the sports media could potentially be used as a source of empowerment for female athletes, traditional approaches are still adopted in their presentation of women where they are trivialised, sexualised and underrepresented. There is evidence of change, however. Biscomb and Griggs (2013) found a shift towards a greater awareness of, and coverage of, female athletes in the sports media and Petty and Pope (2018) noted a removal of the gender marking of women's sport in the media.

Female golfers in the sports media have an equally ambivalent history. Although Billings et al. (2008: 65) highlight that rising audience interest in women's golf has brought about challenges to golf's 'masculine hegemonic entrenchment', both televised and print media coverage of golf have continued to offer representations that reinforce divisions of gender, class, disability and race (Billings et al. 2006, Billings et al. 2008). In examining televised PGA and LPGA golf, Billings et al. (2005) found a multitude of gender differences in on-air golf announcing. They described how luck was a major factor in how female golfer's success or failure was described, whereas men were more likely to be described in terms of their physicality or personality. There are, however, examples that offer some challenges to the gendered norms and traditional depictions of women in golf media. Research on the media coverage of Annika Sörenstam's involvement in the 2003 PGA Colonial Tournament demonstrated ambivalent representations: on the one hand, commentators were likely to highlight Sörenstam's emotions, but on the other, there were also examples of non-gendered explanations of her successes too, such as failing due to a lack of finesse (Billings et al. 2006). More recently, Bowes and Kitching (2019) described the print media representation of professional female golfers as a 'double-edged sword'. They noted positive outcomes in terms of the quantity of print media coverage of the female athletes playing at the GolfSixes but remained critical of the central role that gender played in their representations.

FEMALE ATHLETES AND THE RISE OF ONLINE AND NEW SPORT MEDIA

In the recent emerging dynamic information environment, online media has become central to commentary and presentations of athletes. It has been claimed that social media has given rise to the 'accessible athlete', enabling athletes and organisations to bypass mainstream media outlets and present their product to the audiences unfiltered (Sheffer and Schultz 2013). Since the advent of Twitter and other social media platforms in the early 21st century, there has been a surge of interest in the use of social media by both sports organisations and female athletes. Twitter is considered the most influential social media platform in sport (Gibbs and Haynes 2013). As of April 2019, Serena Williams is the most followed female athlete on Twitter (10.9 million; Twitter 2019a) and, within golf, Paula Creamer (491k; Twitter 2019b), Lexi Thompson (463k; Twitter 2019c) and Michelle Wie (435k; Twitter 2019d) have the most significant following, with Suzann Pettersen (104.6k; 2019e), the most followed female European golfer.

Given the wealth of studies on print media representations of athletes, Hutchins (2014) has criticised how sports media researchers have neglected the rise, effects and meanings of these new, mobile, online media and communication tools. He posits that a mobile research agenda offers the potential for media sport scholarship to make a sustained contribution to the study of mediatisation processes. Bruce (2015) outlines two new rules in how sportswomen are represented in media, firstly through online media, using their own voices on their own terms and, secondly, through the discourse of 'pretty and powerful' over 'pretty *or* powerful'. While Sanderson (2013) suggests that social media can provide a venue for sexist commentary, several commentators have outlined the potential for social media to challenge prevailing hegemonic representations of female athletes, contesting the discourses that devalue sports women and transforming the representation of female athletes (Antunovic and Hardin 2012; Bruce and Hardin 2014).

Online media not only provide opportunities for female athletes to self-represent on their own terms, but also offer sportswomen, fans and commentators a space to share, debate and discuss women's sport (Bruce and Hardin 2014; La Voi and Calhoun 2014). Sanderson and Gramlich (2016) suggest that Twitter has the potential to become the catalyst for advocacy in female sport. However, while LaVoi and Calhoun (2014) ask whether or not digital media could 'free female athletes from the tyranny of traditional media' (ibid: 327), they conclude that it does not provide a platform to contest the status quo of gender narratives in sport. Given the recent growth in online and new media technologies, investigations on how female athletes are represented on social media are still emerging. Notably, Thorpe et al. (2017) found that sportswomen often emphasise their personal lives and sexuality, with little focus on broader gender arrangements influencing their sporting femininities.

FEMALE GOLFERS, ONLINE NEW MEDIA AND NEOLIBERAL FEMINISM

Previous work by the authors in golf environments has been framed using a critical feminist stance, highlighting the marginalisation, underrepresentation and exclusion of females and the simultaneous privileging of men and men's activities (Kitching et al. 2017; Kitching 2017; Bowes and Kitching 2019). In this paper, the authors move away from this second wave outlook to employ the perspective of neo-liberal feminism which moves beyond (or even ignores) gender discrimination, to consider women in the economic space, some of whom have become entrepreneurial agents in control of their own destinies. Banet-Weiser (2015) suggests that in 'economies of visibility' not only are women compelled to assume responsibility for finding innovative solutions to gender discrimination but they are encouraged to demonstrate visibly their entrepreneurial abilities. Gender inequality is still recognised within this perspective, but reactions to such inequalities are framed by individual economic and entrepreneurial discourses (Thorpe et al. 2017). Tofoletti and Thorpe (2018) have outlined how professional sportswomen are internalising neoliberal discourses of self-entrepreneurialism through their self-branding and use of social media. Thorpe et al. (2017: 375) suggest that:

> … critical engagement with neoliberal feminism requires an understanding of the market forces, and particularly neoliberal discourses of entrepreneurialism … it also raises concerns about the effects of such actions for women's positions in the sports-media-industry complex and identifies the necessity for challenging such oppressive power relations.

This perspective is suited to the corporate and commercial world of professional golf, where prize money, tournament/career earnings and athlete endorsements are used as highly prized markers for professionals to strive for. Use of neoliberal feminism in this paper allows the authors an insight into how golf organisations promote, market and commercialise female athletes, which female athletes (if any) are prioritised and who may be excluded.

METHODOLOGY

Given the call by sociologists of sport to consider more carefully the role of online and new media in the presentation of female athletes, this paper uses data collected from Twitter during the GolfSixes tournament. The Twitter profiles chosen for analysis are the accounts of the European Tour and the LET, the organising bodies for professional golf in Europe. The @EuropeanTour account has more than 367K followers (Twitter 2019f), with over 42K following the @LETgolf account (Twitter 2019g). Using Twitter as the data source allows the capture of tweets, along with associated images, videos and article links. As the 2018 GolfSixes event ran over the weekend of 5-6 May, the data collection timeframe was from Tuesday 1 May to Wednesday 9 May, to cover communication from the two Twitter accounts before, during and after the event. The authors used the NCapture tool to download tweets from the @EuropeanTour and @LETgolf accounts and import to NVivo for analysis. Each tweet was sometimes accompanied by an image, video or article weblink, and these were also collected through the NCapture process, along with the quantity of retweets, replies and 'likes' associated with each particular tweet, and the tweet type (e.g. retweet or tweet), related hashtag and tweet weblink.

This data collection resulted in harnessing 218 tweets from @EuropeanTour and 92 tweets from the @LETgolf. Primarily, textual data was thematically analysed, as well as a consideration of the types of videos and images also used. The authors used Ryan and Bernard's (2003) triad test, where both authors read the tweets, coded them and explained our codes to each other. The next step was the co-construction of themes, by making conceptual links between codes, choosing those that were prominent and relevant. Following an initial reading of the data set, irrelevant tweets were removed and as such the data set was reduced to 183 tweets from the @EuropeanTour account, and 81 from the @LETgolf account. The following sections will now present a breakdown of how the two organisations used social media throughout the event, with a specific focus on the involvement of the female players.

RESULTS AND DISCUSSION

There were some similarities in the types of content posted to the Twitter accounts of both the European Tour and the LET. For both tours, many of their outputs was their own original content, with @EuropeanTour retweeting 19 per cent of their output (34 tweets), and @LETgolf retweeting 23 per cent of their output (19 tweets). Both tours used the Twitter platform to promote the innovative nature of the event (@LETgolf, 12 per cent – 10; @EuropeanTour, 11 per cent – 21), centring on the novel aspects such as the six-hole format and the shot clock. Furthermore, both accounts used their Twitter stream similarly over the course of the event to promote the tournament and the tournament venue, offering information on the course and ticket sales (@LETgolf, 11 per cent – 9; @EuropeanTour, 9 per cent – 17). During the tournament, the largest volume of tweets from both accounts was sent regarding the performances of the players and outcomes of the matches. Player, and team, performances were tweeted a total of 66 times by @EuropeanTour (36 per cent) and 24 times by @LETgolf (30 per cent).

Despite some similarities in how the organisations used social media throughout the event, there were some notable differences. The @LETgolf account focused on the 'fun' aspects of the 2018 tournament much more regularly than the @EuropeanTour (21 tweets – 25 per cent compared to 20 tweets – 11 per cent). However, the most obvious difference was the way the two organisations were using the event for different means, specifically regarding the female players. The pre-tournament focus of @EuropeanTour was very active, tweeting pre-event player content across all the players involved (24 per cent – 44), compared to @LETgolf, whose three pre-event tweets (4 per cent) centred solely on the female players' inclusion. Throughout the tournament, again @LETgolf focused mainly on their own tour players, sending only 7 tweets (9 per cent) exclusively about male players, compared to @EuropeanTour, who tweeted about the female players 28 times (15 per cent). @LETgolf focused on the 'state' of women's golf more broadly in 11 tweets explicitly and in a further 14 tweets as a by-line (31 per cent), compared to only 7 tweets from @EuropeanTour (4 per cent). The @LETgolf account's strong focus on their own players is further emphasised when you consider the first tweet they sent about a male player and their performance in the event was at 4:30pm on the last day of the tournament, following the elimination of all female players.

This significance of the female players' involvement in the GolfSixes is further emphasised in terms of the most popular Twitter content seen in the accounts. In terms of likes and retweets of content from the 2018 GolfSixes, the most popular tweet on the European Tour account was the video of and reaction to Hull's opening tee shot when the England women's team played their male counterparts, with 163 retweets and 931 likes. After Hull hit an excellent shot two feet from the pin, the England men's team pretended to run away, seemingly terrified. This was the most popular event on Twitter through the tournament, as was seen in the LET Twitter account also. Saying: 'This is how you start,' the tweet with the same video attached from the LET received 79 retweets.

Following a more detailed thematic analysis of the Twitter outputs, there were a number of significant themes related to the women's involvement in the tournament which featured heavily in both golf organisations' Twitter engagements:

(1) a stage to showcase women's golf;

(2) a conversation starter on women's golf and equality;

(3) a persistence of gendered language.

These will now be explored in more detail, drawing upon the neoliberal feminist framework to help make sense of the ways in which female professional golfers are represented on social media.

A STAGE TO SHOWCASE WOMEN'S GOLF

It has transpired that the female players dominated the print media coverage of the event (Bowes and Kitching 2019) and, likewise, the Twitter dataset demonstrated a similar appreciation for the skills, talent and performances of the female players. On the @EuropeanTour account, female players were often featured in short video clips hitting shots: Hull (1 chip shot, 6 full swing shots), Reid (1 drive, 2 iron shots), Ciganda (2 putts, 1 iron shot), Hall (1 long putt) and Matthew (1 long putt). These clips were often accompanied by phrases outlining their physical power, e.g. 'Stripe show' (Reid's drive), or 'Charley doesn't hold back' (Hull's recoil drive). Reid was also captured as the 'first player on the range' on the first morning of the tournament, indicating the seriousness with which she was taking the event. In terms of the distribution of coverage of all the golfers, it was clear that one of the female players dominated coverage on the European Tour Twitter account, with an emphasis on Hull and her portrayal as a physically powerful and strong player.

While patterns emerged in the distribution of the coverage of the women golfers on the @EuropeanTour account, these patterns were not evident through the @LET account where the coverage of the female golfers was distributed more equally amongst the golfers. This account appeared more proactive in promoting the female golfers' own representations during the event. Acknowledging that Ciganda was not active on Twitter for the tournament, for example, @LETgolf retweeted content from Hull (1), Reid (2), Hall (1) and Matthew (2), whereas @EuropeanTour only retweeted 2 tweets from female players (Reid and Matthew). From a neo-liberal feminist perspective, women are increasingly encouraged to become entrepreneurial agents in control of their own destinies and here, @LETgolf has supported the female golfers' opportunity to elevate their profiles.

As noted, one of the most significant events of the tournament in terms of Twitter engagement was the opening shot from Hull on the first hole for the England women's team in their match against the England men. The @LETgolf account phrased it: 'This is how you start GolfSixes @CharleyHull. See you later @PepperellEddie and @MattsjWallace' and the post was retweeted 79 times. The @European Tour account posted 'Pepperell and Wallace have already had enough. Hull into 2 feet with her first shot…', retweeted 163 times. This made it the most popular tweet on both accounts during the tournament. The shot was featured as one of the @EuropeanTour account's 'Six best shots of the tournament' video. It also resulted in Hull becoming the first woman to win the European Tour's 'shot of the month' award for May (European Tour 2018c).

A CONVERSATION STARTER FOR WOMEN'S GOLF AND EQUALITY

Following the success of the female players in the tournament, it was clear that the women had demonstrated their worth as golfers on an international, mediatised stage, and this was forefronted on the @LETgolf Twitter account. @LETgolf termed the female professionals as 'great role models' (5 May 2018) and popular (4 May 2018), and the account called on fans to 'come and support' the women on the final day of the tournament (5 May 2018). Following the tournament, the account posted that 'they showcased the strength of the women's game…' (6 May 2018). At times @LETgolf went further than just promoting women and gender issues, and on a more politicised agenda, when it posted 'exactly what golf needs' in relation to the fun and energetic atmosphere at the tournament (@LETgolf, 6 May 2018). This evidence outlines how the LET used the social media platform to position and promote female golfers and contributors throughout the event, and differs from historical evidence in golf, where women often positioned themselves against each other (Kitching 2017).

Throughout the week, Reid positioned herself as the spokesperson for women's golf. For example, her European Tour blog took on some sensitive topics such as pay equality and sexism, while many of her interviews during the tournament were forthright and focused on the visibility of women's golf:

> … this is a huge opportunity to showcase women's golf. We don't get the coverage, we don't get supported as I feel that we should, and you know an event like this is huge for us… (interview with Ciganda and Reid, @LETgolf, 5 May 2018).

> Hopefully we've opened up a few more eyes to women's golf, that we can compete and we're pretty good at what we do and we work very hard at what we do … it has been really good exposure for women's golf which hopefully helps it, because it needs help (interview with Reid and Ciganda, @LETgolf, 7 May 2018).

Through the week, she was positioned in the media as assuming the responsibility for speaking out around gender discrimination, similar to Banet-Weiser's (2015) definition of economies of visibility. As Thorpe et al. (2017) outline, reactions to gender inequality are framed by female athletes' individual and entrepreneurial discourses. Reid's comments were retweeted by @LETgolf twice and by @EuropeanTour once. However, in relation to speaking out on women's golf, she was featured four times on @EuropeanTour, and seven times on @LETgolf. Tofoletti and Thorpe (2018) have outlined how professional sportswomen are internalising neoliberal discourses of self-entrepreneurialism through their self-branding and use of social media. While Reid may not be actively pursuing a particular strategy around this, her opinions are recognised by golf's organising bodies. This further demonstrates a neoliberal feminist approach, with the female players taking ownership of their situation, framing themselves as capable and 'letting their golf do their talking'. In this way, the female athletes act as advocates for their sport.

One other interesting aspect of equality as portrayed through the female players was their positioning within a male event, owned and run by the European Tour. At times during the tournament the players spoke about it being an 'opportunity for women's golf', and by the end the players were keen to show their gratitude to the European Tour, with Reid commenting: 'Thank you so much to @EuropeanTour for inviting me to @golfsixes this weekend…' (@melreidgolf, 6 May 2018). Hall also commented that she would 'love to come back' (@LETGolf, 6 May 2018). The LET Twitter account even posted: 'They showcased the strength of the women's game and how good it is to be playing alongside the men' (6 May 2018).

A PERSISTENCE OF GENDERED LANGUAGE

Despite the positive framing of the female players at the event, there were cases where there is a need to think more critically about the language used to represent the women on both of the tour's Twitter accounts. Bruce (2015) writes about the ways female athletes have been historically presented in the media, with gender marking and infantilisation as two key elements. While there is evidence to prove the contrary, 'othering' women in relation to sport has been widespread in the media discourse, while the practice of describing adult sports women as girls or only by their first names is relatively commonplace. This evidence reinforces both points, where the language used to describe the women golfers was archaic, e.g. 'Day 1 at the #GolfSixes belonged to the *ladies*' (@EuropeanTour, 5 May 2018) and 'we all think it's brilliant for the event that the *ladies* are here!' (@EuropeanTour, 4 May 2018).

The second element of gendered language was in differentiating the men's teams from the women's teams, which was visible on both Twitter accounts. For example, 'Team Australia defeat the European Women's Team 2-0' (@LETgolf, 6 May 2018), 'Team Denmark and #GolfSixesEURWomen are tied 2nd in their group with 4 points' (@LETgolf, 5 May 2018), 'The England women beat Team Thailand' (@EuropeanTour, 5 May 2018), and 'England v England Women' (@EuropeanTour, 1 May 2018). Unlike the last example, when the England men's and women's team faced each other, the men's team were also gender marked, particularly on the @LETgolf account, for example, 'Will England Women's and Men's teams meet again in the @golfsixes final?' (@LETgolf, 6 May 2018) and 'watch highlights from England's Women's Vs Men's match' (@LETgolf, 5 May 2018). In contrast, the European Tour used gender marking less frequently, particularly for the men, referring to their '#GolfSixesEng kit' (5 May 2018). They corrected this the following day when they posted about 'the story behind the #GolfSixesENGMen outfits' (6 May 2018).

The final element of gendered language was the way the women golfers were infantilised on the Twitter accounts. For example, 'Here come the girls' (@EuropeanTour, 2 May 2018), and 'The England girls are still undefeated' (@EuropeanTour, 5 May 2018). However, this was sometimes by the female players themselves:

> RT @melreidgolf: Thankyou so much @europeantour for inviting me to @golfsixes this weekend. Had so much fun and hopefully us girls made a statement and put women's golf on the map. As always love playing with @carlotagolf ... (@EuropeanTour, 6 May 2018).

Whilst a neoliberal feminist framework aims to move beyond gender discrimination, it remains important to highlight a persistence of problematic gendered language used to frame the female golfers.

CONCLUSION: HERE COME THE GIRLS – REFRAMING FEMALE GOLFERS AS ADVOCATES?

This paper aimed to explore the representations of female golfers at the GolfSixes by professional golf organisations, shedding light on the way in which these athletes are used, and for what means, by their employers. As mentioned previously, this event transpired as a direct response to the decline in golf participation and including the women professionals in 2018 certainly contributed to the presentation of the event as modern and inclusive. The event was presented as a short, quick form of golf, in a fun and family-friendly atmosphere.

Given these pressures on the golf market, it is clear that the European Tour invited women along for economic reasons, and to present the tour to a new family-orientated crowd. Conversely, the female players were explicitly used by the LET to advocate for their tour (and women's golf more broadly) to a new audience (notably, fans of men's golf). Indeed, the LET strategy was to 'piggyback' on the popularity of the men's tour to raise issues around the status of women's golf in Europe – although these were raised through the players themselves. In this way, the players were presented by the LET as empowered and entrepreneurial, capitalising on their increased visibility due to their involvement on the men's European Tour. Additionally, the fact that the female professionals even agreed to participate in the first place outlines, perhaps, their sense of entrepreneurialism in seizing the opportunity. This aligns with the print media coverage of the event which somewhat positioned the success of the women's teams as a surprise. While this may be seen on the one hand to reinforce ideologies of men's hegemonic positioning within golf cultures, from a neoliberal perspective this can be seen as the women framing themselves in an entrepreneurial way – putting themselves out there against male golfers.

We acknowledge that there are limitations in social media analyses, namely that it is impossible to know the intentions or the editorial decisions made in selecting content for posting by the golf organisations, the market-informed strategies in place, the coordination of posts and press releases by outside social media managers or agents. Despite this, this paper fits in response to Thorpe et al.'s (2017) insistence for more theoretically informed, empirical research on sportswomen's own use of social media, and particularly scholarship that provides space for women's own voices on how and why they are using social media. As they note, '… social media has feminist potential to challenge dominant representational regimes by providing avenues for female athletes to enhance their visibility' (Thorpe et al. 2017: 361) – a strategy that was used by the LET, in the shadow of the women's success in a men's event. Subsequently, 'Here come the girls' seems significant in many ways: the female players were important for both organisations in different ways and were central in promoting the unusual nature of the GolfSixes event. These women, then, are not powerless and at the mercy of their employers but empowered women who seized their opportunity to demonstrate their worth as international competitors in a man's world and, in some cases, used their voices to advocate for and demand positive change.

- This paper was first published in *Ethical Space*, Vol. 16, Nos 2 and 3 pp 12-20

REFERENCES

Allison, Rachel (2018) *Kicking center: Gender and the selling of women's professional soccer*, New Jersey, Rutgers University Press

Antunovic, Dunja and Hardin, Marie (2012) Activism in women's sports blogs: Fandom and feminist potential, *International Journal of Sport Communication*, Vol. 5, No. 3 pp 305-322

Bernstein, Alina and Kian, Edward M. (2013) Gender and sexualities in sport media, Pedersen, Paul (ed.) *Routledge handbook of sport communication,* London, Routledge pp 319-327

Billings, Andrew C., Angelini, James R. and Eastman, Susan Tyler (2005) Diverging discourses: Gender differences in televised golf announcing, *Mass Communication and Society*, Vol. 8, No. 2 pp 155-171

Billings, Andrew, Angelini, James and Eastman, Susan Tyler (2008) Wie shock: Television commentary about playing on the PGA and LPGA tours, *Howard Journal of Communications*, Vol. 19, No. 1 pp 64-84

Billings, Andrew, Craig, Caroline, Croce, Robert, Cross, Kristian, Moore, Kathryn, Vigodsky, William and Watson, Victoria (2006) 'Just one of the guys?': Network depictions of Annika Sorenstam in the 2003 PGA Colonial Tournament, *Journal of Sport and Social Issues*, Vol. 30, No. 1 pp 107-114

Biscomb, Kay and Griggs, Gerald (2013) 'A splendid effort!': Print media reporting of England's women's performances in the 2009 Cricket World Cup, *International Review for the Sociology of Sport*, Vol. 48, No. 1 pp 99-111

Bowes, Ali and Kitching, Niamh (2019) 'Battle of the sixes': Investigating the print media representations of female professional golfers competing in a men's tour event, *International Review for the Sociology of Sport*, Vol. 55, No. 6 pp 664-684. DOI: 1012690219842544

Bruce, Toni (2015) Assessing the sociology of sport: On media and representations of sportswomen, *International Review for the Sociology of Sport*, Vol. 50, Nos 4 and 5 pp 380-384

Bruce, Toni and Hardin, Marie (2014) Reclaiming our voices: Sportswomen and social media, Billings, Andrew C. and Hardin, Marie (eds) *Routledge handbook of sport and new media*, London, Routledge pp 329-337

Cooper, Matt (2019) European golf's Moroccan adventure provides hopes and reveals the difficulties. Available online at https://www.forbes.com/sites/matthewjcooper/2019/04/29/european-golfs-moroccan-adventure-provides-hopes-and-reveals-the-difficulties/#24f783dd4213, accessed on 31 May 2018

Crosset, Todd (1995) *Outsiders in the clubhouse: The world of women's professional golf*, Albany, State University of New York Press

European Tour (2017) Innovative GolfSixes concept unveiled. Available online at http://www.europeantour.com/europeantour/news/newsid=320826.html, accessed on 31 May 2019

European Tour (2018a) 'GolfSixes' attracts new younger fans as short-format golf returns to the European Tour. Available online at http://www.europeantour.com/europeantour/season=2018/tournamentid=2018038/news/newsid=339422.html, accessed on 31 May 2019

European Tour (2018b) GolfSixes set for innovative world first. Available online at http://www.europeantour.com/europeantour/season=2018/tournamentid=2018038/news/newsid=342863.html, accessed on 31 May 2019

European Tour (2018c) Charley Hull wins May shot of the month. Available online at http://www.europeantour.com/myeuropeantour/competitions/charley-hull-wins-may-shot-the-month/, accessed on 31 May 2019

George, Jane (2009) 'An excellent means of combining fresh air, exercise and society': Females on the fairways, 1890-1914, *Sport in History*, Vol. 29, No. 3 pp 333-352

Gibbs, Chris and Haynes, Richard (2013) A phenomenological investigation into how Twitter has changed the nature of sport media relations, *International Journal of Sport Communication*, Vol. 6, No. 4 pp 394-408

Golf World (2019) New world order, March pp 9-11

Hundley, Heather L. (2004) Keeping the score: The hegemonic everyday practices in golf, *Communication Reports*, Vol. 17, No. 1 pp 39-48

Hutchins, Brett (2014) Twitter: Follow the money and look beyond sports, *Communication & Sport*, Vol. 2, No. 2 pp 122-126

Kitching, Niamh (2017) Women in golf: A critical reflection, Toms, Martin R. (ed.) *Routledge international handbook of golf science*, London, Routledge pp 404-413

Kitching, Niamh, Grix, Jonathan and Philpotts, Lesley (2017) Shifting hegemony in 'a man's world': Incremental change for female golf professional employment, *Sport in Society*, Vol. 20, No. 11 pp 1530-1547

LaVoi, Nicole M. and Calhoun, Austin Stair (2014) Digital media and women's sport: An old view on 'new' media?, Billings, Andrew C. and Hardin, Marie (eds) *Routledge handbook of sport and new media*, London, Routledge pp 338-348

McClearen, Jennifer (2018) Introduction: Women in sports media: New scholarly engagements, *Feminist Media Studies*, Vol. 18, No. 5 pp 942-945

McGinnis, Lee and Gentry, James W. (2002) The masculine hegemony in sports: Is golf for 'ladies'?, *ACR North American Advances*, Vol. 29 pp 19-24

McGinnis, Lee, McQuillan, Julia and Chapple, Constance L. (2001) I just want to play: Women, sexism and persistence in golf, *Journal of Sport & Social Issues*, Vol. 29, No. 3 pp 313-337

McGinnis, Lee P. and Gentry, James W. (2006) Getting past the red tees: Constraints women face in golf and strategies to help them stay, *Journal of Sport Management*, Vol. 20, No. 2 pp 218-247

McGinnis, Lee P., Gentry, James W. and McQuillan, Julia (2009) Ritual-based behavior that reinforces hegemonic masculinity in golf: Variations in women golfers' responses, *Leisure Sciences*, Vol. 31, No. 1 pp 19-36

Petty, Kate and Pope, Stacey (2018) A new age for media coverage of women's sport? An analysis of English media coverage of the 2015 FIFA Women's World Cup, *Sociology*, Vol. 53, No. 3 pp 486-502. DOI: 0038038518797505

Reis, Helena and Correia, Antonia (2013) Gender inequalities in golf: A consented exclusion?, *International Journal of Culture, Tourism and Hospitality Research*, Vol. 7, No. 4 pp 324-339

Ryan, Gery W. and Russell, Bernard H. (2003) Techniques to identify themes, *Field methods*, Vol. 15. No. 1 pp 85-109

Sanderson, Jimmy (2013) Social media and sport communication, Pedersen, Paul (ed.) *The Routledge handbook of sport communication*, London, Routledge pp 70-79

Sanderson, Jimmy and Gramlich, Kelly (2016) 'You go girl!': Twitter and conversations about sport culture and gender, *Sociology of Sport Journal*, Vol. 33, No. 2 pp 113-123

Scrivener, Peter (2018) Ladies European Tour: Melissa Reid says players need part time jobs to make living. Available online at https://www.bbc.co.uk/sport/golf/44046293, accessed on 7 June 2019

Sheffer, Mary Lou and Schultz, Brad (2013) The new world of social media and broadcast sports reporting, Pedersen, P. M. (ed.) *Routledge handbook of sport communication*, London, Routledge pp 201-218

Thorpe, Holly, Toffoletti, Kim and Bruce, Toni (2017) Sportswomen and social media: Bringing third-wave feminism, postfeminism, and neoliberal feminism into conversation, *Journal of Sport and Social Issues*, Vol. 41, No. 5 pp 359-383

Toffoletti, Kim and Thorpe, Holly (2018) Female athletes' self-representation on social media: A feminist analysis of neoliberal marketing strategies in 'economies of visibility', *Feminism & Psychology*, Vol. 29, No. 1 pp 11-31

Twitter (2019a) @SerenaWilliams. Available online at https://twitter.com/serenawilliams, accessed on 7 June 2019

Twitter (2019b) @ThePCreamer. Available online at https://twitter.com/ThePCreamer, accessed on 7 June 2019

Twitter (2019c) @Lexi. Available online at https://twitter.com/Lexi, accessed on 7 June 2019

Twitter (2019d) @themichellewie. Available online at https:// twitter.com/themichellewie, accessed on 7 June 2019

Twitter (2019e) @suzannpettersen. Available online at https://twitter.com/suzannpettersen, accessed on 7 June 2019

Twitter (2019f) @EuropeanTour. Available online at https://twitter.com/EuropeanTour, accessed on 7 June 2019

Twitter (2019g) @LETgolf. Available online at https://twitter.com/LETgolf, accessed on 7 June 2019

NOTE ON THE CONTRIBUTORS

Dr Ali Bowes is a Senior Lecturer in the Sociology of Sport at Nottingham Trent University. Her research interests centre on qualitative analyses of sport and gender, focusing specifically on inequalities in elite women's sport. She is the co-editor of two books: *The professionalisation of women's sport* and *Women's football in a global, professional era*. Ali sits on the editorial board for the *Sociology of Sport Journal* and *Managing Sport and Leisure*.

Dr Niamh Kitching is a Lecturer in Physical Education at Mary Immaculate College, University of Limerick. She has a wealth of experience of golf environments and settings, having represented Ireland at amateur level and having worked in Junior Golf Ireland and the PGA in England and Ireland. Her research interests include the sociology of sport and PE, sports pedagogy and coaching, elite sport, sports development and coach education. Her published research focuses on gender equality and sport, with a particular emphasis on female athletes and coaches, and their presence, participation and presentation in sport and sports media. She has published in a number of sociology of sport outputs and edited collections.

Chapter 9

Astroturfing in online comment: An investigation

Murray Dick

This paper investigates 'astroturfing' (the creation of armies of 'sockpuppet' personae towards influencing public opinion) in online news comments. Concerns about this practice and its potential impact on public discourse have been voiced in the press, and across a range of disciplines; but it has been little studied in communications and journalism studies. How is online 'astroturfing' in contemporary online news and current affairs defined (operationally); how is it experienced, and what can be done to mitigate it? Given the difficulties attendant on normatively defining astroturfing, discussion shifts to how alternative frameworks in journalism ethics may help journalists challenge this new phenomenon.

Keywords: astroturfing, journalism ethics, online comments, online journalism, propaganda, user generated content

INTRODUCTION

Astroturfing is an acknowledged but relatively little understood problem in online journalism today. It has been discussed amongst the UK commentariat, particularly those on the left, in recent years (Johnson 2009; Monbiot 2010, 2011; Bienkov 2012). In May 2015, the word was included in dictionary.com (*PRNewswire* 2015); and, indeed, *The Oxford dictionary of journalism* includes an entry on the phenomenon (Harcup 2014). But beyond simple definitions, and in terms of how astroturfing may be identified, mitigated and challenged, there is little guidance in the literature; for example, the word does not even feature in any of the leading texts on journalism ethics (Harcup 2006; Frost 2014; Friend and Singer 2007). New technologies (such as 'persona management software') make the scale of online astroturfing campaigns potentially greater, and their reach potentially wider than their offline equivalent ('Happy Rockefeller' 2011). This may have consequences for the circulation of news and decision-making within the public sphere, especially given that uncivil comments beneath news stories have been found to change readers' interpretation of news stories (Anderson et al. 2014).

This paper intends to establish a clearer understanding of astroturfing in online news comment via recourse to two connected strands of literature; a nascent (and in terms of disciplinary provenance, mixed) body of work concerning the practice of astroturfing, and the literature on online news comments (which sits within the wider literature on user-generated content in the newsroom). Interviews with the Readers' Editor (RE) and the Community Co-ordinator (CC) at the *Guardian* were undertaken towards better understanding astroturfing as experienced. Findings contribute towards a clearer understanding of astroturfing, which is then explored using alternative frameworks in the field of journalism ethics, towards bolstering normative guidelines and regulations in this field.

LITERATURE REVIEW

Most recently, explorations of online astroturfing in the media have concerned its application in geopolitical positioning. In Russia, a secretive organisation known as the Internet Research Agency (Global Voices 2015) is believed to be behind the creation of astroturfing hoaxes across America (Chen 2015), while pro-Kremlin astroturfing has recently been exposed by a whistleblower (Walker 2015). Alternatively the phenomenon (especially at a domestic level) often has a political-corporate aspect. For example, it has been explored in campaigns behind climate change denial (Dunlap and McCright 2011); and in the tobacco industry's backing of the Tea Party (Fallin et al. 2013); and its undermining of local public health policy (Harris et al. 2014).

In the academy, online astroturfing has been studied (and theorised) from a range of perspectives, including political science (Klotz 2007); business studies (Cho et al. 2011); organisational studies (Kraemer et al. 2013); information science (Zhang et al. 2013); and critical linguistics (Gilewicz and Allard-Huver 2013). Experts in law have set out the bounds of commercial practices legislation in the EU with respect to astroturfing (Tigner 2009); while US scholars (e.g. Young 2009) and international anti-corruption groups (Mulcahy 2015) have questioned the robustness of regulation with respect to preventing astroturfing. In journalism studies, one of the few engagements with the phenomenon conceives it as a function of the pernicious, wider influence of public relations on news journalism (Davies 2008: 168-169).

Within the wider literature on the impact of user-generated content on modern networked news, there exists a sub-section with a particular focus on online news comment. Ethical considerations that influence the nature of moderation undertaken have been explored (Trygg 2012). Discussion 'below the line' has been found to be deliberative, and has been seen to contribute to journalists' practice in positive ways (Graham and Wright 2015), albeit the democratic potential has been found to be constrained by incivility (Collins and Nerlich 2014) and even hatred (Loke 2012). Anonymity in user commenting has been found to correlate with higher levels of incivility in online news comment (Rowe 2015). Competing perceptions of online news comment between journalists and the public create a paradox (Bergström and Wadbring 2015): while journalists acknowledge the importance of these spaces in fulfilling the democratic functions of news, they perceive this to be at the expense of damage to the news 'brand' (Canter 2013). This tension has elsewhere been theorised in terms of 'boundary work' (Robinson 2010); with the increasingly contested notion of privilege being seen to be grounded in the values and norms of professional journalism.

RESEARCH QUESTIONS

In the context of reviewing these two sets of literature then, the following two, related research questions were formulated:

RQ1 What is the nature of astroturfing in online news comments?

Given the lack of extant theoretical work in relation to this topic, a grounded theory approach to this problem was chosen.

RQ2 How can astroturfing in online news comments be challenged?

Given the debate concerning the extent to which legal and regulatory frameworks offer adequate protection from astroturfing, I chose to move away from the normative, and towards consideration of different journalism ethics frameworks.

METHODOLOGY

Interviewing after the critical turn is defined by an historic, political and contextual boundedness (Fontana and Frey 2005: 695). The interview cannot be neutral, and any pretensions towards objectivity or scientific method have long lost credence; and in any case, my interviewees have very different experiences of the phenomenon at hand. I employed the 'social scientific prospector' (Holstein and Gubrium 2004: 116) approach, towards establishing validity in the data generated; and I sought 'thick description' of the operationalisation of astroturfing policy in the online newsroom.

In the absence of a suitable literature or pre-existing framework in which to accommodate data about astroturfing in online news comment, it became necessary to ground interview design around the little that is known; and so questions arose during the process of analysing media sources on the phenomenon.

Two semi-structured telephoned interviews were carried out with the *Guardian*'s readers' editor (RE), Chris Elliott (8 July 15) and community editor (CE), Laura Oliver (24 July 15); lasting 40 minutes and 60 minutes respectively. In terms of sampling, my choice of interviewee was circumscribed by various factors; by the specialisms of those sought, and by access.

FINDINGS
DEFINITIONS: THEORY AND PRACTICE

Q. How do you define astroturfing operationally?

RE alludes to an example from the *Observer*, in June 2015, concerning the UK branch of the Shugden Buddhist sect, and their plans to protest and disrupt a UK visit by the Dalai Lama. He said they were inundated with hundreds of emails and complaints (though not comments) from members of the cult and its supporters:

> I don't think they were astroturfing – I think they were all individuals, I mean individuals primed. When is it astroturfing and when is it not astroturfing? In Israel/Palestine, we've often had situations where lobby groups ... who believe profoundly in Israel's cause, and monitor us like mad and take exception and you will find maybe 20 complaints to the *Guardian* readers' editor that say the same thing, and it is quite clear that the person hasn't read it [the story], they've cut and pasted a sentence from some other site and dropped it in there. Now I don't know, is that astroturfing? It's similar to astroturfing, but ... whenever I think of astroturfing I think of a big secret operation that sets out to subvert and so on, but this is just a whole lot of people who haven't read the piece quite willing to believe that we've done something dreadful, and then just cut and paste a sentence. The effect is quite similar.

CC commented:

> It's hard to define sometimes the line ... but then where there are people obviously sharing links that appear to be politically organising, or they are repeating the same tropes and language found amongst other accounts. We have to see a critical mass of it. ... The other difficulty with defining astroturfing on a site like ours is we want to allow as broad a conversation as possible, we want to allow people to challenge what we say, what the *Guardian*'s own politics are. It can be very easy to very quickly say: 'Oh well, that's astroturfing,' when actually it's a lot of commenters disagreeing with a piece or the message we are sending out.

Q. Is astroturfing a chronic problem, in your experience?

CC commented:

> It's not that serious a problem for us. ... I think there's two reasons for that; one is when it crops up it tends to be attached to particular issues; so we are slightly on the front foot. If it is a recurring pattern, then we'll know when to look out for it. It can happen around climate for example or we have had it around ... the Russian/Ukraine issue, so we can spot it that way. ... We had it during the Indian elections [May 2014] ... then suddenly, it wasn't something we'd experienced before, and ... we suspected that there

was organised political astroturfing in favour of not so much individual candidates, but in terms of particular parties. It wasn't unique to us, it was happening a lot elsewhere. So that was a new one for us. But day to day it's not our top problem, it tends to cluster around particular issues.

POLICY: THEORY AND PRACTICE

Q. Do you have a policy on astroturfing?

RE says that while the term may not feature specifically, nevertheless the *Guardian*'s long established (last update in 2009) community guidelines and, in particular, guidelines seven and ten, provide a means of challenging the phenomenon: 'It is implicit that this is about people having a conversation, not groups subverting this by pretending to be someone else.'

Q. Do you have any evidence of (or have you suspected) astroturfing attacks on *Guardian* comments other than the Russia/Ukraine issue (Elliott 2014)?

RE commented:

> I'm sure we've had it before … we [speaking as reader's editor] will only reluctantly take on anything that comes out of moderation. We get maybe 18 to 20 people a week saying 'Why have you put me in pre-moderation' … and we just don't have the resources to look into this. … We want this to be a safe place, a good place for people to come and talk. If you got taken over completely by astroturfers and I'm not saying that some haven't got through, I'm sure they have, but if we are to continue to have a reputation as being a safe place for somewhere to come for a debate … I would be worried …

Q. Has astroturfing had a negative effect on your online community?

CC commented:

> Yes, around certain topics. Around three years ago we were live-blogging events in north Africa and then the Middle East [in connection with the Arab Spring] and we spent a lot of time in the first three months working with our commenting community, because there were people based in those countries contributing, and there was a real interest in the subject, and the spread of 'democracy' … It was a great conversation, and had a lot of our journalists getting involved … it was a really great community. The turning point was March last year [2014 – with the live blog still running] the conflict was then particularly about Libya, it reached a stalemate with terrible things happening on the ground (we could no longer get reporters into the country) information was very scant …it was a difficult story to report … and the effect that had on the community was that they had no anchor … it became a debate around whether the UK should intervene pro- or anti- the Libyan rebels, and those tropes began to take over. So

when commenters off our site discovered we still had this space on our site to discuss it they decided to join, and they squeezed out all of those great commenters. … and it was very difficult to keep those conversations on track once that set in. It started to become organised (on both sides).

Q. How satisfactory have you found the outcome of your investigations into astroturfing?

CC commented:

> …with things like Russia the outcome was slightly unsatisfying. We do all that work … [but on the other hand] we identify new users, or patterns, or words to look out for, so it keeps us up to date, and we are able to spot future attacks. However, because there is no bulletproof technical solution, it still stops us getting totally ahead of the curve. So we may say: 'OK an attack has just happened, some Kremlin trolls were responsible, and because we'd had that we cannot guarantee we will no longer have an attack like that…' It's never going to be that watertight because they will crop up in a different place, on a different server.

METHODS OF DETECTION

Q. What is the basis of your analysis of astroturfing attacks (i.e. the methods used etc.)?

RE commented:

> The mods [comment moderators] have regular meetings at which they discuss these things, and things they've noticed. And they also have internal rules which we don't necessarily publish for all sorts of reasons, about how they work to try to find out whether someone is doing this.

CC said that they considered several factors; whether lots of new accounts had been set up around the same time, using similar names, the extent to which they commented around the same pieces:

> …we have a check-list of things we'd look through. And then we'd take a decision on whether we should take further action. … We have the email addresses of commenting users; so it's that sort of thing where we might look for patterns of emails being set up amongst new users, but that is a very manual process. We've looked into technical solutions… but there don't seem to be many out there, or at least not for an organisation of our scale or indeed purpose. There's lots for moderating for spam, or filtering profanity, but when it comes to dealing with difficult users or problematic discussions on a site that also promotes free speech…

Our moderators and our community teams have access to our discussion back end. We don't share details publicly, and we are very careful internally of how we share information. ... We will try and jigsaw-identify... and that's particularly useful in cases like this where we suspect astroturfing. Search the username. Is it registered elsewhere, and what is their behaviour there, and does it match up? We may search for their email address, or other identifying information, say for example if the same links are being used, or the same language is being used, just to see if these phrases are popping up elsewhere, and in what context. What we do with that information is difficult; but it just helps us build a picture of whether this is isolated behaviour, and whether it is unique to us ... With astroturfing, if all the messages are originating from an IP address that appears to be linked to a company, we'll contact the company and ask them. We have to be careful about the routes we take, just in case we are landing on the wrong individual. ... I'm always incredibly impressed by our moderators ... it might be that we've got a user who's gone rogue, and I'll often say 'Can you go and look into them', and they'll go into the backend of our moderation tool, look at their profile, look at their history, but ... the amount of information they also have at the back of their minds about the users and their passions is incredible ... It really helps, because then you do spot patterns.

WIDER AWARENESS IN ONLINE NEWS INDUSTRY

Q. Have you ever discussed astroturfing with other engagement/communities/journalists at other communities/media titles?

RE has not discussed this issue in the wider industry: 'I personally haven't ... I don't remember being involved in that kind of discussion.'

CC commented: 'Not so much astroturfing; trolling and online abuse more so...' Trolling and online abuse are considered to be much more likely to lead to compromising the safety of discussion-space, and so are of higher priority. Similarly, because astroturfing is an occasional rather than a chronic problem, it is not prioritised.

Q. Have you ever discussed astroturfing with regulators, or branches of government (e.g. GCHQ, the headquarters for Britain's signals intelligence)?

RE admits that, as the *Guardian* is not involved with the new press regulatory body, the Independent Press Standards Organisation (IPSO), he does not know if the topic is being discussed there: 'No, not to my knowledge. There were no discussions about astroturfing with the PCC [the former regulatory body, the Press Complaints Commission].' With respect to GCHQ: 'I really don't know, but I would be absolutely staggered if we had. We barely talk to them at all unless at the point of a gun.'

RE doesn't think astroturfing equates to cyberwarfare necessarily:

> I wouldn't think about it in those terms – that's jacking it up and making it more important than it is. ... I'm not suggesting that you couldn't have an example that wouldn't reach the levels to enable you to describe it thus, but I haven't come across it. If indeed, as we now strongly suspect, that Putin has had this ... does this amount to cyberwarfare?

Q. Does it surprise you that the issue of astroturfing in online news comments is discussed relatively little in UK online media?

RE commented: 'There are websites who care less about astroturfing, they just let it all rip ...'

CC commented: 'We've invested a lot of time and effort in thinking about the positives and negatives of having comments on our site ... we are very invested in commenting, we do a lot with it, it's a crucial part of being a lively and dynamic news site. With others, there is a temptation just to stick comments on ...'

Q. To what extent do you think it likely that the lack of comment and coverage of astroturfing in online news comments in the UK may be because publishers fear that advertising income associated with high engagement may be adversely affected?

RE commented:

> Personally I don't believe that, I've never seen any evidence of it. I think there may be a fear of talking about astroturfing because ... it's such a loaded term, and it's quite hard to prove. And I think that's what puts some people off. I don't know this for certain, but sometimes I wonder if some people in the press really care – if they've got more comments it makes it look like they've got a livelier thread, and I wonder whether they think 'Well, it may be astroturfing, it may be not, but it looks like we've got 500 comments under the piece.' I think it's more likely that than not wanting to talk about it due to advertising issues.

CC commented: '...I doubt that there is as much of a thought process about it as that. Comments are much maligned and understandably journalists are concerned about engaging... I think there's more trepidation [than anything else].'

DISCUSSION

Astroturfing is hard to define; some seemingly 'grassroots' organisations may behave very much like astroturfing campaigns. It can also be hard to detect; many technical factors may collectively point to a likelihood or probability of astroturfing, but there is no collective technical solution for the paradox of policing 'free speech' in an environment where free speech is seen as paramount. Difficulties attendant to the confidence in which judgements may be made about specific examples of astroturfing mean that any normative attempt to deal with the phenomenon is in reality limited, and indeed the globalised nature of online media represents a further challenge to punitive regulation. The uncertainty associated with investigating the phenomenon has a dispiriting effect on investigators; conclusive proof is hard to establish.

Astroturfing is a less pressing issue in terms of online news community safety than other matters (such as trolling and online abuse), and communities play an important, active role in policing suspected astroturfing. It does not appear to be a chronic problem in news comments, and some manifestations are quite predictable. On the other hand, it can drive away valuable commenters and contributors, and some suspected astroturfing attacks appear quite unexpectedly. It is clearly important that a wider debate about the phenomenon (that might involve the sharing of best practice and case studies) is carried out across the wider media industry. This may, in turn, spark still wider debate amongst all stakeholders involved in this issue; educators, journalists, editors, proprietors, regulators and readers.

It is not necessary to define the phenomenon by name in community guidelines in order to challenge it. To this end, the application of alternative ethical approaches may allow journalists to accommodate good decision-making within existing guidelines that shape good community practice. By considering the wider ethical framework of action, it may also be possible to challenge unethical behaviour enacted in the process of following the letter of the law (regulation or guidelines). Here I sketch out two possible routes towards addressing this problem by means of moral philosophy.

The first moral framework I would like to consider is existentialism. The application of existentialism towards thinking about how journalists may view normative imperatives (like the duty to seek out truth, and report truthfully) is long established in the literature (Merrill 1974). More recently, it has been proposed that existentialism is a particularly useful tool in helping to address problems arising out of interactive, online journalism, for example concerning the disputed notion of truth; who is responsible for material carried in comment sections, and the nature of the relationship between media and audience (Singer and Ashman 2009). Central to this approach is the existential ideal of authenticity as something intrinsic, not something that may be acquired (Singer and Ashman 2009: 8); as something that may guide individual decisions and choices in turn.

An appeal to *authenticity* may, therefore, represent a means by which any journalist feeling pressured into permitting what they suspect as being an astroturfing attack in the comment section of their work (or in a comment section for which they are responsible) to remain, for the sake of additional comment, or advertising revenue. On the other hand, an overly-radical approach to existentialism (like Merrill's) may be criticised for its propensity towards moral double-standards. By foregrounding individual choice, authenticity demands tolerance of differences, which in turn undermines the moral absolutism and the notion of some choices being better than others; and yet this very approach valorises rebelliousness over 'going with the flow' (Holt 2012: 13).

The second moral framework to consider relates to virtue ethics, and more specifically, to the Aristotelean notion of *phronesis* or 'practical wisdom'. Various issues may cloud the reliable, positive identification of an astroturfing attack; from the prevalence of 'bots' (Gleik 2015) to rigidly-synchronised campaigning enacted by what may otherwise be described as 'grass-roots' organisations. To this end the verification of comments may comprise an analysis of many variables; linguistic tone (and possible use of rhetorical tropes); registration information, post timings (with corresponding timings of other posters), the nature of subject-matter posted on, and so on. But these factors, no matter how indicative of likelihood, cannot help to definitively establish the authenticity of online community comment. It is proposed that only a much wider debate, informing a deeper immersion in the culture and experience of online comment, a wider understanding of the various (sometimes unpredictable) contingent factors and geo-political events, evinced through dialogue amongst journalists (and with the public), may lead to a more robust means of challenging the problem of astroturfing.

CONCLUSION

Future empirical research is needed to establish more detailed case studies of astroturfing: its manifestation, and the processes and protocols used to deal with it in online newsrooms. Such research would play an important role in informing corporate and regulatory policies throughout industry. Moreover, a more theoretically sustained consideration of astroturfing within the wider literature of frameworks in journalism ethics, than the introductory thoughts contributed here, may profitably inform a debate that is necessary for all stakeholders in news journalism.

- This paper was first published in *Ethical Space*, Vol 13, No. 1 pp 32-38

REFERENCES

Anderson, Ashley A., Brossard, Dominique, Scheufele, Dietram, Xenos, Michael and Ladwig, Peter (2014) The 'Nasty Effect': Online incivility and risk perceptions of emerging technologies, *Journal of Computer-Mediated Communication*, Vol. 19, No. 3 pp 373-387

Bergström, Annika, and Wadbring, Ingela (2015) Beneficial yet crappy: Journalists and audiences on obstacles and opportunities in reader comments, *European Journal of Communication*, Vol. 30, No. 2 pp 137-151

Bienkov, Adam (2012) Astroturfing: What is it and why does it matter?, *Guardian*, 8 February. Available online at http://www.theguardian.com/commentisfree/2012/feb/08/what-is-astroturfing, accessed on 1 December 2015

Canter, Lily (2013) The misconception of online comment threads: Content and control on local newspaper websites, *Journalism Practice*, Vol. 7, No. 5 pp 604-619

Chen, Adrian (2015) The agency, *New York Times*, 2 June. Available online at http://wwwnytimescom/2015/06/07/magazine/the-agencyhtml?_r=0, accessed on 1 December 2015

Cho, Charles, Martens, Martin, Hakkyun, Kim and Rodrigue, Michelle (2011) Astroturfing global warming: It isn't always greener on the other side of the fence, *Journal of Business Ethics*, No. 104 pp 571-587

Collins, Luke and Nerlich, Brigitte (2014) Examining user comments for deliberative democracy: A corpus-driven analysis of the climate change debate online, *Environmental Communication: A Journal of Nature and Culture*, 6 December. Available online at http://www.tandfonline.com/doi/full/10.1080/17524032.2014.981560#.VnW3M0qLTIU

Davies, Nick (2008) *Flat earth news: An award-winning reporter exposes falsehood, distortion and propaganda in the global media*, London, Random House

Dunlap, Riley and McCright, Aaron (2011) Organized climate change denial, Dunlap, Riley and Brulle, Robert (eds) *Climate change and society: Sociological perspectives*, London, Oxford University Press pp 144-160

Fallin, Amanda, Grana, Rachel and Glantz, Stanton (2013) 'To quarterback behind the scenes, third-party efforts': The tobacco industry and the Tea Party, *Tobacco Control*. Available online at http://tobaccocontrol.bmj.com/content/early/2013/02/07/tobacco-control-2012-050815.abstract

Fontana, Andrea, and Frey, James (2005) The interview: From neutral stance to political involvement, *The Sage handbook of qualitative research*, London, Sage, third edition pp 695-728

Friend, Cecilia, and Singer, Jane (2007) *Online journalism ethics: Traditions and transitions*, London, Routledge

Frost, Chris (2014) *Journalism ethics and regulation*, London, Routledge, third edition

Gilewicz, Nicholas, and Allard-Huver, Francois (2012) Digital parrhesia as a counterweight to astroturfing, Folk, Moe and Apostel, Shawn (eds) *Online credibility and digital ethos: Evaluating computer-mediated communication*, Information Science Reference pp 215-227

Gleick, James (2015) Bot or not? *New York Times*, 11 March. Available online at http://www.nybooks.com/blogs/nyrblog/2015/mar/11/twitter-bot-or-not/, accessed on 1 December 2015

Global Voices (2015) Inside the Kremlin troll army machine: Templates, guidelines, and paid posts, *Global Voices*, 14 March. Available online at https://globalvoicesonline.org/2015/03/14/russia-kremlin-troll-army-examples/, accessed on 1 December 2015

Graham, Todd and Wright, Scott (2015) A tale of two stories from 'below the line': Comment fields at the *Guardian*, *The International Journal of Press/Politics*, Vol. 20, No. 2 pp 317-338. Available online at http://hij.sage-pub.com/content/20/3/317.abstract

'Happy Rockefeller' (2011) UPDATED: The HB Gary email that should concern us all, *Dailykos.com*, 17 February. Available online at http://wwwdailykos.com/story/2011/02/17/945768/-UPDATED-The-HB-Gary-Email-That-Should-Concern-Us-All, accessed on 1 December 2015

Harcup, Tony (2006) *The ethical journalist*, London, Sage

Harcup, Tony (2014) *Oxford dictionary of journalism*, London, Oxford University Press

Harris, Jenine, Moreland-Russell, Sarah, Choucair, Bechara, Raed, Mansour, Staub, Mackenzie and Simmons, Kendall (2014) Tweeting for and against public health policy: Response to the Chicago Department of Public Health's electronic cigarette Twitter campaign, *Journal of Medical Internet Research*, Vol 16, No 10, Available online at http://www.jmir.org/2014/10/e238

Holstein, James, and Gubrium, Jaber (2004) The active interview, D. Silverman (ed.) *Qualitative research: Theory, method and practice*, Thousand Oaks, Sage pp 140-161

Holt, Kristoffer (2012) Authentic journalism? A critical discussion about existential authenticity in journalism ethics, *Journal of Mass Media Ethics*, Vol. 27, No. 1 pp 2-14

Johnson, Bobby (2009) Astroturfing: A question of trust, *Guardian*, 7 September. Available online at http://www.theguardian.com/media/2009/sep/07/astroturfing-energy-citizens-us, accessed on 1 December 2015

Jowett, Garth and O'Donnell, Victoria (2006) *Propaganda & persuasion*, London, Sage, fourth edition

Klotz, Robert (2007) Internet campaigning for grassroots and astroturf support, *Social Science Computer Review*, Vol. 25, No. 1 pp 3-12

Kolivos, Eugenia and Kuperman, Anna (2012) Web of lies: Legal implications of astroturfing, *Keeping Good Companies*, Vol. 64, No. 1 pp 38-41

Kraemer, Romy, Whiteman, Gail, and Banerjee, Bobby (2013) Conflict and astroturfing in Niyamgiri: The importance of national advocacy networks in anti-corporate social movements, *Organization Studies*, Vol. 34, Nos 5 and 6 pp 823-852

Lee, Caroline (2010) The roots of astroturfing, *Contexts*, Vol. 9, No 1 pp 73-75

Loke, Jaime (2012) Old turf, new neighbors: Journalists' perspectives on their new shared space, *Journalism Practice*, Vol. 6, No. 2 pp 233-249

Ludlow, Peter (2013) The strange case of Barrett Brown, *Nation*, 18 June 18. Available online at http://www.thenation.com/article/strange-case-barrett-brown/, accessed on 1 December 2015

Merrill, James (1977) *Existential journalism*, New York, Hastings House Publishing

Monbiot, George (2010) These astroturf libertarians are the real threat to internet democracy, *Guardian*, 13 December. Available online at http://www.theguardian.com/commentisfree/libertycentral/2010/dec/13/astroturf-libertarians-internet-democracy, accessed on 1 December 2015

Monbiot, George (2011) The need to protect the internet from 'astroturfing' grows ever more urgent, *Guardian*, 23 February. Available online at http://www.theguardian.com/environment/georgemonbiot/2011/feb/23/need-to-protect-internet-from-astroturfing, accessed on 1 December 2015

Mulcahy, Suzanne (2015) *Lobbying in Europe: Hidden influence, privileged* access, Transparency International. Available online at https://formatresearch.com/img/file/varie/2015/2015_LobbyingInEurope_EN.pdf, accessed on 20 December 2015

PRNewswire.com (2015) Astroturfing, bigender, glanceable, hyperlocal & more new words added to the dictionary, *PRNewswire*, 6 May. Available online at http://www.prnewswire.com/news-releases/astroturfing-bigender-glanceable-hyperlocal-more-new-words-added-to-the-dictionary-300077638html, accessed on 1 December 2015

Robinson, Sue (2010) Traditionalists vs convergers: Textual privilege, boundary work, and the journalist-audience relationship in the commenting policies of online news sites, *Convergence*, Vol. 16, No. 1 pp 125-143

Rowe, Ian (2015) Civility 20: A comparative analysis of incivility in online political discussion, *Information, Communication & Society*, Vol. 18, No. 2 pp 121-138

Singer, Jane and Ashman, Ian (2009) 'Comment is free, but facts are sacred': User-generated content and ethical constructs at the *Guardian*, *Journal of Mass Media Ethics*, Vol. 24, No. 1 pp 3-21

Trygg, Sanna (2012) Is comment free? Ethical, editorial and political problems of moderating online news, *POLIS: Journalism and Society*, January. Available online at http://blogslse.ac.uk/polis/files/2012/01/IsCommentFree_PolisLSETrygg.pdf, accessed on 1 December 2015

Young, Henry (2009) Astroturf lobbying organizations: Do fake grassroots need real regulation? *Illinois Business Law Journal*, 2 November. Available online at http://www.lawillinois.edu/bljournal/post/2009/11/03/Astroturf-Lobbying-Organizations-Do-Fake-Grassroots-Need-Real-Regulation, accessed on 1 December 2015

Zhang, Jerry; Carpenter, Darrell and Myung, Ko (2013) Online astroturfing: A theoretical perspective, *AMCIS 2013 Proceedings*. Available online at http://aisel.aisnet.org/cgi/viewcontentcgi?article=1620&context=amcis2013, accessed on 1 December 2015

NOTE ON THE CONTRIBUTOR

Dr Murray Dick is Senior Lecturer in Multimedia Journalism at Newcastle University. His research concerns visual communication, journalistic praxis and communication ethics.

Chapter 10

News as conversation, citizens as gatekeepers: Where is digital news taking us?

Luke Goode

This paper considers the implications of recent shifts in the digital news landscape for democracy and the public sphere. It discusses the role of participatory news platforms and the claims made about the new elevated role for citizens as participants in and even producers of news. The paper concludes by arguing that rhetoric suggesting a radical upheaval in power relations between citizens and professional news media risks obscuring the real benefits of new modes of audience engagement.

Keywords: news, democracy, citizenship, internet, participatory media

INTRODUCTION: REVOLUTION IN THE AIR?

Consider a scene scarcely imaginable 10 short years ago: of the hundreds of millions of English language blogs tracked by blog engine Technorati, a majority deal in topics that are the traditional preserve of mainstream journalism (politics, technology, business, film, celebrity, sport and so on). Most aren't just confessional diaries or online photo albums (though often those elements are blended in). Technorati's research suggests blogs tend not to be made on a whim and then rapidly abandoned: 85 per cent of them have been active for more than a year. About a third of American blogs have more than 1,000 unique visitors every month (Sobel 2010). On Twitter, Middle East opposition protests, earthquakes and celebrity scandals unfurl in real-time via tweets from innumerable and often uncertain sources, and mainstream media struggle to keep up given their time-consuming responsibilities for fact-checking and analysis. Mainstream media, in turn, are being relentlessly fact-checked (and often found wanting) by dispersed but collectively potent online networks.

So-called 'crowdsourcing' sees once disaggregated citizens pooling resources, poring over British MPs' expenses accounts or scandalous documents released by WikiLeaks – too copious for professional journalism to monopolise. Internet users compile their own news agendas, circumventing the editorial craftsmanship of broadcast news bulletins or print news editions; the very term 'edition' connotes a snap-shot temporality at odds with today's incessant news flows or 'ambient journalism' (Hermida 2010).

News has become *unbundled* and *modular*; tools such as Google News and RSS Newsfeeds allow users to compile a *Daily Me*, a concept prophesied by Nicholas Negroponte (1995) some 15 years ago. Or, via platforms like Facebook or Digg, audiences concoct news diets shaped by friendship and social networks. The expertocracy of news has been radically undermined. This is not to claim that our dependencies upon professional news outlets have loosened (quite the reverse may be true) but only that they have become more intricately mediated. The shift is more profound than one from analogue *table d'hôte* to digital *à la carte*. In terms of their role in shaping our information diets news providers are increasingly in the business of supplying ingredients rather than finished meals. Of particular concern to mainstream media, though, is how all this can function as a business at all when such an abundance of information, analysis and commentary is now available free at the point of delivery, and robust mechanisms for tying content to advertising have so far proven elusive. Murdoch's News Corporation, *The New York Times* and others (in concert with platform providers such as Apple) are, of course, busily engaged in trying to overcome this. It is difficult to see just how exclusively digitisation is responsible for the apparent crisis across newsrooms. As we hear stories from around the world of newspaper closures, newsroom 'restructuring', and circulation, subscription and advertising levels foundering (e.g. Abramson 2010, Deveson 2009, Oliver 2010, Pew 2009), somewhat apocalyptic tones have crept into debates about the future of journalism.

Clay Shirky is a leading US commentator on the rise of digital news and journalism (among other aspects of digital culture). With a rhetorical flourish worthy of the *Communist manifesto*, he says this:

> When someone demands to know how we are going to replace newspapers, they are really demanding to be told that we are not living through a revolution. They are demanding to be told that old systems won't break before new systems are in place. They are demanding to be told that ancient social bargains aren't in peril, that core institutions will be spared, that new methods of spreading information will improve previous practice rather than upending it. They are demanding to be lied to (Shirky 2008).

But isn't it equally plausible to diagnose the reverse, namely an over-eager appetite for tales of revolution? Often we seem to demand to hear all that's solid is indeed melting into air: this certainly makes for better headlines. I suggest that the challenges faced by news media industries, by the journalistic profession and, by extension, by the structures of democracy and public debate are indeed serious but that we are not necessarily in the midst (or on the brink) of a 'revolution' in news media, certainly if we use the term 'revolution' properly to denote a radical change in ends and not merely in means. The future is certainly opaque but not least because the future is still there to be moulded by journalists, editors and owners as well as by citizens and consumers.

CITIZENS, CONSUMERS AND GATEKEEPERS

This paper is concerned with the implications of digitisation for civic, rather than commercial, values. However, whilst the focus will not be on paywalls, advertising revenues or the future of free news on the web, it is vital to recognise that the fates of journalistic business models and of democracy are inextricably linked. This is especially so in our highly commercialised media ecology. It is always tempting for the media analyst concerned with democracy and civic functions of news media to place disproportionate emphasis on the potential of those institutions at one remove from the constraints (for some 'distortions') of the market. In the UK, for example, the BBC and the Scott Trust-supported *Guardian* newspaper, though facing serious pressures (Davoudi and Fenton 2009; Fenton 2010), can seem like beacons of civic purpose amid a sea of cut-throat commercial competition.

Moreover, both institutions have been key innovators in developing digital news platforms. And yet, realistically, the environment in which they operate (and from which they are only partially insulated) is overwhelmingly commercialised. In smaller markets, there is often an inverse correlation between the perceived necessity and viability of public service alternatives to markets dominated by few (often overseas owned) commercial players (Puppis 2009).

In the face of near-ubiquitous commercialism across news media, it is tempting to romanticise the still relatively non-commercialised (or only nascently monetised) domains of citizen journalism, blogging and social media (where content retains relative independence from monetised platforms). The following argument will suggest an ongoing and vitally important democratic role for professional journalism – one that cannot be disentangled from commercialism. A sense of market realism is required for assessing the civic functions of news media in the digital age and advocates for a democratic public sphere need to engage commercial media in critical dialogue and acknowledge their imperatives. If, as I will argue, we should uphold the importance of professional journalism in the era of citizen journalism and social media, then it is unhelpful to treat commercial logic with lofty disdain as defenders of the 'public sphere' (Habermas 1989; Garnham 1992) are often wont to do.

The commercial news market, I suggest, is an insufficient but essential part of the public sphere. To those who believe that the commercial news market is essential *and* sufficient for a democratic media ecology – those who perceive non-market mechanisms such as public funding as distortions not remedies – the concept of 'citizens as gatekeepers' invoked in the title of this paper will seem unremarkable, possibly tautological. The liberal free press dream is one in which citizens determine the news – or get the news they deserve – by voting with their wallets and/or their attention (Curran and Seaton 2003: 346-362). Others, though, would argue that the roles of citizen and consumer, though not intrinsically contradictory, cannot be so easily merged (Lewis, Inthorn and Wahl-Jorgensen 2005). The kinds of news and information that empower us as citizens are not always those we would be drawn to by our immediate desires. Uncomfortable truths are often unpalatable in the short term and their value is only realised in the longer term. In any case, consumers can never be truly sovereign in a commercial news marketplace: citizens have always been partial gatekeepers in a range of complex power-sharing arrangements that include editors and journalists selecting, filtering and framing the news before citizens get to vote with their wallets or time.

This is not a critical claim. As citizens, we require professional newsmakers to exercise good judgement on our behalf about the news agenda, and all the more so in a digital environment now characterised by information overload and by dense and inter-connected news delivery systems. What matters from a democratic perspective is what values and imperatives are driving those selection and filtering decisions and how media literate the public is in terms of understanding newsmaking processes. It is unconvincing and even regressive to hear the gate-keeping functions of professional news media referred to as if they were, by definition, some kind of affront to democracy, a kind of feudal power bloc to be swept away by opening the information floodgates of the internet.

Other agents in this complex power-sharing arrangement include, of course: journalists' sources and PR professionals; advertisers (and their particular target demographics); shareholders and, in some cases, old-fashioned proprietorial powers, though this kind of power has often been over-egged as a product of our appetite for demons – the economic power and market behaviours of large media empires have done more than the eccentric and ideologically-driven personalities of their figureheads to shape the increasingly globalised media landscape of the late 20th and early 21st centuries.

But power-sharing arrangements have started to shift dramatically during the last decade with the rise of the internet and especially Web 2.0 or the 'participatory web' of bloggers, citizen journalists, YouTube and news recommendation engines hooked into social networks such as Twitter and Facebook. Clearly, we can see citizens themselves exercising more gatekeeping power with ever greater choice, personalisation and unbundling of news as well as enriched opportunities to discuss and even shape the news agenda (Deuze 2008; Hermida and Thurman 2008). Clearly, too, we see challenges to the roles of some of the established gatekeepers: editors whose *raison d'être* appears called into question in the era of the *Daily Me* (a strong *raison d'être* can still be argued for but the point is it now needs arguing for and has lost its axiomatic status – see Gans 2010); proprietors and shareholders who see the internet steadily eroding their advertising, subscription and cover-price business models (Harris 2010); and journalists incredulous at the apparent hypocrisy of a blogosphere so acutely critical of 'mainstream media' and yet so often sloppy in its own journalistic standards and ethics (O'Dell 2010).

GOOGLE ISN'T 'JUST A TOOL'

A key issue for public ethics is how transparent (or opaque) are the mechanisms of public sphere institutions including media and information industries. Digitisation is not simply about power shifting between two blocs – citizens and professional media. The emergence of other gatekeeping powers complicates the picture. At an institutional level, this means the major online players – Google, Facebook and Twitter especially. At a professional level, this broadly means software and interface engineers. It is not the case that Google exercises the same kinds of gatekeeping powers as news providers: its influence is at the level of information architecture, not content. And yet it is also not the case that the software driving Google's search and news engines are neutral gateways to information (Beer 2009). Neither, for that matter, are YouTube's search or recommendation engines, or Facebook's Newsfeed algorithms. These are human-made systems designed to sift, rank and filter information flows on our behalf. They are, for the most part, proprietary (and jealously guarded commercial secrets) and subject to less critical scrutiny or public awareness than even the relatively mystified domain of the newsroom.

Neither is there anything intrinsically natural about the 140-character limit on Twitter; nor the assumption made by Facebook that the kind of news I am exposed to should be determined by the things that cause my 'friends' to click a 'like' button. Such features have all sorts of attractions and benefits but they are human-made interfaces that shape the way we consume news. The same holds for conventions of 'traditional' media: there is nothing natural or timeless about daily newspapers or hour-long tea-time news bulletins.

These are historical, human-made artefacts. It does not necessarily mean we should want to get rid of any of them. But it does mean we should always be thinking critically about their benefits and limitations, their usefulness and their fitness for purpose at any particular historical juncture. And at this point in history, just as we ponder the fate of the 'dead tree' newspaper (often misleadingly conflated with, or used as a metonym for, the fate of professional journalism), so our critical scrutiny must also now extend to the various online platforms and news delivery systems that are shaping our news consumption and, by extension, our conversations and our debates.

THE DIGITAL WORLD ISN'T FLAT

An ethical perspective on digitisation requires us, of course, to consider equality of opportunity. It is undoubtedly true that, for all the constraints, features and quirks of these new online delivery systems, citizens are granted unprecedented opportunities to shape the news agenda for themselves and, in many cases, for the peers in their networks. This undeniably represents a form of democratisation. But the idea that there is a broad devolution of power from the few to the many, from professional media to the citizenry at large, is of course simplistic. Power is not distributed evenly among the citizenry and new communication tools can create new forms of inequality just as they can help to level others.

The so-called digital divide is usually viewed from a supply-side perspective, as a primarily socio-economic and geographical (especially urban versus rural) problem requiring redress through infrastructure investment. But one major factor often overlooked (because it lacks clear policy implications) is the divide between the time-rich and the time-poor. An abundance of news sources to navigate and opportunities to 'join the conversation' (whether blogging, re-tweeting stories or commenting on newspaper websites) scarcely 'democratises' news for citizens who work double shifts or have round-the-clock care responsibilities. Of course, we are led to believe that we are all leading increasingly busy and more time-pressured lives. Under time constraints, we look to professional news media to provide packaged digests of the important news of the day: this can be a useful antidote and complement to the more amorphous news flows of the web.

But as and when time allows, active and motivated citizens (motivation is also unevenly distributed) want and need longer-form journalism in order to understand issues sufficiently and this too is a vital antidote and complement to the bite-size chunks of news flowing especially around platforms like YouTube and Twitter. Can mainstream media do both the long and the short well? Both the wide-area survey and the deep-drilling? This seems a tall order, perhaps reflected in much criticism of TV news which stands accused of failing on both counts with both excessive soft news padding and a shortage of in-depth coverage: too long and too shallow are common complaints. In terms of the digital divide, however, the issue is not simply the question of who has sufficient access, time and cultural capital to participate.

There are various power dynamics emerging within online platforms. In blogging, the A-list blogger phenomenon is now well-known: Huffington Post and Instapundit may have challenged entrenched mainstream news power but have become concentrated powers in their own rights (Farrell and Drezner 2008; Sunstein 2007). Compared to mainstream media, there are low barriers to entry to the blogosphere and social media and also fewer instances of producer loyalties divided between audiences and advertisers. And yet there are certainly first-to-market advantages and snowball effects: in an incredibly crowded marketplace like blogging, traffic is driven largely by word-of-mouth (its online equivalent, anyway), by referrals and links, not to mention profiling in the mainstream media: visibility begets visibility in what is essentially an 'attention economy' (Lanham 2006). This is not to claim that top blogs can sustain their position in the long term if audience satisfaction falls significantly (indeed, few mainstream media institutions have ever enjoyed such cushioning); brand loyalty doesn't run too deep in such a competitive market. But it is to suggest that new entrants to the market face considerable hurdles in gaining the kind of visibility required to compete.

We also see power laws at play in other aspects of online news consumption. The social news media site Digg.com has, since its beginnings, had a small fraction of users responsible for submitting a majority of the stories that get voted onto its front page because those power users accumulate visibility and influence and their stories are more likely to be seen and then voted for than those submitted by lower profile users. Under criticism that this looks more like a popularity contest than a platform for deciding the merits and newsworthiness of stories, Digg has made attempts to tweak the algorithm that weights votes for stories to mitigate this snowball effect: in turn, it has then come under fire for using secretive algorithms to undermine the meritocracy of a system that rewards the hard work and success of power users. Either way, 'democratising news', it turns out, is no straightforward business.

Recent research (Cha et al. 2010) shows some striking things about Twitter. It tracked 54 million users and almost 2 billion tweets across an eight month period in 2009, looking at three different measures of network influence: first, who gets the most followers; second, whose tweets are most often re-tweeted through the network; and, third, whose names are mentioned or cited most often in other tweets. The research found little overlap between these measures (less than 10 per cent): the 'million follower fallacy' mistakenly assumes that the Twitter users who recruit the most followers are necessarily the ones shaping the agenda and the conversations on Twitter. It seems Twitter is not just a popularity contest. But the research found strikingly low levels of reciprocity which cautions us against celebrating Twitter as some kind of gigantic water-cooler or digital coffee house. Steep power laws characterise all three measures of influence: the influence of the top 100 users (across all three measures) is exponentially greater than the top 1,000 whose influence is exponentially greater than the top 10,000. Outside the top 10,000, influence becomes statistically negligible – and this from a dataset of 54 million users!

Of course, there are plenty of water-cooler conversations occurring on Twitter but it is structurally closer to a broadcast medium than many realise: many followers and few followed; many tweeters and few re-tweeted; many commentators and few commented upon. There are agenda-setters and gatekeepers. Some of these are mainstream news outlets. In the research just cited, Twitter accounts with most followers include outlets like CNN and *The New York Times*, alongside various celebrities and politicians. But with sources that were most commonly re-tweeted (a better indication of who are the agenda-setters than who has the most followers) it seems traditional news outlets are largely eclipsed by successful new players: news aggregator services are important new gatekeepers in this environment with services like TweetMeme amplifying the power law by aggregating the most popular links and drawing yet more traffic to them in a self-propelling spiral.

Simpler research looking only at the volume (rather than influence) of Twitter traffic found the most prolific 10 per cent of users posting more than 90 per cent of tweets (Heil and Piskorski 2009): most people use Twitter primarily to hear rather than to speak (not necessarily a bad thing as I shall argue later). And there are numerous other examples of how variations on the 80:20 rule prevail in social networks. Social networks are not flat: they are hierarchical and often less conversational than we assume.

Does this matter? There have always been opinion leaders holding disproportionate influence within communities. It is true that their potential reach is greatly extended in online social networks. But this does not render such communities undemocratic in and of themselves. In fact, online social network research is at such an early stage that we do not have a clear picture of whether and how much hierarchies of status and influence among peer networks are artificially bolstered by network design or are merely a reflection of wider social hierarchies. The point is that the resilient myth of blogging, citizen journalism and social media driving us closer towards some kind of egalitarian nirvana in the news where anyone can become newsmaker or opinion leader, where merit has truly triumphed over status, is deeply problematic.

NEWS AS CONVERSATION

Assessing the civic implications of digitisation involves questioning quality and not merely equality of opportunity. It is undoubtedly true that a number of positive things have emerged: greater choice, access and opportunities for participation, and a massive reduction in economic barriers to entry for aspiring amateur and even semi-professional newsmakers. It would be misleading to claim this is not a form of democratisation. Democracy is not simply a quantitative matter of *how much* choice, participation and opportunity is gained, though. The issue is also what citizens can do with these extended opportunities to engage with news and journalism.

Dan Gillmor – champion of citizen journalism and author of the hyperbolically titled book *We the media* (2006) – argues that the internet has been steadily transforming news from a lecture into a conversation. But this risks setting up a false dichotomy. The idea that news should nourish and stimulate conversation is not contentious: without conversation, citizens lack the wherewithal to test, refine and enrich their interpretations of and responses to the news they read, hear and watch. Clearly the internet enhances opportunities for citizens to engage in conversations with peers and with newsmakers. But the idea that news should *become* conversation is deeply problematic. It misses the importance of listening first before expressing opinion. To see journalism itself as conversation smacks of juvenile impatience or attention deficit. We risk celebrating instantaneous feedback and downgrading the values of reading below the fold and processing at a pace fitting for the complex issues news throws up. Tellingly, etymology links the word 'lecture' (for all its contemporary negative baggage) to the act of reading.

Gillmor himself, though, does not run amok with this rhetoric of news as conversation. He is, in fact, deeply concerned with the quality of the conversation and worries about the fate of careful reflection. Recently, he has suggested we might need something like a slow news movement analogous to the slow food movement (2009, see also Shapiro 2010). Notwithstanding the point made already about the constraints on time-poor citizens, there is something useful in this concept. We tend to focus on the supply side of shrunken news cycles and competitive scoop-fests trumping the time-consuming journalistic practices of analysis and even, on occasion, verification. But we often neglect the demand-side: a slow news movement would have to be one that encouraged audiences to slow down, chew their news slowly and moderate their portion sizes rather than assuming more is better, to appreciate dishes that have been marinated and slow-cooked, which is just what the most valuable long-form, investigative journalism tends to be.

The 'morselisation' of news (Atkinson 1994) is, I suggest, not merely a supply-side but also a demand-side issue. This is not to deflect criticism of professional news media nor to support the simplistic claim that outlets serving up morselised news are just giving audiences what they want: supply and demand are shaped by numerous exogenous factors and also by each other. Moreover, it is not to support the claim that market realism dictates an inevitable drive towards faster, softer, more bite-size news. Such a claim constitutes fatalism rather than realism. It is simplistic at best and condescending at worst to fall back on the assumption that few outside the chattering classes want serious long-form news and current affairs any longer. So the point here is not that the public merely gets the news it deserves. However, there are some serious demand-side issues at stake here and we misread the problem, I suggest, if we do not acknowledge them. These issues are about citizenship and civic engagement.

When we hear about trends of declining voter turnouts in Western democracies, declining political party memberships, declining audiences for television news and declining newspaper readership figures, especially among the younger generation, some will proclaim a lamentable deterioration. Others, though, will say that matters are not necessarily deteriorating, only changing. After all, young people in particular may be increasingly disaffected with mainstream national politics but engaging in new and different ways: protests, petitions, online campaigns and the like. So too, a turn away from traditional news sources such as newspapers and national TV news does not signal a decreasing interest in news and current affairs. Quite the contrary, in fact, as an array of new outlets for news, and opportunities to interact with the news, are being tapped into. This may be a cause for optimism unless one believes that, whatever the diverse array of debates and conversations going on at local and global levels, there is also vital importance in the kinds of shared conversations required to keep a democratic light shining on the national polity and its key players (both elected and unelected). If increasing numbers of, particularly younger, citizens are turning away from those conversations then there is a much wider social issue at stake, I suggest, than the quality of the news. To highlight the shortcomings of mainstream news media does not oblige us to single out and scapegoat the media for the state of the contemporary public sphere.

GOOGLE ISN'T EVIL

In a similar vein, it is not helpful to scapegoat the new media players for the perceived crisis in mainstream news and journalism. Google, whose unofficial motto is 'don't be evil' is, of course, the devil incarnate for Rupert Murdoch who argues that it has been brazenly stealing his content. Others, though, cite Google for other sins. In particular, it is seen as one of the major driving forces behind the unbundling of news: it deep links audiences into news stories, bypassing front-page portals with the advertising and branding that brings with it; and it fosters a fragmented, decontextualised approach to news consumption, encouraging greater morselisation and less critical scrutiny of the source behind the content. The tradeoff between unprecedented choice in news and information brought about by digitisation and the unprecedented fragmentation of public life it threatens represents a major dilemma from an ethical perspective.

Google and its rivals have, indeed, impacted on the way news is accessed and consumed. But whilst this allows audiences to skim rapidly across the surface and enjoy superficial engagement with news, the very same platform allows audiences to plumb remarkable depths on a story, issue or event. It takes reading below the fold to new levels and allows citizens to interrogate and assess the credibility of news sources through cross-referencing and fact-checking. It also allows suitably motivated citizens to sift the hard news from the soft, to filter out the infotainment or 'noise' that seems increasingly prevalent in the bundled news of broadcasting and the press. A technology such as Google can have such profoundly contradictory consequences precisely because its consequences are not hardwired into the technology: they are very strongly contingent on users and their social context. Again, this is about the demand-side as much as the supply-side.

As Fallows (2010) suggests, Google is attempting to redress the reputation it is acquiring for damaging both the business models of commercial news outlets (and especially newspapers) and the culture of long-form journalism. He profiles several projects designed to get Google partnering more constructively with mainstream news outlets. One example is the open source *Living stories* experiment designed to allow the automatic collating of reports on a story (one that might develop over a period of time) on a single page that will be prioritised in Google search results. In other words, Google is exploring ways to adapt the information architecture to encourage curation of stories on the producer side and deep reading on the reader side, redressing the decontextualisation or morselisation it is commonly held responsible for. As Fallows points out, not only is Google far from the sole factor driving the fragmentation of news, it also has no vested interest in the corrosion of quality, in-depth journalism: quite the opposite, in fact, as such corrosion is detrimental to its own value as a news gateway.

If it is reassuring that Google would encourage us to access in-depth, credible journalism, this is still under the auspices of the bespoke *Daily Me*. Again, Google can't be held solely responsible for the so-called 'echo chamber' effect where citizens seek out sources that reinforce their own views and prejudices without exposure to alternative or challenging perspectives (Sunstein 2007; Farrell and Drezner 2007). Google's outgoing CEO, Eric Schmidt, has an answer to this that he calls the 'serendipity principle'. In other words, his vision of a healthy online news environment is one in which individuals can get finely grained bespoke news whilst still stumbling across unanticipated topics and perspectives. This sounds like a healthy balance. But it leaves shared conversations about matters of common public interest very much to the whims of trending memes. If personalised news diets and micro-conversations are increasingly dominant, then perhaps the role of mainstream media is increasingly one of complementing (rather than competing with) the *Daily Me*, to regularly draw people out of their news bubbles and to convene debates on matters of public interest fuelled by in-depth coverage of salient facts and perspectives. Such a claim will no doubt appear futile, nostalgic or paternalistic to some.

CONCLUSION: WHO IS IN THE DRIVING SEAT?

One way of drawing citizens out of their micro-conversations into a shared arena is to actively engage with citizen journalists, amateur bloggers and social media rather than seeing them as attempting to encroach on professional territory or merely paying lip service to them – something the *Guardian* online has undoubtedly led the way in. But it pays not to forget the obvious point that for all the committed bloggers (many of whom are either journalists or consider themselves journalists), a majority of citizens relate to mainstream media as audiences first and foremost and not as participants.

Without trying to reduce news and journalism to conversation, it may be possible to encourage more members of the audience to participate and contribute in order to foster greater engagement with the news and, significantly from a market perspective, with particular news media brands. For mainstream media to treat its audience as intelligent citizens and as potential contributors to an ongoing conversation does not mean treating them as equals. As citizens we tend to look to professional journalists to keep us informed about important events and to access newsworthy places and people on our behalf. But we also look to them to interpret, analyse, sift fact from conjecture and opinion, dig beneath the surface, air different voices, and tell us interesting stories. Despite the rhetoric of 'democratising news', citizens do not routinely aspire to be the professional journalist's 'equal' in matters of newscraft, even among those busily blogging and tweeting on a daily basis. Jay Rosen (2006) coined the now well-worn phrase 'the people formerly known as the audience' for these citizens. But as we see in other contexts (theatre, live music, television talk-shows and so forth), increasing audience participation does not in any sense render the concept of audience itself defunct.

Clay Shirky (2009) explores an analogy between journalism in the digital age and driving:

> There is undoubtedly some truth in this claim. But the analogy with driving is an odd one that diminishes the craft and complexity of journalism, whether or not we want to label it a 'profession'. Truly anyone with basic motor, visual and cognitive skills can be a proficient driver; not so a proficient journalist. Good journalism pushes the boundaries, is creative and involves taking risks; not so, good driving.

Perhaps a better analogy would be with music. Many of us enjoy participating in music as well as listening to it. But picking up an instrument, whilst enjoyable and rewarding, also teaches most of us just how big the gap is between great musicianship and our own efforts. Participating in this way sharpens our appreciation (and critical skills) as listeners. Having some competence in music does not make us less respectful of or less interested in listening to expertly produced music – quite the reverse. And perhaps that is the mind shift needed in respect of blogging and citizen journalism. Mainstream news media need not disdain nor fear the growth of amateur journalism, questioning whether it really is 'journalism': it should instead be engaging with it, offering master classes, showcasing the best, and treating it as an opportunity to increase understanding of and appreciation for the journalistic profession.

Again, such idealism should be tempered by a note of realism. Those of us outside the profession should care about the state of journalism because we care about democracy. Journalism is shaped by many forces on the supply-side and also on the demand-side. On both sides of the equation, there are forces which go much wider than journalism itself (including the economic climate on the supply-side and a growing culture of cynicism towards public life on the demand-side). But journalism, new or old, is neither the exclusive cause of nor a potential panacea for the shortcomings of democracy. The internet is bringing citizens greater choices and some extremely interesting opportunities for enriched forms of engagement with, and even participation in, the news. It also brings some risks for citizens: of fragmentation and polarisation, of information overload and dizzying acceleration. But the extent to which the internet can democratise news is a much less important question than the extent to which it can help democratise democracy itself.

- This paper is adapted from a public lecture delivered as part of the University of Auckland's 2010 Winter Lecture Series 'The end(s) of journalism'. It was first published in *Ethical Space*, Vol. 9, No. 1 pp 32-40

REFERENCES

Abramson, Jill (2010) Sustaining quality journalism, *Dædalus*, Vol. 139, No.2 pp 39-44

Atkinson, Joe (1994) The state, the media and thin democracy, Sharp, Andrew (ed.) *Leap into the dark: The changing role of the state in New Zealand since 1984*, Auckland, Auckland University Press pp 152-162

Beer, David (2009) Power through the algorithm? Participatory web cultures and the technological unconscious, *New Media and Society*, Vol. 11, No. 6 pp 985-1002

Cha, Meeyoung et al. (2010) Measuring user influence in Twitter: The million follower fallacy, Association for the Advancement of Artificial Intelligence. Available online at http://twitter.mpi-sws.org/, accessed on 1 May 2011

Curran, James and Seaton, Jean (2003) *Power without responsibility: The press, broadcasting and new media in Britain*, London, Routledge, sixth edition

Davoudi, Salamander and Fenton, Ben (2009) Pressure mounts on *Guardian* strategy, *Financial Times*, 19 September p. 13

Deuze, Mark (2008) The changing context of news work: Liquid journalism and monitorial citizenship, *International Journal of Communication*, Vol. 2 pp 848-865

Deveson, Max (2009) Crisis in the US newspaper industry, BBC News. Available online at http://news.bbc.co.uk/2/hi/americas/7913400.stm, accessed on 2 May 2011

Fallows, James (2010) How to save the news, *Atlantic*, June. Available online at http://www.theatlantic.com/magazine/archive/2010/06/how-to-save-the-news/8095/, accessed on 2 May 2011

Farrell, Henry and Drezner, Daniel W. (2008) The power and politics of blogs, *Public Choice*, Vol. 134, Nos 1 and 2 pp 15-30

Fenton, Ben (2010) BBC unveils downsizing proposals as political pressure mounts, *Financial Times*, March 3 p. 4

Gans, Herbert J. (2010) News and the news media in the digital age: Implications for democracy, *Dædalus*, Vol. 139, No. 2 pp 8-17

Garnham, Nicholas (1992) The media and the public sphere, Calhoun, Craig (ed.) *Habermas and the public sphere*, Cambridge MA, MIT Press pp 359-76

Gillmor, Dan (2006) *We the media: Grassroots journalism by the people, for the people*, Sebastopol CA, O'Reilly Media

Gillmor, Dan (2009) Towards a slow news movement, *Mediactive*, November 8. Available online at http://mediactive.com/2009/11/08/ toward-a-slow-news-movement/, accessed on 3 May 2011

Habermas, Jürgen (1989) *The structural transformation of the public sphere: An inquiry into a category of bourgeois society*, Cambridge, Polity (trans. Burger, Thomas)

Harris, Paul (2010) Rupert Murdoch defiant: 'I'll stop Google taking our news for nothing', *Guardian*, 7 April. Available online at http://www.guardian.co.uk/media/2010/apr/07/rupert-murdoch-google-paywalls-ipad, accessed on 3 May 2011

Heil, Bill and Piskorski, Mikolaj (2009) New Twitter research: Men follow men and nobody tweets, Harvard Business Review Blogs, 1 June. Available online at http://blogs.hbr.org/cs/2009/06/new_twitter_research_men_follo.html, accessed on 4 May 2011

Hermida, Alfred (2010) Twittering the news: The emergence of ambient journalism, *Journalism Practice*, Vol. 7, No. 3 pp 297-308

Hermida, Alfred and Thurman, Neil (2008) A clash of cultures: The integration of user-generated content within professional journalistic frameworks at British newspaper websites, *Journalism Practice*, Vol. 2, No. 3 pp 343-356

Lanham, Richard (2006) *The economics of attention: Style and substance in the age of information*, Chicago, Chicago University Press

Lewis, Justin, Inthorn, Sanna and Wahl-Jorgensen, Karin (2005) *Citizens or consumers? What the media tell us about political participation*, Maidenhead, Open University Press

Negroponte, Nicholas (1995) *Being digital*, London, Coronet

O'Dell, Jolie (2010) How to tell a journalist from a blogger, Jolieodell.com, 21 July. Available online at http://blog.jolieodell.com/2010/07/21/how-to-tell-a-journalist-from-a-blogger/, accessed on 4 May 2011

Oliver, Laura (2010) Journalism job losses: Tracking cuts across the industry, Journalism.co.uk. Available online at http://www.journalism.co.uk/news-features/journalism-job-losses-tracking-cuts-across-the-industry/s5/a533044/#disqus_thread, accessed on 4 May 2011

Pew Project for Excellence in Journalism (2009) The state of the news media. Available online at http://www.stateofthemedia.org/2009/index.htm, accessed on 4 May 2011

Puppis, Manuel (2009) Media regulation in small states, *International Communication Gazette*, Vol. 71, Nos 1 and 2 pp 7-17

Rosen, Jay (2006) The people formerly known as the audience, *Pressthink*, 27 June. Available online at http://archive.pressthink.org/2006/06/27/ppl_frmr.html, accessed on 1 May 2011

Shapiro, Walter (2010) After Breitbart and Shirley Sherrod, we need a slow-news movement, *Politics Daily*, 28 July. Available online at http://www.politicsdaily.com/2010/07/27/after-breitbart-and-shirley-sherrod-we-need-a-slow-news-movement/, accessed on 1 May 2011

Shirky, Clay (2008) Newspapers and thinking the unthinkable, *Edge: The third culture*. Available online at http://www.edge.org/3rd_culture/shirky09/shirky09_index.html, accessed on 1 May 2011

Shirky, Clay (2009) Not an upgrade – an upheaval, Cato Unbound, 13 July. Available online at http://www.cato-unbound.org/2009/07/13/clay-shirky/not-an-upgrade-an-upheaval/, accessed on 1 May 2011

Sobel, Jon (2010) State of the blogosphere 2010, *Technorati*. Available online at http://technorati.com/blogging/article/state-of-the-blogosphere-2010-introduction/, accessed on 4 May 2011

Sunstein, Cass (2007) *Republic.com 2.0*, Princeton, Princeton University Press

NOTE ON THE CONTRIBUTOR

Luke Goode is Associate Professor and Programme Director for Communication at the University of Auckland, Aotearoa New Zealand. His published research relates primarily to themes of digital public spheres and the social impacts of new media technologies. Since the original publication of this paper, his work has increasingly been in the field of critical futures studies. Contact details: School of Cultures, Languages and Linguistics, University of Auckland, Aotearoa New Zealand. Email: l.goode@auckland.ac.nz

Chapter 11

Privacy in Social Network Sites (SNS): The threats from data mining

Yeslam Al-Saggaf and Md Zahidul Islam

This paper explores the potential of data mining as a technique that could be used by malicious data miners to threaten the privacy of SNS users and makes a moral case for the users' right to privacy. It applies a data mining algorithm to a hypothetical dataset of a sample of individuals from Saudi Arabia, Pakistan and Yemen to show the ease at which characteristics about the SNS users can be discovered and used in a way that could invade their privacy. It is hoped by exploring the threats from data mining on individuals' privacy and arguing for users' right to privacy, the study will raise SNS users' awareness about the ways in which information that they reveal online can be used by malevolent data miners to harm them and how to operate in SNS safely.

Keywords: privacy, Social Network Sites (SNS), data mining

INTRODUCTION: SNS AND FACEBOOK

Social Network Sites (SNS) continue to be among the most popular websites on the internet. According to most recent rankings from Alexa (2011a) of the top 500 sites, Facebook is ranked second from the top (in terms of the total number of page views) followed by YouTube in third place, Blogger in the seventh and Twitter in the tenth; suggesting that social networking is one of the popular internet activities among the two billion world internet citizens (Internet World Stats 2011). There are many SNS on the web including MySpace, Twitter, Hi5, Flickr, Orkut, LinkedIn and BeBo, but by far Facebook is the most popular site (Alexa 2011a). Indeed, this observation is consistent with Facebook statistics that showed in less than a year, the number of active users on Facebook has jumped from 500 million to 800 million users, 50 per cent of whom log on to it each day (Facebook 2011). This massive growth in the population size of Facebook is indicative of the huge popularity that Facebook enjoys.

There are not many definitions of SNS in the literature (Al-Saggaf 2011), but the most frequently cited definition is the one proposed by boyd and Ellison (2007: 211) who defined SNS as web-based services that allow individuals to:

1) construct a public or semi-public profile within a bounded system;

2) articulate a list of other users with whom they share a connection, and

3) view and traverse their list of connections and those made by others within the system.

This definition is not just chosen because it is the most frequently used one but also because it incorporates most of the elements found on Facebook such as being a platform where individuals can communicate with each other to form new social connections and/or to maintain existing friendships and in doing so share personal information, photos, videos, thoughts as well as their feelings. This view about Facebook is in line with the results from a recent study which has shown that people use SNS not only to develop new friendships but also to communicate with older friends whom they cannot meet regularly face-to-face (Al-Saggaf 2011). In addition, Facebook allows its members to communicate with others using voice, videos, online chat, offline messages, blogs and 'walling'[1] (Al-Saggaf 2011).

Upon registering with Facebook, the first thing users do is create their own profiles, which they can set to be either private or public. Like any other SNS, Facebook allows its users to upload their photos, videos and emotional states. The site also allows outside developers to build applications which users can then use to personalise their profiles and perform other tasks, such as comparing movie preferences and charting travel histories (boyd and Ellison 2007). In addition, users can also create their own online identities (Jones et al. 2008). To create their identities on SNS, users need to place on their own profiles their personal and biographical data such as name (a real name or alias), date and place of birth, citizenship, nationality, photos, hobbies and so on.

While on the one hand users are increasingly aware and very concerned about their privacy on Facebook (boyd and Ellison 2007; Jones et al. 2008; Young 2009; Al-Saggaf 2011), on the other hand, self-disclosure and revealing private information on the site is very widespread (Jones et al. 2008; Valenzuela, Park and Kee 2009; Al-Saggaf 2011) with users sharing with strangers up-to-the-minute updates of the status of their feelings and thoughts. Given young adults between the ages of 18-24 represent the largest cohort of SNS users (Hoy and Milne 2010), revealing private information such as political views, residential address, date of birth, books read, movies watched, schools went to, sexual orientations and their inner thoughts about their partners, neighbours, colleagues and employers can have serious consequences for these users' informational privacy and possibly also for their financial and physical security.

This paper explores the potential of data mining as a technique that could be used by malicious data miners to threaten the privacy of SNS users and makes a moral case for the protection of users' privacy. By exploring threats from data mining to individuals' privacy and arguing for users' right to their privacy, the study will raise SNS users' awareness about the ways in which information that they reveal online can be used by malevolent data miners to harm them. To achieve this aim, a hypothetical dataset of a sample of individuals from Saudi Arabia, Pakistan and Yemen, as examples of conservative societies, was created. Next, the paper applied a data mining algorithm to this dataset to demonstrate the ease at which characteristics about the SNS users can be discovered and used in a way that could invade their privacy. After that the paper will present a short philosophical analysis to argue for the importance of protecting users' privacy from the threats of data mining. At the end, we will present several recommendations that should contribute to raising users' awareness about how to operate in SNS safely.

PRIVACY AS AN ETHICAL ISSUE

Privacy on Facebook can be threatened in many ways including through the continuous changing of the privacy settings that Facebook does without announcing to users, tracking technologies such as HTTP cookies that gather information about users without their knowledge and Application Programming Interface (API) tools that enable other SNS to share users' information and create complete profiles enabling them, in essence, to sell this information to third parties. Another method that can be used to erode users' privacy is data mining. When a data mining algorithm is applied to a large dataset which can be created by harvesting users' information from SNS, hidden and non-obvious patterns about those users can be unearthed from this dataset (Tavani 2011). Used unethically on Facebook users, data mining can have the potential of incorrectly placing users in newly created categories or groups that could, for example, make them victims of paedophiles or organised crime.

Privacy is one of the most widely discussed topics in the Australian media and in the computer and information technology ethics literature (Al-Saggaf and Weckert 2011). But what is privacy? What is considered as private? And why is privacy valued anyway? There are three theories of privacy (Tavani 2011). The first theory relates to the notion of Accessibility Privacy, which defines privacy in terms of one's physically 'being let alone' or freedom from intrusion into one's physical space. The second theory relates to Decisional Privacy, which defines privacy in terms of freedom from interference in one's choices and decisions. The third, and most relevant theory to this article, is that of Informational Privacy, which defines privacy as control over the flow of one's personal information, including the transfer and exchange of that information (Tavani 2011: 137). In addition, Moor (2000 cited in Tavani 2011) has also introduced an account of privacy that is more comprehensive in that it encapsulates all these three theories. Specifically, it incorporates the elements of the non-intrusion, non-interference and informational views of privacy.

According to Moor, an 'individual has privacy in a situation if in that particular situation the individual is protected from intrusion, interference, and information access by others' (ibid: 137). Tavani also notes that Moor makes a distinction between naturally private and normatively private situations. According to Tavani (ibid), this distinction allows us to distinguish between the conditions required for having privacy (in a descriptive sense) and having a right to privacy in the normative sense. According to this distinction, if a person sees another picking her nose in the library, then that person lost her privacy but her privacy was not violated. But if that other person peeps through the keyhole of her apartment door then her privacy is not only lost but also violated.

What is normally considered to be private? This question has also been raised by Weckert and Adeney (1997) and their answer is that our inner thoughts, our personal relationships, and our personal information such as those relating to our health and finances are all private matters. Informational privacy is seen in different ways. For example, Islam (2008) and Islam and Bronkovic (2011) consider the exact information on any attribute of an individual (such as the disease diagnosis of a patient and income of an employee) as private while Murahidhar et al. (1999) consider any exact information about a group of individuals as private even if it is not clear which individual the disclosed information belongs to.

Privacy is valued for many reasons including for achieving important human ends like trust and friendships (Tavani 2011). For Jim Moor (2004, cited in Tavani 2011), privacy is important because it is the articulation or expression of the core value of security (ibid). On the other hand, for Deborah Johnson privacy is an important social good because when people are watched all the time they take the perspective of the observer. Because decisions will be made on the basis of what they do, they tend to think before acting. This becomes a form of social control which leads to eroding individuals' freedom. This in turn affects democracy (Johnson 2001). In our view, privacy is also important for love, marriage and partner relationships, respect and dignity, freedom of expression and liberty, autonomy, solitude, anonymity and secrecy, data protection and self-confidence to name a few.

Erosion of privacy due to excessive self-disclosure is a problem for participants in SNS and users are more than ever concerned about their privacy (boyd and Ellison 2007; Jones et al. 2008; Young 2009; Al-Saggaf 2011). That said, self-disclosure is rampant on both SNS (Jones et al. 2008; Valenzuela, Park and Kee 2009) and online communities (Dyson 1998; Horn 1998; Kollock and Smith 1999; Markham 1998; Rheingold 2000). There are many reasons for this but the lack of oral and non-verbal cues, and lack of public self-awareness are major factors. Lack of oral and non-verbal cues, and lack of public self-awareness cause abandonment of social inhibitions and detachments from social conventions (Barnes 2001; Joinson 1998; Mar 2000; Preece 2000; Rafaeli and Sudweeks 1997; Wallace 1999).

Trust between online communicators has been found to be another factor that encourages self-disclosure (Valenzuela, Park and Kee 2009). Trust is vital for personal relationships (Cocking and Matthews 2000; Weckert 2003); in fact, one way to show the strength of a friendship between two individuals is by demonstrating they trust each other. At the same time to show my trust in someone I have to reveal more about myself. That is why self-disclosure is also important for personal relationships (Preece 2000; Rheingold 2000; Rifkin 2000; Wallace 1999). Indeed, researchers have found that as people become familiar with others online, they tend to reveal more about themselves (Barnes 2001; Horn 1998; Markham 1998).

But, as online communicators reveal more and more sensitive information about themselves, the chances that their privacy will be eroded or, at least, violated will be increased. For example, women in Saudi Arabia who place their photos (even the ones that show their faces) on Facebook may become subject to sexual coercion by malicious SNS users if these photos fall into these malicious SNS users' hands. They could threaten to release their photos or video clips on the internet or publicly via Bluetooth on mobile phones unless these women submit to their demands. If the women do not comply, the result can cause serious damage to their family's reputation which is a grave matter in Saudi society. While this example suggests that privacy is not valued equally in all cultures (placing photos on Facebook may not be an issue for women in Western societies), it nevertheless shows that privacy has at least some value in all societies (Tavani 2011).

DATA MINING THREATS TO THE PRIVACY OF USERS OF FACEBOOK AND/OR OTHER SNS

There are various data mining tasks including data collection (such as automatic collection of weather data from different sensors), data pre-processing (such as pre-processing of satellite images), data integration/transformation to prepare a suitable flat file containing a range of relevant non-class attributes (such as blood sugar level and cholesterol level of a patient) and a class attribute (such as diagnosis of disease), data cleansing (by identifying and removing/correcting corrupt data, and imputing missing values), and pattern extraction from the clean pre-processed data (Islam 2012). There are a number of pattern extraction techniques including clustering (such as K-means and Fuzzy C-means clustering), classification (such as decision trees and artificial neural networks) and association rule mining such as finding purchase patterns from a market basket dataset.

Data mining has a wide range of applications such as social network analysis, analysis of microarray gene expression data, software engineering, market segmentation, web search result grouping, and irrigation water demand forecasting – just to name a few (Zhao and Zhang 2011; Haung and Pan 2006; Lung, Zaman and Nandi 2003; Tsai and Chiu 2004; Zamir and Etzioni 1999). Data pre-processing techniques can be applied to collect data from various sources including weather stations, satellite images and water usage statements. Various other data mining techniques (such as classification by decision tree and artificial neural network) can then be applied on the collected data to extract patterns that can then be used to predict future water demand for irrigation. Accurate water demand prediction can help us to manage irrigation water more efficiently by reducing the wastage of already limited irrigation water. Data mining can also be applied on huge amounts of data generated from social networking sites (SNS) in order to study contact networks, growth rates and social implications of various SNS (Patton 2007).

Data mining is also used in direct marketing (where targeted advertisements are sent to potential customers), and various business analyses. An example of its application in developing better business strategies and business promotion is association rule mining (Islam 2008). Association rule mining is applied on a huge set of transactions (records), where each transaction consists of a list of items such as milk, bread, butter that are sold together in the transaction. A supermarket chain, for example Wal-Mart, collects each and every sale transaction in a central data warehouse from all its stores (around 2900) situated in around six different countries. From the collected data, they can explore frequent item sets and association rules. When a set of items appear in a huge number of transactions then they are known as a frequent item set. Moreover, when the appearance of one set of items in a transaction increases the possibility of the appearance of another set of items in the same transaction then it is known as an association rule. Based on frequent item sets and association rules a supermarket can design its store in order to increase sales. For example, they can put the frequent items apart in a store so that customers need to walk through the store to find the items. This can often increase the sales as customers tend to buy more items when they walk through them. Moreover, supermarkets can reduce the prices of a set of items and advertise the price reduction. However, they can increase the prices of another set of items when they know from association rule mining that the increased sale of the former set of items will also increase the sales of the later sets of items and, therefore, they will make more overall profit.

Data mining can extract various interesting and hidden patterns (such as logic rules and clusters) from a dataset. Often it is argued that general patterns (logic rules) are public knowledge and should be considered sensitive to individual privacy (Islam 2008; Islam and Bronkovic 2011). For example, the pattern that people from Asia have black hair is public knowledge and therefore should not be considered sensitive. If a person is originally from Asia then it is generally assumed that he/she has black hair and there is nothing wrong with that. However, some general patterns even when they are applicable to many people can disadvantage an individual and therefore need to be considered as sensitive. For example, if a bank discovers that all previous loans granted to the customers living in a specific suburb are defaulted and, therefore, decides to turn down the loan application of an individual living in the suburb just based on his/her address then this pattern can appear to be unfair to the individual. Similarly, if a business learns from its past records that all employees of a race have been found inefficient and, therefore, decides not to offer a job to a new applicant who is from the same race, then the pattern can again appear to be unfair to the applicant.

Tavani (2011) presents an example of such intrusive and privacy threatening data mining where a car loan application, for purchasing a new BMW, was turned down by a bank although the applicant was financially solvent and had an executive position with good salary. The bank mines its data sets and discovers a pattern that executives earning between $120K and $150K annually, who often take expensive vacations and purchase luxury cars generally start their own businesses. The bank then mines another data set and finds that the majority of such entrepreneurs declare bankruptcy within a year. Unfortunately, the applicant for the car loan falls in this category, although neither the applicant nor the bank knows whether the applicant will really start his own business and face bankruptcy in future.

Data mining can be used for extracting various sensitive patterns of activity by the Facebook or other SNS users. The patterns can then be applied on any Facebook (or any other SNS) user resulting in huge user discomfort and serious breach of individual privacy. For example, a malicious data miner can study the Facebook activities of his/her friends. Based on the observation he/she can then prepare a dataset (a table with records and attributes) having information on the users. In the dataset each record can represent a Facebook user and each column/attribute can represent a property of the user. The properties can be learnt from the Facebook use patterns. Examples of the attributes can include: 'Ratio of the number of opposite sex friends to same sex friends' (Col. 6 in Table 1), 'Number of own picture uploads per week' (Col. 3 in Table 1), 'Level of exposure of the pictures (i.e. how exposed the person is in the pictures)' (Col. 4 in Table 1), and 'Number of status changes in Facebook per week' (Col. 5 in Table 1).

The data miner can have some supplementary knowledge on his/her friends in addition to the knowledge learned from their Facebook activities. The data miner can also use the supplementary knowledge to create a class attribute of the dataset. The class attribute can be considered as the label of a record. All other attributes are considered as non-class attributes. Classification task (using techniques including decision tree and artificial neural network) builds logic rules from the dataset to classify the records on the values of the class attribute. An example of a logic rule can be 'if $A = a_1$ and $B = b_1$ then $C = c_1$' where A and B are non-class attributes, C is the class attribute and a_1, b_1, c_1 are the attribute values.

Based on his/her supplementary knowledge on each friend in the Facebook, a malicious data miner can add an attribute, say 'Willingness to date with a male' (Col. 7 in Table 1) as the class attribute having values 'yes', 'maybe' and 'no' for the records of the dataset created from the Facebook observation. All other attributes can be considered as non-class attributes. The data miner can then apply a classifier on the dataset and extract sensitive logic rules to classify a Facebook user as either 'Willing to date with a male' or 'Not willing to date with a male'. Once the logic rules are built they can be used on any Facebook user (whom the data miner might not even know personally) to classify as either 'Willing to date with a male' or 'Not willing to date with a male' simply based on the users' Facebook activities. The malicious data miner can then approach the female users who fall in the category 'Willing to date with a male' for a date. This can be disturbing for a Facebook user especially in a conservative society. If a female Facebook user falls in the category 'Willing to date with a male' serious social problems can arise including extortion, difficulty in finding a partner and even inferior treatment in a job environment.

We now give a hypothetical dataset of a sample of individuals from Saudi Arabia, Pakistan and Yemen, as shown in Table 1, created from Facebook activities and supplementary knowledge of a malicious data miner.

TABLE 1: A SAMPLE DATASET OF FACEBOOK USERS

21	Saudi	7	High	3	0.1	No
19	Pakistan	2	High	2	4	Yes
33	Yemen	7	High	2	4	Yes
35	Saudi	2	High	7	0.1	No
19	Pakistan	2	Medium	12	3	No
25	Yemen	3	Medium	3	4	No
22	Saudi	7	Medium	7	0.1	Maybe
33	Pakistan	8	Medium	8	5	May be
21	Saudi	7	Medium	22	5	Yes
27	Saudi	8	Medium	33	1	Yes
22	Saudi	2	Low	22	7	No
26	Saudi	8	Low	2	2	No
21	Saudi	7	High	3	0.1	No
19	Pakistan	2	High	2	4	Yes
33	Yemen	7	High	2	4	Yes
35	Saudi	2	High	7	0.1	No
19	Pakistan	2	Medium	12	3	No
25	Yemen	3	Medium	3	4	No
22	Saudi	7	Medium	7	0.1	Maybe
33	Pakistan	8	Medium	8	5	Maybe
21	Saudi	7	Medium	22	5	Yes
27	Saudi	8	Medium	33	1	Yes
22	Saudi	2	Low	22	7	No
26	Saudi	8	Low	2	2	No

A data miner can apply a decision tree algorithm (for example, C4.5) on the training data-set shown in Table 1 and build a decision tree as shown below that considers 'Willingness' as the class attribute. The rectangles denote internal nodes and the ovals denote leaves of the tree. There are six leaves and four nodes in the tree. Each leaf of the tree represents a logic rule that classifies the records belonging to the leaf. For example, the logic rule for Leaf 1 is 'If exposure = high, and ratio <= 0.1 then willingness = no'. There are four records belonging to the leaf meaning that four records have 'Exposure = high and ratio <= 0.1' in the training dataset shown in Table 1. In this example, out of the four records all of them have 'Willingness = no'. Therefore, Logic Rule 1 suggests that if a Facebook user uploads pictures with high exposure and the ratio of male friends to female friends is less than or equal to 0.1 then she is usually not willing to date a male. However, Logic Rule 2 (for Leaf 2) suggests that if picture exposure of a Facebook user is high and ratio of male to female friends is greater than 0.1 then she is likely to be willing to date a male since out of four such records in the training dataset all are willing to date a male. Similarly, Leaf 5 and Leaf 6 also represent logic rules that classify records as willing to date.

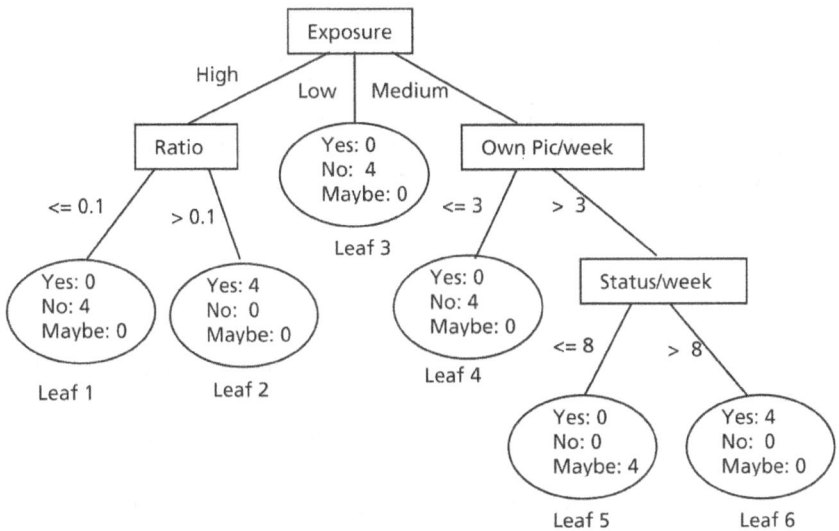

A malicious data miner can then use the knowledge on any other Facebook users whom he/she even does not know. The data miner can learn about the Facebook activities of a user through common friends. Therefore, the data miner may identify a Facebook user as willing to date even though he/she does not know the user. If the logic rules that label a user as willing to date are made public then anyone knowing the rules may classify a user as either willing or not willing to date. This can cause serious social and emotional trouble for the Facebook users who fall in the category of willing to date especially in conservative societies such as in Saudi Arabia, Yemen and Pakistan. This is especially more undesirable for those who are not willing to date but are approached by unwanted people. The logic rules are extracted using data mining algorithms from a sample training dataset and cannot guarantee a correct classification for a new record.

THE APPLICABILITY OF THE STUDY FINDINGS TO WESTERN SOCIETIES

The situation in Western countries is not as striking in many respects. However, the threats of data mining to privacy, highlighted above, are certainly not of concern to the above three conservative societies only. While, on the one hand, the younger generation in Western societies, as this paper has shown, has a greater tendency to have their profiles publicly available, on the other, they are also concerned about sharing personal information on Facebook and about their privacy. Similarly, while the risks associated with the application of data mining techniques on Facebook data to Western societies may be different than the risks to the above three conservative societies, they are certainly not less concerning. Consider the ability of data mining to place users in newly created categories or groups that could make them victims of crimes such as child paedophilia, child pornography, cyberstalking, cyber-bullying, child sexual exploitation and child grooming.

A recent report published by the Australian Institute of Criminology shows online child grooming for sexual offences, for example, is already on the rise in Australia, the UK and the United States because of the misuse of SNS.[2] Data mining of SNS data could further exacerbate this crime which is taken very seriously in Western societies as the damage caused can be enormous and long lasting. So while the risks are different depending on the society one lives in, the harms that can be caused by data mining are no less important.

A MORAL CASE FOR THE SNS USERS' RIGHT TO PRIVACY

The section titled 'Privacy as an ethical issue' above discussed some specific reasons why privacy is valued. The aim of this section is to make a moral case for the SNS users' right to privacy using both utilitarianism and deontology ethical theories. From a utilitarian perspective, it would appear that using data mining to invade SNS users' privacy can harm them. For example, malicious SNS users can use data mining technologies to target women on Facebook and threaten them to either submit to their sexual desires or face the consequences of having hidden but sensitive information about them posted on the internet or distributed publicly, thereby damaging their family reputation. Putting restrictions on the use of data mining (more on this below) can certainly help stop harm from being inflicted upon those women. This shows that data mining can be used to cause harm to people but that privacy can protect individuals from these kinds of harm.

From a deontological perspective it would appear developers of data mining algorithms have a duty of care to the people who are likely to be affected by the algorithms they develop. While it may be difficult to ensure that these value laden technologies cannot be used by malicious data miners to invade people's privacy, developers of data mining algorithms have a responsibility also to develop privacy preserving techniques. Respect for persons entails that people should be treated as ends in themselves, and not just as means to some end. To treat SNS users with respect means they should be treated as persons who have value in themselves, and not only as pieces of information that could be useful, for example, to third party advertisers. SNS owners should exercise caution when selling/sharing their users' data to/with third party advertisers. So a dataset from users' data should not be made available to malicious data miners to mine and use the results against the vulnerable and unsuspecting members of the society and thus breach their privacy.

Privacy protects some freedoms and restricts others. It protects an individual's freedom to be alone, to act without others intruding and to control what others know about him or her. However, it restricts the extent to which an individual can observe others and what he or she can learn about others (Weckert and Adeney 1997); although in the case of the SNS, much to the dismay of the users, this may not be possible. That is, privacy may not be able to restrict the freedom of the malicious SNS users to use data mining algorithms to uncover hidden information about a few people with the mission to target them individually because SNS users' data (necessary for the dataset) and data mining algorithms can easily be acquired. This suggests that privacy in this case may not, when it should, restrict the freedom of the malicious SNS users to harm others. Thus, while it might be argued that the moral value of privacy comes from its specific function in promoting the liberty of individuals by restricting the scope of the power of those in positions of strength (data miners), in the case of these SNS users, this may not happen (Weckert and Adeney 1997).

But why should the SNS users be concerned about their privacy? The number of times they update their status a week or the level of exposure within the photos they share, for example, are the business of nobody except these SNS users but is this information in itself important to the SNS users? Weckert and Adeney (ibid) argue that their preference for unsugared, black coffee rather than the sweet, white variety is also the business of nobody but them and the person making their coffee, but, according to them, worrying about the privacy of this information seems a bit extreme. While much information about the SNS users, like their age, gender, nationality and marital status, which some display on their SNS profiles, might not be much more important than the preference in coffee, the number of times they update their status a week or the level of exposure within the photos they share can reveal a little more about these users when information from other users is also added to the dataset and mined.

CONCLUSION AND RECOMMENDATIONS TO MITIGATE THE RISK

This paper explored the potential of data mining as a technique that could be used by malicious data miners to threaten the privacy of SNS users and made a moral case for the protection of users' privacy. Using a hypothetical dataset of a sample of individuals from Saudi Arabia, Pakistan and Yemen, a data mining algorithm was applied to this dataset to demonstrate the ease at which characteristics about the SNS users can be discovered and used in a way that could invade their privacy. This was followed by a short philosophical analysis which argued for the importance of protecting users' privacy from the threats of data mining.

Privacy is a crucial social good and an instrumental, if not intrinsic, universal value (for the difference between instrumental and intrinsic values see Burmeister, Weckert and Williamson 2011). Privacy is valued for many reasons (as discussed above). While people generally learn about privacy and how to maintain it from their parents, schools and society, the development of technologies has meant that people are operating in environments that did not exist in the past. As a result, on the one hand, people are facing new challenges, on the other hand, they do not seem to get clear guidelines from their parents, schools, and society on how to operate safely in these new environments such as SNS.

Privacy is often not taken seriously by many users especially the young users group. It is essential for SNS users to be careful in maintaining their privacy online for reasons discussed above. Therefore, it is important to raise their awareness about the possible privacy invasions and their implications. One way to preserve privacy online is by masking the individual's data carefully or hiding the sensitive information such as date of birth, address and other identifying information. This way, even if an unknown malicious data miner can classify a user, for example, as 'Willing to date', it can be difficult for the miner to locate the user and thus harass her. At the same time, if the logic rules are known to the users they can deliberately design their activities in a way so that she is not classified as 'Willing to date'. For example, if the exposure of a user is 'medium' in her pictures then she can deliberately keep the number of her own picture uploads per week less than three so that she falls in Leaf 4 and thereby safely classified as 'Not willing to date'.

Another way to protect privacy online is by putting restrictions, possibly in the form of laws and regulations, on the use of data mining for individual purposes. However, restricting malicious data mining by introducing laws can be a difficult job. First it will be difficult to detect that someone is mining data maliciously. Second, even if detection is possible it will be difficult to prove malicious intent. One can always argue that he/she was performing data mining for good intentions such as research and knowledge discovery.

We therefore recommend that the data mining community should develop Privacy Preserving Data Mining (PPDM) techniques specifically catered for online environments. Until such techniques are developed, users should protect themselves by using all possible ways including hiding their identifying information, using SNS privacy settings carefully and masking their online activities to protect them from being identified as potential victims. Ensuring the privacy settings on Facebook are up to date (often they roll back to the default settings) can be another way to keep malicious data miners out of the way.

The threats from data mining on individuals' privacy are serious as the application of a data mining algorithm on the above dataset has shown; and users should have a right to their privacy online as the short philosophical analysis has shown. While the recommendations offered here do not solve the problems, it is hoped the paper has at least begun to raise SNS users' awareness about the ways in which information they reveal online can be used by malevolent data miners to harm them and how to operate in SNS safely in the midst of these threats.

- This paper was first published in *Ethical Space*, Vol. 9, No 4 pp 32-40

NOTES

[1] The participants in Al-Saggaf's (2011) study call the activity of posting comments and other objects on their Facebook wall to communicate with their friends as 'walling'

[2] See http://www.aic.gov.au/en/publications/current%20series/rpp/100-120/rpp103.aspx, accessed on 21 November 2011

REFERENCES

Alexa (2011a) The top 500 sites on the web. Available online at http://www.alexa.com/topsites, accessed on 21 November 2011

Alexa (2011b) The top 500 sites on the web. Available online at http://www.alexa.com/topsites/countries/SA, accessed on 21 November 2011

Al-Saggaf, Y. (2003) *Online communities in Saudi Arabia: An ethnographic study*, PhD thesis, Charles Sturt University, Wagga Wagga, Australia

Al-Saggaf, Y. (2006) The online public sphere in the Arab world: The war in Iraq on the Al Arabiya website, *Journal of Computer-Mediated Communication*, Vol. 12, No. 1. Available online at http://jcmc.indiana.edu/vol12/issue1/al-saggaf.html, accessed on 15 April 2008

Al-Saggaf, Y. (2011) Saudi females on Facebook: An ethnographic study, *International Journal of Emerging Technologies and Society*, Vol. 9, No. 1 pp 1-19

Al-Saggaf, Y. and Weckert, J. (2011) Privacy from a Saudi Arabian perspective, *Journal of Information Ethics*, Vol. 20, No. 1 pp 34-53

Barnes, S. B. (2001) *Online connections: Internet interpersonal relationships*, Hampton Press, New Jersey

Bastani, S. (2000) Muslim women online, *Arab World Geographer*, Vol. 3, No. 1 pp 40-59

Burmeister, O. K., Weckert, J. and Williamson, K. (2011) Seniors extend understanding of what constitutes universal values, *Journal of Information, Communication and Ethics in Society*, Vol. 9, No.4 pp 238-252

boyd, D. M. (2006) Friends, friendsters, and Top 8: Writing community into being on social network sites, *First Monday*, Vol. 11, No. 12. Available online at http://www.firstmonday.org/issues/issue11_12/boyd, accessed on 12 October 2009

boyd, D. M. and Ellison, N. B. (2007) Social network sites: Definition, history, and scholarship, *Journal of Computer-Mediated Communication*, Vol. 13, No. 1. Available online at http://jcmc.indiana.edu/vol13/issue1/boyd.ellison.html, accessed on 15 April 2008

Cocking, D. and Matthews, S. (2000) Unreal friends, *Ethics and Information Technology*, Vol. 2 pp 223-231

Dyson, E. (1998) *Release 2.1: A design for living in the digital age*, Broadway Books, New York

Emerson, D. (2008) Facebook friends not real friends: judge, *Sydney Morning Herald*. Available online at http://www.smh.com.au/news/technology/facebook-friends-not-realjudge/2008/03/27/1206207279597.html, accessed on 6 October 2009

Facebook (2011) Statistics. Available online at http://www.facebook.com/press/info.php?statistics, accessed on 21 November 2011

Fule, P. and Roddick, J. F. (2004) Detecting privacy and ethical sensitivity in data mining results. Paper presented to the 27th Australian Computer Science Conference (ACSC2004), Estivill-Castro, Vladimir (ed.) Vol. 26 of Conference in Research and Practice in Information Technology pp 163-168

Garton, L., Haythornthwaite, C. and Wellman, B. (1997) Studying online social networks, *Journal of Computer-Mediated Communication*, Vol. 3, No. 1. Available online at http://jcmc.indiana.edu/vol3/issue1/garton.html, accessed on 18 September 2012

Hamman, R. (2001) Computer networks linking network communities, Werry, C. and Mowbray, M. (eds) *Online communities: Commerce, community action, and the virtual university*, Hewlett-Packard, New Jersey pp 71-95

Hauben, M. and Hauben, R. (1997) *Netizens: On the history and impact of usenet and the internet*, IEE Computer Society Press, Washington

Haythornthwaite, C. and Wellman, B. (2002) The internet in everyday life: An introduction, *The internet in everyday life*, Wellman, B. and Haythornthwaite, C. (eds) Blackwell Publishers, Oxford pp 1-55

Horn, S. (1998) *Cyberville: Clicks, culture, and the creation of an online town*, Warner Books, New York

Huang, D. and Pan, W. (2006) Incorporating biological knowledge into distance-based clustering analysis of microarray gene expression data, *Bioinformatics*, Vol. 22 pp 1259-1268

Hoy, H.G and Milne, G. 2010. Gender differences in privacy-related measures for young adult Facebook users, *Journal of Interactive Advertising*, Vol. 10 pp 1525-2019

Internet World Stats (2011) Internet usage in the Middle East. Available online at http://www.Internetworldstats.com/stats.htm, accessed on 21 November 2011

Islam, M. Z. (2008) Privacy preservation in data mining through noise addition. PhD thesis in Computer Science, School of Electrical Engineering and Computer Science, the University of Newcastle, Australia

Islam, M. Z. (2012) Explore: A novel decision tree classification algorithm, *Lecture Notes in Computer Science*, Vol. 6121 pp 55-71

Islam, M. Z. and Brankovic, L. (2011) Privacy preserving data mining: A noise addition framework using a novel clustering technique, *Knowledge-Based Systems*, December, Vol. 24, No. 8 pp 1214-1223

Johnson, D. G. (2001) *Computer ethics*, New Jersey, Prentice Hall, third edition

Joinson, A. (1998) Causes and implications of disinhibited behaviour on the internet, *Psychology and the Internet*, Gackenbach, J. (ed.), Academic Press, San Diego pp 43-60

Jones, S. G. (1998) Information, internet, and community: Notes toward an understanding of community in the information age, *CyberSociety 2.0: Revisiting computer-mediated communication and community*, Jones, S. G. (ed.) Thousand Oaks, CA, Sage Publications pp 1-35

Jones, S., Millermaier, S., Goya-Marthinez, M. and Schuler, J. (2008) Whose space is MySpace? A content analysis of MySpace profiles, *First Monday*, Vol. 13, No. 9. Available online at http://firstmonday.org/htbin/cgiwrap/bin/ojs/index.php/fm/article/view-Article/2202/2024, accessed on 18 September 2012

Karpinski, A. C. and Duberstein, A. (2009) A description of Facebook use and academic performance among undergraduate and graduate students, Technology Research Poster Session. Available online at http://researchnews.osu.edu/archive/facebook2009.jpg, accessed on 5 October 2009

Kollock, P. and Smith, M. (1999) Communities in cyberspace, Smith, M. and Kollock, P. (eds) *Communities in cyberspace*, London, Routledge pp 3-25

Lange, P. G. (2007) Publicly private and privately public: Social networking on YouTube, *Journal of Computer-Mediated Communication*, Vol. 13, No. 1. Available online at http://jcmc.indiana.edu/vol13/issue1/lange.html, accessed on 17 October 2009

Lung, C.-H., Zaman, M., and Nandi, A. (2004) Applications of clustering techniques to software partitioning, recovery and restructuring, *Journal of Systems and Software*, Vol. 73, pp 227-244

Mar, J. (2000) Online on time: The language of internet relay chat, Gibbs, D. and Krause, K. L. (eds) *Cyberlines: Languages and cultures of the internet*, South Melbourne, James Nicholas Publishers pp 151-174

Markham, A. N. (1998) *Life online: Researching real experience in virtual space*, Walnut Creek, CA, AltaMira Publications

Mitra, A. (1997) Virtual commonality: Looking for India on the internet, Jones, S. G.(ed.) *Virtual culture: Identity and communication in cybersociety*, London, Sage Publications pp 55-79

Moor, J. (2000) Towards a theory of privacy for the information age, Baird, R. M., Ramsower, R. and Rosenbaum, S. E. (eds) *Cyberethics: Moral, social, and legal issues in the computer age*, New York, Prometheus Books pp 2000-2012

Moor, J. (2004) Reason, relativity, and responsibility in computer ethics, Spinello, R. and Tavani, H. T. (eds) *Readings in cyberethics*, Sudbury, MA, Jones and Bartlett Publishers, second edition pp 40-54

Muralidhar, K., Parsa, R., and Sarathy, R. (1999) A general additive data perturbation method for database security, *Management Science*, Vol. 45, No. 10 pp 1399-1415

Patton, S. (2007) Social networking sites: Data mining and investigative techniques. Available online at https://www.blackhat.com/presentations/bh-usa-07/Patton/Whitepaper/bh-usa-07-patton-WP.pdf, accessed on 18 September 2012

Preece, J. (2000) *Online communities: Designing useability, supporting sociability*, Chichester, John Wiley and Sons

Rafaeli, S. and Sudweeks, F. (1997) Networked interactivity, *Journal of Computer-Mediated Communication*, Vol. 2, No. 4. Available online at http://jcmc.indiana.edu/vol2/issue4/rafaeli.sudweeks.html, accessed on 18 September 2012

Rheingold, H. (2000) *The virtual community: Homesteading on the electronic frontier*, Cambridge, MIT Press, revised edition

Rifkin, J. (2000) *The age of access: How the shift from ownership to access is transforming capitalism*, London, Penguin Books

Tamura, T. (2005) Japanese feeling for privacy, Hongladarom, S. (ed.). Proceedings of the 2nd Asia Pacific Computing and Philosophy Conference, Novotel Hotel, Bangkok, Thailand, January pp 88-93

Tavani, H. T. (2011) *Ethics and technology: controversies, questions, and strategies for ethical computing*, John Wiley, Hoboken, N. J., third edition

Tsai, C. Y., and Chiu, C. C. (2004) A purchase-based market segmentation methodology, *Expert Systems with Applications*, Vol. 27 pp 265-276

Valenzuela, S., Park, N. and Kee, K. F. (2009) Is there social capital in a social network site? Facebook use and college students' life satisfaction, trust, and participation, *Journal of Computer-Mediated Communication*, Vol. 14 pp 875-901

Wallace, P. (1999) *The psychology of the internet*, Cambridge, Cambridge University Press

Weckert, J. (2003) On-line trust, *The impact of the internet on our moral lives*, Cavalier, R. (ed.) Albany, NY, Suny Press pp 95-117

Weckert, J. and Adeney, D. (1997) *Computer and information ethics*, Westport, Connecticut/London, Greenwood Press

Wellman, B. and Gulia, M. (1999) Net-surfers don't ride alone: Virtual communities as communities, Wellman, B. (ed.) *Networks in the global village: Life in contemporary communities*, Westview, Colorado pp 331-366

Young, Y. (2009) Online social networking: An Australian perspective, *International Journal of Emerging Technologies and Society*, Vol. 7, No. 1 pp 39-57

Zamir, O., and Etzioni, O. (1999) Grouper: a dynamic clustering interface to Web search results, *Computer Networks: The International Journal of Computer and Telecommunications Networking*, Vol. 31 pp 1361-1374

Zhao, P. and Zhang, C. Q. (2011) A new clustering method and its application in social networks, *Pattern Recognition Letters*, Vol. 32 pp 2109-2118

NOTE ON THE CONTRIBUTORS

Yeslam Al-Saggaf is an Associate Professor in Computing at Charles Sturt University where he has been an academic since 2003. He is the author of *The psychology of phubbing* (Springer, 2022) and the successful recipient of three Australian Research Council (ARC) grants including in one as the Lead Chief Investigator. Currently, he is leading an Australian government grant in cyber security. He holds a Bachelor of Engineering (with honours) in Computer and Information Engineering from Malaysia and a Master of Information Technology and a PhD from Charles Sturt University. Al-Saggaf is interested in the security side of computing as well as the ethical, sociological and psychological aspects of the technology. For information about his research please visit this page: https://researchoutput.csu.edu.au/en/persons/yalsaggacsueduau.

Md Zahidul Islam is a Research Fellow at the Center for Research in Complex Systems (CRiCS) and Lecturer in Computer Science at the School of Computing and Mathematics, Faculty of Business, Charles Sturt University. He has received his Bachelor's degree in Engineering from Rajshahi University of Engineering and Technology, Bangladesh, Graduate Diploma in Science from the University of New South Wales, Australia and PhD in Computer Science (thesis titled *Privacy preservation in data mining through noise addition*) from the University of Newcastle, Australia. His main research interests include privacy issues for online communities caused by data mining, privacy preserving data mining, application of data mining techniques, and various data mining algorithms including classification, clustering, missing value imputation, data cleansing and data pre-processing. Email: zislam@csu.edu.au. Web: http://csusap.csu.edu.au/~zislam/.

SECTION 3

Professionalisation and media ethics:
Beyond the rhetoric

Chapter 12

Accountable sports journalism: Building up a platform and a new specialised code in the field

Xavier Ramon-Vegas and José-Luis Rojas-Torrijos

Far from its traditional consideration as the 'little brother' of the profession, sports journalism plays a key role in the new information ecosystem and has a huge impact in society. Therefore, sports journalists must gain awareness of their accountability in order to counteract the widespread deficiencies that have not only challenged the normative standards of the profession but have also eroded their credibility. With the aim of helping journalists address these shortcomings, this investigation: (1) has compiled and examined the most relevant ethical codes, stylebooks and other accountability instruments in sports journalism; (2) has created the online platform Accountable Sports Journalism (http://accountablesportsjournalism.org)*; and (3) has produced a new specialised code aimed at covering sports responsibly.*

Keywords: accountability, code, ethics, instruments, sports journalism

In the current cluttered and 'increasingly complex digital media landscape' (Boyle and Haynes 2014: 85), sport content is 'available from a growing range of digital, mobile media and telecommunications companies and intermediaries' (Hutchins and Boyle 2017: 505) as well as from communication departments at clubs and leagues (Suggs 2016). For legacy media, despite its 'perennial dismissal as trivial subject matter' (Weedon et al. 2016: 1), sport remains a pivotal asset to attract advertisers and audiences (Hutchins and Rowe 2009).

In this context of 'digital plenitude' (Hutchins and Rowe 2009), sports journalists face severe challenges, including 'commercial and economic restrictions' (English 2017: 534), 'greater demands in terms of publishing platforms, technology, content and workloads' (English 2016: 1002) and 'growing competition from content aggregators and "social" news specialists' (Hutchins and Boyle 2017: 499). Professionals also struggle with the seemingly endless growth of the PR industry in the world of sport (L'Etang 2013; Sherwood, Nicholson and Marjoribanks 2017).

However, as Hutchins and Boyle (2017: 497) highlight, 'the influence of multiple crosscutting forces does not mean that shared practices of news work no longer exist, or that journalists have voluntarily ceded their cultural authority to "the crowd" in determining what counts as news and how it should be produced and delivered'. Beyond adapting their skills 'to meet the demands of a converged media environment' (Ketterer, McGuire and Murray 2014: 282), sports journalists should maintain the essential principles of ethics at the core of their professional task (Oates and Pauly 2007). Ethics and accountability should be at the centre stage of the 'community of practice' of sports journalism. This is essential to counteract the widespread deficiencies that have not only challenged the normative standards of the profession but have also eroded the credibility and status of its professionals (Horky and Stelzner 2013).

'THE TOY DEPARTMENT': EXPLORING THE ETHICAL SHORTCOMINGS IN SPORTS JOURNALISM

Sports journalism has been labelled as the 'toy department' or the 'sandbox' of the newsroom (Rowe 2007). Its professionals 'have been described as cheerleaders, hero worshippers, fans, homers and sycophants' and as 'biased and responsible for boosterism of athletes, teams, organisations and the sports industry' (English 2017: 532). The dissolution of the frontiers between facts and comments has been commonplace in the field (Boyle 2006). Rumour and speculation have pervaded the coverage, which has also been 'subordinated to entertainment as a way of expression incorporating sensationalist elements that come from the spectacle industries' (Rojas-Torrijos 2011: 18). The use of violence metaphors and images in sports reporting, connected to 'commodification of sport, and its marketing as spectacle' (Holt 2000: 102) has also been frequent.

The limited range of sources has been mainly drawn 'from the ranks of celebrity athletes, coaches and administrators, thus further isolating the sports desk from the world beyond sport' (Rowe 2007: 400-401). Partly because of this interplay between media and the sport industry, sports journalists have failed to cover properly the 'problems, issues and topics that permeate the social world to which sport is intimately connected' (Rowe 2007: 400). Thus, they have proved unable to comply with the essential 'watchdog' and investigative functions of journalism in democratic societies. There are some noteworthy exceptions to this trend, such as the broader perspective shown by US newspapers in the coming out of Jason Collins and Michael Sam (Cassidy 2017); the critical reports in the Australia-India Test cricket series (English 2017); the exposure of child abuse in football (Taylor 2017); the investigation of corruption cases at FIFA (Jennings 2011) or the research on Lance Armstrong, pursued by David Walsh of *The Sunday Times* and the blog *NYVelocity* (Brock 2013). Yet, the amount of critical interrogation on the world of sport is scant compared to other genres.

In addition, as Suggs (2016: 265) highlights, 'news coverage looks surprisingly uniform across different publications and different media'. Moreover, sportswomen, non-white and impaired athletes have been marginalised in the coverage (O'Neill and Mulready 2015; Tulloch and Ramon-Vegas 2017) and have been often presented through the lens of stereotypes. To illustrate, in their recent examination of the US press coverage of Alex Rodriguez, the baseball player, for his alleged use of performance-enhancing drugs, Brennen and Brown (2016: 29) found that newspapers 'dehumanized Rodriguez through repeated use of overtly racist and animalistic imagery'.

THE ROLE OF ACCOUNTABILITY INSTRUMENTS IN SPORTS JOURNALISM

To mitigate the long-held claims of sports journalism being a 'bastion of easy living, sloppy journalism and "soft" news' (Boyle 2006: 1), 'sports journalists must also be accountable to the professional norms that advance the entire profession's credibility' (Hardin and Zhong 2010: 6). The concept of accountability refers to 'the commitment of media organisations and professionals to be held accountable by society for their practices' (Rojas-Torrijos and Ramon-Vegas 2017: 916). According to McQuail (2003: 19), 'accountable communication exists where authors (originators, sources, or gatekeepers) take responsibility for the quality and consequences of their publication, orient themselves to audiences and others affected, and respond to their expectations and those of the wider society'. Traditional and innovative media accountability instruments (Bertrand 2000) – including ethical codes, stylebooks, recommendations issued by organisations, ombudsmen websites and scholars' or citizens' blogs – can play major roles in offering guidance and helping journalists and users monitor and assess the quality of sports content (Ramon-Vegas and Rojas-Torrijos 2017).

OBJECTIVE AND METHODOLOGY

Taking the aforementioned framework into account, the objective of this research has been to compile, examine and disseminate the most relevant accountability instruments in sports journalism. The first stage of the project involved mapping and analysing the most relevant instruments in the field. We first monitored the internet over an 18-month period (October 2015-March 2017) to locate the most relevant instruments across different countries, media systems and journalistic cultures. Through snowball sampling, the instruments were identified and progressively incorporated into the sample. Afterwards, the researchers examined each one of those instruments using the qualitative content analysis technique (Bryman 2016). The categories of the analysis included the following: instruments produced inside or outside of media organisations, description of the specifications for and use of the instruments, and evaluation of the mechanisms from the accountability perspective (Ramon-Vegas and Rojas-Torrijos 2017).

The second stage of the research involved the creation, in April 2017, of the platform *Accountable Sports Journalism* (*http://accountablesportsjournalism.org*) to make the instruments readily accessible to media practitioners, scholars and students. On this site, users can find access to the instruments produced inside the media (in-house stylebooks promoted by major sports media, recommendations for sports journalists in news agencies and general information outlets, ombudsmen and online chats) and to tools implemented outside media companies (external codes, recommendations issued by key stakeholders in the world of sport, the largest publications related to media criticism, as well as several scholars' and citizens' blogs). The range of resources on the platform is being enhanced on an on-going basis. Nowadays, *Accountable Sports Journalism* brings together 42 resources ($n=42$) from 15 different countries, along with those produced by international organisations. Finally, after critically examining all the instruments available, the investigation has produced a new specialised code in sports journalism ('Guidelines for covering sports responsibly').

RESULTS
ACCOUNTABILITY INSTRUMENTS ON A NEW PLATFORM
So far, 42 accountability instruments have been located and uploaded on to the *Accountable Sports Journalism* platform. Those have been classified, as previously noted, into two categories: instruments produced within media organisations and those created outside of them.

INSTRUMENTS PRODUCED INSIDE MEDIA COMPANIES OR MEDIA GROUPS
Stylebooks and guidelines promoted by major sports media

One of the fundamental accountability instruments is in-house stylebooks which establish an implicit contract between journalists and citizens. One of the few sports outlets that has adapted its stylebook to the digital environment is *Bleacher Report* (*http://bleacherreport.com/pages/styleguide*). Another American outlet concerned with accountability is *ESPN*, which has published its *Editorial guidelines for standards & practices* (*http://edge-cache.deadspin.com/deadspin/editorial.pdf*). As their authors note, the purpose of the editorial guidelines 'is the protection of *ESPN*'s journalistic credibility across all platforms'. These recommendations tackle a wide range of ethical issues, including: transparency, commentary, sourcing, attribution, corrections, media criticism, activity on social networking sites and advertising. *Grantland*, a sports and culture website created by Bill Simmons in 2011 and discontinued in 2015, developed useful terminological glossaries on sports like tennis, wrestling, basketball, American football and baseball (*http://grantland.com/tags/grantland-dictionary/*).

Recommendations for sports coverage proposed by agencies and general information outlets

News agencies and general information outlets worldwide have also proposed recommendations for sports journalists. In Europe, the *Reuters sports style guide* (*http://handbook.reuters.com/index.php?title=Sports_Style_Guide*) is one of the key documents available. In Spain, the major public broadcasting corporations have specific sections devoted to sports in their in-house handbooks: namely *RTVE*, the Spanish public broadcasting corporation (*http://manualdeestilo.rtve.es/*); *CCMA*, the Catalan Corporation of Audiovisual Media (*http://www.ccma.cat/llibredestil/*) and *Canal Sur*, the radio and TV corporation in Andalusia. In complying with their remit as public service broadcasters (PSBs), these institutions stress the importance of disseminating the positive values associated with sport.

Moving on to America, the *Ethical journalism handbook* from *The New York Times* (*https://www.nytco.com/wp-content/uploads/NYT_Ethical_Journalism_0904-1.pdf*) outlines three rules (131-333) addressed to the sports desk. More precisely, it mentions that journalists should avoid gambling on sports events and serving as scorers and that they should not 'accept tickets, travel expenses, meals, gifts or any other benefit from teams or promoters'. Further references to conflicts of interest are included in documents issued by *Minnesota Public Radio* (*http://www.mpr.org/about/news_ethics*) and the *Los Angeles Times* (*http://latimesblogs.latimes.com/readers/2011/02/la-times-ethics-guidelines.html*). Conversely, other news organisations such as the *Columbia Missourian* (*http://convergence.journalism.missouri.edu/wp-content/uploads/2009/04/missourian-stylebook.pdf*) focus on providing guidance on sports language.

Online ombudsmen/ombudswomen

The role of ombudsmen/ombudswomen is nearly non-existent in sports media outlets. The exception can be found in *ESPN*'s public editor, a pioneering post created in 2005 to ensure that the content of the network complies with its *Editorial guidelines*. The public editor (*http://espn.go.com/blog/ombudsman*) fosters transparency and helps fans understand *ESPN*'s journalistic culture and the editorial criteria behind the content. He writes a monthly column, reflecting on core aspects such as the loosening of standards with the treatment of *ESPN* Body Issue photographs, the use of sponsored content, the criteria employed by the company to select their anchors or the debates about conflict of interest.

Online chats

Online chats, which help foster live interaction between readers, editorial teams and experts, have expanded in recent years and have proved to be powerful tools for discussing editorial criteria and handling errors (Rojas-Torrijos and Ramon-Vegas 2017). *ESPN*'s programme *Sportsnation* has promoted live chats since 2008. All the live conversations (*http://espn.go.com/sportsnation/chat/ archive*) can be retrieved at any time from *ESPN*'s website.

INSTRUMENTS PRODUCED OUTSIDE MEDIA COMPANIES OR GROUPS
Specialised codes in sports journalism

The range of external codes devoted exclusively to sports journalism is fairly limited. The most recognised document is the *Ethics guidelines* promoted by the Associated Press Sports Editors (APSE) (*http://apsportseditors.com/apse-ethics-guidelines/*). The code, created in 1974 and revised in 1991, is built around seven cornerstones that urge journalists to safeguard professional independence, verify information, be attentive to sources and avoid gender and race discrimination. In 2014, the International Sports Press Association (AIPS) approved its *Code of professional conduct*. The document (*http://www.aipsmedia.com/acopcs/AIPS_CODE_OF_PROFESSIONAL_CONDUCT_STANDARDS.pdf*) provides 13 guiding principles, including the need to be knowledgeable about the law, work with honesty and integrity, provide information about potential conflicts of interest, correct errors and avoid publishing false information. In addition, professionals are reminded about their duty to update their knowledge.

The Football Writers Association of America (FWAA) provides recommendations in four areas: the search for truth, minimising harm, professional independence and accountability (*http://www.sportswriters.net/fwaa/about/ethics.html*). The ethical code of the Automobile Journalists Association of Canada (AJAC) also considers the avoidance of any conflict of interest a cornerstone (*http://www.ajac.ca/web/about/ethics.asp*). The American Auto Racing Writers & Broadcasters Association (AARWBA) has its own code: *The white paper* (*http://www.aarwba.org/aarwbawp.htm*).

In the European context, we should highlight the *Italian media and sports code* (*http://ethicnet.uta.fi/italy/media_and_sports_code*). This code is organised in six chapters that seek to promote justice, dignity and the citizens' right to receive information. Moreover, the eight guidelines presented in 2010 by the German association of sports journalists, the *Verband Deutscher Sportjournalisten* (*http://www.sportjournalist.de/Ueber_uns/Leitlinien/*) are noteworthy.

These recommendations emphasise the public function of sports journalism and call for non-discrimination. The *VDS* also highlights the importance of maintaining independence, respecting individuals' privacy and ensuring accuracy (Horky and Stelzer 2013). In eastern European countries, there's the Serbian Sports Journalists Association (USNS) *Code and sport journalists' club ethics* (*http://www.usns.rs/wp-content/uploads/2016/10/Kodeks-sportskih-novinara-Srbije.pdf*) and the *Moral code* (*http://www.ksn.cz/o-ksn/eticky-a-moralni-kodex*) from the Czech Republic. Both are concise texts focused on standards such as safeguarding independence and verifying information.

There are other relevant codes in Latin America: the *Sports Journalists Association ethics code* (Puerto Rico) (*http://www.wallice.com/apdpur/reglamento.html*), *Manual de Conduta Ética da Associaçao Brasiliense de Cronistas Desportivos* (ABCD)

(Brazil) (*http://abcdesportes.com.br/abcd/manual-de-conduta-etica-da-abcd/*) and the Argentinian Federation of Sports Journalists (FAPED) *Ethics code* (*https://web.archive.org/web/20160328143342/http://faped.org/estatutos.html*).

General codes of media ethics

In addition to specialised codes in sports, professionals can consult the website *Accountable Journalism* (*http://accountablejournalism.org/*) created by the Donald W. Reynolds Journalism Institute at the University of Missouri. The site contains more than 400 general and specialised deontological codes from around the world. Among them, central documents such as UNESCO's *International principles of professional ethics* (*http://ethicnet.uta.fi/international/international_principles_of_professional_ethics_in_journalism*), the International Federation of Journalists' (IFJ) *Declaration of principles on the conduct of journalists* (*http://www.ifj.org/about-ifj/ifj-code- of-principles/*) and the Society of Professional Journalists' *Code of ethics* (*https://www.spj.org/ethicscode.asp*) should be highlighted.

Recommendations for sports journalists issued by key stakeholders

Recommendations issued by key stakeholders in the world of sport should also be taken into account. Among those suggestions, two relevant ones are accessible online: the *Code of sports ethics*, from the Council of Europe (*https://rm.coe.int/16805cecaa*) and the *Charte d'etique et de déontologie du sport Français* (CNOSF 2012). Both emphasise the media's responsibility to promote fair play and set a positive example to children and young people. Moreover, the *Code of sports ethics*, devised by the Portuguese Institute for Sport and Youth (*http://www.pned.pt/media/31485/Code-of-Sports-Ethics.pdf*), includes a section on recommendations with regard to objectivity, truth and privacy.

In addition, the International Paralympic Committee (2014) created an 18-page document entitled *Guide to reporting on persons with an impairment*. This easy-to-use guide provides journalists with general rules and a list of preferred terminology and incorrect terms. Similarly, in 2012 the British Paralympic Association published *Guide to reporting on paralympic sport* (*http://paralympics.org.uk/uploads/documents/ParalympicsGB_Guide_to_Reporting_on_Paralympic_Sport.pdf*). The Special Olympics (2014) *Style guide* is also available to practitioners.

Other external recommendations

Recommendations also come from institutions that promote the appropriate use of language, such as Fundación del Español Urgente (Fundéu), created in 2005 by the news agency EFE and BBVA with the support of the Royal Spanish Academy (RAE). In 2013, Fundéu created a specific section on the language of football, entitled 'Liga BBVA del Español Urgente' (*http://www.fundeu.es/especiales/liga-del-espanol-urgente/*). Recommendations for the whole sports community are included in *Violence in sport* (*http://www.consejoaudiovisualdeandalucia.es/sites/default/*

files/recomendaciones/Recomendaciones_2009_01_Violencia%20 deporte.pdf), a document jointly produced in 2009 by the Andalusian Audiovisual Council and the regional Federation of Sports Journalists (FPDA).

Media observatories and specialised publications in media criticism

Although there is a lack of observatories exclusively devoted to sports journalism, the largest publications related to media criticism around the world examine the good and bad practices of sports media. A relevant example here is *Ética Segura*, a site created by Fundación Nuevo Periodismo Iberoamericano (Colombia), which regularly promotes debates about ethical issues in the sports field (*http://www.fnpi.org/es/keywords/prensa-deportiva*).

Scholars' and citizens' blogs

Finally, other innovative instruments such as scholars' and citizens' blogs also promote reflection on news quality. In Spain, we highlight *La Buena Prensa* (*http://labuenaprensa.blogspot.com.es/*) and *Periodismo Deportivo de Calidad* (*http://periodismodeportivodecalidad.blogspot.com.es/*). In the United States, two key examples should be considered: the blogs from the National Sports Journalism Center at Indiana University (*http://sportsjournalism.org/*) and the Center for Journalism Ethics at the University of Wisconsin-Madison (*http://ethics.journalism.wisc.edu/*).

CREATING A NEW SPECIALISED CODE IN THE FIELD

Bearing in mind that 'sports journalism should not be exempt from scrutiny regarding conventional professional criteria within the news arena' (Rowe 2007: 386), researchers examined all the materials included in *Accountable Sports Journalism* to produce a new ethical code, named 'Guidelines for covering sports responsibly' (*https://accountablesportsjournalism.org/code/*). In order to bridge the gap between the ideal and professional practice and to encourage journalists to use such guidelines, these have been kept as short and operational as possible. The Decalogue, which was first presented in October 2017 at the annual conference of the Institute of Communication Ethics ('Sports journalism: Ethical vacuum or ethical minefield?'), in London, presents the following points:

1. *Public function and right to sports information*

    Sports journalists should report on all areas of sport. As an essential part of their public-service approach, they should not only concentrate on mainstream disciplines but also give exposure to underrepresented sports that generate news and have a large number of practitioners. This can help to broaden the coverage and expand citizens' sporting culture. Media professionals should not report on the private lives of sports people unless the information is relevant to understanding the athletes' performance.

2. *Conflict of interest*

   Sports journalists should avoid taking part in activities that lie outside of their professional realm or in employment that may create conflict of interest. This includes working in the field of public relations (PR) and as advisors for a sports person, club or federation, and writing for a team or league publication. Editors and reporters cannot be sources who are assigned to themselves. Behaving professionally entails remaining loyal to the news organisation for which one works.

3. *Hospitality from sources and independence*

   Sports journalists should reject invitations and gifts from teams or promoters that could call into question their working as independent eyewitnesses. Likewise, they should not use their position as journalists to obtain free tickets for any sports event from sources other than those which customarily make passes or tickets available when a performance has a clear bearing on the journalist's job.

4. *Newsgathering and impartiality*

   Sports journalists should avoid developing a close relationship with sports sources and maintain a critical distance by seeking and using a varied and representative number of arguments and facts on any issue, and presenting them appropriately without bias towards their audiences. They should also avoid misconduct such as 'boosterism' and nationalistic or chauvinistic approaches. Impartiality entails being professional rather than behaving like fans.

5. *Factual reporting*

   Sports journalists are committed to truthful and factual reporting. They should establish a clear distinction between facts and their personal opinions about them, as well as between news and advertising or sponsored content. Reinforcing methods of verification is essential both to the fight against fake news, the pervasiveness of speculation and rumour in sports content, and also to discarding sensationalism and trivialisation in news reporting.

6. *Journalistic quality and use of language*

   Sports journalists are committed to journalistic quality and must, therefore, rely on a correct use of language as their main working tool to enhance their stories. Acquiring a vast vocabulary and developing the ability to use suitable words and phrases in referring to any sportsperson are valuable assets towards improving content quality within the field.

7. *Promotion of positive sports values*

   Sports journalists should contribute to the promotion of positive values, such as fair play, non-discrimination and international peace and understanding through their coverage of sports events among citizens, with special attention for youth and children.

8. *Violence in sports*

   Sports journalists must avoid using warlike language, as well as disseminating expressions and images that emphasise or legitimate any form of violence towards individuals or groups of people within or outside sports venues. Sport is not a substitute for war. Thus, journalists must minimise confrontational narratives and warlike imagery.

9. *Gender perspective*

   To counteract the long-standing under-representation of sportswomen, sports journalists should work with greater dedication to promote equality in their reporting by giving female athletes more exposure when their results deserve it. More women should be incorporated as expert sources into the news agenda. Sexist comments and stereotypes should be avoided when referring to them.

10. *Sports beyond sports*

    Sports journalists should go beyond the dramatic action on the field and raise public awareness about relevant contexts that exist behind the play. Sports should be thoroughly explained from their social, financial, cultural and political dimensions.

This text is not intended to be read in isolation. Sports journalists should also observe the general principles of trustfulness, fairness, social responsibility and respect for the universal values and diversity of cultures that are included in the baseline codes of the profession. These codes are UNESCO's *International principles of professional ethics in journalism*, the International Federation of Journalists' (IFJ) *Declaration of principles on the conduct of journalists* and further documents available on *https://accountablejournalism. org/ethics-codes*. Beyond these general and specific codes, as well as their organisations' in-house guidelines, sports journalists must seek ethical guidance from within themselves, by placing emphasis on their individual conscience.

CONCLUSION

As outlined at the beginning of this paper, many interlinked factors, constraints, debates and tensions contribute to the quality of the media's output in the contemporary 'fluid and commercially volatile context' (Hutchins and Boyle 2017: 496). That said, sports journalism is a very important commercial engine for newspapers and, therefore, its task should be guided by the same professional values, ethical standards and demands for quality that apply to all journalism. The escalating pressures, orientation towards the market and the tensions of immediacy in this high-speed media landscape should not deter journalists from pursuing the goal of an ethical and comprehensive treatment of sports that ultimately links to media's public service mission in democratic societies.

Weedon and Wilson (2017: 22) pose the following question: 'Could sports journalism (and its educative forms) in the future inherit more from the idealist's vision of journalism as a democratic project intended for the betterment of society, than from the allure and prestige of covering sports?' In the light of this question, we contend that all the actors involved in the communicative process (media organisations, citizens and researchers) are responsible in promoting accountability in sports journalism. With the aim of contributing to this task, this investigation has located, examined and made available to professionals, scholars and citizens the most relevant accountability instruments in this field, stemming from different countries and journalistic cultures around the world. Even though there are differences in the ethical practices of sports journalists 'based at least partly on the expectations and cultures within their beats' (Hardin and Zhong 2010: 9), the resources available in the *Accountable Sports Journalism* platform, as well as the 'Guidelines for covering sports responsibly' code, can help current and future practitioners around the globe to be better equipped to develop their task.

To capture an even greater idea of accountability in sports journalism, further work should be carried out. Following the international approach employed so far, future research must track and thoroughly examine the new accountability instruments that emerge in the field. Drawing on these new contributions, which will be progressively incorporated into *Accountable Sports Journalism*, the proposed guidelines will be updated to point journalists in the right direction with regard to language and the highest reporting standards. To maximise the transference of knowledge of the project, the authors will also present the platform and its code to professional associations, media organisations and higher education institutions in different countries..

- This paper was first published in *Ethical Space*, Vol. 15, Nos 1 and 2 pp 15-28

REFERENCES

Bertrand, Claude-Jean (2000) *Media ethics and accountability systems*, London, Transaction Publishers

Boyle, Raymond (2006) *Sports journalism: Context and issues*, London, Sage

Boyle, Raymond and Haynes, Richard (2014) Watching the games, Girginov, Vassil (ed.) *Handbook of the London 2012 Olympic and Paralympic Games, Vol. 2*, Abingdon, Routledge pp 84-95

Brennen, Bonnie and Brown, Rick (2016) Persecuting Alex Rodriguez: Race, money and the ethics of reporting the performance-enhancing drug scandal, *Journalism Studies*, Vol. 17, No. 1 pp 21-38

Brock, George (2013) *Out of print: Newspapers, journalism and the business of news in the digital age*, London, Kogan Page

Bryman, Alan (2016) *Social research methods*, Oxford, Oxford University Press, fifth edition

Cassidy, William P. (2017) Inching away from the toy department, *Communication & Sport*, Vol. 5, No. 5 pp 534-553

CNOSF (2012) Charte d'etique et déontologie du sport Français. Available online at http://franceolympique.com/files/File/publications/Charte%20ethique%20 et%20de%20deontologie%20 du%20sport%20adoptee%20par%20AG%20 CNOSF%202012.05.10.pd

English, Peter (2016) Mapping the sports journalism field: Bourdieu and broadsheet newsrooms, *Journalism*, Vol. 17, No. 8 pp 1001-1017

English, Peter (2017) Cheerleaders or critics? Australian and Indian sports journalists in the contemporary age, *Digital Journalism*, Vol. 5, No. 5 pp 532-548

Hardin, Marie and Zhong, Bu (2010) Sports reporters' attitudes about ethics vary based on beat, *Newspaper Research Journal*, Vol. 31, No. 2 pp 6-19

Holt, Ron (2000) The discourse ethics of sports print journalism, *Culture, Sport, Society*, Vol. 3, No 3 pp 88-103

Horky, Thomas and Stelzner, Barbara (2013) Sports reporting and journalistic principles, Pedersen, Paul M. (ed.) *Routledge handbook of sport communication*, Abingdon, Routledge pp 118-127

Hutchins, Brett and Rowe, David (2009) From broadcast scarcity to digital plenitude: The changing dynamics of the media sport content economy, *Television & New Media*, Vol. 10, No. 4 pp 354-370

Hutchins, Brett and Boyle, Raymond (2017) A community of practice: Sport journalism, mobile media and institutional change, *Digital Journalism*, Vol. 5, No. 5 pp 496-512

International Paralympic Committee (2014) Guide to reporting on persons with an impairment. Available online at https://www.paralympic.org/sites/default/files/docu ment/141027103527844_2 014_10_31+Guide+to+reporting+on+persons+with+a n+impairment.pdf

Ketterer, Stan, McGuire, John and Murray, Ray (2014) Contrasting desired sports journalism skills in a convergent media environment, *Communication and Sport*, Vol. 2, No 3 pp 282-298

Jennings, Andrew (2011) Investigating corruption in corporate sport: The IOC and FIFA, *International Review for the Sociology of Sport*, Vol. 46, No. 4 pp 387-398

L'Etang, Jacquie (2013) *Sports public relations*, London, Sage

McQuail, Denis (2003) *Media accountability and freedom of publication*, New York, Oxford University Press

Oates, Thomas P. and Pauly, John (2007) Sports journalism as moral and ethical discourse, *Journal of Mass Media Ethics*, Vol. 22, No. 4 pp 332-347

O'Neill, Deirdre and Mulready, Matt (2015) The invisible woman? *Journalism Practice*, Vol. 9, No. 5 pp 651-668

Ramon-Vegas, Xavier and Rojas, José Luis (2017) Mapping media accountability instruments in sports journalism, *El Profesional de la Información*, Vol. 26, No. 2 pp 159-171

Rojas-Torrijos, José Luis (2011) *Periodismo deportivo de calidad: propuesta de un modelo de libro de estilo panhispánico para informadores deportivos*, Madrid, Fragua

Rojas-Torrijos, José Luis and Ramon-Vegas, Xavier (2017) Accountability in social networks. Ever-evolving stylebooks and feedback through Twitter, *Revista Latina de Comunicación Social*, No. 72 pp 915-941

Rowe, David (2007) Sports journalism: Still the 'toy department' of the news media? *Journalism*, Vol. 8, No. 4 pp 385-405

Sherwood, Merryn, Nicholson, Matthew and Marjoribanks, Timothy (2017) Controlling the message and the medium?: The impact of sports organisations' digital and social channels on media access, *Digital Journalism*, Vol. 5, No. 5 pp 513-531

Special Olympics (2014) Special Olympics style guide. Available online at http://media.specialolympics.org/soi/files/resources/Communications/StyleGuide-2014.pdf

Suggs, David Welch (2016) Tensions in the press box, *Communication & Sport*, Vol. 4, No. 3 pp 261-281

Taylor, Daniel (2017) One year after football's child abuse scandal broke, stories are yet to be told, *Observer*, 11 November. Available online at https://www.theguardian.com/football/2017/nov/11/andy-woodward-one-year-on

Tulloch, Christopher and Ramon-Vegas, Xavier (2017) Take five: How *Sports Illustrated* and *L'Équipe* redefine the long form sports journalism genre, *Digital Journalism*, Vol. 5, No. 5 pp 652-672

Weedon, Gavin and Wilson, Brian (2017) Textbook journalism? Objectivity, education and the professionalization of sports reporting, *Journalism*, Vol. 21, No. 10 pp 1-26. DOI: 10.1177/1464884917716503

Weedon, Gavin, Wilson, Brian, Yoon, Liv and Lawson, Shawna (2016) Where's all the 'good' sports journalism? Sports media research, the sociology of sport, and the question of quality sports reporting, *International Review for the Sociology of* Sport, Vol. 53, No. 6 pp 1-29. Available online at http://journals.sagepub.com/doi/abs/10.1177/1012690216679835

NOTE ON THE CONTRIBUTORS

Xavier Ramon-Vegas is a lecturer in the Department of Communication of Pompeu Fabra University. He holds a PhD in Communication from the UPF. He is also affiliated to the Autonomous University of Barcelona Sport Research Institute (IRE-UAB). His research focuses on media ethics and accountability and sports communication. He has been a visiting researcher at the University of Stirling, the University of Glasgow, the University of Alabama, the University of Seville and the IOC Olympic Studies Centre. Contact details: Xavier Ramon-Vegas, Pompeu Fabra University, Roc Boronat 138. 08018 Barcelona, Spain. Email: xavier.ramon@upf.edu

José Luis Rojas-Torrijos is a Senior Lecturer in Journalism at the University of Seville. He also participates in the MA programmes in Innovation in Journalism of Miguel Hernández University and in Communication and Sports Journalism of Pompeu Fabra University, European University in Madrid, Pontifical University of Salamanca and San Antonio Catholic University in Murcia. He holds a PhD in Journalism (2010) from the University of Seville. His research focuses on Sports Journalism, Ethics, Media Innovation and Accountability. Contact details: José Luis Rojas-Torrijos, University of Seville, Avda. Américo Vespucio, s/n. 41092 Sevilla, Spain. Email: jlrojas@us.es

Chapter 13

Ofcom: An evaluation of UK broadcast journalism regulation of news and current affairs

Chris Frost

Recent revelations about journalism ethics in the UK have thrown regulation of the media into the spotlight with the Press Complaints Commission found wanting and suggestions of change for the Office of Communication, the broadcast regulator, making this an ideal time to evaluate its performance. Amongst other duties, Ofcom is responsible for accepting and adjudicating complaints about editorial and programme content from viewers and listeners. Ofcom has received between 5,000 and 30,000 complaints a year, depending on whether some incident catches the public imagination. This paper analyses the thousand or so complaints adjudicated by Ofcom in the period 2004 to 2010 to identify how effective Ofcom is at dealing with complaints, particularly those about news and current affairs. The paper also aims to gain some insight into how Ofcom's adjudications affect programme makers' decisions.

Keywords: Ofcom, Office of Communications, regulation, broadcasting, journalism, complaints

INTRODUCTION

Ofcom, the UK's broadcasting regulatory body, came into existence in January 2003, set up by the Office of Communications Act 2002. Its main legal duties as set out by the Communications Act 2003, are:

1. ensuring the optimal use of the electro-magnetic spectrum;
2. ensuring that a wide range of electronic communications services – including high speed data services – is available throughout the UK;
3. ensuring a wide range of TV and radio services of high quality and wide appeal;
4. maintaining plurality in the provision of broadcasting;
5. applying adequate protection for audiences against offensive or harmful material;

6. applying adequate protection for audiences against unfairness or the infringement of privacy.[1]

Ofcom is funded by fees from industry levied for regulating broadcasting and communications networks; and grant-in-aid from the government. It is answerable to the UK parliament but is independent of the UK government.

At a time when UK media regulation is undergoing its most critical assessment from the public and parliament, including the Leveson Inquiry set up by the government in the wake of the Milly Dowler phone hacking revelations and the closure of the *News of the World*, this paper will look at Ofcom's activities. Although broadcasting has so far largely avoided the criticism heaped on the national press for illegal activities it is an ideal time to examine how Ofcom carries out its regulatory duties enforcing its obligation to protect viewers and listeners (especially minors) from harmful or offensive material and to protect those who might appear in programmes from unfair treatment or invasion of privacy. The paper will attempt to identify trends in complaints and to examine particularly any lessons that can be learnt from complaints about news and current affairs.

People wanting to complain about broadcasting standards or unfair treatment in TV or radio programmes in the UK can complain to Ofcom. Ofcom advises them to contact the broadcaster first, complaining to Ofcom only if unsatisfied with the response, but that is not essential. Complainants are required to complete a complaints form that is available online or can be ordered by post or by phone. Once the complaint is received, Ofcom will carry out an initial assessment to decide if there is a case to investigate. If it feels there has been a potential breach of its code, it will proceed to review the programme, providing details of the complaint to the broadcaster and seek a response.

After considering the complaint and the broadcaster's response Ofcom's content board will then reach a decision about whether the complaint is upheld, not upheld or has been resolved. Board decisions are published on the Ofcom website in a fortnightly bulletin. Some more serious breaches may require that the broadcaster broadcast the adjudication at an appropriate time and in the most serious cases the sanction can include a financial penalty or even a suspension or removal of licence to broadcast.

DATA GATHERING

Data for this study were gathered from Ofcom reports (www.ofcom.org.uk). Ofcom publishes two types of report:

1. an annual report of their activities including statistics of complaints;[2]
2. a fortnightly complaints bulletin identifying every complaint adjudicated.[3]

The fortnightly complaints bulletins allow Ofcom to identify the programme complained of, the broadcaster, the clause of the code complained of and the outcome of Ofcom's adjudication. In the case of fairness and privacy complaints it also identifies the complainant. It does not do this for standards cases, partly because it is not significant and partly because there may be more than one complainant. For instance, in the Ross/Brand case there were thousands of complainants. The detailed data contained within the bulletins were all logged onto a database allowing them to be filtered and manipulated in a way that best allowed analysis.

In order to identify programmes that were broadcast by radio as opposed to those broadcast as TV and in order to identify programmes that were news or current affairs each was tagged if it was radio, or if it was news and current affairs. News and current affairs programmes were identified as being programmes that:

- provided a regular news service or;
- regularly commented on or analysed the news or;
- provided topical in-depth analysis of current affairs.

These included *News at Ten, Newsnight, Panorama, Despatches* and local news services. Programmes that although factually based were either reality television, educational programmes or contained no (or very little news) current affairs such as *Motorway Cops, Neighbours from Hell, Police, Camera, Action*, cookery or nature programmes were excluded from this category.

Tables of data were also extracted from Ofcom annual reports to show total complaints made and programmes complained about. These are identified separately in the analysis below. The aim of analysing these data is to identify how effective Ofcom is at dealing with complaints and to gain some insight into how its adjudications affect programme makers and their decision making. Is Ofcom able to address the issues that are of real concern to viewers and listeners?

ANALYSIS OF OFCOM COMPLAINTS

One way of analysing how effective Ofcom is as a regulator of editorial content in programmes broadcast by licence holders in the UK is to measure the number of complaints made and the responses those complainants receive. There are three main categories of complaint:

- those that complain about a programme but that do not allege breaches of Ofcom's broadcasting code;
- those that complain about a programme and that do allege a breach of Ofcom's broadcasting code and that are resolved after some action by Ofcom;
- those that complain about a programme and that do allege a breach of Ofcom's broadcasting code and that are adjudicated by Ofcom.

Those complaints that do not allege breaches of the code cover everything from complaints about schedule changes to irritation at the ending of a favourite series. These are not pursued by Ofcom. Complaints that are potential breaches of the code are identified in Ofcom's fortnightly complaints bulletin.

OFCOM'S BROADCASTING CODE

Ofcom is required by the Communications Act 2003 to draw up a broadcasting code against which it can measure complaints made. This must cover programme standards (minors, impartiality, accuracy, harm and offence) and fairness and privacy.[4] The development of the two types of complaints (standards – and fairness and privacy) is historical but covers the key areas of concern of legislators. Standards, including matters of taste and decency, violence, sex and bad language were under the control of the Broadcasting Standards Council, set up by Margaret Thatcher in 1988 and given statutory authority by the Broadcasting Act 1990. The Broadcasting Complaints Commission had been set up by the Broadcasting Act 1990 to consider complaints concerning unjust or unfair treatment or unwarranted invasions of privacy (Frost 2000: 188-189).

The two were combined by the Broadcasting Act 1996 to become the Broadcasting Standards Commission. This covered the dual role of the two former bodies, looking at both standards – and fairness and privacy. It sat alongside the Independent Television Commission and the Radio Authority who controlled the licensing arrangements for the independent TV and radio providers (ibid: 200). The BSC was obliged under the Act to produce a code and it relied on past codes, the BBC code and codes in use elsewhere to produce a code very similar to the one still in use today. This was taken over by Ofcom when it replaced the BSC, ITC and Radio Authority in 2003. The key difference with regard to the code was the legislative decision to replace 'taste and decency' with 'harm and offence'.

These new terms are more specific allowing measurement by regulators rather than personal judgement. Offence can be determined to have taken place even if one disagrees it is justified and so regulators need only decide if the offence taken was reasonable or unreasonable. Similarly, harm can be measured by the circumstances. Taste and decency is just that, a matter of taste. The new terms also fit much better with the times smacking less of censoriousness seen by many as unsuitable for the 21st century.

The former BSC code was applied by Ofcom for its first year or so giving it time to consult on a new code that was introduced in 2005. This followed a similar pattern to previous codes and although a new consultation followed a couple of years later, the new code introduced for 2011 was little different covering standards (particularly with reference to minors), harm and offence (the newly updated and more specific names for taste and decency) and elections.

The Ofcom code is broken into ten sections (see table 1). The majority of complaints made largely fall under section 1 (under 18s) and section 2 (harm and offence).

Table 1: Ofcom code and its operation

Section 1: Protecting the Under-Eighteens
Section 2: Harm and Offence
Section 3: Crime
Section 4: Religion
Section 5: Due Impartiality and Due Accuracy and Undue Prominence of Views and Opinions
Section 6: Elections and Referendums
Section 7: Fairness
Section 8: Privacy
Section 9: Commercial References in Television Programmes
Section 10: Commercial Communications in Radio Programming

(see http://stakeholders.ofcom.org.uk/broad- casting/broadcast-codes/broadcast-code/)

Over the lifetime of Ofcom there have been three major issues that have drawn a large number of complaints. The first programme to attract large numbers of complainants was the BBC2 programme *Jerry Springer: The opera* broadcast on 8 January 2005. Critics claimed the programme was blasphemous, contained several hundred swearwords and was very damaging to young people. Ofcom received 8,860 post-transmission complaints whilst the BBC received 47,000 or so complaints before transmission and another 900 after broadcast.

Channel Four was the next to trigger widespread protests when Ofcom received more than 45,000 complaints about alleged racism in *Celebrity big brother* (C4) in 2007-2008. This was followed by the *Russell Brand show* (BBC Radio 2) in 2008-2009 in which Russell Brand and his guest Jonathan Ross rang actor Andrew Sachs and left an offensive message on his answer machine. The show was broadcast on 18 October 2008 and two complaints were received by the BBC the next day. The *Mail on Sunday* ran a story that the BBC might be prosecuted for obscenity on 26 October and the number of complaints rose by a further 1,585.

By the end of the week, the BBC had received 30,500 complaints. The final total was 42,851. Ofcom investigated having received 1,939 complaints by 25 October 2008 and in April it fined the BBC £80,000 for breaches of the privacy section of the broadcasting code and £70,000 for breaches of the harm and offence section.[5] These three were the biggest cases in terms of the number of complainants and therefore, presumably, the amount of upset caused.

HOW THE ANALYSIS WAS DONE

The analysis was carried out by compiling information on all the complaints taken up by Ofcom and published in its fortnightly bulletins. The data were compiled into a database giving access to all Ofcom's decisions about complaints made. The database includes information about the outcome, the clause of the code against which the complaint was made, the programme and the broadcaster. Ofcom adjudicates on complaints concerning 200 to 300 programmes drawn from the many thousands of complaints it receives every year. Complaints may be unadjudicated either because they are duplicate complaints or because the complaint does not breach the broadcasting code. There are, therefore, three headline statistics (to March 2011):

- total number of complaints made: 172,191;
- total number of cases (programmes complained about, some of which may attract hundreds or even thousands of complainants): 49,753;
- total number of cases in potential breach: 999.

Ofcom receives a considerable number of complaints each year from viewers and listeners (see table two and figures one and two).

Table 2: Complaints to Ofcom

Year	cases closed	complaints made
2004-5	1,149	4,184
2005-6	1,102	14,227
2006-7	1,483	5,575
2007-8	12,726	67,742
2008-9	13,203	27,549
2009-10	10,888	28,281
2010-11	9,202	24,633

(Ofcom 2004-2011 annual reports)

Although the figures for 'cases closed' is reasonably steady for the first three years and then increases dramatically by more than 10,000 to remain reasonably static again for the next three years, complaints-made numbers can vary wildly from just over 4,000 to more than 67,000.

The number of complaints made reflects the number of complainants in any one year and so it is not possible to make any real judgement about the variation. Some issues spark large numbers of complainants raising the total in any particular year quite dramatically. Most of the very large increases are explained by complaints made about the high profile, controversial programmes mentioned above: *Jerry Springer: The opera* (BBC2), *Celebrity big brother* (C4) and *The Russell Brand show* (BBC Radio 2). If these complaints are factored out, the figures show that complaints made in the first three years are typically around 5,000 and in subsequent years around 25,000 (see Table 3).

Cases closed refer to individual programmes complained about, rather than complaints.

Typically in the first three years there are around 1,200 *cases closed* and subsequently around 12,000. This jump in both cases closed and complaints made is explained by a change in the way Ofcom has collected the data. When Ofcom first started operations, its Contact Centre logged and assessed the broadcasting complaints received by Ofcom and referred any that raised potentially substantive issues under the Broadcasting Code to the standards team for investigation. It was these complaints that were identified in the annual reports. However, from 2007/8 these data were no longer reported separately and so the much larger total number of complaints made to the Contact Centre (not just those referred to the standards team) were reported. An Ofcom spokesman said:

> This change in the way Ofcom reports on its broadcasting complaints was for the purpose of clarity, and to provide a single picture of the work Ofcom undertakes on regulating broadcasting standards. Therefore, while it appears there was a sudden increase in complaints, the number of cases has remained relatively consistent.

Of course, as awareness of Ofcom and its role entered the public consciousness, an increase in complaints might be expected.

Table 3: Complaints received by Ofcom's standards team after redacting major causes of complaints identified above

2004-5	4,184
2005-6	5,367
2006-7	5,575
2007-8	22,742
2008-9	25,610
2009-10	28,281
2010-11	24,633

Figure 1: Complaints made to Ofcom

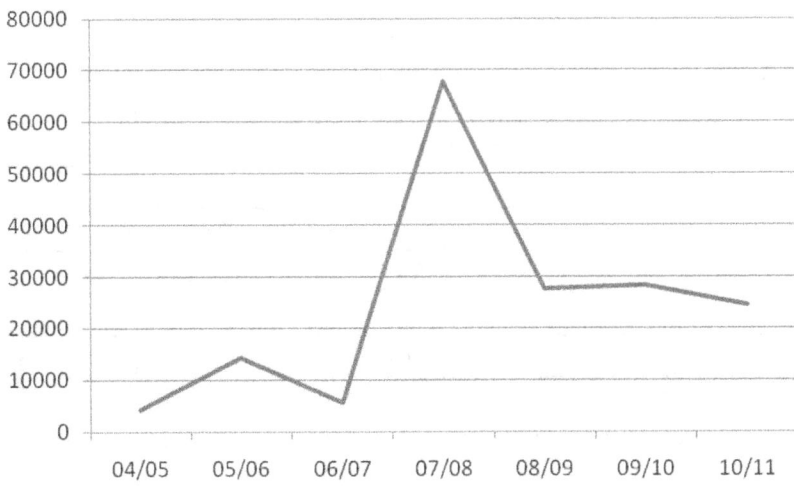

Figure 2: Programmes complained about

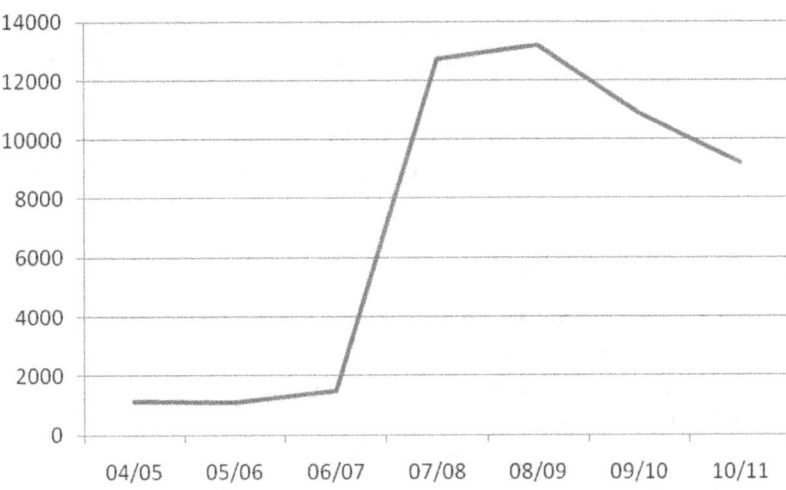

Ofcom investigates complaints made to it after an initial assessment that allows it to reject complaints that are not potential breaches of its code. It then publishes the results of its investigation and whether it has upheld the complaint in its fortnightly broadcast bulletin.[6]

Table 4: All complaints listed in Ofcom bulletins

Year	standards cases		privacy and fairness	
	total	% upheld	total	% upheld
2004	5	60.0	28	28.6
2005	16	0.0	27	37.1
2006	15	26.7	40	37.5
2007	18	66.7	29	20.7
2008	16	50.0	32	37.5
2009	13	81.8	28	10.7
2010	18	46.6	18	16.6

In its first seven years of operation, Ofcom adjudicated 1,522 complaints. These were complaints that allegedly breached its Broadcasting Code and that required Ofcom to reach a verdict. Of these 528 concerned privacy and fairness. Looking at all the complaints, the vast majority are not in breach of the broadcast code and so are rejected. On average each year 7,096 cases are not in breach of the code. An average of 168 standards cases per year are found to be in breach with 61 per cent of the complaints upheld, an average of 15 involving sanctions. The remaining cases are resolved following some action from the broadcaster. An average of 78 fairness and privacy cases are dealt with each year of which 28 per cent are upheld (see Table 4).

NEWS AND CURRENT AFFAIRS

Ofcom does not separate out its decisions on complaints made against news and current affairs and other programming. However, it is possible to identify news and current affairs programmes in the complaints bulletins and flag them in the database so that they can be calculated separately.

For news and current affairs complaints, there is an average of 14.4 standards cases per year of which 47.4 per cent are upheld and an average 28.9 fairness and privacy cases per year of which 27 per cent are upheld. This compares with an average 155.3 standards complaints about non-news programmes per year of which 62.1 per cent are upheld and an average 57.9 fairness and privacy cases per year of which 27.2 per cent are upheld (see Table 5).

The biggest subject of complaint within news and current affairs is fairness closely followed by privacy with 112 complaints (48.5 per cent of the total) being about fairness and 51 complaints about privacy (22.1 per cent). There are fewer news and current affairs programme complaints than for other types of programme with a ratio of standards programmes complaints of 10.8:1 and for privacy and fairness complaints of 2:1. However, without calculating a ratio of transmitted news programmes to entertainment programmes (something that is outside the scope of this research) it is impossible to say whether this is significant.

However, if the ratio of standards complaints in non-news and news are indicative of the ratio of entertainment and news and current affairs programmes, it is clear that the chances of news and current affairs intruding on someone's privacy or treating them unfairly is much higher than for non-news programmes as the ratio of the number of news complaints is much higher. Since many non-news programmes are fictionally based or require active participation, this is probably not too surprising and may not mean anything.

Table 5: Complaints about news and current affairs listed in Ofcom bulletins

Year	standards cases		privacy and fairness	
	total	% upheld	total	% upheld
2004	5	60.0	28	28.6
2005	16	0.0	27	37.1
2006	15	26.7	40	37.5
2007	18	66.7	29	20.7
2008	16	50.0	32	37.5
2009	13	81.8	28	10.7
2010	18	46.6	18	16.6

Table 6: Complaints about other programmes listed in Ofcom bulletins

Year	standards cases		privacy and fairness	
	total	% upheld	total	% upheld
2004	136	47.1	40	17.5
2005	151	35.1	49	25.6
2006	156	31,4	51	17.3
2007	129	74.4	75	39.7
2008	183	78.7	86	35.7
2009	168	83.9	91	31.8
2010	164	84.1	13	23.0

Table 7: Ofcom adjudications of news and current affairs complaints by type from 2004 to 2010

Total complaints: 303

resolved: 37 12 %

Not upheld: 164 54.1 % upheld: 74 24 %

Complaint type	Number	as %	Upheld		As
1 Children:	19	6.27	Uph	7	36.8
2 Harm and Offence:	31	10.2	Uph	6	19.4
3 Crime:	2	0.66	Uph	0	0
4 Religion:	1	0.33	Uph	0	0
5 Impartiality:	10	3.30	Uph	3	30
6 Elections:	4	1.32	Uph	1	25
7 Fairness:	139	45.9	Uph	20	14.4
8 Privacy:	65	21.5	Uph	9	13.8
9 Sponsorship:	16	5.28	Uph	14	87.5
10 Competition:	13	4.29	Uph	12	92.3
Not classified:	1	0.33	Uph	0	0

Figure 3: Fairness and privacy adjudications

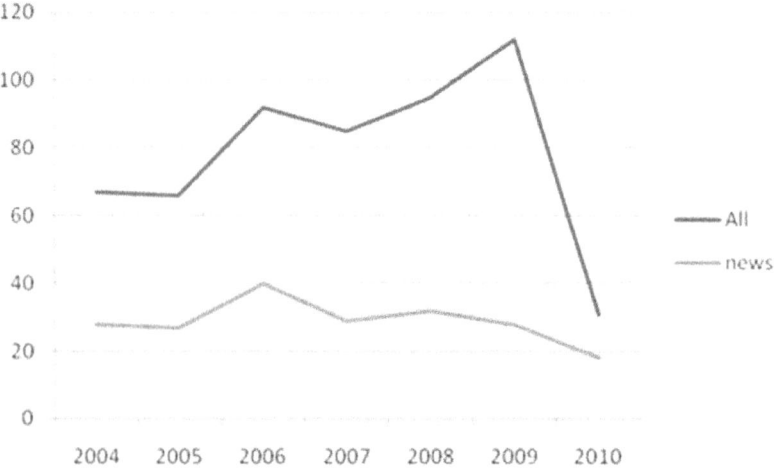

Complaints made against the code sections listed above fall into two categories: those where the harm is done to the subject of the programme (or someone else in the programme) and those where the harm is done to the viewer. The key sections of the broadcast code for news and current affairs are privacy, fairness, impartiality and accuracy, children, harm and offence.

- Fairness and privacy involve complaints that are nearly always made by someone involved in the programme (or someone complaining on their behalf), usually the subject of the programme. There can be two types of complaint involved here: intrusion or unfairness during the making of the programme and/or intrusion or unfairness by broadcasting or by what was broadcast. In this type of complaint, the harm is usually alleged to have been done to the subject of the programme.
- Accuracy and impartiality complaints can be made by someone involved in the programme, but they are more usually made by someone who was not involved in the programme. These types of complaint often concern a harm (inaccurate information) done to the viewer or another but can be a harm to the subject in that it misrepresents them.
- Harm and offence complaints have to be made by others as they concern only the effect a programme can have on viewers.
- Children: complaints concerning children are generally made by viewers about programmes they fear may harm children or offend those responsible for caring for children. If the complaint concerns a child as the subject of a programme these are likely to be made by a parent or guardian of the child and concern intrusion into privacy.

An analysis of all the complaints about news and current affairs adjudicated shows that the number of fairness and privacy cases upheld was fairly small: 20 for fairness and nine for privacy; fewer than one-sixth of the complaints being upheld on adjudication in either case. Looking through the upheld standards cases, there are no obvious lessons to be learned other than continued vigilance over code issues. However, on privacy and fairness it is possible to categorise and consider several types of complaint.

Two of the privacy and fairness complaints concern candid filming that risked being intrusive at the scene: the first a woman filmed during a police drugs raid and the second a woman filmed at the scene of a traffic accident in which her daughter died. In both, Ofcom decided that the broadcasts were unfair and had invaded the women's privacy and should not have been broadcast. Neither was considered to have been intrusive at the time of filming as had there been a strong enough public interest reason for broadcasting then Ofcom might have accepted that transmission was justified. Several of the unfairness complaints concerned interviewee expectations. It is difficult to tell through the filter of the Ofcom bulletin whether these were errors of judgement, different expectations from interviewee and interviewer or simply the news bulletin failing to live up to the promises made. The 18 upheld fairness complaints (some of which were also privacy complaints) covered the following issues that have been split into three main categories:

UNFAIRNESS: PRIVACY AND UNFAIRNESS

Complaints where intrusion into privacy was also judged to be unfair:

1. a woman was filmed handcuffed and in nightwear during a police drugs raid; she was not charged with any offence;
2. an attack victim was promised she could give a description of her attackers, which was not in the end transmitted, and 'body shots' invaded her privacy.

UNFAIRNESS – REPUTATION

Complaints which were unfair because of choice of language:

1. allegations of Saudi Arabian 'sweeteners' were unfair;
2. use of the word 'flop' was pejorative and thus unfair.

Complaints which were unfair because of implications made:

1. a report suggested a council chief executive's job was at risk;
2. a Sikh priest was unfairly maligned;
3. ITV overstated ASA concerns about an advert;
4. coverage of a festival claimed it was a cover for illegal immigration (two complaints).

Complaints which were unfair because there was no right to respond:

1. complainant's radio station was criticised without right to respond;
2. a woman's accusations were said to be false allegations, which treated her unfairly;
3. a report on the collapse of a money transfer company (two complaints).

UNFAIRNESS – SOURCES

Conduct of relationship with source did not go as promised:

1. an interview was not conducted as expected and as promised;
2. the retraction of news piece was unfair to the reporter;
3. a woman agreed to take part in an interview if her identity was obscured but pictures of her were used;
4. surreptitious footage of a hospital was unwarranted;
5. a confidential complaint.

The broadcasters concerned were:

ITV1	4 complaints
Bangla TV	3 complaints
Panjab Radio	2 complaints
STV	1 complaint
BBC1	1 complaint
Radio 4	1 complaint
Sky	1 complaint
Five	1 complaint
Channel 9	1 complaint
Isles FM	1 complaint
Channel S	1 complaint

PRIVACY

Privacy complaints covered the following issues:

1. a woman was filmed handcuffed and in nightwear during a police drugs raid; she was not charged with any offence (as 1 above);
2. an attack victim was promised that a description of her attackers would be given, but it was not, also 'body shots' of her invaded her privacy (two complaints as above);
3. a woman injured in a road accident in which her daughter died was filmed and the film transmitted without permission (two complaints);
4. a programme examining the murder of the complainant's sister without seeking permission should have informed the complainant that the programme was to be broadcast;
5. clandestine filming in a nursery school;
6. a report on the collapse of a money transfer company (as 3 above).

From broadcasters:

ITV1	4
BBC1	3
Bangla TV	1

CHILDREN

Complaints under the children's section concerned either violence or bad language. In two of the three language complaints the words were contained in the lyrics of pop songs. The programme had accidentally played the full version, not the 'radio edit' version of the recording. In one case, a story about child pornography, library footage had displayed website addresses for pornography sites which could have been easily read by children. ITV had three complaints upheld, whilst Sky, GEO News, Isles FM and OneFM each had one complaint upheld. This was considered a significant enough problem for Ofcom to have issued further guidance on 30 September 2011: 'Ofcom warns TV broadcasters to be more careful around watershed.'[7]

Three of the five harm and offence complaints concerned flashing lights, two against BBC1 and one against Sky. The Ofcom broadcast code warns against flashing lights as they may trigger photosensitive epilepsy. The other two complaints concerned a CCTV film of a late night knife attack (GMTV) and murder and an anti-Semitic joke on Radio Faza. Although all of the complaints that were upheld were breaches of the code, none was serious enough to warrant sanctions.

SANCTIONS

One of the major differences between Ofcom and the Press Complaints Commission is the power Ofcom has to levy sanctions against serious breaches of the broadcasting code. Ofcom is able, under statute, to reprimand a licence holder, levy a fine, suspend a licence or remove a licence altogether. It is the last two sanctions, relying on Ofcom's power to grant or refuse licences to transmit, that are seen as particularly controversial when Ofcom is suggested as a model for press regulation. The government is obliged to have some system to regulate the airwaves, which are a finite resource, and so using this as a method to punish licence holders who regularly breach the broadcast code has some logic. Most commentators seem to view this as unacceptable for the press or web-based news outlets.

Ofcom uses these powers infrequently and while it has suspended the occasional licence and even removed one altogether, these have been small specialist digital stations, involved in the soft porn end of the market. The majority of serious sanctions have been fines and, up to the end of 2010, Ofcom had fined stations a total of £6.221m. averaging £135,239 a year. The year 2008 was a particularly punitive year with 19 programmes facing fines of £4,612,500, an average of £242,763. However, this was the year when competitions based on phone-in voting were run with many of them closing voting or being repeat broadcasts allowing the public to vote, even though their votes would not be counted.

Granada Television, LWT and GCap Media Ltd were all fined more than £1m. each. ITV2 and MTV were both fined in excess of £250,000. The BBC was involved in the Ross/Brand affair and also had problems with Sport Relief,

Children in Need Comic Relief and several radio shows and was fined a total of £495,000. Other penalties range from £2,500 to £1.2m. with a typical penalty around the £50,000 level. It is worth noting that no news or factual programme in the study period has breached the code badly enough for Ofcom to consider a sanction.

It is probably impossible to come up with a research method that would show whether penalties are successful in enforcing good practice. However, the general view from the public is that sanctions are likely to promote good behaviour and certainly large fines are not liked by shareholders, or (especially in the case of the BBC) by the public. The fact that sanction penalties fell significantly in 2009 following a number of serious incidents and then rose slightly the following year adds credence to this view, but is hardly incontrovertible evidence.

Table 8: Total sanctions levied by Ofcom

Year	total £	average £
2004	52,500	26,250
2005	185,000	30,833
2006	385,000	12,8333
2007	390,000	78,000
2008	4,612,500	242,763
2009	240,000	40,000
2010	356,000	71,200
Total	6,221,000	135,239

However, the compliance routine of all major broadcasters, particularly but not solely the BBC, does much to maintain high standards. The requirement of evidence of discussion of ethical decision making and a contractual requirement to adhere to guidelines are contained in the BBC's procedures and its compliance forms. Knowledge and proper implementation of the guidelines are central:

> When applying the guidelines, individual content producers are expected to make the necessary judgements in many areas, but some issues require careful consideration at a higher level. The guidelines therefore advise, and sometimes require, reference to more senior editorial figures, Editorial Policy or experts elsewhere in the BBC such as Programme Legal Advice (BBC Editorial Guidelines 2011: 2.2.3).

CONCLUSION

The recent outcries against the tabloid press and the setting up of the Leveson Inquiry have led a number of observers and politicians to wonder if broadcasting also has problems, whether Ofcom ought to be given a role in regulating the press or whether there should be a joint media regulator. The data here make it clear that complaints can be made about news and factual programmes and are taken seriously by Ofcom which is then able to take a serious line against transgressors. This seems to have enormously improved standards of journalism in broadcasting, with no evidence of increasing problems, no increase in complaints numbers and no significant problem complaints in the news and factual programming area.

Most breaches seem to be mistakes, minor errors of judgement or misunderstandings. This is despite an open complaints procedure allowing all to complain and despite accepting complaints that concern harm and offence, neither of which is fully the case with the Press Complaints Commission. Ofcom also has the ability to levy sanctions, but has not needed to do that for a news programme.

The PCC receives complaints mainly about accuracy (approximately 70 per cent) or privacy (20 per cent) whereas Ofcom's biggest complaint category is fairness (46 per cent) followed by privacy (22 per cent) and harm and offence (10 per cent). There is, of course, some crossover between accuracy complaints to the PCC and fairness complaints to Ofcom. Many accuracy complaints made to the PCC are in reality about fairness or about offence. The PCC also does not accept complaints about harm and offence except in very limited circumstances. Tempting though it might be to have a cross-media regulator, these figures do suggest that there are different problems to address in broadcasting to newspapers.

The final question is whether these figures show that Ofcom should have a role in regulating the press. Ofcom's ability to levy sanctions means that the industry certainly seems to take it much more seriously than the newspaper industry takes the PCC, whatever editors say about taking PCC reprimands seriously in their evidence to Lord Justice Leveson. Ofcom's guidance is noted and acted on and there is little evidence of repeat breaches in news programmes. The statutory support that Ofcom can rely on to enforce its decisions on all broadcasters, the openness of the complaints procedure and ability to impose sanctions are all elements that would strengthen press regulation and should be considered by Lord Justice Leveson, but the idea of a media council spanning all media would probably be a mistake.

Despite convergence and the requirement for newspapers, magazines and broadcasters to have websites, a single media council would find it very difficult to give sufficient weight to newspapers and to broadcast news in comparison to the heavy load of TV entertainment programmes in a digital age that will see a steady growth of low-budget specialist channels. Leveson should look to Ofcom for ideas, but should ensure the press, and their websites, continue with their own, but much stronger, regulation.

- This paper was first published in *Ethical Space*, Vol. 9, No. 1 pp 22-31

NOTES

[1] See http://www.ofcom.org.uk/about/what-is-ofcom/statutory-duties-and-regulatory-principles/, accessed on 24 November 2011

[2] See http://www.ofcom.org.uk/about/annual-reports-and-plans/annual-reports/, accessed on 16 October 2011

[3] See http://stakeholders.ofcom.org.uk/enforcement/broadcast-bulletins/, accessed on 16 October 2011

[4] See C4 S319-328 Communications Act 2003. Available online at http://www.legislation.gov.uk/ukpga/2003/21/contents, accessed on 28 September 2011

[5] See http://stakeholders.ofcom.org.uk/binaries/enforcement/content-sanctions-adjudications/BBCRadio2TheRussellBrandShow.pdf, accessed on 28 September 2011

[6] See http://stakeholders.ofcom.org.uk/enforcement/broadcast-bulletins/, accessed on 28 September 2011

[7] See http://media.ofcom.org.uk/2011/09/30/ofcom-warns-tv-broadcasters-to-be-more-careful-around-watershed/, accessed on 28 September 2011

REFERENCES

BBC Editorial Guidelines (2011) Available online at http://www.bbc.co.uk/guidelines/editorialguidelines/page/guidelines-using-roles-responsibilities/#editorial-responsibility, accessed on 21 November 2011

Frost, Chris (2011) *Journalism ethics and regulation*, London, Pearson Education, third edition

Ofcom (2011) The Ofcom broadcasting code, February. Available online at http://stakeholders.ofcom.org.uk/broadcasting/broadcast-codes/broadcast-code, accessed on 1 November 2011

Ofcom (2004-2011) Broadcast bulletins. Available online at http://stakeholders.ofcom.org.uk/enforcement/broadcast-bulletins/, accessed on 1 November 2011

Ofcom (2003-2011) Annual reports. Available online at http://www.ofcom.org.uk/about/

NOTE ON THE CONTRIBUTOR

Chris Frost is Emeritus Professor of Journalism at Liverpool John Moores University where before retirement he was head of journalism. He previously worked as a journalist and newspaper editor. He is a National Executive Council member of the National Union of Journalists and chair of the NUJ's Ethics Council. He is a former President of the NUJ, chair of the Association for Journalism Education and member of the UK Press Council. He has written a number of books, papers and book chapters on journalism including *Journalism ethics and regulation* (now in its fourth edition) and *Privacy and the news media* and has lectured extensively at home and abroad. Contact details: 38 West Park Road, Bramhall, SK7 3JX. Tel: 01618792844; mobile: 07976296777; email: profcfrost@gmail.com.

Chapter 14

A better death in a digital age: Post-Leveson indicators for more responsible reporting of the bereaved

Sallyanne Duncan and Jackie Newton

Reporting death has always been a controversial and sensitive subject for both the bereaved and journalists, but after revelations from the Leveson Inquiry of poor ethical behaviour towards the bereaved this form of reporting is likely to come under greater scrutiny. Research indicates journalists would welcome further guidance, particularly in relation to using social media. The bereaved also would appreciate a more equitable relationship with the media. Through interviews with journalists and bereavement groups, this paper explores their views on the effect the Leveson Inquiry might have on reporting bereaved people, lessons that can be learned, and on any measures which could be adopted in the future.

Keywords: death reporting, bereaved, death knock, Leveson, ethics, regional press

INTRODUCTION

On 29 November 2012, Lord Justice Leveson published the report from his inquiry into the culture, practice and ethics of the press. Many victims of press abuse and intrusion who gave evidence at the inquiry welcomed his proposals for an independent regulator supported by measures for statutory underpinning. A total of 143,704 people had signed a petition set up by the Hacked Off campaign for a free and accountable press by 6 December, calling for Lord Leveson's recommendations to be implemented by the government, which could be taken as a sign of the public's outrage at press treatment of vulnerable people (Hacked Off 2012).

Clearly, many victims, some of them ordinary bereaved families, suffered terribly from the appalling behaviour of certain journalists and their news organisations. Breaches of the Press Complaints Commission's editors' code of practice, and indeed the law, figure regularly in these victims' stories and consequently their calls for tighter regulation would seem legitimate and relevant. Regardless of what form of regulation is introduced it is apparent that a new, more explicit and potentially more stringent set of guidelines will be required for the industry to appear to change its working practices. These are likely to focus on the industry's relationship with the public, and given the evidence presented by victims at the Leveson Inquiry, they are likely to wish to address, in particular how the press treats vulnerable people such as the Dowlers, the McCanns and the Bowles family.

Reporting the bereaved and traumatised is a customary activity for regional media journalists so perhaps there are elements of best practice that could be adopted in any guidelines for the new regulatory body. But between the extreme cases that were outlined at Leveson and the ideal behaviour of a free and faultless press lies a great deal of muddy water where journalists' ethical decision-making can go adrift. Even the most comprehensive guidelines cannot cover every situation. Interpretation will always be left up to the individual, and within that interpretation an errant journalist can stumble. Research has indicated that journalists would welcome greater guidance in death reporting whilst the bereaved would appreciate a more equitable relationship with the media (Duncan and Newton 2010, Newton and Duncan 2012). Thus, it would seem a suitable time to address both the needs of journalists and the bereaved. The authors have conducted a total of 79 interviews as part of a larger death reporting and social media project; 55 with predominantly regional reporters and editors and 24 with bereavement groups and families. A further eight follow-up interviews were undertaken to clarify positions and experiences after Leveson.

WADING INTO MUDDY WATERS

Journalism by its very nature is intrusive (Newton and Duncan 2012) as reporters need to be able to ask questions in order to secure stories. Even when interviewing the bereaved this intrusion generally is accepted as a necessary part of the process, and the death knock is seen to be a legitimate part of a journalist's job (Keeble 2009). However, that intrusion becomes damaging when journalists prioritise the story at the expense of the people they report. Several journalists, news managers and proprietors did this in the publications involved in the hacking scandal when they went after the story and treated people like commodities where the ends justified the means. In his report, Leveson explained that an overarching complaint from victims was that the press 'failed always to treat individuals with common decency'. He said: 'The way in which parts of the press treated the Dowlers, the McCanns, and Christopher Jefferies indicates a press indifferent to individual privacy and casual in its approach to truth, even when the stories were potentially extremely damaging for the individuals involved' (Leveson 2012: 3.2.1: 473).

Here, the morality of the action was based solely on the ends of getting stories and not on the manner in which they were achieved. However, the inquiry may well have left the public with the perception that all intrusion is unwelcome, which is not necessarily the case, and that all newspaper journalists treat the subjects of their stories casually, which is definitely not the case. Many regional and national reporters have received acknowledgements from families who believe they have handled the story of their tragedy well (Willis 2010; Griffiths 2005). Journalists who report traumatic events have to intrude on the grief and shock of those directly affected by the loss but when a grieving relative agrees to an interview they are giving their approval for the intrusion. That said, they are not giving their permission for the journalist to act in an ethically agnostic manner, rather they place a level of trust in the journalist to act responsibly. Sometimes this is misplaced and the journalist can get it wrong by being ethically naïve or by being caught off guard. Thus, they end up in muddy waters where their intentions may have been legitimate but the execution can appear 'indifferent' and 'casual'.

This happened with Kay Burley, a news reporter and presenter at the UK's Sky News, who by her actions in interviewing vulnerable people stirred up a storm of public outrage, mostly on social media site, Twitter. She was covering the disappearance of five-year-old April Jones from her home in Machynlleth, mid-Wales on 1 October 2012. Four days later while reporting live she broke off from interviewing a fellow journalist about the police's view that they did not expect to find the child alive to ask a woman nearby for her reaction. The woman, who had been helping in the search, made it clear she had only just heard the news that the abduction investigation had become a murder inquiry. Her distress was evident and at this point she was joined by another woman, who on hearing the news also became distressed. Within minutes Twitter was inundated with complaints about Burley's conduct, including one from Tom Watson MP, who described her questions as 'insensitive, bordering on cruel' (Sabbagh 2012).

In their guidelines on privacy, the section that deals with the treatment of vulnerable people such as the bereaved, Ofcom, the independent regulator and competition authority for the communications industry in the UK, states: 'Broadcasters should not take or broadcast footage or audio of people caught up in emergencies, victims of accidents or those suffering a personal tragedy, even in a public place, where that results in an infringement of privacy, unless it is warranted or the people concerned have given consent.' It adds: 'People in a state of distress should not be put under pressure to take part in a programme or provide interviews, unless it is warranted' (Ofcom 2012: 8.16-17). Ofcom received more than 300 complaints from viewers and on investigation they found that there was no clear breach of the broadcasting rules and as a result it did not warrant more detailed scrutiny (Faull 2012). This may have been because when adjudicating complaints they consider certain potential pressures on broadcasters covering such stories which might make it difficult to judge at the time whether filming or recording is an unwarrantable infringement of privacy (Ofcom 2012: 8. Foreword).

It is evident that Kay Burley found herself in a difficult ethical place. She was reporting on live rolling news and had stumbled into informing an interviewee of the probable death of the child, and then asked them for their reaction. Much of this would seem contrary to professional standards and strategies in reporting the bereaved. She broke the news of a potential death. She apologised then asked her interviewees for their reaction. She made the classic error in death reporting by asking: 'How are you feeling?' Kay Burley is an experienced journalist, yet she seemed to be wrong-footed when dealing with traumatised people. Was this insensitive reporting? Did she show errors of judgement? Was it right for Kay Burley to keep the cameras rolling? Shouldn't her director have pulled the plug when it was clear she was getting into difficult territory? To be fair, she was also working in the digital environment of live rolling news, where time for reflection is minimal and pressure on reporters is significant

The charity Disaster Action in their submission to the Leveson Inquiry reported an instance of two competing broadcasters both attempting to interview a woman bereaved in a disaster, and squabbling about it in front of her. Burley was perhaps less conscious of ethical constraints because she was interviewing volunteers whom she may have assumed were not vulnerable because they were not April's family. However, this case highlights the need for news teams, regardless of the medium, to assume collective responsibility in their dealings with the bereaved, rather than leaving it to the judgement of the reporter who is face-to-face with a grieving or upset person and consequently, whose judgement may be impaired.

This happened despite guidelines from an apparently robust independent regulator, her considerable experience of live reporting and the consent (albeit implicit) of her interviewees. By contrast, US TV reporter Jeff Gradney says he leaves the cameras behind when first approaching victims of violence or survivors of disaster. He said: 'To hell with taping that first moment of intense emotion. This story will air for a couple of minutes at most; if we do it right, it'll replay for a day or two. But the family lives with this for a lifetime' (cited in Coté and Simpson 2000: 103).

Despite Ofcom's ruling the public perception was that Kay Burley had failed 'to treat individuals with common decency' (Leveson 2012: 2.3.2.1: 473). In a similar situation when a tabloid newspaper journalist broke the news to a grieving family that a body had been found, the Press Complaints Commission (PCC) said in their adjudication on a complaint, which was upheld, that 'newspaper staff should be well-equipped to deal with unexpected situations' (PCC Report 1997: 73). However, as both examples show they are not always. Post-Leveson independent regulation, even with statutory underpinning alone is unlikely to address insensitivity and errors of judgement. Journalists need to develop a robust ethical framework in order to make trustworthy decisions. One regional managing editor interviewed for this study said of Leveson:

> He has been asked to come up with proposals to deal with a problem triggered by 1 per cent of the media which has nothing to do with the rest

of us. I think his role is reactive and doesn't allow him to consider positive ways of building on a lot of great work which is routinely being done in journalism. His focus will be 'how do we stop families being hounded by disreputable reporters' and not 'how can we help families and journalists to frame fitting memorials to their loved ones'.

Thus, it can be deduced that an independent regulator is not the sole solution. A more positive attitude and change of focus in reporting vulnerable people may go some way to modifying the public's perception of the press in these circumstances. Regulation can be a fitting guide but education, training and experiential learning can play a vital role too. Detailed guidance from regulatory bodies which extends beyond a clause or two in a code of practice and transparency in the newsroom about expected and acceptable behaviour would also assist significantly. Engaging journalists in informed discussion of ethical issues to increase their awareness and to encourage a greater understanding of grief, anxiety and bereavement could change the focus from bereaved people as commodities to bereaved people as partners in the story.

CHANGING FOCUS: ETHICAL JOURNALISM IS BETTER

Given the statement by the regional managing editor above it would seem that the media in general could learn from the practices of experienced, ethical journalists in order to adopt a more positive attitude, change of focus and thus improve the profession's image. This was borne out from the interviews undertaken for this research. One daily digital editor said:

> I would hope he [Leveson] will codify the sort of good practice already enshrined in the [PCC] editors' code and followed actively by most regional media, who have always tended to be more sensitive towards victims/ relatives in their community.

This view was supported by other respondents who said that they did not think their approach would be any different after the Leveson Inquiry because, as one regional daily journalist said, she 'always took account of moral and ethical issues during interviews'. The respondents made recommendations for good practice. These included:

- contacting a family only once;
- gathering the story from authoritative sources when the relatives do not wish to participate;
- treating the bereaved with tact, care and sensitivity;
- adhering to the fundamentals of good journalism such as accuracy, and
- building trust with the bereaved through the quality of their reporting.

Limiting contact to one approach, as advised by the PCC's editors' code, was particularly important to reporters. One freelance journalist, and former tabloid news reporter, said:

> If they say no, I would just leave it. In the past, I would be asked by the news desk to return to a door several times, and would do that. Things have changed a lot since then though. For me, being my own boss, I wouldn't put myself in that position.

Some respondents emphasised that accountability could lead to better journalism and if all journalists were in touch with their community – the people they report and those who read their reports – they might behave better. One local newspaper reporter said:

> We realise that we will continue to be in the community so you therefore do not want to step on any toes, whereas a national newspaper can swoop in, do the story, get what they need in any way they can and within reason not have to deal with the consequences.

Although this was a common view among regional journalists, national reporters interviewed said such notions were based on old practices and prejudices and were not necessarily true in recent times, even pre-Leveson.

Autonomy in the manner in which they cover a story about the bereaved was extremely important to reporters. One said she was very lucky to have editors who trusted her to get the facts right and to behave responsibly. This trusted relationship was also acknowledged by a news agency editor who said she listens to any concerns her reporters may have. She said: 'On no occasion have any of them expressed concern about knocking a door. In turn, I have never asked them to go back to a bereaved family's door after an unsuccessful doorstep.' One reporter recognised that not all reporters had a trusted relationship with their editors and this could have a strained effect on the story. She explained that whilst she now had considerable control because she is a freelance this was not always the case:

> It's hard for young reporters to stand up to news desks, especially if they are shouting down the phone to try again, try the neighbours, try the granny, the auntie etc. You knew the story would be reported in a way the news desk wanted, regardless of what you did. Often they had a specific line in mind before you even left the office.

This view was echoed by a former *Sun* reporter who felt that more stringent regulation would not necessarily help reporters to make the right ethical choices and that pressures from the newsroom culture would continue to be detrimental. He said:

> You have to have your own parameters. You have to know what's worth pursuing and what isn't and always do it with sensitivity. People die, and death touched me more than I thought when I was a reporter. Whereas

you used to have time to write a story with details, circumstances and be able to get some kind of picture of the people involved, newspapers don't allow for that anymore. It's like we've got to have quick hits.

Whilst autonomy is important to the journalists they were well aware of the need to recognise a hierarchy of ethical decision-making. Editors, in particular, did not believe that newsrooms needed to be more democratic so that reporters had greater input on the ethics of reporting stories about the bereaved. This was, as one digital editor said, because 'established protocols are drawn up by experienced journalists' who had previously covered such stories. However, he added: 'A good boss will always take account of reporters at the cliff face.' Additionally, a regional daily news editor explained that reporters could exercise control over appropriate conduct during an interview. In her news organisation they could refuse to work on a particular story if they felt it ethically compromised them or they could insist their byline was not used, thus putting the onus back on the news editor. This would seem to be evidence that the conscience clause proposed by the NUJ and by Lord Leveson, which has been dismissed by some journalists as unworkable, is actually being practised in some form within the regional press. She added:

> Newspapers have a strict hierarchy because decisions have to be made very quickly in a busy newsroom. I cannot imagine it would work if individual reporters were involved in making editorial decisions. If the editor and the news editor are good at what they do, this shouldn't be an issue.

Even a local newspaper reporter felt that she did not need to be involved in this decision-making. She said: 'I think my own moral code and the fact that I work for a company who are very respectful of people means that we always handle these stories with care. I don't think I need to have more say in it.'

The national newspaper reporters interviewed felt they also had a degree of autonomy in their practice. 'You are making individual judgements every day as a reporter. I only do what I believe to be ethically sound and in line with the PCC code. I can't speak for others.'

That said, generally the respondents would welcome clear guidelines on the type and scale of activity that is acceptable, providing greater transparency for them as well as the grieving family and the public, although a news agency editor felt there were too many variables amongst news organisations to regulate conduct effectively. She said:

> Even if rules are introduced, will small independent agencies abide by them? Will tabloid journalists, working under immense pressure from news desks to get the scoop, stop and ask themselves if knocking a door for the second time is unethical? Will journalists and desks who abide by rules get sick of not getting the story? They could lose readers.

Training for young journalists who may lack the professional experience to reflect critically on their approach to reporting the bereaved was a recommendation made by one regional editor. She said: 'Being sent on a death knock is a really difficult thing to do and in my experience reporters are left to sink or swim. They are usually thrown into this situation with little or no preparation.'

Further guidance from media regulators on social media would assist in improving behaviour when reporting the bereaved. As noted in previous research the belief is that journalists have a right to use social media material that is in the public domain because it has been placed there consciously by users (Newton and Duncan 2012). However, a daily digital editor thought social media operators should take greater responsibility here, and not merely make this the media's concern. They should 'give overt warnings to their users that their words/images were in the public domain, and thus they had given up rights to reasonable privacy'. The onus could also be placed on news organisations and media interest groups, such as the Newspaper Society, the Society of Editors and the National Union of Journalists, to devise transparent procedures for staff/members. For example, a news agency editor explained that her company did not allow its staff to use photographs from a social media site but a consequence was that sometimes they failed to secure a picture unless the family or the police provided one.

Throughout their comments the respondents emphasised the need to respect the people involved in their reporting, and this had been lacking in the journalists whose disreputable practices led to the Leveson Inquiry. One local newspaper reporter, whilst recognising that many ethical journalists work on national newspapers, observed: 'The basic principles of reporting have been lost. The news agenda has been warped around this need to know more about people's private lives and that is where it all went wrong. I feel there are a lot of ruthless reporters working for these titles who let their ambition overrule human decency.'

National newspaper reporters interviewed for this project were dismissive of the perception that regional journalists were automatically more ethical than their national counterparts – particularly as all those participating had trained on regional papers. One suggested such a notion was simplistic and took no account of the many experienced national reporters who have interacted with vulnerable interviewees without complaint and have won plaudits from the industry for some of their stories. Research (Newton 2011; Disaster Action 2001-2011) and subsequent interviews for this study suggested that complaints from the bereaved were widespread, with regional newspapers, magazines, TV journalists and documentary makers all being named as culpable. Nevertheless, a participant from a red top tabloid said that while he felt his practice was always ethical, the newsroom culture pre-Leveson could sometimes be intimidating. 'I think in the past year journalists have reviewed the way they act and become far less bullish in the way they work.'

FOCUS ON THE FAMILIES

Newton (2011) found that incidences of perceived intrusion after a tragedy came from relatives who objected to being door-stepped shortly after they had been told of their loss. Perhaps the only obvious way any regulator could deal with this is by restricting the death knock altogether. However, the majority of participants did not complain about being approached in such a way, and some were expecting the call, so if the practice were restricted this could arguably disadvantage the majority of bereaved families. One participant said: 'The dangers are families who would like to pay tribute to loved ones, seek redress or go for justice have less of a voice. Not everyone has the confidence and know-how to approach a newspaper.'

Family members participating had an understanding of the reasons journalists approached the bereaved, but shared journalists' concerns about repeated approaches. Newton (ibid) found that support groups were willing to act as intermediaries between the bereaved and the media in the immediate aftermath of a tragedy but lacked the funds and volunteers to do so systematically. However, one national tabloid reporter said journalists were increasingly using intermediaries:

> The recent case of the British students killed in a polar bear attack is a relevant example. My newspaper made no direct approach to families at all. Instead, we went via the travel company in charge of the trip who made it clear no family members of those killed wanted to speak. Later on, however, a surviving victim did wish to talk and gave an interview to us which he and his family were delighted with.

Expert witnesses from victims' organisations felt that greater accountability was important all through the process, from first visit to finished story. Although intrusion can be upsetting, participants were concerned that longer lasting damage can be done by sensational coverage and insensitive portrayal of the victim. One bereaved mother said:

> One thing that should be addressed is how they portray and sometimes slaughter the victim when the story should be about the perpetrator. It is extremely unfair for the victim's family to have to read that or hear it in the case of TV and radio. I felt I had to put forward all sorts of information and pictures to 'defend' my daughter after the things written.

Regulation is too blunt a tool to deal effectively with the majority of problems the bereaved have with coverage, which are more concerned with insensitivity, neglect of families' wishes, lazy labelling of victims, and carelessness with detail than with intrusion. These can be ameliorated to an extent by more informed journalism education, better newsroom awareness of bereaved people's needs and good listening on the part of the reporter. Families have asked that journalists sent out on such jobs act with honesty, sympathy and maturity; honesty about what they are looking for and what the outcome is likely to be, sympathy and sensitivity when carrying out the interview and maturity to understand some of what this tragedy means to the family. One support group organiser said:

> We need the media; what we don't need is sensational coverage that devastates the families. Journalists should imagine the headline they are writing is about one of their family members. How would they like it? How would that affect their family?

A problem with framing guidelines in this area is that families have differing responses to the initial contact with the news media and coverage after a tragedy – and their views can change over time. This often means that practices perceived as being 'ethical' in one case can be disadvantageous in another. One bereaved mother was horrified by the graphic and explicit description of the violence used in the reports of her daughter's death, some of which were extreme by any journalistic standard. Years later she believes those same reports, although still painful, actually fulfilled a purpose; that of demonstrating how horrific the murder was and how her daughter suffered.

> I didn't like that at the time because I felt there was no need for it, especially when her children could be exposed to it, but now I think it did show the perpetrator for what he was, how evil he was. It's difficult. Your view can change.

Several participants at the Leveson Inquiry, who were concerned with the lack of victims' rights, emphasised how necessary the press were to their campaigns. Bereaved parents Audrey and Paul Edwards describe the news media as sympathetic, respectful and courteous and say they are in contact with many more families in similar situations who have been treated well by journalists. They ask that nothing be done which would give extra protection to those in public office against 'legal attempts by the press to make any malfeasance on their part public knowledge' (Leveson Report).

CONCLUSION

Independent regulation with stringent penalties may help curb outright abuses by the press like the ones identified in the Leveson Inquiry; however, these incidences are rare. Many journalists – on both the national and regional media – strive to be ethical practitioners, and that is evident from the respondents' comments. This suggests that those journalists already have a good understanding of ethical practices when dealing with the bereaved. An independent regulator, just like self-regulation, will not be able to address many of the ethical dilemmas faced by journalists on a daily basis; rather these will be left to reporters and editors on the spot to solve. Errors of judgement will occur and given the profession's current public standing and the call for rigorous regulation there could be anxiety, particularly amongst novice reporters, that errors will in the future be interpreted as deliberate unethical behaviour, and punished accordingly.

Regulation alone will not improve professional standards. It needs to be underpinned by journalists developing a rigorous ethical framework. A considerable number already possess this and education and training, discussion and promotion of good practice and a desire to do the right thing could develop this in the future. A key factor is the need to treat people with common decency, which means respecting interviewees, remembering they are not commodities and that it is not all about the story. Respect for people can also be demonstrated by journalists' recognition that the bereaved are not a homogenous group (Newton 2011), and this study underlines the concern that 'ethical' restraints suggested by some would work against the best interests of others. There is a danger acknowledged by both journalists and a number of bereaved families that increased regulation will result in journalists avoiding families rather than be accused of intrusion, harassment or misrepresentation. Therefore, it is important that any regulatory body understands the full extent of media relationships with the bereaved rather than just the shockingly intrusive examples heard by Leveson.

Those bereaved by tragedy are individuals with personal stories to tell, thus journalists should not narrow their approach; they have to be led by the family's needs. Of course, journalists will get it wrong sometimes but they should strive to do the least harm and develop the social skills to deal with emotion and trauma. Bereaved relatives wish to be interviewed by journalists who can act with honesty, sympathy and maturity. Journalists too, need to be clear about their role within the reporting of tragic death. Ultimately, these stories are 'an acknowledgement of what the living owe the dead – of how we must honor [sic] them – of which stories we should tell about their lives, and of what we have learned from them' (Kitch and Hume 2008: xxiv).

- This paper was first published in *Ethical Space*, Vol. 10, No. 1 pp 22-28

REFERENCES

Coté, W. and Simpson, R. (2000) *Covering violence: A guide to ethical reporting about victims and trauma*, New York, Columbia University Press, second edition

Disaster Action (2001-2011) Interviews about disaster experience: Personal reflections and guidelines for interviewers. Available online at http://www.disasteraction.org.uk/support/da_guide11.htm, accessed on 5 December 2012

Duncan, S. and Newton, J. (2010) How do you feel? Preparing novice reporters for the death knock, an exploration of attitudes and approaches, *Journalism Practice*, Vol. 4, No. 4 pp 439-453

Faull, J. (2012) Ofcom drops investigation into Kay Burley following April Jones volunteer interview, *The Drum*. Available online at http://www.thedrum.com/news/2012/11/19/ofcom-drops-investigation-kay-burley-following-april-jones-volunteer-interview, accessed on 19 November 2012

Griffith, J. (2004) Private grief, public kindness, *Insight*, Winter p. 37

Hacked Off (2012) Campaign for a Free and Accountable Press petition. Available online at http://hackinginquiry.org/petition/, accessed on 6 December 2012

Keeble, R. (2009) *Ethics for journalists*, Abingdon, Routledge, second edition

Kitch, C. and Hume, J. (2008) *Journalism in a culture of grief*, New York, Routledge

Leveson Report (2012) *An inquiry into the culture, practices and ethics of the press*. Available online at http://www.levesoninquiry.org.uk/about/the-report/, accessed on 6 December 2012

Newton, J. (2011) The knock at the door: Considering bereaved families' varying responses to news media intrusion, *Ethical Space*, Vol. 8. Nos 3 and 4 pp 7-13

Newton, J. and Duncan, S. (2012) Hacking into tragedy: Exploring the ethics of death reporting in the social media age, *The phone hacking scandal: Journalism on trial*, Keeble, R. L. and Mair, J. (eds) Bury St. Edmunds, Abramis pp 208-219

Ofcom (n.d.) Broadcasting Code. Available online at http://stakeholders.ofcom.org.uk/broadcasting/broadcast-codes/broadcast-code/privacy/, accessed on 4 December 2012

Press Complaints Commission (1997) Report 73: Mrs P Templeton and Miss C Brown v *Daily Record*. Available online at http://www.pcc.org.uk/news/index.html?article=MTkwOA==, accessed on 19 November 2012

Sabbagh, D. (2012) April Jones: Was Kay Burley right to say family 'don't expect to find her alive'? Available online at http://www.guardian.co.uk/media/2012/oct/05/april-jones-kay-burley, accessed on 2 December 2012

Willis, J. (2010) *The mind of a journalist*, Los Angeles, Sage

NOTE ON THE CONTRIBUTORS

Dr Sallyanne Duncan was a senior lecturer in journalism at the University of Strathclyde specialising in journalism ethics. Her research focuses on reporting trauma, suicide and bereavement. She is the author of the third edition of *Ethics for journalists*, co-author with Jackie Newton of the book, *Reporting bad news*, and co-creator of the award-winning Suicide Reporting Toolkit, an online resource for journalists and journalism educators aimed at improving media reporting of suicide.

Jackie Newton is a senior lecturer at Liverpool John Moores University. She previously worked as a feature writer and features editor, senior subeditor and a designer at the *Liverpool Daily Post and Echo* She has also freelanced for national newspapers and lifestyle magazines. Jackie researches comparative ethics in reporting tragedy and media relations with the bereaved. She has co-authored the book, *Reporting bad news* with Sallyanne Duncan.

Chapter 15

Towards responsible journalism: Code of practice, journalist oath and conscience clause

Raphael Cohen-Almagor

This paper draws on the codes of ethics of a wide range of countries to propose an ideal one for a newly constituted press regulatory body in the United Kingdom. It also suggests the adoption of a journalist oath and including a conscience clause in press journalists' contracts which would protect them from being coerced into doing clearly unethical work.

Keywords: journalism, trauma, grounded theory, emotional labour, bystander effect, gender, mental health

INTRODUCTION

When I was a student at Oxford in the late 1980s, a motion was introduced for the Middle Common Room (MCR) members to ban the *Sun*. The MCR received many daily newspapers and the *Sun* provoked controversy due its sensational, racist and chauvinist nature. MCR members were torn between their liberal commitment to freedom of expression and their egalitarian sentiments to minorities and women. After a heated debate, the motion to ban the *Sun* was accepted. The majority of MCR members felt that this red-top tabloid was beyond the pale of tolerance afforded by my fellow graduate students at St. Catherine's College.

Our decision did not inflict much damage on this popular tabloid. It has continued to sell well in the country and has continued to adhere to sensationalist low standards of journalism. The proprietors and editors of the *Sun* think that ethics is one thing, and making profits is another, and that in case of a conflict between the two the latter enjoys the upper hand. Its Sunday sister newspaper, the *News of the World*, had competed with the *Sun* as to just how low professional standards can be set. Both papers concentrated on celebrity-based scoops and populist news. The *News of the World*'s fondness for sex scandals gained it the notorious nickname 'News of the screws'. It celebrated the exposing of national or local celebrities' drug use, scandals and criminal acts, and its editors and reporters did not shy away from setting up insiders and journalists in disguise to provide photographic and audio evidence, thus violating not only ethical standards but also legal directives.

In 2002, 13-year-old girl Milly Dowler was abducted and murdered. In July 2011, it was reported that the *News of the World* had hacked into her telephone while police were still searching for her. Crude reporters gave her parents false hopes that she was alive. Outrage over the tabloid's conduct prompted Prime Minister David Cameron to appoint Lord Justice Brian Leveson to open an official inquiry into the culture, practice and ethics of the press (*Daily Mirror* 2011) and the *News of the World* was closed down by its proprietor, Rupert Murdoch (BBC News 2011). The hot yellow potato was hit hard by the scandal. Advertisers had been pulling away from the Sunday newspaper, and its circulation had fallen from above 6m. to 2.6m. copies. Murdoch decided to sacrifice one newspaper in the hope of sustaining his $46 billion media empire (Edgecliffe-Johnson et al. 2011). It was a cold and calculated business decision.

Leveson (2012) made many important recommendations for a more responsible press that enshrines the basic values of respect for others and not harming others. These principles, it could be argued, are derived from the philosophies of Immanuel Kant and John Stuart Mill. Kant distinguishes between relative value and intrinsic value, explaining that people have intrinsic value, i.e. dignity and absolute inner worth. Kant identifies dignity with moral capacity, arguing that human beings are infinitely above any price: 'to compare it with, or weigh it against, things that have price would be to violate its holiness, as it were' (Kant 1969 [1785]). By virtue of the autonomy of their freedom, people are the subjects of the moral law. Kant wrote: 'Such beings are not merely subjective ends whose existence as a result of our action has value for us, but are objective ends, i.e. things [*Dinge*] whose existence is an end in itself' (ibid).[1] This deontological ethics proscribes a set of actions, with the effect of constraining our range of options, not because the results will be useful, but because this set of actions is incompatible with the concept of justice (ibid: 54-55).[2] Transgression of the rights of others intends to make use of them merely as means, without considering that, as rational beings, they must always be esteemed at the same time as ends.

In turn, John Stuart Mill's 'harm principle' holds that something is eligible for restriction only if it causes harm to others. Mill wrote: 'Acts of whatever kind, which, without justifiable cause, do harm to others, may be, and in the more important cases absolutely require to be, controlled by the unfavourable sentiments, and, when needful, by the active interference of mankind' (Mill 1948).[3] Whether an act ought to be restricted remains to be calculated. Hence, in some situations, people are culpable not because of the act they have performed, though this act might be morally wrong, but because of its circumstances and its consequences. While Kant spoke of unqualified, imperative moral duties, Mill's philosophy is consequentialist in nature (Mill 1971 [1873], 1973 [1867]). Together the Kantian and Millian arguments make a forceful plea for moral, responsible conduct: always perceive others as ends in themselves rather than means to something, and avoid harming others. Both philosophies accentuate the dignity of the person. As Ronald Dworkin (2011) suggests, the concept of dignity needs to be associated with the responsibilities each person must take for her own life. Dignity requires owning up to what one has done.

The dignity of the person should be cherished and respected unless the person in question acted wrongly, in violation of these same basic liberal values. Under all other circumstances, the pursuit of profit, laziness, over-confidence, arrogance, self-indulgence, contempt, the search for glory and any other partisan motive are never justified as reasons for submitting people to invasive reporting and unprofessional conduct, stripped of any regard to the harmful consequences of the unethical conduct.

CODE OF PRACTICE, JOURNALIST OATH AND CONSCIENCE CLAUSE

When I was a member of the Israel Press Council, I visited press councils in the United Kingdom and Canada and analysed their work. Britain, Canada and Israel have sensational tabloid journalism that does not care much for the work of the press councils, and prints whatever story is likely to increase its sales. Competition and sales are in the forefront of their considerations, not ethics and sometimes not even law. The sensational media see the press councils more or less as lightning rods. They exist to show that the press cares about ethics, that it grapples with ethical dilemmas, that it is interested in what the public thinks; therefore there is no need for restrictive legislation. Press councils are designed to receive and deal with public grievances as well as to calm intolerant tendencies on the part of the legislature (Cohen-Almagor 2002, 2005a, 2006).

Furthermore, the press councils are little known in their respective countries. Large segments of all three societies are unaware of their existence, and many of those who are aware of their presence do not appreciate their work. This is because the press councils are voluntary bodies, with little authority and powers, with very limited abilities, and they enjoy only qualified support of the industry. The press industries want the councils to act as preventive bodies, to pre-empt measures that would interfere with press freedom. They do not really want the press councils to represent the public interests (Cohen-Almagor 2003, 2005b, 2007). They fund the work of the councils and through this they secure their independence. The result is that the public conceives their work as a 'sold game', and most of it remain indifferent or uninterested in what the councils do.

During the past fifteen years I have also studied many codes of ethics from different countries, including the United States, Australia, Canada, Israel and Europe and had many conversations with the leading Israeli experts on codes of ethics, Professors Asa Kasher and Yehiel Limor, who have collected such codes for many years.[4] While the successor to the discredited Press Complaints Commission[5] may be considering a new code of practice for journalists in the UK, it is worth bearing in mind that any code should contain the following ethical principles and norms. Moreover, the code of practice should be incorporated into the contracts of editors and reporters. Editors should see that the code is on the desk of every reporter. Reporters should make themselves familiar with its principles.

Fundamentally journalism is like every other profession in that it comprises three groups of people: the first group constitutes a small minority of *ethical* reporters. These are people who care about ethics, who understand the importance of being ethical, and who guide their lives in accordance with ethical principles. Ethical people are blessed with the ability to self-reflect on their conduct. They are concerned about the impact of behaving badly on the character of one's life, and they care about the consequences of their conduct The second group is also small. It consists of people who are blatantly *unethical*. These people could not care less about ethics. They are motivated by zeal for money, profit, fame or some other partisan interest. They are willing to contravene ethical standards to achieve the aims, and they usually do not shun away from seeing people as means to an end, and from harming others when those others stand in their way to fame and glory. They are comfortable with themselves no matter what they do, and they think little about the consequences of their conduct on others. They greatly care about the consequences of their conduct on themselves.

The third group is the largest group. It consists of *aethical* people. These people violate ethical standards without knowing. They have not developed the awareness of ethical norms. They are oblivious to ethics and morality. They cut corners when needed because they are lazy, uncaring, ignorant, selfish or incurious. They harm others without knowing. The introduction of code of practice, journalist oath and conscience clause are important when we bear in mind this large group of people. With their introduction, these people will require cognition. They will not be able to say: 'I did not know.' Hopefully, with the knowledge will come also the realisation that some things are not to be done. Hopefully, with knowledge of the ethical principles and the understanding of their importance, the first group will grow in numbers.

GENERAL PRINCIPLES

- Human dignity of every individual must be respected (*German Press Council Guidelines* 2001,[6] henceforth *German*).
- Respect diversity, pluralism and multiculturalism (Canadian Association of Journalists, henceforth *Canadian*).[7]
- Minimise harm (Society of Professional Journalists 1996 henceforth *SPJ*)[8]: Do not harm anyone unless you have strong moral justification; do not harm people caught up on the fringes of events that are not of their own making.

- Accountability: Be accountable to the public for the fairness, honesty and reliability of reporting (Norms of Journalistic Conduct, India, henceforth *Norms India*;[9] Australian Press Council, henceforth *Australian*;[10] *Canadian*).
- Responsibility: Think about the likely consequences of your report prior to publication and weigh justifications for reporting against important countervailing considerations.
- Privacy is a human right. As a general rule, do not invade personal privacy (*Norms India*; *Australian*; *Editors' Code UK*; Press Council of Ireland henceforth *Ireland*;[11] New Zealand Code: Press Council's Statement of Principles henceforth *New Zealand Code*;[12] Code of Ethics for Press, Radio and Television in Sweden;[13] Cohen-Almagor 2006). You may invade privacy only when you are certain it is in the public interest, to be distinguished from prurient motives. Following the lessons of the Princess Diana affair (Stanyer 2013; Brown 2008; Cohen-Almagor 2002/2003), it is unacceptable to use long-lens photography to take pictures of people in private places without their consent.
- Accuracy: Strive for accurate reporting. Attempt to collect all relevant facts and apply pertinent considerations. Do your homework before writing. Deliberate distortion is never permissible (*Norms India*; *Australian*; *SPJ*; Israel Code: Rules of Professional Ethics of Journalism 1996 henceforth *Israel Code*;[14] *Editors' Code UK*; *Ireland*).

GUIDELINES: DO
- Invite dialogue and criticisms (*SPJ*).
- Always check and recheck your resources and your own conduct (*New Zealand Code*).
- Distinguish between comment, conjecture and fact (*Editors' Code UK*; Barker and Evans 2007).
- Distinguish between editorial text and advertisements (*German*).
- Admit error and strive to correct it promptly with due prominence (*SPJ*; *Israel Code*; *Ireland*).
- Grant fair opportunity to reply to inaccuracies (*Canadian*).
- Give voice to the voiceless (*SPJ*).
- Treat interviewees with respect and fairness. Interviewees have the right to know in advance the context in which their statements will be used. They must also be told if the interview will be used in multiple mediums (*German*). Recording of interviews requires the consent of the interviewee (*Norms India*).
- Protect confidential sources (*Editors' Code UK*; *Ireland*).

- Apply ethical discretion when paying for stories. Paying criminals, terrorists, racists and other anti-social people for their stories is problematic. When payment is made, disclose this to the public and explain how public interest was served (*Editors' Code UK*; *Canadian*).
- Keep the business side of the paper (influence of companies owned by the publisher) from dictating content to the editorial side (news and views) (*Israel Code*; Steel 2012; Schudson 2008).
- Be vigilant and courageous when you seek justice and aim to hold those with power accountable for their deeds (*SPJ*; Himelboim and Limor 2006 and 2011).

DO NOT:
- Never plagiarise (*SPJ*; *Israel Code*; *Canadian*).
- Do not mislead, misrepresent, fabricate or plagiarise (*Israel Code*).
- Avoid altering images and sound in a way that might mislead the public (*Canadian*).
- Do not obtain or seek to obtain information or pictures through harassment, intimidation, extortion, threats, or persistent pursuit (*Israel Code*; *Ireland*).
- Do not aid in staging, promoting, or exaggerating events or rumours (*SPJ*).
- When using social networking sites to obtain information, do not use subterfuge to gain access to private information; verify the credibility of sources; apply ethical considerations and transparency (*New Zealand Code*).
- Avoid undercover, misrepresentation, deceit, subterfuge or other clandestine methods of gathering information except when traditional open methods of information gathering were exhausted and failed to yield information vital to the public (*SPJ*; *Israel Code*; *Editors' Code UK*).
- Every person wishes to protect her good name. Avoid smearing people by innuendo or implying guilt by association. Avoid malicious misrepresentation and unfounded accusations (*Ireland*).
- Avoid publication of material intended to cause grave offence, harm or to stir up hatred against an identified individual or group (*Ireland*). The application and employment of violence, terror and racism should be condemned in explicit language.
- Avoid prejudicial, discriminatory or pejorative reference to a person's race, colour, religion, sex or sexual orientation, and to any physical or mental illness or disability (*Israel Code*; *Editors' Code UK*). Moreover, editors must make concerted, sustained efforts to recruit, retain and develop staffs that reflect the variety of the communities they serve.

- Do not accept gifts, favours, free goods or services, and other benefits from news sources or organisations that the newspaper may cover (*SPJ*; *Canadian*).
- Do not use or pass to others financial information revealed during research.
- Remain free of associations and activities that may compromise integrity or damage credibility (*SPJ*; *Israel Code*).
- Children deserve particular care and consideration. Do not exploit the innocence of children to get information (Guidelines on Media Reporting on Children, India; *Israel Code*; *Editors' Code UK*; *New Zealand Code*).[15]

Furthermore, the press may adopt its own *Journalist Oath*, similar to the Hippocratic Oath in medicine.[16] The oath is a symbolic step to consolidate trust between the journalists and the public whom they are supposed to serve. In whatever the journalists do, the public can rest assured that journalists avoid any voluntary act of impropriety or corruption. So long as journalists maintain their oath faithfully and without prejudice, may it be granted to them to partake life in the practice of journalism, gaining the respect of the public. However, should they transgress this oath and violate it, may the opposite be their fate. The oath should outline in stringent terms values that would not change over the years. It would become public knowledge if any press agency decided not to accept the oath. A tag of honour will be conferred on those who do. Each press should proudly declare on its front page that its reporters signed and subscribed to the journalistic oath.

The contract of press journalists should also include a *conscience clause* which would protect them from being coerced into doing clearly unethical work that negates their conscience. The conscience clause would be an element in individual journalists' contracts that would grant them the ability to refuse any task that breached a specified ethical code without facing disciplinary action or dismissal for doing so. It is noted that the National Union of Journalists (NUJ) has argued for a conscience clause for many years and, in 2003, was backed by the Commons Select Committee on Privacy and the Media. However, the Press Complaints Commission opposed the proposed measure arguing, instead, that editors were the keepers of ethics in the newsroom and that journalists had nothing to fear. Leveson (2012) begged to differ, saying he was struck by the evidence of journalists who felt that they were hard pressed to contravene the code of practice. Leveson was clearly concerned as the journalistic climate of fear became apparent from the testimonials he received. Journalists were unwilling to speak out which resulted in the necessity to hear evidence anonymously through the National Union of Journalists. They feared that speaking candidly would result in their inability to obtain any employment in the national press. Leveson (2012, Vol. 2, Part F, chap. 3: 483) wrote that 'This feature alone raises real concerns about the culture and practices of the press, in closing ranks and refusing to accept and recognise that legitimate debate about its own role and methods of working is not to be shut down but encouraged.'

Indeed, the NUJ's evidence to the Leveson Inquiry details a culture of high stress, tense atmosphere in which reporters fear to speak out and are afraid of dismissal. Let me quote from the testimony of Michelle Stanistreet, general secretary of the NUJ:

> Those who objected were routinely abused verbally publicly. Humiliation was the most minor punishment for failure. Dismissal or relegation to the least favourable shifts, was much more common. A deliberate climate of fear and tension was created by management to improve performance. The only unwritten rule for those subjected to it were never complain publicly and never refuse an order. This included when being ordered to do something illegal, such as steal documents from a car, which I witnessed on one occasion. Another reporter was encouraged to steal a report from a civil servant's briefcase after getting him drunk in a bar. This latter event I did not witness, but I watched as the order was given over the telephone and later read the said report in the office (Stanistreet n.d.).

The word 'fear' appears eleven times in Stanistreet's testimony. It must be difficult for reporters to carry out their tasks professionally and responsibly in such a difficult atmosphere. This culture of intimidation, unrealistic demands, bullying and humiliation confirms the need for a conscience clause. Leveson thus suggested including such a clause in the journalists' contracts (Leveson 2012, Vol. 2, Part F, Chap. 7: 724; Vol. 4, Part K, Chap. 4: 1705). Stanistreet, in the NUJ's evidence to the inquiry, stated that the union is 'clear that journalists should be able to speak out when concerned about unethical practice and pressures to break the Code of Conduct, without the fear of losing their job or suffering adverse repercussions' (DeLong 2012). Rupert Murdoch, being questioned by the NUJ's counsel John Hendy QC, agreed that he thought the conscience clause was a good idea (Leveson 2012, Vol. 4, Part K, Chap. 7: 1799).

CONCLUSION

Freedom of speech and freedom of the press are important values in every democratic society, *sine qua non* for furthering individual autonomy and promoting civic rights. Freedom of speech is a basic human right, a central condition of political legitimacy, crucial for personal development and the uncovering of truth, essential to both human dignity and to democracy (Mill 1948; O'Rourke 2001; Dworkin 1991, 1996, 2009). Freedom of the press is founded upon the principle that the public should have access to information. It is an instrumental good, good as far as it results in the promotion of public interest and the reinforcement of the democratic ideals (Petley 2012: 537). It is certainly not freedom to conduct any business, falsely using concepts like the 'public right to know' as a pretence to transgress law and ethical norms.

Responsible journalism should acknowledge that morality has a role to play in the gathering of information, in reporting and in publishing the news. Responsible journalism should also acknowledge the need for some uniform principles that would guide the work of all papers and news outlets. The adoption of a detailed code of practice will advance the work of the press, promote professional and ethical conduct and enhance the public trust in the work of the media. Journalism is a serious profession that can affect human lives drastically. Thus it should see for itself that its professional standards are shared by reporters, editors and proprietors; that these standards are known and transparent, and that these standards are meticulously kept because otherwise freedom of the press might be undermined, shifting its perception in the public eye from a value to liability. After all, freedom should never be allowed to slide into lawlessness, and democracy should not be exploited and abused to undermine no less important values we cherish and hold dear: respecting others and not harming others.

- This paper was first published in *Ethical Space*, Vol. 11, Nos 1 and 2 pp 37-43

NOTES

[1] For further discussion, see Bayefsky (2013)

[2] See also Dietrichson (1968: 314-330)

[3] For further discussion, see Williams (1976); Urbinati and Zakaras (2007); Miller (2010)

[4] See Kasher (2005); Himelboim and Limor (2006, 2011)

[5] *Editors' Code of Practice, UK*. Available online at http://www.pcc. org.uk/cop/practice.html

[6] *German Press Council guidelines* (2001) Available online at http:// www.mediawise.org.uk/germany/

[7] Canadian Association of Journalists (n. d.) Available online at http://www.caj.ca/?p=1776

[8] Society of Professional Journalists (SPJ) (1996) *Code of Ethics*. Available online at http://www.spj.org/ethicscode.asp, accessed on 19 January 2014

[9] *Guidelines on media reporting on children*, India. Available online at http://www.presscouncil.nic.in/HOME.HTM

[10] Australian Press Council (n. d.) *General statement of principles*. Available online at http://www.presscouncil.org.au/general-principles/

[11] Press Council of Ireland, *Code of Practice*. Available online at http://www.presscouncil.ie/code-of-practice.150.html

[12] *New Zealand Code: Press Council's Statement of Principles*. Available online at HTTP://WWW.RJIONLINE.ORG/MAS-CODES-NEW-ZEALAND-PRESS-COUNCIL

[13] *Code of Ethics for Press, Radio and Television* in Sweden. Available online at http://www.po.se/english/code-of-ethics

[14] *Israel Code: Rules of Professional Ethics of Journalism*, May 1996. Available online at http://www.rjionline.org/MAS-Codes-Israel-Rules, accessed on 19 January 2014

[15] For elaborate rationale and discussion, see Cohen-Almagor (2014)

[16] Hippocratic Oath. Available online at http://www.indiana.edu/~ancmed/oath.htm

REFERENCES

Barker, Ian and Evans, Lewis (2007) *Review of the New Zealand Press Council*, NZ, November. Available online at www.presscouncil.org.nz/articles/press_council_review.pdf, accessed on 17 February 2014

Bayefsky, Rachel (2013) Dignity, honour, and human rights: Kant's perspective, *Political Theory*, Vol. 4, No. 6 pp 809-837

BBC News (2011) *News of the World* to close amid hacking scandal, 7 July. Available online at http://www.bbc.co.uk/news/uk-14070733

Brown, Tina (2008) *The Diana chronicles*, New York, Anchor

Cohen-Almagor, Raphael (2002) Responsibility and ethics in the Canadian media: Some basic concerns, *Journal of Mass Media Ethics*, Vol. 17, No. 1 pp 35-52

Cohen-Almagor, Raphael (2002/2003) Privacy in two episodes: Princess Diana's death and *Les Editions Vice-Versa Inc. v. Aubry*, International Journal of Communication Law and Policy, Issue 7 pp 1-24

Cohen-Almagor, Raphael (2003) Thesis: Granting the Press Council more teeth, *The Seventh Eye* (*Haa'yin Ha'shviit*), Vol. 44 pp 46-47 (Hebrew)

Cohen-Almagor, Raphael (2005a) *Speech, media, and ethics: The limits of free expression*, Houndmills and New York, Palgrave Macmillan

Cohen-Almagor, Raphael (2005b) The Israel Press Council, *Israel Affairs*, Vol. 11, No. 2 pp. 171-187

Cohen-Almagor, Raphael (2006) *The scope of tolerance: Studies on the costs of free expression and freedom of the press*, London and New York, Routledge

Cohen-Almagor, Raphael (2007) Press councils in Canada, Britain and Israel: Window dressing and lightning rods, *State and Society*, Vol. 6, No. 1 pp 43-75 (Hebrew)

Cohen-Almagor, Raphael (2014) After Leveson: Recommendations for instituting the Public and Press Council, *The International Journal of Press/Politics*, Vol. 19, No. 2 (April)

Daily Mirror (2011) Milly Dowler phone hacking: David Cameron shocked by *News of the World* allegations, 5 July. Available online at http://www.mirror.co.uk/news/uk-news/milly-dowler-phone-hacking-david-182626

DeLong, Donnacha (2012) Leveson's support for the Conscience Clause is a significant gain, *Ceasefire*, 2 December. Available online at http://ceasefiremagazine.co.uk/media-ethics-levesons-support-conscience-clause-significant-gain/

Dietrichson, Paul (1968) What does Kant mean by 'Acting from Duty'?, Wolff, Robert Paul (ed.) *Kant*, London, Macmillan pp 314-330

Dworkin, Ronald (1991) Liberty and pornography, *New York Review of Books*, 15 August

Dworkin, Ronald (1996) *Freedom's law: The moral reading of the American Constitution*, Cambridge, MA, Harvard University Press

Dworkin, Ronald (2009) Foreword, Hare, Ivan and Weinstein, James (eds.) *Extreme speech and democracy*, Oxford, Oxford University Press pp v-ix

Dworkin, Ronald (2011) *Justice for hedgehogs*, Cambridge, Massachusetts, Belknap

Edgecliffe-Johnson, Andrew, Fenton, Bden and Parker, George (2011) Murdoch to close *News of the World*, *Financial Times*, 7 July. Available online at http://www.ft.com/cms/s/0/3874c3da-a8b1-11e0-b877-00144feabdc0.html?siteedition=intl#axzz2r1AN7se9

Himelboim, Itai, and Limor, Yehiel (2006) Journalism and moonlighting: An international comparative study of 242 codes of ethics, *Journal of Mass Media Ethics*, Vol. 21, No. 4 pp 265-285

Himelboim, Itai, and Limor, Yehiel (2011) The societal role of journalism – an international comparative study of 242 codes of ethics, *Mass Communication and Society*, Vol. 14, No. 1 pp. 71-92

Kant, Immanuel (1969 [1785]) *Foundations of the metaphysics of morals*, Indianapolis, IN, Bobbs-Merrill Educational Publishers. Available online at http://www.redfuzzyjesus.com/files/kant-groundwork-for-the-metaphysics-of-morals.pdf

Kasher, Asa (2005) Professional ethics and collective professional autonomy: A conceptual analysis, *Ethical Perspectives*, Vol. 12, No. 1 pp 67-97

Keeble, Richard (2001) *Ethics for journalists*, London, Routledge

Leveson, The Right Honourable Lord Justice Brian (2012) *An inquiry into the culture, practices and ethics of the press*, London, Stationery Office, November

Mill, John Stuart (1948) *Utilitarianism, liberty, and representative government*, London, J. M. Dent. Everyman's edition

Mill, John Stuart (1971 [1873]) *Autobiography*, Oxford, Oxford University Press

Mill, John Stuart (1973 [1867]) *Dissertations and discussions*, New York, Haskell House Publishers

Miller, Dale E. (2010) *J. S. Mill*, Cambridge, Polity Press

O'Rourke, K.C. (2001) *John Stuart Mill and freedom of expression: The genesis of a theory*, London and NY, Routledge

Petley, Julian (2012) The Leveson Inquiry: Journalism ethics and press freedom, *Journalism*, Vol. 13, No. 4 pp 529-538

Schudson, Michael (2008) *Why democracies need an unlovable press*, Cambridge, Polity

Stanyer, James (2013) *Intimate politics*, Cambridge, Polity

Stanistreet, Michelle (n.d.) Second Witness Statement on behalf of the National Union of Journalists, In the Leveson Inquiry into the Press. Available online at http://www.levesoninquiry.org.uk/wp-content/uploads/2012/02/MS-Exhibit-11.pdf

Steel, John (2012) *Journalism and free speech*, London, Routledge

Urbinati, Nadia and Zakaras, Alex (eds) (2007) *J. S. Mill's political thought: A bicentennial reassessment*, Cambridge, Cambridge University Press

Williams, G.L. (1976) Mill's principle of liberty, *Political Studies*, Vol. 24 pp 132-140

NOTE ON THE CONTRIBUTOR

Raphael Cohen-Almagor, DPhil, St. Catherine's College, University of Oxford; Professor of Politics, founding director of the Middle East Study Centre, University of Hull, and Global Fellow of the Woodrow Wilson International Center for Scholars. Raphael taught, *inter alia*, at Oxford (UK), Jerusalem, Haifa (Israel), UCLA, Johns Hopkins (USA) and Nirma University (India). He was also Senior Fellow at the Woodrow Wilson International Center for Scholars, Washington DC, and Distinguished Visiting Professor, Faculty of Laws, University College London. In 2022, he was a Public Policy Fellow at the Woodrow Wilson International Center for Scholars, and in 2023, the Olof Palme Guest Professor, Lund University, Sweden. Raphael has published 19 books and more than 300 articles in the fields of politics, philosophy, media ethics, medical ethics, law, sociology, history and poetry, including most recently *Confronting the internet's dark side* (CUP, 2015), *Just, reasonable multiculturalism* (CUP, 2021) and *The republic, secularism and security* (Springer, 2022). He is now writing *Resolving the Israeli-Palestinian conflict: A critical study of peace mediation, facilitation and negotiations between Israel and the PLO*. Raphael was a co-founder of Israel's 'Second Generation to the Holocaust and Heroism Remembrance' organisation, the founder of the University of Haifa Center for Democratic Studies and the Van Leer Jerusalem Institute Medical Ethics think-tank.

Chapter 16

Reporter power: News organisations, duty of care and the use of locally-hired news gatherers in Syria

Richard Pendry

Risk has drastically reshaped the reporting ecosystem in the Syrian conflict. This paper analyses the roles played by commissioning editors, staff reporters and international and locally hired freelance journalists who report the war in Syria. It gathers data from case studies of the reporting of the Sarin gas attacks in the Damascus suburb of East Ghouta in August 2013 and other examples of reporting in Syria which appear to raise ethical questions. The current lack of reporters in Syria has serious ethical implications for news organisations and their ability to inform the public sphere.

Keywords: Syria; duty of care; outsourcing; sub-contracting; freelances; news gathering

INTRODUCTION: RELUCTANCE OF UK NEWSPAPERS TO HIRE FREELANCES

The starting point of this research was to examine whether news organisations, citing safety concerns, were increasingly refusing to commission work from independent journalists while located in an area of conflict, and particularly those who were uninsured. These are the international freelances who travel to areas of conflict and form an increasingly important part of the news gathering ecosystem, as we will explore below. For the avoidance of doubt, this paper will distinguish between international freelances and local journalists: the latter being the Syrian fixers, activists and other news gatherers whose work finds its way into the output of news organisations. They will be referred to as local freelances. The distinction is significant and reflects a hierarchy of power within the foreign news gathering system. As we shall see, there is a separate system for hiring local freelances, that is not subject to the same scrutiny as their international colleagues.

In early 2013 several UK news organisations stated that they would not hire international freelances to work for them in Syria. After the veteran *Sunday Times* reporter Marie Colvin was killed in Homs in February 2012, her newspaper told UK-based freelance photographer Rick Findler that, though he had previously worked for them in Syria, they would no longer take his work, nor that of any other international freelances (telephone interview, 5 September 2013). Later, an executive at the same newspaper told a reporter from *Press Gazette* that neither *The Sunday Times* nor its sister paper *The Times* would be accepting contributions from international freelances working in Syria (Rodgers 2013). *The Sunday Times*, according to the executive quoted, did not want to encourage freelances to take risks:

> After submitting pictures from Aleppo this week Rick Findler was told by the foreign desk that 'it looks like you have done some exceptional work' but 'we have a policy of not taking copy from Syria as we believe the dangers of operating there are too great'. Findler, 28, has been published before in *The Sunday Times* and has been to Iraq, twice, Libya and this is his third trip to Syria. He said: 'Surely it is that photographer's decision to choose whether or not they take the risks. I thought part of photography was the fact that some people in this world do take exceptional risks to show the rest of the world what is happening. I just don't know what else to do any more. I really feel disheartened and extremely let down' (Rodgers 2013).

Four other British newspapers, the *Guardian*, the *Independent*, *The Times* and the *Observer*, then also went on the record to *Press Gazette* to say that they too would not be taking the work of independent journalists (Turvill 2013). A producer for CNN agreed that the rules of engagement between international freelances and their clients, the news organisations, had changed. He put it down to the death of *Sunday Times* correspondent Marie Colvin: 'When Marie Colvin was killed, it scared the s**t out of a lot of [news] executives' (anonymous CNN producer, telephone interview, 24 October 2012).

WHY A BAN ON INTERNATIONAL FREELANCES REPORTING FROM SYRIA MATTERS

Freelances of all kinds have become an increasingly important part of the news gathering community, a trend noted in the mid-1990s by Pedelty (1995). The traditional model of foreign reporting has largely disappeared. Other researchers, such as Richard Sambrook (2010), have noted a trend away from own-staff or own-country correspondents in conflict zones that is part of a wider change in the idea of foreign correspondence. Syria fits into a longer-term picture in this respect. Because the old business models of the news organisations are broken, there is less cash around to pay for staff reporters (Picard 2014; Franklin 2014). The problem is particularly acute in foreign news (Otto and Meyer 2012). This matters because in major conflicts – such as Afghanistan, Iraq and now Syria – because of risk, ever fewer staff reporters cover quite major developments (Cockburn 2013).

The aim of this research was to test evidence that news organisations had become increasingly reluctant to take responsibility for international freelances working in Syria. The results indicated that this may be so, though it must be acknowledged that the conclusions are highly provisional. My research points, however, to a finding that is possibly more significant – that news gathering in the Syrian conflict has been outsourced to local people. These Syrian nationals either work directly for the news organisations or supply user-generated content on social media to them. The data show it is far from clear that news gathered in such a way accords with the core journalistic norms of impartiality, detachment and balance and this current research suggests a mechanism by which this outsourcing has happened. It could also be part of a longer-term trend away from verification and gatekeeping noted by Rosen. The latter's work suggested that in multimedia reporting some of these traditional norms have been discarded. The result has been fierce debate over what journalism is 'for' (Rosen 1999).

METHODOLOGY

The central hypothesis that I wanted to test with this research was: Do such changes – if they have occurred – serve to restrict independent news gathering? And, if news organisations will not hire international freelances to report conflict, then is there a hole in the model for contemporary war reporting? Above all, is the public sphere still being properly served? Specifically, what I wanted to understand is as follows:

1. Whether the rules of engagement for international freelances have, indeed, changed.
2. If true, why this had happened.
3. Finally, whether any such change in the working relationship between international freelances and their employers, the news organisations, had wider implications for conflict reporting and the audience that consumes news.

APPROACH TO THE RESEARCH

The way news organisations, international freelance reporters and other news professionals, including locally-hired reporters, work with news sources on news stories from war zones is complex (see, for example, Venter 2005). I do not come to this subject as a strictly neutral observer. As a UK-based freelance news gatherer myself I am part of the international freelance 'tribe'. This research is my critical reading of the material gathered from a series of interviewees representing international freelances, news executives and staff journalists. It is difficult to disentangle how all the parties really interact, and the public conversations of all sides in respect of the terms of engagement are often somewhat different to those they have in private.

Goffman (1959 and 1969) would have called this the 'dramaturgical dimension'. Goffman is best known for his study of symbolic interaction, which took the form of a dramaturgical analysis of the performances that occur in face-to-face interactions. The insight he offered was that in theatrical performances there is the obvious aspect actors present to the audience. But there is also the hidden, backstage area, where actors can drop the identities they present publicly and be themselves. This is the area I am investigating.

For example, there were certain power struggles below the surface which affected how people answered me. Freelances are generally wary of complaining about the behaviour of their employers. Editors, news executives and staff reporters who commission international freelances are wary of making public pronouncements that may imply legal responsibility for people who are not under their control and whose behaviour may land their organisation in trouble. The result is that many individuals I talked to were reluctant to go on the record. Other researchers (Venter 2005; Pedelty 1995) have found the same thing. I examined three case studies

1. The reporting of the Sarin gas attacks in Damascus in September 2013. At least one news organisation that had previously said it would not hire international freelances in Syria appeared to change its mind when a major news story broke and there were few independent ways of verifying the truth.
2. A report by Hannah Lucinda Smith for BBC Radio's *From Our Own Correspondent* programme.
3. The death of a young Syrian photographer who freelanced for the Reuters news agency, named Molhem Barakat in December 2013. The case highlighted that reporting in Syria had been to a significant extent devolved from international journalists, whether staff or freelance, to local people. An investigation by the National Press Photographers Association gathered evidence that Syrian freelances, again, working for Reuters, had staged photographs. If true, this would be evidence that Syrian news gatherers on whom the news organisations rely – as do their audience – are in some cases insufficiently supported to do their job truthfully and ethically.

GATHERING DATA

I conducted semi-structured interviews with international freelances who report on the Syrian conflict and the staff journalists and news executives who commission them. I interviewed:

- 19 international (i.e., non-Syrian) freelance journalists working in print, online, radio and television. These freelances work for a range of news outlets, including the international news agencies (Associated Press [AP], AFP, Reuters), the BBC, *Die Zeit*, a range of Austrian news outlets (*Wiener Zeitung*, *Profile* magazine and the Austrian broadcasting corporation [ORF]), VICE News, Channel 4 News, CNN, Sky, al Jazeera, the *Los Angeles Times*, the *International Herald Tribune*, the *Guardian*, *Rolling Stone*, *Le Monde Diplomatique*, *VICE* magazine, the New Zealand *Herald on Sunday*, and Swiss radio SRF.

- Seven staff reporters based in Beirut, London and Cairo. (These individuals work for the BBC, the *Daily Telegraph*, Channel 4 News and Reuters.)
- Six desk editors and news executives (working for CNN, the BBC, AP, AFP, Reuters, *The Sunday Times* and the *Guardian*).

Some of the staff reporters have commissioned both international and local freelances to work for them in Syria. One of these staff journalists, BBC producer Stuart Hughes, conducted an investigation into the death of Molhem Barakat (Hughes 2013) which yielded useful data.

Interviews were conducted by telephone, email and using social media. Facebook was by far the most useful social media site for conducting interviews. Facebook interviews are available to download later, which is convenient for a researcher. But the use of Facebook goes far beyond that in contemporary conflict reporting. Murrell (2014) found war reporters and their collaborators use this social media platform to conduct their reporting and discuss aspects of their work. So it is a convenient way to conduct research in this area.

Two of the interviews with international freelances and one with a staff reporter led to face-to-face interviews in London. I conducted one face-to-face interview in Turkey with a freelance cameraman/director, named Mani, who works for Channel 4. I also questioned a news executive from *The Sunday Times*, Sean Ryan, at an event at the Frontline Club in London in order to follow up an earlier phone interview. The face-to-face interviews tended to be more wide-ranging than the interviews on Facebook. Asking a question at a public event was the least useful way of gathering data.

The most 'offstage' (Goffman 1959 and 1969) data came from a series of posts on a closed Facebook site made by staff reporters and commissioning editors trying to solicit international freelances to report on the previously mentioned Sarin gas attack in the hours after it occurred. At the time of writing this Facebook group is used by 932 journalists, workers in non-governmental organisations and other specialists, such as chemical weapons experts, who research, report on and visit Syria. Most of the site's members are journalists. Like the larger, related Facebook group, the Vulture Club (see Murrell 2014 for more on these Facebook groups), it is administered by Human Rights Watch. I have not named it because it is supposedly a secret group and contains logistical information useful to those wishing to do its members harm.

RESULTS

KIDNAP THREAT IN SYRIA

At the time of writing (March 2015) the New York-based Committee to Protect Journalists estimates about 20 journalists who have been abducted by kidnap gangs remain in Syria (CPJ 2014). The journalists who emerge from Syria tell terrifying tales of mistreatment (see Chivers 2013 and Loyd 2014). Two kidnapped international freelances, James Foley and Steven Sotloff, have been murdered on camera by Islamic State, a self-proclaimed Caliphate aiming to unite Sunni Muslims worldwide. Kidnapping is an effective way of intimidating journalists (Beals 2013). Yet for the first two years of the Syrian conflict, from approximately 2011 to 2013, it was on international freelances that the news organisations relied to gather news.

FREELANCES IN SYRIA

At the beginning of the conflict Syria was largely a freelance's war. The number of journalists killed bears this out. According to the Committee to Protect Journalists (2015a), nearly half – 46 per cent – of the 80 journalists killed in the Syrian conflict were freelance. This compares to a global figure of 17 per cent over the same period (CPJ 2015b). The greatest risks in Syria, however (as in most 'new' wars) are to local news gatherers. Locals make up 85 per cent of the journalist deaths in Syria. They also make up the overwhelming majority of the freelance deaths (CPJ 2015a).

I first heard of new restrictions news organisations were imposing on international freelances from photographer and video journalist Robert King, who had previously worked for AP Television News (APTV) and CNN while in Syria (interview via social media, 10 October 2012). He told me that Channel 4 News wanted him to leave Syria before looking at material he had shot in Aleppo. This was later confirmed by a source on the foreign desk at *Channel 4 News* (interview via social media, 16 October 2012). It became apparent that other international freelances also felt they had to jump through more hoops than formerly in order to work with news organisations:

> In a phone conversation, Sky told me No before they even knew who I was, and said we need people to have done hostile environment training. I said I had done such a course in 2007 and they said it needs to have been done within last three years. Al Jazeera said no as well – I can't remember if it was a blanket ban on freelance stuff, but I remember the message being: 'Don't bother approaching us with your stuff' (international freelance journalist, interview via email, 23 May 2013).

> *Die Zeit Online*, the leading German news site for whom I work, sent me a … formal mail the other day. They say they are not ready to endorse my trip to Syria. That they are not ready to admit that they knew in advance I would be going … This was strange, since I have been writing from Syria for them for two years (international freelance journalist Petra Ramsauer, interview via social media, 13 September 2013).

Another international freelance was unhappy that news organisations were refusing to take the work of all his international freelance colleagues, even the responsible ones. He considers himself one of the latter group. He also complains of the 'hypocrisy' of the news organisations in still using freelances (both international and local) who work for the news agencies – of which more later.

> I think it is a bad habit to ban [international] freelance work altogether, like *The Sunday Times* did (and others). As these newspapers still buy photos from the wire – which is often delivered anyway by [international] freelances. So such steps seem to me hypocritical and in the end only minimise the money a[n international] freelance can earn. [This is because] via the wire you often get less money than if you sell it directly to a newspaper – and the newspaper itself pays less money to get wire images (interview via email, 23 May 2013).

International freelance journalist Petra Ramsauer says the traditional rivalry between staff and freelances also plays a part. She says that a foreign desk (staff) reporter who commissions her conceded as such:

> He did admit that he would use each and every opportunity to 'kick [international] freelances' out of an assignment. And pointing out the security risk is such an opportunity. So the safety issue will also be raised and possibly 'used' by people like him against hiring freelances (Ramsauer, interview via social media, 20 September 2013).

Richard Spencer, Middle East correspondent for the *Daily Telegraph*, says *Telegraph* news executives are as concerned as those from rival news organisations about the consequences if things go wrong: 'From a corporate perspective the management of the *Telegraph* are concerned about the costs of getting people out of kidnap situations,' he says (telephone interview via Skype, 23 August 2013). This is not to ascribe solely negative motivations on the part of news organisations to their decisions about international freelance use. Undoubtedly, news executives really do want to protect inexperienced, naive and untrained individuals who unwittingly put themselves in harm's way. Yet news providers who take responsibility for international freelances also face extremely large bills. Online news company *Global Post* commissioned American freelance James Foley to do the reporting from Syria which resulted in him being kidnapped and beheaded. The firm later spent millions of dollars trying to secure his release (Nye 2014).

Nor is there much agreement among international freelances about how much support they should demand from their clients, the news organisations. Independent news gatherers compete intensely with each other, and an exceptional piece might win an award. So freelances do not speak with a single voice when it comes to their terms of employment. The Frontline Club, a body that represents largely international freelance news gatherers who work in areas of conflict, asked its members what they thought of the restrictions that news organisations place on hiring them. Two thirds of those who responded to a survey (Frontline Club 2012) said they would forgo the support of news organisations if it was the only way they could sell their work. Freelances with fewer skills and less experience were more likely to agree with the proposition. Such people were less likely to have done hostile environment training or be able to afford insurance. These are precisely the individuals whom news organisations are likely to be reluctant to employ. One international freelance acknowledged that they were obliged to work responsibly with the news organisations:

> I think it should be natural that if you work on assignment for a special newspaper or magazine to cover an event inside Syria that both sides respect each other's demands. If a newspaper or magazine hires a[n international] freelance on the ground or wants to buy their stuff I think they should for sure put in some of their resources to advance the security of the freelance, like giving him the same protection level like staff members. That means including him in their security assessments … probably providing him with a satellite device (often too expensive for a single freelance), keeping in regular contact with him and try to help him out if there are problems – and working on a risk plan in the case he gets abducted. On the same issue it should be natural for the [international] freelance to listen to the newspaper or magazine and agree to the terms they have, like the security approach etc. It is mutual giving and taking (British freelance journalist and photographer Benjamin Hiller, interview via email, 29 May 2013).

International freelance journalists say that restrictions on hiring them are designed to protect the news organisation from having to take responsibility for freelances if they get into trouble, rather than any other reason. According to another international freelance, the way it works is as follows:

> If you ask someone before they go in you can influence their safety and planning arrangements but you can potentially be considered liable for their safety. If someone is already inside it is:
> - convenient;
> - they have not yet come to harm;
> - you have no control or influence of their safety;
> - are not liable for them as they went of their own volition;

- it's cheaper as you can commission a piece without discussing covering costs as, well, they are there anyway (international freelance, interview via social media, 2 September 2013).

Most of the international freelances voiced cynicism about the motives behind any ban by the news organisations on accepting their work. They surmised that the motive for the news organisations to – as one put it – 'come up with increasingly bigger hurdles' in the way of employment was for their employers to avoid proper responsibility for looking after them. According to this view, the motive was largely legalistic and had to do with concerns over the legal duty of care which may make an employer liable for an employee.

DUTY OF CARE

The impact of concerns over duty of care on news gathering has been little discussed. A briefing paper by BBC reporter David Loyn (2013) remains the best analysis on the subject. But what is duty of care, and how have expectations over what care needs to be provided changed? Duty of care is a longstanding legal obligation under English and United States civil law that governs the responsibility owed by, for example, employer to employee. Such debate over the application of duty of care to conflict journalism as has occurred has coincided with the professionalism of risk management within news organisations described by Loyn (ibid).

Such debates happen at all levels of the news industry and money does not have to change hands to prompt concerns that one is taking responsibility for someone if they supply goods and services. Nor are legal professionals usually involved in such discussions. Few freelances ever sue news organisations over their failure to provide a reasonable duty of care – photographer Tim Page won a case brought against *Time* magazine in 1981 (King 1981). There has been no recent test in court of how far duty of care extends to international freelances and locally-hired journalists. But as reporters become targets, the question has become more pressing for news executives (CPJ 2014).

DID *THE SUNDAY TIMES* REALLY BAN INTERNATIONAL FREELANCES FROM WORKING IN SYRIA?

After speaking to all parties (*Press Gazette*, the newspaper and British freelance Rick Findler), it is still unclear whether *The Sunday Times* really did stop working with international freelances. Sean Ryan, associate editor of *The Sunday Times*, told the author that the ban was 'all a bit of a misunderstanding' (telephone interview, 29 August 2013). Ryan said that, in fact, the newspaper had been open for business all along with 'responsible freelances'. However, he conceded that no work from international freelances in Syria had been published since the *Press Gazette* piece. Ryan also said that the colleague who made the statement to *Press Gazette* was misquoted. When that was put to the *Press Gazette*, the latter said the quote came in an email from the paper (telephone interview, 30 August 2014).

The contradictory statements made by different news executives at *The Sunday Times* perhaps point to concerns over duty of care. But it was difficult to get a clear answer. When asked at a Frontline Club event what *The Sunday Times* lawyers had told him about how far their legal responsibility for duty of care extended to international freelances, Ryan said he personally had never been given any such advice (Frontline Club 2013). While this may be strictly true, he declined to elaborate what the other executives at the paper might have been told. Another broadsheet correspondent, whose newspaper had not 'banned' international freelances, pointed out that any such ban by *The Sunday Times*, its sister paper *The Times* and the rest was never absolute. *The Times* had sent the most famous war photographer of all to Syria during the period of the supposed ban (Loyd 2012).

> As they themselves say it's obviously not really true – they'll send Don McCullin (as they did) and likewise if they get a killer pic whose provenance can be quickly identified they'll use it – what it really means is that the likely need for an offered story or pic and the quality of the person offering is not worth the time and effort that will be required to discuss all the issues involved and take a view on the product. But perhaps, try again when we really need you (Richard Spencer, *Daily Telegraph* Middle East correspondent, interview via social media, 29 August 2013).

In fact, says Spencer, he is not sure the policy on hiring international freelances is so different in Syria now:

> Actually British broadsheets would have that policy re. war zones all the time – we 'generally' only send staffers and retained stringers who have been through our HET [hostile environment training] programmes and are on our insurance ... though we will make exceptions in special circumstances. I'm not sure for most of us that has changed in any way (ibid).

The freelance photographer, Rick Findler, accepts there may be a security reason not to accept work from international freelances while they are in Syria. There had been suspicions that *Sunday Times* reporter Marie Colvin died because her live broadcasts made her easy to locate:

> I think Marie may have been killed by targeting her electronic transmissions when she was filing. So if the pictures will wait and the publication I am working for insists I leave before I file and I think there *may* be a risk, I will file when I am out of Syria ... I don't have a problem with that (Findler, telephone interview, 5 September 2013).

Finally, it may be that a loose or non-existent 'ban' on international freelances is a useful way of filtering out non-staff journalists that a news organisation is unsure about working with – for a range of reasons including but not limited to safety.

Desk editors have a stockpile of useful phrases for fobbing off freelances while trying not to discourage them and this is a quite useful one for this situation. (See also, 'sounds really interesting but we've just got no space what with Syria/royal baby/Miley Cyrus etc.') Saying, 'we generally don't accept freelance copy' to the photographer is what any editor's going to do on any subject, meaning, if you're going to take up my time, make it bloody good (Spencer, interview via social media, 29 August 2013).

CASE STUDY: SARIN GAS ATTACKS IN AUGUST 2013

Some data that reveal how staff reporters and editors actually work with independent journalists – as opposed to how they say they do – came from the reporting of the Sarin gas attack on the people of the Damascus suburb of Ghouta on 21 August 2013. The gas attack was significant because it was a major news story that quickly became a test of whether the United States and its allies should intervene in the Syrian conflict. If it could be proven that chemical weapons had been used, that would appear to cross what US President Obama had said was a 'red line' that would trigger intervention. Very few international journalists – either staff or freelance – were in the area at the time of the attack so it was difficult to find out who was responsible. Again, the data appear to show how ambivalent news organisations are about using international freelances in the most dangerous areas of conflict.

Within hours of the August 2013 Sarin gas attacks, one British newspaper which had previously said it was not going to commission international freelances, but was now desperate for copy and pictures, ended up soliciting them on the closed Facebook group mentioned above. Phoebe Greenwood, assistant foreign editor of the *Guardian*, was one of several editors who went looking for (international) freelances. Others news organisations included the *Mail on Sunday*, *Channel 4 News* and the *Daily Telegraph*. Of those outlets, the *Guardian* had previously stated they would not use (international) freelances working in Syria (Turvill 2013). On 22 August 2013, the day after the gas attacks, Greenwood said that her newspaper was looking for 'any freelances currently working in Damascus'. Greenwood later said that she was only looking for 'corroboration' for the gas story, not to actually hire a journalist (telephone interview, 5 September 2013). Quite how she was hoping to convince a fellow professional journalist to report for her without the individual insisting on either a byline or payment was not made clear.

CASE STUDY: USE OF INTERNATIONAL FREELANCES BY THE BBC

Another case appeared to show how ambivalent news organisations are about working with international freelances in Syria. British freelance reporter Hannah Lucinda Smith scripted and performed a voice piece for the Radio 4 programme *From Our Own Correspondent* about snipers in Aleppo (2013a) after she had left the country. Smith had been commissioned by an executive in BBC radio at a time when BBC staff reporters had been ordered out of the area. However, I had previously been told by a BBC news executive that there was a ban within the Corporation on using international freelances: 'The principle is that we don't want to create a market which encourages people to take risks. It's not fair to encourage people to do that' (telephone interview, 27 June 2013). It then became apparent that my source had had a row with the BBC Radio editor who had commissioned the freelance, because he believed all departments at the BBC should have the same policy. I was referred to the BBC press office: 'We use our own staff on deployments,' they said (via email, 4 September 2013).

So if international staff and freelances are notably absent from large parts of Syria, who is doing the reporting? It turns out to be the locally-hired freelances.

THE NEWS AGENCIES STEP IN

What is remarkable and significant about the reporting of the Syrian conflict is that locally hired news gatherers have almost entirely replaced a large part of the international press corps. And it is international news agencies ('the wires') that have largely enabled this change. After foreign reporters largely had stopped going to Syria (by the summer of 2013), news organisations began to rely on the wire services to fill the gap. Why did that happen? News organisations pay a flat fee to use as much material from the wires as they want and contractual arrangements for staff are handled by the wires. In this way, the news organisations are not responsible for the safety of the people who provide pictures, words and video that fill the foreign pages of their newspapers and their news websites day after day. Loyn says this is by far the safest option for news executives who are concerned about duty of care:

> Few organisations want to ask questions of whether international news agencies were operating with the same ethical standards that newsrooms adopt for material they buy directly. News organisations take risks up to a certain level, and then pull back to rely on the agencies (Loyn 2013: 6).

The outsourcing of news gathering to local stringers in dangerous reporting environments is not new (see Pedelty 1995 for a discussion of the practice in Salvador). Murrell has noted that the same thing happened during the insurgency in Iraq some years earlier. In her analysis, locally-hired news gatherers working for the wires had become a kind of reporting backstop: 'When a news editor doesn't feel able to send their own staff person, there will usually be something available on the wires' (Murrell 2010: 126). But in Iraq the news organisations had international staff in bureaux in Baghdad to supervise the locally-hired news gatherers – and there were coalition troops to guarantee the safety of the bureau staff. In Syria international journalists are operating in unfriendly terrain: no major news organisation has an office in Damascus with international staff to give locally-hired news gatherers daily support. There is also a large number of other Syrians who gather news, including 'activists' and other sources. This raises questions about whether news gathered in this war accords with the core journalistic norms of objectivity and impartiality (see Rodgers 2012: 47 for a discussion of these related areas). There is nothing new in such concerns. Accordingly, organisations such as the BBC have rules warning of the dangers of using news gatherers with a personal involvement in the story: 'Our audiences need to be confident that the BBC's editorial decisions are not influenced by the outside activities or personal or commercial interests of programme makers or those who appear on air' (BBC Editorial Guidelines). The way locally-hired Syrian staff were contracted by the news agencies caused something like a moral panic in the news industry at the end of 2013.

CASE STUDY: USE OF LOCALLY-HIRED PHOTOGRAPHERS BY REUTERS

It is surely asking a lot of Syrians to expect them to be impartial when reporting their own civil war. Yet the death of 18-year-old Reuters photographer Molhem Barakat in Aleppo in December 2013 shone a light on the difficulties facing news agencies relying on local hires to gather news. Reuters faced accusations that the ethical practice of its news gathering had been undermined by the constraints of operating as a news gatherer of last resort. Initially, the focus was on Barakat's youth; Barakat's age was variously reported as 17, 18 or 19. News insiders were scathing: 'We're entering uncharted territory in terms of the "reportability" of Syria and I fear this is the inevitable result. There's no way Reuters would have put a staffer into Aleppo – but they're prepared to give a teenager camera kit and send him on his way' (BBC News producer Stuart Hughes, interview via social media, 24 December 2013).

But it soon also became apparent that Barakat was no neutral bystander and that had implications for his ability to be impartial. Like many other locals working for international news organisations in Syria, Barakat was deeply involved in the conflict. He was killed alongside his brother Mustafa who was a rebel fighter for the Tawhid militia. According to a *New York Times* investigation (Estrin and Shoumali 2014), Barakat would accompany his brother to battles, taking pictures of his brother and his comrades-in-arms. Sometimes Barakat carried a gun. A journalist who befriended Barakat says the latter had considered becoming a suicide bomber for al Qa'eda:

> In the end he didn't join al Qa'eda; he started working as a photographer, hoping to emulate some of the journalists he was hanging around with. He often asked me if he could work with me and I refused, because I didn't want the responsibility of an eager seventeen-year-old with no war-zone training and little experience on my shoulders. Soon afterwards I saw that he was filing photos for Reuters. I hope that they took responsibility for him in a way that I couldn't, and I hope that if he was taking photographs

as he died in the hope of selling them to that agency, they also take responsibility for him now (Smith 2013b).

Reuters, the news agency that hires the most Syrian photographers in Syria, paid Barakat a day rate of $150 to file for them, and provided his cameras and a flak jacket and helmet. Four other Syrian photographers who worked for Reuters said they were not given the medical, safety or ethics training which would be provided for staff photographers and international freelances who regularly worked for the agency. It was claimed that Barakat and other Syrian news gatherers were largely left to work by themselves. There were no foreign photographers in town on the day Barakat was killed (Estrin and Shoumali 2014). BBC News producer Stuart Hughes asked Reuters whether they had checked Barakat's age, and what was Reuters' policy on purchasing freelance material — in this case from locally hired news gatherers — in Syria. The head of PR at Reuters responded:

> We are deeply saddened by the death of Molhem Barakat, who sold photos to Reuters on a freelance basis. To best protect the many journalists on the ground in a dangerous and volatile war zone, we think it is inappropriate to comment any further at this time (Hughes 2013).

Hughes is concerned that the death of Barakat indicates a wider problem. He says locally-hired news gatherers working in other areas of conflict are normally supervised far more closely than they currently are in Syria:

> When Reuters put out statements like the one they gave me I do despair. Big news organisations (mine included) are looking to social media and citizen journalism etc. as a way of telling stories in a different way, increasing access to places like Syria etc., but when they feel threatened they think they can pull the shutters down and say nothing. Hopefully this case will help show that's not an option anymore – they've got to be more transparent (Hughes, interview via social media, 24 December 2013).

The New York Times's investigation also claimed that Syrian photographers had provided Reuters with staged photographs that were in some cases improperly credited (Estrin and Shoumali 2014). Finally, a separate investigation suggested another example where a Reuters stringer had faked pictures, such as those of a ten-year-old boy supposedly working in a munitions factory (Winslow 2014). In all these cases, Reuters denied their photographers had been working unethically.

DISCUSSION AND CONCLUSION

To sum up, the current study looked for evidence that news organisations had become reluctant to take responsibility for international and locally hired freelances working in Syria. It initially investigated news production and hiring processes relating to two specific stories, the gas attacks of August 2013 and a BBC radio piece through interviews with a broad range of freelances, staff reporters and news industry executives. It found that news organisations are sorely challenged by the current situation in Syria. The result is that they are struggling to perform their core duty to inform the public sphere. The focus of the final part of the research shifted away from international freelances, and on to the people who have ended up doing most of the news gathering – locally-hired news gatherers. But it is unclear whether the increased use of the latter is a change of principle rather than simply a change of scale of use in previous conflicts. The conclusion that news organisations find it difficult to find a way through the resulting contradictions concerning ethics and impartiality is supported by the data gathered from all three case studies.

In the end, this study is really about reporter power. International staff reporters are located at the top of the reporting hierarchy and have the most power. International freelances are located lower down the hierarchy than staff reporters and have less power. Local reporters have least status and the least power. This is in line with Pedelty's (1995) findings about the relative status of the staff, freelancers and stringers or locally hired journalists.

Does the data from this research project have broader implications for journalism and conflict reporting? Syria fits Kaldor's (2006) description of 'new wars' in which control of information spaces became part of the war, to the extent that aspects of the conflict become near invisible. The Islamic State group has successfully closed down the information space by killing freelance international journalists, at the same time as it calls attention to its own radical public relations strategy. It is tempting to connect these two elements. If that connection could be proven that would be an interesting development in the debate about the mediatisation of military forces (see Cottle 2006, Maltby 2012). The long-term trend may be away from robust, independent reporting on the ground. Former BBC reporter Martin Bell, for example, paints a bleak future for conflict journalism. Talking to John Simpson, World Affairs editor at the BBC, Bell said: 'I do not believe that war reporting as we used to do it, from among the people, is any longer possible' (Simpson 2012). Indeed, the number of countries where reporting by international journalists on the ground is little practised now includes Afghanistan, the tribal areas of Pakistan, North Caucasus and Somalia and certain areas in the Middle East. In none of these places are international reporters protected by friendly forces. Before the current war in Syria, a generation of war reporters had grown up with the embedding system in Iraq and Afghanistan (Tumber and Palmer 2004). It has been a shock for many reporters working in Syria to discover how exposed they are when not protected by Nato troops. Cockburn (2013) makes the case traditionally made by war reporters – that there is no substitute for on-the-ground reporting. But journalists and their audience are getting used to the idea that increasingly it just isn't possible.

- This paper was first published in *Ethical Space*, Vol. 12, No. 2 pp 4-13

ACKNOWLEDGEMENTS

This work was supported with a small grant from the Faculty of Social Sciences at the University of Kent.

No conflicts of interest have come to light during its preparation.

Disclosure statement: the author has no income to disclose in relation to the research conducted.

REFERENCES

BBC Editorial Guidelines (2015) Conflicts of Interest: Introduction. Available online at http://www.bbc.co.uk/editorialguidelines/page/ guidance-conflicts-introduction/, accessed on 4 November 2013

Beals, Emma (2013) More and more journalists are being kidnapped in Syria, *Vice*. Available online at http://www.vice.com/en_uk/read/its-getting-much-harder-to-report-on-the-war-in-syria, accessed on 4 November 2013

Chivers, Christopher (2013) American tells of odyssey as prisoner of Syrian rebels, *New York Times*, 23 August. Available online at http://www.nytimes.com/2013/08/23/world/middleeast/american-tells-of-odyssey-as-prisoner-of-syrian-rebels.html?_r=0, accessed on 4 November 2013

Cockburn, Patrick (2013) Diary, *London Review of Books*. Available online at http://www.lrb.co.uk/v35/n19/patrick-cockburn/diary, accessed on 4 November 2013

Committee to Protect Journalists (CPJ) (2014) In Syria, fewer journalist deaths but danger has never been greater. Available online at https://cpj.org/blog/2014/12/in-syria-fewer-journalist-deaths-but-danger-has-never-been-gr.php, accessed on 1 May 2014 Committee to Protect Journalists (2015a) 80 journalists killed in Syria since 1992. Available online at https://www.cpj.org/killed/mid-east/syria/, accessed on 13 April 2015

Committee to Protect Journalists (2015b) 746 journalists murdered since 1992. Available online at https://cpj.org/killed/murdered.php, accessed on 9 February 2015

Cottle, Simon (2006) *Mediatized conflict*, Open University Press, Maidenhead

Estrin, James and Karam Shoumali (2014) Questions about news photographers in Syria arise after freelancer's death, *New York Times* Lens blog, 13 March. Available online at http://lens.blogs.nytimes.com/2014/03/13/questions-about-news-photographers-in-syria-arise-after-freelancers-death/, accessed on 1 May 2014 Franklin, Bob (2014) The future of journalism, *Journalism Practice*, Vol. 8, No. 5 pp 469-487

Frontline Club (2012) The first freelance news safety survey, *Frontline Club News*, 29 May. Available online at http://www.frontline- club.com/freelance_safety_survey/, accessed on 1 May 2013

Frontline Club (2013) The changing state of reporting on Syria, *Frontline Club News*, 20 November. Available online at http://www.frontlineclub.com/the-changing-state-of-reporting-on-syria/, accessed on 21 November 2013

Goffman, Erving (1959) *The presentation of self in everyday life*, Garden City, New York, Doubleday

Goffman, Erving (1969) *Strategic interaction*, Philadelphia, University of Pennsylvania Press

Hughes, Stuart (2013) Available online at http://www.twitlonger.com/show/n_1rudf4i, accessed on 1 May 2013

Kaldor, Mary (2006) *New & old wars*, Cambridge, Polity, second edition

King, Wayne (1981) Combat photographer wins $125,000 in a suit against *Time*, *New York Times*, 15 December. Available online at http://www.nytimes.com/1981/12/15/us/combat-photographer-wins-125000-in-a-suit-against-time.html?smid=fb-share, accessed on 1 May 2013

Loyd, Anthony (2012) Don McCullin's last war, *Times*, 29 December. Available online at http://www.thetimes.co.uk/tto/magazine/article3638191.ece, accessed on 1 May 2013

Loyd, Anthony (2014) 'I thought of Hakim as a friend. Then he shot me', *Times*, 17 May. Available online at http://www.thetimes.co.uk/tto/news/world/middleeast/article4092553.ece, accessed on 1 June 2014

Loyn, David (2013) Newsgathering safety and the welfare of freelancers. Available online at https://frontlinefreelance.org/sites/default/files/Safety%20Report_WEB.pdf, accessed on 1 June 2014

Maltby, Sarah (2012) *Military media management*, London and New York, Routledge

Murrell, Colleen (2010) Baghdad bureaux: An exploration of the interconnected world of fixers and correspondents at the BBC and CNN, *Media, War & Conflict*, Vol. 3, No. 2 pp 125-137

Murrell, Colleen (2014) The Vulture Club: International newsgathering via Facebook, *Australian Journalism Review*, Vol. 36, No. 1 pp 15-27

Nye, James (2014) ISIS tortured James Foley's family with emails warning they were planning to execute him last week, *Daily Mail*, 20 August. Available online at http://www.dailymail.co.uk/news/article-2730260/James-Foleys-former-boss-claims-White-House-knew-journalist-held-captors-showed-no-mercy.html, accessed on 1 September 2014

Otto, Florian and Meyer, Christoph O. (2012) Missing the story? Changes in foreign news reporting and their implications for conflict prevention, *Media, War & Conflict*, Vol. 5, No. 3 pp 205-221

Pedelty, Mark (1995) *War stories: The culture of foreign correspondents*, New York and London, Routledge

Picard, Robert (2014) Twilight or new dawn of journalism, *Journalism Practice*, Vol. 8, No. 5 pp 488-498

Rodgers, Gavin (2013) *Sunday Times* tells freelances not to submit photographs from Syria, *Press Gazette*, 5 February. Available online at http://www.pressgazette.co.uk/sunday-times-tells-freelances-not-submit-photographs-syria, accessed on 1 May 2013

Rodgers, James (2012) *Reporting conflict*, Basingstoke, Palgrave MacMillan

Rosen, Jay (1999) *What are journalists for?* New Haven, CT, Yale University Press

Sambrook, Richard (2010) *Are foreign correspondents redundant? The changing face of international news*, Oxford, Reuters Institute for the Study of Journalism

Simpson, John (2012) Life and death on the frontline, Radio broadcast, 4 May, 20.00hrs, London, BBC Radio 4

Smith, Hannah Lucinda (2013a) Aleppo: A city where snipers shoot children, Radio broadcast, 18 August, London, BBC Radio 4

Smith, Hannah Lucinda. (2013b) On the death of another Syrian: Stuff from my notebook blog. Available online at http://hannah-luci.wordpress.com/2013/12/20/on-the-death-of-another-syrian/, accessed on 1 May 2014

Tumber, Howard and Palmer, Jerry (2004) *Media at war: The Iraq crisis*, London, Sage Publications

Tumber, Howard and Webster, Frank (2006) *Journalists under fire: Information war and journalistic practices*, London, Sage Publications

Turvill, William (2013) Broadsheets back *Sunday Times* decision to decline Syria freelance pics, *Press Gazette*, 19 February. Available online at http://www.pressgazette.co.uk/broadsheets-back-sunday-times-decision-decline-freelance-submissions-syria, accessed on 1 May 2013

Venter, Sahm (2005) *The safety of journalists: An assessment of perceptions of the origins and implementation of policy at two international television news agencies*. Unpublished MA thesis, Rhodes University, February

Winslow, Donald R (2014) Reuters denies ethical allegations, while some Syria photographs still questioned, *National Press Photographers Association Blog*, 18 March. Available online at https://nppa.org/news/reuters-denies-ethical-allegations-while-some-syria-photographs-still-questioned, accessed on 1 May 2014

NOTE ON THE CONTRIBUTOR

Dr Richard Pendry is a senior lecturer in Broadcast Journalism at the University of Kent. He was formerly a member of Frontline News Television, a news agency which specialised in reporting conflict. Richard researches how foreign news is produced in the field using a diverse range of newsgatherers, including open-source investigators like Bellingcat and locally-hired journalists.

Chapter 17

Spies and journalists: Towards an ethical framework?

Paul Lashmar

The publication by the Guardian *in the UK from mid-2013 of secret intelligence documents leaked by the former NSA contractor Edward Snowden was highly controversial. The newspaper was attacked by the UK government, intelligence chiefs, some other news media and a range of other critics for publishing the previously secret documents. The Snowden affair was just the latest episode where the news media sought to publish information about intelligence operations, usually revealing some area of significant concern, in the face of government objections. In each case negotiations between the state and the news media have been adversarial. At the heart of this reoccurring problem is the balance in liberal democracies between national security and the freedom of the press to inform the public over matters of concern. This involves a complex set of ethical issues. This paper seeks to lay out the ethical terrain for this discussion incorporating the emergent discipline of intelligence ethics. The paper also takes the first steps in discussing a bipartisan framework for an ethical relationship between intelligence agencies and the news media that would allow accurate information to enter the public domain without recklessly jeopardising legitimate national security. It examines the various bodies that could act as an honest broker between the two sides but concludes that identifying such an organisation that would be trusted at this time is difficult..*

Keywords: spies, journalist, ethics, national security, press freedom

INTRODUCTION

On Saturday 20 July 2013, at the height of the controversy over the UK publication of the documents leaked by the former NSA contractor Edward Snowden, in the basement of the *Guardian*'s King's Cross, London, offices, a senior editor and a *Guardian* computer expert used various tools to pulverise the hard drives and memory chips on which the encrypted files had been stored. The decision was taken after a threat of legal action by the UK government that could have stopped reporting on the extent of American and British government surveillance revealed by the documents. It was only the most absurd moment in the tense negotiations between the *Guardian* and government about what documents would be published. It had been a protracted negotiation.

The Snowden affair is just the latest episode where the news media sought to publish information about intelligence operations, usually revealing some area of significant concern, in the face of government objections. In each case, negotiations between the state and the news media have been adversarial and the government position was that publication would harm national security. In retrospect, government claims largely look insubstantial and reveal a primary intention of seeking to protect them and/or the intelligence community from embarrassment rather than national security. The epitome of this episodic confrontation was the *Spycatcher* affair of the 1980s when the UK government went to the Australian courts to unsuccessfully block publication of a book by Peter Wright, a former senior MI5 officer, revealing profound concerns over the operations of the security service (Wright 1987). However, it is also true that in publication there can be national security issues that journalists are unaware of. Any improvement in relations would have to be based on trust, where often there is little (see Phythian 2005; Lashmar 2013). Following on from the ad-hoc adversarial negotiations at the UK end of the Snowden affair it is not unreasonable to assert there needs to be more mature and responsible approach from Whitehall and the UK news media.

At the heart of this reoccurring problem is the balance between national security and the freedom of the press to inform the public over matters of concern. This paper seeks to lay out the ethical terrain for this discussion. The academic discourse of ethics and intelligence has only been a serious if limited area of study in the last decade or so (see Perry 1995; Herman 2001: 201-227, Herman 2004; Andregg 2007; McCoy 2006; Dover and Goodman 2009; Bellaby 2012). Indeed, the *modus operandi* of intelligence agencies, fuelled by popular fictional representation, are popularly thought to be utilitarian by nature, often characterised as tactical illegality and unethical behaviour undertaken in the over-arching interest of the greater good.

The idea that intelligence agencies should have a more robust ethical dimension has gained traction over the last 50 years. The use of 'Weapons of Mass Destruction' intelligence to justify the invasion of Iraq in 2003, later revealed to be inaccurate or even concocted, was seen to represent the politicisation of MI6 by providing the pretext to support the US President's desire to depose Saddam Hussein and his Ba'athist regime. The reputation of the Central Intelligence Agency (CIA) suffered from this politicisation too (see Lucas 2011). The discussion over intelligence ethics may be limited but it is timely as the methods used by Western nations in the 'the war on terror' have resulted in increasing pressure for consideration of human rights in the intelligence setting especially after cases of the torturing of suspects, drone warfare and rendition.

This author has looked at many of the ethically based confrontations between intelligence and the news media and concludes that there are major ethical issues to consider for both disciplines. This paper attempts to take the first steps in discussing a bipartisan framework for an ethical relationship between intelligence agencies and the news media that would allow accurate information to enter the public domain without jeopardising legitimate national security. It is necessary to map the zone between the two disciplines and discuss how it is best regulated.

INTELLIGENCE AND ETHICS

There can be no doubt that intelligence has to face serious ethical questions in a modern society. In 1995, Perry said:

> The sources and methods of espionage, the goals and tactics of covert action, and the professional conduct of intelligence officers are matters typically hidden from public scrutiny, yet clearly worthy of public debate and philosophical attention.

Perry said that while the ethical questions had been raised they were mostly procedural:

> But what is often missed in such examinations is substantive ethical analysis of intelligence operations themselves (Perry 1995:1).

A leading UK intelligence academic Mark Phythian points out that ethical issues are inseparable from intelligence activities and, like the question of failure, can take in the entire intelligence cycle.

Targeting of 'friendly' states, the very notion of covert surveillance, and the more intrusive forms of collection, together with the question of covert action and other intelligence-led policy responses, all raise fundamental ethical questions. There is a growing body of work on this subject most recently clearly informed by developments in the 'war on terror', specifically the torture debate in the US and the associated question of extraordinary rendition – in effect, the outsourcing of torture by the US. Hence, more than ever before there is a need to adapt the just war paradigm to construct a concept of *jus in intelligentia* (Gill, Marrin and Phythian 2009: 63-64).

Academics are using a range of theoretical concepts to develop a framework. One method has been to adapt the 'just war' concept. Bellaby has outlined a possible ethical structure for intelligence. As he points out:

> As the professional practice of intelligence collection adapts to the changing environment and new threats of the twentieth first century, many academic experts and intelligence professionals call for a coherent ethical framework that outlines exactly when, by what means and to what ends intelligence is justified (Bellaby 2012: 1).

There has been an impact. For example, the US Office of the Director of National Intelligence (DNI) posts an ethics statement online: namely the *Principles of professional ethics for the intelligence community*:

> As members of the intelligence profession, we conduct ourselves in accordance with certain basic principles. These principles are stated below, and reflect the standard of ethical conduct expected of all Intelligence Community personnel, regardless of individual role or agency affiliation (DNI 2015: 1).

Application is everything in ethics but a clear statement can be indicative of a change of approach. Besides issues of legality, competence, politicisation and domain expansion, one of the tension points for the news media is where the intelligence agencies expand from intelligence gathering to proactive covert operations. One of the leading journalism academics writing on ethics, Chris Frost, has said:

> In practice ethics is a way of studying morality which allows decisions to be made when individuals face specific cases of moral dilemma. At their most praiseworthy, the journalist's tussles are going to be between the right of the public to know and some other moral tenet – perhaps the invasion of an individual's privacy – which would militate against publication (2011: 10).

Ethical debates have been a feature of journalism practice since inception. Attempts at resolution have been manifest in terms of regulation, codes and law. Incorporating ethical practice has been a consistent aspiration for journalism since at least the turn of the 20th century (NUJ) but the news media is a heterogeneous entity and has palpably failed to maintain an ethical framework across the industry (Curran and Seaton 1999; Davies 2008 and Davies 2014). In terms of discussion within the discipline this has consolidated around the move to university-level education for journalists. In the United States this began with the foundation of the Journalism School at Missouri University, Columbia, in 1908. In the UK journalism education did not really start until 1970 when University College, Cardiff, launched a journalism course. Ethics have been at the heart of debate between academics and journalists. Certainly academics have seen it as an important part of their role as to bring the more extreme or improper behaviour of journalists to account. While until recently journalists tended to ignore such efforts and dismiss academics as not being of the real world. More recently a middle ground has evolved with the increasing numbers of journalism practitioner/academics who are prepared to reflect and seek improvements in their discipline. The issues are constantly discussed (see Keeble 2009; Frost 2011). Keeble says:

> Ethical inquiry is crucial for all media workers – and managers. It encourages journalists to examine their basic moral and political principles; their responsibilities and rights; their relationship to their employer and audience; their ultimate goals. Self-criticism and the reflective, questioning approach are always required. And journalists need to be eloquent about

ethics and politics, confident in articulating and handling the issues – and imaginative in their promotion of standards, both individually and collectively (2009: 1).

THE INTELLIGENCE AND JOURNALISM ETHICAL BOUNDARY

Aside from the ethics of the intelligence agencies in their general operations and more specifically when dealing with the media, there is the question of the ethics of the media when dealing with intelligence stories. The relationship between intelligence agencies and the news media is complex and often contested.

As a young reporter I became aware that the government's then position to 'neither confirm nor deny' was open to exploitation by unscrupulous journalists. Very early in my career I sat opposite a very ambitious freelance who claimed excellent MI5 sources. He used to make great play of talking to his 'source' on the phone in front of me and then using me to confirm the conversation took place when editors were present. It took me a while to realise he was probably talking to the speaking clock. I also came to suspect that many of the phantasmagorical intelligence sources of 'red scare' stories in the tabloids of the time citing MI5 or MI6 sources were probably fabricated or planted. One of the advantages of the accredited journalist system (see Lashmar 2013) and formal links to the agencies is that falsification on this scale no longer occurs as there is now a check system in place and politicians are much more likely to denounce a wrong or inaccurate story on intelligence issues. This is an important ethical development for journalism given reporting intelligence is such an important part of journalism's fourth estate duty.

It is important to state that reporting of intelligence today is not conducted without restraint. In the heat of the anti-CIA backlash of the 1970s journalists of the left and alternative press took the view that identifying officers of the agency was acceptable given the undemocratic work intelligence agencies had undertaken. Naming names was a point of great tension between the intelligence agencies and parts of the news media. Philip Agee, a former CIA officer, revealed the identities and location of up to 250 people working for the CIA (Moran 2013: 190). For years, the *Covert Action Information Bulletin* published the names of active-duty CIA officers and other intelligence operatives. With the pre-1975 excesses of intelligence agencies in the West laid bare and condemned by inquiry and the slowly improved oversight, the practice of naming intelligence officers was increasingly seen by editors as only justifiable in exceptional cases. On each occasion the UK news media have sought to publish information that suggests inappropriate behaviour by intelligence agencies they have met with condemnation by government. The publication of the Snowden documents puts the recurrent debate into a contemporary light and, therefore, makes for a useful case study to discuss the important issues at stake.

CASE STUDY: SNOWDEN – THE CONTEMPORARY TENSION

American computer specialist Edward Snowden is a former CIA employee and National Security Agency (NSA) contractor who established unauthorised contact with American journalists from late 2012. On 20 May 2013, he flew to Hong Kong, and so was out of US jurisdiction when the initial news stories based on his leaked documents were published. A wide range of Snowden's leaked documents have been published by media outlets worldwide, most notably the *Guardian* (Britain), *Der Spiegel* (Germany), the *Washington Post* and *The New York Times* (US), *O Globo* (Brazil), *Le Monde* (France) and news outlets in Sweden, Canada, Italy, Netherlands, Norway, Spain and Australia (Greenwald 2013). On 23 June 2013, Snowden landed in Moscow's Sheremetyevo International airport. Snowden remained in the airport's transit zone for 39 days until granted temporary asylum by the Russian government on 1 August where he has remained since. These documents reveal operational details of a global surveillance apparatus jointly run by the 'Five Eyes' countries (namely the UK, US, Canada, Australia and New Zealand) in close cooperation with diverse commercial and international partners. Glenn Greenwald, the then-*Guardian* journalist who analysed many of Edward Snowden's documents, summarised his perception of NSA's objective as:

> I think everybody knows by now, or at least I hope they do after the last seven months reporting, that the goal of the NSA really is the elimination of privacy worldwide – not hyperbole, not metaphor, that's literally their goal, is to make sure that all human communications that take place electronically are collected and then stored by the NSA and susceptible to being monitored and analysed (2013).

THE POLITICAL CONTROVERSY

The sheer scale of NSA-GCHQ operations clearly surprised many senior politicians who thought they had been briefed fully on the activities of the intelligence agencies. Other commentators have unreservedly attacked Snowden for his leaks. There are clear political and professional polarities in position taken on Snowden. In the UK Charles Moore, the former editor of the *Daily Telegraph*, said:

> In traditional accounts of Hell, sinners end up with punishments that fit their crimes. Rumour-mongers have their tongues cut out; usurers wear chains of burning gold. On this basis, it will be entirely fitting if Edward Snowden spends eternity in a Moscow airport lounge (Moore 2013).

The UK government and the Prime Minister, David Cameron, attacked the *Guardian* for publishing the Snowden material: 'As we stand today, there are people in the world, who want to do us harm, who want to blow up our families, who want to maim our country. That is a fact, it's not a pleasant fact, but it's a true fact ... .' Cameron maintained that the UK's intelligence agencies are fully accountable:

> So we have a choice, do we maintain properly funded, properly governed intelligence and security services, which will gather intelligence on these people, using all of the modern techniques to make sure that we can get ahead of them and stop them, or do we stop doing that? What Snowden is doing and to an extent what the newspaper are doing in helping him is frankly signalling to people who mean to do us harm, how to evade and avoid intelligence and surveillance and other techniques (Hope and Waterfield 2013).

Sir John Sawers, head of MI6, when appearing in front of a parliamentary committee in November 2013, addressed the impact of the Snowden revelations by questioning the qualifications of journalists and senior editorial staff in deciding what can be published.

> I'm not sure the journalists managing these publications are particularly well placed to make that judgement ... What I can tell you is that the leaks from Snowden have been very damaging, they have put our operations at risk. It is clear our adversaries are rubbing their hands with glee, al Qaida is lapping it up (Marszal 2013).

At the same ISC hearing the head of GCHQ, Sir Ian Lobban, said:

> The cumulative effect of this global media coverage will make our job far, far harder for years to come. ... What we have seen over the last five months is near daily discussion amongst some of our targets (ibid).

The *Guardian* editor, Alan Rusbridger, explained to a parliamentary committee that the paper consulted with government officials and intelligence agencies, including the GCHQ, the White House and the Cabinet Office, on more than one hundred occasions before publication (Rusbridger 2013). There is a considerable amount of material in the Snowden documents on actual UK anti-terrorist operations. Of the estimated 1.5+ million documents said to exist in the Snowden cache, a personal source has told me that almost 60,000 are said to refer to GCHQ. So far (November 2015) only a very small percentage, no more than 1 per cent, has been published by the news media. None has been from documents revealing active anti-terrorist operations.

Even within journalism there are strong differences of opinion about who should be arbiters on national security. Chris Blackhurst, the editor of the *Independent* newspaper at the time of Snowden's revelations, said in response to the *Guardian*'s publication: 'If MI5 warns that this is not in the public interest who am I to disbelieve them?' Blackhurst further commented; 'If the security services insist something is contrary to the public interest, and might harm their operations, who am I (despite my grounding from Watergate onwards) to disbelieve them?' And he wonders; '…what it is, exactly, that the NSA and GCHQ are doing that is so profoundly terrible?' (Mirkinson 2013). In his 2010 book, Gabriel Schoenfeld, a senior fellow at the Hudson Institute, and former Mitt Romney election adviser, challenged the right of the press to make unilateral decisions to 'publish and let others perish' or as he quotes a newspaper editor, to publish 'no matter the cost'. He said that the fourth estate had changed beyond recognition since the era when Roosevelt could speak of the 'patriotic press'.

> Indeed, with a press now wantonly compromising operational counterterrorism programs, things have swung to an extreme without precedent in our history (2010: 275).

In the wake of Snowden, trust would seem to be at an all-time low and not only in the UK. As a reflexive practitioner I recognise that there may be truth in Schoenfeld, Lobban and Sawer's points. Journalists exist in a political economy and are under pressure to publish major exclusive stories. I also recognise that journalists can and have claimed public interest for publishing completely indefensible articles. The UK tabloids have a long track record of such hypocrisy. But in my experience, as a practitioner, many parts of the news media do take their responsibilities seriously. I would also argue that in over three decades of covering intelligence agency activities I have seen many exposés and often the intelligence agencies and their political masters' responses have been to accuse editors and journalists of 'putting lives at risk'. I would observe that in every case I can recall the claim was proven to be without merit.

Nonetheless there have been continuing allegations that the *Guardian* and other news media that published Snowden's document have undermined part of the Five Eyes operations against al-Qaeda. On the other hand their release has created a watershed moment in the discussion over the balance between privacy and surveillance, the public's right to know versus security. No one feels the current *ad hoc* adversarial negotiations over publication are the right way to resolve such tensions. This paper examines the historical and current situation on oversight of intelligence and the news media as a preamble to how an agreed mechanism could be put into place. Changes since the early 1990s to intelligence legitimacy make this possible.

THE TRANSLUCENCY OF INTELLIGENCE

As a result of the many revelations in the 1980s of intelligence service wrongdoing, regulation followed. In November 1993, the government published its Intelligence Bill and simultaneously published, for the first time, the estimates for the intelligence services – then £900m. for the year (Gill 1996: 313). Gill stated the main innovation in the Act, and one which apparently provides some potential challenge to executive information control, is that the Intelligence and Security Committee (ISC) can examine the expenditure, administration and policy of the Security Service, SIS and GCHQ:

> [The Intelligence and Security Committee] has nine members from either Lords or Commons, who will be appointed by the Prime Minister after consultation with Leader of Opposition. The committee will report annually to the Prime Minister, and other times if it wishes, and a copy of the annual report with be laid before each House, subject to any exclusion of 'prejudicial' material made by the Prime Minister but within no specific time limit (1996: 323).

While parliament's ISC is the most high profile of the UK's intelligence oversight mechanisms, there are a number of oversight organisations that intermesh with the intelligence agencies.

The ISC is complemented by three judicial commissioners.

1) The Intelligence Services Commissioner provides independent judicial oversight of the conduct of the Secret Intelligence Service (MI6), Security Service (MI5), Government Communications Headquarters (GCHQ) and a number of other public authorities. The ISC commissioner, Mark Waller, works with the Home Office.

2) There is also the Interception of Communications Commissioner's Office (IOCCO). The commissioner is a judge, Sir Anthony May, and his function is to keep the interception of communications and the acquisition and disclosure of communications data by intelligence agencies, police forces and other public authorities under review.

3) The surveillance commissioner oversees surveillance by police and other public bodies, other than communications interception which is covered by IOCCO.

In addition there is:

1) The Investigatory Powers Tribunal (IPT), a court which investigates and determines complaints of unlawful use of covert techniques by public authorities infringing our right to privacy and claims against intelligence or law enforcement agency conduct which breach a wider range of human rights. In February 2015, for the first time in its fifteen year existence, the tribunal issued a ruling that went against one of the security agencies. It ruled that GCHQ had acted unlawfully in accessing data on millions of people in Britain that had been collected by the US National Security Agency (NSA), because the arrangements were secret (Shirbon 2015).

2) The Independent Reviewer of Terrorism Legislation, David Anderson QC. The independent reviewer's role is to inform the public and political debate on anti-terrorism law in the United Kingdom, in particular through regular reports which are prepared for the home secretary or Treasury and then laid before parliament. The uniqueness of the role lies in its complete independence from government, coupled with access based on a very high degree of clearance to secret and sensitive national security information.

Also exercising accountability are one-off inquiries that take into consideration the role of the intelligence services. The failure to find Weapons of Mass Destruction (WMD) in Iraq caused such public concern that an inquiry was set up by then-Prime Minister, Gordon Brown, under Sir John Chilcot which includes the role of the intelligence services. To much criticism, the inquiry will not report until 2016, thirteen years after the invasion of Iraq. There is growing evidence of MI6 and MI5 involvement in rendition and condoning torture in third party countries (Cobain 2015). After much pressure, Prime Minister David Cameron ordered an inquiry in September 2014 and assigned the task to the ISC. A coalition of nine human rights groups, including Reprieve, Amnesty International and Liberty, challenged the decision. In a letter they said they had lost all trust in the committee's ability to uncover the truth. 'Consequently, we as a collective of domestic and international non-governmental organisations do not propose to play a substantive role in the conduct of this inquiry.' David Cameron had previously promised that the inquiry would be headed by a senior judge (Townend 2014).

There is much evidence that intelligence agencies need to be subject to oversight as there are multiple ethical failures. The official oversight mechanisms have not impressed the wider critical world especially the ISC who were left as fools or knaves by the release of the Snowden documents. Either they knew that surveillance had exceeded that agreed in which case they are knaves or they did not know and were fools.

In my PHD thesis, I argue the that the UK news media, as with those in other Five Eyes countries, have been the most effective oversight mechanism (Lashmar 2015: 71). There is also surprisingly little evidence of the news media causing harm rather than reform by those exposes. Observing that governments do not want to recognise the validity of this aspect of the media's fourth estate role and increasingly take countermeasures, I stated:

> A profoundly serious issue for journalism is the use of surveillance techniques to prevent journalists acquiring and maintaining confidential sources, especially in the public sector. Surveillance is now so pervasive it makes the development of intelligence sources in the sector very difficult, and consequently the news media's duty to provide critical accountability of power is much reduced. In just a few years, journalists have gone from a situation where they could give a reasonable guarantee of protecting a confidential source, to a situation that they have to assume, at least when it comes to investigations into government, the public sector and the related private sector, that such guarantees are hard to give (ibid: 74).

In the US, the Barack Obama administration has been responsible for more prosecutions of sources than any previous administration. *The New York Times* reporter Jeff Stein has asked whether we are at 'The end of national security reporting? ... The upshot is that federal prosecutors have a wide leeway in getting sub-poenas to track reporter's email and telephone calls and compel testimony in court' (Stein 2013). As traditional sources have been closed down there have been massive data leaks such as WikiLeaks and the Snowden documents. So the tension between intelligence and the pro-active news media is likely to continue, each with a very different perspective on publication of intelligence activities.

A RESOLUTION?

How can negotiated arrangement be arrived at in between these two positions? The method used in the UK, mirroring a similar approach used in the US, has been *ad hoc* discussions between the two sides. How to find an agreed ethical process and then create a practical mechanism to create a consensus? Any news organisation publishing secret information takes a great risk. One urgent issue is to find a way of working out what can be published within the greater public interest. Recent evidence suggests a working arrangement will not evolve unilaterally and there clearly needs to be a brokered discussion. How to do this? To devise such an arrangement one has to look at how the current situation functions. There is a legal rather than ethical regime in place where the government can use the Official Secrets Act (OSA) and other statues to deter publication of sensitive material. Government and the judicial system have a marked reluctance to use the OSA as it can be interpreted as government bullying. But it would not have worked in this case as Snowden is not a British subject and not in the British jurisdiction so he cannot be prosecuted. The government could have prosecuted the *Guardian* but that was very unlikely to succeed.

While there is no longer a public interest defence to the OSA it is likely that many damaging documents and issues would be discussed in court. The government could have tried to injunct the *Guardian* but the courts in the UK are hesitant to undertake prior restraint as it is a clear infringement of the freedom of the press. Indeed, there was a threat of injunction if the *Guardian* did not destroy the Snowden hard drives. As things stand, *ad hoc* meetings are the current method of discussion if not resolution between editors, government and intelligence heads on major disclosures. The *Guardian* is considered one of the more ethical and responsible of newspapers with a low rate of complaints to regulators. Other news media are less scrupulous.

In 2015, the relationship between intelligence and the media in the Western world is probably as a fraught as it has ever been. This is as true for the UK as it is for the other Five Eyes countries and their 25-plus third-party partner countries. Exposés of spying on allies, most notably German Angela Merkel's telephone, have been embarrassing. At the time of writing, allegations and counter allegations are still reverberating. Some publications including the *Guardian* and *The New York Times* were accused of serious irresponsibility. The agencies were accused of introducing mass surveillance by stealth but counterattack that media are putting lives at risk. As proven instances of people being killed as a result of media exposés of intelligence are very few and disputed that accusation does not have a lot of traction. Arguments that exposure impacts on reputation and intelligence tradecraft are more compelling. Editors have not published specific details of anti-terrorism operations, that they are known to possess, and have shown restraint. The journalists I have interviewed (2014/15) from the Five Eyes countries, who had nearly all covered national security stories, indeed breaking major stories, were deeply sceptical of this intelligence agency response, seeing a disingenuous response of secretive agencies that have been caught behaving badly. On the other hand it is recognised that journalists can be driven by more than *fourth estate* ideals to publish career enhancing or ratings increasing scoops.

IN THE PUBLIC INTEREST

What has happened at Rupert Murdoch's News International is catastrophic for quality journalism. Public revelation of wholesale phone hacking and bribery of public officials has seriously damaged all of journalism. It has also accustomed the nation to the sight of journalists being arrested and tried. The negative impact of this will be felt by honourable journalists for decades. It will make it far harder to argue a public interest defence to controversial publications like the Snowden documents. What is the public interest? As Allan states '…the emergence of a newspaper press committed to advancing "the public interest" by reporting reality in the social world in a non-partisan manner has been a fairly recent development' (Allan 2010: 32). Public interest journalism is, as Frost puts it, 'a poorly defined device' (2011: 270). The term has a wider context but for the purposes of this thesis I confine the definition to its meaning for journalism. Journalists will argue that putting information into the public domain that enables the citizen to make an informed decision is acting in the public interest. According to the now-superseded Press Complaints Commission (PCC 2011):

The public interest includes, but is not confined to:

(i) Detecting or exposing crime or serious impropriety.

(ii) Protecting public health and safety.

(iii) Preventing the public from being misled by an action or statement of an individual or organisation.

There is public interest in freedom of expression itself (Frost 2011: 270). The concept is very important for journalism, as journalists will sometimes use methods, to obtain information to publish, that would be described as dubious or even illegal and can only be justified if they serve the wider public interest and indeed intelligence agencies might argue the same. There are major differences. The ultimate test of the public interest for journalists may occur in court and is defined by whether a judge or jury accepts that a piece of journalism is in the public interest and finds in favour of the publishers rather than the appellants. Editor of the *Guardian* Alan Rusbridger says in his 2011 Orwell Lecture:

> Why is this agreement over 'the public interest' so crucial? Because, in the end, the public interest, and how we argue it, is not only crucial to the sometimes arcane subject of privacy – it is crucial to every argument about the future of the press, the public good it delivers and why, in the most testing of economic times, it deserves to survive (Rusbridger 2011).

This paper proposes that there should be a more formal set of arrangements with an independent arbiter body. This could either be an individual or committee, suitably experienced, and agreed by both sides in advance of future publications. The role would be advisory but would have the merit that any subsequent publication or legal action will be mitigated by the attempt at an agreement. Is there an appropriate existing regulatory body? Regulation of intelligence has remained within government primarily by cabinet responsibility. The ISC was set up to reassure the public that there is cross-party parliamentary scrutiny, and while it has over the last twenty years proved better than expected, the Snowden revelations have placed it in a poor light.

The news media have a number of regulatory mechanisms. Self-regulation of the print news media was conducted by the PCC but this body was entirely discredited by the phone hacking scandal. The PCC had a less than impressive record of dealing with complaints and allegations since it was dominated by the interests of the big news media companies. The post-Leveson inquiry replacement body, the Independent Press Standards Organisation (IPSO), has been launched but not all major print new organisations have joined. There is evidence that new chair Sir Alan Moses is showing an independence of approach that might work in IPSO's favour and bring more news organisations on board. It is too early to tell whether IPSO would be a suitable vehicle demonstrating a level of independence and judgement that would be respected by editors and Whitehall alike.

For reasons demonstrated above the ISC is generally seen as a sop to the intelligence agencies and unlikely to be seen as a good mediator between the two sides. On paper the office of the UK Intelligence Services Commissioner, Sir Mark Waller, may appear to be a possible mediator. But in March 2014, he was questioned by a parliamentary committee about Snowden's revelations suggesting GCHQ was acting unlawfully. The committee seemed less than impressed when he told them that in response he went to see a senior official at GCHQ who assured him it was not true. His office is staffed by two people (Sparrow 2014). So this body does not seem a promising option.

Another body which could have a role is the DA-Notice Committee. The Defence, Press and Broadcasting Advisory Committee (DPBAC) oversees a voluntary code which operates between the UK government departments which have responsibilities for national security and the media. It uses the Defence

Advisory (DA)-Notice System as its vehicle. The objective of the DA-Notice System is to prevent inadvertent public disclosure of information that would compromise UK military and intelligence operations and methods, or put at risk the safety of those involved in such operations, or lead to attacks that would damage the critical national infrastructure and/or endanger lives. Any DA-notices are only advisory requests and so are not legally enforceable; hence, editors can choose to ignore them. In June 2013, a DA-Notice was issued asking the media to refrain from running further stories related to Prism (a secret surveillance programme under which the NSA collects internet communications from at least nine major US internet companies) and British involvement therein. As it was ignored, questions have been asked as to whether the committee has outlived its use. This all suggests that a new body comprising of independent and qualified experts agreed by representatives of all shades of opinion from both sides needs to be developed.

How can ethics been seen to be central to this process? It is probably fortunate that the newspapers that have published Snowden material are all highly regarded, even if their judgement has been called into question. If such material had been published by a less scrupulous news organisation it is hard to imagine what might have happened.

CONCLUSION

Intelligence ethics theory may be at an early stage but it is a step into the future. I conclude that intelligence community could be more open and accountable without endangering its *modus operandi* and all intelligence operations should be considered in terms of human rights. The quality of reporting of national security is too often simplistic and poor. Journalism ethics should drive professionalisation. The author believes the professions of news journalism and intelligence can move to a more ethical relationship which allows for a greater level of accountability and transparency for intelligence while allowing the intelligence community to operate, without unnecessary constraint in their task of protecting the security of the democratic state. This paper suggests there needs to be an effective mechanism for bringing the two sides together but what organisation would be trusted still needs to be ascertained or created. The existing bodies either have failed on other ethical issues or are at too early a stage to ascertain whether they could incorporate the role effectively into their remit.

- This paper was first published in *Ethical Space*, Vol 12, Nos 3 and 4 pp 4-13

REFERENCES

Allan, S. (2010) *News culture*, Maidenhead, McGraw Hill OUP, third edition

Andregg, M. (2007) Intelligence ethics: Laying a foundation for the second oldest profession, Johnson, L. K. (ed.) *Handbook for intelligence studies*, New York, Routledge

Bellaby, R. (2012) 'What's the harm'? The ethics of intelligence collection, *Intelligence and National Security*, Vol. 27, No. 1 pp 93-117

Cobain, I. (2015) Cooperation between British spies and Gaddafi's Libya revealed in official papers, *Guardian*, 23 January. Available online at http://www.theguardian.com/uk-news/2015/jan/22/cooperation-british-spies-gaddafi-libya-revealed-official-papers, accessed on 23 January 2015

Curran, J. and Seaton, J. (2010) *Power without responsibility*, London, Routledge, seventh edition

Davies, N. (2008) *Flat earth news: An award-winning reporter exposes falsehood, distortion and propaganda in the global media*, London, Chatto and Windus

Davies, N. (2014) *Hack attack*, London, Chatto and Windus

DNI (2015) *Principles of professional ethics for the intelligence community*. Available online at http://www.dni.gov/index.php/intelligence-community/principles-of-professional-ethics, accessed on 25 October 2015

Dover, R. and Goodman, M. S. (eds) (2009) *Spinning intelligence: Why intelligence needs the media. Why media needs intelligence*, London, C Hurst & Co.

Frost, C. (2011) *Journalism, ethics and regulation*, Harlow, Longman, third edition

Gill, P. (1996) Reasserting control: Recent changes in the oversight of the UK intelligence community, *Intelligence and National Security*, Vol. 11, No. 2 pp 313-331

Gill, P., Marrin, S. and Phythian, M. (2009) *Intelligence studies: Key questions and debates*, Abingdon, Routledge

Greenwald, G. (2013) The NSA can 'literally read every keystroke you make', *Open Democracy*, 30 December. Available online at http://www.democracynow.org/2013/12/30/glenn_greenwald_the_nsa_can_literally, accessed on 1 September 2015

Herman, M. (2001) *Intelligence services in the information age*, London, Frank Cass

Herman, M. (2004) Ethics and Intelligence after September 2001, *Intelligence and National Security*, Vol. 19, No. 2 pp 342-358

Hope, C. and Waterfield, B. (2013) David Cameron: Newspapers which publish Snowden secrets help terrorists who want to 'blow up' families. *Daily Telegraph*. 25 October. Available online at http://www.telegraph.co.uk/news/uknews/defence/10406331/David-Cameron-newspapers-which-publish-Snowden-secrets-help-terrorists-who-want-to-blow-up-families.html, accessed on 7 September 2015

Keeble, R. L. (2009) *Ethics for journalists*, London, Routledge, second edition

Lashmar, P. (2013) Urinal or open channel? Institutional information flow between the UK intelligence services and news media, *Journalism: Theory, Practice and Criticism*, Vol. 14, No 8 pp 1024-1040

Lashmar, P. (2015) *Investigating the 'empire of secrecy': Three decades of reporting on the secret state*. PhD Thesis. Brunel University. Available online at http://bura.brunel.ac.uk/bit- stream/2438/11222/1/FulltextThesis.pdf, accessed on 9 September 2015

Lucas, S. (2011) Recognising politicization: The CIA and the path to the 2003 war in Iraq, *Intelligence and National Security*, Vol. 26, Nos 2 and 3 pp 203-227

Marszal, A. (2013) Spy chiefs public hearing: As it happened, *Daily Telegraph*. 7 November. Available online at http://www.telegraph.co.uk/news/uknews/defence/10432629/Spy-chiefs-public-hearing-as-it-happened.html, accessed on 9 September 2015

McCoy, A. W. (2006) *A question of torture: CIA interrogation: From the Cold War to the war on terror*, NY, Metropolitan Books

Mirkinson, J. (2013) Finally, an editor sticking up for the NSA! *Huffington Post*, 15 December. Available online at http://www.huffingtonpost.com/2013/10/15/chris-blackhurst-nsa-mi5_n_4100450.html, accessed on 2 November 2015

Moore, C. (2013) Edward Snowden is a traitor, just as surely as George Blake was, *Daily Telegraph*, 5 July 2013. Available online at http://www.telegraph.co.uk/technology/internet-security/10162351/Edward-Snowden-is-a-traitor-just-as-surely-as-George-Blake-was.html, accessed on 9 September 2015

Moran, C. (2011) Intelligence and the media: The press, government secrecy and 'Buster' Crabb Affair', *Intelligence and National Security*, Vol. 26, No. 5 pp. 676-700

Perry, D.L. (1995) 'Repugnant philosophy': Ethics, espionage, and covert action, *Journal of Conflict Studies*, Vol 15, No1. Available online at https://journals.lib.unb.ca/index.php/JCS/issue/view/467, accessed on 25 October 2015

PCC (Press Complaints Commission) (2011) *Editors' code of practice*. Available online at http://www.pcc.org.uk/assets/696/Code_of_Prac- tice_2012_A4.pdf, accessed on 29 October 2015

Phythian, M. (2005) Still a matter of trust, *International Journal of Intelligence and Counter Intelligence*, Vol. 18 pp 653-681

Rusbridger, A. (2011) Hacking away at the truth: Alan Rusbridger's Orwell lecture, *Guardian*. 10 November 2011. Available online at http://www.theguardian.com/media/2011/nov/10/phone-hacking-truth-alan-rusbridger-orwell, accessed on 9 September 2015

Rusbridger, A. (2013) *Guardian* will not be intimidated over NSA leaks, Alan Rusbridger tells MPs, *Guardian*, 3 December. Available online at http://www.theguardian.com/world/2013/dec/03/guardian-not-intimidated-nsa-leaks-alan-rusbridger-surveillance, accessed on 9 September 2015

Schoenfeld, G. (2011) *Necessary secrets: National security, the media, and the rule of law*, New York, Norton

Shirbon, E. (2015) UK tribunal says intelligence-sharing with U.S. was unlawful, *Reuters*, 6 February. Available online at http://www.reuters.com/article/2015/02/06/us-britain-surveillance-idUSKBN-0LA13320150206, accessed on 6 February 2015

Sparrow, A. (2014) MPs question intelligence services commissioner: Politics live blog, *Guardian*, 18 March. Available online at http://www.theguardian.com/politics/blog/2014/mar/18/cameron-and-clegg-announce-new-childcare-allowance-reaction-politics-live-blog, accessed on 7 February 2015

Stein, J (2013) The end of national security reporting? *IEE Security & Privacy*, Vol. 11, No. 4 pp 64-68

Townend, M. (2014) UK rights groups reject official inquiry into post-September 11 rendition, *Guardian*, 8 November. Available online at http://www.theguardian.com/world/2014/nov/08/british-torture-inquiry-boycotted-rights-groups, accessed on 5 February 2015

Wright, Peter (1987) *Spycatcher*, New York, Viking

NOTE ON THE CONTRIBUTOR

Dr Paul Lashmar is a Reader in Journalism at City, University of London, and is a former head of the department (2019-2021). He has been an investigative journalist since 1978 and has been on the staff of the *Observer*, Granada Television's *World in Action* current affairs series and the *Independent*. Paul has authored or co-authored six books, including *Spies, spin and the Fourth Estate: British intelligence and the media* (Edinburgh University Press, 2020) and with De Burgh, H. (2021) (eds) *Investigative journalism* (Routledge, 2021, third edition). He is working on a history of the Drax family.

Chapter 18

The ethical turn in considering hidden children's Holocaust testimony as historical reconstruction

Julie Wheelwright

How to balance respect for the testimonial quality of post-Holocaust memoirs while critically analysing their value as historical witness statements? This question is explored through the author's experience of collaborating on a memoir project with a Jewish subject who, as a child, was hidden in a Catholic convent in Belgium during the Second World War. Using the concepts of 'collective memory, memory makers and memory consumers', the author argues that witness statements are most valuable when read and understood within broader issues of political and historical structures. Using the example of Hidden Children's testimony, the author examines how a range of historical actors can be acknowledged and appropriately recognised by comparing memories and by including appropriate contextual detail. The paper points to future research questions into how post-Holocaust memoirs are received and understood as historical artifacts by memory consumers.

Keywords: memory studies, hidden children, Belgium, post-Holocaust narratives

INTRODUCTION

In considering the ethics of writing about Jewish child survivors of the Holocaust in Belgium, Misha Defonseca's memoir, *Surviving with wolves: The most extraordinary story of World War II* (2005), is worth our attention. Defonseca's account of her traumatic childhood in occupied Brussels recounts her Jewish parents' deportation to Auschwitz and her search for them when she walked from Belgium to Ukraine, and back. The memoir was a phenomenal commercial success in Europe: published first in English in 1997, it was translated into 18 languages, developed as a French feature film and serialised in the *Daily Mail*. According to Defonseca, she was placed with a Catholic family who Christianised her name to Monique De Wael (her real name) but treated her cruelly, forcing her to find food and shelter in the forest where she was cared for by wolves (Defonseca et al. 2005). Despite its huge sales, however, a series of legal cases (and increasing number of skeptics) forced De Wael in 2008 to admit the memoir was based in fantasy rather than fact. Tellingly, she stated that her invented story 'was not actual reality, but was my reality, my way of surviving …' and that 'there are times when I find it difficult to differentiate between reality and my inner world' (Dearden 2014). Not only had she falsified her religion (she was Catholic) but her parents had been part of Belgium's network of resisters, had been caught and died in prison (Eskin 2008). De Wael's childhood was certainly tragic – but perhaps she felt not tragic enough to garner international attention.[1]

What De Wael violated was the long-accepted principle among writers of narrative non-fiction that in testimonial autobiography there is a 'writer-reader pact' that rests on the centrality and moral significance of the author (Freadman 2004: 30). The realistic aesthetics that De Wael employs through her descriptions of remembered events should have constituted an entirely appropriate perspective for reading a Holocaust memoir. As Freadman argues: 'This is a moral point: we owe those with terrible stories to tell the respect of taking their stories on trust, unless we have good reason for doubting them' (ibid). What should have alerted readers to the disingenuous quality of De Wael's text was its lack of detail, its factual errors and its insistence (in the English translation) on the literary stylisation of the child's voice (Vice 2014: 207).

Although De Wael's memoir is exceptional and extreme, standing in contrast to genuine Holocaust testimonies published in their hundreds since the 1970s (Freadman 2004: 22), it illustrates an important point about the prevailing climate in which memoir is read as historical reconstruction. Since the early 2000s, scholars such as Katharine Hodgkin and Susannah Radstone (2003) have noted the critical weakness in the application of memory and trauma studies by diverse historical actors. Radstone suggested that trauma had 'become a popular cultural script in need of contextualisation and analysis in its own right – the symptom, the cause of which needs to be sought elsewhere' (ibid). The conjoining of the ethical turn that currently informs humanities research more generally (with memory and trauma studies as a transdisciplinary subset), Radstone has argued, still risks obscuring as much as it reveals about the politics of memory (Radstone 2008). Or as Jane Kilby has observed, as memory has arisen as a 'boom' or 'fever', its politics are still poorly understood by historical consumers and by scholars (Kilby 2002: 201).

Adding to these complexities is the discourse around the relation between history and memory that often takes place outside of the academy (Hodgkin and Radstone 2005: 149; Fass 2006). The rise of movements concerned with memorialising experiences has, for example, coincided with the proliferation of online historical sources and technological changes so that historical trauma memoirs can be self-published and made easily accessible as digital texts. However, these new publishing platforms, while allowing witnesses a means to disseminate their accounts and those of others,[2] are, as Radstone describes it, 'always already mediated' (Radstone 2013: 134, 135). One could argue that the gap between the public understanding of this concept by consumers of memoir texts and that of academic critics is growing. For scholars of genocides this question of representation and its reception is particularly sensitive given the paradoxes with which traumatic experience confronts us: as Arruti argues, 'it is imperative to think through the complexities of the relationship between trauma and representation, and to question the extent to which such representation may be therapeutic' (Arruti 2007: 2). De Wael's adoption of a Jewish identity and her insistence that her emotional alternative to 'actual reality', with its own internal logic, should take precedence over fact, is a case in point.

My experience of collaborating on a privately published memoir with Joseph Szlezinger, a retired British Jewish businessman who was hidden in a Catholic convent in Belgium from 1943-1944, provides an opportunity to illustrate this tension between memory as 'lived experience' and as 'historical reconstruction'. In addressing this matter, I placed Mr Szlezinger's recall of events within a broader historical context that involved comparing dozens of memoirs that were either published by small presses, by institutions, privately published (as print, e-books and online) along with witness testimonies. To borrow Freadman's categorisation, such memoirs operate across a spectrum, ranging from witness accounts written at the time, to accounts based on recorded interviews to accounts published with an 'historico-testimonial' impulse. They are rarely given to introspective psychological analysis and are limited in linguistic range (Freadman 2004: 26). The concern then arises from the potential for mis-reading (and mis-writing) personal narratives as substitutes for historical reconstruction that erase the historian's understanding that 'the personal is never the same as the social' (Fass 2006: 111). As historical source texts, they are most valuable when read as part of a larger genre where linguistic patterns, agreement about details of particular historical events and their consequences may broadly coalesce.

Kansteiner's reference to historical agents as those of collective memory, memory makers and memory consumers is helpful in considering the ethics of sharing professional authority within this context (Kansteiner 2002: 179). As an active 'memory maker', I wish to explore, in the first place, how Mr Szlezinger and I provided his memoir with the necessary references to broader historical actors to ensure its complexity and depth. Since Mr Szlezinger was born in 1935 and since the memoir largely covered the years of Belgium's occupation by the Third Reich, it was necessary to provide sufficient background to give meaning and accuracy to his memories. Moreover, the process of gathering this additional material served to memorialise not just Mr Szlezinger's family story but the experience of other Jewish people in Belgium who either died in the camps or survived through a network of resisters. While the resulting text is a first-person, linear narrative, the inclusion of multiple perspectives acknowledges that an individual memoir makes only a single contribution towards a collective one. Richard Freadman, in his examination of Australian Jewish post-Holocaust memoirs, notes that these are 'in the deepest sense purposive narratives' where the need to retain control over the mode of transmission may be made at the expense of accurate recollection and aesthetic sophistication (Freadman 2004: 31). In other words, they may sacrifice nuances of language in articulating their wartime trauma, migrant dislocation and later, their gratitude towards the Australian state where they found refuge.

Freadman's recognition of these memoirs as a grouping, even as a form of collective remembering in print, reveals much about the particularities of post-Holocaust memoirs. For Mr Szlezinger, the link between autobiographical writing and identity construction can be traced to his attendance at conferences devoted to the experience of Hidden Children in 1995 and 2007. The child survivors of the Holocaust shared their representations of the past at this public gathering, stimulating many to begin writing their experiences. In this paper, I wish to examine how the relationship between individual memories, explored within those of the collective (other relevant memoir and witness texts), illuminates the social function of collective memory. My collaboration with Mr Szlezinger points to the need for further research into this third category of 'memory consumers', an idea expressed by Claire and others as 'narrative clusters' where 'stories are connected, sometimes existing in clusters and extend infinitely, crossing cultures and generations' (Claire et al. 2014: 11). The potential of memoirs such as Mr Szlezinger's, produced outside of an academic context, to open up space for the negotiation between individual and collective memory production and its consumption, will be discussed at the end of this paper.

MEMORY MAKING

I first met Joseph Szlezinger (known to me as Joe) in 2010 to discuss collaborating on a memoir about his wartime experiences as a Jewish child, hidden in the Soeurs de Ste. Chrétienne convent boarding school in Chimay, Belgium. As I describe his intentions for a publishing project in *Shattered dreams to new beginnings* (2016), 'Joe had originally talked about something more modest, a pamphlet perhaps'. His readership would be family and friends who would have published details about his father Samuel who was arrested in Brussels in 1942 and deported from the Malines transit camp to Auschwitz while Joe and his mother Gita went into hiding. When Joe described how his mother, seeking sanctuary, demanded that the priest at a Catholic boarding school offer them protection, I was deeply moved. Even decades after the event, hearing and witnessing such a traumatic event was still shocking. My reaction and my historian's instinct was that Joe's description of this event spoke to his mother's courage and to Jewish resistance, and carried an important message that deserved more time and space than a few typed pages.

Thus began a writing collaboration which would span more than five years and pose numerous intellectual and investigative challenges. The first became apparent in gathering information about Joe's wartime memories. Since he was aged five when the German occupation began, his wartime memories were fragmentary and by themselves, not sufficiently detailed to construct a linear narrative. So began the process of researching this historical field where I discovered testimonies of other Hidden Children (a category established in 1991 at the first international gathering of Children Hidden During World War Two[3]), most notably those of Paul Pittermann (2015) and Rachel Benkiel (1968) who were also boarded with the Soeurs de Ste. Chrétienne, which proved extremely useful. Moreover, I had access to Joe's 1996 interview for the USC Shoah Foundation, to correspondence between Samuel Szlezinger and his family during the war and to key primary documents, all of which provided necessary context to Joe's memories.

Although our collaboration took place outside of an academic context,[4] Carolyn Ellis and Jerry Rawicki's recent example of 'collaborative witnessing' as a form of 'relational ethnography' offers a useful parallel. They describe a similar process of 'sharing authority' in gathering oral history mediated by the academic and the witness in analysing and constructing the text. As Ellis found in her work with Rawicki, whose family was deported from Plock to a ghetto in Bodzentyn, Poland (Ellis and Radwicki 2013), interviews were central to the process. The primary source for building the narrative of Joe and his family's wartime experience came from a series of recorded interviews conducted between 2011 and 2014. We began by discussing what Joe knew about his relatives who had lived in shtetls (small Jewish towns) northwest of Warsaw, Poland. Although printed documentary sources were scarce, Joe drew upon a rich vein of oral history. I was impressed with how deeply Joe considered my questions, often adding details, correcting my mistakes or assumptions and building on his own memories. Information about his father Samuel's early life in Drobin and his mother's, in nearby Raciaz, was supplemented by genealogical sources such as the JewishGen and Vad Yashem databases including Yizkor (memorial) books, personal family letters and photographs. To ensure that the memoir was transparent in its construction and to acknowledge the work of other writers and scholars, all sources are acknowledged in endnotes and a bibliography.

In the interviews, Joe provided me with information about his family in Poland that he had learned from his mother while details of his early childhood were more difficult to recall. As Primo Levi comments on the fallibility of memory in *The drowned and the saved*, 'a memory evoked too often, and expressed in the form of a story, tends to become fixed in a stereotype, in a form tested by experience, crystallized, perfected, adorned, installing itself in the place of the raw memory and growing at its expense' (Levi 1988: 24). In this paper, I have identified two memories that arose from my interviews with Joe that could be classified as 'crystallised' but which, used in conjunction with other witness testimony and primary sources, illuminate wider historical questions. This relational process moved the narrative beyond individual acts of heroism and survival to reveal the centrality of collective activities of Jewish and Belgian resistance in subverting the occupying German forces.

There was a powerful theme of saviours in Joe's interviews, the most important of which concerned his mother. Gita had left Poland in 1924 to live with her brother in Bochum, Germany, while still in her mid-teens to learn enough about business to open a haberdasher's shop in Brussels with her husband a decade later. Joe conveyed his sense of a woman with intelligence and character, who was deeply devoted to her son. When Brussels was invaded in May 1940, the Szlezingers fled the city for southern France and despite the terrible conditions of the St-Cyprien camp where they were interned, Gita found a waitressing job and even visited the American embassy in Marseilles to beg the high commissioner for a transit visa (Szlezinger and Wheelwright 2016). After Joe's father was deported to Auschwitz in September 1942, Gita, desperate to find sanctuary for her son, asked her Belgian landlady to foster him. When the woman agreed on the condition that Gita give up all rights to her son and that he convert to Catholicism, she refused (ibid: 53). Mother and son then went into hiding.

The key scene that depicts Gita's courage in the face of her increasing powerlessness springs from Joe's memory of meeting the man he describes as his saviour, Father Clement. Gita had made an arrangement with a sculptor in the Brussels suburb of Uccle to hide Joe in exchange for a monthly payment. This arrangement ended in 1943 when the sculptor asked Gita to pay for her son's upkeep in advance as it had become increasingly dangerous for gentiles to hide Jews. As Joe recalled:

> Whatever the sculptor's motives, my mother told me that one afternoon he had demanded a lump sum, in advance, 'for the duration'. She agreed, saying: 'I'll just take my son out for the day and we'll be back tonight and I'll tell you when I can bring the money.'
>
> The sculptor may well have considered that he would gain more from handing me over to the Germans than from my room and board (ibid: 55).

They walked to a nearby park and sat on a bench. 'My mother had nowhere to go back to and I had nowhere to go. We both began crying' (ibid: 56). When a Belgian woman sitting opposite them asked Joe's mother why she was so distressed Gita turned over the lapel of her coat to reveal the Star of David. Joe remembered this stranger suggesting that he and his mother seek refuge at a nearby boys' Catholic school where they were led to the headmaster's office. When they were introduced to a Father Clement,[5] Gita again revealed her Star of David and asked the priest to save her son. When he refused, saying that it would jeopardise the other children in his care, Gita replied: 'This is a house of God and I am not leaving' (ibid: 56).

Joe had only his fragmentary childhood memories of Father Clement as a lone rescuer but research conducted by Belgian historian Hanne Hellemans revealed that he was not acting independently and had saved three other Jewish children (Hellemans 2012). Secondary sources also gave details of the Comité de Defense des Juifs (CDJ) resistance network to which Father Clement and the Soeurs de Ste. Chretinne belonged; formed in 1942 of ordinary Belgians, they worked to save the lives of Jewish children by placing them in private homes, institutions and convents (Vroeman 2008; Marks 1997). Father Clement's connection to the CJD explains how Joe was provided with identity papers, a ration card and a guardian who accompanied him to Chimay.

A second example where fossilised memory was explored in relation to other historical actors as saviours involved the sisters of Ste. Chrétienne who performed the physical and psychic work of mother figures; caring for Joe's physical needs while operating as a bulwark against the force of mass violence that had brought him to their community. Their actions were rooted in their humanitarian and Christian beliefs; although the Jewish children were compelled to respect the Catholic rituals, the sisters made no attempts to convert Joe. He recalls attending daily mass where he knelt during prayers, genuflected at the altar and even acted as a choirboy. Unaware that other Jewish children were also hidden in the convent, Joe understood his participation in these rituals as necessary to protect his identity (Szlezinger and Wheelwright 2016: 70). Paul Pittermann, an older Jewish child hidden at Ste. Chrétienne, remembered these practices in greater detail and reflected upon their meaning more fully. Pittermann, at first, actively resisted participating in Catholic rituals but was soon warned to comply. 'I was approached by another boy ... who was two or three years older who whispered a little message from the Mother Superior in my ear: "Either you do the same as everyone else, or you return to Brussels"' (ibid: 70-71). Although Pittermann later recognised the need for such stringency, at the time he felt conflicted about his participation in these forbidden practices (Raas 2013). (While there is no evidence the Ste. Chrétienne nuns evangelised to their Jewish charges (baptism, for example, would have required them to bring them up as Catholics) other Belgian orders took a different view (Hellemans 2004: 386).

Moreover, Ste. Chrétienne's links with the CJD and the FI were extensive and during police inspections they were concerned with more than the protection of their Jewish boarders. Testimony from an American War Crimes trial in 1946, the memoirs of Father Jean Cassart, headmaster of the College Saint Joseph, (Ste. Chrétienne's brother school in Chimay), and the convent records,[6] reveal both the importance of these networks in the area and, specifically, the sisters' involvement (Martens 1999: 196). The Mother Superior Marie Mechtilde and her senior nuns ran a supply depot, an ammunitions dump and a makeshift hospital for the local Maquis, along with an illegal press that produced *La Voix de la Resistance* and *Solidarité*, the only local source of uncensored news during the war. Ensuring that these activities remained confidential (they were carried out in the convent basement) ran alongside the need to ensure the Jewish children's safety. Inclusion of references to the nuns' links with the Maquis in *Shattered dreams* moved the memoir beyond Joe's individual experience to the wider issues underlying the Soeurs' willingness to accommodate the Jewish children. This inclusion acknowledged scholarly concerns that memoirs based on traumatic events tend to individualise and over-personalise issues that 'ought properly to be regarded (at least in part) as structural and political' (Radstone 2008: 33). The recognition of the sisters' political stance during the war also challenges their role as purely maternal figures. In fact, they broke away from their contemplative, spiritual life, taking enormous risks to resist the occupying forces. Evidence of these wider activities, therefore, also provides a newly gendered reading of women's war-time activities where female domestic roles are transformed under extreme conditions.

COLLECTIVE MEMORY

Until the 1990s, Joe only rarely spoke with his mother about their traumatic wartime experiences. However, from the age of 10, Joe felt that he and his mother had swapped roles; he helped Gita in the shop, he attended gatherings of returnees from the concentration camps with the hopes of finding his father and was hyper-vigilant of his mother's emotional state. As he describes the time after their reunion in 1945: 'For months I knew that I had to be very quiet and obedient, watching what I said and did because otherwise she would cry hysterically' (Szlezinger and Wheelwright 2016: 83). Although Joe observed that the Jewish people who returned to his Brussels *quartier* were 'all lost souls' the child survivors were schooled to believe that they had no grounds for complaint (Brachfeld 1998: 33; Wolf 2007). Adult children confronted the previous generations' attitude that 'after liberation, what the hidden children had endured was not deemed worthy of attention' (Vromen op cit: 6). In the hierarchy of victimisation, the children occupied a bottom rung. As Belgian historian José Gotovitch, himself a hidden child, has commented: 'For these children, the task of remembering, therefore, came together with the reconstruction of a sense of personality, and in this process the historian often played the role of therapist' (Gotovitch 2010). Joe's attendance at a Hidden Children Foundation conference illustrates Gotovitch's point:

> It was the first time I really remember what had happened to me. ... Two speeches will always remain in my mind. One was from a Jewish lady from Holland whose parents were hidden. She said the children whose parents came back from the camps took over the role of parents to their own parents. I couldn't believe what she was saying, that's exactly what happened to me. From the day I came back from the convent until the day [my mother] died, I was like a father to [my mother]. I looked after her (Szlezinger interview 1996).

Like other Jewish child survivors, his parents' trauma had shaped his post-war life when there was no definitive proof of his father's death, no body to bury, no grave site and, until the 1990s, no public means to express his grief. Through hearing of other testimonies, he was finally able to hear and see his own experience reflected back to him.

This newly acknowledged identity of the 'Hidden Children' resulted in an outpouring of memoirs in the 2000s when Jews whose childhoods had been distorted by the loss of family, of their homes, their culture and even language, were able to articulate and share their experience. The US Holocaust Memorial Museum site now lists 23 memoirs and collective testimonies under this subject heading, the earliest dating from 1982 while many more have been privately published.[7] These narratives, like the international conferences, also performed a collective memorialising function, enabling Jewish adults to thank the people who had saved them from the camps (a sentiment found in other first-generation Holocaust survivor memoirs, according to Freadman 2004: 28) and even to reunite relatives and friends (Anti-Defamation League 2016). Belgian sociologist Suzanne Vromen, author of a major study of the hidden children and their Catholic rescuers, suggests that this shared experience provided a site for a new rhetoric of survivorship and agency (Vromen 2008: 121). Out of this collective experience came a politics which resulted in many members of the Catholic laity and other heroic individuals being remembered as Righteous Gentiles (The Soeurs de Ste. Chrétienne were given this honour in 2015).

My insistence on the inclusion of multiple perspectives in Joe's narrative, extended its purpose beyond that of recording, as much as memory can realistically offer, his witnessing of events. *Shattered dreams*, therefore, memorialised the experiences of other Jewish children who had, through giving written or recorded expression to their trauma, shaped their identity afresh. By including the experiences of Joe's contemporaries[8] the particularities of Belgian history also emerged such as post-war anti-Semitism, the children's gratitude towards the Catholic clergy who had saved them and the extraordinary resilience of Jewish families in rebuilding their lives. This memoir, seen as part of a 'narrative cluster' about hidden children, fulfils the other purposes of narrative, as articulated by Clair: 'to offer resistance, to heal, to emancipate and to grant future possibilities' (Clair 2014: 11). No story stands alone and even as humble a project as a family history reaches deep into roots that extend far across generations and cultures.

MEMORY CONSUMPTION AND AREAS FOR FURTHER RESEARCH

Narratives written by historians, argues Griffiths, must operate within a duality, explaining our epistemology while acknowledging that 'there are things we don't and can't know. Silence, uncertainty and inconclusiveness become central to the narrative' (Griffiths 2015: 17). This argument for the recognition of history's uncertainty as written text echoes Radstone's recognition about the constructedness of memory; 'even personal memory flashes, in all their apparent immediacy and spontaneity, are constructions mediated by means of complex physical and mental processes' (Radstone 2005: 135). Although I have attempted to demonstrate instances where the contextualisation of individual memory, in relation to a collective or shared memory can operate to suggest its constructedness, this addresses only half of the question. The other concerns the need for a deeper understanding of, and better research into 'memory consumption'. Who writes memoirs, from what perspectives and how their intended readers respond to them, have attracted little attention, especially in the burgeoning field of e-publishing. We need to know how the Hidden Child memoirs are received and whether the 'terrible stories' that must be listened to overwhelm the reader's ability to understand the structure of events that produced the Holocaust.

Moreover, fundamental to this process is a need to explore how the inner world of memory operates in relation to the outer world of historical forces; how is experience lived and remembered and how does remembering give shape to the broader contours of influential narratives of events (Radstone 2005: 139). These are all vital and urgent questions that deserve a wider discussion that would extend beyond academia to bridge the gap with the 'memory makers' of self-published autobiographical texts, a concern not only for the trauma of the Hidden Children but writers and readers of all historical narratives.

- This paper was first published in *Ethical Space*, Vol 13, No. 4 pp 4-10

NOTES

[1] See Sue Vice for an exploration of how translations of Defonseca's memoir from French into English are consistent with other false Holocaust testimonies which emphasise their materiality and whose distortions are 'the work of many hands'. Vice, S. (2014) Translating the self: False holocaust testimony, *Translation and Literature*, Vol. 23, No. 2 pp 197-209

[2] 'Memoir and biography' are all featured as categories for e-digital books and online platforms such as Kindle Direct Publishing, iBook authors, Kobo Writing Life and Lulu. As an example, Lulu offers 216 entries under the subject heading 'Holocaust', including memoirs by Dorothee E. Kahn, *Am I a Holocaust survivor?*, Edward Anders, *Amidst Latvians during the Holocaust*, Victoria Benson, *To no man's glory: A child's Holocaust memoir*, George Topas, *The iron furnace: Holocaust survivor stories* and Victor Breitburg and Joseph G. Krygier, *A rage to live* (available online at www.lulu.com, accessed on 4 February 2016)

[3] According to the Anti-Defamation League website, the Hidden Child organisation joined the Braun Holocaust Institute of the ALD after its conference in 1991. Available online at archive.adl.org/hidden/history.html, accessed on 3 March 2016. See also Greenfeld, H. (1993) *The hidden children*, Ticknor and Fields, Boston, and Marks, J. (1993) *The hidden children*, Ballantine Books, New York

[4] Since the project was undertaken privately and solely for the purpose of creating a private memoir initially, the university ethics committee was not consulted

[5] Although Joe met Father Clement several times and he is identified in Hanne Hellmann's research on Catholic rescuers in Belgium, no further identifying details have emerged

[6] As evidence of their involvement with the CJD, the FI and the Red Cross: the Soeurs de Sainte-Chrétienne received an order of merit from the Milices Patriotiques of Schaerbeek on 7 June 1964 and on 12 October 1980 Soeur Marie-Adrienne was given a medal by Le Comité d'Hommage des Juifs de Belgique 1940-1945 for her assistance in saving Jewish children and adults

[7] See www.ushmm.org/research, accessed on 24 May 2015

[8] A few examples of the range of memoirs consulted include: Liebman M. (2005), *Born Jewish: A childhood in occupied Europe*, Verso: London and self-published sources such as Rosenberg, R. (2008) *And somehow we survived*, Bloomington Indiana, AuthorHouse, and Muchman, B. (1997) *Never to be forgotten: A young girl's Holocaust memoir*, Hoboken NJ, KTVA Publishing

REFERENCES

Anti-Defamation League (2016) Reflections on the First International Gathering of Hidden Children. Available online at http://archive.adl.org/hidden/reflections.html, accessed on 5 February 2016

Arruti, N. (2007) Trauma, therapy and representation: Theory and critical reflection, *Paragraph*, Vol. 30, No. 1 pp 1-18

Benkiel, R. (1968) Témoinage de Madame Rachel Arezi [neé Benkiel]', Yad Vashem Archives 03/3294

Brachfeld, S. (1998) Jewish orphanages in Belgium under the German occupation, Michman, D. (ed.) (2007) *Belgium and the Holocaust: Jews, Belgians, Germans*, Jerusalem, Yad Vashem

Cassart, J. (1983-1984) Mes souvenirs de la guerre 1940-1945, *Memoires de la Société Royale D'histoire et D'Archeologie de Tournai*, Vol. 4 pp 25-52

Clair, P. et al. (2014) Narrative theory and criticism: An overview towards clusters and empathy, *Review of Communications*, Vol. 14, No. 1 pp 1-18

Dearden, L. (2014) Misha Defonseca: Author who made up Holocaust memoir ordered to repay £13.3m, *Independent*. Available online at http://www.independent.co.uk, accessed on 3 February 2016

Defonseca, M. with Lee, V. and Cuny, M-T. (2005) *Surviving with wolves: The most extraordinary story of World War II* (trans. Rose, S.), London, Portrait, second edition

Eskin, B. (2008) Crying wolf: Why did it take so long for a far-fetched Holocaust memoir to be debunked? *Slate*. Available online at http://www.slate.com/articles, accessed on 3 March 2016

Freadman, R. (2004) Generational shifts in post-Holocaust Australian Jewish autobiography, *LifeWriting*, Vol. 1, No. 1 pp 21-44

Griffiths, T. (2015) The intriguing dance of history and fiction, Nelson C. and de Matos, M. (eds) *Text* (Special Issue: Fictional histories and historical fictions; writing history in the twenty-first century), Vol. 4, No. 28 pp 1-12

Gotovitch, J. (2010) Hidden children of the Holocaust, *European Historical Review*, Vol. 125, No. 2 pp 244-245

Hellemans, H. (2004) Tot wie behoort de ziel van het kind? Der herintegratie van kinderen in de joodse gemeenschap na de Tweede Wereldoorlog [To whom does the soul of a child belong? The reintegration of children from the Jewish Community after the Second World War], *Journal of Belgian History*, Nos 13 and 14 pp 187-221

Hodgkin, K. and Radstone, S. (2003) *Contested pasts: The politics of memory*, London, Routledge

Kansteiner, W. (2002) Finding meaning in memory: A methodological critique of collective memory studies, *History and Theory*, Vol. 41, No. 2 pp 179-197

Kilby, J. (2002) Redeeming memories: The politics of trauma and history, *Feminist Theory*, Vol. 3, No. 2 pp 201-210

Maerten, F. (1999) Du murmure au grondement. La resistance politique et ideologique dans la province de Hainaut pendant la Seconde Guerre mondiale (mai 1940-septembre 1944) [From whistle to growl: The political and ideological resistance in the province of Hainaut during the Second World War], *Analectes d'histoire du Hainaut*, Vol. 7, No. 1, Mons pp 196-197

Miller, S. (2013) Fantasy, empathy and desire: Binjamin Wilkomirski's *Fragments* and Bernard Schlink's *The reader*, *Modernism/modernity*, Vol. 20, No. 1 pp 45-58

Raats, J. (2013) Sainte Chrétienne Chimay face à la seconde guerre mondiale, Raas – Pittermann email correspondence with Paul Pittermann 20 August 2013. Quoted with permission of Jonas Raats

Radstone, S. (2005) Reconceiving binaries: The limits of memory, *History Workshop Journal* (Rethinking memory special feature) Vol. 59, No. 2 pp 134-150

Singer, F. M. (2007) *I was but a child*, New York, Vad Yashem

Szlezinger, J. (1996) Interview for USC Shoah Foundation

Szlezinger, J. and Wheelwright, J. (2016) *Shattered dreams to new beginnings: A memoir of surviving the Holocaust in Belgium*, self-published

Withius, J. and Mooij, A. (2010) *The politics of war trauma: The aftermath of World War II in eleven European countries*, Amsterdam, Askant

Wolf, D. (2007) *Beyond Anne Frank: Hidden children and postwar families in Holland*, Berkeley, University of California Press

NOTE ON THE CONTRIBUTOR

Julie Wheelwright (PhD) was a creative writing programme director at City, University of London, until 2020, and has taught on the MSt in creative writing at Oxford University. She is currently an honorary research fellow in the department of history at Birkbeck, University of London. Her most recent book is *Sisters in arms: Female warriors from antiquity to the new millennium* (2020, Osprey/Bloomsbury) which was published in Italian in 2021. A former journalist and broadcaster, her research interests include the transmission of history in popular media, gendered readings of women at war and memoir as a historical source text.

SECTION 4

Communication ethics and pedagogy

Chapter 19

Can trolling be taught? Educating journalism students to identify and manage trolling – an ethical necessity

Jay Daniel Thompson

This paper argues that incorporating education about trolling into journalism education is an ethical necessity for journalism educators. This is because trolling has become a significant source of risk for journalists. The paper begins by reviewing existing scholarship on the trolling of journalists, before suggesting ways in which journalism students can be taught to identify and manage trolling in their professional lives. The overall argument is informed by Sue Robinson's model of 'journalism as process' which encourages interactivity and participation from readers. The paper also draws on Ulrich Beck's influential work on risk and Denis Muller's scholarship on journalistic ethics.

Keywords: trolling, journalism education, risk society, media ethics, 'journalism as process'

In February 2014, the Australian television personality, Charlotte Dawson, committed suicide. Her reasons for doing so remain unknown; the trolling she endured could not have helped. In 2013, the British journalist Caroline Criado-Perez publicly described the Twitter trolling that she received following her success in securing a woman's image placed back on English banknotes. Criado-Perez reported receiving threats such as 'I've just got out of prison and would happily do more time to see you berried [sic] #10 feet under' (cited in Nycyk 2019: 584).

These are two examples of how trolling has become a key source of risk for journalists, especially female journalists. This paper contends that because of that risk, there is an ethical necessity for journalism educators to incorporate education about trolling into the journalism classroom. The paper begins with a review of scholarship on the trolling of journalists, in order to contextualise the study at hand. It moves on to describe its engagement with what Sue Robinson (2013) calls 'journalism as process'. Robinson's model usefully conceives of journalism not as a 'finite entity' but as an ongoing process, one that encourages interactivity and participation from readers (Robinson 2013: 8). This model is suitable for journalism education in the digital media era. The paper concludes with suggestions on how students can be taught to identify and manage trolling in their professional lives.

This study appears to be the first to theorise the important role that journalism education can play in equipping future journalists to deal with trolling. Throughout, the term 'trolling' is understood as constituting material that is posted online with the specific purpose of generating a heightened and adverse reaction. This definition is in keeping with the ones provided in other studies (e.g. Jane 2018; Nycyk 2019). This study is conceptual in nature. Conceptual research is useful in that it enables the researcher to identify an area for enquiry *and* clarify the importance of such an enquiry (Dreher 2000: 4). The study lays the ground for more empirical research on the incorporation of education about trolling into journalism curricula. That research is, in turn, part of a broader project on the fraught relationship between trolling, free speech and democracy.

The trolling of journalists has been chosen for two reasons. Firstly, at least in a Western context, journalists have historically played a crucial role in the construction and enforcement of democracy via their 'watchdog role' (Josephi 2016: 16). Secondly, and as suggested by the literature considered in this section, journalists are profoundly vulnerable to trolling. This vulnerability arises from the publicness of a journalist's work activities and their dependence on digital technology to undertake those activities. As Claire J. B. Wolfe points out: 'Being visible online for those working in the media, and particularly for those starting jobs, has become critical for career development' (2019: 11). Journalists establish a social media presence to promote their work, attract future work and interact with followers. Those interactions have been encouraged by the below-the-line comments sections of online publications. Such interactions can be understood as working to democratise journalism and the news reportage process, at least to a small extent. As Beate Josephi points out, 'participation' in news reportage 'is a core value of democracy' (2016: 19).

TROLLING AS A SOURCE OF RISK FOR JOURNALISTS: A LITERATURE REVIEW

There exists a large body of scholarship on online trolling, as well as the trolling of journalists. This literature illustrates some of the ways in which trolling activity can harm its victims. Harms can include trauma and psychological distress (Jane 2018: 588). Emma A. Jane uses the term 'economic vandalism' 'to encapsulate a range of professional and economic harms that result from the receipt of gendered cyber-hate and that do not occur in contexts that can neatly be captured by the term "workplace harassment"' (2018: 576-577). Jane has undertaken extensive research into the harms wrought by online hostility. According to Jane, this hostility can result in 'lost income or productivity; harm to professional reputation, and/or an inability to remain in a particular profession, maintain a professional online presence, engage in business-related networking, or crowdsource/crowdfund for professional reasons' (ibid: 580). Trolling can thus endanger not only the target, but also their employer.

Further, as Catherine Adams points out, trolling demonstrates that 'the much-trumpeted new democracy of the web is failing' (2018: 851). Or, put simply: anyone with internet access can potentially have their voices heard in the digital public sphere, but these voices can just as easily be shut down by other voices. Karen Lumsden and Heather Morgan (2016: 927) elaborate on that point when they describe the tactics deployed by trolls as 'silencing strategies'. Lumsden and Morgan's point is buttressed by the following quote from Emma Barnett (a former women's editor at Britain's *Daily Telegraph* newspaper and currently a BBC broadcaster): 'More people don't want to provoke others, so they start to self-censor what they say if they are trolled. But if you're a journalist, your job is to provoke' (cited in Wolfe 2019: 14). Censorship has traditionally been regarded as anti-thetical to democracy, whether it is enacted by the self or the state (Bradshaw 2019).

In the literature surveyed for this article, there is considerable emphasis placed on the trolling of female journalists (e.g. Gudipaty 2017; Löfgren Nilsson and Ornebring 2016; Lumsden and Morgan 2016). That is unsurprising. As Karen Lumsden and Heather Morgan (2016: 928) write: 'Trolling is situated within the wider social and cultural context of the rise of "lad culture" where sexist and misogynistic language and treatment of women is lauded and admired by peers.' For these authors trolling must be viewed 'within this context, as a means of silencing women's voices online and their participation in virtual public space(s)' (ibid). This is true across the journalism spectrum, and particularly in traditionally male-dominated fields such as sports (Antunovic 2019) and technology (Adams 2018) journalism.

In short, trolling is a major source of risk for journalists, especially female journalists. Conceptualising trolling as risk is useful because it demonstrates how this phenomenon does not simply comprise unrelated, isolated online incidents; it stems from a broader risk society, one in which all journalists work. The term 'risk society' was coined by the late sociologist Ulrich Beck, who famously defined the term 'risk' as 'a systematic way of dealing with hazards and insecurities induced and introduced by modernization itself' (1986: 21):

> In advanced modernity the social production of wealth is accompanied by the social production of risks. Accordingly, the problems and conflicts relating to the distribution in a society of scarcity overlap with the problems and conflicts that arise from the production, definition and distribution of techno-scientifically produced risks (Beck 1986: 19).

Trolling can certainly be classified as a 'techno-scientifically produced risk'; it could not exist without the internet, social media platforms or online publications. Interestingly, Beck did not mention online hostility in his work. In a 2013 interview, he acknowledged that in a digital mediascape, 'individual freedom and privacy' have become casualties. Beck supported this point by referring to data leakages such as those made by the NSA whistleblower, Edward Snowden, in 2013. Similarly, trolling has gone unmentioned in other studies of digital risk (e.g. Lupton 2016).

Beck argues that 'risks open the opportunity to document statistically consequences that were at first always personalized and shifted onto individuals' (1992: 99). This is an important point when critically examining journalistic reportage on trolling. The shifting of risks onto individuals can take the form of blaming victims (explicitly or implicitly) for being trolled. This victim-blaming is suggested by Lumsden and Morgan: 'The advice to women which is propagated in media and popular discourses: "Do not feed the trolls" is a form of "symbolic violence" promoting victim complicity with online abuse' (2016: 927). The Australian journalist, Ginger Gorman, describes the assumption underpinning media coverage of women who are trolled: 'She wouldn't shut up. She was asking for it' (2019: 78). This assumption has been evident historically in media coverage of violence against women (Morgan 2006).

Interestingly, while there have been numerous studies on the trolling of journalists, there seems to be very little research about the incorporation of education about trolling into journalism education. A possible exception is Claire J. B. Wolfe's 2019 study of trolling as an impediment to online discourse. Wolfe interviewed journalism graduates working in the mediascape about whether they had experienced online hostility. Wolfe also interviewed undergraduate journalism students 'about their experiences and what they felt would be helpful to them in [working online]' (Wolfe 2019: 11).

Wolfe's study usefully outlines the support (legal, institutional) that media workers require when they are targeted by trolling activity. Wolfe acknowledges that online hostility is a significant challenge facing journalists, as well as media professionals more generally. She concedes that 'there is little guidance for those entering the media professions to help them navigate their way through the legal and ethical pitfalls of engaging with hostile commentators online' (ibid). Yet, Wolfe does not focus *specifically* on journalism education. This is not so much a criticism of her study as it is an acknowledgement of an area that requires further research. This paper lays the ground for such research when it investigates how and why journalism education can equip future journalists to identify and manage trolling as an inherently ethical endeavour.

CONCEPTUAL FRAMEWORK: 'JOURNALISM AS PROCESS'

This paper's conceptual framework is based on Sue Robinson's model of 'journalism as process'. Robinson borrows that concept from a 2009 blog post by Jeff Jarvis (Jarvis 2009; Robinson 2013: 1). Conceptualising 'journalism as process' is useful because it shifts 'the focus from the journalist as producer to journalist as facilitator, conversationalist, connector, networker and producer' (Robinson 2013: 2). Robinson's model understands the reader as playing an active role in journalism's production and consumption. This audience interactivity is encouraged by digital media outlets, as mentioned, and has facilitated or at least enabled trolling activity (though Robinson does not mention trolling). Simultaneously, the model moves away from the 'sender-receiver model of content production' that has traditionally characterised journalism education (ibid: 3). The term 'process' is crucial; in Robinson's model, the production and consumption of journalism is understood as ongoing, and not something that finishes when the journalist finishes writing an article. Trolling can be part of that process, whether it appears in below-the-line comments or in a journalist's email inbox following the publication of a story.

Robinson frames her 'journalism as process' model as a contribution to research into transforming journalism curricula to equip graduates to work in a digitised workforce. This research has been broad in scope. Studies have examined the benefits of educating journalism students to use blogs (Mulrennan 2017: 328) and social media platforms in researching, producing and/or distributing journalistic content (Kothari and Hickerson, 2016; Larrondon Ureta and Fernandez 2018: 882-886). Bradford Gyori and Matthew Charles (2018) have investigated the use of web design programs in the journalism classroom. The teaching of data journalism has been the subject of several studies (Burns and Matthews 2018; Treadwell et al. 2016).

This paper suggests that teaching journalism students to identify and manage trolling is just as important as teaching them to use social media in their working lives or to produce data journalism. Indeed, the paper contends that incorporating education about trolling into journalism curricula is an ethical necessity for journalism educators. In journalism studies, ethics have commonly been conceived of in terms of the social contract that journalists enter into. Denis Muller describes that social contract:

> By engaging in journalism, a person enters into that contract. The contract says that journalism will provide reliable and relevant information that empowers people to participate in political, economic, and social life. In return, society recognises that practitioners of journalism need certain privileges so they can fulfil that role (2014: 224).

Journalistic ethics include honesty, truth-telling, transparency and care for oneself and one's colleagues (ibid: 226-230). They include a commitment to defending free speech, 'while at the same time recognising that there are times when it yields to other values' (ibid: 230). The question of what constitutes free speech, and the notoriously porous boundary between 'free speech' and 'censorship', are important for journalists and content moderators. That point will be elaborated on in the paper's final section which suggests how those concepts can be integrated into the journalism classroom within the context of educating students about trolling.

Also, journalistic ethics entails a commitment to mitigating harm to oneself and others. This can take the form of anticipating what material is in the 'public interest' (and should, therefore, be reported on) and what might be reasonably cause injury to the reporter and/or readers (and, therefore, should not be reported on, or reported on with great sensitivity) (ibid: 75). In the journalism classroom, educators can demonstrate ethical behaviour by equipping students to avoid (re)traumatising themselves and their interviewees. The provision of teaching about trauma in journalism education has itself been the topic of several studies (see Amend, Kay and Reilly 2012; Dworznik and Garvey 2019). Those studies have recognised the role that the journalism classroom can play in creating future journalists who can effectively manage trauma in their working lives. These studies are important in that they conceive of journalism education as serving an ethical as well as a utilitarian function; indeed, they suggest how a commitment to ethics can *enhance* the utilitarian function. Those studies tend, however, to focus on potentially traumatic areas of journalist enquiry (e.g. violence and murder). They do not mention the abuse that journalists can face in doing their jobs, nor do they mention trolling or online hostility.

The following section suggests ways in which educators can teach students to identify and manage trolling in their working lives. The suggestions encompass learning activities and classroom resources. The latter include academic studies and government reports about trolling, all of which can be obtained via the internet or university library catalogues. Theoretically, the section is animated by Beck's warning that managing risks can have unintended consequences, including the production of further risks (Beck 2001: 271).

The section attempts to illustrate how journalism education can help students avoid risks inherent in addressing trolling, whether as its victim or as a journalist reporting on it.

A disclaimer is needed here concerning the timing of this paper. The piece was completed in March 2020, when the Covid-19 pandemic was forcing education institutions globally to shift to online teaching spaces at a rate, and to a degree, that could not previously have been anticipated. The pandemic will have a panoply of technological and economic ramifications for higher education institutions, many of which are yet to become evident. Thus, the activities suggested below are amenable to online and physical classroom spaces. They are cost-efficient, which is particularly crucial for institutions that have been facing tighter teaching budgets, and will doubtless continue to do so in the wake of Covid-19. The suggestions are broad enough that they can be adapted and modified according to the individual needs of educators and journalism programmes.

YES, TROLLING CAN BE TAUGHT! INCORPORATING TROLLING INTO THE JOURNALISM CLASSROOM

There are several classroom activities that could be used to help students identify trolling activity. These include providing students with real life scenarios involving online hostility, and asking students to identify why or why not this hostility might be regarded as 'trolling'. They can include scanning below-the-line comments sections to identify comments that might be classified as 'trolling' and asking students to explain why this might be so. Activities can also entail online quizzes (e.g. run through Moodle or Kahoot). Online quizzes are useful because they 'allow students to actively participate in their learning processes by self-assessing their progress instantaneously on computers, tablets and/or mobile phones' (Di Meo and Marti-Ballester 2020: 121). These quizzes can alert the student and the educator to the knowledge that the student is retaining, as well as knowledge that they may not yet be fully grasping or may need to revise.

Once trolling has been identified, the following question arises: how does the journalist respond? This is a question that could energise classroom discussions. In Wolfe's study, several undergraduate journalism students reported that 'they did not know where to seek guidance' (2019: 18). The adage 'Don't feed the trolls' is popular in online culture, and correct to the extent that the troll 'wins' when 'discussions descend into virtual shouting matches' (MacKinnon and Zuckerman 2012: 14). Engaging with trolls can compound the distress experienced by victims. Nonetheless, ignoring trolling activity may be futile, and may itself benefit the troll, who is free to continue their abuse.

In other words, not responding to trolls in any manner can mean enabling their activities. Thus, students should be exposed to the policies of international media outlets regarding online hostility, including trolling. These resources could be set as required readings for students, discussed in seminars, and form the basis of assessment tasks. There are many examples to choose from. For example, the 'Editorial Ethics & Guidelines' tab of the Vox Media website states: 'Our editorial guidelines leave no room for indulging harassment on social media. If any Vox Media employee is the recipient of harassment on social media, they should access and review our protocol for reporting online abuse.' Students should also be educated about the various legal and institutional channels to which they have recourse should they be subject to online hostility while working as journalists. The Law Library of Congress's report, *Laws protecting journalists from online harassment* (2019), documents laws from numerous countries and could serve as a useful resource for journalism educators and students. Another useful resource is from Australia: the Media Entertainment and Arts Alliance (MEAA) and Gender Equity

Victoria's *Don't read the comments* (2019). This policy document suggests 'strategies for media organisations to prevent and respond to gender-based abuse on their platforms' (MEAA and Gender Equity Institute 2019: 4).[1]

Educating students to *report on* trolling in an ethical and nuanced manner is crucial. This is firstly because of the victim-blaming entrenched in some media coverage of trolling, especially when the victims are women (e.g. Lumsden and Morgan 2017: 933). Secondly, the word 'trolling' is itself widely misused. For example, in her book *Troll hunting* (2019), Ginger Gorman cites as an example a column published in an Australian newspaper in which the reporter describes the pairing of a 'seemingly unsuited couple' on a television programme thus: 'Now [the programme] is in its fifth season, it's just trolling' (cited in Gorman 2019: 14). The example provided in no way attempts to unsettle or distress the reader; it seems to be a relatively inoffensive ploy for television ratings. The reporter's use of the term 'trolling' may appear merely lazy. Nonetheless, it obscures that term's actual definition, and thus how trolling can be identified and managed.

There are numerous resources that an educator could set as readings for students. For example, organisations such as Our Watch (2019) and the Dart Center for Journalism and Trauma have produced literature regarding the media reporting of violence against women.[2] The Our Watch guidelines specifically recommend that reporters 'name' men's violence against women and girls; 'use evidence-based language' when describing this violence; and be aware that 'that there are certain legal parameters that outline what you can and can't report regarding certain sexual offences, where protection orders have been issued, or where there are children involved' (ibid: 3-4). Drawing on resources such as these, students can be encouraged to write news stories about real-life cases of trolling and online hostility that names this abuse as abuse; that provides facts about online hostility and the damages it causes victims; that does not provide information that may incriminate the journalist or the media outlet for which they are employed; that avoids portraying the victim as deserving/inviting their abuse, and that does not blame the abuse on personal struggles experienced by the abuser (ibid: 4).

In learning to write ethically about trolling, students can be encouraged to develop a range of important skills that can be used in all areas of journalism. These include skills in researching stories and drawing on appropriate sources. In the context of trolling, 'appropriate sources' could include government reports and academic studies on trolling. Students can develop skills in locating interviewees via Google and social media searches. Students can also be encouraged to develop skills when interviewing those who have experienced trolling. Gretchen Dworznik and Adrienne Garvey point out that an absence of trauma training in journalism curricula 'heightens the possibility [of journalists] doing harm to interview subjects ... and often results in insensitive and intrusive behaviors on the part of the reporter' (2019: 370). A 2012 study suggests the use of simulations in the journalism classroom to educate students about ethical trauma reporting practices

(Amend and Reilly 2012: 243). Simulations could be useful in teaching techniques in interviewing trolling victims, as well as dealing with potential scenarios in which students (as journalists) are trolled. The specific forms in which such simulations may take warrant further investigation.

Another crucial aspect of reporting ethically on trolling concerns the representation of trolls themselves. Those responsible for trolling activity are commonly stereotyped as 'ignorant, uneducated and alone' (Gorman 2019: 41). As Ginger Gorman suggests, this stereotype 'serves to diffuse the hate, making us less afraid' of the trolls (2019: 41). Relatedly, that stereotype helps cultivate a comforting distinction/difference between 'them' and 'us' (with 'us' being educated, sensitive to the feelings of others, and not at all prone to trolling activity). The 'ignorant, uneducated and alone' stereotype is, however, inaccurate. This stereotype should be discouraged in the journalism classroom, as it prevents an understanding of the trolls' motives, why they behave the way they do online.

Further to the last point, understanding trolls is a part of developing empathy with them. As Antje Gluck points out: 'Empathy is present in telling the [news] story, in creating authenticity, and in relating to the news source as a human being' (2016: 894). Empathy is thus, crucial to the teaching and production of ethical journalism. In *Troll hunting*, Gorman writes:

> I know with my heart more than my head that we can't leave kids alone in echo chambers of online hate and then wonder why they emerge as socially isolated individuals full of rage. Why they believe the world is an inhospitable place. Why they want to hurt, isolate, damage and enrage other people and laugh at them the way that they've been hurt (2019: 264; and see also Joseph 2019).

Gorman's words are borne out in her book, in which she interviews a number of trolls. This was not an easy endeavour for the author, herself a victim of trolling, who describes the writing of *Troll hunting* as 'harrowing and dark' (2019: 262). That response is unsurprising; as Gluck reminds us, cultivating empathy is an act of 'emotional labour' (2016: 84). Emotional labour can take a psychological toll on journalists. Nonetheless, teaching students to demonstrate empathy when reporting on and/or interviewing trolls is infinitely more ethical than encouraging them to reproduce dehumanising and inaccurate stereotypes of those individuals.

As journalism educators know, many journalism students do not go on to work as journalists. These students may find employment elsewhere in the mediascape, including in content moderation. The latter has been chosen as a case study because of its alignment with the 'journalism as process' model. Robinson argues that in the digital mediascape, readers are 'collaborators with individual members of the public' (2013: 3). This 'collaboration' can take a number of forms, including interactions between journalists and readers on social media and in below-the-line comments sections. Content moderation plays a crucial role in regulating this journalist-reader collaboration. Tarleton Gillespie expands on that point when he writes: 'Platforms must, in some form or another, moderate: both to protect one user from another, or one group from its antagonists, and to remove the offensive, vile, or illegal'. This is in addition to protecting the company's public reputation (Gillespie 2018: 5).

Also, using content moderation as a case study is useful inasmuch as it highlights some of the tensions between 'free speech' and 'online hostility'. Gillespie notes: 'Disgruntled users who have had content removed [from a platform] sometimes cry "censorship"' (ibid: 176). Gillespie rightly suggests that such cries are 'not entirely accurate' (ibid). There is a tradition in libertarian circles of framing all speech as worth defending, even (or perhaps particularly) if it is likely to cause offence (Graefer 2019: 7). In fact, the 'offensive, vile or illegal' material posted online by trolls *encourages* journalists to self-censor. Lumsden and Morgan's study supports that point. Self-censorship 'inhibits the spread of ideas and inhibits diverse opinion' (Bradshaw 2017: 19) and is thus antithetical to democracy.

Nevertheless, Gillespie points to a question that journalists and moderators face, and that journalism students should be encouraged to interrogate in their studies: where is the line between freedom of speech and censorship? This question has been the source of productive debate in the journalism classes run by this paper's author. A hypothetical scenario provided by the author in his seminars is this: a reader announces their opposition to same-sex marriage in the comments section of a pro-same sex marriage article. This reader is articulating an opinion that many readers and, indeed, the journalist who wrote said article may find objectionable. Perhaps the commenter may *want* to distress the author and other readers. Yet, should the expression of this opinion be regarded as trolling (and, therefore, deleted by the moderator) or as free speech (and, therefore, protected)? In considering the scenario, students have been faced with other questions, including: how to balance the offence and distress caused to a journalist with the democratic right of their readers to voice their views, unpopular though such views may be? Will readers be less likely to comment in a below-the-line comments section, or even read the publication hosting that section, if they know that their views may be regarded as 'contentious' and thus deleted? How will this impact on the economic livelihood of the journalist and/or the publication for which they are writing?

The importance of free speech to a democracy was most famously theorised by John Stuart Mill in his essay *On liberty* (1859). This essay is still invoked in critical analyses of free speech (e.g. Bradshaw 2019; Muller 2019), and could be useful as a class reading, if only to introduce students to theories of harm and/in speech. Importantly, Mill does not uncritically celebrate all speech as being inherently valid. A crucial component of his analysis is the Harm Principle:

… a deceptively simple ethical proposition which has generated much debate regarding its practical application. The principle states that 'The only purpose for which power can be rightfully exercised over any member of a civilised community, against his will, is to prevent harm to others' (Mill 1989 [1859]: 13; Bradshaw 2017: 20).

According to Mill, speech becomes problematic when it threatens to cause harm. Thus, journalism educators could encourage classroom discussions about how harm can be defined and measured, and the extent it can be avoided while undertaking work as a journalist or content moderator. Trauma, loss of employment and loss of life would clearly be categorised as 'harm'; the question of whether offence constitutes harm (and if so, how) has been another topic of lively debate in the journalism classes run by this paper's author, with a consensus on the question seldom reached. Potential questions for students to consider within such a debate include: if harm is established, then does reporting the troll to police or deleting their comments from a social media platform constitute 'censorship'? Is harmful speech free speech?

There are many case studies that the educator could use as teaching resources when educating students/future journalists about what constitutes harm. These include Mills' essay and Gorman's *Troll hunting*. They also include studies of journalists who have been trolled (e.g. Adams 2018; Antunovic 2019). Teaching resources could also include academic literature on free speech and censorship in the media.

CONCLUSION

Trolling is a major source of risk for journalists, especially female journalists, and takes a profound economic and psychological toll on victims. This paper has argued that there is an ethical necessity for journalism educators to teach journalism students how to identify and manage trolling in their working lives, without risking their safety or the speech of those with whom they may disagree. The argument for this education has been informed by Sue Robinson's model of 'journalism as process'. That model understands journalism as a process that requires skills in using digital technology, and one in which the reader plays an active role. This is, thus, an appropriate model through which to understand journalism education in the digital era and, specifically, how this education can be enhanced to prepare students for the workforce. Empirical research is required to determine how the suggestions advanced throughout this paper play out in journalism classrooms.

- This paper was first published in *Ethical Space*, Vol. 17, No. 2 pp 30-37

NOTES

[1] The MEAA is the peak union for Australia's creative professionals. Gender Equity Victoria is an organisation dedicated to gender equity and the elimination of violence against women, and is based in Victoria, Australia

[2] Our Watch is a non-profit Australian organisation dedicated to preventing violence against women and their children. The Dart Center focuses on journalistic reportage of trauma and is a project of the Columbia University Graduate School of Journalism

REFERENCES

Adams, C. (2018) 'They go for gender first': The nature and effect of sexist abuse of female technology journalists, *Journalism Practice*, Vol. 12, No.7 pp 850-869

Antunovic, D. (2019) 'We wouldn't say it to their faces': Online harassment, women sports journalists, and feminism. *Feminist Media Studies*, Vol. 19, No. 3 pp 428-442

Amend, E., Kay, L. and Reilly, R. C. (2012) Journalism on the spot: Ethical dilemmas when covering trauma and the implications for journalism education, *Journal of Mass Media Ethics*, Vol. 27, No. 4 pp 235-247

Beck, U. (1986). *Risk society: Towards a new modernity*, London, Sage

Beck, U. (1992) From industrial society to the risk society: Questions of survival, social structure and ecological enlightenment, *Theory, Culture & Society*, Vol. 9 pp 97-123

Beck, U. (2001) Interview with Ulrich Beck, *Journal of Consumer Culture*, Vol. 1, No. 2 pp 261-277

Beck, U. (2013). The digital freedom risk: Too fragile an acknowledgement, *Open Democracy*, 30 August. Available online at https://www.opendemocracy.net/en/can-europe-make-it/digital-freedom-risk-too-fragile-acknowledgment/, accessed on 27 February 2020

Bradshaw, T. (2017) John Stuart Mill: Freedom of expression and harm in the 'post-truth' era, *Ethical Space: The International Journal of Communication Ethics*, Vol. 14, No. 1 pp 15-25

Burns, L. S. and Matthews, B. J. (2018) First things first: Teaching data journalism as a core skill, *Asia Pacific Media Educator*, Vol. 28, No. 1 pp 91-105

Dart Center for Reporting on Journalism and Trauma (2011) Reporting on sexual violence. Available online at https://dartcenter.org/content/reporting-on-sexual-violence, accessed on 27 February 2020

Dreher, A. U. (2000) *Foundations for conceptual research in psychoanalysis*, Oxon and New York, Routledge

Dworznik, G. and Garvey, A. (2019) Are we teaching trauma? A survey of accredited journalism schools in the United States, *Journalism Practice*, Vol. 13, No. 3 pp 367-382

Engelke, K. M. (2019) Enriching the conversation: Audience perspectives on the deliberative nature and potential of user comments for news media, *Digital Journalism*, 1-20, DOI: 10.1080/21670811.2019.1680567

Gardiner, B. (2018) 'It's a terrible way to go to work': What 70 million readers' comments on the *Guardian* revealed about hostility to women and minorities online, *Feminist Media Studies*, Vol. 18, No. 4 pp 592-608

Gillespie, T. (2018) *Custodians of the internet: Platforms, content moderation, and the hidden decisions that shape social media*, New Haven and London, Yale University Press

Gorman, G. (2019) *Troll hunting: Inside the world of human hate and its human fallout*, Melbourne, Hardie Grant

Gluck, A. (2016) What makes a good journalist? Empathy as a central resource in journalistic work practice, *Journalism Studies*, Vol.17, No.7 pp 893-903.

Graefer, A. (2019) Introduction, Graefer, A. (ed.) *Media and the politics of Offence*, Switzerland, Palgrave Macmillan pp 1-20

Gyori, B. and Charles, M. (2018) Designing journalists: Teaching journalism students to think like web designers, *Journalism & Mass Communication Educator*, Vol. 73, No. 2 pp 200-217

Gudipaty, N. (2017) Gendered public spaces. Online trolling of women journalists in India, *Comunicazione politica*, Vol. 18, No. 2 pp 299-310

Jane, E. A. (2018) Gendered cyberhate as workplace harassment and economic vandalism, *Feminist Media Studies*, Vol. 18, No. 4 pp 575-591

Jarvis, J. (2009) Product vs process journalism: The myth of perfection v. beta culture, *BuzzMachine*, 7 June. Available online at https://buzzmachine.com/2009/06/07/processjournalism/, accessed on 24 February 2020

Joseph, S. (2019) Review of *Troll hunting: Inside the world of online hate and its human fallout*, *Ethical Space*, Vol.16, No. 2/3 pp 45-46

Josephi, B. (2016) Digital journalism and democracy, Witschge, T., Anderson, C. W., Domingo, D. and Hermida, A. (eds) *The SAGE handbook of digital journalism*, Los Angeles, CA, Sage pp 9-24

Kothari, A. and Hickerson, A. (2016) Social media use in journalism education: Faculty and student expectations, *Journalism & Mass Communication Educator*, Vol. 71, No. 4 pp 413-424

Larrondo Ureta, A. and Fernandez, S.P. (2018) Keeping pace with journalism training in the age of social media and convergence: How worthwhile is it to teach online skills?, *Journalism*, Vol. 19, No. 6 pp 877-891

Law Library of Congress (2019) *Laws protecting journalists from online harassment*, September. Available online at https://www.loc.gov/law/help/protecting-journalists/online-harassment.pdf, accessed on 28 February 2020

Löfgren Nilsson, M. and Ornebring, H. (2016) Journalism under threat: Intimidation and harassment of Swedish journalists, *Journalism Practice*, Vol. 10, No. 7 pp 880-890

Lumsden, K. and Morgan, H. (2017) Media framing of trolling and online abuse: Silencing strategies, symbolic violence and victim blaming, *Feminist Media Studies*, Vol. 17, No. 6 pp 926-940

Lupton, D. (2016). Digital risk society, Burgess, A., Alemanno, A. and Zinn, J. O. (eds) *Routledge handbook of risk studies*, London and New York, Routledge pp 301-309

MacKinnon, R. and Zuckerman, E. (2012) Don't feed the trolls, *Index on Censorship*, Vol. 41, No. 4 pp 14-24

MEAA and Gender Equity Victoria (2019) *Don't read the comments: Enhancing online safety for women working in the media*, Victoria: MEAA and Gender Equity Victoria. Available online at https://www.meaa.org/download/dont-read-the-comments-enhancing-online-safety-for-women-working-in-the-media/, accessed on 8 May 2020

Morgan, K. (2006) Cheating wives and vice girls: The construction of a culture of resignation, *Women's Studies International Forum*, Vol. 29, No. 5 pp 489-498

Muller, D. (2014) *Journalism ethics for the digital age*, Melbourne, Scribe Publications

Muller, D. (2019) Open discourse: A media theory for the 21st century, *Ethical Space*, Vol. 16, No. 1 pp 3-10

Mulrennan, D. (2017) Mobile social media and the news: Where heutagogy enables journalism education, *Journalism & Mass Communication Educator*, Vol. 73, No. 30 pp 322-333. Available online at https://core.ac.uk/download/pdf/132419351.pdf

Nycyk, M. (2019) Trolls and trolling history: From subculture to mainstream practices, Brügger, N. and Milligan, I. (eds) *The SAGE handbook of web history*, London: Sage pp 577-589

Our Watch (2019) *How to report on violence against women and their children*, Victorian edition, Melbourne, Our Watch

Robinson, S. (2013). Teaching 'journalism as process': A proposed paradigm for J-School curricula in the digital age, *Teaching Journalism & Mass Communication*, Vol. 3, No. 1 pp 1-12

Sreberny, A. (2014) Violence against women journalists, *Media and gender: A scholarly alliance for the global alliance on media and gender*, UNESCO pp 35-39

Treadwell, G., Ross, T., Lee, A. and Lowenstein, J. K. (2016) A numbers game: Two case studies in teaching data journalism, *Journalism & Mass Communication Educator*, Vol. 71, No. 3 pp 297-308

Vox Media (n.d.) Vox Media's Editorial Ethics and Guidelines. Available online at https://www.voxmedia.com/a/vm/ethics, accessed on 28 February 2020

Wolfe, C. J. B. (2019) Online trolls, journalism and the freedom of speech: Are the bullies taking over? *Ethical Space: The International Journal of Communication Ethics*, Vol. 16, No. 1 pp 11-21

NOTE ON THE CONTRIBUTOR

Dr Jay Daniel Thompson is lecturer, Professional Communication in the School of Media and Communication at RMIT University, Melbourne. His research explores ways of cultivating ethical online communication to mitigate digital hostility and networked disinformation. He is the co-author of two books published in 2022: *Fake news in digital cultures* (with Rob Cover and Ashleigh Haw) and *Content production for digital media* (with John Weldon).

Chapter 20

How ethics is taught at leading institutions in the Pacific region

Tom Cooper

This paper includes 1) the previously unpublished findings of a current (2015-2016) study (Part II) about the teaching of ethics at leading English-speaking institutions in the Pacific region, 2) a comparison of those findings with a companion study (Part I) conducted at leading institutions in the Atlantic region in 2008, and 3) the aggregate findings of the two studies considered as parts of a single research project. The purpose of the overall research was to determine how ethics is taught at selected leading English-speaking institutions of higher education, the challenges these ethics teachers and their students face, how individual faculty/staff members enhance their teaching effectiveness over time, and many other related questions. Ideally, the findings can help individuals, institutions and possibly the public better understand and improve ethics instruction.

Keywords: ethics, Pacific region, teaching and learning, higher education, public understanding

BACKGROUND

Field research was conducted in 2008 to determine how ethics and moral philosophy were being taught in six leading English-speaking universities – Harvard, Oxford, Yale, Cambridge, Princeton and the University of Edinburgh – and in five additional top-ranked departments and programmes elsewhere in the Atlantic region. Supported by a Page grant, by sabbatical endorsement from Emerson College, and by guest scholar-in-residence status at the University of Edinburgh, Union University, and field locations above, this researcher visited and/ or corresponded with scholars at eleven British and US campuses in a study titled 'Part I – Atlantic Region'. A complete summary of the findings was published in 2009 in *Teaching Ethics* (Vol. 10, No. 1 pp 11-42) while an abridged overview also was published in *Ethical Space* (Vol. 6, No. 1 pp 12-16).

A companion study ('Part II – Pacific') was conducted in 2015-2016 to determine how ethics and moral philosophy were and are being taught at leading Pacific region English-speaking institutions in the United States, Canada, Singapore, Australia,

New Zealand and Hong Kong. Within this latter study, the 'Pacific region' of the United States meant California, Hawaii, Oregon and Washington. This study is reported below for the first time. It was supported by an anonymous invited grant, by guest scholar status at Stanford, UC-Berkeley, the East-West Center, and the University of Hawaii and by full-year sabbatical endorsement by Emerson College.

PURPOSE

Although the purpose of Part I was to study Atlantic region ethics instruction and Part II was to inspect Pacific region instruction, both studies constitute a larger project with these purposes:

1) to determine how ethics classroom instruction is taught in many leading English-speaking institutions;

2) to learn from respected ethics teachers how many enhance their teaching effectiveness over time;

3) to gather an inventory of creative teaching tools and resources potentially helpful to other ethics faculty;

4) to ascertain in what sense of the word 'ethics' may be successfully taught within higher education;

5) to ascertain collective views on primary pedagogical issues within ethics; and

6) to compile statistical data on these and related questions.

After interviews with forty selected ethics faculty were recorded, coded, analysed and amalgamated to determine discernible patterns, then two further purposes of the study could be completed:

7) to share the study with other instructors, administrators and educators to better publicise findings about the teaching of ethics; and

8) ideally, to add tools and recommendations for improvement to a larger inventory This report not only includes 2015 findings from Pacific region institutions (Part II) and refers to 2008 primary findings from the Atlantic region (Part I), but also contains comparisons between the two studies.

SUMMARY OF PRIMARY FINDINGS

Here are the 'headlines' about findings of the 2015-2016 study listed in bullet point format only:

- Participant use of short papers, classroom discussion, the teaching of applied ethics, bringing new ideas from the field into the classroom, discussing 'hot' issues (e.g. hate speech, racism, genetic manipulation, sexual morals, etc.) are all trending upward since the 2008 study.

- A strict adherence to canonical (e.g. Aristotle, Kant, Mill, Rawls, etc.) texts, case studies, assigning self-authored texts and formal debates are all trending slightly downward since 2008.
- Faculty think that both ethics students and teachers now face the same greatest obstacle within the educational process – a perceived lack of time.
- Far more women and a somewhat more racially diverse faculty are increasingly prominent contributors to teaching ethics than in 2008.
- Faculty remain divided about whether ethics teachers should be 'neutral' referees in the classroom or should 'take a stand' and reveal their 'biases'.
- Although faculty also remain divided about whether the ethics of 'moral improvement' (i. e. 'being a better person') may be taught in schools, the majority now feel it should not or cannot be taught at the university level. One third disagree.
- The most frequently mentioned reason ethics faculty now teach pertains to 'service to society' rather than other reasons often reported such as enjoyment, passion for learning, fulfilment, love of students, etc.
- There is currently a push back against PowerPoint-type technologies by many ethics professors for both philosophical and pedagogical reasons. The minority defending PowerPoint was smaller than in 2008.
- More faculty are minimising or banning the use of cellphones and laptops by students in their classrooms than in 2008.
- Over time, newer faculty tend to move from a single (course content) to a dual (student-driven and personal research influenced) emphasis compared with the previous study.
- As in 2008, most ethics faculty typically and Socratically consistently challenge students' assumptions, opinions, beliefs and the status quo.
- As in 2008, while students frequently find the mode of ethical and philosophical thinking challenging and unsettling to their desire for closure and moral simplicity, often they later find this approach to thinking rewarding and relevant.
- As in 2008, graduate ethics courses tend to be 1) smaller, 2) less formal, and 3) more student-driven. Graduate pedagogies more frequently include 4) student presentations, 5) textbooks/articles written by the professor, 6) allusions to the professor's research, and 7) more expansive discussion supplanting the media projections, debates, cases and lectures prominent within undergraduate classes.

- Just as the Oxford/Cambridge traditional tutorial system provided a minor influence on the overall 2008 study outcomes, even so the Confucian/Taoist Eastern tradition has a minor influence overall in the teaching of ethics in English-speaking institutions in the Pacific. However, the primary curricula in both studies are similar.
- While for some participants ethics is only subject matter or a mental process, for many it is also a potential means for both students and faculty to raise the bar in public discussion if not to bring pro-social change in civic moral decision-making.

THE PARTICIPANTS AND THEIR SELECTION

The participants from Harvard, Oxford, Cambridge, Yale, Princeton, and their selection process for the first study were previously listed in *Teaching Ethics* and *Ethical Space*. For the 2015 companion study 60 potential participants were chosen by reputation and referral by advisors within germane leading professional organisations and institutions and by selected ethics 'elders', then compared for frequency of mention, location and for balanced demographics. This process narrowed the group to 54 which then self-selected for participation according to availability and choice.

Major advisors to the selection process consisted of appropriate American Philosophy Association (APA) officers and selected academic leaders in the field. Initially 43 of the 54 at leading Pacific institutions (Stanford, Berkeley, UCLA, the Australian National University, etc.), responded that they were available to participate. When six of these dropped out or could not meet a deadline, alternates who had been similarly selected were invited to fill vacancies until the group again came to a total of 40 participants.

More teachers from larger high echelon universities were selected for the study whereas only one or two were typically chosen from smaller and lower ranked universities including those within tiny nations. Thus factors of scale, reputation, ranking, advisory input, representation, demographics, sub-discipline and 'quota' were all taken into account when both institutions and individuals were selected. Those interviewed included a wide spectrum of roles and experience including former and current deans, department chairs, centre and programme heads; recently retired faculty and professionals currently teaching ethics including journalists, lawyers and health professionals. A few relatively new staff members who had taught ethics for fewer than eight years were included to add generational scope, representativeness and 'new blood'. Some 52 per cent were full professors, 28 per cent were associate, and 20 per cent were either assistant professors (15 per cent) or instructors (5 per cent) if one uses US academic nomenclature. Some 23 per cent were or had been academic administrators.

Invitations to a large number of women and those from a spectrum of races and cultures were extended. Although only eight women (20 per cent of participant total) accepted the invitation for the Atlantic study in 2008, twice as many (40 per cent) participated in the Pacific study. In 2008, only one diversity participant was available while in 2015 this number had grown to seven (18 per cent) diversity (including disability) staff members. These increases were roughly proportional to the increasing numbers of women and individuals from diverse cultures within relevant disciplines in higher education.

In the 2008 Atlantic study, 52 per cent taught in the US and 48 per cent in Great Britain. In Part II, 72 per cent of those interviewed taught in the US and the remainder at other English-speaking countries in the Pacific (although several have taught in both environments and a few have taught in at least three countries). As of 2015, twenty-nine had taught within institutions in the US Pacific region; four in Australia; two each in New Zealand, Canada (Pacific coast) and Hong Kong, and one in Singapore.

On average, the 2015 participants had taught an average of 51 ethics and moral philosophy classes yielding an estimated total of 2,040 classes taught before and during 2015! Of these, on average 58 per cent were undergraduate classes, 27 per cent graduate, and 15 per cent mixed classes, almost the same as in 2008.

Approximately 42 per cent of these courses were taught in philosophy departments, 40 per cent in professional (e.g. medicine, law, journalism and business) colleges and (ethics) institutes, while 18 per cent were taught in other departments or mixed (e.g. interdisciplinary institutes, cross-listed courses, humanities programmes) venues.

APPROACH AND METHODS

Adapting questions used by Kenneth Bain in his Harvard University Press award-winning book, *What the best college teachers do* (Bain 2004), the researcher created a 40-question interview that was uniformly administered to all eighty participants whether in person (35 per cent), online (60 per cent) or by phone (5 per cent) according to their preference, geographic distance (including during travel) and availability. In both years almost one third of all participants also provided additional materials such as relevant syllabi or hand-outs. Twenty-two were also observed during lecture or seminar teaching some 'live' and some via recordings.

Of the 40 questions, 10 focused upon general teaching (e.g. 'What are your teaching methods?', 'How do you prepare to teach?') as developed by Bain, while the remaining 30 were created for this study by the researcher to focus upon:

1) how teaching effectiveness is enhanced and evolves over time (10 questions);

2) how ethics and moral philosophy courses are specifically taught by these faculty (10 questions); and

3) empirical data about teaching experience (e.g. 'How many years have you taught ethics courses?').

Classroom observation of participants included undergraduate and graduate ethics, moral philosophy and next-of-kin courses offered within philosophy departments and professional colleges based upon availability, logistics and permission.

SUMMARY OF FINDINGS: TEACHING ETHICS (QUESTION 31)

Clearly one cannot ask if ethics instruction can be improved without considering whether ethics can and should be taught in the first place. Indeed, one long-standing debate within the educational domain and indeed within society expands upon the question 'Can ethics be taught?'

According to responses from the participants the answer may depend upon what is meant by 'ethics' and within which culture, age group, or context. When they were asked 'What have you to say to those who feel that ethics cannot be taught?', most participants in the Pacific study responded that:

1) it depends upon what is meant by ethics and may depend upon age and culture;

2) if ethics means thinking more clearly, systematically, or knowledgeably about moral decision-making, then most (88 per cent) say ethics can be taught; and

3) if ethics means the improvement of moral character or becoming a 'better' person, then only one third (33 per cent) believe that 'moral growth' can be 'taught' within a university-level ethics classroom. Some 53 per cent feel that such educators cannot teach students to be 'better' people while 14 per cent are not sure.

The first two findings immediately above were similar to the 2008 study. However, finding 3) showed a marked difference from the Atlantic region research in which participants were evenly divided (40 per cent positive; 40 per cent negative, 15 per cent unsure, 5 per cent other) about whether moral improvement could be taught in universities. Figure 1 below indicates how the question 'Should "ethics", meaning moral improvement, be taught within higher education?' was answered by participants in 2008, in 2015, and on the whole (see 'average').

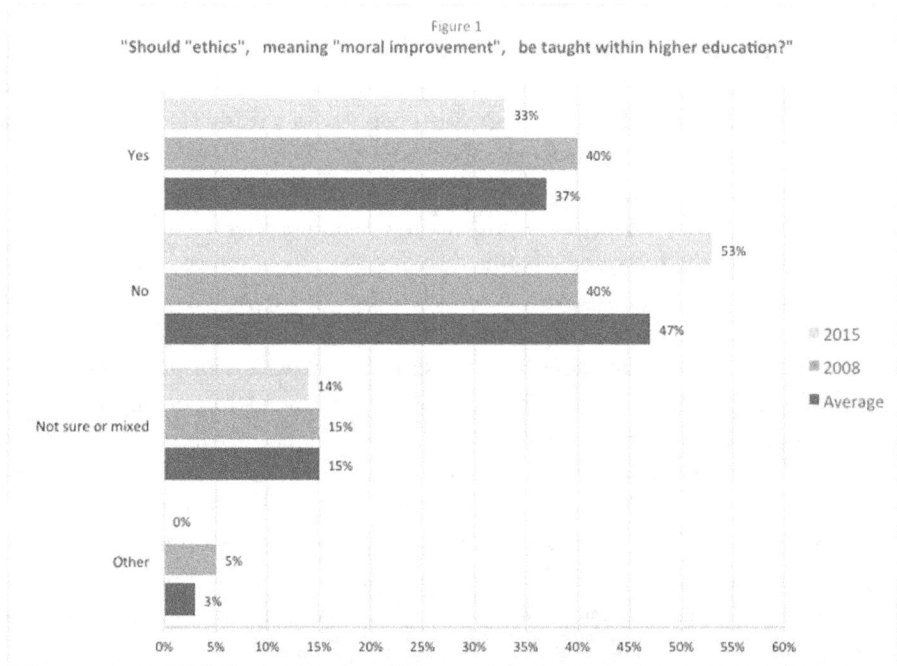

Figure 1
"Should "ethics", meaning "moral improvement", be taught within higher education?"

In both studies most thought that ethics instruction can and should effect improvements in moral reasoning. Yet 2015 participants did not feel that changes in moral action should be taught (53 per cent negative; 33 per cent positive), thus indicating an increase or difference of 13 per cent in the negative response since 2008.

In the recent Pacific study Debra Satz, Senior Associate Dean of Humanities and Arts at Stanford, commented: 'Ethics can certainly be taught; it's a discipline like many others. But teaching ethics as a way of making people ethical is not the best route.' Dr Sara Goering, at the University of Washington, explained: 'I'm not teaching them an ethical view, but ... how to evaluate a wide variety of ethical arguments.' Professor Mark Schroeder, at the University of Southern California, stated: 'Students can come to be better at recognising when a situation is morally fraught ... what can't be taught is a method or way of solving moral problems.'

The majority expressed the view that classroom ethics is not a moral 'fix-it kit': one participant said: 'If people are not already inclined to be ethical, studying ethics will probably not persuade them.' Dr Scott Anderson, of the University of British Columbia in Canada, added: 'I don't expect an ethical sceptic or the ethically indifferent to change their minds.'

Some participants pointed out that the matter is not one of opinion and that valid studies may be consulted. Professor Deborah Rhode, Founding Director of Stanford's Ethics Center, observed that 'there's a fair amount of research literature that concludes that young adults do develop in their ethical reasoning ... well designed courses can have a positive effect'. Others noted the value of ethics pedagogy whether or not it can 'make people better'. Professor Glen Pettigrove, at the University of Auckland, wrote that college instruction 'will not turn a sociopath into a philanthropist ... but it will provide people who already care about certain values with tools they might use to deliberate ...'

Not everyone agrees. Both in the 2008 and current studies, there are also those who think that moral development can or should be initiated, advanced or enhanced within the classroom. Is this thinking more pronounced in parts of the Pacific region due to the legacy of Asian philosophy? Professor Grace (Lai Kuen) Leung, at the Chinese University of Hong Kong, commented: 'It is easier to teach ethical behaviour in Asian societies because the Confucius culture backs up the importance of being moral and ethical.' However, many institutions in the North American part of the Pacific region have not been discernibly impacted by Asian philosophies. It is hard to know how much weight to give this factor, say, in states such as Oregon and Washington or in the Canadian province of British Columbia.

In both studies participants overwhelmingly affirmed the importance of teaching ethics as moral reasoning, reflection, the application of key philosophers' principles and a lens for better understanding moral dilemmas. See Figure 2 below for the overall replies in 2015, 2008, and on the whole ('average').

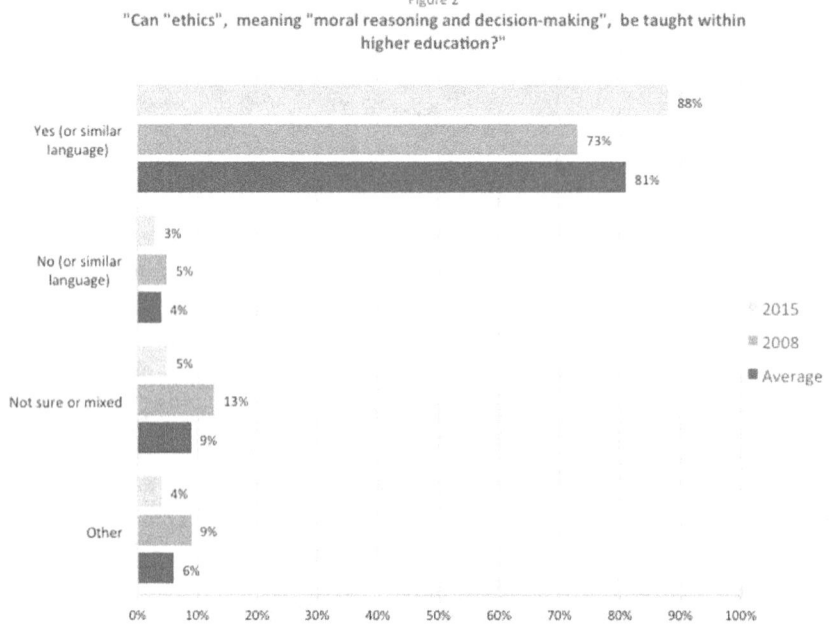

Figure 2
"Can "ethics", meaning "moral reasoning and decision-making", be taught within higher education?"

Where they differed was that in 2015 a majority (53 per cent) took the position that teaching moral behavioural growth at the university level should not be undertaken while only 40 per cent took this position in 2008. There were articulate spokespersons on both sides of each set of interviews. On the one hand, David Smith, Margaret Farley and Elizabeth Anderson argued similarly in 2008: 'You may not change students' overall behaviour, but you can give them corrective lenses' (David Smith, Yale) 'You can't make every student a good person but increasing students' moral insight is helpful' (Margaret Farley, Yale), and 'Does [classroom ethics] make people more virtuous? I doubt it. But it may make them more responsible, thoughtful decision-makers when hard decisions arise' (Elizabeth Anderson, University of Michigan).

Those voicing support for normative and corrective ethics in the Atlantic study included appeals to Kant '… since ethics is not inbred, it must be taught' (Stephen Latham, Yale); or to modelling: 'When showing is better than telling, thinking about ethics is best taught and displayed by who you are in students' presence' (Nick Adams, Cambridge); or to social necessity: 'Given the state of the world, ethics must be taught' (Julian Savulescu, Oxford, 2008).

TOWARD WHAT END? (QUESTIONS 12, 13)

Let us suppose that ethics, at least by some definitions of that word, can be taught? What then? What might a student learn in such a course? What would successful teaching of an ethics course look like? All participants were asked two questions (12 and 13) about such 'success'.

When asked 'What do you expect students will be able to do perceptually and conceptually upon completion of your class which they could not do upon entry?', they answered as rank-ordered below left (top nine responses only) in Figure 3.

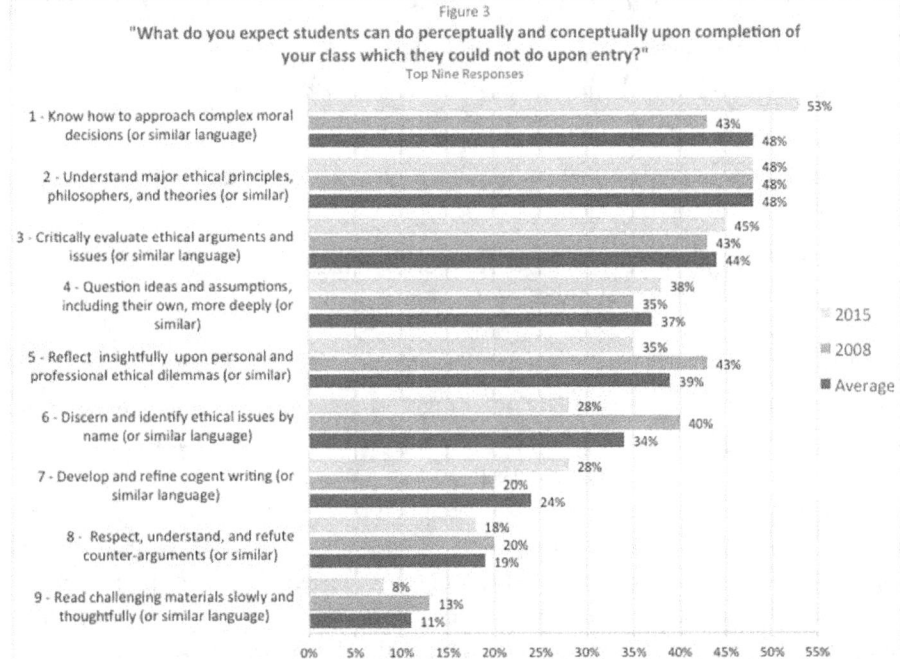

A large range of less frequently mentioned teaching aspirations were also articulated including: speaking persuasively (8 per cent), moving beyond opinion (8 per cent), reading slowly and thoughtfully (8 per cent), and more. In 2015, 27 per cent of all participants also listed goals that might be unique to their own classroom such as 'learn how to counsel executives about ethics' (2 per cent) and 'take these ethics theories from the textbook into their science labs' (2 per cent).

An overview of the statistics above suggests that while a large majority see themselves as primarily teaching critical thinking and moral theory, some go further into more specialised areas. Professor Margaret McLean, who teaches within a historically religious institution (Santa Clara University), added to her list of goals 'to recognise the role that religion and faith play in ethical decision-making historically and currently'. Professor Ann Auman, at the University of Hawaii, who is teaching future journalists, commented: 'Students are faced with many ethical issues in the world of social media and online information. … I want them to learn that they need a set of standards to follow because they are both consumers and producers of news and information. It is their responsibility to create and maintain a moral compass.'

When asked: 'What do you expect of your students' learning if you are to regard it as successful?', the Pacific region participants replied that their students should be able to:

53 per cent – identify ethical issues and explain them;

45 per cent – make better ethical decisions;

38 per cent – apply tools for ethical decision-making to their lives and careers;

35 per cent – engage in more sophisticated thinking/reasoning;

35 per cent – know the major ideas of the course content;

35 per cent – articulate moral views more clearly;

33 per cent – converse more intelligently and respectfully with those with whom they disagree;

25 per cent – develop ethical sensitivity and courage;

18 per cent – become more self-critical/aware.

HOW TO TEACH ETHICS? (QUESTIONS 11, 18, 19, 20, 28, 29, 32, 33, 37)

In the Pacific study, on the surface teaching staff seemed to use standard teaching tools. For example, although 18 per cent opposed the use of final exams, 38 per cent gave finals. Some 90 per cent assigned and graded long (53 per cent) or short (75 per cent) papers. Some 23 per cent assigned both. Other exercises which were graded included discussion/participation (35 per cent), responses to readings (33 per cent), quizzes (28 per cent), mid-term exams (18 per cent), group projects (18 per cent), class presentations (18 per cent), homework (18 per cent), case study analysis (15 per cent) and rewriting assignments (15 per cent).

When answering the question of whether teachers should use and sometimes profit from the sale of texts and articles they themselves have written, Pacific region participants revealed that they have always (13 per cent), frequently (10 per cent), sometimes (24 per cent), rarely (25 per cent), or never (28 per cent) used publications they have (co-) authored themselves. Most (85 per cent) also used new ideas and literature in the field, whether frequently (63 per cent), sometimes (20 per cent) or only in graduate courses (10 per cent).

This new material was often (70 per cent) balanced with an emphasis upon traditional 'canon' texts by seminal moral philosophers such as Aristotle, Kant and Mill, and sometimes included more modern thinkers (e.g. Rawls, Parfit, Korsgaard) or in some cases more traditional Eastern (e.g. Confucius, Lao-Tzu) or feminist (e.g. Gilligan, Noddings) voices. Some (20 per cent) opposed the use of textbooks, anthologies, thumbnails and commentaries as primary resources. But others used topical texts (15 per cent), philosophical excerpts (15 per cent), diversity anthologies showcasing under-represented voices (10 per cent), standard textbooks (10 per cent), online and printed commentaries (10 per cent), traditional anthologies (10 per cent) and mixed (case study, philosophy, commentary) volumes (8 per cent).

The data indicates a steady increase in adoption of new technologies since 2008. However, what is surprising is a reverse trend with two technologies: 1) a sharp increase (from 25 per cent to 45 per cent) in the objection to laptop and hand-held devices in the classroom; 2) increased concerns about PowerPoint (see below). Some 55 per cent of those who once used PowerPoint stated that they were either phasing out PowerPoint-type technologies or they had already done so.

Half of the 20 per cent who use PowerPoint-type technologies defend them as 'student friendly', an 'eyeball focus', 'organisationally superior', 'easier and cheaper for students than buying Cliff Notes', 'no less interactive than using film and videos' and 'good creative pressure upon us faculty to really outline and clarify our thinking ... which in turn helps students'. Those who welcome laptops and cell phones are also persuasive: 'The laptop and smart phone bring almost all available knowledge right into the classroom'; 'We can't live in the past; thinking is no longer primarily silent reflection', and 'I bring mine to work; this is their work zone – how can I forbid them from bringing theirs?'

Still others have adopted a PowerPoint policy or adjustment ('I still use it ... only a lot less'; 'It's for the first part of class only ... but then we turn up the lights and have great discussions.') Some also use a laptop policy such as 'They can use it only if they sit in the back row so no one else is distracted' and 'Their Wi-Fi access must be turned off so then cannot zoom in on baseball scores, email and porn during class ... they know in advance my penalty for their losing focus.'

When asked: 'How do you prepare to teach?' the most frequent replies were rereading class reading assignments (55 per cent), reviewing notes (53 per cent), thinking about and searching for new examples, questions and topics (38 per cent), writing a new outline or plan (38 per cent), reading widely from related texts and journals (38 per cent), preparing media clips, PowerPoint, and other technologies (23 per cent), finding topical tie-ins to class readings (20 per cent), collecting and updating materials (20 per cent), writing the entire lecture afresh (15 per cent) and originating and adapting key questions (13 per cent). Less frequently mentioned forms of preparation were unique to individuals such as 'preparing spatial organisation on blackboard', 'seeking input from senior professionals', 'following up on student questions' and 'getting enough sleep'.

PRIMARY TEACHING PROBLEMS (QUESTIONS 15, 16, 34, 35)

Faculty in the current study discussed both the problems they face in the classroom and also the problems they perceive that students face. When asked: 'What problems do you face working with students?', staff members replied as in Figure 4.

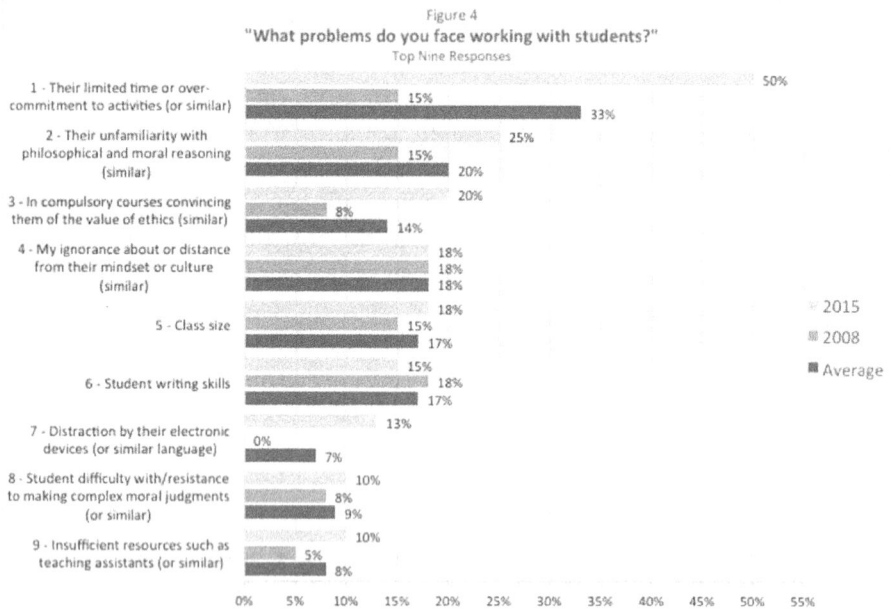

When asked the same question only from a student perspective (i.e. 'Which problems do you perceive that students face in learning from you?'), staff members replied as in Figure 5.

These two charts, in which faculty and students share overlapping problems, reveal just a few of the challenges. Depending upon geography other reported problems faculty and students may face include dependency upon drugs and alcohol, preference for skills (rather than cognitive) training, grade inflation, blind acceptance of 'relativism', a factory approach to teaching, mono-cultural bias, dogmatic religious or political beliefs (by either party), the teacher's hand-writing, class conversation 'bullies', speed-driven lecturing and many others.

How ethics is taught at leading institutions in the Pacific region

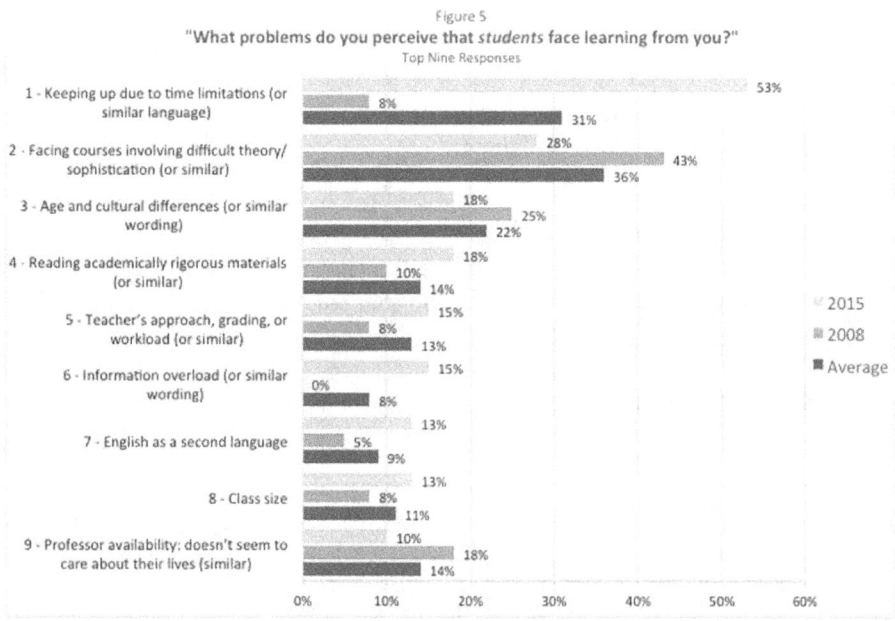

In response to this debate, participants were quizzed: 'How does your ethics instruction impart a free and rational inquiry without bias?' They replied as within Figure 6 below.

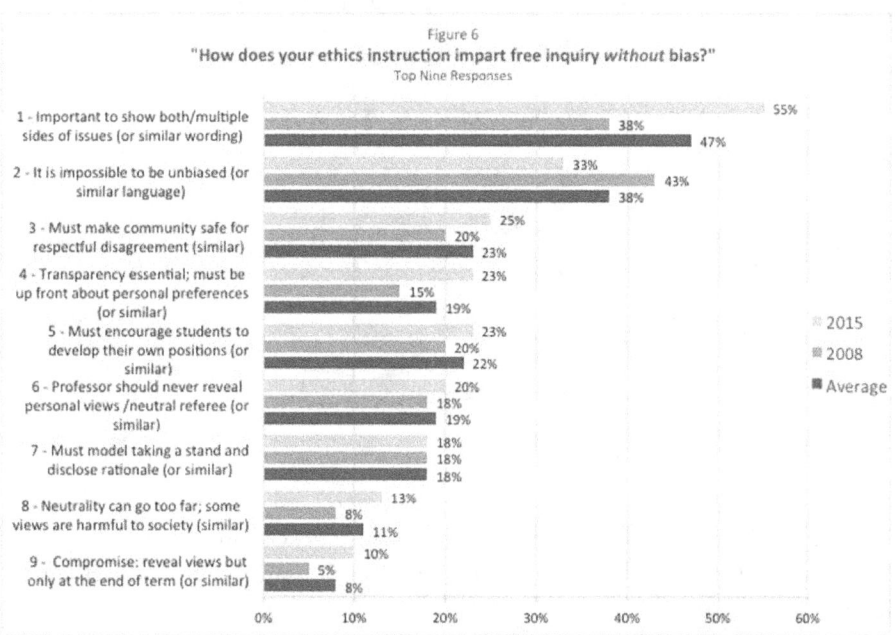

319

While the field is still divided about whether modelling one's positions constitutes 'bias', there is near unity about the importance of engaging in honorable disagreement and respecting students' diverse views. In the debate about 'neutrality' vs 'advocacy', those leaning toward being an 'even-tempered referee' had much to say. Mark Schroeder, at USC, explained:

> I don't reveal any of my own views when I teach. I'm pretty successful with this as evidenced by the fact that I take open questions about what I think during the last day of classes. Students are always obviously surprised by many things ... there is no implication that students must come to think anything in particular.

OUTSTANDING TEACHING (QUESTIONS 30, 40)

Questions 30 and 40 seemed most important to many teachers because they were asked if there were keys or secrets to both excellent teaching at large (Question 30) and to drawing forth 'the best ethical thinking, passion for learning, and growth' (Question 40) from ethics students. Only two staff members by-passed these questions and most spoke or wrote passionately and at great length.

In the recent 2015 study when asked: 'Are there any keys and secrets to outstanding teaching?' participants responded as in Figure 7.

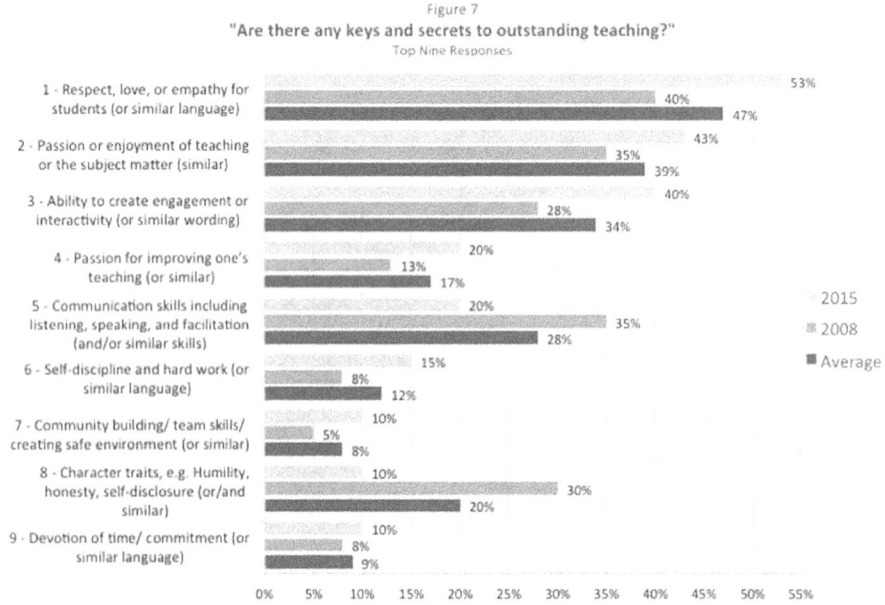

When asked the similar, but more ethics-specific, question about 'What draws forth the best ethical thinking, passion for learning and growth?' participants replied as in Figure 8.

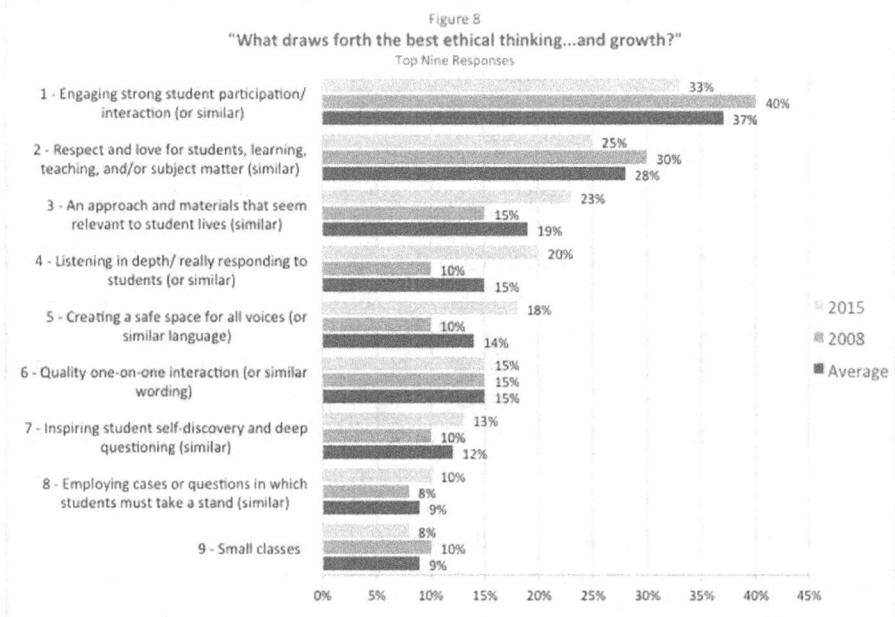

Figure 8
"What draws forth the best ethical thinking...and growth?"
Top Nine Responses

There were many aspects to what participants considered excellent teaching. One involved modelling: 'The more relaxed you are, the more relaxed they can be which helps with your first job – building community,' Stanford/ MIT Professor Tamar Schapiro explained. At the Australian National University, Tamara Browne agreed: 'When *you* enjoy it, the students enjoy it too. You must have a passion for the subject ... and enjoy the performance aspect.'

The final question on the survey asked: 'Given that the Latin root of education, *educare*, means to rear or draw forth, what have you discovered draws forth the best ethical thinking, passion for learning and growth from your students?' Although it was the longest question, in 2008 it drew the shortest, and possibly most important reply. At Cambridge, Professor Simon Blackburn replied with only one word: 'Honesty.'

ENHANCING PEDAGOGICAL EFFECTIVENESS (QUESTIONS 21, 22, 23, 24, 25, 26, 27)

One of the most important areas of research pertained to how teachers improve teaching over time whether through trial and error, feedback from students and peers, or more formal mechanisms such as workshops, mentors, teaching centres, video playback and assessment. Faculty in both surveys relied more upon student feedback and personal reflection than upon other approaches.

In the Pacific study, most participants (90 per cent) reported making temporary or long-term changes in their approach to teaching. Almost two thirds (65 per cent) of all changes were made to accommodate student (including graduate assistant 15 per cent) feedback.

Most student-directed changes (70 per cent of all changes made) pertained to adjusting to the students' 1) self-reported thinking capacity, 2) media preferences, 3) learning pace, homework saturation point, and 5) other forms of feedback. Faculty respondents disclosed becoming 'more relaxed', 'more varied in approach', 'less didactic', 'more aware of students as individuals', 'more conversational', and 'less ambitious' and thus many teachers often reduced the amount, speed, or level of course presentation, reading material, home-work or lecturing. Often participants increased the amount of 1) discussion (28 per cent), 2) spontaneity (20 per cent), 3) newer media (20 per cent), 4) reading and homework incentives (15 per cent), 5) online presence (15 per cent) and 6) updated material (15 per cent). They also decreased the length of lectures (15 per cent), essays/papers (15 per cent) and readings (13 per cent) in response to student feedback.

Student written (formal) and spoken (informal) feedback effected instructor changes 'frequently' (65 per cent) or 'sometimes' (33 per cent) although one instructor (2 per cent) felt that feedback was unnecessary and unimportant. Seven (18 per cent) deliberately initiated additional student input by creating their own feedback forms and processes or by using college-wide mid-term evaluation forms.

Student feedback coupled with the passing of time seems to have had a tempering effect on many rigidities and possibly unrealistic expectations of some younger staff members. Bill Damon, at Stanford, revealed: 'I've become a better improviser and more fluid ... and I require less reading.' Berkeley's Tom Goldstein has become a 'little looser about the lesson plan ... and a little less doctrinaire about when the plan gets covered'.

A second means for potentially enhancing pedagogical effectiveness is the input of other faculty. While 10 per cent felt that their courses were 'not influenced' by faculty colleagues and 20 per cent felt they had 'only rarely learned' from their peers, almost three fourths (73 per cent) felt they had either 'frequently' (30 per cent) or 'sometimes' (43 per cent) accrued teaching insights from colleagues. Many of those felt they had learned:

1) informally, by observing their own teachers, guest lecturers and other faculty (40 per cent);

2) from collaborative or team-teaching processes (20 per cent);

3) by sitting in on each other's classes (15 per cent), and

4) by more formal peer evaluation (10 per cent).

To a lesser extent participants also learned from other formats such as teacher surveys, conference panels, correspondence and instructor supervision.

Participants were asked not only how they evaluated their teaching via student and faculty input, but also via their own reflection and independent analysis. Almost all (98 per cent) reported some mode of self-inspection whether they described it as 'self-criticism' (38 per cent), 'thinking about my teaching' (35 per cent) or 'continual assessment' (25 per cent). Some 23 per cent took the practical approach of quickly discarding what had not been working in class, but others (13 per cent) first utilised either graduate assistant feedback, informal student feedback such as after class or during office hours, or requested a meeting with CITL (a campus programme for teacher training) personnel. Still others (10 per cent) said that they welcomed peer classroom visitation.

Some 20 per cent reported some additional means of evaluating their work. A participant at the University of Southern California said: 'Every class ... I hand out a sheet that asks them to "name two things about the class you would change ... and two things you would not change". I then aggregate these results, share the trends with the class, and make relevant adjustments.'

WHY TEACH? (QUESTIONS 14, 17)

Figure 9 below shows not only how current participants answered the question 'Why do you teach?' but also shows how this question was answered in 2008 and the averaged answer when the two surveys are treated as one.

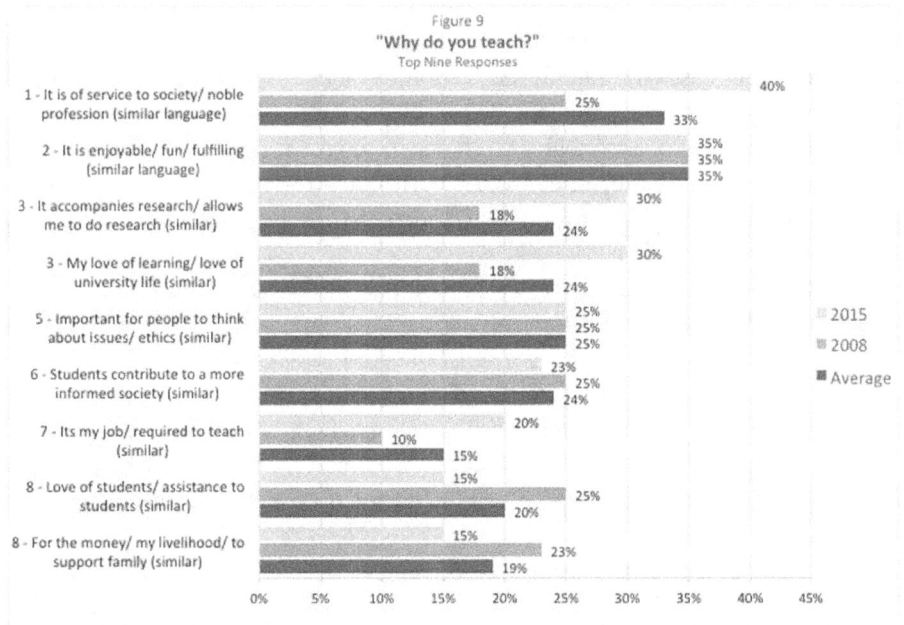

Many other reasons were articulated in both parts of the study such as 'relating theory to practice', 'I'm good at it' and 'it is important for its own sake'. Many teachers teach ethics for the gratification of engaging in an effective or rewarding job. When asked 'How do you know when you've done a good job teaching?', the largest number of 2015 participants answered 'the degree of student engagement with the material' (43 per cent), including in class, in assignments, by e-communication and during office hours. Positive feedback about the course and teacher, whether informally (40 per cent) such as students rushing the podium at the end of class, ovations, thank you notes and spontaneous comments, or more formally (28 per cent) such as through mandatory written evaluations, were also key indicators.

Other important 'signs' of perceived effective teaching included the increased comprehension of material (23 per cent), greater quality of student contributions (20 per cent), unexpected positive feedback such as via holiday cards, requests for recommendations, and invitations to student events (20 per cent); increased retention of ideas (15 per cent), greater sophistication of discussion (15 per cent), depth and refinement of final papers (15 per cent) and more independent thinking (10 per cent).

To be sure, almost one quarter of the participants (23 per cent) stated that they were not certain when they had been successful in their teaching. Nevertheless, the majority experienced positive perceptions that they translated as momentary if not sustained success. As Bill Damon, at Stanford, indicated: 'You can really tell … they have those visible "Eureka" moments.'

ANALYSIS AND INTERPRETATION

When analysing the two studies seven years and several thousand miles apart, there are clearly factors of both time and space which separate the two studies. In some cases it is hard to be certain which differences might be caused by time, space, a mixture of the two and other factors both known – such as the participants and their backgrounds – and unknown – including hidden influences upon each participant and institution.

The introduction of specific new technologies in the classroom might well be partially explained by 'time' since some technologies were unavailable in 2008. On the other hand, a greater emphasis upon Taoist, Buddhist and Confucianist ethics in the curriculum of some Pacific institutions might seem more due to a 'bias' of 'space' or geography. Yet other differences such as the number of faculty who, for example, now prefer Aristotle to Kant or vice versa, who did not before, may have little to do with time or space and might be explained by yet other factors or remain unknown.

The ongoing expansion (from 28 per cent to 40 per cent) of ethics taught within the professional schools and other expansion within programmes, institutes and departments other than philosophy, might be seen as a product of time if that growth pattern may be shown to be part of a national or international trend. However, such 'growth' might not be a trend at all but rather an accidental over-representation of participants from such applied programmes. They might constitute a sample not likely to be replicated by the demographics of other samples. More and different research is needed to find out. Moreover, one must be very careful about the interpretation of data based upon only eighty participants.

'Time' refers to far more than a literal eight-year interval and also includes movement into an age of 'super-speed-up'. Does this sort of 'time change' help explain why it seems that both students and faculty find the primary limitation to their learning is a perceived or real 'lack' of time? Might this 'time starvation' also have bearing upon the trend toward 'short' papers, faster technologies and smaller content 'dosages?' Or not? Common sense and research alike suggest that technology and socio-cultural trends 'link' to the psychology of time and its perceived quantification and speed.

The reaction to PowerPoint, laptop use by students and cell phones in the classroom seems more driven by time than space since many faculty welcomed these technologies initially, then reacted to their impact upon students over time. Such a pattern happened across many regions and cultures and the impulse to react seemed largely based upon first-hand experience rather than geographic accent. More faculty than not who phased out PowerPoint or who banned laptop and cell phone use did so following an initial trial phase, that is, over time. And their objections were based more upon over-arching general philosophical and pedagogical concerns, not derived from national or cultural belief systems which were location-specific (i. e. 'space').

Another dimension of time pertains to the age of the participants' institutions. When one considers the history, standards and traditions of universities in the Atlantic region and remembers that the average age of Oxbridge and Ivy institutions taken together is more than 4000 years old, then the other Pacific institutions – which average a little more than one hundred years each – look quite young by comparison.

Although Stanford and Berkeley, among others, stand somewhere in between the 'older' and 'younger' institutions, throughout their development and those of the surrounding schools in California, western Canada, Oregon, Washington and Hawaii, such universities also felt the need to emulate if not compete with the prototypical Oxbridge and Ivy cultures.

Many of these 'parent' Atlantic institutions sought to define and to some degree transplant curricular templates not only for higher education writ large but also for the ethics classroom. Nevertheless, the degree of influence varies from institution to institution and cannot be seen as homogenous or conclusive.

What about 'space'? One participant in Asia wrote directly about the decades of influence of Buddhist, Hindu, Confucian, Taoist and even Maoist ethics upon institutions of the Asian Pacific and their curricula. One is more likely to find a higher proportion of courses about Confucian or Taoist ethics taught in Hawaii and California (not just Singapore or Hong Kong) than in Rhode Island or Scotland. Space matters.

Moreover, evidence seems to suggest that, despite exceptions, teaching styles, student requirements and even university dress codes are somewhat more relaxed and 'pacific' in the Pacific. Overall the 2015 participants, despite notable exceptions, did appear to be somewhat but not substantially less formal, demanding and competitive.

But how much of that may be accounted for by 'space'? Many other factors, not just time, space, culture and their mixture, are often more subtle or undetected. For example, the selection, training and predispositions of each participant, the time that each allotted the interview (some were laconic, others comprehensive), what they ate and drank the night before, and a host of other factors, had unmeasured impact upon the outcome of both studies.

All researchers must stay humble in the light of uncertainty, the likely misinterpretation of culture and many types of possible human error. Moreover, it is impossible to calculate the interplay of seen but misunderstood influences, not to mention invisible factors not perceived until years later. Would 40 different participants from the same institutions answer the 40 questions identically to those in 2008 or 2015? That seems unlikely. Would 40 participants from neighbouring institutions or fields answer identically? That too is unlikely. Would these same 40 or 80 answer identically one year later or earlier? Also unlikely. But in general would most if not all of the over-arching patterns emerge despite variations? That seems more likely.

So the comparisons seem noteworthy, but neither absolute nor permanent. Nor has their reliability and validity been tested by other researchers choosing different samples.

- Graphics by Angela Carlson-Bancroft assisted by Michael Duggan.

- This paper was first published in *Ethical Space*, Vol 14, No. 1 pp 4-14

REFERENCE

Bain, K. (2004) *What the best college lecturers do*, Cambridge, MA, Harvard University Press

NOTE ON THE CONTRIBUTOR

Dr Tom Cooper has been a guest scholar at Stanford, Berkeley, the East-West Center and the University of Hawaii. He is Professor Emeritus of Visual and Media Arts at Emerson College. The Association for Responsible Communication, which he founded, was nominated for the Nobel Peace Prize and he has received many awards and scholarships. Cooper taught at Harvard, where he graduated *magna cum laude*, and at Temple University, the University of Hawaii and at the University of Maryland. A former assistant to Marshall McLuhan, he is the author, editor or co-author of eight books and more than one hundred academic and professional published articles on media ethics and related topics. Musician, poet, playwright and Black Belt in Tae Kwon Do, he was also one of the speech writers and editors for Jochen Zeitz, former CEO of Puma. He was a consultant to the Elders Project which involved global 'elders' such as Nelson Mandela, Kofi Anan and Jimmy Carter.

Chapter 21

Supervisors' perspectives on the ethical supervision of long form writing and managing trauma narrative within the Australian tertiary sector

Sue Joseph and Carolyn Rickett

Miller and Tougaw observe: 'If every age has its symptoms, ours appears to be the age of trauma.'[1] Their observation may help explain the emergence of memoir and autobiographical or autoethnographic creative works, not just commercially but also within the tertiary sector. Almost all of this work is appearing within journalism, English and creative writing schools as students turn to creative practice degrees as a means to write through traumatic events. The focus of this paper is to share various perspectives from experienced academics gathered during a qualitative research project where a range of scholars supervising trauma narrative Higher Degree Research (HDR) candidates within Australian universities were interviewed regarding what their needs are in relation to the ethical supervision of their candidates. We anticipate this paper may also contribute to a better understanding of the supervisory relationship pertinent to candidates undertaking their own personal trauma narrative research and the ways in which academics might provide a safer space for both themselves and their Higher Degree Research students.

Keywords: ethical supervision, long form writing, trauma narrative, Australian tertiary sector

> Writing is a form of therapy; sometimes I wonder how all those who do not write, compose or paint can manage to escape the madness, the melancholia, the panic fear which is inherent in the human situation.[2]

INTRODUCTION

The research for this paper is shaped by the field of literary journalism, a long-debated and critiqued scholarly arena in the northern hemisphere though it is far less debated and critiqued in Australia. Away from this global debate concerning the naming of this genre, we contend that memoir/life-writing/autoethnography sits comfortably within this burgeoning field of journalism research, also found nestled within creative writing schools.

Our concern with current practices pertinent to supervising this mode of literary journalism is twofold: firstly, is the commodification of trauma in the tertiary sector in order to gain a degree, without proper safeguards for the student, an ethical practice? And secondly: linked to this concern is also the possibility of vicarious traumatisation for academics managing these kinds of student testimonial projects. There is clear documentation of 'vicariously induced PTSD in therapists who talk to traumatised clients' (Littrell 2009: 308). Witnessing student repackaging of traumatic narrative in a supervisory role might produce the same effect in academics (Joseph and Rickett 2010: 4) and, therefore, they too need safeguards.

Building on previous scholarly work focusing on the benchmarking of Australian doctoral standards (Webb, Brien and Burr 2012), this paper aims to develop an understanding of the institutional framework supervisors require to support and empower them and their candidates to safely produce literary journalism texts of trauma narrative. Can there be a generic form of doctoral supervision applicable across the disciplines? Debate around this issue has been on-going for some decades. We argue that, indeed, there is a generic scaffolding around doctoral supervision, but that the space within this scaffolding must be fluid, depending on many elements, both professional/disciplinary and personal. In this way, we agree with Frick et al. when they contend: 'The pedagogic relationship between the doctoral student and research supervisor(s) forms an important *relational* learning space. This relational learning space exists regardless of the doctoral programme format' (Frick, Brodin and Albertyn 2014: 1). This is a quasi-private space between supervisor and candidate, with periodic and eventual institutional and community accountability.

What we have learnt from our own research is that the canon around supervision literature is growing but none of it attests, or tests, what we recognise as the fraught issues around supervising trauma narrative in this quasi-private and fluid relational space. Catherine Manathunga (2007) comes close to echoing a broad warning: 'For both supervisors and students, there are additional risks associated with the blurry boundaries between acting upon students' disciplinary subjectivities and providing advice and guidance about aspects of students' personal lives' (ibid: 219); as do Aitchison and Mowbray (2013: 859) when they observe that: '… the role of emotion in the doctoral undertaking is often subsumed in the passionless language of bureaucratic rationalisation and economic imperatives'. Again, while not directly addressing the writing of trauma narrative as creative artefact, they are articulating some of our supervisory concerns. They argue: '…governments and institutions demand efficiency and productivity, and favour "countables" such as research outputs, completions and competencies rather than the more subjective and elusive aspects of experience such as emotion' (ibid: 859-860).

While Aitchison and Mowbray lean towards recognition of this seemingly unspoken gap of emotion within the learning space, again their approach, while non-specific, is still important: '… the emotional aspects of doctoral education are rarely openly discussed during candidature. The research culture of higher education is deeply rooted in notions of scholarship that favour objectivity, disembodied rationality and autonomy' (ibid: 861). Indeed, their research, as with Manathunga's eight years earlier, finds that candidates rarely felt able to confide in their supervisors about emotional issues affecting their lives and candidature. Two years later Aitchison (2015) insists:

> … discourses that view the ability to write as a 'given', ensure writing is silenced, that it is not explicated in curriculum or supervisor training, and is therefore situated as incidental to doctoral scholarship. Thus, discussions about pedagogical practices of writing remain peripheral, even subversive – except at times of crisis, when writing comes very much to the fore (Aitchison 2015: 1294).

Psychology professor James Pennebaker (2000: 8) argues that 'converting emotions and images into words changes the way a person organises and thinks about trauma…'. He further explains: '… by integrating thoughts and feelings … the person can more easily construct a coherent narrative of the process'. But as taboos are broken down by society and the marketplace explodes with memoir, students look towards the academy to write about their own crises. Joseph asserts this allows '…for the discussion of formerly proscribed subjects' where 'people write their life stories in an attempt to heal, to expose, to indict, to rebalance an injustice, as a community service, to help other victims, to empower', and that increasingly 'many turn to the university as a framework to execute their work' (Joseph 2011).

Doctoral supervision in the Humanities and Social Sciences has become a focal point for debate, growing in magnitude in the past decade. There are various reasons for this, but one of the integral explanations is the emergence of the creative PhD and, attendant to that, differing definitions of what constitutes 'research' in this space. Hamilton and Carson conclude that it was the publication of the Strand Report,[3] formally recognising practice-led research in 1998, which led to the acceptance of the creative PhD throughout Australia (Hamilton and Carson 2013: 1). Our research[4] examines a particular category of creative doctoral investigation – life writing/memoir/autoethnography shaped by the narration of trauma. It is clear from the cumulative literature reviews on supervisory practices[5] that issues around the safety or, otherwise, danger zones of such endeavours – and the resulting ethical tensions – have not been adequately addressed within the academy. We believe both issues are of paramount importance both to the professional and personal approaches within supervision in the Australian tertiary sector and, we argue accordingly, further afield.

This paper, while one of several we are producing from our research to date, aims to draw attention to what supervisors of HDR candidates writing trauma narrative believe may be lacking pedagogically on an institutional level, and what strategies could be implemented for 'safer' supervision of such projects.

THE STUDY: METHODOLOGY

Ethical approval for this research project was granted by the University of Technology Sydney's human research ethics committee,[6] and thirteen supervisors drawn from the Humanities and Social Sciences within the Australian academy were interviewed between 13 October 2015 and 6 May 2016, either by Skype, telephone or face-to-face. The qualitative interviews were semi-structured, drawing on a set of five inter-related questions in an attempt to answer our over-arching question: do supervising academics of long form trauma narrative doctoral research within the field of literary journalism (memoir, life-writing, autoethnography) feel professionally and emotionally equipped to supervise ethically and safely such work, and what further resources and training are needed to support ethically and safely their role?

Interviews were recorded, including consent, and academics were given the opportunity to be on-the-record or de-identified; two of the thirteen academics chose de-identification during the course of the interview. In these two cases, it was to protect the identity of candidates, since what was discussed may have led to recognition. Interviews were then transcribed. This research was funded by the Journalism Education and Research Association of Australia (JERAA) as part of the JERAA Research Grant 2015. It was also conducted in accordance with the Australian Media, Entertainment and Arts Alliance Code of Ethics.

A major indication from the data is that the majority of interviewees believe there is an opportunity for more explicit addressing of the life-writing of trauma narrative with its attendant triggers for psychic injury. Within the HDR supervisory pedagogy in their own institutions, many flagged existing ethical and supervisory protocols, but nothing which had a specific focus on the creative and autobiographical rendering of trauma narrative, and its ramifications. Having identified trauma narratives as a potentially fraught space for both candidate and supervisor (Joseph and Rickett 2010; Joseph 2011), we hope that the long-term objective of this research project promotes a further discussion throughout the academy, with the future goal of developing strategies for redress.

As a starting point, this paper immediately focuses on the final two questions of the five we asked the thirteen academics taking part in our research project. The following selected data will be presented in a raw, Question and Answer format (edited only for space) to provide an authentic voicing of how our interviewees, all highly experienced HDR supervisors within creative or journalism disciplines, initially and instinctively responded to the selected questions:

1. What are your recommendations for improving the pedagogy and practices around supervising HDR trauma narrative?
2. How can institutions further support both the student and supervisor working within this field?

We acknowledge that given the word limit constraints of this paper, we have not been able always to provide the supervisor's responses to these two questions in full, but as part of the qualitative interview process we have selected the most representative observations to build a collegial picture of current and possible future practice.

SUPERVISORS' PERSPECTIVES ON QUESTION 1
PROFESSOR CATHERINE COLE, WOLLONGONG UNIVERSITY

I think it's really important that less-experienced supervisors get the protocol thing right, get the support thing right and also have a forum in which to discuss, without breaching confidentiality too much, some of the things they've had to deal with and how they're managed. I think that's really, really important. … But there are always things that slip under the radar. Know where the support is. Be very clear, as a supervisor, about your own feelings about the whole process. If you've experienced similar trauma, this can be a good thing…

…I don't want to make the protocol thing sound too bureaucratic. I think it's just more that ensuring people are aware of what's required legally, what's available as support and where to go for help. How to ensure the annual report or the biannual report process is honest and fair and the student can talk about it. But I do think also being aware of your own psychopathology within this is important.

… this is something that maybe in the past was dealt with, a long time ago, by the students either failing or becoming so unhappy they just left so the university didn't have to worry too much about it. But now, more and more people are coming – especially through the creative and visual arts. It isn't just unique to them. Other areas as well are taking more and more international students, for example, where they've often come from very, very traumatised places. Of course it's important that at least these matters are discussed and protocols and supports set in place that is respectful of both student and teaching while meeting the organisational response. … It just seems you can't pretend it's not happening. It's happening and it's happening very much within these areas (interview, Cole, 2015).

DR FIONA GILES, UNIVERSITY OF SYDNEY

I'm wondering if rather than a set of guidelines about how to manage the relationship that the supervisor follows and ticks boxes, it might be better to build it up ... between the candidate and the supervisor ... and to write an ethics of engagement to some extent. So it's not just the supervisor saying: 'I've done this, I've ticked the box' but there're two of them understanding together what the process is. At least having a road map of some kind, a broad road map of where they're headed and what they might encounter along there.

There are things like history that people ... might be doing which might be written in narrative form, not as memoir. But they still cover traumatic material. And then in psychology people writing PhDs on child abuse or incest or self-harm. In cultural studies, I met a PhD student a few years ago who'd worked as a prostitute and was writing about prostitution and self-harm and drug taking. So there were trauma elements there. So I think it comes up in ... different contexts (interview, Giles, 2015).

PROFESSOR KEVIN BROPHY, UNIVERSITY OF MELBOURNE

I think [the] suggestion that there be explicit training around the ethics concerned with that is a good suggestion, that's specifically for supervisors ... I think it would be very important if you did focus on trauma narrative to make it, for any kind of training, involve awareness that this applies at any moment to all, or can apply at any moment to all kinds of creative writing, even film scripts.

I think, maybe rather than subjecting theses of a non-fiction kind that are dealing with narratives of trauma, rather than subjecting them to an ethics clearance process, maybe it needs to be framed as an ethics awareness process to make sure that the student is aware of as many of the ethical implications. I'm wary about the term clearance because I don't think you're going to eliminate the ability of creative writing to hurt, to reveal, to run a very dangerous line between offence and revelation, and I wouldn't like to see creative writing become anodyne in the face of needing clearance. I'd rather that the clearance was framed as a process of increasing awareness of the ethics of the project such as this (interview, Brophy, 2015).

PROFESSOR MATTHEW RICKETSON, UNIVERSITY OF CANBERRA

The practices need to be written up in projects of this kind and in other places so that people become more aware of them. Within institutions, one thought might be to have a more ... overtly ... balanced and mindful supervision team so that you have, let's say, someone's come to you as the primary supervisor because of your experience in this kind of area. Well, maybe the other people on the panel are not simply a junior colleague or a very, very senior colleague who's just filling in the numbers, but someone who is more attuned to the kind of issues here so that you've got more than one port of call.

Different places place different weight on the primary as distinct from the secondary. ... I think it's an area where having two people who are quite closely involved will be of benefit to the student and will be of benefit to the supervisor because – it's like a co-author – you've just got that ability to bounce things backwards and forwards and to hopefully complement each other. One person is, say, really strong on the content of the area to do with the trauma. Then you've got someone who's got a stronger mental health background, or a background that complements so you build from the original supervision model. If you're weak on theory, get a good theory person; if you're weak on the content well then get a strong content person and so on. You build your supervision panel – or you should – so that it complements your needs as a student and your weaknesses and strengths. Apply that idea to this so that you are explicitly understanding and recognising there are mental health issues involved for both student and supervisor. That's what it's referred to at the Uni of Canberra. It's a supervision team ... the primary supervisor is the only person who gets a workload allocation; you will then have a secondary supervisor and you might have an associate depending on what the student wants. The idea is to build it a little bit more as a team that will provide complementary input (interview, Ricketson, 2015).

DE-IDENTIFIED INTERVIEW 7

There's really very little at our university of any kind of advanced standing on how to supervise or be a supervisor; it's all very operational. I was going to say I'm now supervising a number of projects with a professor of mental health nursing and that's actually really great because even though they're not even that kind of project – we're actually working quite a lot on history and other kinds of things, but it's really fantastic when those issues come up, because there's actually an expert that can deal with things. When questions come up in the ethics forum, it's really great.

Well I think it [trauma narrative] is a quite risky-in-a-way form of supervision and I don't think that fledgling supervisors should be just thrown into it. I don't believe that for any kind of supervision. I think it would be really great if there was maybe not a mandated module, but resources available that people could go to and find. One of the troubles with OLT[7] is that all of these resources are developed, but often you don't know about them and often they're these cumbersome, difficult websites. I think a little ready-reckoner kind of thing, something like a booklet or something. A little resource that was just a checklist or something (de-identified interview 7, 2015).

DE-IDENTIFIED INTERVIEW 8

If there was some kind of basic workshop, a three-hour basic workshop or something, that someone getting into this territory could do, online or something, text – certain texts to read, warn – certainly the warning areas, key discussion points. I think something like that would just be fabulous. We all have to do these supervision workshops, which are a lot of the general stuff about supervision, but to have one dedicated to people who are going to deal with trauma narratives or even creative writing more generally ... that would be fabulous, I reckon. If you could distribute it maybe even via an organisation like AAWP or something (de-identified interview, 2015).

ASSOCIATE PROFESSOR DEBRA ADELAIDE, UNIVERSITY OF TECHNOLOGY SYDNEY

I would think that if there isn't some kind of statement or set of guidelines or protocols, or whatever you like to call it, then there should be, but it shouldn't be too extensive because we don't need more paperwork. If supervisors are taking on a student who's writing a trauma narrative and they feel that they don't really understand what will be involved – it should be made available to them in the form of a statement.

If there was something that a student was working on and for some reason – and I can't imagine why – this would affect me really, really personally to the point where I felt that I was myself suffering or traumatised, I suppose I would go and talk to someone more experienced. In the past I would've gone and talked to ... really, really experienced supervisors.

I suppose as confronting as some of the material is ... I mean, I read this piece [of a life-writing candidate] and just wept. It was such an awful story. So things do have the ability to affect me like that. It's hard not to be moved by – sometimes by what your students are writing, but I don't feel that I am affected to the point where I ever need to seek any help. I don't feel that at all. I suppose if I did I would see what support was available at the – through Student Services, for a start. I know they're very good for students. I don't know how helpful they are for staff (interview, Adelaide, 2015).

PROFESSOR NIGEL KRAUTH, GRIFFITH UNIVERSITY

My recommendations for pedagogy and practice are not formulistic. For the kinds of knowledge that trauma narratives uncover, the frameworks need to be flexible, agile and capable of innovation.

- Supervisory teams need to be solid in their supervisory capacities and insights, and in their caring and communicative skills.
- A crucial factor is the trust the student has in the supervisor, and vice versa, and the commitment of the supervisor. If there is a breakdown of trust or commitment, then there needs to be quick action to find alternative supervision arrangements. This requires a culture in the school where the student feels safe about speaking freely regarding their supervision.

- Common sense, caring, and a general understanding of defamation and other publishing laws and practices need to pertain in supervisory advice.

Get to know your HDR students very well in the supervisory process through personal discussions and friendly email exchanges. Go out to lunch, regularly, in HDR groups and one-to-one (interview, Krauth, 2015).

ASSOCIATE PROFESSOR DOMINIQUE HECQ, SWINBURNE UNIVERSITY, MELBOURNE

I think it's very important for supervisors to know themselves first of all, so I would recommend supervisors to answer a list of questions for themselves before they embark into such a difficult territory. So basic questions about what makes them tick, what are their master signifiers, whom they identify with and what makes them distressed, what makes them angry, what makes them identify with people or what are the triggers of empathy for instance. Sometimes we identify with victims without knowing why we are doing it, but it's important to know why we do it. So that's the rational aspect of it, but also I think that supervisors need to have an analyst – a therapist. I don't like the idea of therapist because there is the idea of normality attached to it, but a psychoanalyst is better because he always flicks back the question to you.

And then the student needs to do the same work independently of their supervisor, and I think the student needs a therapist or somebody they can turn to if there is a crisis because trauma never goes away.

I've written a … paper for *TEXT* about problems and mistakes I made and what I did about it and how I learnt from my mistakes. However, what has helped me in this process is this reflecting upon it and writing and working through the problem, through writing actually was to think about another person I might like on the supervisory team. So it has been to broaden the supervisory panel and I have found that immensely useful (interview, Hecq, 2015).

PROFESSOR GAIL JONES, UNIVERSITY OF WESTERN SYDNEY

I've supervised a lot of trauma narratives and a lot of trauma work – there's not a lot of institutional recognition of what this means as an area of investigation. So I guess I've just developed my own protocols and my protocols are to deal with reading and discussing particular works … talking about what is empathy, what is empathetic unsettlement, what is the distinction between historical and structural trauma, giving some sort of rather great examples. So talking about the way in which levels of generalisation are offensive to the victims of trauma and to historical victims of violence. So ideas about levels of discussion, but being historically specific and contextualising is more likely to lead to an ethical outcome, but also more likely to lead to one's own caution and hesitation I think. I don't know anybody has ever investigated this before. There's so much theoretical work, you know, I can give anyone a bibliography on trauma settings, but I doubt anyone's actually asked these questions about the academy (interview, Jones, 2015).

ASSOCIATE PROFESSOR KATE DOUGLAS, FLINDERS UNIVERSITY

I think I'm increasingly thinking that it would be good – everybody, I think, feels kind of slightly undermined when you create more kind of guidelines to support supervisors. … I work in RHD for a portion of my job and every time we try and do something that we think is more supportive, people feel as though it's an increased level of kind of surveillance or something like that, which is not what I think this is. But I do really feel no supervisor should be going into these kinds of projects without … either a very experienced supervisor working with them, perhaps two other supervisors working with them, or some sort of set of guidelines that can be talked through with the candidate in the initial meeting perhaps with at least two supervisors present. I think there has to be something like that (interview, Douglas, 2016).

SUPERVISORS' PERSPECTIVES ON QUESTION 2
PROFESSOR CATHERINE COLE, UNIVERSITY OF WOLLONGONG

One way or another, supervisions – and I speak here from having worked at three unis now on different experiences of supervision. I think most universities are aware from a number of points of view. One is their own liability issues, including vicarious liability around supervision and expectation of completion and so on. I think there are a whole lot of just straight organisational matters which made people say: if we take this person on, are they going to complete within three years? Most universities now [are] introducing this element that if you don't finish in time, you start paying, all these sorts of things. So there are legal issues. I think also universities are mindful of who's a – and I say this in inverted commas – 'good supervisor' and who's not. People who get too close to students, who don't supervise well through protocol because they don't know the best ways to do it. That's why those annual reports or biannual reports are always important to be done honestly.

I suppose there are other elements too. But if you said to a university do you really sit down and think about what this might mean, I don't know. There are so many elements of what constitutes trauma. But I do think most universities, to be fair, do have enough internal mechanisms to say: all right, the student's distressed. Let's get them student support or student counselling or international studies or supervise – they do provide supervisor training around these issues, if not directly, then certainly peripherally. They'll talk about it through supervisor training programmes. I've heard it at UTS. I've been in seminars where people have talked about what happens when a person starts to break down for a range of reasons, not just trauma.

... I've been doing some work with Liverpool Uni in the UK and UEA and so on. Do you know some of these universities actually specialise in trauma narratives and have units which are looking at trauma from the point of view of the post-colonial and so on? So they must, in themselves, have a whole range of protocols. I haven't looked into it in depth. But if you've got a cohort of 15 people who are all people who've experienced some pretty remarkable things, how do they manage a group like that? You've almost got to kind of gestalt, haven't you, where there's this conversation around a particularly painful area (interview, Cole, 2015)

DR FIONA GILES, UNIVERSITY OF SYDNEY

I'm a bit torn about whether or not more ethics. Just that I don't want more in my life. ... I'm really wary of requiring more documentation and compliance requirements of ourselves and our students. On the other hand, I can see in certain instances why it's important to have that.

You're responsible for your own fate. If you make a mistake it's you who made the mistake, not the institution that can support you to prevent the mistake happening. So I'd really like the institution to support you to prevent the mistake. Not make you fill out another form (interview, Giles, 2015).

PROFESSOR KEVIN BROPHY, UNIVERSITY OF MELBOURNE

Maybe there needs to be – maybe institutions need to be a little bit more sophisticated and targeted in the kind of counselling services that are offered and specifically employ people who are capable and knowledgeable enough to supervise the highly intelligent but perhaps fragile people who are doing PhDs, and not send them to the same counsellors that other graduates are talking to (interview, Brophy, 2015).

DR WILLA MCDONALD, MACQUARIE UNIVERSITY

Just to recognise it as a potential issue and to make sure supervisors know they can access support. And where they can access it, and also for students. I don't know if this is related or not, but we do have nominated people who are students' representatives that students can go to if they have issues with their supervision, that's not you. They have to have someone they can go to, to bypass you if they have complaints or concerns.

I think there not only needs to be support for the supervisor who may recognise what the student is going through, but perhaps somebody independent within the department or faculty that the student can go to if they feel they can't come to you, but something is going on. Because you've got this double role of having to keep them on track with the project (interview, McDonald, 2015).

PROFESSOR MATTHEW RICKETSON, UNIVERSITY OF CANBERRA

I don't think academia as an institution or as an enterprise, deals with the muck of human emotions very well at all ... they're head people, they're intellectual people. When I say 'they' I mean 'we' you know, so it's just not where they go to naturally.

It used to be a kind of once-a-year, one-day workshop. It's now a continual series of workshops on all different aspects: examination, ethics committees, writing workshops. When I arrived there it was mandated, you had to do one a year; now I don't think it is mandated, but they're actually offered all the time. They are face-to-face. There's some materials online for some of the stuff, but they did that because they were responding to 'I can't make it on this day' whereas if we just continually are offering them, you just come along as you need ... the process that you're in and having struggles with at the moment.

There are modules on dealing with the examination process; the supervisor/student relationship; the confirmation seminar and getting you ready for ... writing ... but I don't recollect trauma.

The hope is that I think it's probably fair to say that five or ten years ago, there wasn't much in the way of workshops about the student/supervisor relationship and how important it is and how potentially difficult it can be and how much management it requires from both parties and from the university to support both parties. Like at least there is some understanding now that that is a key relationship ... that lots of PhDs, if they fall over, it's because the relationship between the supervisor and the student has broken down. This is the next thing which is to do with the content of what you're researching about and not just seeing it through a 'rats and stats' mindset, but understanding, you know ... there are disciplines that are quite attuned to this, like anthropology and ethnography and you would presume, psychology and psychotherapy and so on (interview, Ricketson, 2015).

PROFESSOR JEN WEBB, UNIVERSITY OF CANBERRA

I'd like to see them work together. When someone's doing a PhD that's engaging with trauma narratives then I think that the supervisor and the candidate together, or supervisors because we have panels, should actually be in conversation maybe with a specialist trauma psychologist who's trained in the field, and talk every six months – you touch base and you debrief and then you go on from there. That means you're getting an outside – the cold, calm, outside – view of it who will see if there's risk – people go slow enough, do the first years, but I think six months is probably long enough. I think by the time you get to your six months if there are serious problems you can catch them then before it becomes a disaster. But that would have to be mandated and then there would have to be some sort of sign off by the research students' office. They need to see the document; they need to see the confirmation document. They need to see all the other documents to be sure that you're going – that you're going about it the right way.

I think it's that failsafe button and the failsafe would be something like knowing that there is a system in place to back me up, knowing there's a system – I'm not a trained psychologist. I don't have time to go to the doctor and say I feel a little bit stressed because one of my students is having a bad time. What are they going to do about that?

I think it's probably fairly obvious in the writing disciplines because we are pouring ourselves out in a way. I think the problem is we supervise them and say I'm not a therapist, you're having issues, let's get you into counselling, let's get a professional to deal with you and that. So I think that students may expect that supervisors be the grown-ups and to be responsible. [Supervisors need to] understand if they did try to counsel them, they're going to be in legal trouble. Because you've given them advice and you've got no idea what you're talking about (interview, Webb, 2015).

DE-IDENTIFIED INTERVIEWEE 7

Well, I think really authentic support and really knowledge-based training delivered by experts. That's my answer to lots of these kind of projects because often we get people supposedly offering us training, but they know a lot less than us and then I think that becomes quite – what is it called when you're distanced? Yes, it makes you feel alienated. It's very alienating, but there really are pools of experts out there that have done a lot of work in these areas (interview, 2015).

DE-IDENTIFIED INTERVIEWEE 8

I think maybe there needs to be a kind of more open process between the research deans and – when they're allocating students, or when you accept a student, maybe there does need to be a kind of area where you can declare whether you think this is an area that you need support or not, but yes, that would be suggesting again a kind of counselling approach and I'm not sure that is the best approach. Might just want to talk to colleagues or talk to someone about what you might do under certain circumstances (interview, 2015).

ASSOCIATE PROFESSOR DEBRA ADELAIDE, UNIVERSITY OF TECHNOLOGY SYDNEY

… The fundamental thing about being a creative writer – not that I'm setting them all up to be basket cases; I'm not trying to set up anything except preparing them for the confronting things they're getting in workshopping. They do. It's very confronting putting your work out there and getting feedback. It can be really confronting, and I always tell them how affected I was the first time I ever got feedback on my work. Felt sick for a month, but I realise that that was necessary.

The other thing that absolutely has to be taken into consideration, I think, in this sort of discussion, is that our postgraduates are experienced writers, and if they're not they don't get into the programme. It's basic, they should be. We'd only accept them if they've got a track record. Basically by the time I would get a DCA student, that student is an experienced writer, so they've gone through a lot of this stuff anyway. So they may not need the help. They may not need any help, and they may find that the writing of the story is sufficient to – difficult though that may be – it is sufficient to help them. Just thinking of the students I've got at the moment, they're all experienced. They've all been well published (interview, Adelaide, 2015).

PROFESSOR NIGEL KRAUTH, GRIFFITH UNIVERSITY
A school needs a flexible reporting and support system within its culture, in conjunction with a dependable university counselling service (interview, Krauth, 2015).

ASSOCIATE PROFESSOR DOMINIQUE HECQ, SWINBURNE UNIVERSITY
I used to think they [ethics committees] were a pain in the ass because they'd ask questions and so forth, but I think it's a good thing that they go through the ethics committee. It helps us think through the dangers. But you're right about particularly autobiographic projects, you never know what you are going to find, there are always skeletons in the closet and you don't know whom you are going to upset but it's important to at least cover your bases from the academic point of view. Even if the person upset is a family member, it can be disastrous. I think it's an important part of the process. I think the forms are not devised for our kinds of projects, and I think a lot of work needs to be done in the policy department. The questions they ask are not particularly addressing the problems we are encountering. So yes, there is an area there that needs to be addressed.

I think there should be a team of therapists or analysts who are attached to the university but not part of the university. So a team of people we can trust and that are not, how shall I say, traceable through human resources for instance. Something that is really confidential or para-institutional. It [trauma] pops up everywhere, even in straight doctorates. But certainly in poetry a lot of trauma comes, but not only lived trauma but also witnessed trauma. It's everywhere, yes (interview, Hecq, 2015).

PROFESSOR GAIL JONES, UNIVERSITY OF WESTERN SYDNEY
Ethics committees seem to be very much based on social sciences rather than the humanities and don't always have a sensitivity to language and to the kind of things that we do. What I would like is for there to be instruction to supervisors. So not an ethics committee that clears the project, because we don't really ever know where a project will go, and there are privacy issues and intimate disclosure makes people very vulnerable, and I'm not sure I would want some of my students

to have to lay out before an ethical committee whatever exactly they're doing, or to describe it before it's thought through. But I think if we insist that supervisors need some training and ethical circumspection and some strategies, psychological strategies, to help students. Kind of a language. Language is things like projection, transference. Even to talk to students about something like denial, how that works in being in the university. So vocabulary, ethical vocabulary and ethical strategies for dealing with real people and their experience, they would seem to me more useful.

And I think actually having awareness of the discourses of psychology and psychoanalysis and all of those things because we're dealing with psychic damage often. And then with recovery, you know, how does one recover, how does one use language and intellectual strategies for a restorative purpose? I mean, don't you think that we need a restorative ethic? We need to believe that there's some good that comes from this. I really think the idea of a humanistic discourse about self-growth, identity and inferiority, you know, recognising the irreducible inferiority of your students, that seems to me so much more important than the risk assessment model (interview, Jones, 2015).

ASSOCIATE PROFESSOR KATE DOUGLAS, FLINDERS UNIVERSITY

… I think that we had a community of practice at Flinders for a little while and we had kind of interdisciplinary people working together and talking through these issues and I found that very supportive. But like everything else that's organised for academics, it's fine for the first couple of meetings and then everyone says I don't have time to attend these meetings anymore. But we had people from law and politics and sociology and English and creative writing and it was really good. And so I thought these kinds of interdisciplinary conversations are very supportive because people all of a sudden realise that this is not an issue that just they are dealing with alone, which is fantastic. But I don't know, I think every time you feel like you can offer some kind of support, people always just see it as some kind of invasion on their time. So I don't know. I feel like I can micromanage all this stuff with a couple of really close colleagues and I find that very helpful (interview, Douglas 2016).

CONCLUSION

The important perspectives drawn from the representative supervisors' lived experiences not only demonstrate the commitment these academics have to their candidate's ultimate success, but also testify to the impulse to manage ethically projects borne out of trauma narratives. Those of us working in the fields of humanities, journalism and creative practices are perhaps more likely to increasingly encounter candidates who seek to write personally about traumatic events that have disrupted their lives and caused psychic distress. As one of the interviewees, scholar and novelist Gail Jones observes:

> And to be alive is to be wounded, and that doesn't have to incapacitate you. It can become another kind of capacity for imagining the humanity of other people. I'm sure that's why we're all in the field, or why we all care about it (interview, Jones, 2015).

Writers often turn to writing projects as a response to wounding. Another of the experienced interviewees, writer Debra Adelaide, makes this particular observation about candidates: 'If they're going to be creative writers, they are going to be vulnerable' (interview, Adelaide, 2015). It would seem vulnerability is part of the creative process when rendering authentic autobiographical experiences. We return again here to echo Kevin Brophy's observation and warning: '…the ability of Creative Writing to hurt, to reveal, to run a very dangerous line between offence and revelation, and I wouldn't like to see Creative Writing become anodyne…' (interview, Brophy, 2015). These notions allude to the somewhat nebulous core of creative practice and the more political heart of journalism; notions which do not always neatly align with an empirical paradigm of traditional modes of ethics clearance or academic writing.

There is a general consensus amongst those we interviewed that further onerous and time-consuming protocols for already time-poor writing project supervisors are not necessarily the best strategy for improving pedagogical and supervisory practices relating to autobiographical trauma projects, and there is a sense from some interviewees that further bureaucratisation and compliance might adversely affect creative output. However, we do wish to signify that many of the interviewees signalled the need for more intentional institutional work to be done by way of educating and establishing a shared model of best practice that involved developing tailored training modules for academics supervising HDR projects dealing with traumatic narration. Aitchison reminds us: 'In the humanities and social sciences, writing is the major pedagogical activity that dominates, even defines, interactions between students and their supervisors … our understanding of what goes on in supervision around writing is still relatively limited' (Aitchison 2015: 1295-1296). To advance our shared understanding of supervisory practice and support, several interviewees flag that at their universities, candidates have supervision panels, with more than one supervisor. But several also acknowledge that this can also create tensions – frequently, only a principal supervisor is allocated work-load credit, which may create a disincentive to already overworked and time-poor academics from taking part as a panel member. Reflecting on the possible incentive for being on a panel without a workload allocation, Matthew Ricketson, of the University of Canberra, comments:

> Well look here's the trade-off … at the point at which the student graduates with their PhD or their Master's, the secondary supervisor is acknowledged, not only acknowledged in the same way that the primary is at the graduation ceremony, but you as a secondary supervisor or second

member of the panel can count it as a completion and because of the metric which says in your performance and development review meeting each year, one of the measures that you are judged by, is how many HDR completions you have (interview, Ricketson, 2015).

Regardless of possible 'trade-offs', we would argue there is a strategic opportunity for institutions to more formally address this possible inequity (and lost opportunity in some cases) to create a more robust and safer HDR experience by affording workload allocations to all panel members, and include trauma experts, or psychotherapists, on panels if necessary.

We offer this preliminary research paper as a starting point of collegial dialogue undertaken with expert HDR supervisors working in the Australian tertiary sector. In voicing some of their perspectives, we hope this paper serves to generate an ongoing nation-wide conversation devoted to addressing the issue of how to create safer boundaries around trauma narrative projects. Our future work, in dialogue with colleagues and experts, will turn attention to how tertiary institutions might go about implementing practical strategies to further support both the supervisor and candidate because as Gilmore concludes: 'Trauma inflects so much autobiographical material that we should probably admit that it has already chosen us and acknowledge this demand' (Gilmore 2007: 368). Finally, we hope to further this research internationally, as a potentially comparative and discursive model.

- This paper was first published in *Ethical Space*, Vol. 14, Nos 2 and 3 pp 61-71

ACKNOWLEDGEMENTS

We would like to thank the thirteen academics who gave freely of their time and expertise. The generous sharing of insightful responses to the selected research questions have added to a deeper understanding of supervisory practices in the area of autobiographical writing projects shaped by trauma. We also acknowledge the Journalism Educational and Research Association of Australia's Research Grant scheme (2015) of which we are the grateful recipients.

NOTES

[1] Greene, G. (1980) *Ways of escape*, London, The Bodley Head p. 9

[2] Miller, N. and Tougaw, J. (2002) *Extremities: Trauma, testimony, and community*, Illinois, The University of Illinois pp 1-2

[3] Australian government-funded inquiry into research in the creative arts, Strand Report, 1998

[4] JERAA grant 2015: The ethical HDR supervision of literary journalism: Managing long form trauma narrative within the Australian tertiary sector

[5] See Baker and Buckley (2009) Evans, T., Macauley, P., Pearson, M. and Tregenza, K. (2003) and Brien, D. L., Burr, S. and Webb, J. (2012)

[6] UTS HREC No. 2015000377

[7] Office for Learning and Teaching

REFERENCES

Aitchison, C. (2015) Writing the practice/practise the writing: Writing challenges and pedagogies for creative practice supervisors and researchers, *Educational Philosophy and Theory*, Vol. 47, No. 12 pp 1291-1303

Aitchison, C. and Mowbray, S. (2013) Doctoral women: Managing emotions, managing doctoral studies, *Teaching in Higher Education*, Vol. 18, No. 8 pp 859-870

Baker, S., Buckley, B. and Kett, G. (2009) Future-proofing the creative arts in higher education: Scoping for quality in creative arts doctoral programs, *Australian Literature Review*, Effective supervision of creative practice higher research degrees, 2013, Government Office for Learning and Teaching Project Final Report. Available online at http://www.olt.gov.au/project-futureproofing-creative-arts-melbourne-2007, accessed on 28 April 2016

Evans, T., Macauley, P., Pearson, M. and Tregenza, K. (2003) A brief review of PhDs in creative and performing arts in Australia, Jeffrey, R. and Shilton, W. (eds) *Conference proceedings of the Australian Association for Research in Education* pp 1-14. Available online at http://dro.deakin.edu.au/eserv/DU:30004959/evans-brief-review-2003.pdf, accessed on 28 April 2016

Frick, L., Brodin, E. M. and Albertyn, R. M. (2014) A conceptualisation of the doctoral student-supervisor relationship as a negotiated learning space, Nygaard, C., Branch, J. Scott-Webber, L. and Bartholomew, P. (eds) *Learning spaces in higher education*, Oxfordshire, Libri Publishing pp 241-262

Gilmore, L. (2007) What do we teach when we teach trauma? Fuchs, M. and Howes, C. (eds) *Teaching life writing texts*, The Modern Language Association of America pp 367-373

Hamilton, J. and Carson, S. (2013) *Literature review in effective supervision of creative practice higher research degrees*. Available online at http://supervisioncreativeartsphd.net/?page_id=197, accessed on 28 April 2016

Joseph, S. and Rickett, C. (2010) The writing cure?: Ethical considerations in managing creative practice life writing projects, Cole, C., Freiman, M. and Brien, D. L. (eds) *Strange bedfellows: Refereed conference papers of the 15th Annual AAWP Conference*. Available online at http://www.aawp.org.au/the_strange_bedfellows_or_perfect_partners, accessed on 26 April 2016

Joseph, S. (2011) Supervising life-writing of trauma in a tertiary setting, Krauth, N. and Brophy, K. (eds) *TEXT*, Vol. 15, No. 2. Available online at http://www.textjournal.com.au/oct11/joseph.htm, accessed on 26 April 2016

Littrell, J. (2009) Expression of emotion: When it causes trauma and when it helps, *Journal of Evidence-based Social Work*, Vol. 6, No. 3 pp 300-320

Manathunga, C. (2007) Supervision as mentoring: The role of power and boundary crossing, *Studies in Continuing Education*, Vol. 29, No. 2 pp 207-221

Pennebaker, J. (2000) Telling stories: The health benefits of narrative, *Literature and Medicine*, Vol. 19, No. 1 Spring pp 3-18

Ricketson, M. (2005) Literary journalism, *The Media Report ABC*, interview by Julia May, 23 June

Strand, D. (1998) *Research in the creative arts: Evaluations and investigations programme*, Department of Employment, Education, Training and Youth Affairs, AGPS, Canberra

Webb, J., Brien, D. L. and Burr, S. (2012) *Examining doctorates in the creative arts: A guide*, Australasian Association of Writing Programs. Available online at http://d3n8a8pro7vhmx.cloudfront.net/ theaawp/pages/20/attachments/original/1384907948/Examiners_booklet_final_0.pdf?1384907948, accessed on 28 April 2016

INTERVIEWS

Catherine Cole, University of Wollongong, 13 October 2015: Skype; France

Fiona Giles, Sydney University, 22 October 2015: Skype; Sydney

Willa McDonald, Macquarie University, 29 October 2015: Skype; Sydney

Kevin Brophy, University of Melbourne, 29 October 2015: Skype; Melbourne

Matthew Ricketson, University of Canberra, 27 November 2015: face-to-face; Melbourne

Jen Webb, University of Canberra, 30 November 2015; face-to-face; Melbourne

De-identified interview 7, 15 December 2015: telephone

De-identified interview 8, 17 December 2015: telephone

Debra Adelaide, University of Technology Sydney, 18 December 2015: telephone; Sydney

Dominique Hecq, Swinburne University, 29 January 2016: telephone; Melbourne

Nigel Krauth, Griffith University, Queensland, 26 January 2016: email; Queensland

Gail Jones, University of Western Sydney, 29 January 2016: telephone; Sydney

Kate Douglas, Flinders University, 6 May 2016: telephone; Adelaide

NOTE ON THE CONTRIBUTORS

Sue Joseph is an Associate Professor who holds an Adjunct position at Avondale University, is a Senior Research Fellow at the University of South Australia and is a doctoral supervisor at the University of Sydney, Central Queensland University and the University of Technology Sydney. She is currently Joint Editor of *Ethical Space: The International Journal of Communication Ethics* and co-editor with Willa McDonald and Matthew Ricketson of the Literary Journalism Palgrave book series.

Carolyn Rickett is an Associate Professor and Dean of Learning and Teaching, senior lecturer, researcher and creative arts practitioner at Avondale University. Utilising her background in arts, medical humanities and healthcare chaplaincy, she currently teaches undergraduate students and supervises postgraduate candidates in the fields of communication, creative writing, education, nursing and chaplaincy. Along with co-editing several poetry anthologies, she is the coordinator of the *New Leaves* writing group.

Chapter 22

Communication and globalisation: A justification for critical pedagogy

Andrea Patterson-Masuka and Omar Swartz

This paper, situated in critical pedagogy, argues that communication educators need to examine the basic communication course, a general education requirement for many undergraduate students, in the context of globalisation. The paper first explores the concept of globalisation and its adverse impact on college students. It contends that the model of intercultural praxis can be utilised for curriculum development to revise the basic communication course. It concludes by challenging readers to envision transformative models of teaching, engaging and developing curricula for a new globalised critical praxis of citizenship education in introductory communication courses.

Keywords: basic communication course, globalisation, communication education, power, intercultural praxis, critical pedagogy, oral communication, general education

The 'free market' ideology is the reigning viewpoint of our time (Centeno and Cohen 2012). Its success in withering criticism has not entirely thwarted growing moral repugnance to the gross injustices it is spawning, particularly its callous indifference to human suffering and contribution to vast environmental degradation. Increasingly, questions are raised regarding the erosion of democratic accountability in the 'new world order' in which corporations wield so much power over the basic conditions of life on the planet (Shapiro 2006: 201). Globalisation, however, is not new. For centuries, Europeans in particular, but others as well, have traversed the globe to buy and trade, invading and upsetting local ways of life and traditions. In some ways this is positive, as civilisation clearly advances along with trade and the liberalising effect of interacting with diverse people. For these and other reasons, some view globalism as inevitable and desirable and willingly embrace it (e.g., Friedman 2007; Lechner 2005; Nye 2002).

On the other hand, many people around the world regard globalisation with suspicion, viewing it as a threat to jobs, culture and the environment. As critics point out, globalisation increasingly leads to inequality between countries, wealth for a few, and mounting poverty for many. Moreover, globalisation is linked to such environmental disasters as global warming, deforestation and accelerated reduction in biodiversity (Nye 2002, 2009; Gore 2013). Sorrells and Nakagawa (2008) argue that the current wave of globalisation, deeply rooted in an ideology of European colonisation and Western imperialism, has thrust people from different countries and cultures together into shared physical and virtual workplaces, schools and communities in unprecedented ways, often benefiting the stronger over the weak. The inequities in our society are evident in how communication technology is allocated in our world. Sorrells (2008) reports that while technological advances enable about 15 per cent of the earth's inhabitants to connect to the world on wireless laptops at home or in our favourite coffee spots, more than 50 per cent of the earth's population lives below the poverty line. These people start their day without the basic necessities of sufficient food, clean water and safe shelter. They have become an exploited population whose lands, resources or labour is the engine of world economic growth but who see few of the benefits that are produced.

The problem, notes Sorrells (ibid), is that for many in the US, their continuing belief in their 'exceptionalism' and moral superiority as a civilisation influences how they understand and interpret their world and other cultures, rendering social injustice invisible: 'These hidden assumptions mask historically inequitable relations of power that contribute to the maintenance of social, political, and economic injustice' (ibid: 21). To remedy this situation, Sorrells advocates:

> ... [a] critical approach to culture, sense-making, processes, and everyday lived practices [which] challenges these ethnocentric attitudes and nurtures the ability to understand cultures from within the cultures' frame of reference rather than interpreting and negatively evaluating other cultures from one's own cultural position (ibid).

Thankfully, educators have begun to take note of the impact that the market and social forces of globalisation have had on schools and colleges (Currie and Newson 1998; Slaughter 1997). Some argue that the market and social forces of globalisation have had an adverse impact on schools and colleges (Torres 2002; Wang, Lin, Spalding, Odell and Klecka 2011). Smith (2002), for example, points out that many schools have become locations for branding and sites for policy-market solutions and corporate expansion. Ritzer (2000) contends that education has become a victim of McDonaldisation which is the 'process by which the principles of the fast food restaurant are coming to dominate more and more sectors of American society as well as the rest of the world' (ibid: 1). The four principles are efficiency, calculability, predictability and control. Ritzer (2000, 2004) argues that these principles can be found in a variety of industries within US society. The principles can also be applied to higher education.

The principle of *efficiency* is the concept of finding the most favourable and fastest method of achieving your desired result. In higher education, the use of multiple choice tests and scantron sheets allow professors to grade tests with less expenditure of time and energy. The second principle is *calculabilty*, the method of reducing all or most decisions down to numbers. The use of multiple choice questions, scantron sheets, and the use of grading rubrics helps reduce subjectivity and reflection, and thus time. The third principle is *predictability*, in which the options and choices are set, therefore being more efficient. Students only have the option of enrolling in a freshman composition course to meet the general education requirement for written communication instead of the option of a course on African American playwrights that is writing intensive. The fourth principle of *control* is the precise management of all these duties that entails the careful training of personnel and the aid of technology. Control not only involves the flow of production but the consumption of this as well. Entering freshers are taught to be efficient with the advisor's time by perhaps working in a small group with a professional advisor before being assigned to a faculty advisor. Some schools are even more clever and efficient and students are advised in a freshers orientation course. They are trained to come to the advising session prepared with a selection of courses and make maximum use of their allotted time.

Communication educators do not always acknowledge the role we play in endangering our democracy and our planet. It is imperative that we reevaluate communication curricula through the lens of globalisation. We argue that communication can be employed to assist students in learning how to use cultural critique to question the existing power structures within our society that disempower and disenfranchise certain groups. Communication educators can help realise this vision by developing a pedagogy that encourages an appreciation and understanding of diverse and marginalised voices in our world and focus on how to use rhetoric to foster social justice, advocacy and peace (see Swartz 1997).

Below, we examine the need to reevaluate and redescribe communication-related courses in the context of globalisation. We argue that the standard method for teaching these courses is limited in its approach to helping students communicate competently in a global society. Students must be able to critically examine the world around them and use communication to co-create a more peaceful and equitable world for all the earth's inhabitants. More specifically, our purpose is to develop a pedagogy in which students become more effective communicators in a global society. This vision can be realised through *intercultural praxis*, developed by Kathryn Sorrells (2013). This intercultural praxis model calls for 'critical, reflective, engaged thinking and action' (ibid: 15) that enables educators to help their students understand other cultures, find their voice, engage in critical dialogue and become empowered to use communication to advocate for social justice. We argue that this model, originally developed for studying intercultural communication in the context of globalisation, can also be used as a curriculum development framework to teach the basic communication course and highlight how the classroom can be a place of social change and provide a powerful environment for creating dialogue, emancipation and empowerment. The next section of the paper provides a closer examination of globalisation, exploring various definitions, descriptions and its adverse impact on education.

GLOBALISATION: IDEOLOGY, PATHOLOGY OR JUST SOMETHING WE DO

Globalisation is not one thing or even a common experience or phenomenon. Its experiences are uneven and continuouly changing. In India, China or Vietnam, globalisation may look like economic prosperity and opportunity, at least on the surface, while in regions such as Central America it may look like greed, exploitation or empire (Blum 2005; Hardt and Negri 2001).

President Barack Obama, in his June 2009 speech in Cairo, Egypt, said the purpose of his visit was to forge a new relationship between the US and Muslims worldwide. This was important for the new American president given the two on-going wars against predominantly Muslim nations in Iraq and Afghanistan (as well as the long-threatened war against Iran). Yet Obama's speech was much more than that. He addressed several key international issues, including economic development, opportunity and globalisation – the inequality of which animates much US adventurism:

> I know that for many, the face of globalization is contradictory. The internet and television can bring knowledge and information, but also offensive sexuality and mindless violence. Trade can bring new wealth and opportunities, but also huge disruptions and changing communities. In all nations – including my own – this change can bring fear. Fear that because of modernity we will lose control over our economic choices, our politics, and most importantly our identities – those things we must cherish about our communities, our families, our traditions, and our faith (*AmericaNews.com* 2009, para. 62).

The competing and in some cases contradictory descriptions of globalisation – the fear, the lack of trust the developing world reasonably has about this reinvigorated Western project – suggest that the experience of globalisation is built on deeply embedded historical and philosophical experiences arising from strikingly different views or assessments. US citizens, after all, forget their history. The subaltern, however, have long memories. What Nye (2009) defines as globalisation, 'the increase in worldwide networks of interdependence' (ibid: para. 3), others may see as networks of *dependence* as in colonialism or neo-colonialism.

In this section we follow Sorrells (2008) in examining three dimensions of globalisation: social/cultural, political and economic. We acknowledge there are other facets of globalisation, including environmental and military which, while important, are outside the scope of our study.

The first type of globalisation, *social/cultural globalisation*, includes the dissemination, infusion, or exchange of ideas, images, artifacts, customs, cultures and interactions of people. The dimensions of social/cultural globalisation impact on people's ways of thinking, believing, behaving and communicating. As people travel across the world, they take their culture with them and, even if inadvertantly, recreate a sense of the familiar or home. In addition, people returning home from their travels take artifacts or reminders of the places they have visited. While the complicated notion of culture cannot be reduced to an item packed in a suitcase, the mementos we take or leave are important in representing our cultures, the languages we speak, the beliefs we hold and the practices we carry out.

The second type of globalisation is *political*. Sorrells (2008) argues there is a growing trend toward political globalisation. She cites an increased interconnectedness between nation-state politics, the development of bodies of global governance, and a global development of resistance in response to increased inequities in political power. Following the fall of the former Soviet Union in 1990, there has been a growing assumption that capitalism and democracy together will bring about global prosperity and peace. This assumption of 'democratisation', however, is highly suspect (Leys 2001; Nsouli 2008; Nye 2009; Palley 2006), as some observers and sceptics of globalisation conclude that the political agendas associated with 'democratisation' are closely related to the free-trade agreements of the World Trade Organisation (WTO), the World Bank and the International Monetary Fund (IMF), none of which deliver democracy in the sense of ensuring substantive equality for all (Swartz 2004).

Political globalisation, however, does not necessarily lead to democracy. As Barber (1992) elucidates, there is another tension, that between tribalism and globalism. He characterises tribalism and cultural terrorism such as *jihad* to describe approximately a hundred faiths that oppose 'every kind of interdependence, every kind of artificial social cooperation and civic mutuality' (ibid: 53). In contrast, Barber characterises capitalistic, corporate seduction with fast food, computers, technology, popular music and television as *McWorld*. These two clashes of culture and ideology create a dialectic in which the 'planet is falling precipitately apart and coming reluctantly together at the very same moment' (ibid: 53). He refers to this cultural clash 'as the two axial principles of our age' and argues they are both 'threatening to democracy' (ibid).

Finally there is *economic globalisation*: many economists, businesspeople and journalists view globalisation and the world economy as one (Nye 2002). Friedman views it as the international system that replaced the one established by the Cold War involving the integration of capital, technology and information across national borders, creating a single global market or 'village' (Friedman 2007). What the champions of this view overlook is that the rules and regulations that govern this virtual community are displaced and unconnected from the actual world in which people live. Few object, after all, when the costs of development occur far away, but feel differently when the factory or waste site is in their backyard. When government ceases being local, the human costs of our politics are rendered invisible.

GLOBALISATION AND ITS DISCONTENTS: EMPOWERING OUR STUDENTS

Life is seldom fair; nevertheless, we take hope in institutions (such as struggling public universities) that at least help prevent or ameliorate grave injustice by keeping the *idea* of a critical citizenry alive. Globalisation, at least potentially, removes this hope from us when it undermines institutions that ensure/support democratic, constitutional or human rights. On the other hand, we find hope in the many acts of resistance to globalisation by young people as they represent a reassertion of the spirit animating democracry (i.e., the Occupy and Black Lives Matter movements).

Clearly, resistance to globalisation and its adverse effects are erupting around the globe (most recently, for example, with the negative example of Brexit). Protestors are angry about the inequities between rich and impoverished countries, the policies of the Group of Eight (G-8), IMF and the World Bank, the lack of intervention from the United Nations, and the increasing militarisation and domination of foreign countries in the name of 'democracy' and 'freedom'. In recent decades, anti-globalisation protests have disrupted meetings around the world, including those of the IMF, World Bank and WTO, among others. Demonstrations were held during the annual meetings of the IMF and the World Bank in 1988 in West Berlin. Since then, protesters against globalisation have marched faithfully during WTO, IMF and World Bank meetings. The first mass anti-capitalist, anti-globalisation protest took place on 18 June 1999, when thousands of militant protesters took to the streets in more than 40 cities around the world including London, England, and Eugene, Oregon, in a mass movement known as the Global Carnival against Capital (Dodson, 2003). The event also came to be known as the J18.

The second major anti-globalisation protest, known as the Battle of Seattle or N30, occurred some five months later on 30 November 1999, in Seattle, Washington. With an estimated 50,000 to 100,000 protesters in attendance, the massive gathering turned violent, more than 600 people were arrested, and opening ceremonies of the WTO meeting were cancelled. The protest, however, continued throughout the four-day meeting. On 26 September 2000, 9,000 protesters in Prague voiced their fury and frustration over economics. The *Seattle Times* reported at least 69 people were injured and 44 hospitalised. News reports called Prague a 'smoky battle zone' (*Seattle Times* 2000: para. 4) filled with the chants of demonstrators yelling: 'London, Seattle, continue the battle' (ibid: para. 3) as they converged on Prague's Wenceslas Square, where peace protesters had gathered more than 10 years earlier to speak out against communism.

A later protest against the WTO in Seattle in 2001 resulted in more than 1,300 trade organisations and social movements from more than 80 countries. Since 2001, additional protests held in Quebec, Canada, Davos, Switzerland, and other places have become symbols of the festering and growing feelings of frustration and resentment about the unfair gap between rich and poor and the power inequities that exemplify globalisation (Sorrells 2008). These meetings, rallies and protests are being held around the world to develop programmes, strategies and oppositional forces to combat the various forms of globalisation – environmental, military, economic and others. The patchwork quilt of forces has formed a loosely-woven blanket of resistance: 'This decentralized, multi-headed swarm of a movement has succeeded in educating and radicalizing a generation of activists around the world' (Klein 2002: 2).

During 2011-2012, the movement against the inequities of globalisation experienced a burst of new energy with the 'Occupy Wall-Street' or, more generally, the 'Occupy Movement' (Balardini 2012). Watching these protests from our classrooms was invigorating – we cheered and spoke words of encouragement to our students, even giving academic credit for those who chose to be involved or excused their absence from class. As professors, we can think of no higher calling than to urge our students out of the classroom and on to the streets to apply and live the principles of social justice we profess. More recently, the Black Lives Matters movement has captured the attention of people living in the United States, as millions of Americans confront the ugly reality of systemic poverty, injustice and racism experienced by minority communities. Many of our students are actively involved with our blessing and occasional strategic advice. In a class taught by one of our colleagues, students founded a non-profit organisation to resist gentrification and related injustices to minority communities in Denver, CO, getting news coverage in the *Guardian* (see Tracey 2016).

Below we more systematically examine the influences of globalisation, power, consumerism and their adverse impact on youth and higher education. We conclude with the question: how do we envision a new globalised and critical praxis of citizenship education in the communication classroom? Or, more bluntly, how do we prepare the next generation of student protesters, keeping alive the spirit that animates our students today?

POWER, DISNEYISATION OF HIGHER EDUCATION AND GLOBALISATION

Essential to our understanding of the consequential grip of globalisation on higher education is the consideration of the notions of power and consumerism. Power can be viewed as something that is imposed on or held over someone that other people do not have. In this sense power can be seen as coercion, control, or manipulation through language, thought, or action. In some cases, people are rendered helpless, defenceless and unable to respond or escape – physically or mentally (Swartz, Campbell and Pestana 2009). Power can also mean something different. For instance, Foucault challenges us to critically examine the relationship between power and the way it is understood, how it develops, its intricacy, how it functions and how it is formed. He notes that power is not something that is only hierarchical in nature, uniform or top down only in its approach; it is something that is pervasive, insidious, and grows and manifests itself within society. Power not only rests on the elements of repression and ideology, but goes a step further:

> Power is taken above all carrying the force of a prohibition. Now I believe that this is a wholly negative, narrow, skeleton conception of power, one which has been curiously widespread. If power were never anything but repressive, if it never did anything but to say no, do you really think one would be brought to obey it? (Foucault 1984: 61).

Foucault further argues that power can be understood in terms of discipline and the function of rule, norms and regulations, reified through policies and procedures. It is through this normalisation of power that it becomes a process, it is enforced, and the language becomes codified:

> What makes power hold good, what makes it accepted, is simply the fact that it doesn't only weigh on us as a force that says no, but that it traverses and produces things, it induces pleasure, forms knowledge, produces discourse. It needs to be considered as a productive network which runs through the whole social body, much more than as a negative instance whose function is repression (ibid).

An example is Barber's (1992) concept of *McWorld*, which he uses to describe the capitalistic spell that mesmerises consumers from fast food like McDonald's to MTV, fast computers, fast music and glamorous makeup and clothes. Ritz also observed this concept of 'McDonaldisation', as cited in Swartz et al. (2009). Ritz's critique also extends to mainstream America where 'McMansions' are becoming more prevalent in the suburbs – a sign of progress and affluence. The McDonald's mentality has become embedded in American culture. Bryman (1999) compares this idea to the policies, procedures, operations and marketing of the Disney theme parks, whose practices are being adopted across America as well as around the globe. Disney's amusement parks consist of fantasy worlds that transport the visitor to a different global location and even to outer space.

The bigger-than-life theme is also evident in oversized malls such as the Mall of America in Bloomington, Minnesota. The casinos and hotels of Las Vegas, also often built around a theme, transport the visitor to another world. Hotel visitors can travel around the globe: Caesar's Palace becomes Italy; New York, New York becomes a cosmopolitan city; Circus Circus becomes the ultimate children's three-ring circus event. Visitors are constantly surrounded by merchandise, food courts, casinos and amusement. Bryman (1999), who refers to this as the 'dedifferentiation of consumption', argues that the 'general trend of consumption associated with different institutional spheres becomes interlocked with each other and increasingly difficult to distinguish' (ibid: 33). This is apparent in Las Vegas where, he argues, guests may enter the hotel through a lobby filled with merchandise and a casino. Like Disney World, Las Vegas hotels offer themes and settings that carry the consumer into a make-believe universe. Bryman goes further to say that in this process, 'conventional distinctions between casinos, hotels, restaurants, shopping, and theme parks collapse' (ibid: 36).

The interlocking elements of globalisation have become weapons in what Giroux (2003b) characterises as 'the war against youth' (ibid: 145).

He argues that neoliberal capitalism has created weapons to destroy our youth: inadequate healthcare, food, education, unemployment, corporate downsizing and corporate deregulation, among other basic necessities. These 'youth' are our students, our children, our friends. Unfortunately for many, culture has become a product to purchase as consumers and they are fluent in the language of capitalism.

The economic and market forces of capitalism and consumerism have changed the language we use in how we present ourselves and how we assess the behaviour of others (Fassett and Warren 2007; Giroux 2003b; Smith 2002; Sorrells 2008; Swartz 2006; Swartz et al. 2009). Stars such as Michael Jordan, Beyoncé, Martha Stewart, Kim Kardashian and Queen Latifah market themselves as a brand. We are conditioned through advertising and the media to consume the products being sold for self-gratification and to be accepted by society. Giroux (2003b) argues that no longer defined as a form of self-development, 'individuality is reduced to the endless pursuit of mass-mediated interests and pleasures' (ibid: 154).

Zygmunt Bauman warns: 'Globalization is on everybody's lips, a fad word fast turning into a shibboleth, a magic incarnation, a passkey meant to unlock the gates to all present and future mysteries.' 'For some,' he continues, '"globalization" is the cause of our unhappiness' (cited in Ibrahim 2007: 102). Bauman's stance astutely characterises the tensions that surround globalisation. Advocates such as *New York Times* journalist Thomas Friedman, Yahoo founder Jerry Yang, global corporate leaders and world organisations such as the WTO view it as an avenue for possibilities, profit, opportunity and expansion. However, sceptics of globalisation and public intellectuals such as McLaren, Giroux, Shapiro, Sorrells and many others are angered by the devastation, destruction and despair that globalisation has caused our youth, society, democracy and planet. We find compelling Giroux's question that educators must ask themselves in the context of globalisation:

> Under this insufferable climate of increased repression and unabated exploitation, young people become the new casualties in an ongoing war against justice, freedom, citizenship, and democracy. What is happening to our children in America and what are its implications for addressing the future of higher education? (Giroux 2003a: 145).

In the context of globalisation, many critical educators continue to envision a different world and engage in a critical pedagogy that is transformative and helps students imagine that another world is possible. In the words of Paulo Freire (1994), teachers and students become 'critical co-investigators' and create projects of social justice, emancipation, peace, economic equity, global citizenship, cultural critique, dialogue, democracy, empowered voices and those yet to be imagined. For example, we teach variations of the following throughout our courses as appropriate: that is, issues of law, diversity and community as they have been played out historically in the construction of US culture. We immerse students in hundreds of primary source historical documents (such as advertisements, archival newspaper articles, comics, court decisions, old photographs, personal letters from historical figures, statutes, videos and other cultural artifacts), along with critical, historical, legal, narrative, philosophical and sociological approaches to study diversity and the conflict that often surrounds the quest for economic, moral and social inclusion in this country. The overarching method of exploration is our and our student's *moral imaginations* – our ability to conceptualise and name the constraints placed on us by language and/or conceptual barriers so as to become morally intelligent agents in our relationships with others as well as to be more conscientious citizens in our increasingly heterogeneous and interdependent society.

In this way, we follow Freire, and help our students to envision a new 'globalized and critical praxis of citizenship education' (ibid: 89) in all that we do, but particularly in the undergraduate basic communication course. We argue that *parrhesia*, the Greek concept of 'fearless and bold speech', in the context of globalisation is fading (Patterson and Swartz 2014). The future of democracy, dissent, fearless and bold speech and educating for critical consciousness is being threatened around the globe. It is critical for communication scholars to examine our pedagogical practices and explore multiple and competing ways of knowing and learning in the college communication classroom.

THE NEED FOR A GLOBAL PERSPECTIVE IN COMMUNICATION EDUCATION

Deanna Sellnow and Jason Martin (2010) contend that one of the questions that 'continually perplexes basic communication course teacher-scholars is simultaneously simple and complex: just what is the basic course in communication?' (ibid: 33). We define the basic communication course as 'that course required or recommended for a significant number of undergraduates or that course which the department has or would recommend as a requirement for … all or most undergraduates' (Morreale, Hanna and Gibson 1999: 3). Beyond this general definition, there are many opinions that surface regarding the content, how it should be taught and who should teach this course. One frequently asked question is: 'Should the course be focused more for skills for the workplace or to help students function as citizens in a democracy?'

In view of the above question, it is important to evaluate the course for several reasons. First, the basic communication course is included in the majority of two- and four-year colleges and universities and assists institutions in meeting its general education requirements. The Association of American Colleges and Universities (AACU) reports that 56 per cent of the institutions surveyed showed that general education has become an increasing priority among their institutions, while only 3 per cent report that it is diminishing in importance (Glenn 2009). The survey also indicated that 89 per cent reported their colleges were either reevaluating or making modifications to their general education requirements. Carol Schneider, Association of American Colleges and Universities president, argued that a general education should produce graduates with 'a deep and flexible set of skills' and hence not rely too heavily on a narrow, technical, pre-professional model of education (cited in Glenn 2009: A8). Furthermore, Schneider, citing a 2006 survey conducted by employers, noted that businesses also wanted colleges to emphasise written and oral communication, cross-cultural team communication skills, and other skills not directly linked to a specialised field of study (cited in Glenn 2009).

Second, it is important to assess the ideological shifts in rhetoric in the context of globalisation. In higher education before 1885, public speaking was a skill used to engage in academic discourse and for citizenship issues. And although in the beginning public speaking was recognised as a skill to engage in critical issues, the course later developed into a focus on the basic skills of public address and elocution (Cohen 1994). This shift from the perspective of public speaking as a social- and critical-performance class to a class focused on standard, universal (i.e., Anglo-middle-class) delivery skills is an important shift that needs acknowledgement. Increased scholarship interest in areas such as feminist theory, intercultural communication and critical theory has increased. The absence of these perspectives in the most basic communication course, however, signals a gap between vision and reality as it relates to helping our students become competent communicators in the global village.

Furthermore, understanding how people use messages to create meaning and communicate across various contexts, cultures and media is of critical importance in a global society (Korn 2000). Scholars outside of the field of communication also attest to the centrality of communication education. McCloskey, a professor of economics, presents three primary reasons to support her argument: 'A nation of new minorities needs better communication skills; we are existing in a communication revolution with the same magnitude as the invention of printing; and many people earn their living through the use of talk' (as cited in Morreale, Osborn and Pearson 2000: 225). Hence, McCloskey concludes that the field of communication studies is critical to interdisciplinary teaching and research, but its theories must match the diverse identifications of our students.

A nationwide study conducted by Bollag (2005) concurs with this assertion. Results show there is a growing consensus among educators, business leaders and accreditors on what skills are necessary for all undergraduates. These include good written and oral communication skills, critical-thinking skills and the ability to work in teams. The data suggest, however, that many students finish college with serious deficiencies in these areas.

The fourth reason is that being a culturally competent communicator will help participants become responsible in the world, socially and culturally (Berry 2005; Fassett and Warren 2007; Gamble and Gamble 2008; Jaffe 2001; Jenefsky 1996; Morreale et al. 2000; Scudder 2004). There is a growing recognition among educators and business leaders that working, worshipping and living among people of other cultures will be inevitable for many in our society. 'Communication can be easy at play. It's harder at work, especially when there are significant differences in cultures, goals, and perspectives' (Scudder 2004: 559).

Scudder acknowledges that technological advances have made it easier to talk to one another but have not necessarily resulted in more effective communication. He argues too much communication is 'me to me'. The method leads to failure. In this context there is much work to be done in the area of globalisation. Consequently, in the 21st century, an increasing number of employees will be required to adjust their communication skills to the competency level of their communication partners. Therefore, communication educators must teach their students to become culturally competent communicators in a global society. To this end it is important to unmask 'white privilege' and undermine its normative power in limiting citizenship so narrowly, particularly in the critical arena of education (Matias 2016).

Many communication educators articulate that utilising critical pedagogy is a liberating and empowering classroom concept; however, in the classroom it may be more complex to implement from a practical perspective on a daily basis (Carter 2005; Cooks 2010). Those who do engage their students in the 'analysis and critique of power, identity, culture and schooling toward social justice and social change' (Cooks 2010: 296) find it to be transformative. Giroux (1994) states that critical pedagogy connects the intricate relationship among structures, identities and pedagogies. Giroux states that critical pedagogy '... signals how questions of audience, voice, power, and evaluation actively work to construct particular relations between teachers and students, institutions, and society, and classroom and communities. ... Pedagogy in the critical sense illuminates the relationship among knowledge, authority, and power' (1994: 297).

INTERCULTURAL PRAXIS

In this section, we will briefly explain the model or concept of intercultural praxis and how it can be applied as a pedagogical framework for our study of the basic communication course. Sorrells (2016) contends that the concept of intercultural praxis is useful as a pedagogical tool to help guide students and provide them with an alternative 'way of being in the world that joins critical, reflective, and engaged analysis with informed action for socially responsible action for global justice' (ibid: 234). We further extend Sorrells's belief that intercultural praxis can develop students' intercultural competency to the notion that this concept can also be used to develop communication competency for students enrolled in the basic course in the context of globalisation. The following six entry points of inquiry, framing, positioning, dialogue, reflection and action were used as concepts to deconstruct the basic communication course in the context of globalisation.

INQUIRY

As a place of entry for intercultural praxis, inquiry means a desire to know, ask and learn. Exploratory inquiry about those who are unlike us leads us to engaging with others. We are willing to take risks and be open to other perspectives. In relation to curriculum, inquiry is viewed as an invitation to question. It is used as a space for exploration (Patterson 2011). Questions are asked such as whose knowledge is presented? What ideologies are reinforced? (Sorrells 2010). Inquiry in the basic course may encourage your students to develop an informative speech on the Black Lives Matter movement in the United States, or the Brexit vote in the UK, and to engage the *causes* of both. It may also increase a student's willingness to invite someone who is different from them to join their group for a class project and to explore collectively the *reasons* why certain social tensions exist.

FRAMING

When we think about the concept of framing, we reflect upon how our thoughts and our actions – our very sense of vision of the world – are limited by our conscious and unconscious frames (Patterson 2011). As a port of entry in intercultural praxis, framing means that we are able to zoom in and focus on the particular details of a specific exchange or interaction. Engaging in framing allows us to become more audience-centred in the basic course. In developing a speech assignment, the educator may consider requiring the student to develop a persuasive presentation from the perspective of an immigrant group in our society. Entering the port of framing would encourage the student to develop more sophisticated inquiry skills and require them to interview someone such as a Hispanic immigrant in order to conduct research on the Deferred Action for Childhood Arrivals programme (DACA).

POSITIONING

Sorrells (2010) contends that positioning refers to curriculum as a politics of location. It is critical to be able to locate 'knowing' in one's body/experience. It makes one mindful of the material, intellectual, and practical consequences of curriculum and how it relates to ourselves. Moreover, it allows the educator to look at different ways of helping students develop a way of knowing – other than the textbook. Positioning allows us to explore how to use our access to power, privilege, status and education to speak out for those who do not have access to the resources, cultural capital and audience, starting with our students. The entry port of positioning allows us to model for our students how to reflect upon whose voice is heard and whose voice is silenced depending upon the situation and the audience. The concept teaches students to interrogate critically sources beyond the traditional scholarly references that we teach from an academic standpoint but also whose 'truth' is being represented from the various media outlets and how those intersect and possibly contradict our students' lived experiences. Once students are able to make connections between reality as portrayed to them and the reality of their experiences, we can move our students to engaging in meaningful dialogue.

DIALOGUE

The entry port of dialogue invites the educator to view curriculum as a site of dynamic and substantive meaning-making. Regardless of the student's discipline or field of study, a dialogic form of education is essential in helping students problematise and understand their world. It is through dialogue that educators can reinvent our classroom and create spaces of freedom (Patterson 2011) in which students can begin to inquire about global issues or their impact. One of our students attended a protest rally for six African American teenagers convicted of beating a white student at Jena High School in Louisiana. The student travelled with other campus students. When he returned he was excited to reflect upon his experiences and then develop a persuasive speech for his classmates, animating life into what might have been a mere news story.

REFLECTION

The concept of reflection allows the educator to review their pedagogy, what was effective that day, what was not effective. It allows us to consider our pedagogy for areas of synergy and growth. In participating in reflection as an educator, we are better able to help our students step back and reflect upon their assignments and readings beyond the current class and make connections. Reflection may mean keeping an instructional journal or developing a pedagogy circle with other instructors or even taking the time out of our research commitments to pen essays on pedagogy. Once we have informed our pedagogy and engaged in reflection, we can then help our students and our colleagues use their newly developed communication tools for action.

ACTION

Intercultural praxis challenges us to move beyond curious inquiry, framing, positioning and reflecting, but to also take action (Patterson 2011). In curriculum as in teaching itself, action is a site for engagement. It allows us to connect what we are with what we know and with the needs of our students and to exemplify the engaged knower in the learning process. Curriculum planning involving action looks at how can we encourage and engage our students to make a difference in society and to encourage them to make being a change-agent a priority. In intercultural praxis educators are able to push beyond the boundaries of the textbook and the standard syllabus to help students see that education is not about preparation for a future life, but a life-affirming act of self-creation in the here-and-now with immediate impact on the community.

CONCLUSION

It is time to collectively and critically interrogate the impact of globalisation on our educational process. We must first understand the geopolitical history and forces that shape society and our world – globalisation. This paper is our attempt to encourage engagement in this critical discourse. We have explored the concept of globalisation and its various definitions and descriptions as well as the influences of globalisation, power, consumerism and its adverse impact on youth with an emphasis on higher education. Within this context, how do we envision a new globalised critical praxis of citizenship education in early level communication-related university courses? The classroom is representative of our world; it can be a site of social change, self-reflection and development of our critical consciousness. The lessons learned in our schools can either help us create a more peaceful society or lead to more destruction and demise.

We can connect our students and classrooms to issues that impact our local community, nation and world. We must revision the basic course in a way that can aid with the evolution of this course in a world that is coping with the myriad faces of globalisation.

- This paper was first published in *Ethical Space*, Vol 13, No. 4 pp 18-28

REFERENCES

AmericaNews.Com (2009) Text of President Obama's speech in Cairo, *Voice of AmericaNews.Com*, 4 June. Available online at http://1.voanews.com/english/news/a-13-2009-06-04-voa7-68693602.html, accessed on 24 July 2016

Balardini, F. (2012) The self-destructive logic of capitalism and the Occupy movement, *Socialism and Democracy*, Vol. 26, No. 2 pp 35-38

Barber, B. (1992) Jihad vs McWorld, *Atlantic Monthly*, Vol. 269, No. 3 pp 53-65

Bauman, Z. (2011) *Collateral damage: Social inequalities in a global age*, Malden, MA, Polity Press

Berry, L. (2005) What's so important about communication? Plenty! *Mississippi Business Journal*, Vol. 27, No. 11 pp 30-31

Blum, W. (2005) *Rogue state: A guide to the world's only super-power*, Monroe, ME, Common Courage Press, third edition

Bollag, B. (2005) Consensus grows on basic skills that colleges should teach, but gauges of those abilities are poor, *Chronicle of Higher Education*, Vol. 50, No. 7 pp 13-16

Bryman, A. (1999) The Disneyization of society, *The Sociological Review*, Vol. 47, No. 1 pp 25-41

Centeno, M. A. and Cohen, J. N. (2012) *Global capitalism: A sociological perspective*, Malden, MA, Polity Press

Cohen, H. (1994) *The history of speech communication: The emergence of a discipline, 1914-1945*, Annandale, VA, Speech Communication Association

Currie, J. and Newson, J. A. (eds) (1998) *Universities and globalization: Critical perspectives*, Thousand Oaks, CA, Sage

d'Inverno, R., Davis, H. and White, S. (2003) Using a personal response system for promoting student interaction, *Teaching Mathematics and its Applications*, Vol. 22 pp 163-169

Dodson, S. (2003) History of anti-capitalism protests, *Guardian*. Available online at https://www.theguardian.com/world/2003/apr/30/mayday.seandodson, accessed on 24 July 2016

Fassett, D. and Warren, J. (2007) *Critical communication pedagogy*, Thousand Oaks, CA, Sage

Foucault, M. (1984) Power/knowledge: Selected interviews and other writings, 1972-1977, Rabinow, P. (ed.) *The Foucault reader*, New York, NY, Pantheon Books pp 51-75

Freire, P. (1994) *Pedagogy of the oppressed*, New York, NY, Continuum

Friedman, T. L. (2007) *The world is flat: A brief history of the twenty-first century*, New York, NY, Picador

Gamble, T. and Gamble, M. (2008) *Communication works*, New York, NY, McGraw Hill

Giroux, H. A. (2003a) *The abandoned generation: Democracy beyond the culture of fear*, New York, NY, Palgrave Macmillan

Giroux, H. A. (2003b) Youth, higher education, and the crisis of public time: Educated hope and the possibility of a democratic future, *Social Identities*, Vol. 9, No. 2 pp 141-168

Glenn, D. (2009) College seeks new ways to give students a general education, *Chronicle of Higher Education*, Vol. 55, No. 38 p. A8

Gore, A. (2013) *The future*, New York, NY, Random House

Halloran, L. (1995) A comparison of two methods of teaching: Computer managed instruction and keypad questions versus traditional classroom lecture, *Computers in Nursing*, Vol. 13, No. 6 pp 285-288

Hardt, M. and Negri, A. (2001) *Empire*, Cambridge, MA, Harvard University Press

hooks, b. (1994) *Teaching to transgress: Education as the practice of freedom*, New York, NY, Routledge

Ibrahim, A. (2007) Linking Marxism, globalization, and citizenship education: Toward a comparative and critical pedagogy post 9/11, *Educational Theory*, Vol. 57, No. 1 pp 89-104

Jaffe, C. (2001) *Public speaking: Concepts and skills for a diverse society*, New York, NY, Wadsworth Publishing

Jenefsky, C. (1996) Public speaking as empowerment, *Communication Education*, Vol. 45, No. 4 pp 343-354

Klein, N. (2002) *Fences and windows: Dispatches from the frontlines of the globalization debate*, Toronto, Vintage Canada Edition

Korn, C. M. (2000) Defining the field: Revisiting the ACA 1995 definition of communication studies, *Journal of the Association for Communication Administration*, Vol. 29, No. 1 pp 40-52

Lechner, F. (2005) Globalization, Ritzer, G. (ed.) *Encyclopedia of social theory*, Thousand Oaks, CA, Sage pp 330-333

Leys, C. (2001) *Market-driven politics: Neoliberal democracy and the public interest*, London, Verso Books

Matias, C. E. (2016) *Feeling white: Whiteness, emotionality, and education*, Rotterdam, Sense Publishers

McLaren, P. and Farahmandpur, R. (2005) *Teaching against global capitalism and the new imperialism: A critical pedagogy*, Lanham, MD, Rowman and Littlefield

Morreale, S. P., Osborn, M. M. and Pearson, J. C. (2000) Why communication is important: A rationale for the centrality of the study of communication, *Journal of the Association for Communication Administration*, Vol. 29 pp 1-25

Morreale, S. P., Hanna, B. R. and Gibson, J. (1999) The basic communication course at US colleges and universities: Study VII, *Basic Communication Course Annual*, Vol. 11 pp 1-36

Nsouli, S. (2008) *Ensuring a sustainable and inclusive globalization*. Speech delivered at Universal Postal Union Congress, Geneva, International Monetary Fund pp 1-4

Nye, J. (2002) Globalism vs. globalization, 15 April. Available online at *http://www.theglobalist.com*

Nye, J. (2009) Which globalization will survive? *realclearworld.com*, 12 April. Available online at http://www.realclearworld.com/articles/2009/04/nye_globalization_will_survive.html

Palley, T. (2006) Could globalization fail? *Yaleglobal*, 13 April. Available online at http://yaleglobal.yale.edu, accessed on 24 July 2016

Patterson, A. (2011) *Revisioning the basic communication course in the context of globalization*, Ann Arbor, MI, UMI ProQuest

Patterson, A. and Swartz, O. (2014) Social justice and the basic course: A central student learning outcome, *Basic Communication Course Annual*, Vol. 26 pp 44-56

Ritzer, G. (2000) *The McDonaldization of society*, Thousand Oaks, CA, Pine Forge

Ritzer, G. (2004) *The globalization of nothing*, Thousand Oaks, CA, Pine Forge

Scudder, V. (2004) The importance of communication in a global world, *Vital Speeches of the Day*, Vol. 70, No. 18 pp 559-662

Seattle Times (2000) Prague protests renew 'Battle of Seattle', 20 September. Available online at http://community.seattletimes.nwsource.com/archive/?date=20000927&slug=4044799, accessed on 24 July 2016

Sellnow, D. D. and Martin, J. M. (2010) The basic course in communication: Where do we go from here? Fassett, D. L. and Warren, J. T. (eds) *The Sage handbook of communication and instruction*, Washington, DC, Sage pp 33-53

Shapiro, H. S. (2006) *Losing heart: The moral and spiritual miseducation of America's children*, Mahwah, NJ, Lawrence Erlbaum

Slaughter, S. (1997) *Academic capitalism: Politics, policies, and the entrepreneurial university*, Baltimore, MD, Johns Hopkins University Press

Smith, M. (2002) Globalization and the incorporation of education, *infed.org*. Available online at http://www.infed.org/biblio/globalization_and_education.htm

Sorrells, K. A. (2008) *Linking social justice and intercultural communication in the global context*, Portland, OR, Intercultural Communication Institute

Sorrells, K. A. (2013) *Intercultural communication: Globalization and social justice*, Thousand Oaks, CA, Sage

Sorrells, K. A. and Nakagawa, G. (2008) Intercultural communication praxis and the struggle for social responsibility and social justice, Swartz, O. (ed.) *Transformative communication studies: Culture, hierarchy, and the human condition*, Leicester, UK, Troubador pp 23-61

Sorrells, K. A. (2016) *Intercultural communication: Globalization and social justice*, Thousand Oaks, CA Sage

Swartz, O. (1997) Toward critical education in the communication classroom, *New Jersey Journal of Communication*, Vol. 5 pp 20-29

Swartz, O. (2004) Toward a critique of normative justice: Human rights and the rule of law, *Socialism & Democracy*, Vol. 18 pp 185-209

Swartz, O. (ed.) (2006) *Social justice and communication scholarship*, Mahwah, NJ, Lawrence Erlbaum

Swartz, O., Campbell, K. and Pestana, C. (2009) *Neo-pragmatism, communication, and the culture of creative democracy*, New York, NY, Peter Lang

Torres, C. A. (2002) Globalization, education, and citizenship: Solidarity versus markets? *American Education Research Journal*, Vol. 39, No. 2 pp 363-378

Tracey, C. (2016) White privilege and gentrification in Denver, 'America's favourite city', *Guardian*, 14 July. Available online https://www.theguardian.com/cities/2016/jul/14/white-privilege-gentrification-denver-america-favourite-city, accessed on 24 July 2016

Van Dijk, L. A., Van Den Berg, G. C. and Van Keulen, H. (2001) Interactive lectures in engineering education, *European Journal of Engineering Education*, Vol. 26, No. 1 pp 15-28

Wampler, P. J. and Clark, K. (2006) *Clickers in the classroom: Rewards and regrets of using student response systems in a large enrollment geology course*. Available online at http://faculty.gvsu.edu/wamplerp/GSA%20Poster%2010-18-06.pdf, accessed on 24 July 2016

Wang, J., Lin, E., Spalding, E., Odell, S. J. and Klecka, C. L. (2011) Understanding teacher education in an era of globalization, *Journal of Teacher Education*, Vol. 62 pp 115-120

NOTE ON THE CONTRIBUTORS

Andrea Patterson-Masuka (PhD, University of North Carolina at Greensboro, 2011) is an Associate Professor in the Department of Communication and Media Studies at Winston-Salem State University. She is the co-editor of three books and author or co-author of more than 15 essays and book chapters.

Omar Swartz (PhD, Purdue University, 1995; J.D., Duke University, 2001, *magna cum laude*) is Director of the Master of Humanities and Master of Social Science programmes at the University of Colorado Denver. He is the author or editor of 12 books and more than 120 essays, book chapters, and reviews.

Chapter 23

Journalism education after Leveson: Ethics start where regulation ends

David Baines and Darren Kelsey

Theory and practice in journalism education are not separate, binary entities; they are interlinked, interrelated and interdependent. This paper argues that a crisis of trust in British journalism, which led to the 2012 Leveson Report, highlights the need for an ethical and practical turning point in British journalism education. By considering more nuanced, active, informed notions and understandings of ideology and political economy we argue that incorporating critical frameworks into journalistic education provides the reflexive, philosophical and theoretical tools necessary for developing future journalism education, post-Leveson. In conclusion, we propose that attention to Aristotle's concept of phronesis *– usually translated as 'practical wisdom' – has much to inspire journalism educators, encouraging a 'culture of informed dialogic engagement', which offers the promise of eroding the often prevailing 'cult of the leader'.*

Keywords: journalism education, ethics, Leveson Inquiry, political economy, ideology

INTRODUCTION: CRISES IN CONTEXT

Business schools have realised that preeminent among those who bore responsibility for the current global financial crisis were their graduates and are reflecting on the manner in which they have prepared those graduates for leadership roles in industry, commerce and finance ('Schumpeter' 2010). Journalism in Britain in 2012 faced a crisis of trust. What has become known as 'the phone hacking scandal' (Keeble and Mair 2012a, 2012b) resulted in a public inquiry led by high court judge Sir Brian Leveson QC, and exposed opaque and manipulative relationships between, primarily the News International media organisation, and both police and politicians. Did journalism graduates in Britain contribute to this crisis of trust?

This paper puts the case that Leveson presents journalism schools with an opportunity to reflect critically on how journalism is taught, why it is taught in the ways it is and the philosophical and ideological contexts which inform journalism education and training. Through more critical engagement with theoretical concepts in journalistic training, we conclude that attention to Aristotle's concept of *phronesis* demonstrates the culture of more active agency in journalism as a way of progressing ethical practices beyond Leveson.

It is tempting for journalism educators to say: 'We give our journalism students an ethical grounding and if something goes wrong later, that is the fault of employers.' Tom Watson and Martin Hickman tell us in *Dial M for Murdoch* (2012: 17): 'Rupert Murdoch promoted [Rebekah Wade] to deputy editor of the *Sun* in 1998 and in May 2000 to editor of the *News of the World*, a heady position for a 32-year-old with no journalism training.' Journalism educators might well say: 'Had she been trained properly things might have been different.' But the problems which emerged in evidence to Leveson and associated police and parliamentary inquiries exposed networks of hidden and potentially corrupt relationships which involved big media, government and public service from the chief executives, chief police officers and prime ministers to lowly reporters, constables and MPs.

Following 'Operation Motorman', an investigation by the UK Information Commissioner into the use by journalists and others of private investigators to obtain personal information in breach of the Data Protection Act 1998, the report to the UK parliament (Thomas 2006) listed 32 national newspapers and magazines on which 305 journalists had been identified as customers 'driving the illegal trade in confidential personal information' (the *Guardian, Independent* and *Telegraph* were not on the list). Those 305 journalists were not named – but it is likely that the majority will have held a National Council for the Training of Journalists (NCTJ) qualification. Between April 2011 and December 2012, more than 47 journalists were arrested as a result of these investigations (Turville 2012). It is reasonable to assume that many of them will have had an NCTJ qualification.

PROBLEMS CLOSE TO HOME: NATIONAL CRISIS INCLUDES LOCAL JOURNALISM

While there is no evidence of local papers indulging in phone hacking and the paying of bribes to police and other public servants there is a continuum across the press (in particular) of practices, processes and structures which demand attention from a moral perspective. Wendy Weinhold's 2008 study of a local newspaper in the US found 'American community newspaper journalists forced to negotiate their values and internalise business demands in order to answer their employers' profit motives' (Weinhold 2008: 476). She concluded: 'I contend the managers rarely placed stories' newsworthiness above their market potential ... Each of these stories was selected for its ability to sell papers over its news value' (ibid: 484). Weinhold equated news value with relevance to the needs of the community. But in the local newspaper business model, the 'community' becomes a commodity to sell to advertisers. This is not an ethically neutral state of affairs. From a Kantian perspective, people are being treated as means to the commercial organisation's ends, rather than ends in themselves (Kant 2002 [1785]: 45).

Two examples demonstrate how this is exemplified by the local press. First, Danny Schechter points to the role the local press played in the property bubble which led to the global financial crash as it placed business interests before those of its readers: 'The newspaper industry became, in some communities, the marketing arm of the real-estate industry' (Schechter 2009: 21). Secondly, let us apply Kant's thinking to issues that local journalists face in a practical sense. Research by Nick Davies (2008) and the Cardiff School of Journalism demonstrated how journalism had become a production line process in which PR copy was directly reprinted in local newspaper articles. Traditional, investigative and reporting processes of journalism had been replaced by a culture of 'churnalism', as Davies called it; fewer journalists under increasing pressure to produce more copy became means to the end of churning out news from pre-packaged resources. As Davies points out: 'It is a common experience among young journalists that they leave university with a degree in journalism, bursting with enthusiasm, only to end up chained to a key board on a production line in a news factory, churning out trivia and cliché to fill space in the paper' (ibid: 56).

Such examples demonstrate that the ethics of journalism, business and economics have more of a bearing on the local press than we are often led to believe. The press owners' 'human resources', their journalists and communities which they ostensibly serve are commodified: both become means to corporate ends.

SHARED CRISIS, SHARED SOLUTIONS? PARALLELS IN JOURNALISM AND BUSINESS ETHICS

The issues above demonstrate the cross-disciplinary nature of ethical issues that journalism and business schools both face. Our thoughts on ethics and journalism education have been informed in part by perspectives on ethics and the education of business students set forth in a paper delivered to business school academics by Stewart Clegg, Professor of Management at the University of Technology Sydney (Clegg 2012). In criticising the traditional (Anglo-American) models of business education, he said:

> No clear consensus emerged as to what constitutes the public good in university-based management education. The typical undergraduate business school curriculum still looks like a trade school preparation for vocational purposes. It has no broad-based disciplines constituting it – and many MBAs, perhaps the vast majority of MBAs, offer a functional and shallow smorgasbord' (ibid: np).

There are uncomfortable parallels here with a form of journalism education which is in large part informed by a craft model maintained and directed in Britain by such organisations as the National Council for the Training of Journalists. The

NCTJ is, in its turn, directed by the newspaper industry with the aim of producing entry level recruits with a skill set stipulated by current editors. This model tends to be self-perpetuating: it is not constituted of broad-based disciplines, nor does it generate a clear consensus as to what constitutes the public good in university (or college or private-sector) journalism education.

Many professions restrict membership through monopoly control of conditions of entry enforced through a professionally-defined curriculum taught at university, and whose exclusivity is sanctioned by the state. Clegg makes the point that 'whereas doctors and lawyers for instance must be professionally qualified to practise legally, anyone, almost anyone, can call themselves a manager and thus become one'. The same is true of journalists. And he continues: 'It is for this reason that the legitimatory role of business schools is important. In an organisation field that is open to malpractice on a catastrophic scale, and in which the gatekeeper function, such that it is, resides in a variety of for-profit, not-for-profit and public business schools, no other organisation comes close to assuming the mantle of responsibility.' For business schools, we might read journalism schools. But if journalism educators are to assume the mantle of responsibility, and their schools a legitimatory role, key tensions need to be addressed. They and their students need to critically interrogate the ideological bases of the models of journalism they embrace. They need to address inequality and imbalances of power in organisational practice. And inherent in each of these tensions are ethical or moral concerns.

Subsequent to this lack of resonance, we suggest that more nuanced, active, informed notions and understandings of ideology and political economy are crucial to progressive ethical practices in the media field.

Solutions to such imbalances of power and the ability to reorientate organisational power do not, of course, lie solely in the hands of individual journalists or journalism educators. But we suggest that journalists are able to take a lead in developing solutions if they can bring to the field the necessary knowledge, understanding and wisdom to do so – and if they have the confidence, individually and collectively, to deploy these in an ethical manner. We argue that it is up to journalism educators to endeavour to ensure that their students enter careers with that knowledge, understanding and confidence; encourage them to develop that collectivity and equip them to develop that wisdom. This is not to say that the skills to find and tell stories are not critically important. But journalism educators need to give equal parity to criticality; to encouraging a praxis which provides honest and ethical brokerage of information and analysis; which helps us all to make more sense of the increasingly complex and diverse society in which we live.

Clegg (2012) pointed to a critical failing in business schools. James O'Connor (1974) and Jürgen Habermas (1976) both set out analyses of the financial and economic systems which explored their flaws and presciently predicted how those flaws would precipitate a crash: analyses which closely correspond to the manner in which the current financial crisis developed. But, Clegg noted that:

... neither O'Connor's political economy nor Habermas's political philosophy would have found much resonance in the strategy literature of the day or since because the provenance of these tools in Marxist accounts with their apocalyptic focus on capitalism's necessary crisis hardly suited the rhetorical purposes of the business school as an institution – vision was truncated. Business school academics lacked a systematic analysis of the crisis, or the tools with which to make one. The assumptions of conventional economic approaches cut strategy and strategic management off from, not only some of the most interesting and creative currents in organisation theory, but also from the broader currents of social analysis, especially sociology (ibid).

Subsequent to this lack of resonance, we suggest that more nuanced, active, informed notions and understandings of ideology and political economy are crucial to progressive ethical practices in the media field.

REDISCOVERING IDEOLOGY: CRITICAL THEORY FOR ETHICAL PRACTICE

As McLellan (1995) demonstrates, there are various social, historical and political contexts and ways of understanding ideology. He also states: 'Any examination of ideology makes it difficult to avoid the rueful conclusion that all views about ideology are themselves ideological. But avoided it must be – or at least modified by saying that some views are more ideological than others' (ibid: 1-2). Although we are stating that ideology should be realised more consciously in both self-reflective and accusatory contexts, we still keep McLellan's caution in mind. We propose that rather than recognising ideological critiques as inherently Marxist – oppositional, revolutionary idealist, economically reductionist, *destructive* perspectives – a more *constructive* account would apply the suggestive nature of critical theory in a reflective context that informs and intellectualises media practice, as it does for media theory. In the same way that media theorists should be encouraged to consider journalists as media workers and recognise the structural pressures and conditions in which they work (rather than destructively criticising the work they produce), the ethics of practitioners would also benefit from recognising the constructive contributions of media theorists. But among some of the fundamental problems we recognise in this relationship between theory and practice lies the common (negative) perceptions of a particular word: 'ideology'.

We propose that ideology should not be used solely in accusation or criticism (a fault that often lies with media critics and theorists) but in observation and recognition – even in one's proposed political arguments and solutions. If you criticise something for its ideological intentions, a progressive approach to ideology would accept that your counter-argument might be equally ideological. This approach immediately welcomes (rather than suppresses) the possibility of discussions about structural issues involved in, for example, news production.

Since the rhetoric of Tony Blair and New Labour, we in Britain have often faced constructions of 'post-ideology' politics and an economic system that deals with 'reality' over ideology; for example, the 'third way' of New Labour supposedly overcame the pulls and persuasions of left and right wing ideology. As recently as 2011, Blair spoke of post-ideological societies in the 21st century: 'We live today in a post-ideological era of government. The fundamental political divide between left and right is a phenomenon of the 20th century' (Blair 2011). Of course, Blair's vision of a Third Way always remained ideologically constructed, and maintained, but its perception of socio-economic 'compromise' suppressed the salience of ideology at work. As Fairclough observed in his critique of New Labour's rhetorical strategies, 'the pamphlets, speeches and newspaper articles of New Labour politicians are full of descriptions of how the "Third Way" of New Labour differs from the "old left" and "new right"…' (2000: 9). As Blair stated in *New Labour's annual report* of 1998: 'The Third Way is a new politics that helps people cope with a more insecure world because it rejects the destructive excesses of the market and the intrusive hand of state intervention' (ibid: 10).

As we have since learnt, market forces in both business and journalistic contexts, are far from the bliss of post-ideological harmony evoked by Blair. Nonetheless, a more engaged cultural and political awareness of ideology, in journalistic (and business) education, we argue, would stimulate a more active and negotiated process of ethical thinking and practical decision-making. If media practitioners (journalists *and* editors) of the future, and theorists alike, were more open to the relevance of ideology and political economy on an observational level then we create possibilities for more progressive ethical thinking in practical and professional contexts.

Rediscovering ideology, so to speak, increases the potential for a more critical, structural awareness and reflective engagement among media practitioners. This is where ideology, in a working and ethical context, becomes intrinsically linked to political economy: when workers – be it journalism graduates or their counterparts from business schools – are increasingly aware (and potentially critical) of the structural systems they work within and the economic, political and social (ideological) interests that they influence and represent. In agreement with Fowler, through the analyses that media theorists provide, critical work on journalism seeks to be descriptive rather than destructive (1991: 10). Media workers need to be able to adopt similar frameworks in the discussions they have in the newsroom and the way they reflect on their work; we argue that an awareness of ideology and political economy in such a context is descriptive rather than destructive. Reflective and descriptive ethical encouragement can only be a healthy progression for media industries, post-Leveson. To only observe ideology in a destructive context is naïve: it assumes that identifying ideology and criticising the bias of another party makes one's self unbiased or uninfluenced by ideology. The latter provides, arguably, a vulgar application of Marxist thinking that has at least contributed to the negative (albeit, inaccurate) impression of other neglected models discussed above. Fowler provides a useful analogy of naïve perceptions of ideological bias in the press:

> … There is an argument to the effect that biases do exist as a matter of fact, but not everywhere. The *Daily Express* is biased, the *Socialist Worker* not (or the other way round). In a good world, all newspapers and television channels would report the unmediated truth. This view seems to me to be drastically and dangerously false. It allows a person to believe, and assert, complacently, that *their* newspaper is unbiased, whereas all the others are in the pocket of the Tories or the Trotskyites; or that newspapers are biased, while TV is not (because 'the camera cannot lie'). The danger with this position is that it assumes the possibility of genuine neutrality, of some news medium being a clear undistorting window. And that can never be (Fowler 1991: 12).

Incorporating critical frameworks into journalistic education provides the reflexive, philosophical and theoretical tools of thinking necessary for developing the future of journalism practice beyond Leveson. Theory and practice are not separate binary entities; they are interlinked, interrelated and interdependent. Their binary separation is an artificial conflict that suppresses intellectual thinking for the convenience of ideological interests that, pre-Leveson, went unchecked in their control of media production. To develop the work of Kant that we referred to earlier, the critically engaged and theoretically enriched minds of young journalists can redirect journalism away from the production tendencies of top-down pressures and the persuasions of ethically disinclined practices. This redirection can provide journalism with the answers (post-Leveson) that the business and banking sectors have arguably lacked since the economic crisis.

One thing we have become increasingly aware of is the need to clarify our own political and theoretical intentions when introducing students to traditionally Marxist disciplines of cultural theory. When we present particular theoretical models to students, some of them are prone to a binary perception of the Marxist teacher arguing against the dominant order of contemporary capitalism. This should not be the case. Rather, as we often need to clarify, using Marxist theory does not mean we are dogmatic or idealistic Marxists; rather, Marxist theory is suggestive and provides a critical and reflective awareness that ethically minded journalism graduates can benefit from in the long, gradual quest for responsible journalistic practice. The latter reasserts the point made earlier regarding scholars such as O'Connor and Habermas who foretold the current financial crisis in the 1970s.

Yet, in British journalism there is a fault line of suspicion, defensiveness and anti-intellectualism which is evident in repeated disparagements of media and journalism studies as legitimate disciplines and this fault line is often reflected in an uneasy relationship between those who teach journalism practice and those who teach journalism – and media – studies. Of course, this is not true of every institution – but the NCTJ does not demand that reading lists feature journals such as *Ethical Space* or *Journalism Studies* on courses it accredits. Just as Marxist critiques of capitalism which predicted the crash were shunned by business schools in pursuit of legitimacy in the eyes of employers in commerce and industry, there is a danger that a lack of a wider sociological perspective on the media cuts off much of journalism education – or training – from broader currents of critical media theory and wider social analysis. And this can deprive some journalism students – and educators – of the tools they need to analyse the crisis which led to Leveson.

The Academy of Management, the European Academy of Management the European Group for Organisational Studies are all pushing business schools to reassess what they teach and how. Who, to paraphrase Stewart Clegg, is 'pushing an agenda *in journalism schools* for a more ethical and more responsible mode of practice in what and how *journalism schools* teach'? We suggest that there is a role in the field of journalism for the Institute of Communication Ethics, the Association for Journalism Education and similar organisations around the world to press for a reassessment of journalism education.

But engaging with the critical paradigms which help us to understand media's place in society, while necessary, is not sufficient. Journalism education and business education show a degree of correspondence in their pedagogical approaches to ethics. These discussions are, in both, couched in terms of the individual. It is individuals who require reformation, rather than structures. Indeed, some quite lowly individuals are now being held to account for structural and organisational failings at the *Sun* and other titles. But individual action always takes place within social structures which both encourage and facilitate and discourage and restrict individual agency – so we need to understand these structures.

Accrediting bodies demand that our students learn the relevant industry-body codes of practice. Whether or not our programmes are accredited by industry bodies, ethical elements of journalism education and training are at best heavily informed by, at worst limited to, such codes. While codes of practice are useful in some respects, there is a danger that they define – and confine – the boundaries of journalistic ethics. If it is not in the code, it may not be regarded as an ethical issue. However, industry-led questions of ethics have a narrow focus – and so questions relating to ethics are often foreclosed. Clegg says: 'It is as if all that is needed is to know the right rule in order to do the right thing: ethics becomes a question of following the rules' (2012).

But when rules run out we are still faced with moral choices. Clegg numbers among issues which are not touched upon by business school ethics the ideas behind contracts of employment, equity and poverty, shareholder and stakeholder conflicts (ibid). In journalism, we might number the lack of diversity in the workforce; commodification of public and employee; a business model that drove a property price bubble; the muting and marginalisation of minority voices. Such matters are not morally neutral, but they also arise out of the structures of, and ideological influences within, the industry. They do not feature in codes of professional practice intended to regulate the conduct of journalists. They are rarely reflected upon by the press. Weinhold on US community journalism concludes:

> Journalists' training and education should be restructured to incorporate an understanding of the economic imperatives at work in newspaper decision-making, and a rearticulation of journalists' principles that accommodates increased transparency in the connection between journalists and their labor is needed (Weinhold 2008: 485).

Understanding that furthers greater transparency of economic imperatives is necessary, but not sufficient if we are to encourage the development of ethical organisations. So where do we look for a way forward?

CONCLUSION: THINKING THROUGH *PHRONESIS*

There has been a revival, in the interrogation of ethical behaviour in the professions, of attention to Aristotle's concept of *phronesis* – usually translated as 'practical wisdom' – and this is the case in journalism (Glasser and Ettema 2008; Quinn 2007). Aristotle conceives of *phronesis* as 'concerned with things human and things about which it is possible to deliberate'. It is applied when there are variables to consider, it is applied to an end or purpose and that end or purpose is a good that can be brought about by action (Ross 1925: 1141b, 9-13). *Phronesis* is thus a practical ethical form of knowledge, always grounded in experience and context. It foregrounds the 'common sense' of, in our case, working journalists. It is primarily dialogical – it comes from discussion and argument, it melds inquiry with value and reflection and a programme for action. It calls on theory and practice, but Aristotle resolves and synthesises theory and practice within praxis where actions taken are uniquely shaped by practical wisdom. Clegg (2012) sets out the process through which practical wisdom is applied – suggesting three questions – plus a fourth:

1. Where are we going?
2. Is this desirable?
3. What should be done?
4. And – who gains and who loses?

In the fourth question he further suggests, although Aristotle does not, that *phronesis* must address power relations. Power relations – and the abuse of power – in and by media organisations have featured prominently in evidence put before Leveson and are relevant to any consideration of journalism education, and praxis, post-Leveson. If we are concerned here with dialogical practice – within the newsroom and between the newsroom and the wider organisation in which it sits – then power lies in shaping an environment in which there is confidence in being able to express views which might be at odds with doctrine of the day.

We do not lay claim to great originality in this suggestion. Clearly it is informed by Clegg (2012), Quinn (2007), Glasser and Ettema (2008), Frost (2011) and others. Indeed, Richard Keeble, in *Ethics for Journalists*, acknowledges in a note:

> … John Tulloch for stressing the importance of 'eloquence'; to me during our many discussions on media ethics and other matters. Kovach and Rosenstiel (2003: 181) make the same point: 'Every journalist, from newsroom to boardroom, must have a personal sense of ethics and responsibility – a moral compass. What's more, they have a responsibility to voice their personal conscience out loud and allow others around them to do so as well' (Keeble 2009: 37).

And this is, indeed, how journalists decide the moral course of action – when the culture in which they work allows them to do so. British broadcasters have told us of the often intense discussions they have in the newsroom about how to cover a particular story – discussions involving all levels of seniority. But the British popular press is renowned for adopting a dictatorial model of editorship, more cult of the leader than a culture welcoming of open and critical dialogue (e.g. Chippendale and Horrie 1992: 88). and this culture is also manifest in some local and regional newspapers (e.g. Aldridge 1998: 121).

Journalism educators encourage dialogical exploration in students. They need to encourage students to carry this practice to the workplace. That is necessary, but not sufficient in journalism after Leveson. They also need to take into the newsroom a commitment to collective and mutual support to enable such discussion and reflection. This requires a major cultural shift within the workplace and the acceptance by British newspaper managements of the journalists' trade union, the National Union of Journalists. Harcup (2007: 122), Frost (2011: 237) and Keeble (2009: 70) among others point to occasions on which NUJ chapels (office branches) have collectively opposed their managements on specific points of unethical publication, or sought to moderate more general unethical practice, something which can be difficult for journalists acting individually.

If journalism education after Leveson is to assume the mantle of responsibility for developing a restorative and legitimatory role in a field of endeavour where malpractice has led to the current crisis of trust, it must set out on a (long) road to change the culture of, to better inform, to democratise that field. Codes, rules and regulations can take us so far, but when the codes are silent on an issue of concern, or when they demand interpretation, ethics come into play and journalists, as writers and broadcasters, or as managers, must rely on their critical understanding of the field, on discussion and practical wisdom.

- This paper was first published in *Ethical Space*, Vol. 10, No. 1 pp 29-35

REFERENCES

Aldridge, Meryl (1998) The tentative hell-raisers: Identity and mythology in contemporary UK press journalism, *Media, Culture and Society*, Vol. 20 pp 109-127

Blair, Tony (2011) Tony Blair speaks on globalisation and religion at national university of Singapore. Available online at http://www.tonyblairfaithfoundation.org/news/2011/03/25, accessed on 3 December 2012

Chippindale, Peter and Horrie, Chris (1992) *Stick it up your punter! The rise and fall of the* Sun, London, Mandarin

Clegg, Stewart (2012) Strategy, organizations and society. Talk delivered to the Strategy Organisations and Society Summit at Newcastle University Business School, 31 May 2012 (unpublished)

Davies, Nick (2008) *Flat earth news*, London, Random House

Fairclough, Norman (2000) *New Labour, new language?* London, Routledge

Fowler, Roger (1991) *Language in the news, Discourse and ideology in the press*, London, Routledge

Frost, Chris (2011) *Journalism ethics and regulation*, London, Pearson, third edition

Glasser, Theodore L and Ettema, James S (2008) Ethics and eloquence in journalism, *Journalism Studies*, Vol. 9, No 4 pp 512-534

Habermas, Jürgen (1976) *What does a crisis mean today? Legitimation problems in late capitalism* (trans. McCarthy, Thomas), London, Heinemann

Harcup, Tony (2007) *The ethical journalist*, London, Sage

Kant, Immanuel (2002 [1785]) *Groundwork for the metaphysics of morals* (trans. Wood, Alan W.), New Haven, Yale University Press

Keeble, Richard Lance (2009) *Ethics for journalists*, London, Routledge, second edition

Keeble, Richard Lance and Mair, John (2012a) *The phone hacking scandal: Journalism on trial*, Bury St Edmunds, Abramis

Keeble, Richard Lance and Mair, John (2012b) *The phone hacking scandal: Journalism on trial*, Bury St Edmunds, Abramis, second edition

Kovach, Bill and Rosenstiel, Tom (2003) *The elements of journalism: What journalists should know and the public expect*, London, *Guardian*/Atlantic Books

McLellan, David (1995) *Ideology*, Bristol, A. W. Arrowsmith

O'Connor, James (1973) *The fiscal crisis of the state*, New York, St Martin's Press

Quinn, Aaron (2007) Moral virtues for journalists, *Journal of Mass Media Ethics*, Vol. 22, Nos 2 and 3 pp 168-186

Ross, William David (1925) *Aristotle's* Ethica Nicomachea, Oxford, Oxford University Press

Schechter, Danny. (2009) Credit crisis: How did we miss it?, *British Journalism Review*, Vol. 20, No. 1 pp 19-26

'Schumpeter' (columnist: pseudonym) (2010) A post-crisis case study: The new dean of Harvard Business School promises 'radical innovation', *Economist*, 29 July. Available online at http://www.economist.com/node/16691433?story_id=16691433, accessed on 22 October 2012

Thomas, Richard (2006) *What price privacy now? The first six months progress in halting the unlawful trade in confidential personal information*, London, Stationery Office, December

Turville, William (2012) The accused, *UK Press Gazette*, October pp 28-30. Available online at http://www.pressgazette.co.uk/accused-least-46-journalists-arrested-uk-police-last-16-months, accessed on 23 October 2012

Watson, Tom and Hickman, Martin (2012) *Dial M for Murdoch: News Corporation and the corruption of Britain*, London, Pearson

Weinhold, Wendy (2008) Newspaper negotiations, *Journalism Practice*, Vol. 2, No. 3 pp 476-486

NOTE ON THE CONTRIBUTORS

David Baines is a lecturer in journalism at Newcastle University. His PhD was on journalism education and changing practices in journalism and his research focuses on local and community journalism. He has published in *Journalism Practice*, *Local Economy*, *The International Journal of Sociology and Social Policy* and *Ethical Space*. He is a founding member of the Media Communication and Cultural Studies Association research network on Local and Community Media and is a trustee of the youth charity, Headliners. He spent 28 years in daily newspaper journalism before joining the academy in 2007. Email: David.Baines@newcastle.ac.uk.

Darren Kelsey is Reader in Media and Collective Psychology at Newcastle University and Deputy Head of the School of Arts and Cultures. His BA was in Journalism, Film and Broadcasting, his MA in Political Communication, and his PhD from the School of Journalism, Media and Cultural Studies at Cardiff University. His research and teaching combines theories of mythology and psychology with discourse analysis to study the role of moral storytelling in society. Recent projects have studied narrative, psychology, philosophy and storytelling in relation to themes and topics such as mental health, philosophy for life, military advertising, celebrity persona and surveillance culture. Darren's other research interests focus on the role of media and journalism in society and the relationships between media, culture and politics.

AND FINALLY:

Speaking out on ethics

Chapter 24

How consumer journalists can help restore public trust in the profession

Angela Rippon, who became the BBC's first regular woman newsreader in 1976 and was awarded an OBE for her services to broadcasting in 2004, argues that one of the most vital roles of the journalist is to protect the consumer.

On my very first day as a journalist I was called into the office of my senior reporter, Wilfred Cox, who told me: 'Over the next three years you will learn a great deal. But there are three words I want you to remember all your professional life and I want them to be the foundation of your career as a journalist. They are honesty, accuracy and integrity – be honest in your dealings with whoever you meet; be accurate in the facts you put into your story, and have integrity in your motives – and in everything you do.

Those three words have stayed with me all my professional life. They are, I believe, three of the most important words in any journalist's lexicon. They should be printed above your desk or computer screen. They are a tripod of values on which to build your career – a solid foundation of principles on which to establish a peerless reputation.

A recent MORI poll asked the public who were the professionals that they trusted. Out of some 20 professions doctors came out on top – politicians, not surprisingly, grubbing along at the bottom, but journalists below even them. Just 17 per cent trusted journalists and that means 83 per cent of the population does not. Some 72 per cent said they did not believe that journalists told the truth. What a terrible indictment on our profession.

JOURNALISM: A POTENT AND INFLUENTIAL FORCE IN SOCIETY

I am proud to have on my passport that I am a journalist and broadcaster. Because I know that for the most part journalists can be and, indeed, should be a potent, powerful and influential force in society – especially when they do their job well. They can be especially effective when working on behalf of the consumer whether it's trying to sort out a grievance or perceived injustice by banks, the health service, shops on the high street, the government or large corporations. There are always in our communities individuals who, on their own, feel helpless and need the support of a more powerful voice to help them fight a wrong or social injustice. That voice is the voice of the media – powered by journalists prepared to do battle on their behalf.

Consumer journalism – in its broadest sense – is without doubt one area where journalists can and should be able to re-build the public's trust in our profession. We can make a real difference to people's lives. We do make a difference to people's lives.

Recently I presented a new series of consumer programmes for the BBC, *Rip-off Britain*. Our brief was to expose those areas where the British consumer was being ripped off; to right wrongs where we could – and to inform consumers not just of their rights but how best to ensure that they avoided rip-offs themselves in the future. We looked at banking, travel, shopping, utilities and housing.

INDIVIDUALS FIGHTING AN INJUSTICE ON THEIR OWN

When we began assembling our case studies one thing became very clear. All over the country there are individuals facing a problem, fighting an injustice on their own. Because they are on their own, they often believe the problem is confined just to them. And that, as an individual, they are pretty powerless against a large company or organisation. But an organ of the national media – a television or radio programme or national newspaper – can see the bigger picture. It can collate all the individual studies and present not an isolated case, but a national scandal – and that's when the power of the media clicks in.

I suppose you could say that Charles Dickens was one of the earliest of the great investigative, consumer journalists as his books highlighted so many of the social scandals of Victorian Britain and gave them a wider audience.

But for a more contemporary and legendary example, let me take you back to the late 1960s. In 1958 a company called Distillers launched a drug called Thalidomide to help pregnant women suffering with morning sickness. More than 400 babies born to those mothers were born with major physical deformities. The Ministry of Health refused a public enquiry – so 62 families were forced to take private legal action. In England, once that happens the details of the case become *sub judice* – and so could not be discussed or published in public. The case dragged on for years.

One very brave father, David Mason, held out for years as Distillers offered small sums of money as compensation. He knew the families and the children were entitled to more than the few hundred pounds they were being offered. But he was for the most part fighting alone. He received hate mail – even death threats.

In 1967, enter Harold Evans – newly appointed editor of *The Sunday Times*. He took up the case on behalf of the families. He printed stories and photographs knowing that he was breaking the law. In his recently published memoir, *My paper chase*, he says: 'We had the power to do something that only a popular newspaper could do.' Not only the power – also the money. Litigation is not cheap. But here was a newspaper fighting on behalf of consumers: in this case, consumers who had been let down by Distillers, by the government and by law. After years of bitter legal argument, and continued coverage in the press, the case went to the European Court of Human Rights in Strasbourg – and in 1973 they won.

Not only did Distillers have to set up a fund of £20 million so that each of the 400-plus children would have an income of £18,000-a-year to help fund medical needs, for the public at large – the general consumer – there were implications. Because that victory forced a change in the law on freedom of speech in Britain. It is now possible to publicise cases in law where a 'manifest injustice' is judged to be occurring. And that opened the way for consumers to have their grievances aired publicly in cases where otherwise they would have remained hidden and unreported.

THAT'S LIFE: CHANGING THE FACE OF CONSUMER REPORTING

That same year 1973 saw the birth of yet another consumer milestone. BBC1 aired a programme called *That's life*. It was fronted by Esther Rantzen – and it changed the face of television consumer reporting in this country. The programme ran for 21 years and in that time British consumers not only got a better understanding of consumer law and their rights, the programme also campaigned on their behalf in a whole raft of areas that affected the everyday lives of just about every consumer in the country. In fact, if people were having problems with a consumer issue, it became something of a national catch phrase to say: 'I'll have Esther Rantzen after you.' She and her programme were the threat that kept a lot of companies in line – that was the power of the media in full cry.

The programme was an eclectic mix of entertainment and information – everything from peculiar shaped vegetables and a dog that said 'sausages' to hard core journalism about health and safety, financial scams, bullying, and so on. It was often criticised because of that mix. Esther Rantzen always says she was happy to seduce the audience into watching with the promise of a bit of fun, but knowing that they would also get something of value. That's the secret of good programme making. As a direct result of that consumer programme:

- concrete in all children's playgrounds was dug up and safe surfaces were laid;
- the law on car seatbelts was amended after the Department of Transport was commissioned to film in slow motion what happened to children in cars without specialist seatbelts when involved in head-on crashes.

Moreover, it was the first programme to use DNA testing on air to ascertain the parentage of children. One day a researcher took a telephone call from a woman who said: 'My name is Debbie Hardwick. I have a two-year-old son called Ben who is normal in every way – except that next month he will be dead' – her son had a rare liver complaint and needed a transplant. That launched a campaign through the programme to highlight the need for organ donation. Groups of mothers alerted the programme to bullying since they could get no action from schools or local authorities. That led to the setting up of Childline.

Not just big stories. For individuals who were being intimidated by authority and could not afford a solicitor the programme produced information leaflets and pre-written letters to deal with specific problems.

It's what we do on *Rip off Britain*: helping, for instance, the family who were charged thousands of pounds for probate after the death of a family member. Or the couple who invested all their life savings – £200,000 – into a scheme recommended by the bank only to find that it was high risk, not low risk as they'd been promised and lost everything. We exposed water companies who were charging for services they didn't provide. I won't give a complete catalogue – suffice to say each day after the programme we received around 300 emails from viewers and sacks of letters – all from individuals who need the media to help fight their battles.

WHEN CONSUMERS FEEL THEY ARE BEING TAKEN FOR A RIDE

In other areas, it's almost impossible to open your newspaper these days without reading yet another story of some failure in, or discontent with, the services provided by the National Health Service, social services, local councils and the law. In fact, I doubt that there is any area of life in Britain where some consumers don't feel that they are either being let down or taken for a ride.

So where do we come in – we journalists – why are we so important? Because companies have a whole armoury of sneaky ways to ensure that you the consumer does not get an answer or satisfaction. You complain and get what? – a *pro forma* letter that is meaningless with a scribbled signature at the end from someone who probably does not exist. Companies regularly hide behind a smokescreen of call centres. They fail to tell you what your consumer rights actually are – hoping you won't have a clue about the law and once fobbed off will go away because it's all too much bother.

Or they blind you with science and complicated legal jargon leaving you feeling helpless and ignorant – and so intimidated that you walk away rather than take them on. You end up feeling that you are banging your head against a brick wall. They win. You lose.

But as journalists, we don't fall for any of that. Or we shouldn't. For a start we can call on genuine legal advice to get the facts. We can also legitimately go to the press office to get answers. Often just the whiff of bad publicity and national exposure is enough to put the fear of God into them and get a response. Often a newspaper or broadcaster can get to the very top – to the head of a company. Think of it like a dinosaur: a huge corporation where the head is so far up in the clouds that it does not know that its feet are trampling people. Companies such as Ryanair and easyJet are, for the most part, indifferent to criticism. They know that people want cheap flights and just keep on being annoying and do things to infuriate us.

But it's when you, as a journalist, hit the brick wall that you have to start getting tough if you want the story to stick – and you want to do your best for the consumer. First check your facts. Begin with the complainant. Be devil's advocate and make sure that the facts presented to you are correct.

Make sure that the consumer has not misread a letter, or misunderstood a situation, or is simply attention-seeking. Then look for corroboration: is this an isolated case or are there others? Is it a rare case or not? Go to an expert – arm yourself with as much information on the situation as you can – then lay your story before the company or individual against whom the complaint has been made. Give them a chance to respond – and then go for it. Go for the jugular.

SOME OF THE DANGERS OF INVESTIGATIVE CONSUMER JOURNALISM

I need to warn you that there are dangers in this line of investigative consumer journalism. Roger Cook, of the *Cook report*, tackled everything from counterfeit consumer goods, to loan sharks, mock auctions, drug dealing, child pornography. He and his crew were regularly beaten up or threatened. *That's life* got a single letter from someone bemused by charges from his double glazing company – the team followed it up and uncovered a massive nationwide money laundering scam. A detective turned up at the offices in TV Centre and told Esther Rantzen that she had been threatened with a concrete overcoat and trip to Romney Marsh. Later, someone turned up on her doorstep at home and threatened to push her teeth down her throat. As she says: 'Then we knew we were on the right track.'

So if you are going to take up the cudgels on behalf of consumers, you as a journalist must be above reproach. Your story must be accurate – no room for loopholes or innuendo. You cannot give people false hope. Never make an assumption and pass it off as fact – check your facts. Don't fall foul of the old Fleet Street adage: 'Never let the truth get in the way of a good story.' The truth will always be the best story. Anything else is just comic book material.

Piers Morgan, former editor of the *Sunday Mirror*, famously didn't bother to check his facts when offered photographs supposedly of the Queen's Lancashire Regiment abusing prisoners in Iraq. It was a good story, but it wasn't the truth. They were a hoax. He lost his job (though he then went on to become a huge media star in America – that's another story). And finally, if you believe in the story, believe in what you are doing to protect the consumer – you have to stick with it. Don't lose heart. Martin Lewis, of Moneysavingexpert.com, took on – amongst other things – the challenge of excessive bank charges on overdrafts. Thousands of people got rebates, and the case went all the way to the High Court. The banks finally got a ruling in their favour, albeit rather a Pyrrhic victory. And Martin Lewis has not given up: he's found a loophole and is still advising people on how not to be ripped off by their bank. He recognises the power of the media and uses it to benefit consumers every single day.

During an interview last year, Harold Evans talked about his campaign for the victims of Thalidomide: 'I fear a certain commitment to the public good has vanished in the race for circulation.' I hope not. The *Daily Telegraph* increased its circulation last year – but did so by exposing the scandal of MPs' expenses: a story of enormous importance to all of us, as consumers and tax payers. At last we know how and where our hard-earned taxes are being spent. It was, ultimately, a piece of valuable consumer journalism.

The media does have a vital role in protecting the consumer, representing the consumer and standing up for the consumer. The fact is that as journalists we have a powerful tool in our armoury: we have a spotlight that can be trained on those areas that some people would prefer to keep in the dark. We can shine that light into dark and dismal crevices and expose the crooks and charlatans, the malpractice and injustice that are lurking in the shadows.

That's our job. And if you do manage to work following the principles of honesty, accuracy and integrity, you will gain the trust of the public – a trust that you must not violate. It's a trust that will help you to build a personal and professional reputation that is beyond question. And if you can do that then you won't just become journalists, you will become great journalists – and that's something that I hope will apply to every one of you.

- This is an edited version of a talk Angela Rippon gave to a public meeting at the University of Lincoln's School of Journalism on 15 February 2010.
It was published in *Ethical Space*, Vol. 7, Nos 2 and 3 pp 7-10

Chapter 25

Challenges of journalism training in developing countries

Fernando J. Ruiz argues that Latin American communication scholars have relied for too long on Anglo-Saxon theoretical texts. They need to develop their own theory to explain the workings of the media in developing countries – as well as their own strategies to promote higher standards of journalism.

FIRST CHALLENGE

In Latin American schools of journalism and communications we have a distinct 'theory challenge'. On the one hand, we have the Anglo-Saxon literature about media and journalism that focuses on post-industrial societies. It is useful – but of only limited value for the understanding of Latin American media. It is First World theory, but we don't live in the First World. Underdeveloped countries are significantly different in their politics, economies and cultures.

The media systems are also substantially different. In those Anglo-Saxon texts we learn about news values, relations with sources, journalism routines, audience reception, and other topics in modern and democratic societies. But these issues are very different in Latin America. For example, news values never focus on political power. In advanced democratic societies, governments and other political actors have very narrow opportunities to enforce censorship. But in the Latin American media, censorship by the powerful is one of the major factors in the construction of news. The first question of a Latin American journalist is not if he or she *wants* to broadcast a specific news item, but if he or she *can* broadcast that news.

On the other hand, there is the critical theory of communications which sees the media as tools of domination where journalists have little or no autonomy to inform audiences. These approaches are very popular in Latin America. But such analyses tend to exaggerate the threats to good journalism – and are certainly difficult to teach to future reporters.

In other words, we lack a body of theoretical texts which help us to define the role of the profession in our continent. Latin American scholars need to develop a theory that helps us to teach the future journalists. We need a theoretical corpus that understands the power realities in our region but, also, understands and develops the skills we need to practise our profession.

SECOND CHALLENGE

We have to improve the relations between the profession and the academy. 'Academy' is a bad word in newsrooms just as 'journalist' is a bad word in academy. It is impossible to cooperate constructively without resolving these huge misunderstandings.

FOPEA is a professional association which brings together journalists and academics to promote higher standards in journalism (see www.fopea.org). Currently it includes some of Argentina's most famous journalists and has members from all the provinces of the country. FOPEA has approved an ethical code which has become one of the main reference points in the discussion of ethics in Argentina.

In addition, FOPEA has organised the only national system of monitoring freedom of the press in Argentina with more than twenty monitors at work in different parts of the country. Reports are prepared assessing press freedom – and these have been found helpful by press associations in other Latin American countries.

Significantly FOPEA's last national congress, in November 2009, focused on the social responsibility of journalists. At that congress, we invited a wide range of spokespeople to come and debate the current state of journalism. Politicians, religious leaders, trade unionists, social workers, minorities, businessmen and educators all put their views in front of three hundred journalists and students of journalism.

THIRD CHALLENGE

The third challenge is more difficult. We need good jobs for journalists. We can improve the theory, we can improve the links between professors and journalists, but it is much more difficult to improve the quantity and quality of journalist jobs. Increasingly universities are becoming themselves media outlets. That is very useful for the universities because they instruct students in real work, but they are probably in the process reducing the number of jobs their graduates can move on to. If the universities are going to become media outlets, local media are likely to find it more difficult to survive.

There is a huge problem of journalist unemployment in Latin America. Universities provide many places for journalism students but few, when they graduate, are likely to work as journalists. Probably less than 10 per cent of graduates make a career in journalism.

Universities can respond in a number of ways to these challenges. For example, they can improve their teaching of management and entrepreneur skills. The new media landscape is a paradise of opportunities for new journalists, but students need more management skills to produce sustainable outlets.

FOURTH CHALLENGE

This is the most difficult one: we need professionals who are dedicated to promoting quality journalism. Democracy in our countries needs professionals profoundly committed to (and aware of) their social responsibilities. And journalism, in any democracy, has the crucial role of improving the public conversation and of telling something near the truth. We need journalists to expose the corruption of the powerful and to give a voice to the voiceless.

Ideally, a Unesco programme should be launched to help Latin American journalists face these challenges. They are so enormous – and so important – that they can only be resolved through some kind of international coordination.

- **This paper was first published in *Ethical Space*, Vol. 7, No. 4 pp 5-6**

NOTE ON THE CONTRIBUTOR

Fernando J. Ruiz is Professor of Journalism and Democracy at Austral University, Buenos Aires. He is a former president of the Argentine Journalists' Organisation and his current area of research focuses on journalism and human rights in his country. Email: fruiz@austral.edu.ar.

Chapter 26

Defending John Pilger's journalism on Israel and Palestine

Jake Lynch (with additional research by Catherine Dix and Stuart Rees)

No sooner had the journalist and film-maker, John Pilger, been named the 2009 winner of the Sydney Peace Prize, than a chorus of criticism broke out from Jewish groups objecting to his coverage of the Israel-Palestine conflict. This was conducted in public media and included several contributions from Philip Mendes, a social work academic from Monash University, Melbourne, and a writer on Australian Jewish affairs. Mendes drew attention to a scholarly article he had published a year earlier, in the Australian Journal of Jewish Studies (AJJS), *a critical analysis of Pilger's 'views and sources'. However, Mendes's analysis was, this paper argues, based on misunderstandings of key concepts and debates in journalism, and flawed by highly selective representations of both Pilger's reporting and important historical events. This, and subsequent interventions, by Mendes and others, in public debates – including those dealing with calls for an academic and cultural boycott of Israel – attempted to demonise certain points of view, consigning them and their proponents to what Hallin (1989) called the 'sphere of deviance'. This paper argues that this is not an ethical scholarly activity, since it risks reducing the scope of public debate, rather than expanding it, whereas Pilger's journalism exemplifies a value-explicit teleological ethic in favour of peace with justice.*

Keywords: Pilger, Mendes, Israel, Palestine

John Pilger's best-known piece of broadcast journalism on the Israel-Palestine conflict is a programme originally made for Carlton TV, in the UK, and released in 2002, called *Palestine is still the issue* (*PISTI*). In the tradition of authored documentary film-making, it ends with a long in-vision commentary by Pilger himself, framed against the Jerusalem skyline. His concluding words were:

> Israelis will never have peace until they recognise that Palestinians have the same right to the same peace and the same independence that they enjoy. The occupation of Palestine should end now. Then, the solution is clear. Two countries, Israel and Palestine, neither dominating nor menacing the other.

In an earlier sequence, Pilger made it clear that Palestinian independence meant a state in East Jerusalem, the West Bank and Gaza Strip, the territories occupied since 1967:

> [The establishment of the State of Israel] cost the Palestinians 78 per cent of their country. Today, they are seeking only the remaining 22 per cent of their homeland. For 35 years, that homeland has been dominated by Israel.

It was for films such as this – along with his books and his regular column for the *New Statesman* magazine – that Pilger was named the peace prize winner in succession to previous laureates including Archbishop Desmond Tutu, Professor Muhammad Yunus and, in 2003, the Palestinian legislator, Hanan Ashrawi. The last of these was met with a campaign of criticism in public media and political discourse – and behind-the-scenes arm-twisting – led by groups that speak for Australia's self-defined 'mainstream Jewish community'.

Given Pilger's well-known output on the Israel-Palestine conflict, executive members of the Sydney Peace Foundation, which bestows the award, were braced for a similar reaction this time. A post on a well-known blog, The Sensible Jew, seemed to presage controversy, albeit in the form of a warning to community leaders to 'tread carefully' and avoid 'frothing at the mouth'. It described Pilger as a 'far more odious character' than Ashrawi, however, and attacked his journalism as 'a joke among the serious-minded' (Sensible Jew 2009).

One of the first to respond with a comment on this blog was a scholarly writer on Australian Jewish affairs, Philip Mendes. In it, he described Pilger as 'a much worse choice than Ashrawi' and recommended his refereed research article in the contemporary edition of the *Australian Journal of Jewish Studies*: John Pilger on Israel/Palestine: A critical analysis of his views and sources (2008). In it, Mendes does not mention the passages from *PISTI*, quoted above, however; and they appear to contradict one of his central claims:

> Pilger adopted what I have termed an anti-Zionist fundamentalist perspective. This perspective regards Israel as a racist and colonialist state which has no right to exist, and should instead be replaced by an Arab State of Greater Palestine (ibid: 99).

The source relied on for support is a 2007 article by Pilger in the *New Statesman* magazine, which reports the view of the historian, Ilan Pappé, that 'a single, democratic state, to which the Palestinian refugees are given the right of return, is the only feasible and just solution, and that a sanctions and boycott campaign is critical in achieving this'. Pilger's article continues:

> ... A boycott of Israeli institutions, goods and services, says Pappé, 'will not change the [Israeli] position in a day, but it will send a clear message that

> [the premises of Zionism] are racist and unacceptable in the 21st century. ... They would have to choose. And so would the rest of us' (Pilger 2007b).

To equate this piece of reporting with the adoption or espousal, by its author, of the view being reported, shows confusion over the role of journalism, defined as 'disseminating newsworthy information' (Goc 2008: 45) and a form of public communication distinguished in being chiefly actuated by the pursuit of 'internally defined ... goals' (Hanitzsch 2008: 73) such as 'fairness and accuracy' (Lynch and McGoldrick 2010: 91). Pilger's columns for the *New Statesman* state his opinions, but they are his opinions *as a journalist*: an understanding which, it is reasonable to assume, is shared by his readers. They are clearly recounted and framed from a reporter's perspective. The introduction to the article as stored on Pilger's own website states:

> In a column for the *New Statesman*, John Pilger describes his first encounter with a Palestinian refugee camp and what Nelson Mandela has called 'the greatest moral issue of our age' – justice for the Palestinians. 'Something has changed,' he writes, referring to the world view of sanctions and a boycott against Israel (ITV 2007).

There are good reasons why a journalist might choose to report, as a witness, the growing debate over a single, bi-national state, and the views of prominent contributors to that debate, at this time. The continued expansion of Jewish settlements and the construction of Israel's 'separation fence' had already created 'facts on the ground' leading even some well-known advocates of a two-state solution to express doubts as to its feasibility: 'With the buttressing of seized land ... [t]he idea of separating Palestinians from Israelis, and establishing two states, becomes virtually impossible to do' (Tamari 2004).

Those remarks were made shortly before the International Court of Justice issued its advisory opinion that the wall was in breach of international law. Israel's decision to defy the court ruling might therefore have the effect, on the same argument, of further downgrading the prospects for an independent Palestinian state on the 22 per cent of Mandate Palestine that lies beyond Israel's internationally recognised borders.

BOYCOTT

In his *AJJS* article, Mendes characterises the call for an academic boycott of Israel as 'based on the racial or ethnic stereotyping of all Israeli Jews as an oppressor people'. This claim is not sourced, but it, too, is apparently contradicted by evidence whose omission, from Mendes's article, is significant, given its provenance. Omar Barghouti and Lisa Taraki, the founders of the Palestinian Campaign for the Academic and Cultural Boycott of Israel (PACBI), issued their own clarification of this issue in 2005:

> The fact that we go out of our way to 'exclude from the above actions against Israeli institutions any conscientious Israeli academics and intellectuals opposed to their state's colonial and racist policies' follows from our realisation that there is always a grey area where an academic may be perceived as representing her/himself rather than her/his institution (2005: np).

Clearly, if an Israeli academic can be exempted from the boycott, then it cannot logically be based on racial or ethnic stereotyping. Indeed, the other text on which Mendes relies, to sustain this point, is another *New Statesman* column from 2002, also reporting Pappé's views, which highlights the support he received from other Israelis over the threat to his position at Haifa University. This, Pilger sees as upholding 'the bravest traditions of Jewish humanity' and as a way to support 'the cause of justice in both Israel and Palestine' (Pilger 2002a). Again, Pilger is careful not to stereotype all Israeli Jews as oppressors.

Naomi Klein, in an influential article for *The Nation*, described the international campaign for Boycott, Divestment and Sanctions as an effort to 'boycott the Israeli economy but not Israelis' (Klein 2009). Mendes cannot have been expected to consider this text in his article for *AJJS*, since it appeared months later, but it is worth noting that he continued, afterwards, to characterise the case for boycott in these same terms.

In an article for the *Australian* newspaper, Mendes and co-writer Nick Dyrenfurth (2009) complain about the 'discriminatory singling out' of Israel when others, such as 'China in Tibet, the US during Vietnam, Indonesia in Aceh and formerly East Timor, and Russia in Chechnya' have been guilty of more 'brutal' behaviour. Again, this article failed to consider several prominent comments, by its supporters, setting out the rationale for the call to boycott Israel: 'a tactic', in Klein's words, 'not a dogma', and certainly not tantamount to ignoring the rights records of other countries: 'The reason why it should be tried on Israel is that it might work' (op cit).

The article by Mendes and Dyrenfurth was a contribution to public media, rather than a scholarly article, but, according to the Monash conduct and compliance procedures, such activities should still embody 'the university's key values' including 'excellence in ... research and scholarship' and 'fairness' (Monash nd: np). An article in the *Australian* by a Monash academic such as Mendes should, therefore, exhibit ethical scholarly virtues, and criticism of an idea and its exponents is validated, in scholarly ethics, by giving fair consideration to what they actually say.

No critical analysis can, or should be expected to, consider in detail the entire *corpus* of works put out by its subject, of course. In context, however, the concluding in-vision commentary of *Palestine is still the issue*, and the statements by Taraki and Barghouti and Klein should, for reasons explained above, be considered prominent and clearly important pieces of evidence. That Mendes omits such evidence from any consideration whatsoever, on a consistent basis, suggests the application of a particular method, manifest in both scholarly and public writings. An attempt appears to be underway to represent both John Pilger's journalism, and calls for a boycott of Israel, as racist in character. This is a serious charge, and one that threatens to propel its targets into what Daniel Hallin called the 'sphere of deviance … exposing, condemning, or excluding from the public agenda those who violate or challenge the political consensus. It marks out and defends the limits of acceptable conflict' (op cit: 117).

PEACE WITH JUSTICE

The citation by the jury of the Sydney Peace Foundation, in awarding Pilger the Sydney Peace Prize, singles out his 'commitment to peace with justice by exposing and holding governments to account for human rights abuses' and 'enabling the voices of the powerless to be heard'. Pilger himself has characterised the purpose of journalism as 'an antidote … [to] the insidious propaganda of authority' (2009).

This is to adopt a teleological ethic (Butler et al. 2003: 5), in which journalists take on responsibility for countering what Jowett and O'Donnell, in their well-known definition of propaganda, call 'the deliberate and systematic attempt to shape perceptions, manipulate cognitions and direct behaviour' (1999: 6). It is for this reason that a 'propaganda orientation' is one of the four chief defining characteristics of war journalism, in the peace journalism model conceived by Johan Galtung (1998). 'War journalism' is so defined because the forms of representation of conflict denoted all serve to legitimise violent responses. The list is headed by a 'focus on the conflict arena; two parties, one goal (victory); general zero-sum orientation' (ibid.). To reduce the number of parties to two – a structure Lynch and McGoldrick describe as a 'tug-of-war' formation (2005: 8) – is automatically to construct a built-in dominant reading in favour of violence, since 'anything that is not "winning" must be "losing"' and 'defeat being unthinkable, each has a readymade incentive to step up, or escalate, efforts for victory'. As Majid Tehranian writes:

> We live in a largely mediated world ruled by government media monopolies or commercial media oligopolies that construct images of 'the other'. Promotion of particular commodities and identities are the main preoccupations of both commercial and government systems. The two systems thus tend to exacerbate international tensions by dichotomising, dramatising, and demonising 'them' against 'us' (2002: 58).

Pilger's declared vocation to bring to readers and audiences the perspectives of the marginalised and oppressed – 'them' in Tehranian's equation – can be construed as a contribution to peace journalism, a form based on a 'critical self-awareness' (Lynch and McGoldrick op cit: xvi) and applying insights from the value-explicit discipline of peace research to 'predict ... the influence' of particular media responses on 'the actions and motivations of parties to conflict' (ibid: 218).

The ethical validity of peace journalism therefore depends on being able to identify who and what can legitimately be regarded as 'them' – as the subjugated terms in binary oppositions constructed and/or evoked in attempts to manipulate cognitions. It is in the nature of conflict, of course, that agreement on such points is at a premium, and Mendes criticises Pilger for declaring that, in pursuing this purpose in the reporting of this conflict, it is his 'duty to rectify' an imbalance, in which Palestinian perspectives and versions of events routinely receive less – and less favourable – coverage than those of Israel and its supporters (op cit: 104).

This is wrong-headed, Mendes argues, since the 'picture' of Western media representations of the conflict should be seen as 'greyer' than Pilger allows (ibid: 105). Perhaps the best-known piece of research on this is a peer-reviewed study by Greg Philo and Mike Berry of the Glasgow University Media Group, which is based on interview data from 800 subjects, including senior professional journalists, and content analysis of television news over a period of two years. Its conclusions are nuanced, but, on every significant analytical factor, it finds a pattern of 'Israeli dominance' (Philo and Berry 2004: 259), both in the choice of developments to report and in the way they were described, interpreted and framed. Interview subjects showed a profound ignorance of key points, to the general disadvantage of Palestinian experiences and perspectives. At one point, the study found, 'Many believed that the Palestinians were occupying the occupied territories ... the great bulk of those we interviewed had no idea where the Palestinian refugees had come from' (Philo 2004).

Against this, Mendes cites a book chapter by the London correspondent for the *Jerusalem Post*, Douglas Davis, which is not peer-reviewed, and relies on anecdotal reporting of particular broadcasts by the BBC and disputes arising from them. He does allow that this chapter is by a 'pro-Israel advocate' but does not specify that the contribution dates from 2003, when the paper was still owned by Conrad Black's Hollinger Group, and had undergone a pronounced shift to the right. This perhaps accounts for the intemperate language in the study, such as 'the BBC's relentless, one-dimensional portrayal of Israel as a demonic, criminal state and Israelis as brutal oppressors responsible for all the ills of the region' (Davis 2003: np); language which is not supported by any systematic analysis.

To support his argument, Mendes also relies on an internal BBC study by Malcolm Balen, a former deputy editor of the main evening news programme on domestic television who was subsequently appointed to oversee the BBC's reporting of the conflict, and responses to representations received in public debate. Mendes implies that the 'nature of [Balen's] investigation' enables it to be used to refute Philo and Berry (2008: 105). However, several significant facts are ignored. The Balen study has never been published, indeed the BBC has successfully resisted attempts to obtain it under UK Freedom of Information legislation, so no-one, except Balen himself and a small group of BBC news managers, knows what it actually says.

A still more significant omission from Mendes's account is the context in which the Balen study was commissioned and produced. For some time, BBC News' coverage of the conflict had been under investigation by the corporation's own governors. The eventual report found that the BBC was in a 'straitjacket of balance' and, therefore, misrepresented a situation that was inherently unbalanced – a conflict between an occupying power, 'in control' of events, and an occupied people who were effectively rendered powerless. As Pilger himself observed:

> The panel's conclusion was that BBC reporting of the Palestinian struggle was not 'full and fair' and 'in important respects, presents an incomplete and in that sense misleading picture'. This was neutralised in BBC press releases (Pilger 2007b).

There is some evidence that BBC News management saw this as an attack on them: Lynch records how Balen stepped in to prevent him, as a BBC News presenter, from publishing an opinion column in a magazine sent to members of a journalists' club, which quoted and supported these findings, because it would be 'very odd for a BBC presenter to be overtly siding with the report' (Lynch 2008: 122).

An unpublished internal BBC study, compiled as a 'defence document' for an under-fire news management, and an anecdotally-based book chapter by a reporter for a right-wing newspaper, can hardly be set alongside the peer-reviewed, book-length study by Philo and Berry, and for Mendes to imply that its key findings should, therefore, be regarded as questionable is profoundly misleading. There is abundant evidence of injustice in Western media representations of the conflict, the Palestinians are on the receiving end of it and, in so far as it can be regarded as a legitimate stance for a journalist to set out to rectify such injustices, this represents a solid target. As Pilger comments:

> The media 'coverage' has long reversed the roles of oppressor and victim. Israelis are never called terrorists. Correspondents who break this taboo are often intimidated with slurs of anti-Semitism – a bleak irony, as Palestinians are Semites, too (Pilger 2002b).

In another significant nuance missed in the criticisms by Mendes and others, Pilger's ethical stance gives his journalism a valid and important role in the UK system of public service broadcasting, in which his films are commissioned and produced for Carlton Television, and screened on the ITV network. Carlton and ITV have to comply with licence conditions set and overseen by the Office of Communication, which regulates the industry. The Ofcom programme code contains a section on news and current affairs, which obliges 'licensees [to] ensure that justice is done to a full range of significant views and perspectives' (Ofcom 2003: np). *Palestine is still the issue* was a necessary corrective to the imbalance diagnosed by Philo and Berry, as well as other studies, to help ITV to comply with its licence conditions. Mendes also omits to mention the investigation by the Independent Television Commission, Ofcom's predecessor, into complaints about the film:

> In January 2003, the Independent Television Commission announced that it rejected all complaints against *Palestine is still the issue*. The commission praised the film's 'journalistic integrity', the 'care and thoroughness with which [the film] was researched' and the 'comprehensiveness and authority' of its historical and other factual sources (Pilger 2006: 143).

THE 'MENDES METHOD'

The 'Mendes Method' is evident in his treatment of other evidence in and about Pilger's journalism on the Israel-Palestine conflict. He claims that what he calls Pilger's 'anti-Zionist fundamentalism' is 'reflected through a number of reporting frames or themes'. They include:

1. Palestinians as ordinary human beings and victims (Mendes 2008: 100)

Pilger in *Distant voices* (1994), as referenced by Mendes, documents the suffering of Palestinian children, with original interviews supported by quotes from an independent research report by the Swedish Save the Children and also a UN report. Both document large numbers of child deaths and injuries. The Swedish official for Save the Children 'describes research conducted over two years with 14,000 cases of child injuries. She said the shooting of children was contrary "to official military orders", but there was a "second set of orders, understood by the soldiers"'. This is not the only frame for the conflict, of course, but its significance and salience are well-attested by the most reputable sources. Mendes implies, without explicitly stating, that there is something objectionable about Pilger's application of this frame, but it clearly merits a place in a *corpus* of professional journalism whose legitimate intention is to compensate for its habitual omission or marginalisation.

Further developing his complaint about the alleged lack of 'balance' in Pilger's reporting, Mendes goes on to imply that Pilger does not attach sufficient weight or seriousness to the Israeli victims of Palestinian suicide bombers:

> Pilger never balances his presentations by reporting on Israeli children or other civilians who had been killed or injured or traumatised by Palestinian suicide bombers or rockets. His compassion appears to be limited to one side of the conflict (op cit: 101).

The use of the word, 'never' imposes a heavy evidentiary burden and, again, the claim is easily refuted. In *Palestine is still the issue*, in another passage ignored by

Mendes, Pilger records a moving interview with a Jewish Israeli, Rami Elhanan, whose daughter was killed by a suicide bomber. 'Someone who murders little girls is a criminal and should be punished,' Mr Elhanan says. 'But if you think from the head and not from the guts and you look what made people do what they do, people that don't have hope, people who are desperate enough to commit suicide, you have to ask yourself, have you contributed in any way to this despair and craziness … the suicide bomber was a victim the same as my girl was … understanding [that] is part of the way to solving the problem.'

The second in the list of Mendes' complaints:

2. Stereotyping Israelis as racist oppressors (ibid: 101)

'Pilger has rarely attempted to present the full social and political diversity of Israeli society,' Mendes complains. 'In his early reports, Pilger did at least speak to ordinary Israelis, but seemed intent on essentialising their views and attitudes. They were depicted as a harsh people living in a fortress-like Sparta who either ignored the Palestinians, or held racist views towards them.'

Mendes refers to Pilger's book *Heroes* (1986), which includes a range of Israeli voices, who are certainly not depicted as 'harsh' or 'racist'. For example, the Israeli photographer, Dan Hadarni, originally a Pole, whose family were gassed in Nazi camps, comments: 'I am full of confusion. I wish I had not seen the camp or the kibbutz. ... In my heart, I want them to be free, to go home, but I am afraid, and I know I have to stop them!' An Israeli farmer's wife who wrote a letter to Moshe Dayan is quoted: 'Our treatment of the Arabs, right down to our personal dealings with workmen and others, sends shivers up my spine' (Pilger 1986: 360-363). These, again, are ignored in the Mendes method. As with Pilger's supposed views on a one- or two-state solution to the conflict; as with the esteem for suffering on all sides; as with the nature and effect of the proposed academic boycott of Israel, Mendes's claims are sustainable only by ignoring important and prominent counter-vailing evidence.

Mendes continually uses selective quotations from Pilger's columns in the *New Statesman* to represent them as 'picking on' Israel. Many of the articles do discuss Israel, but also include a range of references to other regimes that commit human rights abuses, such as Iraq, Iran and Venezuela. The impression arising from Mendes' critique, that Pilger unfairly singles out Israel, is misleading, and in a substantive way, since it obscures his journalistic orientation in disseminating newsworthy information, whatever its provenance, in order to highlight injustice.

Mendes accuses Pilger of rejecting 'any nuanced political or ideological distinction between left and right Zionists or Israelis', relying on another *New Statesman* article in which Pilger states:

> In understanding Israel's enduring colonial role in the Middle East, it is too simple to see the outrages of Ariel Sharon as an aberrant version of a democracy that lost its way. The myths that abound in middle-class

Jewish homes in Britain about Israel's heroic, noble birth have long been reinforced by a 'liberal' or 'left-wing' Zionism as virulent and essentially destructive as the Likud strain (Pilger 2004).

Pilger is making an observation about a particular diasporic narrative of the conflict in the UK. This may sustain the claim that he rejects distinctions among adherents of Zionism, but Mendes again, by appending the qualifier, 'or Israelis', projects on to Pilger an essentialisation of this argument that is not supported by the evidence. There are, of course, significant political and ideological distinctions among Israelis, and Pilger does not dispute this.

Mendes concedes that 'many of the historical facts [Pilger] cites are true, and may be inconvenient for partisans of Israel. But nowhere does he document or condemn the long history of Palestinian terror and violence against Israeli civilians. His moral censure applies only to one side'. Pilger does not condone Palestinian attacks on Israeli civilians. He does attempt to explain why such attacks occurred, as in showing the continued violence experienced by Palestinians, as in this passage from another *New Statesman* article:

> 'Some say,' said the Channel 4 reporter, that 'Hamas has courted this [attack] …' Perhaps he was referring to the rockets fired at Israel from within the prison of Gaza which killed no one. Under international law, an occupied people has the right to use arms against the occupier's forces. This right is never reported. The Channel 4 reporter referred to an 'endless war', suggesting equivalence. There is no war. There is resistance among the poorest, most vulnerable people on earth to an enduring, illegal occupation imposed by the world's fourth largest military power, whose weapons of mass destruction range from cluster bombs to thermonuclear devices, bankrolled by the superpower. In the past six years alone, wrote the historian Ilan Pappé, 'Israeli forces have killed more than 4,000 Palestinians, half of them children' (Pilger 2007a).

Another Mendes bugbear – number 5 on his charge-sheet – is the occasional comparisons, in Pilger's writing, of Israeli policies towards the Palestinians with the Nazi holocaust. Again, Mendes fails to reflect adequately Pilger's remit as a reporter, since these are always in the form of journalistic accounts of comparisons drawn by others.

Mendes's complaints that Pilger misrepresents the view of Hamas, as being prepared, in certain circumstances, to recognise the legitimacy of the State of Israel, also founder in the face of the evidence. Once again, the criticism is trumped by the sheer robustness of Pilger's journalistic methods: the disarmingly simple expedient of carrying out his own interviews, with primary sources, and telling his readers what they say:

Moreover, Hamas's long-standing proposals for a ten-year ceasefire are ignored, along with a recent, hopeful ideological shift within Hamas itself that amounts to a historic acceptance of the sovereignty of Israel. 'The [Hamas] charter is not the Quran', said a senior Hamas official, Mohammed Ghazal. 'Historically, we believe all Palestine belongs to Palestinians, but we're talking now about reality, about political solutions. ... If Israel reached a stage where it was able to talk to Hamas, I don't think there would be a problem of negotiating with the Israelis' [for a solution] (Pilger 2007a).

PUBLIC INTELLECTUALITY

As this account has shown, Mendes's method is one of attack, which relies on selective quotation. Selectivity is unavoidable, of course, but what is distinctive about this method is that it depends on ignoring even prominent and clearly important evidence which flatly contradicts the claims being made about the target of the attack. Step two is to take this mis-characterisation of arguments and use it as the basis to attach demonising labels to their exponents: 'fundamentalist' is a word he does not scruple to use in a scholarly article; 'loony left' is a term of abuse handed out in his column in the *Australian*, mentioned above, about the call for an academic boycott of Israel.

Indeed, these *apercus* have found a ready resonance in newspapers and blogs, recalling Herman and Chomsky's observations (1988: xi) about the media fixing 'the premises of discourse, to decide what the general populace is allowed to see, hear and think about'. This is the opposite of what should be the effect of scholarship and public intellectuality. Pilger, at the time of writing, was preparing his City of Sydney Peace Prize lecture, under the title, 'Breaking the Australian silence'. Such a contribution becomes, in the context set out here, an overdue signal that we are entitled to know what we know, and say what we want to say about it.

- This paper was first published in *Ethical Space*, Vol. 7. No. 4 pp 48-55

REFERENCES

Barghouti, Omar and Taraki, Lisa (2005) Academic boycott and the Israeli Left, *Electronic Intifada*, 15 April. Available online at http://electronicintifada.net/v2/article3763.shtml, accessed on 4 June 2010

Davis, Douglas (2003) Hatred on the airwaves: the BBC, Israel and anti-semitism, November. Available online at http://www.aijac.org.au/review/2003/2811/essay2811.html, accessed on 16 October 2009

Goc, Nicola (2008) *Media and journalism: Theory to practice*, Melbourne, OUP

Hallin, Daniel (1989) *The 'uncensored' war*, Berkeley, University of California Press

Hanitzsch, Thomas (2008) Situating peace journalism in journalism studies: A critical appraisal, Kempf, Wilhelm (ed.) *The peace journalism controversy*, Berlin, Regener

Herman, Edward and Chomsky, Noam (1988) *Manufacturing consent: The political economy of mass media*, New York, Pantheon Books

ITV (2007) Introduction to John Pilger column. Available online at http://www.johnpilger.com/page.asp?partid=451, accessed on 26 February 2010

Jowett, Garth S. and O'Donnell, Victoria (1999) *Power and persuasion*, London, Sage

Klein, Naomi (2009) Enough: It's time for a boycott, *Guardian*, 10 January

Lynch, Jake (2008) *Debates in peace journalism*, Sydney, Sydney University Press

Lynch, Jake and McGoldrick, Annabel (2005) *Peace journalism*, Stroud, Hawthorn Press

Lynch, Jake with McGoldrick, Annabel (2010) A global standard for reporting conflict and peace, Keeble, Richard Lance, Tulloch, John and Zollmann, Florian (eds) *Peace journalism, war and conflict resolution*, New York, Peter Lang pp 87-103

Mendes, Philip (2008) John Pilger on Israel/Palestine: A critical analysis of his views and sources, *Australian Journal of Jewish Studies*, Vol. 22 pp 97-112

Mendes, Philip and Dyrenfurth, Nick (2009) Racism risk in calls for Israeli boycott, *Australian*, 19 September

Monash (nd) Conduct and compliance procedures, Monash University website. Available onlineat http://www.adm.monash.edu.au/advancement/media-advice/advice.html, accessed on 26 February 2010

Ofcom (2003) *ITC programme code*. Available online at http://www.ofcom.org.uk/tv/ifi/codes/legacy/programme_code/pc_section_three, accessed on 26 February 2010

Philo, Greg (2004) What you get in 20 seconds, *Guardian*, 14 July

Philo, Greg and Berry, Mike (2004) *Bad news from Israel*, London, Pluto Press

Pilger, John (1986) *Heroes*, London, Pan Books

Pilger, John (1994) *Distant voices*, London, Vintage

Pilger, John (2002a) John Pilger sees Israel denying its past, *New Statesman*, 3 June

Pilger, John (2002b) John Pilger on Israel and the media, *New Statesman*, 1 July

Pilger, John (2004) John Pilger on terror in Palestine, *New Statesman*, 22 March

Pilger, John (2007a) Children of the dust, *New Statesman*, 28 May

Pilger, John (2007b) Israel: An important marker has been passed, *New Statesman*, 23 August

Pilger, John, (2009) In conversation with Professor Richard Keeble at Lincoln University. Available online at 26 February 2010 from http://thelinc.co.uk/2009/10/john-pilger-explains-why-journalism-matters/, accessed on 27 February 2010

Tamari, Salim (2004) Speaking in *News from the Holy Land*, Jake Lynch and Annabel McGoldrick, Hawthorn Press/Films for the Humanities.

Tehranian, Majid (2002) Peace journalism: Negotiating global media ethics, *Harvard International Journal of Press/Policy*, Vol. 58, No. 7 pp 58-83

NOTE ON THE CONTRIBUTOR

Jake Lynch is the most published and most cited author on Peace Journalism (seven books and over sixty articles and book chapters). His work has appeared in field-leading scholarly journals, and been translated into languages including Korean, Spanish, Portuguese, Italian, Arabic and Bahasa Indonesia. He served as Secretary General of the International Peace Research Association, 2010-2012. Jake has devised and delivered training courses for professional editors and reporters in many countries, for clients including major official aid agencies. For contributions to both theory and practice, he was awarded the 2017 Luxembourg Peace Prize, by the Schengen Peace Foundation. Before joining the University of Sydney, in 2007, Jake was in journalism, with spells as a political correspondent for Sky News and Australia correspondent for the *Independent*, culminating in a role as on-air presenter at BBC World TV News. He won five international awards for his documentary film, *Soldiers of peace*, narrated by Michael Douglas. In 2020, Jake was Leverhulme Visiting Professor at the Centre for Trust, Peace and Social Relations of Coventry University. His debut novel, *Blood on the stone*, an historical mystery thriller set in Oxford of the 17th century, was published 2019 by Unbound Books.

Chapter 27

Boris and the press dogs that didn't bark

We are witnessing not just irrationality in public discourse but also unprecedented immorality in the British political classes, argues John Mair. And the press are largely failing in their responsibility to expose it.

ETHICS IS A COUNTY TO THE EAST OF LONDON FOR BRITISH POLITICIANS AND THE PRESS

It seems fitting that on this, the twentieth anniversary of *Ethical Space*, we should be witnessing a new age of the irrational (AI) – especially in British politics and media. One man embodies that – Boris Johnson – but more of him and his moral compass (or distinct lack of one) later: his warped world view promoted and still kept alive by a compliant British press.

What is AI? We can date its start to precisely 24 June 2016 when the referendum on Europe was narrowly won by the Brexiteers. Since then, it has been a helter-skelter trip towards the irrational, the outré or just the simply bonkers.

I recall reading a book fifty years ago called *The British political fringe*, by George Thayer. Fascinating, full of the insights of those outside mainstream politics looking in. Today, some of that fringe is very firmly the mainstream. They control the Conservative Party and the government and (too) much of the public discourse. Remainers are labelled 'Remoaners', views that are not popular are called 'woke' to deride them. Any dissent is actively discouraged. The centre of discourse simply has not held.

The centuries-old Age of Enlightenment, liberal thinking and free speech may be coming to an end. Watch *GB News* or *talkTV* if you want to see irrationality in action. Presenters are given a licence to spout, usually unchallenged, utter tosh: public ranting on the airwaves. The British printed press, right wing at the best of times, has gone even 'righter' towards AI. Many of them have become the megaphones for the Brexiteers and Boris Johnson. Any attempt at or scintilla of objective reporting is out of the window.

THE SOCIAL MEDIA SEWER

Now let's look at the populists' sewer – social media. Anybody with a keyboard, phone or laptop and a Wi-Fi signal can become a culture warrior. The content and arguments they 'create' is beyond the Wild West. Anything goes especially on unmoderated sites, specialist alt-right places or in the dark web. There are rabbit holes in which the irrational live but they can also emerge blinking into the light on mainstream social media – Facebook, Twitter, Instagram and TikTok. If you have not swum that swamp, then look at the comments beneath many online newspaper articles. Especially from those with *noms de guerre* rather than real names. Toxic rubbish does not describe the language or too often the poor spelling and grammar.

THEIR 'BELIEFS'

These keyboard warriors coagulate around transient causes. It may have been the 'danger' of covid vaccines two years ago or of an Islamic takeover of Britain or the threat posed by immigrants arriving on cross-Channel boats. The sites may be local – like the *Oxford Mail* – but with a national cast. Take a simple example – the imaginative plan by Oxfordshire County Council to install traffic filters/bus gates on main roads into and out of Oxford (where I live) and the low traffic neighbourhoods created in some of them. Designed to make streets more liveable. Simple common sense you may think but look at the social media traffic around it. The bus-gates are slammed as 'Checkpoint Charlies'. Every Tom, Dick, Harry and Laurence (Fox, one of the UK AI'S 'intellectual leaders') has a point of view on this simple local issue. I am told that *Fox News* in the USA has run stories critical of the Oxford traffic filters. Even Jordan Peterson, the Canadian guru of AI, has recently pronounced on them: 'The idea that tyrannical bureaucrats can decide where you're "allowed" to drive is the worst imaginable perversion ... and make no mistake it's part of a well-documented plan.'

Marshall McLuhan may have been proved right. The media is global but a global sewer thanks to the internet.

'MR AI' BORIS JOHNSON

If we want to find the AI embodied in one person let's look at Alexander Boris de Pfeffel Johnson, the deposed and disgraced Prime Minister of the UK. To put it bluntly, Boris is a liar, a cheat, a charlatan, an adulterer and a total chancer. Yet, his ghost still overhangs much of the day-to-day political life of the country. He is gone but not forgotten. The BBB (Bring Back Boris) movement of rich supporters may yet achieve their dream in 2023. That would be the icing on the cake for the AI.

I could appear on *Mastermind* with BoJo as my special subject. I curated and edited *Boris Johnson: Media creation, clown and casualty* published between his resignation in July 2022 and his leaving office in September 2022. The book treats BJ as a comedy actor and a cracked one at that with his comedy used to disguise much deceit. BoJo was raised to the heights of Downing Street thanks to a cacophony of support from the *Daily Express*, *Daily Mail* and even from the bible of suburbia, the *Daily Telegraph*.

A JOURNALIST WHO LIES

Let's start with his 'profession' – journalism, the only proper job he has ever had. Boris has a fatal flaw as a hack – he has an 'interesting' relationship to the truth. He just ignores it when inconvenient. Sacked from his first paper, *The Times*, for making up quotes from his godfather (!), then to Brussels as the European correspondent for the even then increasingly Eurosceptic *Daily Telegraph*. There his 'stories' were embellishment in whole or part. Bent bananas banned, Italy 'failing to measure up' on condoms and more. Some Boris stories did not have even a scintilla of truth in them. But Boris had rolled the intellectual pitch for the Eurosceptics in his party and the country whom he later led to 'victory' in 2016.

Despite the shaky start in journalism – or maybe because of it – he later emerged as one of Britain's best-paid journalists and commentators. Paid more than £250,000-a-year for dashed-off *Daily Telegraph* columns which often verged on the racist and sexist, Boris used the platform created by his newspaper to carve out a firmly A1 manifesto.

ON TO THE POLITICAL STAGE: BOJO ENTRANCES THEM

Somehow the clown/politician/'journalist' became the Mayor of London. Twice. There to cause chaos with plans for garden bridges, airports on an island in the Thames whilst continuing his philandering ways. The 'outside families' of Boris are such that it is hard to ascertain whether BJ is the father of six, seven, eight or nine children. Only he and the various mothers know. Much of the British press has been incurious about this aspect of his character.

The Tory party and the Tory press became – and still is – entranced with the 'BoJo magic'. They generated much of the BoJo hysteria. To the party and press he is a winner. Winner of the London Mayoralty (twice) and the 2016 Brexit Referendum when Boris won with false promises or lies especially on the side of that battle bus. Then, winner in the campaign to undermine Theresa May as Prime Minister, he gets that prize when he eventually triumphs, by a landslide, at the 2019 General Election. And with many false promises of extra hospitals, more police on the streets and a spurious concept of 'levelling up' the North of England with the South. The press were, mainly, his lapdogs in much of that.

You can clearly fool some of the people for much of the time.

MINISTERIAL IR/RESPONSIBILITY?

Under Johnson as PM for three years the abnormal became the norm. He got through more heads of communications – four – than any other previous prime minister. The revolving door from Derry Street/the *Daily Mail* to Downing Street was ever at work. Their job? Spinning Boris out of trouble constantly. Mainly it worked. Boris stayed the hero of the Eurosceptic press. His ministers grew to believe they could act with impunity. BoJo would not censure them. Johnson burned through two ethics advisers by ignoring the advice of Sir Alex Allan in the case of Priti Patel's bullying or simply ignoring them in the case of Lord Geidt (who quit in June 2022 after saying there was a 'legitimate question' about whether Johnson broke ministerial rules over 'Partygate'). They both left shouting and screaming. Ethics and morals have no place in the Boris AI universe.

The nadir of Boris's AI was his attempt to save the parliamentary career of Owen Paterson, his fellow right-winger and friend, from the judgement of his peers for blatant disregard for the Commons rules on outside interests. Paterson was a paid lobbyist whilst an MP. The move came after a conversation with Charles Moore, Johnson's former editor at the *Daily Telegraph*. That BJ ruse failed, shot down partly by his own MPs and it marked the high (or rather low-)-water mark for BoJo riding his luck as PM.

LOCKDOWN PARTIES 'R' US

It was journalists who got him in the end. Not the Boris fan club but two 'diggers': Pippa Crerar, then of the *Daily Mirror* (now of the *Guardian*), and Paul Brand, of *ITV News*. Week after week their revelations about the breaking of lockdown rules came tumbling out of Downing Street like so much tumbleweed.

That truth problem came back to haunt him throughout 2022 with his various evasions and more on 'Partygate'. The lies could not hold after party after party held in lockdown came to light thanks to simple good journalistic probing, senior civil servant Sue Gray's inquiry report and some shallow Metropolitan Police work. The emperor now had few clothes.

The culmination? Simple untruths on his knowledge of the sexual peccadillos of his deputy chief whip Chris Pincher. His transgression with younger men in the Carlton Club proved the last straw. Revealed by, of all papers, Rupert Murdoch's *Sun*. Even Johnson could not lie his way out of this tight corner once it became clear that his judgement was bad and his lying blatant. He was left with a tsunami of ministerial resignations: close to 60, half the government, in one day. Even Triple Teflon BoJo could not withstand that mass protest movement. In his own words in his resignation speech, 'when the herd moves, it moves' and it trampled him on the way. The cheerleaders in the national press still found it difficult to let him go.

With Johnson called before the House of Commons privileges committee for telling untruths in July 2022, the *Daily Mail* kept arguing that this properly constituted committee was a 'kangaroo court'. They still do. Down but not out. BBB (Bring Back Boris) is still a distinct possibility.

BORIS'S ETHICAL LEGACY

The moral after-effect of BoJo's (lack of) morals can still be seen today. Think of the early 2023 behaviour of minister and Tory Party chairman Nadhim Zawahi. Fined by HMRC for not declaring – avoiding – all his earnings for tax: £3.7m. worth. He was fined a further £1m.-plus for his 'careless' act. Trouble was it was paid by him when he was Her Majesty's chancellor of the exchequer in charge of the UK's taxes, collection and avoidance. Worse, he did not think to tell those who gave him the high offices of state that the fine had been levied and paid. He was, eventually, forced to resign after a coruscating report from the third prime ministerial ethics adviser in three years.

Only some of the national press – the usual suspects – played any part in exposing Zahawi's behaviour to the oxygen of scrutiny.

So, we are witnessing not just irrationality in public discourse but also unprecedented immorality in the British political classes. There appears to be no ethical space in the modern Conservative party.

The British press has not proved a watchdog on this. It is the 'dog' that did not bark.

NOTE ON THE CONTRIBUTOR

John Mair is on the editorial board of *ES*. He was a TV producer for the BBC (where he helped to invent *Question time*), Channel Four and ITV. He has taught journalism and over the last decade has edited more than 50 books. The latest is *Oil Dorado? Guyana's black gold*, now in its fifth edition. His book *Boris Johnson: Media creation, clown and casualty?* is available on Amazon.

Index

Accountability 18, 189, 190, 191, 192, 194, 199, 225, 228, 236, 271, 275, 328, 346

Accuracy 21, 89, 194, 205, 206, 212, 213, 218, 224, 236, 280, 379, 384, 390

Adelaide, Debra 334, 339-340, 342

Al Jazeera 89, 248, 249

#AllLivesMatter 20

Al-Saggaf, Yeslam 171-186

Anderson, Patrick D. 74-99

Anti-capitalist 351

Anti-globalisation 351

Assange, Julian 74-93

Astroturfing 144-153

Attlee, James 123-124

Australian 391, 398

Bain, Kenneth 311

Baines, David 6, 7, 364-375

Barakat, Molhem 247, 248, 256, 257

Barnes, Lyn 60-73

BBC 159, 205, 206, 207, 215, 216, 217, 233, 247, 248, 252, 254-255, 256, 257, 258, 295, 379, 380, 393, 394

Berry, Mike 393, 394, 395

#BlackLivesMatter 20

Blogs/blogger 46, 48, 49, 57, 65, 75, 137, 148, 157, 159, 160, 161, 162, 164, 167, 168, 172, 190, 191, 192, 193, 196, 297, 389, 398

Bowes, Ali 129-143

Bradshaw, Tom 6, 8, 10, 26-44, 295, 302, 303

Brophy, Kevin 332, 337, 342

Buddhist ethics 3, 48, 55, 102, 324, 325; right concentration 56; right conduct 52-53; right effort 54; right intent 50-51; right living 53-54; right mindfulness 54-56; right speech 51-52; right views 50

Burley, Kay 222-223

Capitalism 18, 348, 354, 368, 370, 371

Censorship 18, 20, 26, 28, 29, 30, 31, 32, 35, 40, 41, 85, 86, 87, 91, 295, 302, 303, 385; see also self-censorship

Christians, Clifford 1-5, 10, 13, 18, 19, 74-93

Citizen journalist/s 47, 48, 49, 57, 160, 167

City, University of London 6, 9, 28, 38

Close travel 115-125

CNN 163, 245, 248, 249

Codes of ethics 23, 47, 48, 51, 53, 56, 57, 60, 68, 189, 191, 192, 194-199, 203, 204, 205-206, 210-213, 216-217, 220, 224, 226, 232-241, 265, 274, 330, 371-372, 373, 386, 394

Cohen-Almagor, Raphael 26, 31, 37, 232-243

Cole, Catherine 331, 336-337

Colvin, Marie 245, 253

Committee to Protect Journalists 249

Communist manifesto 158

Consumer journalism 10, 379-384

Convivial technology 79, 89

Cooper, Tom 307-326

Cronin, Michael 117, 118, 125

Cultural pluralism 79, 80

407

Cypherpunk ethics 74, 76, 77, 78, 79, 82, 86, 90, 92, 93

Daily Express 28, 370, 403
Daily Mail 28, 278, 403, 404, 405
Daily Mirror 233, 403
Daily Telegraph 248, 250, 254, 267, 295, 384, 403, 404
Data mining 171-182
De Botton, Alain 121-122
Defonseca, Misha 278, 279, 287n1
De Maistre, Xavier 118, 119, 120, 121, 124
Democracy 13, 14, 19, 20, 26, 28, 81, 86, 91, 103, 148, 157, 158, 159, 160, 164, 168, 174, 239, 240, 294, 295, 302, 348, 350, 351, 359, 4, 355, 387, 396
Descartes, René 2, 3
Dewey, John 15, 17, 37
Dick, Murray 144-156
Distillers 380, 381
Diversity 32, 33, 38, 198, 235, 311, 317, 355, 371, 396
Douglas, Kate 336, 341
Dowler, Milly 203, 221, 233
Duncan, Sallyanne 8, 63, 220-230
Duty of care 180, 244, 252, 253, 255

Elliott, Chris 146-151
Ellul, Jacques 78, 88, 90
Empathy 301, 335
Ethical rationalism 1, 28

Facebook 19, 34, 41, 158, 160, 171-173, 175, 177, 178, 179, 180, 182, 183n1, 248, 254, 402
Fact-checking 41, 157, 166

Fairness 21, 45, 46, 198, 204, 205, 206, 210-213, 218, 236, 390, 391
'Fake news' 21, 27, 28, 30, 40, 41, 197
Freadman, Richard 279, 280, 281, 286
Freedom of expression 26-41, 174, 232, 273
Freelance journalists 225, 244, 245, 246-255, 257-258, 266
Freud, Sigmund 83
Frost, Chris 27, 36, 144, 202-219, 265, 273, 373

Gandhian conundrum 105, 106, 110, 111
Giles, Fiona 7, 332, 337
Gillmor, Dan 164, 165
Glasgow University Media Group 393
Global ethics 75, 84
Globalisation 9, 56, 84, 346-358, 360
GolfSixes 129, 131, 132, 134, 136, 137, 138, 139, 140
Goode, Luke 157-170
Google 19, 158, 161, 166-167, 300
Gorman, Ginger 296, 300, 301, 303
Grand Tour 115, 116
Grounded theory 60, 61, 64, 65, 66, 70, 104, 105, 146
Guardian 27, 126, 145, 146, 147, 148, 159, 167, 245, 248, 254, 262, 263, 267, 268, 269, 272, 274, 352, 365, 404

Habermas, Jürgen 14, 103-104, 111, 159, 367, 368
Harcup, Tony 22, 144, 373
Harm Principle 26, 31, 35-37, 41, 233, 302
Hecq, Dominique 335, 340
Hermida, Alfred 27, 28, 158, 160

Hidden children 278, 281, 282, 285, 286, 287, 287n3

Holocaust 278, 279, 281, 286, 287, 287n1, 2, 3 and 8, 397; post-Holocaust narratives 278, 281

Hume, David 1

Hybrid journalism 22

Ideology 61, 346, 347, 349-350, 353, 364, 367, 368-369

Impartiality 13, 18, 22, 197, 205, 206, 212, 213, 246, 256, 258

Independent 245, 268, 365

Independent Press Standards Organisation (IPSO) 150, 274

Independent reporters 19, 21, 246, 247, 251, 254, 258, 324

Integrity 28, 53, 110, 194, 238, 379, 384, 395

Intercept 85, 87

Intercultural praxis 346, 348, 357-358, 360

International Federation of Journalists 195, 198

Islam, Md Zahidul 171-186

Israel 147, 388-398

ITV News 404

Jarvis, Jeff 30, 40, 41, 297

Jerusalem Post 393

Johnson, Boris 10, 401-405

Jones, Gail 340-342

Joseph, Sue 7, 10, 301, 327-345

Kant, Immanuel 1, 4, 23, 233, 309, 315, 317, 324, 365-366, 370

Keeble, Richard Lance 6, 9, 10n1, 23, 221, 265, 364, 373

Kelsey, Darren 364-375

Kitching, Niamh 129-143

Krauth, Nigel 334-335, 340

Lashmar, Paul 7, 262-277

Leveson Inquiry 27, 46, 47, 53, 203, 218, 220, 221, 223, 224, 227, 229, 239, 274, 364

Libertarian theory 15, 16, 17, 18, 46

Locke, John 2, 17, 23

Lynch, Jake 10, 47, 48, 52, 56, 75, 84, 388-400

Mair, John 9, 10, 364, 401-405

Marx/Marxism 368, 369, 370, 371

Matheson, Donald 6, 7, 10

McDonald, Willa 7, 337

McDonaldisation 347, 353

Memoir 278, 279, 280, 281, 282, 284, 286, 287, 287n1, 2, 4 and 8, 327, 328, 329, 330, 332, 381

Memory studies 278

Mendes, Philip 388, 389, 390, 391, 392, 393, 394, 395, 396, 397, 398

Mill, John Stuart 2, 14, 17, 18, 21, 26, 28, 30, 31, 32, 33, 35-41, 46, 233, 239, 302, 303, 309, 317; see also Harm Principle

Milton, John 14, 16, 18, 21, 26, 27, 28, 30, 37, 46

Mindful journalism 45, 47, 54, 56-57

Misinformation 27, 30, 40

Morgan, Piers 383

Muller, Denis 13-25, 293, 297, 302

Multiculturalism 235

Murdoch, Rupert 158, 166, 233, 239, 273, 365, 404

Murrell, Colleen 248, 255

Nambiar, Prithi 100-14

National Union of Journalists (NUJ) 219, 227, 238, 239, 265, 373

Neoliberal feminism 129, 133, 134

News of the World 46, 47, 203, 232, 233, 365

New Statesman 389, 390, 391, 396, 397

Newton, Jackie 8, 63, 220-230

New York Times 48, 158, 163, 193, 256, 257, 267, 271, 272, 354

Nietzsche, Friedrich 1, 2, 3, 4

Ofcom 202-218

Oliver, Laura 146-151, 158

Ombudsmen/ombudswomen 192, 193

Open discourse theory 13, 15, 19, 21-23

Outsourcing 244, 246, 255, 264

Oxford Mail 402

Palestine 147, 388-398

Patterson-Masuka, Andrea 346-363

Peace journalism 47, 48, 52, 56, 392, 393

Pearson, Mark 45-59

Pendry, Richard 244-261

Pettinger. Alasdair 117, 118, 124

Philo, Greg 393, 394, 395

Pierce, Charles Sanders 4

Pilger, John 9, 10, 76, 388-400

Pluralism 13, 22, 79, 80, 235

Political economy 61, 269, 364, 367, 368, 369

PowerPoint 309, 317, 318, 325

Press Complaints Commission (PCC) 150, 202, 216, 218, 220, 223, 224, 226, 234, 238, 273, 274

Press Gazette 245, 252

Privacy 47, 74, 76, 77, 82, 86, 90, 91, 92, 171-177, 179, 180-182, 194, 195, 203, 204, 205, 206, 210, 211, 212, 213, 214, 215, 218, 221, 222, 227, 236, 238, 265, 267, 269, 270, 274, 296, 340

Professional journalism 74, 75, 78, 83, 85, 86, 87, 88, 90, 146, 157, 159, 395

Propaganda 10, 76, 88. 89, 90, 92, 144, 392

Ramon-Vegas, Xavier 189-201

Rawls, John 2, 37, 309, 317

Reporting death 220-230

Responsible journalism 8, 17, 45, 51, 56, 80, 116, 220, 232-240, 250, 252, 263, 272, 370, 371

Reuters 85, 193, 247, 248, 256, 257

Ricketson, Matthew 7, 332-333, 338, 342, 343, 345

Rickett, Carolyn 7, 327-345

Rippon, Angela 10, 379-384

Robinson, Sue 146, 293-294, 297, 300, 303

Rojas-Torrijos, José-Luis 189-201

Rosen, Jay 47, 168, 246

Rousseau, Jean-Jacques 4

Rowe, David 190, 196

Ruiz, Fernando J. 385-387

Seattle Times 351

Self-censorship 26, 28, 32-34, 40, 41, 85, 302

Shirky, Clay 158, 168

Snowden, Edward 90, 91, 262, 263, 266, 267, 268, 269, 271, 272, 273, 274, 275, 296

Socialist Worker 370

Social media 13, 15, 19, 20, 22, 23, 27, 28, 32, 33, 34, 40, 41, 71, 116, 129-138, 140, 159, 162, 164, 167, 220, 221, 222, 227, 246, 248, 249, 250, 252, 254, 256, 257, 294, 296, 297, 299, 300, 301, 303, 316, 402

Sorrells, Kathryn 350, 352, 354, 357, 358

Sports journalism ethics 189-199

Stubbs, Ben 115-125

Stylebooks 189, 191, 192

Sun 28, 225, 232, 365, 371, 404

Sunday Mirror 383

Sunday Times 190, 245, 248, 250, 252-254, 380

Sustainable development 100, 101, 102, 103, 104, 108, 109

Swartz, Omar 346-363

Sydney Peace Prize 388, 392, 398

Syria 8, 244-277

Szlezinger, Joseph 280-285

The New York Times 48, 158, 163, 193, 256, 257, 267, 271, 272

The Times 245, 253, 403

Thompson, Jay Daniel 293-306

Thoreau, Henry David 120

Tourism 106, 115, 116, 118, 121; dark tourism 116

Trauma 55, 60-71, 221, 222, 223, 230, 232, 278, 279, 280, 281, 285, 286, 287, 294, 298, 300, 303, 304n1, 327-343, 395; supervising trauma narrative students 327-345

Trolling 293-303

Trump, Donald 21, 27, 76

Truth 1, 4, 14, 15, 16, 17, 18, 21, 22, 27, 28, 29, 30, 31, 32, 39, 40, 41, 45, 46, 47, 48, 49, 50, 51, 52, 55, 57, 78, 79, 80, 86, 87, 88, 89, 90, 92, 152, 160, 168, 194, 195, 197, 221, 239, 247, 271, 297, 359, 370, 379, 383, 387, 403, 404; 'post-truth' 26, 27, 28, 30, 402

Tulloch, John 9, 373

Twain, Mark 120

Twitter 33, 129-140, 157, 160, 161, 162, 163, 164, 171, 222, 293, 402

Unfairness 203, 213, 214

Utilitarianism 39, 80, 180

Watson, Meg 122-123

Webb, Jen 338-339

Wheelwright, Julie 278-292

WikiLeaks 74-99, 157, 272

YouTube 160, 161, 162, 171

www.ingramcontent.com/pod-product-compliance
Lightning Source LLC
Chambersburg PA
CBHW071944220426
43662CB00009B/980